BRITISH POLITICAL PARTIES

R. T. McKENZIE

BRITISH POLITICAL PARTIES

THE DISTRIBUTION OF POWER WITHIN THE CONSERVATIVE AND LABOUR PARTIES

SECOND EDITION

FREDERICK A. PRAEGER, *Publishers*

New York • Washington

For

FRANCES AND PATRICIA

FREDERICK A. PRAEGER, PUBLISHERS
111 Fourth Avenue, New York, N.Y. 10003
77-79 Charlotte Street, London, W.1, England

Published in the United States of America in 1964
by Frederick A. Praeger, Inc., Publishers

Second printing, 1966

The original edition of this work was first published
in 1955, by St. Martin's Press, Inc.

© R. T. McKenzie, 1963
Library of Congress Catalog Card Number: 64-10619

Printed in the United States of America

PREFACE

THE scope of this book is indicated by its sub-title; its purpose is to examine the distribution of power within the two major British political parties. It is not concerned with party ideologies or programmes, nor does it deal in any detail with the minor parties. The Liberal Party has been relegated to an Appendix. In view of the party's long and distinguished history, this may seem unnecessarily cruel. But there can be no escaping the fact that in the last election the Liberal Party received only 2½ per cent. of the popular vote and won only 1 per cent. of the seats in the House of Commons. The most important conditioning influence on the internal life of any British political party is the fact that it is either responsible for the government of the country or has a reasonable prospect of winning such responsibility. If the party accepts the conventions of cabinet and parliamentary government, then the prospect of office is of far greater importance in determining the distribution of power within the party, than are any of the party's internal constitutional arrangements. But if a party has no such prospects, if, in other words, its Leader is not a potential Prime Minister, and if his senior colleagues do not constitute a potential cabinet, then the party's domestic arrangements are of only very limited interest. This, I submit, is the justification for my almost exclusive concern in this book with the two major parties which between them have shared responsibility for the government of this country in recent decades and appear likely to continue to do so for some decades to come.

Although I am primarily concerned with the working of the Conservative and Labour Parties in our own day, I have nevertheless made extensive use of historical material. This perhaps requires some explanation, since it accounts for what may seem the inordinate length of the present book. I have found that before I could attempt to explain the institutional arrangements of either party I have had to try to repair some of the gaps left by the historians. There is, for example, no history of the Conservative Party since Peel; this is an appalling gap since the modern structure of the party has been built almost entirely on foundations laid in Disraeli's day. The Labour Party has been better served by the historians, notably, of course, by Professor G. D. H. Cole, to whose work I am greatly indebted. But he would admit, I am sure, that his historical studies of the Labour movement have dealt only incidentally with problems of major concern to me, such as the evolution of the party's conception of the rôle of its Leader or the history of the relationship between the Parliamentary Labour Party and the party's mass organization outside Parliament. I could not attempt, of course, to incorporate complete histories of the two parties within this single volume, but I have treated each institution of each party historically; thus, to take but one example, in Chapter II I have traced the way in which each Conservative Leader since Disraeli has won office in order to provide a basis on which I could attempt to generalize about the process by which Leaders emerge in the Conservative Party. A similar historical approach has been adopted in each subsequent chapter. I could have written a briefer book on the contemporary structure of the two parties had I omitted much of my historical material; but this seemed inadvisable since the material is not readily available elsewhere.

Reference is made in the bibliography and in the footnotes throughout the text to the principal manuscripts and printed sources on which I have relied. But in addition, I must express my gratitude to the many hundreds of men and women in British political life who have discussed with me the problems of party organization with which I have been concerned. They range from those who have held, or now hold, high political office, through all levels of party activity in Parliament and outside. In order to obtain first-hand knowledge of the working of British political parties I have spent a great many hours in conversation at the House of Commons, at the party head offices, at the annual party conferences (most of which I have attended since the war) and in the regional and local offices of the parties. I value, not least, my contacts with those extremely important citizens who devote their spare time and energy to party work in the constituencies. I have been privileged to observe at first-hand the " front line " party activity in the electoral battles of 1945, 1950 and 1951. I know of no better place to get the " feel " of party activity than in conversation over a cup of tea with a team of canvassers who have spent a chilly evening spying out the land on behalf of their party's cause. But wherever I have gone, whether among the politically lowly or the eminent, I have met with an invariably friendly and helpful response.

I must thank in particular those practising politicians—there have been more than fifty of them—who have taken part in the post-graduate seminar on political parties which my colleagues, Mr. D. G. MacRae and Mr. R. H. Pear, and I have conducted at the London School of Economics and Political Science. During the past four academic sessions, our students (who have been drawn during this period from a score of countries) have met weekly to discuss the nature and the problems of party organization and of political behaviour. In the course of our work we have drawn heavily on the knowledge and experience of those who are active at every level in British political organizations. We have invited men and women from the front and back benches of both major parties in Parliament, from the Whips' offices, from the party central offices, and from the regional and local organizations; almost without exception, however busy they may have been, they have set aside several hours of their time to take part in our seminar sessions. I know that the members of the seminar would wish me to express their gratitude; and, for my own part, I must acknowledge that these discussions have provided an invaluable opportunity to test out, under the critical scrutiny of our guests and of the members of the seminar, the ideas I have elaborated in this book.

It will be evident that I cannot possibly thank by name all of those who have contributed at least indirectly to the preparation of this book. But I must mention those who have been kind enough to read portions or all of the manuscript. The Viscount Davidson (formerly Mr. J. C. C. Davidson) has read and discussed with me in detail the section on the Conservative Party. As secretary to Bonar Law and subsequently as Chairman of the Conservative Party Organization, as an intimate friend of Baldwin and a member of the National Government, Lord Davidson has an almost unrivalled knowledge of Conservative politics in the inter-war years; I hope he will forgive me if I remind him here of the half-promise he made in the course of our conversations to write a history or political memoir of the period. Sections of the manuscript on the Conservative Party have been read by officials of the party's Central Office, of the National Union, of the Research Department and of the Conservative Political Centre. They have chosen, conforming to their usual practice in these circumstances, to remain anonymous; but each of them took such pains in helping me to understand the working of their party organization, that I must express my gratitude. Officials and prominent members of the Labour Party have been equally helpful. Those who have read and discussed with me one or more Chapters of the section on the Labour Party include my very old and valued friends, Mr. G. R. Strauss, M.P., the former Minister of Supply, and Mrs. G. R. Strauss, L.C.C.; Mrs. Margaret I. Cole, who has contributed so much to the literature of the Labour Party; Mr. Kenneth Robinson, M.P., a former Labour Whip; Mr. Carol Johnson, the Secretary of the Parliamentary Labour Party; Mr. Gwilym Williams, of the Secretary's Department at the Labour head office.

I must also record my debt to the late Professor Harold Laski who encouraged me in this project and whose friendship I so greatly valued. He would have disagreed, I suspect, with much that I have written, but I deeply regret that I have not had the opportunity of arguing my case with him in what I know would have been an exhilarating series of discussions. Amongst my other academic colleagues, Professor W. A. Robson has read the manuscript, discussed it with me, and made a number of suggestions for its improvement. Mr. D. G. MacRae, one of the most helpful and stimulating colleagues I have known, must bear a good deal of the responsibility for inspiring the project in the first place; he has provided invaluable advice and assistance at every stage in the writing of the book. To Mr. David Butler of Nuffield College I also owe a particular debt. He has placed his great knowledge of British political parties unhesitatingly at my disposal and has read the manuscript and discussed it with me in detail. I have, incidentally, been content to deal with the regional and local aspects of party organization more briefly than I might otherwise have done because I am aware that they will be definitively treated in his own forthcoming book on the local basis of national politics. Finally, I must acknowledge a great debt of friendship to Mr. George Ffitch for his tireless labours and for his kindness in bearing a large part of the responsibility for seeing the manuscript through the press during my absence from the country.

I bear sole responsibility for any errors of fact or judgment.

R. T. McKENZIE

September 1954

PREFACE TO THE REVISED EDITION

A NEW chapter (X) in this revised edition deals with the profoundly important changes which have occurred in the two major British parties since the publication of the first edition eight years ago. At that time, Sir Winston Churchill and Clement Attlee (now Lord Attlee) still led their respective parties. Both, however, were to retire during 1955 and, since then, each party has had two Leaders. In Chapter X I have examined the career as Conservative Leader of Sir Anthony Eden (now Lord Avon) and the process by which Harold Macmillan won power as his successor. The eight years covered in this chapter almost exactly span the career in office of Hugh Gaitskell; his experience as Leader is of the first order of importance for the light it throws on the distribution of power in the Labour Party.

I have revised the main body of the text throughout to take into account recent research into the history and workings of the two parties. The analysis of the distribution of power in the Conservative Party is largely unaltered; that of the Labour Party has been modified in certain respects, and I have spelled out in Chapters X and XI, in particular, certain differences between the parties which were, perhaps, taken too much for granted in the first edition. But the basic argument remains: regardless of the claims the parties themselves may make about their own internal organization, their power structure is determined, in practice, by their acceptance of the rules and conventions which govern the exercise of power by the Prime Minister, the Cabinet and Parliament in the British political system. Despite the vast differences in origin, social composition and formal structure of the Conservative and Labour parties, their acceptance of the rules and conventions of the governmental system ensures that the distribution of power, as between the Leader and his frontbench colleagues, the parliamentary parties, their mass organizations and professional machines, will be (and is) fundamentally similar.

One phrase in the preface to the first edition, to the effect that this book was " not concerned with party ideologies or programmes ", undoubtedly proved misleading. I meant to say only that I was not attempting to provide a systematic history or analysis of the ideologies, philosophies or programmes of the two parties. But, of course, this book is deeply concerned with the ideological issues and policy disputes which have racked the parties, and the ways in which they have debated and resolved these controversies. Balfour's struggle over Tariff Reform, Austen Chamberlain's attempt to build a new and permanent Coalition party in 1922, Baldwin's battle with his followers over India, the Labour Party's ideological turmoil in 1929–31 (and at many other critical moments in the party's history), Hugh Gaitskell's contest with the unilateralists in 1960–61, these are among the ideological and policy controversies which have been examined for the light they throw on the policy-decision process in the parties.

I regret that I have had to leave the Liberal Party in the ghetto of an Appendix. It was not possible, if this edition was to be kept within manageable limits, both to incorporate the extensive new material on the Conservative and Labour parties, and to undertake a full-scale treatment of the Liberals. Faced with this choice I have had no doubt that it was preferable to retain the original framework of the book.

In any event, it is by no means clear that the domination of the British political scene by the Conservative and Labour parties is approaching its end. The Liberals managed to increase their popular following in the early 1960s to the point where the opinion polls reported that they had the support of approximately one-quarter of the electorate. But the penalizing consequence of the British electoral system seemed likely to ensure that their position in Parliament, where they still hold only one per cent. of the seats, was unlikely to improve dramatically.

In conclusion, I must acknowledge again the invaluable assistance I have continued to receive from " practising politicians " at every level in British public life. Several hundred, in all, have now taken part in the post-graduate seminar on political parties, pressure groups and the political process, which Mr. R. H. Pear and I have conducted for the past thirteen years at the London School of Economics and Political Science. The members of the seminar, incidentally, have " taken apart " the first edition of this book (and its author) on many occasions; any improvement in this second edition is in part the result of their efforts.

I wish also to acknowledge my debt to Miss Karla Wetherall and Miss Susan Schwartz who, in turn, have assisted me on various research projects and, in addition, have devoted time to checking references and to the other work involved in preparing this edition for publication.

I wish to record further that Mr. Alan Hill of Heinemann's is probably the most persistent, stimulating, exasperating and helpful publisher in the business.

R. T. McKENZIE

THE LONDON SCHOOL OF ECONOMICS
AND POLITICAL SCIENCE
June 1963

CONTENTS

PART III

The distribution of power within the two party
organizations—The continued ascendancy of the
parliamentary parties—Some causes for concern—
The relevance of the theory of oligarchy—British
political parties and the democratic process.

ABBREVIATIONS USED IN THE TEXT

ILP   Independent Labour Party.

LRC   Labour Representation Committee.

NAC   National Administrative Council (of the ILP).

NEC   National Executive Committee (of the Labour Party).

PLP   Parliamentary Labour Party.

SDF   Social Democratic Federation.

ACKNOWLEDGEMENTS

The author and publishers gratefully acknowledge the permission of the following to use extracts from copyright books: Messrs. Cassell & Co. Ltd. for Sir Austen Chamberlain's *Politics from Inside* and Sir Charles Petrie's *The Life and Letters of Austen Chamberlain* and Sir Winston Churchill's *The Second World War, Vol. I*; Messrs. Collins, and Lord Elton for his *Life of James Ramsay MacDonald*; *The Daily Telegraph and Morning Post* for extracts from *The Morning Post*; Messrs. Victor Gollancz Ltd. for C. R. Attlee's *The Labour Party in Perspective* and Kingsley Martin's *Harold Laski*; Messrs. Constable & Co. Ltd. for W. A. S. Hewins's *Apologia of an Imperialist*; Messrs. G. Harrap & Co. Ltd. for David Kirkwood's *My Life of Revolt*; Messrs. Rupert Hart-Davis Ltd., and G. M. Young for his *Stanley Baldwin*; Her Majesty's Stationery Office for the *Official Reports of the House of Commons Debates*; Messrs. Hodder and Stoughton Ltd., and the Executor of the late Lady Gwendoline Cecil for her *Life of Robert Marquis of Salisbury*; Messrs. Hutchinson & Co. Ltd. for L. S. Amery's *My Political Life*, Francis Williams's *Ernest Bevin*, Mrs. Blanche Dugdale's *Arthur James Balfour* and J. R. Clynes's *Memoirs*; the Independent Labour Party for W. J. Stewart's *J. Keir Hardie*; Messrs. Longmans, Green & Co. Ltd., and the Passfield trustees for *Beatrice Webb's Diaries*, 1918–24 (ed. Margaret Cole), also for extracts from the unpublished diaries of Beatrice Webb for the years 1924–31; Messrs. Macmillan & Co. Ltd. for Henry Pelling's *Origins of the Labour Party*, Keith Feiling's *Life of Neville Chamberlain* and Lord Newton's *Lord Lansdowne*; The Macmillan Company (New York) for A. L. Lowell's *The Government of England*, M. Ostrogorski's *Democracy and the Organization of Political Parties*; Messrs. Frederick Muller Ltd. for Hugh Dalton's *Call Back Yesterday*; Messrs. John Murray Ltd. for *The Letters of Queen Victoria* and Lord Hemingford's *Back-Bencher and Chairman*; Sir Harold Nicolson for his *King George the Fifth*; Messrs. James Nisbet & Co. Ltd. for Wickham Steed's *The Real Stanley Baldwin*; Penguin Books Ltd. for Quintin Hogg's *The Case for Conservatism*; Raleigh Press for E. S. Riley's *Our Cause*; Messrs. Martin Secker and Warburg Ltd. for L. MacNeill Weir's *The Tragedy of Ramsay MacDonald*; The Times Publishing Co. Ltd. for extracts from *The Times*; Messrs. Ivor Nicholson and Watson Limited and the Executors of Viscount Snowden for extracts from his *Autobiography*.

CHAPTER I

INTRODUCTION

" PARTY," said Lord Holland in February 1830, " seems to be no more." And, writing at almost the same time, the Duke of Wellington remarked: ". . . there is (now) very little difference of principle among public men in general. The opposition," he added, " is, generally speaking, *personal*." [1] These comments were made, of course, at a particularly confused and fluid moment in the history of British politics. In the immediately preceding years Parliament *had* been divided on a great issue of principle, namely Catholic emancipation. And in the year after these statements were made Parliament was again to be deeply divided on another issue of principle: parliamentary reform. But on neither issue was there a clear division along strict party lines; at the end of the third decade of the nineteenth century it was still almost impossible to identify within Parliament or outside it anything that resembles the modern party system. The contrast in this regard with the politics of our own day could hardly be more complete.

Two party names, " Whigs " and " Tories ", had been current since the latter part of the seventeenth century, but as Professor Namier has argued, it is a dangerous illusion to assume that anything remotely resembling a two-party system existed in the eighteenth-century House of Commons.[2] Namier shows that in reality the Members of Parliament during that period may be

[1] Cited in Aspinall, A., *Three Early Nineteenth Century Diaries*, London, 1952, p. xxvi.

[2] Namier, Sir Lewis, *Monarchy and the Party System*, Oxford, 1952, p. 19. Keith Feiling speaks of the existence of two distinct parties with more assurance (in his *History of the Tory Party 1640-1714*, Oxford, 1924). He refers (p. 13) to " two twin schools of thought . . . decisively opposed to each other on the causes which most divide mankind—on religious truth and political power." In the preface to a later study (*The Second Tory Party 1714-1832*, London, 1938) Feiling acknowledges Namier's work in this field and is almost apologetic for using the word *party* in his title. Feiling adds, however (p. v): " I have kept a title which may serve as a reminder that there was none the less a continuous tradition and some elementary framework of party, and a descent of political ideas. . . . " On the rise of parties, see Jennings, Sir Ivor, *Party Politics*, Vol. II, *The Growth of Parties*, London, 1961.

classified under three broad divisions " based on type and not on
party." He lists these as, first, the followers of the Court and
Administration, the " placemen " *par excellence*, a group of permanent " ins "; and second (on the opposite side), the independent
country gentlemen, who were of their own choice permanent
" outs "; and finally, in between, occupying as it were the centre
of the arena, stood the political factions contending for power.
Among this last group, as Namier points out, are to be found
the true forerunners of parliamentary government based on the
party system.

But even this rough threefold classification in itself gives little
indication of the enormous complexity of the loose groupings of
cliques and factions which dominated the House of Commons
until well into the nineteenth century. After the election of July/
August 1830, for example, the situation was so confused that it
was impossible to get agreement between government and opposition as to which side had gained and which had lost as a result
of the election. Government spokesmen were claiming gains of
up to 22 seats, but according to opposition calculations they had
lost very nearly 50 seats.[1] The Treasury list of the election returns
compiled in September 1830 is the best indication of the state of
politics immediately prior to the Reform Bill of 1832. The Treasury
list of 656 M.P.s (out of a total membership in the Commons of 658)
is divided under the following heads: (1) Friends . . . 311, (2)
Moderate Ultras . . . 37, (3) Doubtful favourable . . . 37, (4) Very
doubtful . . . 24, (5) Foes . . . 188, (6) Violent Ultras . . . 25,
(7) Doubtful unfavourable . . . 23, (8) The Huskisson party . . . 11.[2]

Here then is a picture of a House of Commons split into factions
which the government Whips themselves could classify only vaguely
on the basis of the consistency of their support for, or opposition
to, the government. Party organization (if that is not too strong
a term) was of the most rudimentary; it consisted of a loose and
sporadic co-operation between like-minded people to achieve
some common purpose. It was the duty of the Whips' office to try

[1] *The Life and Times of Henry Lord Brougham*, London, 1871, Vol.
III, pp. 54-9.

[2] The list was compiled by a Junior Lord of the Treasury and included
(for the benefit of Peel) supplementary comments written by Joseph Planta,
(Parliamentary) Secretary of the Treasury. It is interesting to note that
the latter fairly frequently dissented from his junior colleague's judgments.
Against the group of 37 " Moderate Ultras ", for example, Planta wrote
"nine of which at least I should call friends." And significantly against
the name of one of the " Moderate Ultras " he wrote: " Asks for patronage: don't give it." *Brit. Mus. Add. MS.* 40401 (Peel Papers), folios
182–95. Cited in Aspinall, *op. cit.*, xxi–xxii.

to ensure sufficient co-operation and loyalty to the government of the day to enable it to survive and win elections. It was the Whips' office indeed (and, particularly after 1832, the political clubs[1]) which constituted all there was in the way of formal party organization.

The 656 M.P.s in the Commons of 1830 who are classified above represented an electorate of 465,000 (in a total population of 24 million in the British Isles). Manchester, despite its population of 180,000, had no representatives, nor had Birmingham, Leeds, Sheffield, Wolverhampton, Huddersfield or Gateshead, while eight members sat for the whole of London. On the other hand, " Old Sarum with its bare field " had two members.[2] In the circumstances, any large-scale party organization *outside* Parliament was obviously unnecessary and there was none. It was sufficient that the Whips and M.P.s should keep in as regular contact as possible with the handful of influential citizens who determined the outcome of elections. On the eve of the first Reform Bill there was nothing that could seriously be called a party system either inside or outside Parliament.

The contrast between the Parliament of 1830 and that of to-day is striking. In its numerical size the House of Commons has remained almost unchanged; it has shrunk in numbers only slightly from 658 to 630. But in most other respects there are enormous differences, and the most marked is the fact that party is now the overwhelmingly dominant factor in British politics. Within Parliament, party lines are drawn with rigid strictness. In most important divisions the Whips can predict with confidence how every member present will vote. The tiny band of Liberals may split (as they did so often in the Parliaments of 1945 and 1950) but, if they do, they are the subject of much derision. A minority of the Labour Party may fail to vote with the majority of their party on an issue such as re-armament, but if they do they are subject to the sternest sort of reprimand; indeed by doing so they succeeded in the Parliament of

---

[1] As early as 1690 the Tory Members of Parliament dined together to draw up plans for the general election campaign. It is thought that similar meetings were held by the Whigs during the elections of 1679-81. Emden, C. S., *The People and the Constitution*, Oxford, 1933, pp. 128-9. The Whig Club and Brooks's were formed in the late 18th century, the Carlton Club in 1832 and the Reform in 1836. For an excellent description of the work of these clubs, see Gash, N., *Politics in the Age of Peel*, London, 1953, Chapter 15, " Club Government ".

[2] Butler, J. R. M., *The Passing of the Great Reform Bill*, London, 1914, p. 236. See also Porritt, E. & A. G., *The Unreformed House of Commons*, Cambridge, 1909, 2 Vols.

1951 in provoking the re-imposition of a stern code of party discipline. Just beyond, there lie grimmer sanctions: the withdrawal of the party Whip within the Commons and expulsion from the national party organization. The party managers of either great party can now warn the heretics (in paraphrase of their medieval ecclesiastical predecessors): " Outside *the party* there is no salvation."

All but one of the 630 M.P.s elected in 1959 owed his election to the support of one or other of the three party organizations.[1] And of the six Liberal M.P.s returned only three had had to face Conservative opponents; they were in fact the only M.P.s who could claim to have withstood a combined assault of the two great party organizations. In all, at the 1959 election, some 210 Liberals, 18 Communists and 56 others had unsuccessfully attempted to break the Conservative-Labour domination of the House of Commons which was now as nearly complete as it had ever been.

In addition to the rigorous party discipline within the House, there is this further striking contrast between the Parliament of our own day and that of 1830: the party organizations outside Parliament have now emerged to a position of great importance. In 1830, as we have seen, they were almost non-existent; now they boast a total membership of almost nine million.[2] The explanation of course is simple. An electorate (in 1830) of 465,000, or about 2 per cent. of the adult population, has expanded on the basis of universal adult suffrage to one of almost 35 million. While each M.P. in 1830 represented on the average about 330 voters (and a few represented none at all), by 1959 the average M.P. represented 56,000 electors. To win and maintain support among that number of people is of course an expensive process, far beyond the resources of all but the well-to-do. And even for a wealthy candidate who could afford to pay all his own election expenses, the task of winning

---

[1] The only M.P. describing himself as " Independent " was Sir David Robertson who had been a Conservative M.P. until he resigned the Whip in January 1959. He was not opposed by a Conservative candidate at the general election in October of that year.

[2] For a detailed discussion of party membership see Chapters IV and VIII below. One of the points of contrast between the party organizations in Britain and those in the United States and certain other countries is that British parties have fairly accurate rolls of paid-up party members. Yet despite their size and importance British parties are almost completely unacknowledged in law. There is no formal recognition of their rôle either in electoral law or in the proceedings of Parliament. Party labels do not appear on the ballot papers nor in the official reports of parliamentary debates.

and holding a seat without the support of one or other of the great parties appears to be all but hopeless. All the great organs of opinion, including the press, radio and television, are devoted during an election to presenting and dramatizing the issues between the two great parties. The Independent, with little access to the press and none at all to radio or television, simply cannot make himself heard. Nor can he claim that a vote for him would help in any direct way to settle the highly publicized and exciting conflict between the two great parties.

It is not only the *Independent* candidate who has suffered an eclipse in the modern electoral battle; so in a sense have all individual candidates irrespective of party. Most observers are now fairly firmly agreed that a particular candidate, whatever his merits, is not likely to add or subtract more than about 500–1,000 votes to the total his party would win, regardless of who had been nominated.[1] A large number of electors appear now to agree with one voter in the election of 1951 who said, " I would vote for a pig if (my) party put one up." [2]

Lord Holland's remark in 1830—" Party seems to be no more "— has a mocking echo in our day. Superficially at least, party now is everything; certainly it has emerged across 130 years as the dominant factor in British politics. It is not the purpose of this study to re-tell the story of the emergence of the mass party during the nineteenth century; this task Ostrogorski [3] did superlatively well, even though the impetuosity of his judgments led him to distort his

---

[1] After a very detailed study of the 1951 election, David Butler came to a similar conclusion. See his *The British General Election of 1951*, London, 1952, pp. 273-5. Elsewhere, Butler shows the amazing uniformity of the " swing " in popular support from one party to another. In the 1951 election, for example, not a single candidate of the defeated party (Labour) was able to overcome the " swing " against his party (which over the whole country averaged only 1.1 per cent.) and capture a seat from the Conservatives. See Butler, D. E., *The Electoral System in Britain 1918–51*, Oxford University Press, 1953, for a further discussion of this phenomenon. The uniformity of the swing in popular support from one party to another seems to underline the lack of importance attached by the voters to the calibre and personal opinions of the particular candidates from among whom they have to choose.

[2] Cited by Maddick, Henry, in " A Midland Borough Constituency," *The British General Election of 1951*, p. 173.

[3] Ostrogorski, M., *Democracy and the Organization of Political Parties*, London, 1902, Vol. I. Appropriately, Ostrogorski's study stands almost exactly mid-way in time in the evolution of the party system since 1832. (It was published in this country in 1902 but it does not carry the history of British party organizations beyond 1895.)

narrative at many points.[1] Nor is it intended to take up the chrono-
logical narrative where Ostrogorski left it in the 1890s and bring
it up to date. This study will merely examine certain aspects of the
history of the Conservative and Labour parties since Ostrogorski's
day where this will help to illustrate the working of the modern
party system. But it is necessary in this introduction to make one
or two broad generalizations about the emergence and evolution
of the mass party since 1832 to provide an historical setting for the
study of the contemporary structure of the two major parties of
to-day.

The modern party system is of course a direct product of the
expansion of the electorate. The Reform Act of 1832, even though
it increased the number of those entitled to vote by approximately
49 per cent.,[2] had little immediate impact on either the social composition of the House of Commons or the legislation which it
passed.[3] But the Act of 1832 did nevertheless mark the beginning
of the end of the House of Commons as a closed arena in which
cliques and factions within the ruling classes contended for power.
As the electorate was expanded in successive waves beginning in
1832, and as corrupt election practices were gradually eliminated,[4]
the parliamentarians had to turn increasingly to the task of organizing popular support for themselves among the newly enfranchized
voters. Their task was to organize such support *without sacrificing
their own freedom of action within Parliament*. Some, no doubt,
sought to retain their freedom of action because they realized that
the newly enfranchized would ultimately bring pressure on them to
modify the economic and social structure of the nation in a way
that they themselves might think undesirable. Others, for nobler
reasons, sought (with Burke) to ensure that the Member of Parlia-

[1] There is much to be said for J. L. Garvin's comment on Ostrogorski's
analysis of the Birmingham Caucus. Garvin said that Ostrogorski's study
left him with " a singular impression as of mathematics tinged with melo-
drama ". Although " a massive feat of research and arrangement, (the
book) is not unprejudiced but pervaded by preconceived hostility."
(Garvin, J. L., *The Life of Joseph Chamberlain*, London, 1932, Vol. I,
p. 252.) This is not to say, however, that Garvin himself is a reliable guide
to a study of the Caucus.

[2] Seymour, C., *Electoral Reform in England and Wales*, p. 533.

[3] Thomas, J. A., " The House of Commons, 1832-1867. A Functional
Analysis," *Economica*, No. 13, March 1925, pp. 49–61. Gash (in his
Politics in the Age of Peel) also emphasizes that the Reform Act had a
more limited effect on the electoral process than has sometimes been
assumed.

[4] For a discussion of the importance of this factor see pp. 164 ff.
below.

ment should not be forced to sacrifice his judgment to that of his constituents. But certainly after 1832 the self-interested and the high-minded could agree—had they sufficient foresight—that the new extra-parliamentary party organizations must not be allowed to become Frankenstein's monsters which might destroy (or at best enslave) their creators.

Towards the end of the nineteenth century there were many who feared that this was in fact taking place. As early as 1877 Lord Hartington, then leader of the Liberal Party, acknowledged with some reluctance that " The Birmingham Plan (Joseph Chamberlain's caucus system) is perhaps the only one on which the Liberal Party can be sufficiently organized in a great constituency." But he feared the consequences; would not a federation of such local associations put effective control of the party in the hands of " the most advanced men "? . . . . " though we have all been preaching organization," he added, " I think we may sacrifice too much to it." [1] The result surely would be the belittlement of Parliament. Others shared these fears.[2] Chamberlain himself had a ready reply to all such fears. " Those who distrust the people and do not share Burke's faith in their sound political instinct—those who reject the principle, which should be at the bottom of all Liberalism, that the best security for good government is not to be found in *ex-cathedra* legislation by the upper classes for the lower, but in consulting those chiefly concerned and giving shape to their aspirations whenever they are not manifestly unfair to others—these all view with natural apprehension a scheme by which the mob, as they are ever ready to term the great bulk of their fellow-countrymen, are for the first time invited and enabled to make their influence felt." [3]

[1] Lord Hartington to Lord Granville, 23rd November, 1877, cited in Holland, Bernard, *The Life of Spencer Compton, Eighth Duke of Devonshire*, London, 1911, Vol. I, p. 245. Holland summarizes Chamberlain's innovation (on which Hartington was commenting) as follows (p. 244): " Hitherto the choice of candidates and management of electoral affairs had been in the hands of quite independent and self-nominated local committees, who corresponded when necessary with the party Whips, but formed no part of any larger association or federation. Mr. Chamberlain's plan was twofold. He proposed the formation of large local associations on a representative basis in each constituency, and the subsequent federation of these associations in a central organization."

[2] Cf. Gardiner, A. G., *The Life of Sir William Harcourt*, London, 1923, Vol. II, pp. 407-8. The students of politics no less than the active politicians were apprehensive. See Wilson, E. D. J., " The Caucus and its Consequences," *The Nineteenth Century*, Vol. IV, October 1878, pp. 695–712; and Broderick, G. C., *Political Studies*, London, 1879, Chapter X, " The Liberal Organization."

[3] Chamberlain, J., " A New Political Organization." *Fortnightly Review*, Vol. XXII, July 1877, p. 134.

None the less by 1892 Goldwin Smith for one was convinced that the caucus was enthroned in the ruins of the old British constitution.[1] Ostrogorski, after his elaborate survey of the British party system, quoted Goldwin Smith with qualified approval; there were forces still at work which might yet prevent the total destruction of the old parliamentary system which Goldwin Smith felt had already occurred, but Ostrogorski feared these forces were fighting a losing battle. Parties would soon, he feared, " live only by and thanks to a machine like the Caucus." [2]

The beginnings of the mass party had been safe enough; the Registration Societies set up after 1832 were intended solely to ensure that those entitled to vote should see to it that their names were placed on the voters' list. As Ostrogorski put it, ". . . registration became, so to speak, a gap through which the parties, hitherto confined to Parliament, made their way into the constituencies and gradually covered the whole country with the network of their organization." [3] Ostrogorski did not find much cause for concern either in the work of Peel (and later of Disraeli) in setting up a more formal party organization outside Parliament. The trouble, as he saw it, began in earnest with Joseph Chamberlain and the Birmingham Caucus,[4] with their attempt at popular control by the constituency parties of their elected representatives; it spread to the Conservative Party when Lord Randolph Churchill (for his own purposes) attempted to " democratize " the Tory Party [5] and to ensure that the parliamentary leaders should be accountable

[1] Smith, G., *A Trip to England,* London, 1892, p. 120.

[2] Ostrogorski, *Democracy and the Organization of Political Parties,* Vol. I, pp. 618-23.

[3] *Ibid.,* I, p. 142. See also Seymour, C., *Electoral Reform in England and Wales,* Chapters V and VI. For a more recent study of this subject see Thomas, J. A., " The System of Registration and the Development of Party Organization, 1832-1870," *History,* Vol. XXXV, February and June 1950, pp. 81-98.

[4] See Ostrogorski, M., " The Introduction of the Caucus into England ", *The Political Science Quarterly,* Vol. VIII, June 1893, pp. 287-316. Also his *Democracy and the Organization of Political Parties,* Vol. I, and Garvin, J. L., *The Life of Joseph Chamberlain,* especially Vol. I, Books II and III. For contemporary discussions of the issues raised by the emergence of the Caucus see also Chamberlain, J., " A New Political Organization," *Fortnightly Review,* Vol. XXII, July 1877, pp. 126-34, " The Caucus," *Fortnightly Review,* Vol. XXIV, November 1878, pp. 721-41; Wilson, E. D. J., " The Caucus and its Consequence," *Nineteenth Century,* Vol. IV, October 1878, pp. 695-712. For the most recent account of the rise of the caucus, see Hanham, H. J., *Elections and Party Management: Politics in the Time of Disraeli and Gladstone,* London, 1959, Chapter 7.

[5] See Chapters II and IV below and also Ostrogorski, M., *Democracy and the Organization of Political Parties,* Vol. I, Part II, Chapters 7, 8 and 9, Churchill, W. S., *Lord Randolph Churchill,* Vol. I, Chapter VII and

to the rank and file of the party outside Parliament. Finally Ostrogorski feared that the disease had become endemic when he found that the emergent Labour and Socialist movement of his day seemed bent on electing a group of M.P.s who would serve in Parliament as its servants. He was convinced that this trend toward " caucus control " of Members of Parliament was bound ultimately to swamp all that was best in the British parliamentary system. Parliament could no longer function as a national forum in which enlightened and independently-minded M.P.s could discuss great issues on their merits. As he saw it, M.P.s as individuals and the parties in Parliament were almost certain to become the slaves of the mass party organizations outside Parliament.

Before a detailed examination of the structure of present-day British parties is attempted it should be noted that, so far as the Conservative and Liberal parties were concerned, the worst apprehensions of Ostrogorski and others who shared his fears were not fulfilled; the leaders of the two older parties had recognized the principal danger against which Ostrogorski preached as soon or sooner than he did. It is worth underlining the fact that the parliamentary leaders of each of these parties had originally called their extra-parliamentary organizations into being primarily as vote-getting agencies. But the Liberal parliamentary leaders after their experience with Joseph Chamberlain, and the Conservatives, as a result of the escapades of Lord Randolph Churchill, quickly recognized the danger to themselves if their mass party organization got out of hand. They did not need Ostrogorski's frantic jeremiads to warn them that the monster might easily destroy its creators; by the turn of the century the leaders of both parties had shackled the monster they had created. Thereafter with occasional growls of protest (and some of these were of considerable importance in the histories of the two parties) it obediently served the purpose of its masters.

Lord Salisbury had put the matter bluntly. In reproving Lord Randolph for his attempt to " democratize " the Conservative Party by instituting a system of " popular " control of the activities of the party in Parliament, Salisbury reminded him, in effect, that the true rôle of the extra-parliamentary organization of the party was to serve and support the party in Parliament. Each organization had a specific set of jobs to do (among the responsibilities which belonged exclusively to the parliamentary party was the formulation

Appendix II; Balfour, A. J., *Chapters of Autobiography*, Chapter XIII; and Herrick, F. H., " Lord Randolph Churchill and the Popular Organization of the Conservative Party." *Pacific Historical Review*, No. 15, June 1946, pp. 178-91.

of policy); Lord Salisbury saw no reason at all why their paths should cross.[1] The Liberal leaders, despite their fears, rarely spoke so bluntly. But after their sad experience with the " Newcastle Programme " of 1891 (which—as Ostrogorski put it—the Liberal leaders had to drag about with them for years after, like a convict's chain), they proceeded to re-establish effective Central Office control over the activities of the mass organization of their party. Reviewing the structure of British parties only six years after the publication of Ostrogorski's work, A. L. Lowell noted that caucus control of the parties in Parliament had clearly failed to materialize.[2]   A major danger against which Ostrogorski warned had been effectively circumvented. And as far as the two older parties are concerned, this danger has never reappeared in any really serious form.

The parliamentary leaders of the two older parties were so successful in shackling and controlling their mass organizations that the emergent Labour Party managed to convince itself that this was crowning proof of the undemocratic nature of the two older parties. This conviction has remained a cardinal feature of Labour doctrine ever since. The official and unofficial literature of the party abounds with condemnations especially of the Conservative Party leaders for their refusal to hold themselves responsible to their mass organization outside Parliament. The Labour Party appears to have convinced itself that the Conservative conference is a sham and that the Conservative Leader stands in a very nearly dictatorial relationship to his followers inside and outside Parliament. Thus, on the first of these propositions, Clement Attlee wrote: ". . . Conservative conferences . . . simply pass resolutions that may or may not be acted upon. . . . (They) are generally more like demonstrations than conferences. Leaders come down and make speeches, but they do not really depend on these gatherings to lay down lines of policy; far less do they in any way feel bound to follow them." And to emphasize the contrast between the Conservative and Labour organizations in this regard, Attlee added that the Labour Party conference " lays down the policy of the Party and *issues instructions* which must be carried out by the Executive, the affiliated organizations and its representatives in Parliament and on local authorities. . . . The Labour Party Conference is in fact a parliament of the movement."[3]

---

[1] See pp. 172 ff. below.
[2] Lowell, A. L., *The Government of England*, New York, 1908, Vol. I, p. 497.
[3] Attlee, C. R., *The Labour Party in Perspective*, London, 1937, p. 93. [Italics mine.] Reflecting on his experience in office, Attlee took a very different view; see Williams, F., *A Prime Minister Remembers*, London, 1961, p. 91.

The Labour Party head office (in its *Handbook* prepared for the use of party speakers in the 1951 election) adds: " In all other English political parties (except the Conservatives) policy is made by the party members. Only the Tories prefer the personal infallibility of a Leader to the collective wisdom of their members. . . . The Leader of the Conservative Party is all-powerful. He is beyond the control of the Party Conference and of the National Union. His word is law." [1] In another publication, the Labour head office offered a more reasoned view of its conception of the Conservative Party organization and of the way in which it contrasts with that of the Labour Party:

> " The Tory Party has always been primarily a *parliamentary* party, supported financially and in other ways by business interests outside Parliament, but organized round a parliamentary leader, and owing no allegiance to any party organization in the country. The local Tory associations and their national federation are mere adjuncts to this parliamentary machine: they have no power to govern the party, nor do they, in effect, claim such power, for they are not, as the Labour Party is, founded on democratic notions. The Tory Party is a grouping of Tory politicians round a parliamentary leader ; whereas the Labour Party is a collective expression of democratic sentiment based on the working class movement and on the constituency organizations of the workers by hand and brain. Accordingly, in the Labour Party, the final word rests with the Annual Party Conference, and between conferences the National Executive Committee is the administrative authority. The Parliamentary Party carries through its duties within the framework of policy laid down by the Annual Party Conference to which it reports each year. The Parliamentary Party has no power to issue orders to the National Executive, or the Executive to the Parliamentary Party. *Both are responsible only to the Party Conference."* [2]

It will be seen from these quotations that Labour writers are in effect taunting the leaders of the Conservative Party for their success in escaping the dangers which Ostrogorski foresaw as the inevitable by-product of the emergence of the mass party. Labour writers appear to imply that no political party has any right to call itself democratic unless its parliamentary leaders are effectively controlled by the mass membership of the party; and they argue that on this test the Conservatives fall down lamentably. It is part of the purpose of this study to assess the validity of this charge against the Conservative Party and to determine whether its mass

---

[1] *Handbook* (Facts and Figures for Socialists) 1951, prepared by the Labour Party Research Department, pp. 303-4.

[2] *The Rise of the Labour Party*, 1948, p. 14. [Italics mine.]

organization is as totally impotent as its critics suggest. In addition, however, a further problem is raised by the Labour Party comments quoted above. Taken at their face value, they would appear to suggest that Ostrogorski's fears have proved fully justified at least as far as the Labour Party is concerned. Attlee very nearly borrows the language of Joseph Chamberlain, who spoke in 1877 of his plan to form " a truly Liberal Parliament outside the Imperial Legislature " which would formulate party policy and control the actions of Liberal Members of Parliament.[1] Attlee wrote of the Labour Party conference as " a Parliament of the movement " which " lays down the policy of the Party, and *issues instructions* which must be carried out by . . . (Labour) representatives in Parliament and on local authorities." If this were in fact the relationship between the Labour conference and its Members of Parliament, this would be " caucus control " indeed; it would appear to embody in gravest form a fulfilment of the threat to parliamentary institutions which the pessimists were convinced was bound to be a consequence of the emergence of the mass party.

Without prejudging whether this is so, it must be noted that the circumstances of the origin of the Labour Party were bound to raise the issue of extra-parliamentary control of the party in Parliament. As was noted above, the Conservative and Liberal Parties in Parliament deliberately created their organizations outside Parliament to recruit support among the mass electorate provided by the Reform Acts. It was never intended that the mass party should become the master of the party in Parliament; consequently, the experiments in this regard which were attempted under Chamberlain and Lord Randolph Churchill were firmly suppressed and thereafter the parliamentarians resumed their accustomed authority. But the pattern of development of the Labour Party as a mass political movement was not nearly so simple. The extra-parliamentary organs of the Labour Party were not called into being by a party oligarchy in Parliament; almost exactly the opposite was in fact the case.[2] The real predecessors of the Labour Party are not the Registration Societies with their very limited political

---

[1] Cited in Ostrogorski, M., *Democracy and the Organization of Political Parties,* Vol. I, p. 175.

[2] A difference in the terminology used by the two parties themselves is of interest. The term " The Conservative Party " applies strictly only to the party *in* Parliament; it is supported outside Parliament by its creation, " The National Union of Conservative and Unionist Associations ". The term " The Labour Party " is properly applied only to the mass organization of the party *outside* Parliament; it supports in Parliament a distinct and separate organization, " The Parliamentary Labour Party ".

objectives, but the great nineteenth-century mass movements for political and economic reform: Chartism, the Anti-Corn Law League, and the early trade union and co-operative movements. At its actual inception in 1900 [1] the Labour Party (or Labour Representation Committee as it was called at first) was established as a federation of a number of trade unions and socialist societies. Their declared purpose was to elect working-class representatives to Parliament; in their impatience with the existing political parties they sought to *extend into Parliament* the movement to improve the lot of the working population, a movement which had already achieved notable successes in other fields. The founders of the Labour Party did not think of themselves as establishing a third or fourth political party broadly similar in organization and function to the existing parties. [2] They had decided rather to carry into Parliament the campaign for social and economic change which they were already waging through their trade union and co-operative organizations.

It followed naturally that the Labour M.P.s and the Parliamentary Labour Party itself were from the beginning considered to be " the servants of the movement ". Any other relationship, and in particular one which recognized that Labour in Parliament was independent of the control and direction of the movement outside Parliament, would have seemed intolerable. Labour in Parliament was not merely a political party; it was the parliamentary emanation of the Labour Movement. It became an article of faith in the Labour Party that the ultimate subservience of the Parliamentary Labour Party to the party outside Parliament was proof of the democratic structure of " the Movement ".

The Conservatives have stood this argument on its head; they have been just as diligent as their Labour counterparts in exposing what they claim to be the undemocratic nature of their opponents' organization. They charge that the Labour Party in Parliament is no more than the mouthpiece of the extra-parliamentary organization of the party which in turn is manipulated either by a caucus or by a clique which is beyond the control of the electorate. The most spectacular attack in this vein on the Labour Party organization was delivered by Churchill himself in the course of the 1945 campaign. It will be recalled that Churchill (then Prime Minister of the Caretaker Government) had invited Attlee as Leader of the Opposition to accompany him to the Potsdam conference, which

---

[1] See Chapter VIII for a discussion of the origins of the Labour Party.

[2] See Chapter VII on the early years of the Parliamentary Labour Party.

was to take place after polling day in Britain but before the announcement of the election results three weeks later. Harold Laski, then chairman of the National Executive of the Labour Party, had promptly issued a statement which said in part: "It is, of course, essential that if Mr. Attlee attends this gathering he shall do so in the rôle of an observer only." The next day Churchill formally drew Attlee's attention to Laski's statement and suggested that it would be derogatory to Attlee's position to attend under these conditions. In the course of a lively exchange between the two party leaders Churchill commented: ". . . the constitution (of the Labour Party) would apparently enable the Executive Committee to call upon a Labour Prime Minister to appear before them and criticise his conduct of the peace negotiations." Churchill subsequently broadened the attack and alleged that if a Labour Government were returned at the election it would be responsible not to Parliament but to an " unknown body "—the National Executive of the Labour Party; in his final election broadcast he spoke about what he described as " the dictatorship of the Labour caucus ".[1]

It is difficult to believe that after his experience of the War Coalition in which a number of Labour Ministers had served, Churchill could have believed that a Labour Ministry would be subject to the control of the National Executive of the mass organization of the Labour Party; perhaps his charges were no more than an election stunt. Yet similar allegations echo through every Conservative comment on the structure of the Labour Party. An even more lurid charge is to be found in *The Case for Conservatism*, an otherwise excellent and persuasive statement of the Conservative position, written by Lord Hailsham (then Quintin Hogg, for many years a Conservative M.P.).

> " The Labour Party almost admittedly aims at the establishment of a single-party system ; and it may be said at once that they are almost within striking distance of their goal . . . . The Labour Party is at first sight singularly well placed to complete its task. Already organized minorities dominate the Trade Union and Co-operative Movement. The Communist Party and ILP have been denied independent or even separate subordinate existence. The vast machine, designed not to hammer out an adequate foreign or domestic policy but to further industrial and co-operative ends, lies almost completely at the mercy of Transport House and its capable political bosses . . . Never since the days of Cromwell

---

[1] Attlee's replies to these charges and other aspects of the controversy are discussed below, pp. 330-1.

has a single force in this country constituted a more formidable menace to political liberty."[1]

It may be suggested that too much attention should not be paid to the caricature offered by each party as a portrait of its opponent. Undoubtedly their efforts are inspired mainly by a desire to incite their own followers and the uncommitted elector to rally to the task of keeping their wicked and " undemocratic " opponents out of office. But the fact remains that there is good reason to believe not only that each party caricatures the other but that *it caricatures itself* in its official description of its own organization. This would not perhaps be of any serious consequence were it not for the fact that no intensive effort has been made to probe the inner working of British political parties in the half-century since Ostrogorski wrote.[2] In the following pages an attempt will be made to analyse the distribution of power within each of the two great parties in the hope that it will provide a more realistic appraisal of the working of these parties than has so far been provided by the polemical exchanges about party organization that are conducted between them.

An attempt will also be made to assess the relevance of certain theories concerning the nature of political parties of which perhaps the most provocative and interesting is that elaborated by Robert Michels in his *Political Parties; a Sociological Study of the Oligarchical Tendencies of Modern Democracy*.[3] Michels' theories need not be recapitulated in detail here but it should perhaps be noted first that he took it for granted that conservative and " reactionary " parties by definition are not genuinely " democratic "; their claim to be democratic he considered no more than an " ethical embellishment " and a necessary concession to public opinion in the era of the mass electorate. Michels devoted his attention mainly to those political organizations (particular social democratic parties

---

[1] Hogg, Q., *The Case for Conservatism,* London, 1947, pp. 304-5.

[2] Two books dealing with the British party system have appeared since 1902. One was a brief symposium published by the Hansard Society in 1952 entitled *The British Party System*; another, by Ivor Bulmer-Thomas, was entitled *The Party System in Great Britain* (London, 1953). The latter provides an extremely useful review of many features of the party system but makes only a very limited attempt to examine the distribution of power within the parties themselves. The author is too ready to see the parties as they see themselves, rather than to probe behind the façade which they present to the public.

[3] This study was originally published in Germany in 1911. The first English translation was published in 1915; the latest edition by Collier Books (New York, 1962) has a valuable introduction by Seymour Martin Lipset.

and trade unions) which had set out seriously to challenge the established order of society and which, initially at least, had made a sincere attempt to ensure that their own internal organization was fully democratic.

After an intensive analysis (in which he drew primarily on the experience of the German Social Democratic Party and German trade unions) Michels concluded that these organizations inevitably fall victim to what might be termed the " iron law of oligarchy ". Michels nowhere defines his law very precisely, but he appears to mean by it that individuals who hold positions of authority within an organization are not (and in the nature of things cannot be) controlled by those who hold subsidiary positions within the organization.[1] Michels did not mean to imply that the leaders of an organization can completely ignore the wishes of their followers. Leaders are restricted (in the sense that sculptors are restricted) by the nature of the material with which they work; but the " material " (which for the political leader is the mass membership of his organization) can have no more than a somewhat remote and negative influence on the activities of the leaders. Michels identifies two main groups of causes of this state of affairs; he suggests that there are both " technical " and " psychological " reasons for the strong oligarchical tendencies in all organizations. The " technical " causes relate to what might be termed the inevitable division of labour within any large-scale organization. Certain individuals must be accorded the right to act in the name of the mass membership; they come to devote most if not all of their time to the affairs of the organization and become, in this sense, professional leaders. The mass membership is capable of no more than " yes " or " no " responses to initiatives which come from their leaders. He concluded that the " psychological " causes related to the widespread sense of need among members of a large organization for direction and guidance and to the sense of gratitude with which they respond to those who guide and direct them. Over a period of time leaders win recognition for what they readily assume is their own indispensability and they tend inevitably to devote themselves to consolidating their own positions of power; they come to regard both the organization itself and their own rôle in it as more important than the professed goal of the organization. These views would appear of course to be of particular relevance to an analysis of the Labour Party; but one need not dismiss the Conservative organiza-

---

[1] For a useful analysis of Michels' ideas see C. W. Cassinelli, " The Law of Oligarchy," in *The American Political Science Review*, Vol. XLVII. September 1953, pp. 773–84, and Lipset, S. M., Introduction to Michels' *Political Parties*, Collier Books edition, New York, 1962.

tion as abruptly as did Michels himself. His law of oligarchy will be re-examined in Chapter XI for the light it may throw on the working of both party organizations.

An examination of the Conservative organization must obviously begin with the rôle of the Leader since, as is shown in Chapters II and III, he is formally accorded what seems at first to be almost overwhelming power and authority. Chapter II is therefore devoted to a discussion of the process by which Conservative leaders since Disraeli have emerged and Chapter III to a discussion of the relationship between the Conservative Leader and his followers in Parliament and outside. The experiences of Balfour, Austen Chamberlain and Baldwin as Conservative Leader are examined in considerable detail since they throw much light on the realities of the position of Leader in the Conservative Party. In Chapter IV the emergence of the Conservative mass organization (known as the National Union of Conservative and Unionist Associations) is traced from its earliest beginnings at a remarkable meeting in November 1867. This story has already been told in part by Ostrogorski, but he appears sadly to have misunderstood the position of the National Union at the close of the nineteenth century, and some reassessment of the record is necessary if one is to understand the work of the National Union in the modern period. Chapter IV also deals with the regional and local organizations of the party, but the treatment is comparatively brief since this study is concerned primarily with the distribution of power at the national level. Chapter V deals with the origin and modern development of the Conservative Central Office, the body of professional party workers. The Conservatives have never hesitated to acknowledge that the Central Office is in effect the " personal machine " of the Leader, an arrangement which has laid the party open to scathing criticism from its opponents; it is therefore necessary to assess the real rôle played by the party bureaucracy in the Conservative Party.

The various sections of the Labour Party organization are examined in the same sequence, beginning again with the rôle of the Leader. One chapter rather than two, however, is devoted to this topic; as is shown in Chapter VI the party has had only two Leaders (MacDonald and Attlee) in the sense that that term is used in other parties,[1] and it is therefore possible to examine the Leader's rôle in briefer compass. A full chapter (VII) is, however, devoted to the Parliamentary Labour Party since it is a more highly organized

---

[1] Since 1955 it has had a third, Hugh Gaitskell, whose career as Leader is examined on pp. 601 ff. below.

body than is its Conservative counterpart, and it has had a more spectacular history. Chapter VIII traces the emergence of the mass organization of the Labour Party and examines its principal organs including the National Executive Committee, the annual conference and the regional and local sections of the party. The professional staff of the Labour Party (which is responsible to the National Executive rather than to the Leader) is examined in Chapter IX. The principal developments in the two major parties since 1955, mainly at the leadership level, are considered in Chapter X. The conclusions (Chapter XI) are devoted to a comparison of the distribution of power in the two parties and to some general reflections on the nature of the British party system.

PART I

POWER IN THE
CONSERVATIVE PARTY

CHAPTER II

THE EMERGENCE OF THE LEADER

" Great leaders of parties are not elected, they are evolved.
. . . I think it will be a bad day [when we] have solemnly to
meet to elect a leader. The leader is there, and we all know it
when he is there."—*Capt. the Rt. Hon. Ernest Pretyman, M.P.*[1]

THE most striking feature of the Conservative party organization
is the enormous power which appears to be concentrated in the
hands of the Leader. Once he has been elected, he is not required
to submit himself for periodic re-election. Nor is he required to
report in any formal way on his work as Leader either to the party
in Parliament or to the National Union. When his party is in office
he chooses his own ministerial colleagues (as of course does the
Leader of any other party when he is the Prime Minister); but
even when the Conservative Party is in opposition the Leader
chooses his own " Shadow Cabinet " associates who become in
effect the ruling oligarchy of the party. The Conservative Leader,
whether in power or in opposition, has the sole ultimate responsibility for the formulation of the policy and the electoral programme
of his party. The resolutions of the annual conference and the other
organs of the National Union are " conveyed " to him for his
information; however emphatic these resolutions may be, they are
in no way binding upon him. Finally, the party secretariat (the
Central Office) is in effect the personal machine of the Leader.
He appoints all its principal officers and therefore has effective
control over the main instruments of propaganda, research and
finance.

This, as Nigel Birch has suggested, is a system of " leadership by
consent ".[2] Others, however, have taken a harsher view. Some have
claimed that the Conservative Party " is democratic until it reaches
the top"; [3] or, as two American political scientists put it, " essenti-

[1] Moving the resolution (at a meeting of Conservative M.P.s, 21st March
1921) inviting Austen Chamberlain " to assume the leadership of the . . . Party
in the House of Commons." The resolution was passed unanimously. Cited in
Gleanings & Memoranda, April 1921, p. 301.

[2] Birch, Nigel, *The Conservative Party*, London, 1948, p. 42.

[3] Marsden, Sir Charles, in a letter to *The Times*, 22nd November, 1929.
See also p. 134 below.

ally the system is one of autocracy tempered by advice and information."[1] But a more careful examination of the Conservative Party
organization suggests that a bald statement of the Leader's powers
can give a highly misleading impression. Although there are few
formal democratic checks on his authority, it is important to note
that the Conservative Leader achieves office and retains power only
with the consent of his followers; *and there is ample precedent for
the withdrawal of that consent.* Indeed it can be argued from the
history of the Conservative and Labour parties since the turn of
the century that the Conservative Leader has often been on a
less secure pedestal than has his Labour counterpart.[2]

But whatever the merits of this argument, it seems clear that
the key to an understanding of the Conservative Party organization
lies in an examination of the rôle of the Leader and the obvious
starting-point is a study of the way in which the Leader is selected.
Nominally he is elected by a body constituted (since the election of
Neville Chamberlain in 1937) as follows : the Conservative and
Unionist[3] members of the House of Commons and the House of
Lords, all prospective Conservative parliamentary candidates, and
the Executive Committee[4] of the National Union. But in practice
when the party is in power the Leader is in one sense selected in
effect by the monarch.[5] If a Conservative Prime Minister retires
or dies, the monarch (after consultation with those best qualified
to advise him) calls as Prime Minister the Conservative front-
bencher who is most likely to be able to command the support of
the party. Thereafter the new Conservative Prime Minister has
invariably been elected Leader of the Party. Alternatively, if the
leadership falls vacant while the Conservatives are in opposition,
then the position of Leader of the Party has in the past been left
vacant. The Conservative M.P.s have merely elected a Leader in
the Commons while their colleagues in the Lords have done the
same for their House. When the party has eventually been returned
to power whoever is called as Prime Minister has been subsequently

---

[1] Ranney, J. C., and Carter, G. M., *The Major Foreign Powers*, New York,
1949, p. 74.

[2] Cf. p. 299 below.

[3] Hereinafter " Conservative " will be taken to include " Conservative &
Unionist." The word " Unionist " derives of course from the breakaway from
the Liberal Party of the Liberal Unionists who were opposed to Home
Rule for Ireland. The Liberal Unionists and Conservative Party organizations were formally fused in 1912.

[4] See p. 206 below.

[5] For the one exception to this procedure see p. 35 below in which the
election of Bonar Law to the leadership in 1922 occurred immediately
before the King called him to the Palace.

elected Leader of the Party. But the process by which the Conservative Party chooses its Leaders is more subtle and complex than this summary might suggest. This can best be illustrated by a review of the rise to power of the men who have led the Conservative Party since Disraeli.[1]

After the Conservative defeat of 1880 it became clear that Lord Beaconsfield (then 76 and in declining health) could not long continue as Leader of the Party. During his final year in office he had indicated that he would prefer as his successor the Marquis of Salisbury (1830-1903), then his lieutenant in the House of Lords.[2] But on Disraeli's death in April 1881, the office of Leader of the Party was not immediately filled. It was decided instead to elect a party leader in each of the two Houses of Parliament. Lord Salisbury was unanimously elected by the Conservative peers to be their leader in the House of Lords while Sir Stafford Northcote was re-elected by the Conservative M.P.s to lead them in the House of Commons;[3] the office of " Leader of the Conservative Party " was for the time being left vacant and the public was given to understand that Salisbury and Sir Stafford Northcote would lead the party in the country as a duumvirate with equal power.[4] There

---

[1] Strictly speaking only eight men have held the title " Leader of the Party " since Disraeli: Salisbury, Balfour, Bonar Law, Baldwin, Neville Chamberlain, Winston Churchill, Eden and Macmillan. But for the purpose of this study, Austen Chamberlain is considered a Leader of the Party although he was never formally elected to that office because he never served as Prime Minister. He was however Leader of the Party in the Commons for 18 months in 1921-22. See table p. 52 below.

[2] He wrote to Salisbury on 27th December, 1880: " One of my dreams was that in February (1881) I should be sitting behind you in the House of Lords and that you would be leading H.M.'s Opposition . . . " Cited in Monypenny & Buckle, *The Life of Benjamin Disraeli, Earl of Beaconsfield*, Vol. VI. p. 595.

[3] Sir Stafford Northcote had led the Conservative Party without much distinction in the House of Commons since Disraeli's elevation to the peerage. See Balfour, A. J., *Chapters of Autobiography*, London, 1930, pp. 143 ff.

[4] Cecil, Lady Gwendolen, *Life of Robert, Marquis of Salisbury*, London, 1931, Vol. III, p. 41.
Queen Victoria wrote in a confidential letter to Northcote, 15th May, 1881: " (The Queen) is anxious to say that *she* will look on Sir Stafford Northcote as the Leader of the great Conservative Party, though it may not be necessary to *announce* this *now,* and she wished that Sir Stafford, who is so old and kind a friend, should *know* this." *The Letters of Queen Victoria,* (Second Series), London, 1928, Vol. III, pp. 218-9. But as Balfour was to remark in retrospect, " none of these decisions (respecting either Salisbury or Northcote) could bind the (party) as a whole, and neither the practice of the Constitution nor party loyalty debarred any Conservative from endeavouring to obtain a position which, when the time came, would

was general reluctance to confer on Salisbury the Leadership of the Party at that time; the reasons were partly personal (some felt he was too reactionary and too immune to criticism), but a more important explanation would appear to have been the jealousy of the Commons men for the prerogatives of their own House. W. H. Smith, M.P., reflected the latter view when he wrote to a friend deprecating the suggestion that Salisbury should be made Leader of the Party: " No one can have any doubt that, if his health remains good, Lord Salisbury is the natural leader of the Conservative Party in the House of Lords, and I do not doubt that in all questions of policy which affect the interests of the party as a whole, he will consult with Northcote and his late colleagues in the House of Commons in order that we may present a united front to the enemy. (But) it is in the House of Commons that the great battle will have to be fought, and there the policy of the party will from time to time have to be announced and asserted. I am sure Lord Salisbury will recognize this." [1]

Salisbury himself did not press for recognition as Leader of the Party. He wrote (3rd May, 1881) of " the expediency of leaving alone for the present all questions of ' party ' leadership . . . The difficulties in the way of any other course would be considerable." [2] When on occasion the Conservatives in the Commons were later to become impatient with Northcote's leadership, Salisbury refused to intervene against him. " I will gladly do all I can to help " he wrote to Lord Randolph Churchill on one such occasion, " but always with one reservation—I am bound to Sir Stafford Northcote as a colleague, by a tie not of expediency but of honour, and I could not take part in anything which would be at variance with entire loyalty to him." [3]

Lord Randolph himself was, of course, bitterly exasperated by the failure of the Conservative Party to name a new Leader. He claimed in letters to *The Times* in April, 1883, that the Tory Party would be ruined if its leadership was left " in commission ".[4] He argued that the party had ample talent to choose from: he mentioned Salisbury, Northcote and one other (Cairns) by name and indicated a clear preference for Salisbury. In his famous article

justify him in hoping for the place left vacant by Lord Beaconsfield's death." Balfour, A. J., *Chapters of Autobiography*, p. 152.

[1] W. H. Smith to Lady John Manners, 4th May, 1881, cited in Cecil, *The Life of Robert, Marquis of Salisbury*, Vol. III, p. 41.

[2] Cited in Cecil, *The Life of Robert, Marquis of Salisbury*, Vol. III, p. 41.

[3] *Ibid.*, Vol. III, p. 132.

[4] Balfour, A. J., *Chapters of Autobiography*, p. 154.

in the *Fortnightly* on 1st May, 1883 ("Elijah's Mantle") Lord Randolph again attacked the system of "Dual Control" of the party, but he now appeared to be seeking a more colourful heir to the mantle of the prophet.[1] The new Leader must be a man "who fears not to meet, and who knows how to sway, immense masses of the working classes," and who "by all the varied influences of an ancient name can move ' the hearts of households '." These phrases were applied to Lord Salisbury but he had given no sign of response to Lord Randolph's letters to *The Times* and it had become clear that the latter was now prepared (although he was only 34) to press his own candidature.[2]

To demonstrate his own capacity to move the masses, Lord Randolph did two things: he undertook to contest a seat in Birmingham, the very stronghold of Radicalism, and he set about his spectacular campaign to remodel and "democratize" the machinery of the Conservative Party.[3] The first of these projects was widely approved within the party; the second stirred a good deal of resentment. Balfour, who had been closely associated with Lord Randolph, had a cynical interpretation of his motive . . . "questions of organization were raised," Balfour wrote, "not in order to make the political machine work more efficiently, but in order to replace those who were endeavouring to work it." [4]

In any event, after a rather hectic winter of dispute over the functions of the National Union, Lord Randolph made his peace with the party leaders. In the course of the dispute his popular following within the party had increased enormously. He apparently became more than ever convinced that "Elijah's mantle was not far beyond his reach" and this conviction, as Balfour concludes, forced Lord Randolph to recognize the folly of his scheme to transfer executive control of the party to the National Union. "If he was a potential leader," Balfour wrote, "it behoved him to look at party problems from a leader's point of view; and how could any man do so, whatever his prejudices, without perceiving that if all executive powers and all financial control were transferred to an independent body (outside Parliament), leadership in the ordinary sense would cease." For this reason or some other, Lord Randolph took little further interest in the affairs of the National Union. He had used it to elevate himself into the ruling

[1] Churchill, Lord Randolph, "Elijah's Mantle", *Fortnightly Review*, Vol. XXXIII (New Series), May 1883, pp. 613-21.

[2] Churchill, W. S., *Lord Randolph Churchill*, Vol. I, p. 252.

[3] See pp. 8-10 above and pp. 166-73 below.

[4] Balfour, A. J., *Chapters of Autobiography*, p. 158.

oligarchy of the party; once there he soon adapted his veiws concerning party organization to those of his colleagues.

Salisbury meanwhile was steadily establishing his own immediate
claim to the mantle of Elijah. Northcote's prestige continued to
decline as a result of his ineffectiveness in the House. And it is
significant that during the winter of 1883/4 Salisbury replied for the
duumvirate when Lord Randolph challenged their control of the
party on behalf of the National Union. Salisbury's letters carefully preserved the formalities of dual control (" it appears to *us*
that. . . . " " The field of work seems to *us* large " etc.). But
Salisbury clearly established his own ascendancy in the councils of
the party, both in the course of his correspondence with Churchill,
and in his public speeches. With the defeat of the Liberal Government in 1885, the Queen called Salisbury to the office of Prime
Minister; her selection was accepted " not only with unanimity
but as a matter of course ". Salisbury himself was apparently
reluctant to take on the assignment. Lord Randolph wrote: " It
was most distasteful to him to be brought into any conflict with
Sir Stafford (Northcote), to be preferred above him—thus shatter-
ing what had been Sir Stafford's great and honourable ambition."[2]
But under considerable pressure from his supporters[3] Salisbury
agreed to accept the Queen's commission. He was subsequently
unanimously confirmed as Leader of the Conservative Party.

Seventeen years later (in July, 1902) the leadership of the Conservative Party passed from Salisbury to his nephew, A. J. Balfour.
The Conservatives were of course in office at the time and the
leadership in effect passed automatically from Salisbury to Balfour
along with the office of Prime Minister. Salisbury resigned on
10th July, 1902, and King Edward VII called Balfour two days
later. On the 14th, at a joint meeting of the Conservative member

---

[1] Cecil, *The Life of Robert, Marquis of Salisbury*, Vol. III, p. 41.

Lord Randolph readily agreed to serve under Salisbury with whom he
had made peace a year earlier. He did however succeed in eliminating
Northcote from his path; he made it a condition of his joining the Salisbury
Government that Northcote should cease to lead the party in the Commons.
Salisbury, with great reluctance, therefore elevated Northcote to the Lords
and Sir Michael Hicks-Beach was appointed Leader of the House of
Commons.

[2] Cited in Churchill, W. S., *Lord Randolph Churchill*, Vol. I, p. 407.

[3] The other explanation of Salisbury's reluctance was the fact that he
would have to carry on in Parliament for some time without a majority,
since an election could not be held for several months. " The pressure,
however, from the local (Conservative) organizations in the country was
strong to cause him to undertake the unattractive duty, and the prevalent
feeling of the Party in Parliament was in accord with this pressure."
Churchill, W. S., *Lord Randolph Churchill*, Vol. I, pp. 410-11.

of both Houses of Parliament, Balfour was elected Leader of the Party. He succeeded to the two offices of Prime Minister and Leader without any hint of opposition or serious rivalry within the party. Balfour had first entered Parliament 26 years earlier and two years later in 1878 he accompanied his uncle, Lord Salisbury, then Foreign Secretary, to the Congress of Berlin as his parliamentary private secretary. Balfour first claimed public attention in the years immediately following the Conservative defeat of 1880 when he was associated for a time with the spectacular " Fourth Party " group which attempted to re-vitalize the Conservative Party in opposition.[1] But when the Fourth Party's most colourful member, Lord Randolph, came into conflict with Lord Salisbury during the period of the duumvirate Balfour remained loyal to his uncle. He attempted however to act as a mediator in the dispute over the functions of the National Union and this unquestionably enhanced his standing in the party. In Salisbury's first short-lived ministry in 1885, Balfour, then 37, served without particular distinction as President of the Local Government Board. In the subsequent Salisbury administration Balfour served first as Secretary for Scotland, and then as Chief Secretary for Ireland.[2] In this latter post he made his parliamentary reputation in a great series of clashes with the Irish parliamentary party. When the office of Leader of the House of Commons fell vacant with the death of W. H. Smith in October, 1891, the Conservative M.P.s " insisted on (Balfour) for Leader in the Commons."[3] Salisbury writing to Queen Victoria (15th October, 1891) explained the problem:

> "The choice of successor to Mr. Smith involves very serious difficulties. Sir M. Beach has expressed his wish not to succeed to the leadership which he held before. The choice therefore lies between Mr. Goschen and Mr. Balfour. Mr. Goschen's age and reputation commend him greatly, and it would be inconvenient to take Mr. Balfour from Ireland at this moment. But against these considerations must be set the almost unanimous view of the members who support the Government in the House of Commons. So far as Lord Salisbury can judge he fears he would run

[1] Gorst, H., *The Fourth Party,* London, 1906.

[2] With reference to Balfour's appointment as Chief Secretary for Ireland, one of Balfour's biographers has remarked: " The country saw with something like stupefaction the appointment of the young dilettante to what was at the moment perhaps the most important, certainly the most anxious office in the administration. Salisbury knew, however, very well what he was about. . . . His (Balfour's) personal triumph was indubitable." Cecil, A., " A. J. Balfour," *Dictionary of National Biography* (1922-30), pp. 46–7.

[3] Dugdale, Mrs. Blanche, *Arthur James Balfour*, London, 1936, Vol. I, p. 200.

great risk of breaking up the party, he certainly would dishearten it very seriously if he were to recommend Mr. Goschen. Lord Salisbury . . . as at present advised thinks circumstances are concurring to make Mr. Balfour an inevitable choice, though the objections to it from many points of view are considerable."[1]

Balfour was duly named Leader of the House in 1891 and also became in effect Leader of the Conservative Party in the Commons. He thus served an eleven years' apprenticeship to Lord Salisbury until the latter's retirement in 1902. Lord Randolph Churchill's early death had long since eliminated him as a possible rival. The other powerful personalities in the Conservative (then Unionist) ranks, Joseph Chamberlain and the Duke of Devonshire, made no effort to contest the leadership. The King's action in calling Balfour on 12th July, 1902, was again accepted "not only with unanimity but as a matter of course". When the joint party meeting of Conservative members of both Houses assembled two days later (oddly enough in the Foreign Office) Balfour was unanimously elected Leader of the Party after several speeches had been made pledging loyalty to him. As is so often the case on these occasions, the new Leader's most powerful associates were at particular pains to affirm their allegiance. The Duke of Devonshire pledged the support of the Liberal Unionists. Joseph Chamberlain could not be present but he sent a message through his son, Austen, who said: " I am to say how greatly disappointed (my father) is that he cannot be here to welcome Mr. Balfour to the leadership and to say with what pride and pleasure he will give all the assistance in his power to Mr. Balfour in the responsible task which lies before him." With these happy reassurances of loyalty Balfour was launched on his stormy career as Leader of the Party. Within two years both the Duke of Devonshire and Joseph Chamberlain had resigned from Balfour's Cabinet on the issue of Tariff Reform. Nine years later, having grown tired of the endless struggle to maintain party unity, Balfour resigned as Leader in November, 1911.[2]

Again, as in 1881, the Conservative leadership fell vacant with the party in opposition and again the office was for the time being left unfilled. There loomed however the prospect of a sharp struggle for the leadership in the Commons.[3] Support seemed fairly evenly divided between the two leading contenders, Walter Long (afterwards Viscount Long) and Austen Chamberlain. It was a

---

[1] *The Letters of Queen Victoria,* (Third Series), Vol. II, p. 76.

[2] For a discussion of Balfour as Leader, see Young, Kenneth, *Arthur James Balfour,* London, 1963, Chaps. 10–13.

[3] For a full account of the emergence of Bonar Law see Blake, R., *The Unknown Prime Minister,* pp. 71–86.

matter of some importance that the post should be filled as soon as possible after Balfour's resignation on 8th November, 1911; there were urgent political issues on which the party should, if possible, take a united stand and since the National Union was due to meet at Leeds the following week it was agreed that a new party leader in the Commons should be chosen before then. There was apparently some fear that if a new leader had not been chosen by then, the National Union might decide to take a hand in the matter. In a letter to his family, Austen Chamberlain explained why he pressed hard for an immediate decision on the leadership.

" *Any* decision taken early was better than leaving the question indefinitely open. The position would be intolerable for those whose names would be canvassed and most injurious for the Party where every difference would be sharpened and exacerbated. *Besides if the M.P.s didn't decide on Monday, the Leeds Conference* (of the National Union) *would take it out of their hands;* there would be resolutions, speeches, every kind of lobbying and intrigue. The Party must be summoned to decide at once."[1]

A meeting of Conservative and Unionist M.P.s was accordingly arranged by the party whips for the Carlton Club on 13th November, five days after Balfour's resignation.

Chamberlain himself has summarized with remarkable fairness the prospects for both himself and Long on the eve of that meeting.

" I think it is true to say that my colleagues in the late Government, including the Whips, the keener Tariff Reformers, and many of the younger men, thought that I was the better fitted to fill the vacancy, but I still called myself a Liberal Unionist, I had only joined the Carlton Club a little time before, and the part which I had taken in recent events had certainly aroused some passing antagonism. Long, on the other hand, was a life-time Conservative, a typical country gentleman, and senior to me both in length of service in the House and in Cabinet rank, and he aroused none of the jealousies or doubts which were inseparable from my position." [2]

[1] Chamberlain, Sir Austen, *Politics from Inside*, London, 1936, p. 384. [Italics mine.] In the event the National Union conference of 16th and 17th November, 1911, appears to have been fully satisfied with the method used in selecting the new Leader. They passed the following resolution: " That this Conference desires to convey to the Rt. Hon. A. Bonar Law, M.P., its heartiest congratulations on his election as Leader of the Unionist Party in the House of Commons, and begs to assure him of the loyal and undivided support of every member of the party throughout the country." Cited in *National Union Gleanings,* December, 1911, p. 589.

[2] Cited in Petrie, Sir Charles, *The Life and Letters of Sir Austen Chamberlain,* London, 1939, Vol. I, p. 295. Lord Balcarres, the Chief Whip, told Chamberlain: " The squires wanted (Long) because he was a squire." Cited in Chamberlain, A., *Politics from Inside,* p. 387.

Chamberlain was naturally not unmoved at the possibility that he might succeed Balfour, but he was frankly apprehensive about the prospect.[1] " I wish," he wrote, " there were another Balfour, clearly superior to us, and obviously marked out for the post. How gladly would I play second fiddle to him! But there is no such man at present, and having given my life to this work and got to the position I now hold, I cannot shirk fresh responsibilities or heavier labours if they fall to my lot."[2]

Walter Long for his part was not eager to contest the election with Chamberlain. " We owed so much to his father," he said, somewhat surprisingly, " that it would be proper to pay him the tribute of electing his son."[3] Nevertheless Long's friends brought strong pressure on him to stand, some of them arguing that there was an important section of the party which would not follow a Liberal Unionist like Chamberlain.

Almost at the very moment when Balfour was announcing his resignation to a meeting of the Council of his constituency association on 8th November, Chamberlain and Long met by accident in the Commons.[4] They then retired to Balfour's own room to discuss the situation. Chamberlain proposed that rather than permit the issue to come to a vote at the end of what might be a rather bitter series of nominating speeches, they should both retire in favour of a compromise candidate (if one could be found) on whom everybody could agree. Long immediately fell in with this proposal and when Bonar Law's name was put forward, Chamberlain proposed they should both endorse him. Long readily agreed, saying later that he had done so with " considerable relief, for I did not believe that it was possible for either Chamberlain or myself to reunite the Party in its present condition."[5] Chamberlain was later to console himself in somewhat the same vein. In a letter to his family he wrote: " I cannot have as much or as direct an influence on policy as a follower as I might have had under happier circumstances as leader, but I believe that I can now exert more influence

---

[1] Chamberlain seems to have received the news of Balfour's resignation with genuine regret. "The blow has fallen," he wrote to his family, " and I am as sick as a man can be . . . . (it is) sad news to me whatever happens for I love the man . . . . and to no other man can I feel again what I have felt towards him." Chamberlain, Sir Austen, Politics from Inside, pp. 377-8.

[2] Chamberlain, A., Politics from Inside, p. 381.

[3] Cited in Petrie, Life and Letters of Sir Austen Chamberlain, Vol. I, p. 298.

[4] For Chamberlain's account of this meeting see his Politics from Inside, pp. 384-6.

[5] Petrie, Life and Letters of Sir Austen Chamberlain, Vol. I, p. 302.

on the policy of the Party and do more for the causes I have at heart than if I had been promoted to the first place by a narrow majority after an angry fight leaving bitter memories and unappeased enmities behind it."[1]

The more militant followers of both Chamberlain and Long were exasperated at the compromise. There were cries of "hear, hear" when Chamberlain, in seconding Walter Long's nomination of Bonar Law at the party meeting on 13th November, said: "I know . . . there has been a little feeling that the matter has been taken out of the hands of the Party, and too much settled for you before you came to this gathering." But both Chamberlain and Long strongly urged the meeting to give its wholehearted support to Bonar Law. Since all other candidates had by then withdrawn themselves the meeting had little alternative and the 232 M.P.s present elected Bonar Law as their Leader in the Commons "unanimously and by acclamation." Thus what Sir Charles Petrie has described as the most interesting contest for the leadership in the long history of the Conservative Party was settled at a meeting which began "at mid-day" and terminated (in good time for lunch) at 12.55 p.m.[2] The two strongest contenders for the leadership had withdrawn in favour of a man much their junior in parliamentary experience and public recognition, who had never held Cabinet office. "The fools," said Lloyd George, "have stumbled on their best man by accident."[3] But even King George was, according to Harold Nicolson, "puzzled by the fact that this almost unknown iron merchant from Glasgow should have unanimously

---

[1] Chamberlain, A., *Politics from Inside,* p. 396. Chamberlain was convinced however that had a ballot been taken he would have won (p. 392). On the other hand, Balfour's secretary wrote that Chamberlain's support of Bonar Law was due to the fact that Long "up to some few hours ago appeared to be winning". Cited in Young, Kenneth, *Arthur James Balfour,* p. 316.

[2] The Conservative Chief Whip told Austen Chamberlain in a private letter that "People (and Press too) are urging me to publish the full text of our proceedings. . . . The meeting was so harmonious that with the most subtle malice it will prove difficult to misrepresent the proceedings . . ." However the Chief Whip questioned the wisdom of publication first, because the speeches of Chamberlain and Long in the necessary process of editing would "lose the authenticity as well as the charm." Second, the Chief Whip said, he "would like to retain the vagueness which in the future will magnify rather than depreciate the *personality* of our proceedings." And, finally, to publish the record would "set a precedent which might haunt us in future." Cited in Chamberlain, *Politics from Inside,* p. 400.

[3] Cited in Jones, T., "Bonar Law," *Dictionary of National Biography,* (1922-30), p. 485.

been acclaimed as the Leader of the Conservative Party." [1] Lord Derby, on 16th November 1911, wrote to the King by way of explanation: " Bonar Law is a curious mixture. Never very gay . . . still he has a great sense of humour—a first-class debater—and a good, though not a rousing platform speaker—a great master of figures which he can use to great advantage. He has all the qualities of a great leader except one—and that is he has no personal magnetism and can inspire no man to real enthusiasm." Lord Derby was convinced that when the Conservatives came to fight the Home Rule Bill they would regret having dispensed with the leadership of A. J. Balfour. " And I hope," he added, " that they will be ashamed of themselves." [2]

Bonar Law himself appears to have been suitably impressed by the magnanimity of Chamberlain and Long in stepping down in his favour. Speaking to the National Union annual conference a few days after his election he said: " In the whole personal history of the Conservative party, or indeed in any party, there is nothing of which we have more reason to feel proud than the spirit of self-sacrifice which was shown by Mr. Austen Chamberlain . . . and by Mr. Walter Long . . . . As soon as the proposed solution of the leadership was mentioned to me, I at once saw both of those gentlemen . . . . I should never have undertaken the duties of my new position if I had not known . . . that they had made the proposal not only in the interests of the party, but with a feeling of goodwill and of personal friendship towards myself." [3]

It seems clear that Bonar Law did not share any of the apprehensions of Chamberlain and Long about accepting the Leadership. Chamberlain in his diary records that J. L. Garvin had told him that three days before the Carlton Club meeting he (Garvin) " had been with Law trying his hardest to persuade him not to allow his name to go forward. He reported that he had found Law inflexible, quite determined to get the position if he could and quite satisfied that he was fully qualified for it."

After he had won the leadership, Bonar Law was in the next three years to reveal himself as an able fighter in the Conservative cause;[4] subsequently (after 1916) he worked with Lloyd George in

---

[1] Nicolson, H., *King George the Fifth*, London, 1952, p. 165.

[2] Cited in Nicolson, H., *King George the Fifth*, p. 165. For an analysis of Bonar Law's character and abilities, see Amery, L. S., *My Political Life*, Vol. II, pp. 261–2 and Blake, R., *The Unknown Prime Minister*, *passim*.

[3] *National Union Gleanings*, December, 1911, p. 580.

[4] Within a few days of assuming the leadership Bonar Law denounced Home Rule, the disestablishment of the Welsh Church and free trade

what Baldwin described as "the most perfect partnership in political history".[1] But throughout these years there seems to have been no question of granting Bonar Law the title of Leader of the Party. He remained Leader in the House while Lord Lansdowne led the party in the Lords. The fact that Bonar Law was not made Leader of the Party even after he took a senior Cabinet post in the War Coalition would appear to confirm the principle that the Leader of the Party is elected only after he has been called to the office of Prime Minister.

In March of 1921 while the Conservatives were still in the Lloyd George Coalition, Bonar Law was forced on grounds of ill-health to resign both as Leader of the House of Commons (a ministerial appointment) and as Leader of the Conservative Party in the Commons. Lloyd George appointed Austen Chamberlain to succeed Law as Leader of the House of Commons; the Party Leadership in the House followed almost automatically. A meeting of Conservative M.P.s was held at the Carlton Club on 21st March, 1921; messages were read from several party leaders who were either elder statesmen of the party or who might conceivably have been considered as rivals to Chamberlain. They were unanimous. Arthur Balfour: . . . "I cannot doubt that Austen Chamberlain would be asked to undertake the heavy responsibilities which our Leader has been so unfortunately obliged to lay down."[2] Walter Long: . . . "You are good enough to ask for my views . . . , surely with one voice our party in the House of Commons will acclaim Austen Chamberlain as his successor, and pledge ourselves to give him our most loyal support."[3] Sir Edward Carson: "I understand that Austen Chamberlain will be proposed as leader of the party in the House of Commons, and I can assure you of my warm approval of such a selection if made."[4]

The resolution put before the meeting read as follows: "That this meeting extends a hearty invitation to the Rt. Hon. Austen Chamberlain to assume the Leadership of the Unionist Party in the House of Commons, and in the event of his acceptance, it desires to assure him of its loyalty and support in maintaining the high traditions of the Party and the best interests of the nation as a whole." This resolution was proposed in a speech by Capt. the

---

"with a swinging directness which contrasted sharply with Balfourian subtleties." Jones, T., "Bonar Law," *Dictionary of National Biography* (1922-30), p. 485.

[1] Cited in Jones, T., *Lloyd George*, London, 1951, p. 96.
[2] *Gleanings and Memoranda*, April, 1921, p. 300.
[3] *Ibid.*, p. 300.
[4] *Ibid.*, p. 301.

Rt. Hon. Ernest Pretyman, M.P. His speech throws a remarkably interesting light on the emergence of Leaders within the Conservative Party. Speaking of the 1911 meeting of Conservative M.P.s which had elected Bonar Law, Pretyman said:

" There were many who then held doubts when we were asked to elect a leader of the Unionist Party in the House of Commons. There were doubts in two directions. There were doubts as to whether a comparatively untried man was going to prove himself a real leader, and there were doubts on the more general point as to what was involved in the election of a leader of the party in the House of Commons; and people thought that we needed to elect a leader of our party as a whole. I venture to suggest that any who held that opinion then have since realized that *great leaders of parties are not elected, they are evolved.* Our leader (Bonar Law) who has just laid down his sword for the moment was never elected formally leader of the party at all; he was evolved, and I venture to hope it will not be necessary—and I think it will be a bad day for this or any party to have solemnly to meet to elect a leader. *The leader is there, and we all know it when he is there.*

" There is no necessity either now or at any future time to hold a competition for the leadership of the whole party. But it is necessary immediately that we should elect somebody to lead us in the House of Commons, as we have no leader at the present time, and I feel sure that we shall all agree that it is desirable that we should elect our leader with unanimity. (Hear, hear.) There may be doubts in people's minds as there were ten years ago. It mattered less then than it matters now. If one voice of doubt is raised now it will be seized upon and will be magnified into party disunion at a most critical time. That I sincerely hope we may avoid . . . "[1]

Sir Edward Coates, M.P., in seconding Pretyman's resolution, described himself as " a back-bencher and one of the rank and file "; he said (in part):

"many of us here were present at that meeting in 1911, when there was every chance . . . of (Austen Chamberlain) becoming leader of our party in the House of Commons. But when he saw that there was any trouble ahead he and that grand veteran, Walter Long, stepped aside, and we had our beloved Bonar Law to lead us. Ten years ago Austen Chamberlain had the chance of leadership. During those ten years what has he done? He has been a good, gallant, honest follower of his leader . . . In my opinion it is our duty to put no pebble of discord in his path, but

[1] *Gleanings and Memoranda*, April, 1921, p. 301. [Italics mine.]

it is our full bounden duty, if there is any pebble of discord, to use our united endeavours to sweep it away."[1]

The resolution calling on Chamberlain to lead the party in the Commons was carried unanimously; "the Party meeting was very cordial," wrote Chamberlain, "and (they) gave me a great reception." [2] Yet within 18 months his path was completely blocked by the "pebbles of discord" to which Sir Edward Coates had referred and Chamberlain (not the pebbles) was to be swept away by another meeting of the same Conservative M.P.s who had elected him with such warm unanimity in March, 1921 ; even the very Capt. Pretyman who had moved the resolution calling on him to lead the party was amongst the rebels. But this is to anticipate a later discussion (in Chapter III) of the process by which Conservative leaders have been unseated. Chamberlain resigned the leadership of the party in the Commons following his defeat at the famous meeting of Conservative M.P.s at the Carlton Club on 19th October, 1922. This meeting had rejected Chamberlain's views on the future of the Coalition; he therefore resigned as Conservative Leader, the Coalition fell and Bonar Law (who had played a decisive rôle in defeating Chamberlain at the Carlton Club) was called to form a Conservative Government.

The exact sequence of events on this occasion is of considerable interest. The Carlton Club meeting had taken place on the morning of 19th October, 1922; by 5 p.m. on the same day Lloyd George had tendered his resignation at the Palace. Lord Stamfordham (the King's private secretary) was at once despatched to consult with Bonar Law at his home. There, according to Harold Nicolson's account, Bonar Law explained "that he was not now the official Leader of the Conservative Party and that in any case that party for the moment had broken up. Lord Stamfordham pointed out that unless a new government were constituted immediately and elections held, it would be impossible to ratify the Irish Treaty by 6th December and that the Treaty would therefore lapse. Mr. Bonar Law was with no unnecessary delay re-elected Leader of the Conservative Party, and kissed hands as the new Prime Minister at 5.30 p.m. on Monday, 23rd October." [3]

The party meeting to elect Bonar Law was held in fact on the afternoon of 23rd October at the Carlton Club four days after Lloyd George's resignation and immediately *before* Bonar Law went to the Palace. This is the only occasion in the history of the

[1] *Gleanings and Memoranda*, April, 1921, pp. 302–3.
[2] Cited in Petrie, Sir Charles, *The Life and Letters of Sir Austen Chamberlain*, Vol. II, p. 157.
[3] Nicolson, H., *King George the Fifth*, pp. 370-1.

Conservative leadership in this century in which the title " Leader of the Party " has been conferred on anyone before he has become Prime Minister. The meeting is interesting in another respect. For the first time a meeting to elect a new leader was open not only to all Conservative members of both Houses of Parliament, but also to all prospective Conservative candidates.[1] The latter appear to have been included because of the imminence of the forthcoming election. But the inclusion of prospective candidates was not treated as a binding precedent; they were not invited to the meeting which chose Baldwin a few months later. They have however been invited to the subsequent party meetings called to choose a new leader.

In other respects, the meeting which invited Bonar Law to resume the leadership ran true to form. Lord Curzon, Leader of the Party in the House of Lords, presided. There were the usual messages from elder statesmen of the party and possible rivals. Viscount Long (formerly Walter Long) sent a message saying: " I earnestly hope the whole Party will unite in giving cordial support to our new Chief." [2] Lord Curzon paid tribute to the labours of Austen Chamberlain, but added that this was

> " a great day in the history of our Party, for it is the day on which the Conservative and Unionist Party, which for more than seven years has been loyally willing to subordinate its interests and, to a large extent, to merge its identity in a national party and a national cause, resumes its freedom and *proceeds to re-elect its old leader*." [3]

Continuing, Lord Curzon explained why the re-election of Bonar Law had become inevitable.

> " At that meeting (in the Carlton Club four days ago) from the moment that Mr. Bonar Law had completed his speech there could be little doubt as to what would be the result ; and if I may say so, on his part there was no choice left for him but to accept the burden if it was laid upon his shoulders. But that meeting was confined to members of one House of Parliament ; and to make the action complete it was necessary that the members of the other House should take part in the choice. That is

---

[1] The composition of the meeting at the Carlton Club on 23rd October, 1922, was as follows: 152 members of the House of Lords, 220 members of the House of Commons, and 67 parliamentary candidates. Smellie, K. B., *A Hundred Years of English Government*, London, 1950, p. 232.

[2] *Gleanings and Memoranda*, November, 1922, p. 496.

[3] *Gleanings and Memoranda*, November, 1922, p. 496. [Italics mine.] The chairman's statement, it will be noted, completely pre-judges the issue; it is a striking evidence of the extent to which meetings such as this are no more than a formality.

why we are all here to-day, members of the Conservative and Unionist Party in both Houses of Parliament and the candidates who are standing for the approaching election, so that that invitation which will presently be extended to him shall come from those who have a right to speak for the Party as a whole."

Lord Curzon then read the resolution (" which I have been asked to move "): " that this meeting extends a hearty invitation to the Rt. Hon. A. Bonar Law to resume the Leadership of the Unionist Party, and in the event of his acceptance it desires to assure him of its loyal support in maintaining the high traditions of the Party in the best interests of the nation as a whole." In speaking to his own resolution Lord Curzon added:

> " We invite Mr. Bonar Law once again to become our leader, not merely because of his services in the past, great and unforgettable as they are; not merely because during the last year and a half we have all been waiting, if his health improved, to see him return to the scene of his former triumphs ; nor again, although there is much point in this, merely because we regard him as the best and most faithful exponent and spokesman of our views ; but because we see in him, as I believe the nation sees in him, the kind of man which it wants for the crisis with which we are at present confronted. We see in him a man with a strong sense of public duty, a man who is utterly innocent of self-seeking, a man who possesses just those gifts and qualities which the nation requires in its trusted leaders."

Significantly, the resolution was seconded by another member of the party whose star had lately risen with startling rapidity, Stanley Baldwin, M.P. The resolution was carried unanimously as was a vote of thanks to Austen Chamberlain for the work he had done as Leader of the Party in the Commons. Bonar Law in his acceptance speech spoke warmly of the work of his predecessor: " I am convinced," he said, " that the greatest political genius who ever lived could not have avoided the difficulties into which Mr. Chamberlain fell." Bonar Law then emphasized that the Carlton Club meetings of a few days ago assured that the Conservative Party would remain united; he explained that this was not the occasion for an elaborate declaration of policy, contenting himself with the promise that his administration would not be " a Government purely of reaction ". Finally the new Leader closed with a warning about the uncertain condition of his health.[1]

In the election that followed Bonar Law's Government was returned with a comfortable majority. But within seven months the Prime Minister's health had so far deteriorated as to make his

[1] *Gleanings and Memoranda*, November, 1922, pp. 496-500.

resignation inevitable. By common consent the leading contenders for the succession to the leadership were Curzon and Baldwin, the two men who had moved and seconded the resolution offering the leadership to Bonar Law at the meeting on 25th October. Each had impressive claims. The former, Lord Curzon, had been, of course, one of the great pro-consuls of the modern British Empire;[1] in the Bonar Law Government he had retained the office of Foreign Secretary which he had held under the Coalition. When Bonar Law on medical advice had left in late April, 1923, for a sea voyage, Lord Curzon had been appointed Deputy Prime Minister. It is not surprising that Curzon himself assumed that his claim to the succession was irresistible.

Baldwin until recently had been a comparatively obscure back-bench politician.[2] After undistinguished service on the Worcester-shire County Council he had virtually inherited a seat in Parliament (at age 41) following his father's death in 1908. In the next six years he spoke only five times. He was well liked but little known. G. M. Young quotes Asquith's judgment: " One of the nicest fellows in the House," and adds Baldwin's own judgment: " No use to God or man." In 1917 Bonar Law, then Chancellor of the Exchequer, had made Baldwin his Financial Secretary to the Treasury largely, according to G. M. Young's account, because of the Chancellor's affection for Stanley Baldwin's late father.[3] After four years in this junior office (aged 50-54) he served briefly as President of the Board of Trade in the latter stages of the Coalition Government. On Baldwin's appointment to the Board of Trade Bonar Law (then in temporary retirement) wrote to him: " You have what I am told was one of my defects, too much modesty; so

[1] Ronaldshay, Earl of, *The Life of Lord Curzon,* and Nicolson, Harold, *Curzon, The Last Phase,* London, 1934.

[2] Speaking of his own youth with what can be described either as frankness or becoming modesty, Baldwin once wrote: " I thought I was making a modest success on my own, but I have *never* made any real impression on a woman. I may have had a modest success for an evening if the party was particularly dull, but to be remembered next day, much less next week, NEVER." Cited in Young, G. M., *Stanley Baldwin,* London, 1952, p. 23. For other interpretations of Baldwin, see Steed, Wickham, *The Real Stanley Baldwin,* London, 1930; Wylie, A. G., *Stanley Baldwin,* London, 1926; Baldwin, A. W., *My Father: The True Story.* See also Churchill, R., *Lord Derby,* London, 1959, Chapter XIII, " The Advent of Baldwin".

[3] Lord Beaverbrook, an intimate friend of Bonar Law, has a slightly different account: " As a matter of fact I recommended Mr. Baldwin to Bonar Law as his Parliamentary Secretary—the first step in his upward career." Beaverbrook, Lord, *Politicians and the Press,* London, (*n.d.*) p. 62. For another account see Steed, W., *The Real Stanley Baldwin,* p. 26.

my advice to you is to get rid of that defect as soon as possible." [1]
As President of the Board of Trade, Baldwin was popular with
businessmen (" they felt he was one of themselves "). In the House
he showed patience, good humour and an unexpected readiness in
answering questions.[2] Baldwin, according to Lloyd George's account,
rarely opened his mouth in the Cabinet. There is no way of knowing, as Wickham Steed has commented, whether he was ruminating
or merely inarticulate. But when at length he spoke and acted—
outside the Cabinet—his speech and action were decisive.[3]

Baldwin had decided by the autumn of 1922 that it was urgently
necessary that his party should be detached from the Coalitions
Whether in arriving at this decision Baldwin had calculated his own
prospects, whether he ever reckoned " how many steps were between him and the highest place ", his principal biographer is unable
to decide. Baldwin had said on one occasion: " I should like to
be Chancellor of the Exchequer; that is the limit of my ambitions." [4]

He had achieved that " limit " within a matter of months. His
speech at the Carlton Club meeting of 19th October, 1922, along
with the stand taken by Bonar Law, was a decisive factor in the
downfall of both Austen Chamberlain and the Coalition Government. In the new Bonar Law administration, Baldwin was
Chancellor of the Exchequer, and in the view of *The Times* parliamentary correspondent of the day he was " in some respects the
outstanding personality " in the Government. Certainly he was
the best liked man in the House of Commons.[5] When Bonar Law
went on his cruise leaving Lord Curzon as Deputy Prime Minister,
Baldwin became Leader of the House of Commons. On the Prime
Minister's return to England it was found that his health was
deteriorating rapidly and on 20th May, 1923, he resigned.

When a Prime Minister resigns through personal reasons (other
than his defeat in the Commons) it is of course for the monarch,
after he has taken advice, to decide who shall be called as his
successor. As Harold Nicolson has pointed out, " there is seldom
any doubt who among possible successors has the confidence of the
party in power."[6] In addition the monarch may ask the advice of
the retiring Prime Minister if the latter is in a position to give it.
But in this case there was genuine room for doubt as to which of

[1] Quoted in Young, G. M., *Stanley Baldwin*, p. 27.
   Young, G. M., *op. cit.*, p. 28.
[2] Steed, W., *The Real Stanley Baldwin*, p. 33.
[4] Young, G. M., *op. cit.*, pp. 30–1.
[5] Cited in Steed, W., *op. cit.*, p. 42.
[6] Nicolson, H., *King George the Fifth*, p. 376.

the main contenders was most likely to win the confidence of the Conservative Party in Parliament, and the retiring Prime Minister, who was dying of cancer of the throat, was too ill to discuss the matter with the King.[1]

The King did discuss the issue with a number of his privy councillors including among others Lord Salisbury, the Lord President of the Council, and Lord Balfour. The latter urged that despite the fact that Baldwin's public career had been " more or less uneventful and without any signs of special gifts or exceptional ability ",[2] he should be appointed for one over-riding reason: the Prime Minister ought to be in the House of Commons.[3] The King decided " on the strength of this advice, and in conformity with his personal judgment ", to send for Baldwin on 22nd May, 1923.[4]

This was a savage blow for Curzon who had convinced himself that he was bound to be called to the Palace. When the King's Private Secretary came to tell him that the King had decided to call

---

[1] This interpretation is based on Nicolson's *King George the Fifth*. He quotes (p. 377) a memorandum by the King's Private Secretary saying: " owing to the condition of Mr. Bonar Law's health, His Majesty was deprived of consultation with him."

G. M. Young has a different account in his *Stanley Baldwin*, pp. 48-9: " By constitutional usage an outgoing Prime Minister cannot proffer advice on the choice of a successor, but he must give his advice if asked. Bonar Law was not asked. ' If I were,' he was reported to have said, ' I am afraid it would have to be Baldwin.' To Curzon he wrote: ' I understand it is not customary for the King to ask his Prime Minister to recommend his successor in circumstances like the present and I presume he will not do so." But see also Blake, R., *The Unknown Prime Minister*, pp. 508-27, for the fullest account of these events.

[2] Cited in Nicolson, H., *King George the Fifth*, p. 376.

[3] *Ibid.*, pp. 376-7. L. S. Amery has another account of these events. He writes: " King George V's decision in 1923 to send for Mr. Baldwin instead of Lord Curzon (Mr. Bonar Law declining to make any recommendation) is often referred to as having been the natural consequence of the latter's being in the House of Lords and so under modern conditions disqualified. As a matter of fact Lord Curzon's appointment was practically settled when two junior Members of the Cabinet, the late Lord Bridgeman and myself, intervened with Lord Stamfordham and urged reconsideration in favour of Mr. Baldwin, as likely to be more acceptable to his colleagues and to the rank and file of the Party. Lord Balfour, who was called up from the country, agreed and suggested Lord Curzon's peerage as a sound reason for passing him over. The final decision was, to the best of my belief, made mainly on the issue of the personal acceptability of the two candidates. If a constitutional precedent was created, it was largely as the *ex post facto* cover for a decision taken on other grounds." Amery, L. S., " The Nature of British Parliamentary Government," in *Parliament: A Survey*, London, (1952), p. 62. See also Amery's *My Political Life*, Vol. II, pp. 259-60.

[4] Nicolson, H., *King George the Fifth*, pp. 376-7.

Baldwin, Curzon replied that this " was the greatest blow and slur upon him and his public career, now at its summit, that he could have ever received." He protested vehemently against the principle implied in the King's decision—that no member of the House of Lords could be Prime Minister; . . . " with that protest," he told Lord Stamfordham, " (I will) retire from public life."[1]

But on 28th May (six days after Baldwin became Prime Minister) Lord Curzon presided over a meeting of Unionist members of both Houses of Parliament and moved a resolution that Stanley Baldwin " be elected Leader of the Conservative and Unionist Party ". Rather pointedly, Curzon remarked in the course of his speech:

> " In a sense it may be said that the choice of Mr. Stanley Baldwin as Leader of the whole Conservative Party has been determined by the action of the King. But we all felt, and I am sure you will agree, that it was right that the choice of the Sovereign should be ratified and confirmed by the vote of the entire Party, so that Mr. Baldwin in taking up his task may feel that he is a leader who is acclaimed by every section of the Party . . . "

Then Curzon undertook an analysis of the virtues of this man who had snatched the highest prize from him:

> " . . . what manner of man is it whom the King has delighted to honour and whom we are about to accept, I hope, for our leader? The rise of Mr. Stanley Baldwin to the highest position in public life has been one of phenomenal, and I believe quite unexampled, rapidity. Only a few years ago he was a private serving in the ranks in the House of Commons, and I daresay there were not many, except among his personal friends, who saw the field-marshal's baton peep out of the corners of his knapsack." Nevertheless he was . . . " a man of shrewd and vigorous intellect, great independence of character . . . and an infinity of courage. Never did he show those qualities more than in the troublous days of last October, when you will recollect it was largely his action and his speeches, both in the Carlton Club and in this hall, which gave the push to a fabric already toppling to its fall."

Other achievements were listed by Lord Curzon and then he added:

> " . . . lastly (I breathe this almost *sotto voce*), Mr. Baldwin possesses the supreme and indispensable qualification of not being a peer . . . "[2]

A back-bencher seconded Lord Curzon's motion and Baldwin was elected by acclamation.

[1] Cited in Nicolson, H., *King George the Fifth*, pp. 378-9.
[2] *Gleanings and Memoranda*, June, 1923, pp. 633-4.

Baldwin spoke of his predecessor, Bonar Law, in moving terms ("I love the man") and concluded with a plea for party unity. Referring to the old dispute with Austen Chamberlain and the former coalitionists he said: "There may be symptoms in the Press for a few days of a fire burning up, but it is a fire that will die down if no fuel is added. There will not be a faggot thrown on it by me, and I trust all members of the party will avoid any discussions at this moment that may prevent or delay, let me say a final and complete reunion inside the party which I am convinced can be brought about at no very distant date . . . " Curzon continued to serve under Baldwin;[1] Austen Chamberlain eighteen months later agreed to do likewise. There was to be trouble enough from other quarters later on, but Baldwin was firmly in the saddle, surprisingly firmly when one reflects on the precipitous way he had got into it. As he himself later put it in a letter to Asquith: "The position of leader came to me when I was inexperienced, before I was really fitted for it, by a succession of curious chances that could not have been foreseen. I had never expected it: I was in no way trained for it."[2] Yet an opposition Liberal paper commented a few months later: "The great office of Prime Minister fits Mr. Baldwin like a glove . . . . A man little known to the general public called suddenly . . . . is found to be entirely adequate to the exacting rôle. The remarkable evolution of Mr. Baldwin's character and his rapid growth in authority is the outstanding feature of the Session."[3]

The emergence of Baldwin's successor was a much less spectacular process. Neville Chamberlain was first elected to the Commons in 1918; at about that time he wrote: "My career is broken. How can a man of nearly 50, entering the House with this stigma upon him, hope to achieve anything?" The stigma was of course his failure during his brief service as Minister of National Service in the first Lloyd George Government.[4] Subsequently he served as Postmaster-General in the Bonar Law Governments, and then despite

---

[1] In accepting Baldwin's invitation to remain at the Foreign Office, Curzon wrote: "As my retirement at this moment might be thought to involve distrust in your administration, which would be a quite unfounded suspicion, I will for the present continue at the Foreign Office." Cited in Young, G. M., *Stanley Baldwin*, p. 49.

[2] Cited in Young, G. M., *Stanley Baldwin*, p. 52. Young adds by way of comment: "(Baldwin's) name was associated with no famous law, no national debate; he had left no mark on any department; he had never really fought an election. He was Prime Minister because none better could be thought of" (pp. 53–4).

[3] The *Daily News*, 3rd August, 1923.

[4] Lloyd George in his *War Memoirs* (London, 1934, pp. 1367-8) gives this explanation of Chamberlain's failure; the task required "a great breadth and boldness of conception, a remorseless energy and thoroughness

his protest that he had " no gift for figures " he was moved suddenly by Baldwin to the Exchequer. During the 1924-29 Government Chamberlain served with distinction at a lesser post, the Ministry of Health. After the party had returned to opposition (1929-31) he superseded Churchill as the Conservative's main financial critic when the latter broke with his own front bench over Imperial affairs. Thereafter Chamberlain returned briefly to the Ministry of Health following the formation of the National Government in 1931 and on the re-organization of the Government after the election of that year he succeeded Snowden as Chancellor of the Exchequer. During the '30s Chamberlain grew steadily in stature and when Baldwin, old and weary, decided to retire it seems to have been accepted by all concerned that Chamberlain would succeed automatically to the premiership and the leadership of the party.

Yet, until the closing stages of his apprenticeship, Chamberlain seems to have moved almost reluctantly towards the leadership. " (I) have done nothing to increase my reputation with the public," he wrote in his diary in December, 1919, " (and) at present I feel very little inclination to try." [1] The next year he wrote " . . . I believe I have a steadily growing position as a man of judgment among M.P.s," but added " . . . I have plenty of friendly acquaintances in the House, but no one whose views accord sufficiently closely with my own to tempt me into joining forces." [2] Reflecting on the events of the following year (1921) he wrote: " A very trying year. I have spoken more often this year than last, but my speeches have rather been solid contributions to information than debating successes, which are really what count with the House. But indeed I feel less and less inclined to take office, even if it were offered, and I certainly shall never go out of my way to get it. Sometimes I wish I were out of the House altogether . . . " [3] When offered the Chairmanship of the Party Organization in 1922 he declined on the grounds that it was a " soulless job," adding that for party " I care very little." [4] It was not until that same year indeed that

of execution, and for the exercise of supreme tact." But Neville Chamberlain, he said, was " a man of rigid competency . . . . lost in an emergency or in creative tasks at any time," a man with " . . . A vein of self-sufficient obstinacy." This may be an unfair explanation of Chamberlain's failure on this occasion but it does underline some of Chamberlain's weaknesses which were later to prove fatal when he assumed supreme political power.

[1] Feiling, K., *The Life of Neville Chamberlain*, p. 88.

[2] *Ibid.*, p. 89.

[3] *Ibid.*, p. 92.

[4] *Ibid.*, p. 90. See also Macleod, Iain, *Neville Chamberlain*, London, 1961, Chapter 8.

" he cross(ed) the party rubicon by joining the Carlton Club." [1]
Subsequently (in 1930-31) Chamberlain did accept the office of
Chairman of the Party Organization, but only on the understanding
that it would be for a limited period during which he undertook
a major re-organization of the party machine. When Baldwin's
leadership was so vigorously challenged during the period 1930-31,
Neville Chamberlain stood by him and earned the gratitude of his
Leader. But Chamberlain was still a man of limited enthusiasms;
Lord Beaverbrook thought it necessary to warn him: " you, like
the late Bonar Law, always understate your case. That is part of
your character. But you do not make headway on this understate-
ment. You make it on the character. So do not be deceived." [2]

When Baldwin began to tire of the turmoil of party activity in
the mid- '30s Chamberlain took on more and more of the burdens.
He stimulated the work of research and publicity in the party's
Central Office; he arranged meetings of Conservative Ministers to
underline the independent identity of the party within the National
Government. Chamberlain grew, too, in self-confidence. He wrote
to his sisters during 1934: " There are some who think I am over-
cautious—timid, Amery calls it—humdrum, commonplace, and
unenterprising. But I know that charge is groundless, or I should
not have been the one to produce the Unemployment Assistance
Board, the policy of regulation of production now generally
adopted, the slum and over-crowding policy now accepted by the
Minister of Health, the sending of commissioners to the derelict
areas." [3] But Chamberlain was still very much aware of the shortcomings of his own personality as far as politics was concerned;
when Hilton Young retired in 1935, Chamberlain wrote to his
wife that Young had received little gratitude for much good work
" because, like me, he can't unbutton ". By the autumn of 1935
Chamberlain had become what Churchill [4] was to call " the pack-
horse " of the National Government. Yet at times he still seriously
contemplated quitting politics altogether and, when he asked himself why he did not do so, he supposed the answer was " I know no
one I would trust to hold the balance between rigid orthodoxy and
a fatal disregard of sound principles and the rights of posterity."
In any case Chamberlain decided it was not " as if I had ambitions

---

[1] Feiling, K., *The Life of Neville Chamberlain*, p. 88.
[2] Lord Beaverbrook to Neville Chamberlain, 7th June, 1934. Cited
Ibid., p. 121.
[3] *Ibid.*, pp. 235-6.
[4] Churchill, W. S., *The Second World War*, Vol. I, p. 172. Churchill notes
that Chamberlain considered his comment to be a compliment.

which might be ruined by present unpopularity. I believe (Stanley Baldwin) will stay on for the duration, and by next election I shall be 70 and shan't care much, I daresay, for the strenuous life of leader, even if someone else hasn't overtaken me before then." [1] But early in February, 1936, Baldwin began to speak privately to Chamberlain of retiring during 1938; in the event he did so on 28th May, 1937, following the Coronation of King George VI; "loaded with honours and enshrined in public esteem," as Churchill has put it, "(Baldwin) laid down his heavy task and retired in dignity and silence to his Worcestershire home." [2] In the previous year when Baldwin had taken a long rest on his doctor's advice, Chamberlain had deputized for him. On 2nd October, 1936, (at Baldwin's request) he had also given the address normally delivered by the Leader of the Party to the mass meeting immediately following the annual conference of the National Union; "the main result" as Chamberlain noted in his diary 7th October, 1936 "appears to be a general acceptance of my position as heir-apparent." [3] In March, 1937, he wrote " . . . I should not greatly care if I were never to be Prime Minister. But when I think of Father and Austen, and reflect that less than three months of time, and no individual, stands between me and that office, I wonder whether Fate has some dark secret in store to carry out her ironies to the end." [4]

On the day Baldwin resigned as Prime Minister, 28th May, 1937, Chamberlain kissed hands as his successor.[5] As Churchill wrote later: "There was no doubt who his successor should be. Mr. Neville Chamberlain had, as Chancellor of the Exchequer, not only done the main work of the Government for five years past, but was the ablest and most forceful Minister, with high abilities and an historic name." [6] But writing in his own diary Chamberlain echoed phrases used by Baldwin on a similar occasion fourteen years earlier: "it (the Leadership) has come to me without my raising a finger to obtain it, because there is no one else "; (then, an afterthought) "and perhaps because I have not made enemies by looking after myself rather than the common cause." [7]

[1] Extract from Diary for 8th December, 1935, quoted in Feiling, K., *The Life of Neville Chamberlain,* pp. 275-6.

[2] Churchill, W. S., *The Second World War,* Vol. I, p. 16.

[3] Feiling, K., *The Life of Neville Chamberlain,* p. 287.

[4] *Ibid.,* p. 294.

[5] There is no firm evidence as to whether Baldwin advised the King to call Neville Chamberlain, but there is no reason to doubt that he must have been consulted; nor is there any doubt as to what his recommendation must have been.

[6] Churchill, W. S., *The Second World War,* Vol. I, p. 172.

[7] Feiling, K., *The Life of Neville Chamberlain,* p. 294.

Three days after Chamberlain became Prime Minister the party meeting was held to confer on him the leadership. The distinctive feature of this meeting was its composition. Traditionally the Leader of the Party had been elected by a joint assembly of those peers and M.P.s taking the Conservative whip. In 1922 at the meeting called to offer the leadership of the party to Bonar Law, it will be recalled that prospective Conservative candidates in the forthcoming election had also been invited to attend; apparently because an election was not believed to be imminent the candidates were not invited to attend the meeting in May, 1923, which elected Baldwin. But for the meeting called to elect Chamberlain invitations were sent not only to Conservative peers and M.P.s but also to all prospective candidates and members of the Executive Committee of the National Union.[1] The meeting was presided over by Lord Halifax and the resolution in favour of electing Chamberlain to the leadership was moved by Lord Derby. Interestingly enough, the seconder of the resolution was none other than Winston Churchill, M.P.; in three years' time he was to succeed the man who on that day was elected to the leadership by acclamation.

Winston Churchill was the seventh Leader of the Conservative Party since Disraeli. It would be pointless to recall here the details of his political career since he first entered Parliament in 1900. As Conservative, then Liberal, then Conservative again he had by 1929 held most of the great cabinet offices except Foreign Secretary and Prime Minister. During the period 1929-31 he had broken with the Conservative Party primarily over their Imperial policy.[2] Thereafter his points of difference with the party leadership had widened on a number of issues, notably foreign policy and defence. He had found Baldwin a " wiser, more comprehending personality (than Chamberlain), but without detailed executive capacity . . . . I should have found it easier to work with Baldwin, as I knew him, than with Chamberlain," Churchill has since written, " but neither of them had any wish to work with me except in the last resort." After Chamberlain assumed the leadership, he adds, " our relations continued to be cool, easy and polite

---

[1] *Politics in Review,* April-June 1941, p. 121. It is not possible to establish with certainty on whose authority the membership of the meeting was so extended but it is entirely likely that Chamberlain himself, because of his personal interest in recent years in the party organization outside Parliament, may have recommended this action to the Party Whips who were responsible for calling the meeting.

[2] " So far as I could see," Churchill has remarked sadly, " Mr. Baldwin felt that the times were too far gone for any robust assertion of British Imperial greatness . . . " Churchill, W. S., *The Second World War,* Vol. I. p. 26.

both in public and private."[1] Chamberlain as Prime Minister was in many ways a more lonely, remote figure than Baldwin; he had not, as Baldwin had, someone like himself as second-in-command. Chamberlain was reluctant, too, to give any indication of his own preference among the possible candidates for the succession to the leadership. In any case, as the international crisis deepened, Chamberlain could not entertain the thought of stepping down from the leadership. In 1939 he wrote: " I believe that if I am allowed, I can steer this country through the next few years out of the war zone into peace and reconstruction. But an interruption would be fatal, and I should have then to leave it to someone else to try some quite different line." [2] The interruption, (which did not prove fatal) came in May, 1940. In the winter of 1939-40, Churchill had already proved himself the shining figure in Chamberlain's dull, lack-lustre Cabinet; yet there was little evidence that the Prime Minister had any intention of making full use of Churchill's talents. The disasters of the campaign in Norway led the opposition to demand a debate on the war situation on 7th/8th May, and it was soon evident that the tide had set in heavily against Chamberlain. He nevertheless dared to call for a vote of confidence. " No government," he said, " can prosecute a war efficiently unless it has public and parliamentary support. I accept the challenge . . . and I call upon my friends." Churchill (as he himself admits) [3] had " volunteered to wind up the Debate". He belaboured the opposition with all his might (" I did this with good heart when I thought of their mistakes and dangerous pacifism in former years "); this drove the Labour benches to wild anger. But clearly their anger was directed more against the Prime Minister than against his stubborn defender. The decisive blows had come, of course, from Chamberlain's own back-benchers. L. S. Amery, a friend and colleague of the Prime Minister over many years, borrowed Cromwell's ringing words to the Long Parliament: " You have sat too long here for any good you have been doing. Depart, I say and let us have done with you. In the name of God, go! "

---

[1] Churchill, W. S., *The Second World War*, Vol. I, pp. 173-4. It is interesting that Churchill, in describing his relations with Chamberlain, makes no reference to the fact that he seconded the resolution offering the leadership of the party to him. Nor does he mention this incident in March, 1938: " That month a round-robin, collected haphazard from some 150 Conservative members who chanced to be in the House, in wishing (Neville Chamberlain) joy of his 69th birthday *assured him of their wholehearted confidence;* the fourth name on that list was that of Churchill." [Italics mine.] Feiling, K., *The Life of Neville Chamberlain*, p. 306.

[2] Feiling, K., *The Life of Neville Chamberlain*, p. 412.

[3] Churchill, W. S., *The Second World War*, Vol. I, p. 521.

When the division bells rang it was clear that Chamberlain's "call to his friends" had fallen on many pairs of deaf ears. The Government's majority, which was normally more than 200 over all other parties combined, fell in this division to 81; 33 Conservatives voted with the opposition, while 60 more abstained. Strangely, Chamberlain seemed able to grasp only part of the significance of this result. He now recognized there must be a National Government, but his first move was to ask Labour if they would serve under him. Rebuffed, he then hoped momentarily that Halifax might prove acceptable.

Churchill tells how he and Halifax were together called on 10th May to discuss the matter with Chamberlain:

> "(Chamberlain) told us that he was satisfied that it was beyond his power to form a National Government . . . . The question therefore was whom he should advise the King to send for after his own resignation had been accepted."

Churchill adds that he himself remained silent and

> "a very long pause ensued. It certainly seemed longer than the two minutes which one observes in the commemorations of Armistice Day. Then at length Halifax spoke. He said that he felt that his position as a Peer, out of the House of Commons, would make it very difficult for him to discharge the duties of Prime Minister in a war like this . . . by the time he had finished it was clear that the duty would fall upon me—had in fact fallen upon me."[1]

Later that day the King called Churchill and in a broadcast that evening Chamberlain said: "In the afternoon of to-day it was apparent that the essential unity could be secured under another Prime Minister, though not myself . . . . you and I must (now) rally behind our new leader . . . "[2] Churchill's first act on returning from the Palace was to write Chamberlain to thank him for his promised support. The letter contains a significant phrase: "With your help and counsel, and with the support of *the great party of which you are the Leader*, I trust that I shall succeed."[3]

Thus for the first time a Conservative M.P. became Prime Minister without automatically assuming the office of Leader of the Party. It was agreed between Churchill and Chamberlain in an exchange of letters that this arrangement was advisable in the interests of unity; there were three parties in the new National Government and it was apparently at first considered preferable

[1] Churchill, W. S., *The Second World War*, Vol. I, pp. 523-4.
[2] *The Times*, 11th May, 1940.
[3] Cited in Feiling, K., *The Life of Neville Chamberlain*, p. 442. [Italics mine.]

that the Prime Minister should not carry the title of Leader of any one of them. Churchill's letter to Chamberlain ended: " The relations of perfect confidence which have grown up between us makes this division of duties and responsibilities very agreeable to me." Keith Feiling records Chamberlain's private comment to the effect that this arrangement was " essential, if Winston was to have wholehearted support", as many Conservatives were sore and some were disappointed.[1]

During the summer of 1940 Chamberlain became seriously ill; on 9th September, after a major operation, he wrote in his diary: " . . . I have still to adjust myself to the new life of a partially crippled man, which is what I am. Any ideas which may have been in my mind about possibilities of further political activity, and even a possibility of another Premiership after the war, have gone." [2] But Chamberlain apparently remained convinced of his own authority within the Conservative Party. Later in September he wrote in his diary: " If I did get well enough, I could give (Churchill) more help personally, and ensure him more support politically, than anyone else." [3] And on 14th October, he wrote in a letter to the Archbishop of Canterbury: " Only a few months ago I saw no limit to my physical strength and endurance and until the Norway withdrawal (which of course was right) I seemed to have an unshakable hold over the House of Commons. (If my health had permitted) I could have survived my political fall and perhaps come back like others before me." [4]

Meanwhile even before Chamberlain's death on 9th November the leadership of the party had been formally transferred to Churchill. On 30th September, six weeks before he died, Chamberlain resigned from the Government; several days later he gave up the leadership of the party.[5] On 9th October a party meeting was called to name the new Leader. As in 1937, the meeting was attended by Peers and M.P.s who received the Conservative Whip, by prospective candidates who had been adopted by constituency associations, and by members of the Executive Committee of the National Union of Conservative and Unionist Associations from England and Wales, Scotland and Northern Ireland.[6] Lord Halifax, the Leader of the Party in the House of Lords, presided [7] and moved

[1] Cited in Feiling, K., *The Life of Neville Chamberlain*, p. 444.
[2] *Ibid.*, p. 450.
[3] *Ibid.*, p. 451.
[4] *Ibid.*, p. 455.
[5] *The Times*, 4th October, 1940.
[6] *The Times*, 10th October, 1940.
[7] Churchill later wrote : " Lord Halifax, who might have been an alternative choice of the party if I had declined, himself proposed the motion . . . " Churchill, W. S., *The Second World War*. Vol. II, p. 439.

two resolutions; one thanked Chamberlain for the " eminent services that he has rendered to the nation " and expressed the hope that " having laid down his office, he (might) rapidly recover his health and enjoy the rest which he has so well earned." The other resolution proposed that Churchill " be elected Leader of the Conservative and Unionist Party " and promised him loyal support. Sir George Courthope, M.P., one of the senior back-benchers of the party, seconded the resolutions and they were supported by Sir Eugene Ramsden, M.P., Chairman of the Executive Committee of the National Union. The resolutions were carried unanimously and as Churchill entered the hall he was given " a tumultuous reception, the meeting rising to its feet and cheering enthusiastically." [1] His speech was more than the platitudinous affair which such occasions had often produced in the past. He explained that before he had decided to accept the position he had asked himself two questions. " The first is whether the leadership of a great party is compatible with the position I hold as Prime Minister of an Administration composed of, and officially supported by, all parties." He admitted there were arguments both ways but added:

> " Considering, however, that I have to be in daily relation, in matters of much domestic consequence, with the leaders of the other two parties who are serving in the Government, I felt that it would be more convenient that I should be able to speak for the Conservative Party with direct and first-hand knowledge of the general position which they occupy upon fundamental issues, and also to speak with their authority. It also seemed to me that as leader of the House of Commons at a time when the Conservative Party enjoys a very large majority over all other parties, and when, owing to the war and grave dangers and peculiar conditions amid which we live, no General Election is possible, I could discharge my task with less difficulty if I were in formal relation with the majority of the members of the House of Commons." [2]

Subsequently in his war memoirs Churchill considerably sharpened the argument he advanced in October, 1940. " I should have found it impossible to conduct the war," he wrote, " if I had had to procure the agreement . . . not only of the Leaders of the two minority parties but of the Leader of the Conservative majority. Whoever had been chosen and whatever his self-denying virtues *he would have had the real political power.* For me there would have been only the executive responsibility. These arguments," Churchill added, " do not apply in the same degree in time of peace; but I

[1] *The Times,* 10th October, 1940.
[2] *Ibid.*

do not feel I could have borne such a trial successfully in war."[1] Churchill elaborates a further argument as to why he felt he ought to accept the leadership of the party ; . . . " in dealing with the Labour and Liberal Parties in the Coalition it was always an important basic fact that as Prime Minister and at this time Leader of the largest party I did not depend upon their votes and I could in the ultimate issue carry on in Parliament without them."

A review of the rise to the leadership of the Conservative Party of the nine men who have held the office since Disraeli[2] shows that the process has few parallels in the struggle for power that goes on within other democratic political organizations. The most striking fact, of course, is that each Leader has been elected by acclamation; no ballot, nor any formal contest of any kind, has ever taken place. Indeed, except in the case of the election of Bonar Law in 1911, no other possible contenders (apart from the man ultimately chosen) appear even to have been canvassed. When in 1911, two strong rivals did emerge and a clash (followed by a ballot) seemed inevitable, both withdrew in favour of an apparently weaker and lesser known candidate; these remarkable proceedings reached their culmination in a meeting at which the two strongest rivals moved and seconded the nomination of the victor. In objecting to the suggestion that he should publish the verbatim record of these proceedings it will be remembered that the Conservative Chief Whip used the fascinating argument that he " would like to retain the vagueness which in the future will magnify rather than depreciate the *personality* of our proceedings." [3] That these proceedings have (to use the Chief Whip's word) " *personality* " there is not a shadow of doubt. It will be noted that at each of the meetings called to elect a new Leader it appears to be established practice that the most important of his possible rivals (as well as the elder statesmen of the party) should either send messages urging his election or else they should move or second the resolution offering him the leadership.

[1] Churchill, W. S., *The Second World War,* Vol. II, p. 439. [Italics mine.] Churchill's view that whoever was chosen Leader of the Party "would have the real political power", greater even than that of the Prime Minister, throws an extremely interesting light on the importance he attached to what might otherwise seem to be the routine process by which the Conservative Party has traditionally conferred the party leadership on whoever emerges as a Conservative Prime Minister. It also seems to suggest (although there is no other evidence to confirm this) that Mr. Churchill had not been satisfied with the arrangement which was in operation between 10th May and 9th October, 1940, whereby Chamberlain retained the leadership of the party while Churchill held the office of Prime Minister.

[2] For the emergence of Eden and Macmillan see pp. 582 ff. below.

[3] See p. 31, note 3 above.

TABLE 1

LEADERS OF THE CONSERVATIVE PARTY
1885–1955

Name	Length of service in Parliament before elected to leadership*	Age at election to leadership	Length of service as Leader
The Marquis of Salisbury (1830–1903)	28 years (15 in Commons) (13 in Lords)	51	18 years
A. J. Balfour (1848–1930)	26 years	54	9 years
Bonar Law (1858–1923)	11 years	53	11 years
Austen Chamberlain (1863–1937)	29 years	58	1½ years
Stanley Baldwin (1867–1947)	15 years	55	14 years
Neville Chamberlain (1869–1940)	19 years	68	3 years
Winston Churchill (1874–)	38 years	66	15 years
Average	24 years	58	8 years 9 months

* " Leadership " refers here to leadership of the Conservative Party in the Commons or leadership of the party as a whole. Cf. p. 23, note 1 above.

Captain Pretyman, M.P., appears to be one of the few people ever to try to put into words a description of the strange process by which the Conservatives choose their Leaders: " great leaders of parties are not elected, they are evolved . . . I think it will be a bad day [when we] . . . have solemnly to meet to elect a leader. The leader is there, and we all know it when he is there." This is of course precisely the point: none of the nine leaders was in any serious sense " elected ";[1] each of them was " evolved ". The Leaders served on the average 24 years in Parliament before their election to the leadership;[2] each of them had already emerged (except in the case of Bonar Law in 1911) as the most powerful figure in their own party in the Commons. Thus Balfour had been Leader of the Party in the Commons for 11 years before he became Leader of the Party as a whole. Bonar Law, it is true, was comparatively inexperienced when he first won the leadership of the party in the Commons in 1911. (He had served only as a junior minister in the last Conservative Government, though he had shown a good deal of skill in debates.) But Bonar Law was, to put it simply, a very lucky man. Balfour had retired fairly abruptly and had made no effort to groom a successor; two rivals were threatening a head-on clash. All concerned happened to be more eager to preserve the unity of the party and the decorum of the proceedings than they were to win power for themselves.

Austen Chamberlain appears to have inherited the leadership of the party in the Commons in 1921 mainly because he was generally accepted as ranking second to Bonar Law in the councils of the party on the eve of the latter's first retirement. It was also widely felt that Chamberlain had earned a reward for his great act of self-abnegation in 1911. When Bonar Law re-emerged from retirement to accept the leadership of the party as a whole for the first time in 1922 he was easily the dominant figure in the anti-Coalition faction of his party. Baldwin's rise to power was in many ways the most spectacular of any. But he, like Bonar Law, was lucky; most of the more powerful figures in the party (except of course Curzon) were still nursing their grievances in the wilderness after their defeat on the Coalition issue; and it is important to note that Baldwin had already served for a few weeks as Leader of the House during Bonar Law's absence. Neville Chamberlain, as " pack-horse " of the National Government, had established his right to the succession many years before the retirement of Baldwin. The emergence of Winston Churchill in 1940 is of course a special case; apart from his obvious suitability as a war leader the most important consideration was the fact that he was the only prominent Conservative who was acceptable to the Opposition as a Coalition Prime Minister.[3]

[1] That is why there appears to be so little concern about who, in addition to Conservative M.P.s and Peers, are included in the meeting which nominally elects the Leader.

[2] See Table, p. 52.

[3] It is important to note that Chamberlain in effect proposed both himself and Halifax for the rôle before, by a process of elimination, he turned to Churchill. See also p. 48 above.

Although Lloyd George's phrase may have been applicable when he used it in 1911, it is certainly not true that " the fools stumble on their best men by accident "; neither however do they elect them by any procedure which would ordinarily be called democratic. A potential Conservative Leader in the process of his " emergence " first establishes his prowess in oratorical battle in the Commons; he is called into the councils of the party by the current Leader (into either the Cabinet or the Shadow Cabinet). Increasingly he is groomed by the old Leader and recognized by the party as the heir apparent.[1] If the emerging Leader has rivals they must either outshine him or supersede him in the affections of the old Leader and of the party. And they must do so *long before the party meeting assembles to elect a new Leader*. There can be no question of forcing a contest at that late date. Convention requires that on that occasion all potential rivals should affirm their unswerving allegiance to the tribal chief. The tribe then speaks with one voice and the new Leader has " emerged ".

[1] For the unusual circumstances of Macmillan's emergence see p. 587 below.

CHAPTER III

THE LEADER AND HIS FOLLOWERS

THE Leader of any major British political party is either a potential or an actual Prime Minister; by virtue of this fact alone, he is bound to have enormous authority over his followers whatever the checks and limitations his party's constitution may attempt to impose on him. Either at present (if his party is in power) or at some time in the future he will be able to distribute ministerial offices; he will be able to make and break the careers of his colleagues and rivals almost at will. Since, as was suggested in the introductory chapter, there now appears to be so unpromising a political future for the man who is expelled from or falls out of favour with his own party,[1] every M.P. must ponder deeply before he challenges or condemns his Leader. And, above all, of course, he must think very deeply indeed before he joins anything which might be classified as a rebellion against him. If he falls too far out of favour with the Leader his political career may be ruined.

These considerations apply to both the Labour and Conservative parties; they are the direct consequence of the enormous increase which has occurred in recent decades in the powers of the Prime Minister and his Cabinet, coupled with the drastic tightening of party discipline which has occurred over the same period. However "democratic" the Labour Party may claim its party constitution to be, nothing can alter the fact that the Leader of the Parliamentary Labour Party is either the Prime Minister or the potential Prime Minister of the country; in either case he will wield enormous authority in his relations with his party followers. When the Labour Party is in opposition, however, the Leader is not only bereft of the powers of the Prime Minister, he is also formally subject to many more restraints on his authority.[2] By contrast the Conservative Party, even in opposition, places few such formal restraints on the authority of its Leader.

The administrative arrangements of the Conservative Party in

[1] The prospect even for those who cross the floor of the House and join the rival party is now much dimmer than it used to be. No M.P. who has crossed the floor since 1945 has subsequently been able to secure re-election.

[2] See p. 297 below.

opposition [1] are as follows: the Leader (whether he is Leader of the Party or merely Leader of the Party in the Commons) selects from among his followers those he wishes to have as regular advisers. This group is known technically as the Consultative Committee and popularly as the "Shadow Cabinet".[2] The Conservative Members of Parliament (unlike their Labour opposite numbers; see p. 413 below) play no part in the selection of those of their number who are to become members of the Shadow Cabinet. The Leader alone chooses the oligarchy which controls the affairs of the party while it is in opposition;[3] he has in fact the same authority to choose his Shadow Cabinet as he has to choose his Cabinet when the Conservative Party is returned to power.

In addition to the Shadow Cabinet, the Leader is also advised by a larger Business Committee which consists of the principal officers of all the main "functional" committees of the parliamentary party. There are normally about twenty of these committees, each dealing with a major field of government activity such as foreign affairs, defence, finance, and education; the chairman of each committee (while the party is in opposition) is normally a front-bench member.[4] The committees have no fixed membership; any Con-

[1] This description is based on the organization of the Conservative Party while it was in opposition during the period 1945-51. There were some minor variations from the arrangements in operation during previous periods in opposition.

[2] Sir Ivor Jennings traces the origin of this institution as far back as 1876 when Sir William Harcourt objected to the "late Cabinet" deciding the policy of the Liberal Opposition. Jennings, W. I., *Parliament*, p. 71. The actual term "Shadow Cabinet" appears in one of Austen Chamberlain's letters in May, 1907: . . . "We are to have a (shadow) cabinet on this and other matters on Wednesday . . . " Chamberlain, Sir Austen, *Politics from Inside*, p. 84. In the late 19th century the Shadow Cabinet was known for a time as the Central Committee. See Balfour, A. J., *Chapters of Autobiography*, p. 158, and Churchill, W. S., *Lord Randolph Churchill*, Vol. I, Chapter VII, *passim*.

[3] The Leader usually of course invites the senior members of the last previous Cabinet formed by his party, but some may be dropped and others who have never served as Ministers may be added. Mrs. Dugdale writes of Balfour's Shadow Cabinet in 1911: . . . "there were no definite rules as to who should be summoned. Thus Mr. Chaplin continued to be invited, although he had left the Government before the reconstruction of 1903. Mr. F. E. Smith, who had never served in a Ministry, was usually present, as were the ex-Law Officers . . . ; Lord Balcarres, and Mr. Steel-Maitland attended in their capacities as Chief Party Whip and Party Organizer." Dugdale, Blanche, *Arthur James Balfour*, Vol. II, p. 68 (n.1). For a description of the rather remarkable circumstances in which F. E. Smith became a member of Balfour's Shadow Cabinet see Birkenhead, *Life of Frederick Edwin, Earl of Birkenhead*, Vol. I, pp. 222-3.

[4] When the party is in office the members of the Government no longer serve as chairmen of the party's "functional committees". The list of

servative M.P. is free to attend their meetings, though naturally there tends to emerge a hard core of " regulars " who are specially interested in the subject with which a particular committee is concerned.

Whether the Conservatives are in power or in opposition, the Leader is kept informed of the views of his back-bench followers through the activities of one of the most important organs in the structure of the Conservative Party, the Conservative (Private) Members Committee, or " 1922 Committee " as it is popularly called. This committee is the nearest equivalent on the Conservative side to the Parliamentary Labour Party, although there are significant differences in the structure and functions of the two organizations. There is also the further difference that the activities of the 1922 Committee are much less highly publicized than those of the Parliamentary Labour Party, which may help to explain why so many legends have grown up about the 1922 Committee.

The hostile press has often portrayed the Committee as a somewhat conspiratorial and essentially " reactionary " body which attempts to control the strategy and policies of the Conservative Party in the House of Commons. The original inspiration for this view came no doubt from Lloyd George and others who placed a sinister interpretation on the famous Carlton Club meeting of Conservative M.P.s of October, 1922, which led to the downfall of Austen Chamberlain as Leader of the Party in the House of Commons and to the disruption of the Coalition. The circumstances of this meeting are analysed below [1] but it is perhaps sufficient to note here that the Carlton Club meeting was not the " backstairs conspiracy in a West End club " which its foes attempted to suggest. It was in fact a vigorous assertion of " intra-party democracy ".

As will be shown in greater detail below, the Conservative Party in Parliament was until 1922 almost completely devoid of any formal organization. The Leader and his colleagues (with the aid of the Whips) were in exclusive command of the affairs of the party. This system seems to have worked smoothly enough except in periods of crisis; but on such occasions the Leader sometimes

Conservative Party Committees in the House of Commons for the session 1952-53 was as follows: Agriculture and Food; Civil Aviation; Commonwealth Affairs; Defence (with sub-committees for Naval, Army and Air Force affairs); Education; Finance, Trade and Industry; Foreign Affairs; Fuel and Power; Health and Social Security; Home Affairs; Housing, Local Government and Works; Labour; Transport; Scottish Unionist Members. Each committee has a chairman, one or two vice-chairmen and one or two honorary secretaries. All of these posts were held by back-bench Conservative M.P.s. See *Press Release 3921*, Conservative and Unionist Central Office, 5th December, 1952.

[1] See below pp. 97 ff.

found himself dangerously isolated from the rank and file of his supporters in the House. The dramatic downfall of Austen Chamberlain at the Carlton Club in October, 1922, convinced the more thoughtful members of the party that some permanent form of organization in the House of Commons was essential. The initiative in the formation of the 1922 Committee was taken by a group of back-benchers returned to Parliament for the first time in the election of 1922 which was held immediately after the fall of the Coalition. Sir Gervais Rentoul, who was chairman of the committee for the first ten years of its life, has recalled that the decision to form the committee was a direct result of the feeling of " ineffectiveness and bewilderment " among the newly elected Conservative M.P.s. The advent of the 1922 Committee was not, he wrote, " exactly welcomed by the powers that be. The leaders of the party considered it rather a nuisance. It is always so much easier to deal with either supporters or opponents individually than collectively. The 'Whips' feared it might be a ' cave ', an opportunity for the ventilation of criticism, which it would be better should not exist." The committee at first did little more than provide instructions for new members " on matters of parliamentary procedure and general policy". In this capacity they proved their usefulness and at the end of their first year of operation they received a personal letter of thanks from Stanley Baldwin who had succeeded to the Leadership of the party.

But a few months later, after Baldwin had taken the party to the country on the issue of protection, the survivors of the Conservative debacle returned to Parliament in a mood of considerable dissatisfaction. Rentoul recalled that there was a strong feeling of exasperation with the " lack of cohesion in the Party". A delegation from the 1922 Committee saw Baldwin, Austen Chamberlain and the Chief Whip and urged that there should be " regular Party meetings under the chairmanship of the Leader, or some deputy appointed by him, at which from time to time an indication would be given to the rank and file of the general policy of the Party, and an opportunity afforded to members to raise any questions or points that seemed to them of importance. We complained (Rentoul adds) of being left too much in the dark regarding the purposes and policies of the Government, which ultimately we, as private members, would have the responsibility of supporting and fighting for in the constituencies, and pointed out that such a state of affairs could only lead to weakness and confusion." Baldwin expressed sympathy but added that " Party meetings would be a mistake, mainly because of the inevitable leakage to the Press." Rentoul adds that the delegation was " finally flattened out by the remark from Sir Austen that we must trust our leaders, and that when we had been longer in the House we would take a different view." The deputation withdrew "entirely unconvinced"; it had to content itself with the compromise that one of the Whips would in future attend all meetings of the Committee and report direct to the Leader the views that were expressed at the meeting. It was further decided to throw open the doors of the 1922 Committee to all Conservative private members, and this arrangement has persisted ever since.[1]

The 1922 Committee is in effect therefore an organization of the entire back-bench membership of the Conservative Party; it is intended to serve as a sounding board of Conservative opinion in the House of Commons, just as the National Union serves as a sounding board of Conservative opinion in the country. Neither the National Union nor the 1922 Committee is authorized to formulate policy for the party[2]; neither do they control in any direct sense the activities of the Leader and his colleagues; both are intended merely to keep him informed of the state of Conservative opinion. But there is this difference in the relationship of the Leader to the two organizations: the Leader must of course strive to win the confidence (and if possible the enthusiastic support) of the National Union if he is to lead his party to victory at the polls; but his position as Leader and ultimately as Prime Minister is solely and directly dependent on his ability to retain the confidence of the back-bench Conservative M.P.s who constitute the membership of the 1922 Committee.

In comparison with those of the Parliamentary Labour Party, the meetings of the 1922 Committee are surprisingly informal and unspectacular. There are no written rules of procedure and, as one member of the Committee put it to the writer, they operate "on the basis of common law rather than statute law". The Committee normally meets once a week and its sessions are from one to two hours in duration. When the party is in opposition (and all Con-

---

[1] Rentoul, Sir Gervais, *Sometimes I Think,* Chapter XXXIII ("The 1922 Committee") *passim.* Rentoul's account is now the only available source of information about the early meetings of the 1922 Committee since the first minute book of the committee has been lost. The writer has discussed the work of the committee with several of its prominent members and this account is based substantially on these discussions. There are also some references to the work of the committee in Lord Winterton's *Orders of the Day,* London, 1953, *passim.*

[2] Although it is important to note that the 1922 Committee like the National Union names a number of representatives to sit on the 16-man Policy Committee which is responsible to the Leader (see p. 211 below). The 1922 Committee also, incidentally, names four members to sit on the Executive Committee of the National Union (see p. 206 below) and in addition, all members of the 1922 Committee are members of the Central Council of the National Union.

servative M.P.s are therefore private members) the whole member-ship of the party is eligible to attend, but by custom the Leader attends only on those occasions when arrangements have been made for him to address the Committee. Members of the Shadow Cabinet and Whips do attend the meetings of the Committee but they are not considered eligible for office and have no voting rights. When the party is in power neither Ministers nor Junior Ministers attend meetings of the 1922 Committee; the Whips do continue to attend but, again, without voting rights. The Commit-tee annually elects a chairman (who is usually one of the most prominent back-benchers), two vice-chairmen, two secretaries and a treasurer. These officers (together with 12 others elected by the Committee from among its members) constitute an Executive Com-mittee; they meet weekly immediately before the meeting of the Committee. The agenda for the latter normally includes reports from the functional committees of the party (described above); an announcement of the business of the House for the following week (this announcement is given by a Whip on duty for this pur-pose and he may be questioned with respect to whipping arrange-ments); the Committee then usually proceeds to a discussion on any major issues of party or government policy which concern the mem-bers of the Committee. Votes are not taken and it is therefore the duty of the chairman to interpret " the sense of the meeting".

The chairman has direct access to the Leader of the Party (whether he is Leader of the Opposition or Prime Minister) and it is the chairman's duty to report the views of the Committee to the Leader, particularly if there has been extensive criticism of a par-ticular policy being pursued by the Leader and his colleagues. As one prominent member of the 1922 Committee has explained, there may be circumstances in which the chairman will have to report to the Leader that " the boys won't have it". No formal sanctions are of course threatened but naturally under these cir-cumstances the Leader must take immediate steps to discuss his policy with the members of the Committee; if strong criticisms persist he may have to modify it. When the system is working at its best the chairman of the 1922 Committee need not make special representations to the Leader, since the latter receives regular reports on the mood of the Committee from the party Whips who attend its meetings.

On occasion the 1922 Committee may serve, in a sense, as a court of appeal from one of the functional committees. During the 1952-3 session for example the members of the Fuel and Power Committee of the party urged a certain line of action upon the Minister of Fuel and Power. The Minister was not prepared to accept the advice of the Committee and on the initiative of the chairman of the Fuel and Power Committee the matter was raised at a full meeting of the 1922 Committee. There both the Minister and members of the Fuel and Power Committee presented their points of view, with the result that the 1922 Committee endorsed the views of the Minister and rejected those of the Fuel and Power Committee.

In recent years especially, the 1922 Committee has not been the scene of continual factional battles of the sort that have plagued the Parliamentary Labour Party.[1] Since the Tory Reform group virtually suspended its activities in 1945 few organized Conservative pressure groups have attempted to win over the 1922 Committee to their point of view. Indeed even in the 1930s Winston Churchill appears to have made comparatively little effort to convert the Committee to his point of view either on the issue of India in the early 1930s or on the issues of rearmament and appeasement in the late 'thirties. This is in a sense surprising since one would have been inclined to assume that the Committee would be the logical place in which to launch a campaign to win over the Conservative Party in Parliament to an alternative policy; but Churchill apparently preferred to conduct his campaigns primarily in the press and on the public platform.[2] This isolated incident should not however be thought to detract from the great and continuing importance of the work of the 1922 Committee; it is the most important forum for the expression of Conservative opinion within the House of Commons. For that reason alone its deliberations are of vital concern to the Leader of the Party.

The management of the affairs of the party in the House of Commons is of course in the hands of the Chief Whip and his associates. The function of the Whips within the British parliamentary system has been examined in detail elsewhere,[3] and need not therefore be treated at length here. The only important point to note is the fact that on the Conservative side the Chief Whip, his deputies and associates are all appointed by the Leader of the Party personally (on the Labour side the Chief Whip is elected annually by the Parliamentary Labour Party and he appoints the junior Whips);

[1] But for a valuable analysis of currents of opinion in the Conservative Party in Parliament see Finer, S. E. (*et al.*), *Back Bench Opinion in the House of Commons 1955–59*, Chapter 3.

[2] He may have felt that had he fought his case before Committee and lost, he would have been under some obligation to refrain from criticizing the policies of his party in public.

[3] Morrison, H., *Government and Parliament: A Survey from the Inside*, pp. 93 ff. See also Chilston, *Chief Whip*, London, 1961, and " Whips of Parliament," *The Economist*, 15th July 1961.

this provides a further addition to the enormous list of major offices within the party organization which are filled by personal appointees of the Leader.

In 1945 the party established a Conservative Parliamentary Secretariat to be responsible to the Leader through the Whips' Office. Its function was two-fold: first, to provide official secretaries (M.P.s serve as honorary secretaries) to the functional committees referred to above. These official secretaries prepared briefs on each measure brought before Parliament which concerned their particular committee; they drafted amendments proposed by their committees and sought out the best technical advice available on behalf of the committee. They were to act in fact as " a miniature civil service " when the party was in opposition and were " organized on the lines of the Cabinet Offices ".[1] Subsequently in 1948, however, the duties of the parliamentary secretariat were transferred to the Conservative Research Department. (Again it is important to note that the chairman of the Research Department is appointed by the Leader and is responsible to him.)[2]

In the House of Lords there is no Conservative Committee equivalent to the 1922 Committee although meetings of Conservative peers are held and there is of course a party leader in the Lords and a Conservative Whip. The party leader in the Lords and several other Conservative peers are normally included in the Shadow Cabinet. The Conservative peers who wish to be members of the Central Council of the National Union have to make application annually and one of their number is appointed to sit on the Executive Committee of the National Union.

Whether the Conservative Party is in office or in opposition the Leader (after his initial election) is not normally required to subject himself to any system of re-election; nor is he formally required to report on his work to the party organization inside or outside Parliament. As is explained above, however, he makes periodic appearances at meetings of his parliamentary colleagues to explain and discuss his policy. In addition, although the Leader does not normally attend the annual conferences of the National Union, he customarily addresses a mass meeting of the delegates immediately after the conference has adjourned. The Leader on these occasions frequently refers to the deliberations and resolutions of the conference and may, indeed, indicate that he approves of some or all

[1] See *The Party Organization*, Conservative and Unionist Central Office Organization Series, No. 1, 1947, p. 20.
[2] *The Party Organization*, 1950, p. 16, and see p. 284 below.

of their decisions. But he is, of course, in no way bound by these decisions; they are merely " conveyed "[1] to him so that he may be kept constantly aware of the mood and opinions of his followers. References made to the Leader (particularly after Winston Churchill assumed that office) in the course of the National Union conference deliberations are usually in extravagantly laudatory terms. At the 1947 conference, for example, a representative who seconded the Chairman's motion to adopt the Annual Report of the National Union said: " . . . I believe that with Lord Woolton to guide us and with Mr. Churchill to lead us we have no fear of the future." [2]

The Leader also has exclusive responsibility for the formulation of party policy. He may consult whom he wishes; he may (and obviously does) pay attention to the resolutions passed by the various organs of the party, but he remains (as the Maxwell Fyfe Committee put it in its review of the Conservative Party structure) " the main fountain and interpreter of policy."[3] The Maxwell Fyfe Report explains (p. 36) that there are " three phases in the evolution of a Party's intentions . . . Principles, Policy and Programme." The first of these is not subject to change; " the Disraelian principles [4] are as valid to-day as when they were first propounded." The second, the party's *policy*, " relates Conservative principles to the national and international problems of the day, usually in general terms." In the formulation of policy the Leader is "*served*" by the party's various policy committees and " these in their turn

---

[1] This is the term used in the pamphlet *The Party Organization* (Organization Series, No. 1) published by the Conservative and Unionist Central Office (revised January, 1961), p. 7.

[2] *Report of the 68th Annual Conference of the National Union of Conservative and Unionist Associations*, 2nd to 4th October, 1947, London, 1947, p. 34. (Subsequent references to these reports will be abbreviated, e.g. *1947 Conservative Annual Conference Report*.)

[3] *Interim and Final Reports of the Committee on Party Organization*, 1948 and 1949, London, the National Union, 1949, p. 32. This committee which met under the chairmanship of Sir David Maxwell Fyfe, was set up by the Executive Committee of the National Union in June, 1948. Its final report which is discussed in Chapter IV was approved by the Central Council of the National Union on 15th July, 1949. (It will be referred to throughout as the Maxwell Fyfe Committee and its report as the *Maxwell Fyfe Report*.) The Report provides a very valuable " official " review of the structure of the party; however the passage on the "*History of the Election of the Leader*" pp. 32-3 is full of inaccuracies.

[4] The reference here is no doubt primarily to Disraeli's great Crystal Palace speech of 24th June, 1872: " The Tory party has three great objects . . . . to maintain the institutions of the country . . . . to uphold the Empire of England . . . the elevation of the condition of the people." Cited in Riley, E. S., *Our Cause*, Exmouth, 1948, p. 123. See also White R. J., (ed.) *The Conservative Tradition*, London, 1950.

are *influenced* by the views of the Party as revealed in the various resolutions at the Part Conferences." But, the Report adds: " *Endorsements and pronouncements on Party policy are the prerogative and responsibility of the Leader."* The third phase in " the evolution of a Party's intentions," the *programme,* is defined as " the specific plans for the application of policy". Its preparation " must be a continuing process; but, as the final document has to be related directly to circumstances existing immediately before a General Election, *the final proposals are normally presented in a Party Manifesto by the Leader on the eve of a General Election, and are his responsibility."* [1]

Thus, as the Maxwell Fyfe committee saw it, Disraeli gave the definitive statement of the party's basic *principles* and it is the responsibility of each succeeding Leader to elaborate the party's *policy* and *programme* in light of these principles. In undertaking this task the Leader is expected to listen to the advice of various policy committees and to take into account the resolutions passed by the various organs of the party. But final responsibility for the formulation of policy and programme rests solely with the Leader. Since 1945 much has been done, of course, to encourage the extra-parliamentary organizations of the party to feel that they have some part to play in the formulation of policy. R. A. Butler (Chairman of the party's Advisory Committee on Policy) reassured the 1948 conference of the National Union: " Gone are the days when policy is brought down to us from Mount Sinai on tablets of stone, so that we are blinded by the light when it is brought to us! The Conservative Party is now helping . . . . to give its own contribution to the making of policy." [2] But Butler had already underlined the word " helping " the previous year. " We are " (he said) " *helping* our Leader who must take the final decisions on all those matters and must himself promulgate the policy when the time comes." [3] Again and again the literature of the party

[1] *The Maxwell Fyfe Report,* p. 36. [Italics mine.] The Leader's own Election Address long served as the Conservative party manifesto. In the 1945 election the party took its stand on *Mr. Churchill's Declaration of Policy to the Electors.* In 1950 however the Conservative manifesto took a more impersonal form. It was called *This is the Road* and carried no indication that it was written by the Leader himself. (See Nicholas, H. G., *The British General Election of 1950,* London, 1951, pp. 117 ff.) In the 1951 election the Conservatives reverted to their earlier practice and presented their programme in the form of a personal statement from their Leader. It was followed a few days later by a longer (and anonymous) statement of party policy, *Britain Strong and Free.* (See Butler, D. E., *The British General Election of 1951,* p. 44.)

[2] *1948 Conservative Conference Report,* p. 34.

[3] *1947 Conservative Conference Report,* p. 53. [Italics mine.]

and the speeches of its leaders return to this theme.

Repeated attempts have been made (usually after the party has suffered defeat in an election) to force the Leader to share his responsibility for the formulation of policy. This happened, to take but one example, after the great defeat of 1906. Under pressure from the National Union, an advisory committee was set up to ensure a better flow of information between the Leader and the party both inside and outside Parliament. The suggestion was made that this committee might be given certain executive responsibilities in the formulation of policy. Sir A. Acland-Hood, the Chief Whip, emphatically rejected the suggestion, saying that he " could not imagine anything more disastrous to the party welfare than to have the party managed by a committee. The party could stand many things, but it would not, in his judgment, ever stand a caucus. (Cheers.) The policy of the party must be initiated by its leader, who would, without doubt, receive valuable advice and assistance from the advisory committee. But they could never submit to have the policy of the party dictated by a committee. No leader and no Whip would ever submit to it."[1] As on that occasion, the party has invariably acquiesced in this view. As the Chairman of the Party Organization said in 1947, in explaining the Leader's responsibility for policy: " This method suits us, and has suited the succession of great men we have been proud to have as our leaders." [2] The same theme recurs in the opening address of the Chairman at the 1952 Conservative conference: " We are met here to-day, *not to form policy*, but to review the progress of the nation and the Empire under our Conservative Government, and to consider the affairs of our Party. You will have an opportunity of expressing your opinions, of hearing the views of the Ministers concerned, and of recording your own decisions." [3]

A final evidence of the authority of the Leader is his control over the Central Office [4] (or civil service) of the party. This organization (whose equivalent on the Labour side is responsible to the National Executive Committee of the party) is in a sense the personal machine of the Leader. He appoints the Chairman of the Party Organization,[5] the senior official of the party; he appoints also the two Vice-Chairmen, the Treasurers of the Party and the Chairman and Deputy-Chairman of the Advisory Committee on

[1] *The Times,* 28th July, 1906.
[2] Cited in Ranney, J. C., and Carter, G. M., *The Major Foreign Powers* New York, 1949, p. 74.
[3] *1952 Conservative Conference Report,* p. 26. [Italics mine.]
[4] See Chapter V.
[5] This office was first established in 1911. The duties of the Chairman of the Party Organization are also discussed in Chapter V.

Policy. All of these officials are responsible to the Leader alone and to no other individual or group within the party. Thus through these appointments the Leader directly controls the entire Central Office organization with its research and policy-forming committees, its educational and propaganda functions, and the spending of party money. Further, it must be remembered that this enumeration of the powers of the Leader does not represent an archaic accumulation of nominal powers which might long since have fallen into desuetude. As recently as 1948-9, the entire party organization and the rôle of the Leader within it was thoroughly re-examined; with a few recommendations for minor changes the Leader was confirmed in his powers.[1]

Supporters of the Conservative Party can hardly be surprised if their critics and even comparatively detached observers find much to criticize and question about the rôle which the party apparently assigns to its Leader; indeed if one takes the Conservative Leader's position and powers at their face value he appears to have greater authority over his followers and to be less subject to their restraint and control than the leader of any other political organization calling itself democratic. The extent to which the situation misleads even comparatively friendly observers may be illustrated by reference to an article in *The Times* on party organization.[2] " The whole Constitution of the Conservative Party (*The Times* comments) tends to exaggerate the isolation of the leader from the rank and file." But then a remarkable sentence follows: " It is difficult to imagine (the article continues) how a revolt against the leader of the Conservative Party would be conducted." Clearly, the author of this article was overwhelmed by the formal description of the powers of the Leader of the Conservative Party; he apparently overlooked the fact that the Leader holds these powers with the consent of his followers in Parliament and (to a lesser extent) of the popular organization of the party outside. And as has already been emphasized, there is ample precedent in the modern history of the Conservative Party for the withdrawal of that consent. Of the Leaders since Disraeli, no less than three—Balfour, Austen and Neville Chamberlain—were, in effect, driven from the office of Leader by their own followers. A fourth, Baldwin, had to fight a bitter battle to retain his leadership. Indeed of the first seven Leaders after Disraeli, only Salisbury, Bonar Law and Winston Churchill were relatively free from concerted moves by their followers to drive

---

[1] *The Maxwell Fyfe Report,* Chapter III.
[2] " The Party Conference; Reality and Illusion of Popular Control," *The Times,* 29th September, 1952.

them from office. (The question whether Churchill or Eden may have resigned under pressure from certain of their colleagues to do so is discussed on pp. 581-6 below.)

The fall of Neville Chamberlain in 1940 has already been described in some detail. He was not of course defeated in the House nór was he deposed from the leadership of the party. He resigned the office of Prime Minister because in a vote of confidence some 93 of his followers failed to support him; presumably they no longer considered him a suitable war leader. In other words, a large minority of Chamberlain's party withdrew their consent to his continued leadership. He was not immediately removed (or forced to resign) from the leadership of the party because his successor as Prime Minister apparently felt at first that his own position as leader of a three-party war coalition would be strengthened if he did not become the leader of one of the parties in the coalition. But it is evident that Churchill soon found this arrangement unsatisfactory. It would seem fair to assume that had Chamberlain not been forced to resign the party leadership through ill-health Churchill would in any case eventually have brought strong pressure on him to do so. There can be no other interpretation of the sentence: " I should have found it impossible to conduct the war if I had had to procure the agreement . . . not only of the Leaders of the two minority parties but of the Leader of the Conservative majority."[1] There seems little reason to doubt that once Churchill had established his authority as war leader the leadership of the Conservative Party would have been his for the asking even if Chamberlain had not been forced for personal reasons to retire from the party leadership. It therefore becomes clear that as soon as Chamberlain had lost the confidence of a sizeable proportion of his followers in the Commons his powers as Leader of the Party (which seem on paper so impressive) were of no great importance. The vast powers of the Leader of the Conservative Party are exercised only with the consent of his followers; when there is clear evidence that this consent is withdrawn then the Leader has no real alternative but to resign. However powerful he may be while he enjoys the confidence of his followers his authority evaporates the moment he loses that confidence. The position of the Conservative Leader is much more precarious and much less invulnerable than any formal reading of the party constitution would suggest.

It might be argued that too much emphasis should not be placed on the downfall of Neville Chamberlain as evidence of the precarious position of the Conservative Leader. Certainly the cir-

[1] Churchill, W. S., *The Second World War*, Vol. II, p. 439.

cumstances were highly unusual in that his followers who withdrew
their consent to his continued leadership did so at a moment of
national peril. It might be claimed that in a grave emergency
they were merely putting country before personal political loyalties
and that this incident in no way modifies the proposition that in
normal circumstances the ascendancy of the Conservative Leader
over his followers is complete. An examination of the downfall of
Balfour and Austen Chamberlain (and of the unsuccessful revolts
against Baldwin's leadership) does not bear this out. The first two
lost the confidence of their followers and resigned the leadership;
the third retained his position but only after a stubborn and ultimately successful battle against the malcontents in his party. The
experiences of Balfour, Austen Chamberlain and Baldwin are invaluable case studies in Conservative leadership; they are examined
here in some detail because they provide by far the best illustrations of the relationship of the Conservative Leader to his followers
inside and outside Parliament.

BALFOUR AS CONSERVATIVE LEADER

A. J. Balfour's nine years as Leader of the Conservative Party
(1902–11) were in many respects the least happy period in his long
political career[1]. It is an open question whether he was suited by
temperament to lead a political party. Lord Birkenhead had
described him as " the finest brain that has been applied to politics
in our time". And one of his biographers has claimed that he enjoyed
a social prestige " perhaps unequalled by any statesman since the
days of Fox". But, as Sir Harold Nicolson has put it, Balfour was
" a dexterous rather than a compelling leader". Nicolson adds:

> "His patrician temperament rendered him unsympathetic to
> the cruder men who were by then ousting the old territorial
> aristocracy from the control of the Conservative Party. His
> philosophic aloofness had induced in him the habit of mind, so
> dangerous in any politician, of being interested in both sides of a
> case. It was not that he lacked the courage of his convictions: few
> statesmen have manifested such physical and moral audacity: it
> was rather that he classed convictions with deliberate forms of
> belief and much disliked all deliberate forms of belief. Moreover
> he was unlucky."

Some would no doubt claim that this interpretation is unduly

[1] Kenneth Young's *Arthur James Balfour*, London, 1963, appeared
immediately before the publication of this edition of *British Political Parties*.
It illuminates this account at a number of points but does not differ in its
interpretation of Balfour's rôle as Leader.
[2] Nicolson, Harold, *King George the Fifth*, pp. 90–1.

kind to Balfour. There are certainly grounds for charging him with indecision and procrastination, and these are defects which might have proved fatal however good Balfour's luck had been. But certainly the least that could be said in justification of his comparative failure is that he took over the leadership at a singularly difficult moment in his party's history.

Within eighteen months after Balfour succeeded Salisbury as Prime Minister and Leader of the Party in July, 1902, a number of Ministers, including two of the most powerful figures in his Government, had resigned. Both Joseph Chamberlain and the Duke of Devonshire were dissatisfied with his handling of the issue of tariff reform. Chamberlain had returned from a visit to South Africa in 1902 a passionately convinced supporter of Imperial Federation; as a first step towards that goal he advocated the complete abandonment by Britain of the traditional policy of free trade and the introduction of a system of tariff preference for colonial products. Chamberlain tried to get Cabinet endorsement of these new policies, but others in the Government (including C. T. Ritchie, the Chancellor of the Exchequer, and the Duke of Devonshire, the party leader in the House of Lords) were strongly opposed. Balfour himself adopted a somewhat vague mid-position in an attempt to maintain party unity. He insisted, however, that his own policy rather than those of either Chamberlain or the extreme Free Traders should prevail. As a result he ultimately lost the sympathy and support of both groups. Chamberlain quit Balfour's Government because he could not win endorsement for a wholehearted policy of tariff reform; Devonshire and three other free trade ministers resigned because Balfour would not disavow his own modest proposals for tariff reform.

Balfour hoped that by accepting the resignations of the extremists on both sides of the controversy he would be able to retain the remainder of his followers on the basis of an agreed middle-of-the-road programme.[1] But subsequent division lists showed a wide rift in the party's ranks; Balfour, haunted by the ghost of Peel, strove at all costs to avoid a final split. He continued to procrastinate on the issue of tariff reform to the annoyance of extremists on both wings of the party. Finally as the situation continued to deteriorate Balfour resigned the premiership in December, 1905, without asking for a dissolution. In January, 1906, he and

[1] See Churchill, W. S., " Arthur James Balfour," in *Great Contemporaries,* London, (1937), pp. 243 ff. for an account of this incident. See also Holland, Bernard, *Life of the Duke of Devonshire,* Vol. II, pp. 352-3, and Spender, J. A., *The Life of the Rt. Hon. Sir Henry Campbell-Bannerman,* London, 1923, Vol. II, pp. 112-15.

his party met overwhelming defeat at the hands of Campbell-Bannerman and the new Liberal administration.

Even with the full panoply of power accruing to him as both Prime Minister and Leader of the Party Balfour had been unable to assert his authority over his followers, who were bitterly divided on a major issue of policy. In opposition his position was in many respects even more difficult. In the 1906 election he lost his own seat by some 2,000 votes and his party in the House was reduced to a shadow of its former strength. But these setbacks in no way dampened Balfour's enthusiasm for politics. In reply to a letter expressing condolence at the Conservative defeat he wrote: " If you had asked me when we last met whether I should much mind permanently leaving politics, I should have answered in the negative. But I am so profoundly interested in what is *now* going on that I should return a very different answer to-day."[1]

Until a safe seat could be found for Balfour, Joseph Chamberlain led the remnant of the party in the Commons.[2] This was soon arranged and Balfour was returned for the City of London on 27th February, 1906. Meanwhile he had been earnestly engaged with Chamberlain in an attempt to work out a common policy on which the party could unite. The negotiations between the two men throw an important light on the relation between the Leader and his followers. At a private meeting on 2nd February, 1906, Balfour and Chamberlain managed to establish the will to agree but little more; thereafter for the next twelve days they continued their negotiations in an important series of private letters. Chamberlain urged that a meeting of their followers in the House should be called to discuss the issues between them. Balfour replied in a remarkable letter:

"You know how strong my objection is in ordinary circum-

---

[1] A. J. Balfour to Lord Knollys, 17th January, 1906. Cited in Dugdale, Blanche, *Arthur James Balfour*, Vol. II, p. 20. Balfour was referring not to the Liberal victory, nor to the disputes within his own party, but to the emergence of socialism as a political force in the election of 1906. " If I read the signs aright," he wrote elsewhere, " . . . what is going on here is the faint echo of the same movement which has produced massacres in St. Petersburg, riots in Vienna, and Socialist processions in Berlin." (*Ibid.*, Vol. I, pp. 438-9.)

[2] There is no evidence that Chamberlain sought to take advantage of Balfour's difficulties to supplant him as Leader. Chamberlain's sole and overriding desire at this stage appears to have been to advance the cause of tariff reform which he believed to be in the best interests of his own party and of the country. He wrote to Alderman Salvidge, a powerful local figure in the party, " . . . I believe I have taken the right course to keep the party together . . . " J. Chamberlain to A. T. Salvidge, 12th October, 1903, cited in Salvidge, S., *Salvidge of Liverpool*, London, 1934, p. 52.

stances to a Party Meeting, and how reluctant I am to have all our differences dealt with in a manner which is certain to be published, and will probably be irritating. But, on carefully thinking over the whole situation, I have come round to your view that, *if you desire it*, a Party Meeting must be held . . . .

" The most difficult of the questions we have to settle . . . relates to the procedure to be adopted when it does meet. *There is no case in history, as far as I am aware, in which a Party Meeting has been summoned except to give emphasis and authority to a decision at which the Party have informally already arrived ; still less is there an example to be found of a vote being taken at such a Meeting.* How then are we to proceed on the present occasion? Are you and I to agree upon some question on which the Meeting can vote Aye or No? If so, what is this question to be, and how is it to be formulated? . . . These things puzzle me greatly, and I should be glad to have your opinion about them."[1]

This passage is the most striking evidence available of the extraordinary rudimentary nature of Conservative Party organization within Parliament at this time. Party meetings, on the rare occasions when they were held, appear to have been of no greater importance than the perfunctory meetings of M.P.s and Peers which, as we have seen, are customarily called to offer the leadership of the party to a Conservative who has been called for the first time to the office of Prime Minister. Lowell in his classic analysis of British government and politics just after the turn of the century gives this description of the parliamentary organization of the two great parties of the day:

" The whips may be said to constitute the only regular party organization in the House of Commons, unless we include under that description the two front benches. The very fact, indeed, that the ministry and the leaders of the Opposition furnish in themselves the real party machinery of the House, avoids the need of any other. The ministers prepare and carry out the programme of the party in power, while a small coterie of leaders on the other side devise the plans for opposing them. The front bench thus does the work of a party committee or council, and in neither of the great parties is there anything resembling a general caucus for the discussion and determination of party policy. Sometimes a great meeting of the adherents of the party in Parliament is called at one of the political clubs or elsewhere, when the leaders address their followers. But it is held to exhort not to consult . . . " [2]

[1] Cited in Dugdale, Blanche, *Arthur James Balfour*, Vol. II, p. 23. [Second italics mine.]

[2] Lowell, A. L., *The Government of England*, Vol. I, pp. 455-6.

Chamberlain in his reply to Balfour's baffled enquiries appeared to be proposing nevertheless that the party should in fact be consulted. He reassured Balfour: " Of course there will be no question whatever as to Leadership." But he added: " . . . I think the Party as a whole should be asked to express freely their opinion as to the best policy for the future, and to vote as between the alternatives suggested." He then referred directly to formal statements which he himself and Balfour had previously made outlining their respective attitudes to tariff reform; the party meeting would be asked to choose between these. But then, amazingly, Chamberlain added: " It will be clearly understood that the decision is not binding on the leaders, or any of them, but is merely taken for information . . . "[1] The vote, Chamberlain argued, " would furnish all of us with a really valuable indication of what is practicable, as well as of what is desirable."

Balfour could see little merit in Chamberlain's suggestion. He conceded that " the members of the Party must have an opportunity of ' blowing off steam '." But if they were to be asked to choose between Chamberlain's and Balfour's own policies with respect to tariff reform, then inevitably the one whose views were favoured would have to become Leader of the Party. " There is something amounting to absurdity (Balfour added) in asking a Party to give an opinion upon an important question of policy, and, when it has given that opinion, perhaps against its titular leader, asking that leader to be good enough to continue his work on their behalf." Balfour proposed instead that the meeting should occupy itself " merely in hearing and expressing various opinions " (on the subject of tariff reform). But if, against his advice, a vote were taken and that vote indicated that Chamberlain's views were preferred to his own then, he hinted broadly, he would resign and Chamberlain would have to consider his decision not to contest the leadership.[2] In this letter and elsewhere Balfour consigns to the party meeting a rôle not unlike that of the annual conference of the National Union. He seems to conceive of it as, at best, a sounding board for the party leaders; at worst, he thinks of it as a tiresome (but perhaps inevitable) process of " blowing off steam". In either case there is no question of permitting a party meeting (or a party conference) to take any active part in the formulation of policy.

Chamberlain in his reply appeared to accept the logic of this argument; he dropped his reference to the need to offer a clear choice of policies to the party meeting and enclosed instead a fresh

[1] Cited in Dugdale, Blanche, *Arthur James Balfour,* Vol. II, pp. 23-4.
[2] Dugdale, Blanche, *Arthur James Balfour,* Vol. II, p. 25.

statement of policy on tariff reform which he hoped would prove acceptable to Balfour. After further exchanges agreement was finally reached on the very eve of the party meeting. Austen Chamberlain gives this account of the final negotiations:

> "At the last moment (before the party meeting) I drafted a letter which was approved by Akers-Douglas, formerly Lord Salisbury's trusty Whip and latterly Home Secretary in Balfour's Government, and by Alec Hood our Chief Whip. Jack Sandars, Balfour's secretary, made some additions to it, and it was accepted by Balfour and my father and published . . . on 14th February . . .
>
> "It was heralded with relief by everyone except the extreme Free Fooders, and enabled my father to continue his co-operation with Balfour."[1]

The party meeting[2] was subsequently held but since Balfour and Chamberlain were now (nominally at least) in agreement, it was not necessary to ask the meeting to choose between their respective policies. The party meeting became therefore what Balfour had always intended: an " opportunity for blowing off steam". Balfour, who presided, appealed for a " united constructive policy". There were some lively exchanges as to what this should entail. The Duke of Devonshire was prepared to continue to work under Balfour's leadership " if a *modus vivendi* during the present Parliament could be devised on the fiscal question." He complained, however, of the " compromise " on the tariff issue reflected in the Balfour-Chamberlain correspondence and indicated that he and his friends would continue to act independently. Joseph Chamberlain urged that the " constructive policy " referred to by Balfour " must be the policy of the majority "; to Devonshire he said that the letters involved " a definition, not a compromise". The meeting closed with a vote of confidence in Balfour's leadership which was carried unanimously.[3]

[1] Chamberlain, Austen, *Politics from Inside*, p. 37.

[2] Austen Chamberlain in describing this meeting notes: " As we had succeeded in winning only 150 seats, it was decided, on my father's urgent insistence, that the defeated candidates should be invited with the successful ones so as to make the gathering more representative." Chamberlain, Austen, *Politics from Inside*, p. 37. *The Annual Register for 1906* (p. 15) reports that some 650 peers, M.P.s and defeated candidates attended the meeting.

[3] For an account of the meeting see *The Annual Register for 1906*, p. 15. One of those present, who was sympathetic to Balfour, later wrote: " My recollection is that the audience appeared to be almost wholly in favour of Tariff Reform; that the proceedings were amicable, and that Mr. Balfour appeared somewhat in the character of a captive, it being the general belief that he had yielded at the last moment in consequence of the pressure put upon him by numerous members of the party. Certainly the general impression was that Mr. Chamberlain had practically got his way." Lord Newton, *Lord Lansdowne, A Biography*, London, 1929, p. 352.

On his return to the House in March, 1906, Balfour began to rally his supporters by a militant campaign of opposition to the new Liberal Government's legislative programme. This raised the spirits of his followers for a time, but they soon grew dissatisfied. Balfour's private secretary wrote warning him:

> "The rank and file clamour for some broad line of policy above and beyond resisting and denouncing (the) Government no matter how pernicious it may be. . . . They thoroughly appreciate your great services to the Party, your ripe experience, and the extraordinary skill you exhibit in leading the Party in Parliament. But they are not proof against the blandishments of those who promise that they can sweep the country with a fiscal policy that will be of enormous national benefit. . . . If you do not speak on the fiscal question, then the malcontents will declare that their contention is well founded and that you are indifferent to the Tariff issue. . . . The bulk of the Party do not for a moment desire that you should commit yourself to details . . . but they do want a statement on broad lines . . . . A speech on these lines would, in (the Chief Whip's) opinion, pull the Party together. The point is —are you disposed to make it? It may in your judgment be unwise to make it. Be it so—but then, says (the Chief Whip), we shall practically lose our army—very likely not all at once, but by degrees, until anarchy is succeeded by a new authority . . . "

Balfour's private secretary adds that he sees the folly of some of the malcontents who want Balfour to propose " a constructive policy " regarding tariffs which would provide " just the target that (our) opponents want." But, he concludes,

> " you have to take men as you find them and if they will choose the path of difficulty it still behoves you—their leader—to guide them, doesn't it? How best to do it is the question."[1]

Balfour replied that he was " well acquainted " with the situation as described by his private secretary and that he proposed " telling the Party the ' truth in love ' " in a forthcoming public address.

In that address he warned the party that either group of extremists on the issue of Tariff Reform could destroy the party. And then he expounded his classic argument against formulating " programmes " while in opposition. " I am sure (he wrote) that no competent politician has ever done what I have been asked by some people to do except under duress, and no politician who has done it in duress has ever done so without repenting what he did for the rest of his natural life." [2] This was the " truth in love " as

---

[1] Cited in Dugdale, Blanche, *Arthur James Balfour*, Vol. II, pp. 43-4.
[2] *Ibid.*, p. 45.

Balfour saw it; but a great many of his followers were quite unconvinced and they kept him in continual " duress ".

Clearly Balfour had the greatest difficulty in adjusting himself
to the changed circumstances of opposition. For the best part of
twenty years he had been almost continuously a prominent member
of the Government side and he had served briefly as Prime Minister.
But now he was in a much more exposed position; even though the
Conservative Party constitution in theory guarantees to the Leader
the sole right to declare party policy even when the party is in
opposition, it is very clear from Balfour's experience that in opposition the Leader has nothing like the same authority as he has when
his party is in power. His followers expect (and may well demand)
that their views should be taken seriously into account. And it is
important to note, that in circumstances such as these, the party
organization *outside* Parliament may play an important rôle.

The 1906 conference of the National Union had unanimously
passed a resolution commending the tariff policy laid down in the
exchange of letters between Balfour and Chamberlain in February,
1906. In the following year the conference again unanimously
passed a resolution in favour of tariff reform after L. J. Maxse, an
extreme Tariff Reformer, had denounced the inaction of the leaders
and the Whips in the cause. A letter was read from Balfour commending the resolution, but it is evident from the debate that there
was a good deal of dissatisfaction with Balfour's advocacy of the
tariff reform policy.

In a speech at the 1907 conference of the National Union,
Balfour went farther than he had ever done before in the direction
advocated by the Tariff Reformers, although it also became clear
that if there was to be a major change in the party's tactics there
would have to be a change of leadership too. He declared that
" precision of doctrine as to party loyalty " was impossible. He
deprecated therefore the exercise of " tyrannical jurisdiction " over
those who felt difficulties with particular items in the party's programme. There was a lively difference of opinion in the press as
to how far Balfour had moved in acceptance of tariff reform doctrines. Liberal and Free Trade papers declared mockingly that
he had " again evaded his Tariff Reform pursuers[1]."

But in the following year (1908) Balfour pledged that " the establishment of a moderate general tariff on manufactured goods, not
for the purpose of raising prices or giving artificial protection
against legitimate competition, should be adopted if shown to be
necessary," and the Conservative Central Office hinted that in
future candidates who could not support his view were unlikely to

[1] *Annual Register for 1907*, p. 251.

be regarded with official favour.[1] Early in 1909 Bonar Law wrote
in a private letter:

> " . . . from our point of view—the point of view, that is, of those
> who are in earnest about Tariff Reform—this difficulty is prac-
> tically solved. The step taken by the Central Office, which I am
> sure would not have been taken without Balfour's approval, will
> inevitably have the effect, without our making any fuss about it,
> of bringing candidates into line on this question." [2]

Meanwhile during 1909 the intra-party argument on tariff reform
dwindled in importance as the shadow of the great constitutional
crisis of that year fell over British politics.[3] The repercussions of
that crisis within the Unionist Party were ultimately to undermine
Balfour's leadership to the point where he felt he had no alternative
but to resign. Again Balfour's problem was his inability to assert
his authority over his more extremist followers.

Balfour had always been eager to co-ordinate the activities of his
party in the two Houses of Parliament. In April, 1906, he had
written to Lansdowne, then Unionist Leader in the Lords: " The
real point is . . . to secure that the party in the two Houses shall not
work as two separate armies . . . " And he added: " . . . I incline to
advise (as a general policy) that we should fight all points of importance very stiffly in the Commons, and should make the House
of Lords the theatre of compromise." [4] The first part of this strategy
was implemented in the battle over the budget of 1909; the party in
the Commons fought it almost line by line from April until it
finally passed the Commons in November. But the second part of
the strategy was certainly not implemented in the Lords; the peers
threw the budget out after a three-day debate. There were reports
that this action of the upper chamber was taken on the insistence

---

[1] Cited in Salvidge, S., *Salvidge of Liverpool*, p. 83.

[2] A. Bonar Law to A. T. Salvidge, 28th January, 1909, cited *Ibid.*, p. 83.

[3] For an excellent account of these events see Jenkins, R., *Mr. Balfour's
Poodle;* an Account of the Struggle between the House of Lords and the
Government of Mr. Asquith, London, 1954.

[4] A. J. Balfour to Lord Lansdowne, 13th April, 1906. Cited in Lord
Newton, *Lord Lansdowne*, pp. 354-5. This letter was written in reply to a
memorandum by Lansdowne (p. 353) proposing closer co-operation between members of the party in the two Houses. Lansdowne proposed
setting up a committee composed of four or five members of each House.
Balfour objected on the grounds that this committee would almost certainly
duplicate the work of the Shadow Cabinet. It is interesting that Lansdowne's
biographer (himself a Conservative peer) writing in 1929 comments that
the close co-operation which Lansdowne urged " though manifestly
essential, is still lamentably lacking after the passage of twenty-three years."
(p. 353.)

of certain powerful peers and against the advice of Balfour,[1] but there is no evidence to support this view; Balfour defended the action of the Lords as " abundantly justified ".[2] In the subsequent election (January, 1910) Balfour led a united party into battle and succeeded in regaining over one hundred seats.[3] This unity was largely maintained through the second election of the year in December, 1910, but thereafter it began to crumble. As Parliament moved from the budget dispute to the Liberal proposals for parliamentary reform there were deeply divided counsels within the Conservative Party.[4]

Balfour did not learn until July, 1911, that the new King had privately promised Asquith before the election of December, 1910, that he was prepared (if the Liberals won that election) to create enough peers to ensure the passage of the Parliament Bill. Balfour was deeply indignant both with the King's advisers and his Ministers [5] and immediately called his Shadow Cabinet colleagues into session on 7th July, 1911, to discuss the situation in light of this new knowledge. There was a sharp difference of opinion as to the policy which should be pursued. The split grew wider at a subsequent Shadow Cabinet meeting on 21st July, when eight of the twenty-two present were for continued resistance while Balfour and thirteen others were for capitulation.[6] The resisters (or " Die-Hards " as they became known) included the party's Chief Whip, Lord Balcarres; he apparently feared the repercussions within the

---

[1] *The Annual Register for 1909*, p. 246.

[2] Cited in Cecil, A., " A. J. Balfour," *Dictionary of National Biography*, 1922-30, p. 51.

[3] With the election of 1910 the tariff reform issue receded (for the time being) almost completely into the background as a source of friction within the party. The members of the small Free Food group lost their seats with the result that (as Austen Chamberlain recorded) the Conservative Chief Whip was able to boast " that he had 273 members, including the Speaker, and that he could count on 272 of them ". Chamberlain, A., *Politics from Inside*, p. 190. But in the second election of 1910 Balfour backslid considerably on the issue of tariff reform promising only that he would if successful submit it to a referendum. Chamberlain confessed that he was " broken-hearted and protested vehemently." *Ibid.*, p. 195.

[4] It will be recalled that at one stage in these controversies Lloyd George proposed informally that an all-party Coalition might be established to deal with the great problems facing the country. Balfour was initially favourable to the suggestion, but he dismissed the idea when he was told by his former Chief Whip Akers-Douglas that the Conservative back-benchers would be bitterly hostile (cf. Jenkins, R., *Mr. Balfour's Poodle*, p. 113). This provides further evidence that the Conservative Leader is by no means free to take his party in any direction he wishes.

[5] See letter from A. J. Balfour to Lord Stamfordham, 1st August, 1911, quoted in Nicolson, H., *King George the Fifth*, p. 149.

[6] Dugdale, Blanche, *Arthur James Balfour*, Vol. II, p. 68.

party if the Shadow Cabinet were to recommend acquiescence in the passage of an unamended Parliament Bill. There were demands in the Carlton Club and elsewhere that Balfour should make a strong public statement defining the party's position. Again as in 1906 some urged Balfour to call a party meeting. But this, as Mrs. Dugdale notes, he would not grant, " being always convinced that such advertisements of difference of opinion during crises did more harm than good."[1] Balfour drafted a memorandum for circulation to his Shadow Cabinet colleagues which was intended to clarify his position. Several colleagues to whom he showed it took exception on the grounds that it took a stronger line than he had adopted at the Shadow Cabinet meeting of 21st July, and that it might therefore encourage the spirit of resistance; as his biographer records, he consented reluctantly to suppress it. And from that occasion, " a sense of isolation began to grow in him, which could only lead him to one inevitable conclusion." [2]

The situation within the party was soon, from Balfour's point of view, out of hand. Lord Lansdowne, the Conservative leader in the Lords, advocated capitulation and in a letter published in *The Times* on 26th July, Balfour backed him:

> " let us then, (he wrote in part) if we can, agree. Let the Unionists in the Upper House follow their trusted leader. But if this is impossible, if differ we must, if there be Peers who (on this occasion) are resolved to abandon Lord Lansdowne, if there be politicians outside who feel constrained to applaud them, let us all at least remember that . . . unless the forces conducting (this campaign for constitutional liberty) possess unity and discipline, ultimate victory is impossible." [3]

Austen Chamberlain, a prominent Die-Hard, wrote Balfour a

---

[1] Dugdale, Blanche, *Arthur James Balfour*, Vol. II, p. 69. Again it should be noted that the Leader felt no responsibility to consult the rank and file of his colleagues in the parliamentary party. Such a meeting for Balfour could only be an occasion for " blowing off steam " and that he obviously felt would add to, rather than diminish his troubles.

[2] *Ibid.*, pp. 69–71.

[3] *The Times,* 26th July, 1911. It is interesting to note that in effect this letter in *The Times* took the place of an address to a party meeting, a meeting which Balfour was unwilling to call on the grounds that it would advertise differences within the party.

The letter purported to be an open letter to a perplexed peer who required advice.   The peer chosen as " recipient " was Lord Newton, who claims that the letter was written " at the instigation of Lord Curzon ". (See Lord Newton, *Lord Lansdowne*, p. 425.) Again Balfour gives the impression that he was responding to pressures from his colleagues rather than leading them.

private reply the next day. He deeply resented the charge of " abandoning our Leader " and added:

> " I think we have deserved better treatment at your hands. You cannot say that those whom you thus pillory have ever been wanting in loyalty to yourself. Might they not have asked in return at least for such ordinary consideration and frankness as a leader customarily extends to his followers? I have (often) discussed this matter with you . . . . Nothing that you have said . . . has prepared me for the line you have now taken up or given me a hint of your intention to treat this as a question of confidence in the leadership of either yourself or of Lansdowne. . . . Till this morning you had given no lead . . . . You have confronted us not with a reply to our arguments but with a denunciation of our conduct, and to make the pill more bitter you have addressed that denunciation not to us but to the public Press."[1]

This was Chamberlain's personal answer to Balfour; that evening the whole Die-Hard group gave theirs. They assembled six hundred strong at a banquet in honour of the Earl of Halsbury, the pugnacious old Die-Hard leader in the Lords. They cheered him to the echo when he denounced all suggestions of compromise or capitulation; only the intervention of his family saved the 87-year-old Earl from being drawn in a carriage down the Strand and to his house in Kensington.[2] It had been stated by its organizers that this Die-Hard rally was not intended as a demonstration against Balfour and Lansdowne but as Lord Newton has remarked: " the underlying tone, however, (was) complete repudiation of Balfour's advice." [3]

In his reply to Austen Chamberlain's letter of 26th July, Balfour explained that he had not intended to impugn the loyalty of the Die-Hards. But he protested that with the Shadow Cabinet split wide open and with the Die-Hards launched on their campaign against compromise he had been forced to act. He had therefore published the letter backing Lansdowne; he could not, he said, " remain a mere spectator."[4] But in the closing stages of the struggle over the Parliament Bill, Balfour was hardly even a spectator. On the very day before the Bill was returned to the Lords he left the country for a holiday in Germany! Before he left he

---

[1] Cited in Chamberlain, Austen, *Politics from Inside,* pp. 348-9. The final sentence of Chamberlain's letter seems to underline Balfour's folly in refusing to call a party meeting at which he could present his views.

[2] Fox, A. W., *The Earl of Halsbury,* London, 1919, p. 254.

[3] Lord Newton, *Lord Lansdowne,* p. 426.

[4] Cited in Chamberlain, A., *Politics from Inside,* p. 351.

spoke privately of his deep unhappiness about the condition of
his party and of his relations with it:

> " On a question which is not one of principle, but of mere Party
> tactics, I am confronted with a deep schism among my leading
> colleagues. In a Cabinet, if there is a division of opinion, the
> rule is that the majority must prevail; and if the view of the
> majority is not accepted, those who will not accept it have no
> alternative but to leave the Government. But here, after a full
> discussion, a minority decline to accept my advice, which commanded
> the majority of votes at the Shadow Cabinet, and the dissentient
> members have gone out into the world and have embarked upon
> a policy of active resistance. I confess to feeling that I have been
> badly treated. I have no wish to lead a Party under these humili-
> ating conditions. . . . If they think that someone else is better able
> to discharge the duties of leadership, I am quite willing to adopt
> that view."[1]

Clearly there were some of Balfour's followers who did think
there were others " better able to discharge the duties of leadership ". Maxse, a colourful Conservative firebrand and editor of
the *National Review,* launched a campaign in the September issue
of his journal with the slogan: " Balfour Must Go ".[2] Balfour's
biographer insists that this campaign in itself had no effect on
Balfour's decision.[3] But on his return to England in early September, Balfour learned from the party managers that there was widespread dissatisfaction within the party. One of his oldest colleagues
and best friends, Walter Long, wrote to Balfour severely criticizing
his leadership. Balfour himself called the letter " a bold and brutal
invitation to retire ". Then on 7th October, the " Halsbury Club "
was formed. The prospectus circulated by one of the leading Die-
Hard peers said: " Some of those who took an active part in supporting Lord Halsbury in his action over the Parliament Act . . .
have met together and agreed that the spirit of the ' Halsbury
Movement ' should become a permanent force in the Party. There
is no idea of forming an organization hostile to the official Party,
but the necessity is strongly felt of keeping together that mass of
opinion both in and out of Parliament that is looking for a definite
lead." [4] This scheme ultimately came to nothing: but when Balfour

---

[1] Cited in Dugdale, Blanche, *Arthur James Balfour,* Vol. II, p. 85.

[2] Maxse expressed his view very forcibly in a private letter to Alderman
Salvidge of Liverpool. " I own to being simply appalled by the attitude of
the people at the top of our party, and above all by their total failure to
realize that a continuance of Balfourism means general ruin." L. J. Maxse
to A. T. Salvidge, 23rd October, 1911, cited in Salvidge, S., *Salvidge of
Liverpool,* p. 113.

[3] Dugdale, Blanche, *Arthur James Balfour,* Vol. II, p. 86.

[4] Cited in Fox, A. W., *The Earl of Halsbury,* p. 286.

first heard of the plans of the Halsbury Club he was deeply indignant; he saw it as a frontal challenge to his leadership.

Balfour was convinced that he could have clung to the leadership had he chosen. " I know I cannot be evicted,"[1] he wrote to the Chief Whip. In fact of course he could have been " evicted " had a majority of the party so decided. But there is little evidence that his critics were prepared as yet to go to such lengths. Austen Chamberlain, a leading Die-Hard, had written (on 20th August, 1911), " I confess that Balfour's leadership at times makes me despair of the fortunes of a Party so led. He has no comprehension of the habits of thought of his countrymen and no idea of how things strike them. . . . (But) I am too much attached to him ever to join any combination against him or his leadership." [2] And two months later (after Balfour had decided to resign, but before his decision was made public) Chamberlain wrote: " Balfour is my leader as long as he will lead." [3] This, incidentally, despite the fact that Chamberlain had already indicated his willingness to join the Halsbury Club.[4]

There was talk among Balfour's friends of calling a party meeting at which a vote of confidence would be proposed. But again there were warnings that this would magnify any divisions of opinion on the issue. In any event, Balfour had already made up his mind to retire and he announced his decision at a meeting of the Executive Committee of the City of London Unionist Association on 8th November, 1911. Although Balfour was then only 63 (and as one journalist put it, his subsequent activities " gave no evidence of his need of repose " [5]) he put forward as the reason for his resignation the condition of his health. He reminded his constituents that he had been an M.P. for thirty-eight years and that he had led his party in the House for twenty years. He wanted to resign before he became " petrified " and inelastic; he feared he had not the vigour to conduct another ministry. He referred to " a certain feeling of unrest in the party " but denied that, in the circumstances, the party was in such a bad condition. A new leader of the party in the Commons would have to be chosen (not " I am glad to think," he added, " a Leader of the Party as a whole ") and that new leader would have no easy task " because leadership is never an easy business ". " But," he added, (and here he permitted himself a touch of irony) " the Unionist Party have always been faithful

[1] Cited in Dugdale, Blanche, *Arthur James Balfour*, Vol. II, p. 88.
[2] Chamberlain, Austen, *Politics from Inside*, p. 352.
[3] *Ibid.*, p. 370.
[4] *Ibid.*, p. 359.
[5] Mackintosh, Sir Alexander, *Echoes of Big Ben*, a Journalist's Parliamentary Diary, London, (1945), p. 60.

to their leaders, and I am quite sure that that ancient tradition will not be violated on the present occasion."[1]

Austen Chamberlain in a letter to his father quoted both Balfour and Balfour's secretary as claiming that the " Halsbury Club movement had nothing to do with his decision " but Chamberlain adds: " . . . I think the restlessness in the Party, *particularly outside the House*, has affected him, as requiring more labour than he can give to deal with it satisfactorily and as indicating demands on the leader's strength and time to which he no longer feels equal . . . . (Balfour) therefore feels that the dissatisfaction . . . is not confined to one section of the Party, but that on all sides demands are being made which he has not the strength to satisfy."[2]

Chamberlain's interpretation, which is probably as sound as any, is particularly interesting for its emphasis on the importance it suggests that Balfour attached to the " restlessness " in the party *outside* Parliament. Balfour had always taken a somewhat patronizing view of the National Union [3] and he is alleged on one occasion to have said that he would as soon take advice from his valet as from a Conservative annual conference. But clearly he could not ignore entirely the mounting evidence of impatience with his cautious tactics which was reflected in the debates at the annual conferences of the National Union. These debates provided ammunition for Balfour's critics within the parliamentary party who claimed that he was failing to express the will of the party. Balfour's experience is a useful reminder that the powers of the Conservative Leader, which may on paper seem almost dictatorial, are wielded only with the consent of his followers. When the Leader loses the confidence of any considerable body of his followers, then the formal possession of those powers in no way ensures his continued authority within the party.

Balfour may well have been, as Asquith claimed, " by universal consent the most distinguished member of the greatest deliberative Assembly in the world ";[4] but the hard fact was that he had clearly lost the confidence of a great many members of his party both inside and outside the House. There was no formal move to depose him and he might have been able to hold on to the leadership much longer; perhaps, in the rush of events in 1912 and especially in 1914 he might have survived indefinitely. But this is at best a de-

---

[1] Cited in *National Union Gleanings*, December, 1911, pp. 573-6.

[2] Cited in Chamberlain, Austen, *Politics from Inside*, p. 380. [Italics mine.]

[3] *Cf.* Balfour's, *Chapters of Autobiography*, Chapter XIII.

[4] Asquith speaking at Lord Mayor's banquet on 9th November, 1911, the day after Balfour's resignation. Cited in Spender, J. A., and Asquith, Cyril, *The Life of Lord Oxford and Asquith*, London, (1932), Vol. I, p. 351.

batable proposition. It is important to remember that the tariff reform dispute broke out with renewed force within the party not long after the Parliament Bill controversy subsided. The difficulties reached their climax after the annual National Union conference in 1912 at which Lord Lansdowne announced the decision to retain as part of the party programme the duty on foreign wheat, subject to certain conditions. This, according to Lord Lansdowne's own account, " split the party from top to bottom " and, he added:

> " Both to Bonar Law and myself it seemed that the only course open to us was the resignation of our leadership—amongst other reasons for this, that it appeared virtually certain that as soon as the food duties were dropped, those who were against Tariff Reform of any kind would immediately agitate for its complete abandonment. But practically the whole Unionist Party in the House of Commons sent a memorial to Bonar Law in which they undertook, if food taxes were dropped, the rest of the tariff programme should be loyally supported. We did not think that we had a right to resist the appeal which was made to us, and the situation was saved upon this basis; but we had to put our pride in our pockets, and I do not think that either of us would do so a second time."[1]

It is highly doubtful also whether Balfour would have " put his pride in his pocket " for a second (or would it have been a third?) time. He was a sensitive man who was alternatively bored and exasperated by the dogmatic enthusiasms of his more militant followers. As he saw his authority crumbling he chose to abdicate rather than to fight a long rearguard action to defend his position.

AUSTEN CHAMBERLAIN AS CONSERVATIVE LEADER

Austen Chamberlain served as Leader of his party in the Commons for only 18 months, from March, 1921, to October, 1922. But his brief, tempestuous career as Leader and his dramatic downfall throws important additional light on the relationships between the Conservative Leader and his followers both inside and outside Parliament. Chamberlain, it will be remembered, succeeded Bonar Law as Leader of the Party in the Commons following the latter's first retirement on the grounds of ill-health in March, 1921. Chamberlain inherited a party deeply divided on two main issues: the problem of Ireland and the future of the Coalition. On both issues he had clear-cut views. He supported the Irish Settlement of 1921 (which indeed he helped to negotiate) and he favoured the

---

[1] Cited in Lord Newton, *Lord Lansdowne*, pp. 434-5.

continuation of the Coalition. On the first issue he managed after
a great struggle to defeat the Die-Hard opponents of the Irish
settlement within his own party. On the second issue he himself
was defeated; his followers, in open revolt, rejected his advice
and he immediately resigned[1].

Chamberlain had had few personal enemies within the party
when he was unanimously elected to lead his party in the Commons
at a meeting of Unionist M.P.s on 21st March, 1921. It will be re
called that he wrote: " The Party meeting was very cordial, and
gave me a great reception." But in his acceptance speech Cham
berlain struck a note which must have been received with anything
but unanimous enthusiasm by his audience: " I am not going here
and now (he said) to attempt to forecast the future of our party
or even of the Coalition; but there are moments when insistence
upon party is as unforgivable as insistence upon personal things
when the difficulties which the nation has to confront call for a
wider outlook and a broader union than any that can be found
even within the limits of a single party, and when the traditions
of more than one party, the ideas of more than one party need to
be put into the common stock, so that the country may be safely
piloted through the hours of crisis and of danger."

With the prestige of the Coalition sagging steadily, a great many
of Chamberlain's listeners already believed that the hour had
come for " insistence upon party ". If the Coalition was, as they
feared, drifting onto the rocks it would be a case of *sauve qui peut*
and many believed that the only prospect of saving the fortunes of
the Unionist Party was to get it out of the Coalition at the earliest
opportunity. The case was first made publicly by the Marquis of
Salisbury in a letter to the press on 20th June, 1921 (three months
after Chamberlain had succeeded Bonar Law):

> " The fact is, (he wrote) the Coalition Government no longer
> possesses the full confidence of the Unionist Party. . . . As it appears
> to me, then, the duty of every Unionist association in the country
> is to approach its Unionist member or candidate, as the case may be
> and request that henceforth he shall consider himself free from any
> binding obligation to support the Coalition Government. If the
> request is made and he assents to it . . . there would be no reason why
> he should not continue to vote with the Government upon issues
> where he might agree with them. But the assent would be a clear
> indication in the name of his constituents that he would prefer
> Unionist Government."[2]

[1] Since the preparation of this edition of *British Political Parties* a new and
very stimulating account of the Coalition and its downfall has been provided by
Lord Beaverbrook in his *Decline and Fall of Lloyd George*, London, 1963.

[2] The *Morning Post*, 20th June, 1921. Cited in *Gleanings and Memo
randa*, July, 1921.

The letter appeared the day before Chamberlain was scheduled to speak for the first time as Leader before the Central Council of the National Union. The timing was no doubt deliberate and although Chamberlain made no direct reference to Salisbury's letter he obviously thought it necessary to reply. He emphasized that he was no " despiser of party ". It " has its place and it has its time. I know not," he said, " how soon the party system will revive." But, he added:

> " I conceive that those men of (our) party who at the present time would deliberately break up a national combination and a national Government in face of all the difficulties, foreign and domestic, with which we are confronted, without clear necessity, would deserve ill of their countrymen, and would meet with condemnation at the hands of their countrymen."[1]

There for the moment the matter rested; there was for a time no further overt sign of rebellion within the party against the Coalition. But Chamberlain faced trouble enough over Ireland. He had become convinced that there was no alternative but to come to terms with Sinn Fein and in October, 1921, he was one of the British delegates who met the Sinn Fein representatives to negotiate the Irish Treaty which was ultimately signed on 5th December.[2] As the negotiation dragged on throughout this period Chamberlain was under continual fire from the Die-Hard wing of his own party. They were opposed to negotiations of any sort with Sinn Fein and were deeply uneasy about their Leader's rôle in the conference. Chamberlain wrote (17th October): " The Conference drags, and a section of our Party grows more restless every day. If we fail to make peace, I suppose that the Party will reunite and I think that the country will be behind us. But if we succeed . . . we shall have serious trouble with a section of our own people—with how many I cannot say." [3] But before very long the Die-Hards stood up and were counted. Some of their number tabled a motion in the Commons which was tantamount to a vote of censure on the Government for entering into the Irish negotiations. In the debate which ensued on 31st October [4] the Government (and, by implication, Austen Chamberlain) were under bitter attack from a number of Unionist back-benchers; Chamberlain himself, when he rose to speak, was continually interrupted by his own supporters. But

---

[1] Cited in *Gleanings and Memoranda*, July, 1921, pp. 88-9.

[2] For Chamberlain's own account of these events see Chapter IX (" The Signature of the Irish Treaty "), in his *Down the Years*, London, 1935.

[3] Cited in Petrie, Sir Charles, *The Life and Letters of Austen Chamberlain*, Vol. II, pp. 163-4.

[4] *House of Commons Debates*, 31st October, 1921.

when the vote was taken it became clear that the Die-Hards were more noisy than numerous. The Government was sustained by a vote of 439 to 43.

The Die-Hards in a bold move then decided to lay their case before the annual conference of the National Union which was due to meet at Liverpool on 17th November. Chamberlain was genuinely and deeply worried about the prospects for this meeting. In the House there had been no real risk of defeat; the Liberals and Labour stood with Chamberlain's own supporters among the Unionists. But at the Liverpool conference the situation was different.[1] The city itself was in any case a hot-bed of Orange Toryism and the delegates to Conservative and Unionist conferences have traditionally stood well to the Right of their leaders where Imperial affairs and constitutional issues are concerned. Chamberlain wrote just before the meeting: " I am fighting for my political life. What Liverpool has in store I don't know. The Die-hards are organizing fiercely and strenuously. *If we are beaten there it won't be the end, but it will be very unpleasant.*"[2]

" Not since the great Liberal split over Home Rule in 1886," wrote one eye-witness, " had feeling within a party reached the intensity evident amongst the Conservative politicians who poured into Liverpool on the eve of the National Unionist Conference of 1921."[3] There were ominous forebodings in the press. The *Daily Express* predicted: " Unless some great personality arises to sway the audience towards unity, the minority and the majority will part company and the great and historic Conservative Party will be left in ruins." [4] As the conference turned to the problem of Ireland [5] a deputation from Ireland was introduced to report on the wrongs suffered by Unionists in the south at the hands of the Irish extremists. The conference listened, deeply moved, and there was loud cheering when General Prescott-Decie, a Southern Loyalist,

[1] For the best description of the atmosphere of the city and the conference see Chapter XV (" Salvidging Ulster ") in Salvidge, S., *Salvidge of Liverpool.*

[2] Cited in Petrie, Sir Charles, *The Life and Letters of Austen Chamberlain,* Vol. II, p. 164. [Italics mine.] This quotation is the best indication of the importance which may be attached by the Leader to a Conservative Party conference held at a critical moment in the party's affairs. Chamberlain knew that if he were defeated it would not be " *the end* "; he would not necessarily have to resign. But it would be " *very unpleasant* " since it would enormously strengthen the position of his foes and critics within the party in Parliament.

[3] Salvidge, Stanley, *Salvidge of Liverpool,* p. 205.

[4] *Ibid.,* p. 207.

[5] For a full summary of the debate see the *1921 Conservative Annual Conference Report,* folios 15–25.

demanded an end to " all parlance with the murder junta . . . .
Given fifty thousand additional troops and a free hand," he claimed
they could be crushed " in from three to nine months ". The Die-
Hards then moved their resolution calling for " the condemnation
of the long-continued ascendancy of crime and rebellion in Ireland."
The resolution was more moderate in tone than had been expected
but the mover accused Chamberlain and other Unionist leaders
of " agreeing to at least the moral if not the physical coercion of
Ulster." Until lunch-time on the first day of the conference the
Die-Hards had dominated the proceedings; no voice had yet been
heard in support of Chamberlain and his policies.

Chamberlain's supporters opened their counter-attack in the
afternoon; it was led most effectively by Alderman Archibald
Salvidge, who was by far the most powerful figure in Liverpool
Conservative politics. He moved an amendment which, in effect,
expressed confidence in the work of Chamberlain and his colleagues
in their Anglo-Irish conference:

> " The real issue (Salvidge claimed) is whether you condemn
> or support your own elected leader (uproar). Some members may
> try to shout me down—(cheers and counter-cheers)—but I tell you
> I am going to divide this Conference on a vote of confidence in
> the leadership (loud applause) . . . . Always, as many of you will
> remember, there has been this group of fractious and discontented
> critics amongst us. I recollect the time when the cry was ' Balfour
> must go '. Then it was ' Bonar Law must go ' and now it is
> ' Chamberlain must go' (cries of ' Never '). How can we be led—
> how can we survive—under such conditions? No sooner is a
> new man in the saddle than there is a howl to drag him down
> . . . . I ask you to say, once and for all, that you will have no
> more of it. (Cheers). Did Mr. Chamberlain seek the position he
> holds? (' No '). Who put him there? (' All of us '). And who
> will stand by him?" (Cries of " We will ", and renewed cheering).[1]

Salvidge turned then to the Irish issue and argued skilfully for the
party to stand behind its Leader. " Only by keeping the Conservative Party intact could they be sure of enforcing [their] pledges to
Ulster . . . . It would be playing into De Valera's hands to exhibit

---

[1] Cited in Salvidge, S., *Salvidge of Liverpool*, pp. 209-10. A note in
Archibald Salvidge's own diary gives some indication of the mood of the
conference: " I knew I was carrying the Conference on loyalty to the
leader, but I was not quite sure how to bring them to the main issue. A
free fight in the middle of the hall, about half-way through my speech, provided a moment or two in which to think out the right approach. One of
the delegates shouted that I was a traitor, and I could see little Tommy
Dowd (Alderman T. Dowd, afterwards Lord Mayor of Liverpool) swing round
in the seat in front and give him a clip on the jaw." *Ibid.*, p. 213.

disunity in the midst of the present negotiations," etc. Other strong speeches were made in support of Chamberlain's Irish policy and it became clear that the tide had set in strongly in his favour.

Salvidge's diary records the last dramatic moments of the debate: " Before the vote was taken there was a hurried pow-wow with Col. Gretton (who had moved the Die-Hard resolution) to get him to withdraw his resolution. Lord Derby was all for this being done so that an appearance of complete unity might be presented. But Gretton, game to the last, retorted that it required a division to convince him that the Conference was overwhelmingly against him, whereupon I replied (writes Salvidge), ' Then, damn you, you shall have your division '."[1] When the vote was taken, of the 1800 delegates representing the Conservative and Unionist Associations of the United Kingdom, fewer than seventy sided with the dissentients.[2]

Chamberlain was not of course in attendance when the vote was taken; even on an issue of this importance the Leader does not normally appear to make his case before the conference. But the result was flashed out to him at Knowsley where he is said to have been anxiously waiting with the notes of two speeches before him —one in case he had to face that night's mass meeting after an adverse decision, the other " sounding a clarion call " to a party which had endorsed his policy.[3] In the event he was to give the latter speech and it proved to be one of the best of his career.

Alderman Salvidge moved the resolution thanking Chamberlain for his speech; he concluded with an earnest appeal for party unity : " whatever their prejudices of the past might have been, he appealed to them at this juncture to put country first. As loyal members of the Unionist Party, having ' had it out ' fairly and squarely, let them close up their ranks and stand solidly behind their Leader in the difficult task he had before him. (Cheers.) "[4] But the newly-elected President of the National Union, the Earl of Derby, had warned (in an earlier speech at the conference) that this would not be easy. He had said: " I do not disguise from myself the fact that

---

[1] Cited in Salvidge, S., *Salvidge of Liverpool*, p. 213.

[2] For a Die-Hard explanation see Hewins, W. A. S., *Apologia of an Imperialist*, London, 1929, Vol. II, p. 244. Hewins claims that a large number of the delegates did not vote and adds: " Gretton took the modest view that about 40 per cent. were really in his favour. The cabinet were afterwards told that they were greatly mistaken if they thought the victory lay with them, it was really a victory of the Die-Hards. The feeling of the Conference according to all reports was strongly against the Coalition, Lloyd George's name was scarcely mentioned."

[3] Salvidge, S., *Salvidge of Liverpool*, p. 213.

[4] *1921 Conservative Annual Conference Report*, folio 42.

at the present moment it will require any tact and any intelligence one possesses to keep together the Conservative Party." [1]

The defeat of the Die-Hards and Chamberlain's personal triumph at Liverpool shows that there are circumstances in which the party conference can be of vital importance in the affairs of the party. As the official Conservative Party monthly magazine (*Gleanings and Memoranda*) claimed at the time: " It is the fashion to decry the usefulness of party conferences, but the Unionist Conference at Liverpool effected a real purpose. It showed clearly that the vast bulk of the party supported the Unionist leaders in their endeavour to arrive at a peaceful settlement of the Irish question. The policy of exhausting every possibility of conciliation and agreement before turning to the grim alternative was endorsed by an overwhelming majority."[2] The Leader, not the Conference, makes policy, it is true; but if on this major issue his policy had been rejected by the party conference, Chamberlain's position would almost certainly have proved untenable. In effect however he had won a double vote of confidence by defeating the Die-Hards both in the House and in the party conference.

Chamberlain's victory on the Irish issue gave him only the briefest of respites from internal party conflict. His own belief in the need for continuation of the Coalition grew steadily firmer;[3] he began, indeed, to think of it as a permanent feature of British politics. In the course of his speech to the Liverpool conference he had said: " I don't hesitate to say that out of (this) Coalition, formed in the midst of war, at a time of national necessity, cemented by common action in years of difficulty and danger . . . will come a new party, constitutional, democratic, national." [4] In a private memorandum to Lloyd George in January, 1922, Chamberlain was even more specific: " My object has been to lead the Unionist Party to accept merger in a new Party under the lead of the present Prime Minister and including the great bulk of the old Unionists and old Liberals so as to secure the widest and closest

---

[1] *1921 Conservative Annual Conference Report,* folio 11.

[2] *Gleanings and Memoranda,* December, 1921, p. 441.

[3] Chamberlain's motives in supporting the Coalition need not be cast in too noble a light. Reflecting on the events of the years since 1918 he wrote Lord Long on 27th April, 1922: " Had we formed a purely party Government (in 1918), the Party would have borne the blame for all of which the country now complains. As it is ' Coalition ' has to shoulder the burden, and there is at least this to be said—that the shoulders of the Coalition are broader than the shoulders of the Party . . . . " Cited in Petrie, Sir Charles, *The Life and Letters of Austen Chamberlain,* Vol. II, p. 180.

[4] Cited in *Gleanings and Memoranda,* December, 1921, p. 536.

possible union of all men and women of constitutional and progressive views. This requires time and careful preparation. No one except myself has ever begun to touch it." [1]

This memorandum is a document of vital importance. In it Chamberlain declared in the most unequivocal terms his intention to lead his party into a complete merger with the Liberals; he acknowledges that at the moment he is almost alone in his purpose and that it will take " time and careful preparation " to win the party over to his point of view. He even seems to envisage the possibility of a party split on the issue: he speaks of carrying " the great bulk of the old Unionists " into the new party. [2] Chamberlain was presumably within his rights in attempting so bold and revolutionary a scheme, though clearly it tested to the limit the Leader's theoretical right to formulate policy. But so also were other members of the party within their rights in resisting the scheme if they preferred to retain the identity of their party. There would certainly seem to be no reason to question the loyalty (either to their party or their Leader) of those who resisted Chamberlain's plan. This needs to be kept in mind in examining the revolt against Chamberlain's leadership which culminated in his defeat at the Carlton Club in October, 1922.

There is ample reason to doubt whether at any period in the controversy a majority of the party sympathized with Chamberlain's merger scheme. In the very period in which his memorandum to Lloyd George was written one ardent Die-Hard wrote in his diary (19th January, 1922): " The striking thing about the last fortnight is the disintegration of the Coalition . . . , the prevailing feeling amongst Conservative M.P.s and still more in the constituencies is that they will not have another Coalition election . . . . Fusion is out of the question." [3] There was evidence from less prejudiced quarters to back this up. Lord Balfour recorded a conversation with Bonar Law following the latter's return to London after the parliamentary recess in February, 1922. Bonar Law said that he found " a complete change of opinion " among the Con-

[1] Cited in Petrie, Sir Charles, *The Life and Letters of Austen Chamberlain*, Vol. II, p. 171.

[2] Subsequently however, (in March, 1922) Chamberlain became aware of the dangers of a party split. Alderman Salvidge told him that " it would be impossible to carry the policy of a continued alliance with Lloyd George without giving such a firm lead as to entail shedding some of the Die-Hards . . . . " Chamberlain upheld that " one thing, and one thing only, deterred him from giving such a lead. The Conservative Party was intact when its leadership had been placed in his hands. . . . He was not prepared to have it recorded of him that he split the party which had been handed over to him as a united force." Salvidge, S., *Salvidge of Liverpool*, p. 233.

[3] Hewins, W. A. S., *Apologia of an Imperialist*, Vol. II, p. 247.

servatives with regard to Coalition. He had spoken to the Prime Minister on the subject, telling him that in the present mood of the Conservatives it was impossible that things should go on as they were. Lloyd George, according to Bonar Law, did not express dissent.[1] Disaffection was clearly spreading throughout the whole party. The Chairman of the Party Organization wrote to Alderman Salvidge protesting against what he felt was the latter's imputation that he (the Chairman) was lukewarm in his support for the Coalition: " If you mean to imply that the Central Office has in any way been supporting hostility to the Coalition you are entirely mistaken. No one has worked harder than myself, during the last six months, to smooth difficulties and maintain the alliance, *but I am met everywhere by revolt . . .* " [2]

Open revolt was not long in appearing. Col. Gretton, M.P. (who had led the Die-Hard revolt on Ireland) wrote to the press (3rd February, 1922) saying that he had been asked by " a considerable number of Conservatives in the House of Commons " to place a few considerations before " those who still consider that Conservative principles should have a voice in determining the policy of the Government of their country."

> " It is evident, (he added), that an effort is being made to merge the Conservative Party and their organizations permanently in the Coalition, either by continuing the existing Coalition, or under some new name. . . . We are therefore of opinion that the time has come when we should have a clear declaration from the leaders of the Conservative Party as to their views of the future of the Party that they were chosen to represent, and how far they are prepared to co-operate in the maintenance of a consistent Conservative policy, which, in our belief, can alone secure that stability and confidence in the Government of the country which has been its greatest asset in promoting the progress and welfare of the people. We would therefore appeal to all Conservatives in the country, who still believe in their principles, not to pledge themselves to support any Coalition candidates until the position of the party and its future policy are made clear." [3]

Ten days later Col. Gretton led a delegation of 35 M.P.s which saw Chamberlain and other Unionist Ministers to put the case against continued association with Lloyd George and the Coalition. Chamberlain, in talking with the delegation, made no secret of his goal: ultimate fusion between Coalition Liberals and Unionists. Meanwhile he promised that when the election came each of the

---

[1] Cited in Dugdale, Blanche, *Arthur James Balfour*, Vol. II, p. 345.
[2] Sir George Younger to Alderman A. Salvidge, 14th February, 1922. Cited in Salvidge, S., *Salvidge of Liverpool*, p. 228. [Italics mine.]
[3] Cited in *Gleanings and Memoranda*, March, 1922, p. 282.

partners to the Coalition would issue its own manifesto. Speaking subsequently to a meeting of the Central Council of the National Union on 21st February he had explained that he did not envisage an exact replica of the " coupon " procedure of 1918: " I think it more likely that we shall follow the older example—let us say of Mr. Balfour and my father—and each address our own constituents, but not without an undertaking between ourselves, both as to what we want to do and as to the method by which it may be accomplished."[1]

In a series of public speeches Chamberlain pressed his case for continuation of the Coalition. At the Oxford Carlton Club on 3rd March, 1922, he said: " The minds of my (Unionist colleagues in the Government) and myself are clear. We see our duty and we will fulfil it. We tender our advice to our Party. We hope they will be persuaded of its wisdom. But for ourselves we mean to continue that co-operation in Government and out of Government until some question of principle arises—if it does arise—which clearly separates us (from our Liberal allies)." In the same speech there is the first indication that Chamberlain realized he might not succeed in carrying his party with him: " No leader is indispensable, and no leader would or could desire to remain leader unless he could continue to receive the confidence of his Party in such a measure that in any great questions of this kind they would listen to his advice."[2]

One passage in Chamberlain's Oxford speech stirred considerable concern within the party. He had used the sentence: " when we go to the country, we go as a Government." The Chairman of the Central Council of the National Union (Sir Alexander Leith) took the unusual step of writing to Chamberlain on 4th March to ask whether this sentence implied that he had gone back on his previous declaration that the two parties to the Coalition would go to the polls as separate parties. To this Chamberlain replied that it was a misapprehension to think that he had gone back on his declaration to the National Union, and that the policy he advocated at Oxford was the same as followed by Balfour and his father in 1900. But he added: " I regard Unionists and National

---

[1] Cited in Petrie, Sir Charles, *The Life and Letters of Sir Austen Chamberlain*, Vol. II, p. 174. Chamberlain's willingness to consider fusion seems to have been much influenced by his early experience of fusion between the Conservatives and Liberal Unionists.

[2] *Gleanings and Memoranda*, April, 1922, pp. 392-4. This passage reflects the traditional theoretical assumptions that underlie the Conservative conception of the rôle of the Leader. On " great questions of this kind " the Leader assumes the party will accept his " advice "; Chamberlain does not suggest here that he has any responsibility to reflect the views of his followers. In the event, of course, they rejected his advice and his leadership collapsed.

Liberals as, under present circumstances, two wings of one great constitutional and progressive Party."[1]

Few among his followers seemed to share Chamberlain's conception of " one great constitutional and progressive Party ". On 14th March there was a special meeting of 200 Unionist M.P.s at the House of Commons to discuss the idea of a new centre party to be formed by the Unionists and Coalition Liberals.[2] Resolutions to this effect received little support. Hewins recorded the Die-Hard view of this result: " This scheme ended ingloriously and the adjournment of the meeting was carried unanimously. This was virtually a vote of no confidence in the Coalition, Lloyd George and the present Unionist leaders. I found the Die-Hards jubilant about the meeting. It seems to have been very amusing. There were not more than a dozen Die-Hards present. I hope the fiasco ends this business . . . "[3]

But the argument over the future of the Coalition was by no means ended. It now became increasingly reflected in the party outside Parliament as well. Chamberlain wrote to Lord Long (27th April, 1922): " The feeling in favour of a return to a purely party fight is strongest . . . in London and the Home Counties, and in those constituencies where our Party or candidate standing alone is powerful enough to be certain of victory. But in the industrial districts of the North and Midlands and in Scotland feeling in favour of continuing the Coalition is strong both among our Members and among our supporters. For some time past I have received many indications of the strength of this feeling, which was at first slow to express itself, but now comes to me in numberless Resolutions from Associations in nearly all parts of the country, but especially in those which I have named."[4]

As the year wore on the Coalition limped from one crisis to another; its sagging prestige in the country was reflected in a series of by-election defeats. By June the extremist section of the Die-

[1] The exchange of correspondence was made public on 9th March, and is reproduced in *Gleanings and Memoranda*, April, 1922, p. 394. This exchange shows that although the Leader is in no way accountable to the extra-parliamentary organs of the party, his actions are kept under close scrutiny and he may be asked questions which are so phrased as to express the anxiety of his followers.

[2] *Gleanings and Memoranda*, April, 1922, p. 400.

[3] Hewins, W. A. S., *The Apologia of an Imperialist*, Vol. II, p. 249.

[4] Cited in Petrie, Sir Charles, *The Life and Letters of Austen Chamberlain*, Vol. II, p. 180.

This is one of the first of many indications that the views of the constituency associations were an important factor in determining the course of the struggle waged by Chamberlain to carry his party into fusion with the Coalition Liberals.

Hards was in open revolt. The Marquis of Salisbury who had fired the first shot a year earlier (see p. 84 above) again took the lead. On 2nd June the press carried a manifesto from a body calling itself the " Conservative and Unionist Movement ". It stated:

> " The time has come when the British people should be fully informed of the sources of the evils which cause the grave peril and chaos in Ireland, the confusion and misdirection of foreign policy, the vacillation and errors in dealing with our great dependencies ; unemployment on an unprecedented scale, languishing industries, an overgrown bureaucracy, and an overwhelming burden of taxation. The immediate need and the remedy is a rally of the deep-seated Conservative feeling in the country and the application without delay of a policy based on true national principles. To drift further with ever-changing policies must quickly produce chaos, disaster, and ruin. Our purpose is not to break up the Conservative and Unionist Party, but to rally and revive the true Conservative and Unionist principles, and we appeal to all Conservative and Unionist associations and all who agree with us to give us their support."[1]

The manifesto was signed by the Marquis of Salisbury, ten other peers and a group of commoners (none of whom were M.P.s). In July Salisbury was unanimously elected " Leader of the Conservative and Unionist Movement " and a few weeks later he acknowledged a fund of £22,000 raised by the *Morning Post* to advance his cause. That cause he summarized: " In a word, we stand for the spirit of Conservatism and against the spirit of the Coalition."[2]

The Chairman of the Party Organization (Sir George, later Viscount Younger) had earlier made an effort to stop the rot. Speaking to a conference of the Association of Conservative Clubs, 16th June, 1922, he had said:

> " Although we shall go independently to the country, and in that way restore our own identity, if our leaders think it essential to make some kind of working arrangement with the friends they are working with now, I beg of you to follow them trustfully. You may be sure they are not doing it without a very good reason. They regard it as in the best interests of the country and the party cause. If we get at one another's throats and oppose one another

---

[1] Cited in *Gleanings and Memoranda*, July, 1922, p. 97.

[2] Cited in *Gleanings and Memoranda*, September, 1922, p. 309. See also Hewins, W. A. S., *The Apologia of an Imperialist*, Vol. II., p. 253, and Chapter XXII (" The Wreck of the Coalition ") *passim*. It is important to note that this rebel group called itself a " movement " and not a " party " but it could hardly have been a more overt challenge to Chamberlain's leadership. Compared with Salisbury's " movement ", the abortive Halsbury Club scheme pales into insignificance.

in the constituencies, the only result would be to give up those seats to Labour."[1]

But Chamberlain seemed to have little idea of how to meet the situation. He had confessed in a private letter to his sister:

> "I know what I want. My colleagues (his Unionist colleagues in the Cabinet) are agreed with me and Younger intends to carry out my policy; yet they all seem to conspire to prevent it. Younger humiliates the (Prime Minister) publicly, F. E. (Lord Birkenhead) attacks Younger personally; Bonar Law tries on the crown, but can't make up his mind to attempt to seize it, won't join us and share the load, but watches not without pleasure the troubles of his friends, and the Die-Hards instead of responding to my advances, harden in their resistance."[2]

In September, Chamberlain again wrote privately to his sister predicting in this letter that even after an election " No Govt. is possible without Coalition. (But) no Coalition on present lines and *in present conditions* is possible with Co-Libs. (Coalition Liberals), except under a Ll. G. premiership." But there was another complication . . . " the National Union in November may declare (a) Against Coalition of any sort; (b) Against Coalition, except under a Unionist P.M. What a kettle of fish! (the letter concludes) Envy me my job ! . . . ." [3]

Amongst Chamberlain's own colleagues, revolt began first among the Unionist junior ministers. They had seen him as a group in July and expressed to him their uneasiness and their apprehensions about the position of the party. They then asked and were permitted to meet the Unionist cabinet ministers.[4] Birkenhead and other staunch Coalitionists severely reproved them (which did no good at all); but there was much evidence that their uneasiness was now reflected throughout the party organization. Sir George Younger wrote on

[1] *The Times,* 17th June, 1922.

[2] Cited in Petrie, Sir Charles, *The Life and Letters of Austen Chamberlain,* Vol. II, p. 181.

[3] Cited in Petrie, Sir Charles, *The Life and Letters of Austen Chamberlain,* Vol. II, p. 193. This letter again shows that the Conservative Leader is forced to take into account the views of the extra-parliamentary organs of his party.

[4] L. S. Amery (a junior minister at the time) quotes an interesting passage from his diary describing this meeting. Birkenhead, he says, berated the junior ministers " for their impertinence in having asked for a meeting at all, when they had already been informed of the Cabinet Ministers' views . . . " Amery added that " Whatever chances (Birkenhead) may have had of the Unionist leadership of the future they are not likely to have survived this unfortunate performance." Amery, L. S., *My Political Life,* London, 1953, Vol. II, p. 233.

16th September to Chamberlain: " . . . undoubtedly the feeling in the constituencies is becoming more and more pronounced against any continuation of the present situation . . . . to attempt to continue as at present would appear to be courting certain disaster." [1] This latter warning was obviously in Chamberlain's mind when he went next day (17th September) to a crucial meeting of senior Coalition ministers of both parties at Chequers. There Chamberlain advocated an immediate dissolution, and his colleagues agreed to go to the country as a Coalition under Lloyd George's leadership.[2] All but one of Chamberlain's Unionist cabinet colleagues—including Balfour, Birkenhead and Curzon—endorsed this decision; the one exception was Baldwin who, according to Chamberlain's own account, " clearly showed his dislike but did not definitely refuse assent." But elsewhere in the party the decision was received very badly indeed. The senior party officials were unanimously hostile. Sir George Younger, the Chairman of the Party Organization, was " frankly appalled "; Sir Malcolm Fraser, the Chief Agent, saw " much trouble ahead, all round " and Sir Leslie Wilson, the Chief Whip, was " very disturbed ". According to Chamberlain's own account, " Younger and Leslie Wilson . . . wrung their hands and lamented—and proceeded to work against me." [3]

Opposition within the extra-parliamentary organs of the party was also mounting rapidly. On 10th October, the Executive Committee of the National Union was to consider a motion which struck squarely at Chamberlain's own policy towards the Coalition. It read: " The Executive Committee of the National Unionist Association desires to call the attention of the Leaders of the Party to the grave conditions of unrest in the Party, and to represent to them the necessity of bringing the Coalition to an end on friendly terms before the General Election which may be in the near future." Chamberlain was so eager to prevent this resolution from coming

[1] Sir George Younger to Austen Chamberlain, 16th September, 1922. Cited in Petrie, Sir Charles, *The Life and Letters of Austen Chamberlain,* Vol. II, p. 195.

[2] Amery claims that " By now it was clear, even to the inner circle of the Cabinet, that the Coalition could not survive the Unionist Annual Party Conference due to meet in October. The only way out was to forestall the Conference by an immediate dissolution." Amery, L. S., *My Political Life,* Vol. II, p. 234. (The conference was, in fact, due to meet in November, but Amery's comment is still valid.)

[3] Cited in Petrie, Sir Charles, *The Life and Letters of Austen Chamberlain,* Vol. II, pp. 198-9. Chamberlain's charge—that the party officials " proceeded to work against me "—is the first hint of the theory that he was victim of a conspiracy which reached its climax in his destruction at the Carlton Club meeting on 19th October, 1922. This theory is examined below.

to a vote that he called its proposer (a Miss Fardell) to come to see him, when, according to his biographer, " he put to her the arguments which had convinced himself and his colleagues at Chequers, stressing especially the probability of extensive Labour victories at the polls if the Coalition was dissolved before the General Election took place."[1] Sir Charles Petrie describes Chamberlain's action as being " true to his policy of hearing all points of view . . . " It might be fairer to say that he was eager to ensure that the National Union was prevented (or at least discouraged) from entertaining any point of view other than his own. In any event Miss Fardell withdrew her motion in deference to Chamberlain's request.

On 15th October in a speech at Birmingham, Chamberlain made his last plea to his followers to stand by the Coalition. He emphasized that in all he had done and said since he became Leader he had acted and spoken with the full assent of his Unionist colleagues in the Cabinet; the advice which he had tendered to the party he had tendered in agreement with them. He added that in the judgment of others and of himself there was no possibility that in the new Parliament any government could be formed except by a Coalition drawn from more than one of the old parties. " Let us see, if that be so (he concluded), that it is the constitutional Conservative Coalition which prevails, and do not let us hand over for experiments of wildly subversive, if not of violently revolutionary type, the institutions, the industry, the welfare and the greatness of this country and of the Empire of which it is the heart." [2]

But even this impassioned argument, which might have been expected to appeal strongly to the most Die-Hard of Chamberlain's opponents, left most of his followers within Parliament and in the party outside unconvinced.[3] The Unionist cabinet ministers had, three days earlier (10th October), re-affirmed their intention to go to the country as a Coalition under Lloyd George's leadership, but at that meeting Sir Leslie Wilson, the Chief Whip, urged that before an election was held the Coalition issue should be discussed at the annual conference of the National Union in November. On 15th October Wilson repeated the argument at a private dinner meeting

---

[1] Petrie, Sir Charles, *The Life and Letters of Sir Austen Chamberlain*, Vol. II, p. 199.

[2] *Birmingham Post*, 14th October, 1922.

[3] Lord Salisbury as Leader of the Conservative Unionist Movement replied to this speech on 16th October. He accused Chamberlain of using the " Bolshevist bogey " in arguing for a continuation of the Coalition. He said that he and his friends " trusted Labour " and " believed in the good sense of the working-classes, and intended to appeal to them to give the country . . . a good Government", (under the Unionist Party). Cited in the *Annual Register for 1922*, p. 113.

of most of the Unionist ministers at the home of Winston Churchill. Here is Austen Chamberlain's account of what ensued:

> " (Wilson) had been pressing hard that I should either wait for the meeting of the National Union or call a special meeting. I refused, saying that this would certainly split the Party in two for I and the colleagues who agreed with me would have to attend and debate the question, and you couldn't debate in a gathering of three or four thousand without bringing out temper on both sides, and in the end we might be nearly equally divided, and at best there would be a large minority with heightened tempers, confirmed prejudices and a resolve to continue the struggle throughout the constituencies."

Then, as Chamberlain put it: " I offered [Wilson] a compromise. I would summon all the M.P.s to the Carlton. I asked (Wilson) point blank after others had spoken: ' Now are we all agreed? Leslie [Wilson], do you accept that? ' and he replied, ' Yes, I accept that '."[1]

For four feverish days until the Carlton Club meeting on the 19th there was a furious round of discussions among the leading figures in the party. The Executive Committee of the National Union was exasperated that it had not been consulted. The junior ministers were in open revolt; they reluctantly agreed to a compromise suggested by one of their number, L. S. Amery, that the Coalition should go to the country as a government, provided that the Unionist Party preserved its right to reconsider its position at a party meeting as soon as the election result was known.[2] Chamberlain was sympathetic to the proposal but the sterner Coalitionists among his colleagues (notably Birkenhead and Balfour) were strongly opposed and persuaded him to reject it. Baldwin meanwhile pressed hard for a clean break with the Coalition and several other ministers began to waver in his direction. The decisive factor was Bonar Law. The anti-Coalitionists needed a major figure in the party as alternative Leader; late in the afternoon of the 18th, Bonar

---

[1] Cited in Petrie, Sir Charles, *The Life and Letters of Sir Austen Chamberlain*, Vol. II, p. 200. Petrie also records (p. 200 Note 1) Wilson's own account: " I replied, ' I do ', having gained my point as to the Party being asked to give their opinion, but I also added, ' I have not, however, changed my own opinion.' From that hour to the Wednesday of the meeting (i.e. at the Carlton Club) I tried to get Austen to change his views and, having failed, I had no alternative but, as Chief Whip, knowing the facts and the views of over 180 Conservative Members of Parliament, to speak at the meeting."

[2] Amery, L. S., *My Political Life*, Vol. II, pp. 235 ff.

Law decided, apparently with some reluctance,[1] to accept the rôle. He told Chamberlain privately of his decision and the latter knew at once that his own defeat was almost certain.

Even before the party meeting assembled on the afternoon of the 19th two more nails were driven into the coffin of the Coalition. On the afternoon of the 18th the Executive Committee of the National Union decided unanimously to call an emergency conference of the National Union to discuss the future of the Coalition. Alderman Salvidge, the only executive member present who abstained, described the meeting in his diary as " extremely acrimonious ". He added (and this is the only available record of the meeting):

> " The Die-Hards, who as usual were present in great force, were obviously afraid that the Carlton Club gathering on the morrow would decide against them. They argued that it was merely a sectional meeting and its conclusions, whatever these might prove to be, would not represent the views of the party as a whole. As a counterblast they demanded that Younger should be empowered to summon a special conference (of the National Union) forthwith. In the end a resolution to this effect was passed and a deputation appointed to lay it before Chamberlain."[2]

The Executive then adjourned *for twenty-four hours*. The clear intention appeared to be to provide the strongest possible evidence of the Executive's unhappiness about the Leader's intention to take their party into the election in partnership with the Lloyd George Liberals. The very brief adjournment was apparently meant to underline this warning.[3]

[1] There seems no reason to question Bonar Law's sincerity in this matter despite Chamberlain's caustic observation (p. 95 above) about his " trying on the crown ". Bonar Law told Salvidge on the eve of the Carlton Club meeting that in his view " there was a tidal wave of feeling in favour of a United Conservative Party. To ignore it would mean ignoring his duty to the State, as the disintegration of the Conservative Party would be a national disaster." Cited in Salvidge, S., *Salvidge of Liverpool*, pp. 237-8.

[2] Cited in Salvidge, S., *Salvidge of Liverpool*, p. 237. The Die-Hard argument which Salvidge quotes (to the effect that a full meeting of M.P.s is " merely a sectional meeting . . . (which) would not represent the views of the party as a whole ") and, indeed, the Executive decision to call for a special conference are extremely interesting since they reflect one of the few occasions in the party's history in which the extra-parliamentary organs of the party have appeared willing to challenge the autonomy of the party in Parliament.

[3] When the Executive reassembled the following day the results of the Carlton Club meeting were known and the following resolution was passed: " That in view of the resignation of the Government and the consequent change in the political position, it be decided to abandon the Special Con-

The second and final blow to Chamberlain's hopes came in the morning of the 19th when news was received of the unexpected[1] by-election victory at Newport of a Conservative (anti-Coalition) candidate over his Labour and Liberal opponents. This victory appeared of course to belie Chamberlain's argument that the Conservatives could not win the election if they fought as a separate party.[2] The case for the Coalition had fallen to the ground; the party was in revolt both inside and outside the House; the rebels had found themselves a new Leader—or rather an old and respected Leader who was prepared to come out of retirement to lead into battle a reunited and independent party. Chamberlain's case was now hopeless and he undoubtedly knew it when he faced the party meeting at the Carlton Club at 11 a.m. on 19th October, 1922.[3]

In the course of his speech to the Carlton Club meeting, Chamberlain explained why he had rejected the Chief Whip's advice that the future of the Coalition should be settled at the forthcoming National Union meeting (cf. p. 98 above). His explanation provides an important definition of the responsibility of the Leader to his followers in Parliament (rather than to the party organization outside).

> " Nor can I, gentlemen," Chamberlain said, " accept on this matter an appeal from you to any other tribunal. With my friends I have carefully considered that question beforehand, and in the interests of the Party no less than for personal reasons, I thought that my confidence was due to you, and to you only, and you I have invited to meet me in order that I might make (my) declaration of faith. It is you deriving your authority from the electors who conferred my authority upon me and made me what I am, and in such a matter as this I can accept no appeal from you to any other authority than that of the electors who are the masters of us all."[4]

ference and to postpone the Annual Conference summoned for 15th November to a later date." Cited in *Gleanings and Memoranda*, November, 1922, p. 487.

[1] Hewins, a Die-Hard, claims in his diary: " This day (the 19th) was chosen (for the Carlton Club meeting) because the Newport poll would be in the papers that morning and a Labour victory was expected." Hewins, W. A. S., *The Apologia of an Imperialist*, Vol. II, p. 260.

[2] *The Times* commented: " The country will see in (this result) a most complete condemnation of the Coalition Government . . . " (19th October, 1922). *The Times* had privately pledged its support to Bonar Law if he took the lead in opposing the Coalition at the Carlton Club meeting, cf. *The History of the Times*, Vol. IV, Part II, p. 754.

[3] For a full account of this meeting see Blake, R., *The Unknown Prime Minister*, pp. 436–61, and Beaverbrook, Lord, *The Decline and Fall of Lloyd George*, pp. 191 ff.

[4] This and the subsequent speeches at the Carlton Club meeting are

The electors were not however the " masters " of some of those present at the Carlton Club; it had been decided to invite Unionist peers who were members of the Government.[1] But otherwise Chamberlain's point was valid: he appeared now before the men who had conferred his authority upon him and he proceeded to make his " declaration of faith " and to offer them his advice at a profoundly important moment in the history of the party. Chamberlain re-stated the full case for the Coalition and urged that " we should maintain the closest most cordial co-operation in the constituencies and throughout the fight and after the fight with the men who have stood by us in the difficult years." He agreed that every " Unionist and Conservative, every Liberal Coalitionist should stand under his own Party name, and should retain his Party loyalty unimpaired." But " As for the members of the present Government, we must go (to the country) as a Government." [2]

quoted from *Gleanings and Memoranda,* November, 1922, pp. 488 ff. Chamberlain appears in this statement to have been attempting to preclude the possibility that his opponents, if defeated in the Carlton Club vote, might attempt to appeal their case to the annual conference of the National Union. He no doubt had in mind the actions of the Die-Hards the previous year when, defeated in the Commons on the issue of Ireland, they carried their case to the annual conference of the National Union. But whatever motive prompted Chamberlain's statement on this occasion it provides one of the few definitions by a Conservative Leader of his conception of his responsibilities to his followers.

[1] A letter was read out from Lord Curzon to Austen Chamberlain saying: " I have been a good deal concerned at the idea of Ministers who are members of the House of Lords, and particularly myself as Leader, being present and very likely being called upon to speak .... Considerable feeling has been aroused at the limitation of this meeting to members of one House of Parliament alone, and although the situation is quite clear as it affects yourself (Chamberlain) and your leadership of the Party in your House, since you are appealing to the body by which you were elected, it is different as regards myself and my House. I have received several protests from peers against my taking part as Leader of the House of Lords in a meeting from which the peers are excluded and seeking by anything that I may say to influence the judgments of members of the House of Commons, and I think in the circumstances that it will be better that I should abstain." Cited in *Gleanings and Memoranda,* November, 1922, p. 487.

[2] One of those present at the Carlton Club meeting, Lord Hemingford, (then Sir Dennis Herbert, M.P.) gives an interesting sidelight on Chamberlain's performance that day: " The uncompromising and somewhat aggressive attitude adopted by Austen Chamberlain surprised many of us, and even before Bonar Law's speech, tended to make us support the break-up of the Coalition: I believe it was partly due to an unfortunate misunderstanding on Austen's part. The meeting was somewhat excited and at one point there were loud murmurs of ' traitor ' from some of those present; this was meant for Birkenhead, who had just come in late to the meeting, and with whom some of the anti-Coalition members were very angry: but Austen is said to have thought it was meant for him and an accusation

Three other speeches of importance were made after Chamberlain had spoken. One of them, by Balfour, appears to have carried very little weight[1] but it is of interest because of the obvious link it provides with the last previous occasion on which the party rejected its Leader. From the beginning of the argument over the Coalition Balfour had stood by Chamberlain, and on the eve of the Carlton Club meeting at an informal discussion at 10 Downing Street, he was (according to Salvidge's diary) the most militantly eager of all of Chamberlain's colleagues to fight the anti-Coalitionists. " To me," Salvidge records, " the biggest surprise of the whole evening was Lord Balfour. When I had finished my tale (Salvidge had brought the news that Curzon intended to swing against Coalition) he banged the table with his fist and shouted, ' I say fight them, fight them, fight them! This thing is wrong. The Conservative Party has always acted on the advice of its leaders. Is the lead of Law and Curzon to count as everything, and the advice of the rest of us as nothing? This is a revolt and it should be crushed '."[2] Balfour spoke somewhat similarly at the Carlton Club meeting:

" The leader of this Party, I thought, was Mr. Austen Chamberlain, and I really listened with surprise and with some pain to the lip service we all pay to the loyalty of our leaders when compared with the actual practice . . . . What is the use of saying one thing to the country about our leader when much that is done has for its inevitable result not merely to increase the embarrassments and the difficulties of that leader, but to weaken his authority? That is not the way to carry on the great Conservative principles. . . . I, therefore, strongly urge this meeting to support its leader. I understood that by a unanimous vote he was made our leader, and the only legitimate way in which you can make a leader is to treat him as a leader."

The fact that this argument appears to have carried no weight whatever with the meeting is a matter of very considerable importance. It reflects of course the decline to zero of Balfour's influence

of that kind was one which he with his sensitive disposition was certain to feel keenly resentful about." Lord Hemingford, *Back-Bencher and Chairman*, London, 1946, p. 42. For another account, see Amery, L. S., *My Political Life*, Vol. II, pp. 238 ff.

[1] " His speech at the Carlton Club did not sway a vote," says Mrs. Dugdale, (*Arthur James Balfour*, Vol. II, p. 357.)

[2] Salvidge, S., *Salvidge of Liverpool*, p. 239. It is of course highly ironical that Balfour of all people should say, " The Conservative Party has always acted on the advice of its leaders." Salvidge commented on Balfour's outburst: " Nothing could have been less like the dreamy Balfour of tradition . . . . I thought of how, in the long years I had served him, there had been times when I would have been thankful for instructions containing a touch of the fire and temper he showed that night."

in the party. But more than that it suggests that appeal to the principle of unquestioning allegiance to the Leader carries very little weight with the Conservative Party when its members are deeply stirred on an issue of principle.[1]

The decisive speeches at the Carlton Club meeting were made by Baldwin and Bonar Law. The former defined his purpose very simply: " Mr. Chamberlain has called this meeting as he has . . . told you, to put before you the views of the majority of the Unionist members of the Cabinet; and it is my duty . . . to put before you, very briefly and very clearly, the views of the minority in the Cabinet—that is of myself and of Sir Arthur Boscawen." Then, in a frontal challenge to Chamberlain's leadership, Baldwin said: " . . . it seems to me that a fatal mistake was made in agreeing to go to an election without consulting the party as to whether they were willing or not to continue the arrangement which they entered into in 1918." He warned that Lloyd George (" that dynamic force ") had smashed the Liberal Party to pieces, and he added: " . . . it is my firm conviction that, in time, the same thing will happen to our party . . . . if the present association is continued, and if this meeting agrees that it should be continued you will see some more breaking up, and I believe the process must go on inevitably until the old Conservative Party is smashed to atoms and lost in ruins." [2] No mention here of loyalty to the Leader, but an urgent appeal to the survival instincts of the Conservative Party.

Bonar Law in his speech did however deal with the leadership issue:

> " What I would like if it were possible . . . but I am afraid it is too late even to discuss it now, was to say this: ' This is a question in regard to which our system (and a good system it has been) has hitherto gone on this principle: that the party elects a

---

[1] A similar appeal by Salvidge at the 1921 conference of the National Union had appeared to carry more weight. But it would seem reasonable to assume that the conference had swung against the Die-Hards because of the weakness of their case rather than out of loyalty to Chamberlain.

[2] Cited in Young, G. M., *Stanley Baldwin*, pp. 40-2. For a further description of the occasion see also Steed, Wickham, *The Real Stanley Baldwin*, pp. 39-42. Although Baldwin's biographers do not stress this point, there can be little doubt that he was deeply apprehensive about the extent to which corrupt practices (involving, among other things, what amounted to the sale of titles) were alleged to be spreading among the higher reaches of the party. One of those present at the Carlton Club meeting (who supported the Baldwin-Bonar Law line) has told the writer that he believes that if the Conservative Party had not freed itself from the Coalition, political corruption might have come to play as large a part in its affairs as it has in the history of American political parties.

leader, and that the leader chooses the policy, and if the party does not like it they have to get another leader ' . . . . If it were possible, even at this last moment—I am afraid it is not—I would say, ' Let Mr. Chamberlain and those who think with him and those who disagree with him submit to the party the question: ' Shall we or shall we not continue the Coalition ? ' and let us abide by their decision.' If that is possible I would gladly adopt that . . . . (But) now we are faced with, I am sorry to say, an inevitable split, and I am afraid the suggestion I have put cannot be adopted. I confess frankly that in the immediate crisis in front of us I do personally attach more importance to keeping our Party a united body than to winning the next election."

Bonar Law explained that he saw no danger of a Labour victory but added that " having a party composed of everyone who was not Labour, with Labour as the only alternative, will inevitably have the effect of making a Labour Government some day." Then he used a subtle and interesting further argument:

> " The feeling against the continuance of the Coalition is so strong that [if we follow Austen Chamberlain's advice] our Party will be broken, that a new party will be formed; and, not the worst of the evils of that is this, that on account of those who have gone, who are supposed to be more moderate men, what is left of the Conservative Party will become more reactionary; and I, for one, say that though what you call the reactionary element in our party has always been there, and must always be there, if it is the sole element, our party is absolutely lost. Therefore if you agree with Mr. Chamberlain in this crisis, I will tell you what I think will be the result. It will be a repetition of what happened after Peel passed the Corn Bills. The body that is cast off will slowly become the Conservative Party, but it will take a generation before it gets back to the influence which the Party ought to have . . . very reluctantly (therefore), I shall vote in favour of no Coalition."

Bonar Law's speech, which was in many respects the best of those delivered at the Carlton Club meeting, shows clearly the dilemma of the Conservative leadership system, as it functioned then and to a large extent still does now. The Leader is solely responsible for the formulation of party policy. Normally he confers with his Cabinet (or Shadow Cabinet) associates and if he is wise he takes into account the views of his followers in Parliament and in the party organization outside. But there is (or rather there was at this time[1]) no effective machinery to ensure a regular exchange

---

[1] Partly as a result of the Carlton Club meeting the 1922 Committee (see p. 57 above) was set up to ensure more effective liaison between the back-benches and the Leader and his associates. Similarly, arrangements for ensuring that the Leader is kept informed of the views of the party

of views between the Leader and his immediate associates on the one hand and their followers in Parliament and in the country on the other. Above all, there was (as Bonar Law regretfully pointed out) no established procedure for polling the Conservative Members of Parliament on a major issue of party policy. Chamberlain, like Balfour, inevitably considered it an intolerable affront when the party rejected his " advice "; he was bound therefore to resign.

The party signalized its rejection of his views by passing a resolution moved by Capt. Pretyman, the same M.P., no less, who had nominated Chamberlain only eighteen months earlier. His resolution read: " That this meeting of Conservative Members of the House of Commons declares its opinion that the Conservative Party, whilst willing to co-operate with Coalition Liberals, fights the election as an independent Party, with its own leader and its own programme." The Chief Whip, Sir Leslie Wilson, in a speech which merely repeated the arguments which had gone before, threw his weight on the side of the anti-Coalitionists. One speaker tried to adjourn the meeting till the following day. Another urged that the National Union ought to be consulted at its forthcoming emergency meeting. But Chamberlain impatiently brushed aside all suggestions for delay and he underlined the fact that the resolution on which the meeting was to vote excluded " the possibility of any but a Tory Prime Minister ". The vote was then taken, with this result: for the resolution, 187; against, 87. After this decisive defeat, Chamberlain announced: " My friends and I will consider the course we have to pursue." Within three hours of the conclusion of the meeting the Coalition Government had resigned, and Austen Chamberlain and twelve of his leading associates issued a statement which said in part:

> " It is true that the resolution upon which the decision was taken was not in its expressed terms such that it might not have been modified so as to secure agreement, but it was made absolutely plain in the course of the discussion that its authors regarded it as involving us all in an undertaking that here and now we should give notice to the Prime Minister that in no circumstances would the Conservative Party, if it rested with them, consent to his retaining the Premiership after a successful election, however much he and his party might have contributed to the result. Of such a message we could not be the bearers."[1]

Thereafter Chamberlain and his friends adopted an attitude towards

organization outside Parliament have been greatly improved. But the problem discussed subsequently below has by no means been entirely overcome.

[1] Cited in *Gleanings and Memoranda*, November, 1922, p. 503.

the new leadership of their party which *The Times* described as
" benevolent independence ". Chamberlain himself did not return
to office until the formation of the second Baldwin Government in
1924.

Many legends have grown up around the famous Carlton Club
meeting of 19th October, 1922. One can argue as Chamberlain did
in reporting the meeting to his constituents that his anti-Coalition
opponents had decided to put party above nation;[1] this is a possible
interpretation of events although it is at best a dubious proposition. But it would appear to be a quite indefensible view to claim
that Chamberlain was the victim of a conspiracy or plot organized
by his jealous rivals or by a reactionary clique in the Carlton Club
to deprive him of the leadership. No doubt there were envious men
among the anti-Coalitionists (and especially perhaps among some
of the junior ministers) who coveted the positions held by Chamberlain and the Coalitionists. This is no doubt a factor in the shift of
power from one group to another in any intra-party struggle. But
the blunt fact is that in a major issue involving the whole future of
his party Chamberlain failed to carry his party with him. In the
previous year in a debate on Ireland he had fought and defeated
those who disagreed with him; he fought and won first in the House
and then in the party conference. But in the second great dispute
—on the future of the Coalition—he was defeated by his parliamentary colleagues and would probably have been defeated even
more decisively had he debated the issue before the annual conference of the National Union.

There is important evidence on the latter point which has been
largely overlooked. It is provided in a speech by Sir George
Younger at Weston-super-Mare (7th November, 1922); this speech
throws light not only on the reasons for Chamberlain's downfall but
also on the rôle of the extra-parliamentary organs of the party in a
crisis such as this. Younger was replying in effect to the charges by
Lloyd George and others that the Coalition was destroyed by a
powerful little band of reactionaries centred in the Carlton Club. He
explained that as far back as December, 1921, the Central Office had
warned Chamberlain that there was a rising tide of opposition to

---

[1] Lloyd George went one better. He said (20th October at Sheffield): " The
national unity which won the War has been deliberately and wantonly
smashed by the Carlton Club. It was done merely in the hope of snatching
a party advantage. . . . They provoked the fight. I am sorry. I would have
avoided it if I could in the interests of the nation, but they have thrown
the gauntlet into the ring. That is what the reactionaries have done, and
I mean to pick it up and to go on fighting the old battle for a steady but
progressive England." Cited in *Gleanings and Memoranda*, December,
1922, p. 515.

the Coalition "not so much in the House of Commons as in the constituencies". This dissatisfaction grew steadily, Sir George claimed, during the winter and spring of 1922. In order to meet it, Chamberlain, he recalled, had made his declaration to the Council of the National Union that there would be no "coupon election" but rather a reversion to the electoral policy pursued by Balfour and his father. This had quietened fears for a time but they sprang up again after Chamberlain's Oxford speech in March when he appeared to whittle away his previous pledge by saying that the Government would go to the country as a Government. Again an attempt was made to allay fears in the constituencies, but uneasiness grew steadily. Finally, in September came the decision taken at Chequers to go to the country at the earliest opportunity under Lloyd George's leadership.

Sir George then described his own reactions to this decision:

> "I [have recently] turned up the file which I have at the office to see what I said when I got the news. My letter was a short one. 'I am,' I said, 'appalled to hear this decision has been taken. It will break our Party in twain if persisted in'. [Of] that I am satisfied and know now it would have done."

Younger then described his own rôle in the events that followed:

> "What was my duty? I am Chairman of the Party Organization . . . . I tried to build every conceivable bridge—to get any change in the policy which these senior members had decided in our Party . . . . from my knowledge of the constituencies which I get every morning . . . I knew the constituencies were dead against this policy. I knew that if a special conference of our Party was called they would show to our Ministers that that was the view of the country. I said to my leader: 'If you find it absolutely necessary to have a General Election before the National Union Conference of 15th November you will be tricking the Party out of their rights if you don't have a special conference of these people, and give your reasons for this policy before you plunge into disaster.' . . .
>
> "So I made up my mind that if there was going to be a split it should split from the top, and not from the bottom, and that the leaders who were responsible for pushing such a disastrous policy were the men to go, and not the tail. We have to maintain the solidarity of the Party. I consider as nothing the result of an election in comparison with the vital necessity of maintaining our Party intact. To lose an election is a temporary thing; to smash a party is an appalling disaster. I would remind you that our great Party is the only great political party which stands between the constitution of this country and those who believe in subversive policies. It is no use Mr. Chamberlain saying to you, as he

said to his constituents, that he was all for the nation and the others were all for a party. I say the interests of both are synonymous, and we stand for the nation as much as him. I took care to see that the Party should not be wrecked."

Younger then dropped a broad hint that he personally had sent " an SOS " to Bonar Law asking him " to come forward and re-establish unity ". And in final comment on his own rôle Sir George added that " when a skipper was driving the ship on the rocks it was not a bad idea to have a cabin boy there to see that a new skipper and crew were provided for the barque ".[1]

No one was in a better position than the Chairman of the Party Organization to know the mood of the party outside Parliament. Even though he owed direct allegiance to the Leader, Younger warned him that he would split the party down the middle if he persisted in his intention to go to the country as a Coalition Government under Lloyd George's leadership. Younger's account fully corresponds with a statement by Sir Alexander Leith, the Chairman of the National Union (then called the National Unionist Association). In the course of the election campaign which followed the fall of the Coalition, he said:

"I find that a certain number of people think Mr. Chamberlain was badly treated at the Carlton Club meeting, and that there was a sort of plot among some members of the Ministry now in power to get rid of him. I speak with authority and full knowledge of the facts, as Chairman of the National Unionist Association, and I say this is absolutely untrue. Mr. Chamberlain has been warned and advised several times during the last year by Sir George Younger, myself, and others of the rank and file that the majority of the Unionist Party would not agree to another Coalition Government, and, therefore, he knew that in forcing an issue he risked splitting the Conservative Party from top to bottom. Let me say at once that I do not believe Mr. Chamberlain realized that he was being used by certain clever people with first-class brains to call that meeting at the Carlton Club, and so forestall the National Unionist Conference, fixed for 15th November, at which 6,000 delegates would attend from all parts. For these people with first-class brains well knew the Unionist Party would declare itself wholeheartedly against a continuance of the Coalition. But I consider Mr. Chamberlain must realize now how things stood, and should not have allowed this story of a West End club to be used as a red herring in the present election.

[1] *Bristol Times*, 8th November, 1922. Cited in *Gleanings and Memoranda*, December, 1922, pp. 510-11. The significance of this statement as an illustration of the rôle of the Chairman of the Party Organization is discussed pp. 279 ff. below.

"Even Mr. Lloyd George says that a West End club broke up the Coalition Government. It is quite a useful political story, and it has, I suppose, served its purpose, but again I say, it is not true. I am sorry Mr. Chamberlain has allowed it to be used without saying that he called the Carlton Club meeting, that he decided who should be there, that he hoped to get a majority vote for another Coalition Government, and that he failed. He should have had the frankness to say this."[1]

Bonar Law himself underlined the arguments of Leith and Younger: "The cause (of the downfall of the Coalition) was not intrigue. It was not mutiny . . . . It was deep-rooted feeling in the constituencies."[2] This is no doubt an oversimplified view. The party in Parliament, as the Chief Whip, Sir Leslie Wilson, testified, was at least as uneasy as the party outside. But it is perfectly clear that wherever Chamberlain chose to fight, at a meeting of the parliamentary party or at a conference of the National Union, he was bound to be defeated. In the event he chose—rightly and for sound constitutional reasons—to fight at a meeting of the parliamentary party. By chance (or at worst by custom) that meeting was held in the premises of the Carlton Club and this contributed enormously to the legend that the Conservative Party is ruled by what one writer has misleadingly called its "demi-king and little sovereign",[3] the Carlton Club. But in fact the meeting which took place at the Carlton Club on 19th October, 1922, represented a thoroughly healthy manifestation of internal party democracy. It does not matter for the purposes of this study whether the decision to withdraw from the Coalition was an act of gross disloyalty to a great wartime Prime Minister or whether on this occasion the Conservative Party callously sacrificed the national interest for partisan advantage. The simple fact is that Austen Chamberlain tried to lead a party in a direction in which the great majority of its members both inside and outside Parliament did not want to go. They therefore rejected his leadership and his authority collapsed. There could be no more vivid proof that a Conservative Leader is no autocrat; in the last analysis, he can neither force nor lead his party in a direction it does not want to go.[4]

---

[1] *Gleanings and Memoranda,* December, 1922, pp. 512–13.
[2] *The Times,* 3rd November, 1922.
[3] Catlin, George, "Contemporary British Political Thought," *American Political Science Review,* Vol. XLVI, No. 3, September, 1952, p. 646 (n.1).
[4] For another comment on the significance of the downfall of Austen Chamberlain, see Beer, Samuel, "The Conservative Party of Great Britain," *Journal of Politics,* Vol. XIV, No. 1, February, 1952, pp. 47-9.

BALDWIN AS CONSERVATIVE LEADER

As astute an observer as Sir Winston Churchill has described Baldwin as "the greatest Party manager the Conservatives ever had";[1] yet even Baldwin on many occasions during his fourteen years as Leader had great difficulty in holding his followers in line.[2] In May, 1923, he inherited from Bonar Law a party which was of course far from united. The bitterness over the Coalition struggle still rankled; Austen Chamberlain, Balfour, Birkenhead and a number of the best minds in the party were outside the Government; the party bureaucracy had lost the services of Sir George Younger who retired from the office of Chairman of the Party Organization and of Sir Malcolm Fraser who had resigned as Principal Agent;[3] and the new Prime Minister and Party Leader was himself still very much of an unknown quantity. "The question soon arose," as Wickham Steed put it, "whether the new man would take charge of events or be taken charge of by them." Baldwin himself provided the answer; he boldly decided within a few months of taking office that the one thing which would bring the party together was a general election.

The manner in which Baldwin brought about the election of 1923 is of considerable interest. His Cabinet colleagues became aware that he had begun to feel himself hamstrung by Bonar Law's pledge that Protection would not be introduced within the lifetime of the present Parliament;[4] Baldwin had apparently become convinced that a general tariff was the only possible solution to the

---

[1] Churchill, W. S., *The Second World War*, Vol. I, p. 26.

[2] As G. M. Young has put it: "throughout his public career Baldwin was harassed by a group—always forming, always quelled, always re-forming—demanding (of him) something more than a continuous parade of good intentions garnished with quotations from Disraeli . . . " Young, G. M., *Stanley Baldwin*, p. 100. See also Amery, L., *My Political Life*, Vol. III, pp. 22 ff., and Blake, R., "Baldwin and the Right" in Raymond, R. (ed.), *The Age of Baldwin*, London, 1960, pp. 25 ff.

[3] *1923 Conservative Annual Conference Report*, p. 5.

[4] Bonar Law had promised in the course of the election that the new Parliament "will not make any fundamental change in the fiscal system of the country". W. A. S. Hewins, who was a Conservative candidate at Swansea in the 1922 election comments: " . . . during the election, for reasons which I have never heard, (Bonar Law) gave a new pledge which was not even properly communicated to Conservative candidates. I never heard of it at Swansea." Hewins, W. A. S., *Apologia of an Imperialist*, Vol. II, p. 265. This comment provides further interesting evidence of the extent to which a Conservative Leader is in some circumstances free to act independently of his followers.

intractable problem of unemployment.[1] Many of his colleagues did not share his conviction and in any case most of them were against calling an early general election merely for the purpose of releasing the Government from Bonar Law's pledge. They therefore sought, surprisingly, to bind the Prime Minister to promise that any statement he should make on the issue should be a personal one which would not commit his colleagues.[2] Baldwin apparently agreed to this condition and his reference to Protection in his speech at the close of the annual conference of the National Union at Plymouth on 26th October, 1923, was carefully phrased:

> "To me, at least, (he said), this unemployment problem is the most crucial problem of our country . . . . I can fight it. I am willing to fight it. I cannot fight it without weapons. *I have for myself come to the conclusion* that . . . . the only way of fighting this subject is by protecting the home market."[3]

The phraseology seems intended to make it clear that on this occasion at least the Leader of the Conservative Party was not exercising his exclusive right to formulate party policy; true to his pledge to his colleagues, he claimed to be speaking only for himself. Baldwin had apparently agreed also that the country should be given an opportunity to contemplate and digest his proposals before an election should be held. One of his Cabinet colleagues had written to him privately: " . . . I think we should be acting both unwisely and wrongly . . . if we were to attempt to snatch a verdict, and that, if this is so, the appeal should be deferred." He was careful to add, however: " All this in great deference, recognizing that fixing these matters is your special perquisite." [4]

But to all such comment and advice, Baldwin seems to have been largely oblivious. Certainly he appears to have made little or no

---

[1] Amery claims (*My Political Life*, Vol. II, p. 280) that " . . . what had really prompted so sudden a decision (on Baldwin's part) was the report which had reached him that Lloyd George was coming home from his visit to the United States and Canada full of ideas of a bold Empire policy with Imperial preference well in the forefront. So far from welcoming a convert Baldwin only saw the danger of Lloyd George consolidating his hold over Austen Chamberlain and the old Coalition Unionists, and so re-asserting his influence over the Tory Party as a whole." Amery quotes in support of this interpretation a statement which Baldwin made to Dr. Tom Jones in 1935.

[2] Young, G. M., *Stanley Baldwin*, p. 65.

[3] A full summary of this and other speeches on the subject by Baldwin along with press and opposition comment is contained in the " Plymouth Policy ", a special supplement of *Gleanings and Memoranda*, December, 1923. [Italics mine in the above quotation.]

[4] Cited in Young, G. M., *Stanley Baldwin*, p. 66.

effort to sound out his supporters in the country about the party's prospects in an election fought on the Protection issue. Salvidge's diary provides a fascinating illustration of Baldwin's almost Olympian detachment. A few days after his Plymouth speech Baldwin had repeated the argument for protection in a major speech in the Manchester Free Trade Hall. Lord Derby (who had taken the chair) and other local party stalwarts had warned Baldwin of the dangers of a tariff election in Lancashire. Yet, Salvidge records " . . . Baldwin had not made a single inquiry as to whether Derby was willing to shoulder the delicate task of trying to preserve the allegiance of the numerous influential Unionist Free Traders in Lancashire." [1] Following the meeting, Baldwin spent the week-end at Knowsley and Derby invited Salvidge to join them at a luncheon at which it was intended they should attempt to obtain from Baldwin some idea of what he actually contemplated doing.

> " With this good intention (Salvidge records) we went in to lunch. During most of the meal Mr. Baldwin talked about how to grow raspberries. He said the raspberry was ' a jolly little fellow ' and provided an interesting hobby for anyone who took the trouble to cultivate him. Mrs. Baldwin listened with rapt attention, and from time to time beamed in appreciation of the Prime Minister's remarks. Later, over coffee in the library, Lord Derby and I were alone with the P.M. He was fairly definite about his conviction that to fight unemployment properly he must have weapons, and that the only effective weapon was the tariff. But as to whether such a policy would carry the country he asked for no opinion, and never allowed the conversation to get down to practical politics from the point of view of electioneering. There seemed nothing to be gained by prolonging the conversation, and when Derby came out to see me off I told him my impression was that the P.M. hardly contemplated an appeal to the country before next year, thus giving some chance of educating the new electorate, especially the women, on the subject of Protection. As it turned out, I was hopelessly wrong. Nine days from then Parliament re-assembled only to learn from Mr. Baldwin that he had advised the King to dissolve . . . " [2]

When he met Parliament on 13th November Baldwin explained the situation: " . . . it seemed to me that my only course as an honest man was to place my views before the country and take my chance. As soon as I had done that it became perfectly obvious from speeches that were made by my opponents that an election

---

[1] Cited in Salvidge, S., *Salvidge of Liverpool,* p. 253.
[2] *Ibid.*, p. 254. Randolph Churchill has provided a very valuable account of " Baldwin's Tariff Election " and its aftermath in his *Lord Derby*, Chapter XXIV.

would have to take place before very long . . . "[1] He then announced that the election would in fact take place on 6th December. This caused a good deal of consternation among his Cabinet colleagues. Those who had opposed him both on the Protection issue and on the timing of the election apparently feared that he intended to force them out to make way for the return of Austen Chamberlain and Birkenhead. But Baldwin assured them that this was not the case and, after a private exchange of memoranda, a statement of the party's new tariff policy was drafted which proved acceptable to all sections of the party leadership. Thus equipped and apparently united the party marched into battle and was resoundingly defeated on 6th December, 1923, just six weeks after Baldwin's Plymouth speech.

When the smoke of battle cleared it was revealed that the Conservatives had suffered 107 casualties and their defeat had paved the way for the formation of the first Labour Government. Not unnaturally, there were some bitter recriminations within the Conservative Party. Baldwin's old foes whom he had defeated at the Carlton Club just over a year earlier were convinced that their worst apprehensions were now being fulfilled. In the *Daily Mail*, 7th January, 1924, Lord Birkenhead wrote:

> "An election was challenged by a Government which had a majority sufficient to keep it in office for three or four years. No one wanted to turn the Government out . . . for some utterly incalculable reason the Prime Minister, several of his colleagues and the party managers decided that there must be an election.
> "I am myself a Protectionist, and I have reached an age at which it is little likely that I shall revise my economic views, but I confess I shuddered at the rashness which flung this issue without preparation and without education on an electorate which had either never heard of or had forgotten Mr. Chamberlain's campaign."[2]

Even Austen Chamberlain, the epitome of the perfect gentleman in politics, could hardly restrain himself:

> "It is not so very long since I was pleading with my friends of the Unionist Party, at the famous meeting in the Carlton Club, not to break up the Coalition which had then existed for many years. . . . I was answered by Mr. Bonar Law. He said that if you teach the country that there are but two parties capable of Government, one comprising all that is most liberal in the Liberal Party and all that exists in the Unionist Party, and the other comprising the Socialist Party, then is it not certain that

---

[1] *House of Commons Debates,* 13th November, 1923.
[2] Cited in *Gleanings and Memoranda,* February, 1924, p. 126.

sooner or later, some day, the Socialist Party will come into power? Yes, ' some day ', if we had continued the Coalition. But barely a year has passed and to-morrow a Socialist Government enters office." [1]

There were rumours (started perhaps by Baldwin's friends) that the fatal decision had not been his, that he had yielded to the persuasion of some of his colleagues. But Baldwin, to his credit, made no attempt to shift the blame. He told the House (21st January, 1924):

"I think it is only fair I should make a statement with regard to the policy on which the Government went to the country. Responsibility for that policy was mine and mine alone. It was the decision of a united Government when we went to the country, but any reports anyone may have read, that I was driven by anyone else—I am not quite so malleable as that—is entirely wrong . . . . I have myself and for myself no regrets."

But there were others within the party who *had* regrets. In particular, Mr. Baldwin's luncheon companions at Knowsley (who had been treated on the eve of the election to a disquisition on the growing of raspberries) decided to register their deep unhappiness about the subsequent course of events.

Lord Derby and Salvidge proceeded to mobilize and register the resentment of their local associations against Baldwin's handling of the election of 1923. A special meeting of the Council of the Lancashire and Cheshire Division of the National Union was called at Manchester on 9th February " to discuss the political situation ". This meeting provides the best available illustration of the working of the regional organization of the party at its most effective; it is therefore considered in greater detail in the appropriate section of Chapter IV (see pp. 238 ff. below). It need only be noted here that the meeting of the Lancashire dissidents passed by " an overwhelming majority " a resolution recording that:

"This meeting . . . believing that the verdict of the country at the recent election was against a change in the fiscal system, respectfully represents to the leaders of the party that it is undesirable that Protection should be included in the programme of the Conservative policy at this juncture. Further, it respectfully protests against the methods adopted previous to the recent General Election when an appeal was made to the electors on the issue of Protection without affording the party organizations throughout the country an opportunity of expressing their opinions thereon ; and urges that, with a view to securing in the future greater harmony and better to obtain the representative

[1] *House of Commons Debates*, 21st January, 1924.

opinion of the party, a satisfactory method of *liaison* be established between the leaders of the party, the Central Office, and the local organizations."[1]

Lord Derby, who had presided at the meeting, was careful to explain in an interview with the *Morning Post* that this resolution " should on no account be looked upon as a vote of censure on the leaders of the party." He particularly desired it to be understood that " there was no thought of disloyalty to the Head Office . . . and that the main thought pervading the meeting was to restore the feeling of mutual confidence and to arrive at the best methods of giving expression to the principles for which they stood and from which they had never wavered."[2]

Derby's statement reflects the general mood among Baldwin's critics. They were exasperated with his handling of the Protection issue and with his timing of the election and the more militant of them were prepared to record their exasperation publicly. But there was no suggestion of overt rebellion. Baldwin with his pipe and his homely mannerisms had suddenly become a national figure of great public popularity. As G. M. Young puts it: . . . " the instinct of self-preservation alone compelled the body of the party to range themselves under the only leader who could restore them to office." [3]

This they proceeded to do at a special meeting in London on 11th February, 1924,[4] of all Conservative peers, M.P.s and candidates who had been defeated at the recent election. Although this meeting is described in his diary by one of the defeated candidates who was present as " a dull affair ",[5] it is none the less of very considerable interest in the study of Conservative leadership since it is one of the comparatively rare occasions on which the Leader of the Party has voluntarily presented himself before his followers for a renewal of his mandate. Baldwin himself presided over the meeting and opened the discussion with a review of the recent election and a re-statement of Conservative policy. He conceded that the electors had given a clear verdict against Protection and he added that

---

[1] *Gleanings and Memoranda*, March, 1924, pp. 242–3. See also Churchill, R., *Lord Derby*, Chapter XXIV.

[2] The *Morning Post*, 11th February, 1924.

[3] Young, G. M., *Stanley Baldwin*, p. 73.

[4] The Manchester meeting of the Lancashire Division had been held, it will be noted, only two days earlier. The timing was presumably deliberate and intended to impress on the party leaders the extent of uneasiness within the party. On the other hand Derby's statement in the *Morning Post* renouncing any suggestion of rebellion against the leaders was made on the very morning of the London meeting.

[5] Hewins, W. A. S., *The Apologia of an Imperialist*, Vol. II, p. 282.

in the circumstances he " did not feel justified " in advising the
party again to submit the proposal for a general tariff until there
was clear evidence that public opinion was disposed to reconsider
its judgment. There followed an examination of alternative policies
which might serve similar ends and an exhortation to the party:
" in the next two or three months, inside the party and in consultation with experts outside, there should be examined in the light of the
present, a number of the pressing problems that have presented
themselves since the war—problems of housing, education, and the
relationship between master and man. The conclusion of such an
investigation . . . might well form part of the Party's social policy
by the time the next election comes."

After this conciliatory speech the following resolution was moved
by the Earl of Balfour: " That this meeting, having heard the statement by the Leader of the Party, desires to express its confidence
in him and its agreement with the policy he has outlined." The resolution was seconded by a back-bench M.P. and supported by Austen
Chamberlain amongst others. It was carried with acclamation and
the singing of " For He's a Jolly Good Fellow".

It will be noted that this meeting conformed to the customary
pattern where leadership issues are concerned in the Conservative
Party: elder statesmen and possible rivals joined in praise of the
Leader and the voting was unanimous. But there were certain
distinctive features of the meeting. One speaker (J. C. Gould, M.P.)
did seize the opportunity to vent some of the grievances which had
been reflected at the Manchester meeting and elsewhere. He said
that he had not come there " in view of the fact that they had at
last a united party, for the purpose of opposing any resolution
appointing Mr. Baldwin as Leader." But there were issues he
felt that had to be faced:

" . . . they must take immediate and effective steps to bring their
organization more up to date and more into touch with the electorate . . . Unfortunately, there had been a tendency in the councils
of leadership of the party for the chief advisers to be men who
sat in cloistered seats and who led more or less sheltered exis-
tences. . . . Another point he wished to stress was that decisions
of importance should not be taken without consulting the leaders
of the party in the country (cries of ' hear, hear ' from some sections of the meeting). It might be a time-honoured tradition that
the Prime Minister, or the Leader of the Party, might see fit to
take a decision unto himself, or perhaps in consultation with certain members of his Cabinet, or his Cabinet, without consulting
those who had to deal with the electorate, or knew the feeling of
the electorate. But in this democratic age it was desirable that a
more democratic spirit should prevail in their councils if they

wished to attain success. He hoped that in the future the advice of the agents as to the feeling in the country would be accepted, and that Mr. Baldwin and those who were leading the party would provide that more democratic control should take place."

Another speaker (a defeated candidate) endorsed Gould's remarks and added that " there was an old practice in the House by which the Whips ascertained from the members what their opinions were on a certain given point "; he thought that " if that practice had been adopted last November, the party would have to-day been still in power." [1]

Austen Chamberlain in his speech supporting the resolution of confidence in Baldwin replied to these suggestions that the Leader should in some way submit himself to the effective control of his followers:

> " Let me say that I do not for one moment conceal from myself, or attempt to conceal from you, that our organization is not perfect. (Hear, hear.) I have never known in my thirty odd years of active political life a moment when it was perfect; I have never known the time when good and well-founded criticism could not be made upon it. But that is rather matter for smaller gatherings, more confidential meetings, more conversational meetings, than one of this kind; and all I would venture to say to you—and once again I plead that I have had some experience when I venture to tender advice—is this: *Do not weaken the hand of the man whom you choose for your Leader (hear, hear), and do not ask of him or of any of us that we should remit executive decisions to be debated in public meetings.* That way confusion and disaster lie. That has been the practice of the Labour Party, and unless their arrival in power leads to a direct breach with their past traditions, leads to their giving to their leaders a confidence, a responsibility, and a power that they have never been entrusted with so far, they will come to an early and speedy disaster.
>
> " Mr. Clynes in the last Parliament, in two speeches which I recall of great wisdom and of great courage, warned them of their danger. Do not let us at this hour, with all our traditions, with all

[1] The same speaker added: " Mr. Baldwin had been accused of being responsible for this disaster which they had sustained. He happened to know that Mr. Baldwin was against an election taking place last year. He was urged on by some of his colleagues (cries of ' Names ') and he thought that (they) ought to-day to bear a little of the blame." In *The Times* (12th February, 1924) the Parliamentary Correspondent wrote: " One point is not made clear in the official report of the meeting. One of the speakers had suggested that Mr. Baldwin was not in favour of an early election after his Plymouth speech and had been forced into it by some of his colleagues. In replying to the vote of thanks, Mr. Baldwin insisted that this was not the case, adding that he was not the kind of man who was driven into any course of action against his will."

our experience behind us, fall into the error which that new party has committed, and of which it is trying to shake itself free."[1]

This statement is of particular interest when one recalls that at the time Chamberlain was in no sense a close personal friend or ally of Baldwin. The latter had taken a leading part in destroying Chamberlain's own position as Leader just over a year before and since then Chamberlain had been languishing in the political wilderness. Yet in this speech he made no effort to capitalize on dissatisfaction with Baldwin's leadership: instead he seized the occasion to re-state the traditional Conservative view that the Leader must not be forced to submit himself to the supervision and control of his followers. The party meeting (which of course had no desire to use its ultimate authority to destroy Baldwin) accepted Austen Chamberlain's advice and made no effort to halter him.

It appeared at first that the popular organization of the party outside Parliament would not be quite so easily satisfied. The Central Council met the next day (12th February) and heard speeches by Baldwin and Col. Jackson, the Chairman of the Party Organization. Baldwin reaffirmed his declaration to the party meeting with respect to the protection issue [2] and Col. Jackson explained that it was proposed to consider the advisability of " setting up a Central Committee consisting of representatives nominated by the Leader of the Party and the National Unionist Association, in order to keep the Leader in more direct touch with the feeling in the constituencies." But to underline its concern the Council passed the following resolution: " That in the opinion of this meeting it is desirable that more democratic methods should prevail in the Councils of the Party, and that a re-organization should take place in the Constituencies and in the Central Office wherever it is found to be desirable."[3] In the event, nothing appears to have come either of Col. Jackson's suggestion or of the Central Council resolution. The report of the Central Council for 1924 stated: " The (Executive) Committee (of the Central Council) has given particular consideration to the following matters arising out of the Council Meeting held in February last: . . . the advisability of

[1] *Gleanings and Memoranda*, March, 1924, pp. 227–37. [Italics mine.]

[2] Salvidge records in his diary: " After Baldwin's speech to the Central Council, as he was leaving the platform he paused in front of me, and with quite a twinkle in his eye inquired, ' Well, anything to say?' Feeling that I had been given pretty well all I had been asking for, I replied, in military fashion, ' No complaints, sir.' ' Come now, that's a bit of a change and at least something to be thankful for in these hard times,' remarked Baldwin, with his whimsical smile as he moved on." Cited in Salvidge, S., *Salvidge of Liverpool*, p. 267.

[3] Cited in *Gleanings and Memoranda*, March, 1924, pp. 241–2.

setting up a Central Committee in order to keep the Leader in more direct touch with the Constituencies. . . . The committee came to the conclusion that another Central Committee was not required so long as the Chairman of the Party Organization remained Chairman of the Executive Committee, and decided to take no further action on the point."[1]

Baldwin's performance in the election of 1923 continued however to cause uneasy reverberations even after the party was returned to power in 1924. At the 1928 conference of the National Union, for example, a delegate moved:

> " That this conference respectfully urges that in the event of a substantial departure from the recognized policy of the party being contemplated on any of the major political issues, an opportunity be given the Executives of all Conservative and Unionist Associations to discuss in confidence such proposed departure, and to forward their conclusions for the consideration of the Central Council of the National Union of Conservative and Unionist Associations."

The mover explained that his object:

> " . . . was to give responsible representatives of the party throughout the country an opportunity of considering any vital proposal which might be brought forward before any such proposal was incorporated in the policy of the party . . . . " And he added that:

> " The lesson of the General Election of 1923 should teach them that it was courting disaster to appeal to the country on a programme which had not been fully considered before its adoption. He welcomed Mr. Baldwin's announcement that the next election was not to be fought on any great departure from the principles laid down in the election of 1924. He hoped that the conference would agree with him that it would be to the advantage of the party if they could encourage co-operation between their leaders and the responsible rank and file."

In reply, the then Chairman of the Party Organization (J. C. C. Davidson, now Viscount Davidson) said that although the officials of the party

> " had great sympathy with the objects of the resolution, he thought that they could take it more or less like this: *When you elect your leader, you must trust him.* If the resolution was carried into effect they would have very much the same position as existed in Russia, where they governed by committees. . . . They had, as was well known, a vast organization in the National Union. There was

---

[1] *1924 Conservative Annual Conference Report,* folio 6. (Report of the Council.) It should be noted that the Chairman of the Party Organization ceased to be Chairman of the Executive Committee in 1930. See p. 271 below,

no subject upon which any branch of any association might not pass any resolution and submit it, through the Council, to the provincial division, thence right up to the Executive of the National Union, and so to the leaders. It was the most democratic organization in the country, and they must give a lead to the country and to their leaders who had led them so well."[1]

The resolution according to the conference report was " overwhelmingly lost ".

What then were the final consequences of the strange election of 1923? For Baldwin personally and for the office of Leader which he held there appear to have been no lasting adverse consequences at all. He had deliberately, and in a sense gratuitously, provoked an election which most of his colleagues considered unnecessary. He had chosen to fight on a complex and difficult issue without any serious attempt to explain the issue as he saw it to the electorate. He had led his party to resounding defeat and opened the gates to the formation of the first Socialist Government in this country. Yet, strangely enough, in the process Baldwin appears greatly to have increased his own stature as a national figure and, in addition, to have unified his party. He gave an interesting retrospective justification for his action in 1923 in a speech to the Constitutional Club in January, 1925:

> " (In the autumn of 1923). . . . our Party then was not wholly united. . . . What would have happened . . . if we had attempted to run for our full term? . . . Having come into power as we did, and not being a wholly united Party, we should have lacked that impetus, that popular will behind us. . . . I am not at all sure . . . that there was not beginning a dry rot in our Party that might have led to disaster two years hence.
>
> " What was the result of our all fighting together (in the election of 1923)? The result was that, when we were beaten, we had exactly the shock that was wanted to pull us together, and that nothing else could have done, and the opportunity was taken to overhaul our Party and its mechanism from the top to the bottom, and to infuse and to instil into it a new life and new ideals . . . as so often happens to those who have the courage to do what they think right, the fates themselves took a hand in the game and they fought on our side from that moment." [2]

In fact of course there is no real evidence to support Baldwin's claim that the " opportunity was taken to overhaul our Party from the top to the bottom ". A few minor changes were made in the composition of the Executive Committee of the National Union [3]

---

[1] *1928 Conservative Annual Conference Report,* folio 18. [Italics mine.]
[2] Cited in Steed, W., *The Real Stanley Baldwin,* pp. 65-6.
[3] See *1924 Conservative Annual Conference Report.*

but no fundamental re-organization was attempted.   Above all, despite the loud grumbles of the Lancashire dissidents and others, *there was no modification whatever in the relationship between the Leader and his followers either inside or outside Parliament.* Despite the rather foolish efforts of his colleagues in the Government to extract a promise from Baldwin that in espousing Protection he would speak only for himself, he did, on the occasion of his Plymouth speech, exercise his right within the party constitution to formulate policy. That he did so in such an abrupt fashion (and with such disastrous consequences) was bound to stimulate some of his followers to call for a more effective system of liaison between the Leader and his followers. But in the end all such suggestions were either ignored or side-tracked. Baldwin *did* make the pledge that was expected of him: he would not go to the country again on the same issue (Protection) until there was clear evidence that the electorate had changed its mind. But he made no pledge that he would in future give greater weight to the views of his followers either inside or outside Parliament when it came to determining either the timing of the next election or the issues on which it would be fought. And—an important point—in avoiding such commitments Baldwin was supported and protected by the principal elder statesmen and senior officials of the party. It is fair to assume, however, that Baldwin must have learned from his experience (if he had not already learned from the history of the downfall of Balfour and Austen Chamberlain) that the Conservative Leader, whatever his rights within the party constitution, ignores at his peril the moods and opinions of his followers.

Yet there is a good deal of evidence that on many issues Baldwin was more sensitive to, and concerned about, the mood of Parliament as a whole and of the country than of his own immediate followers in his party. This is perhaps the measure of whatever greatness there was about him as a statesman; it is also the explanation of some of his subsequent difficulties as Leader of the Party. Certain of these difficulties arose as a result of his attitude to the Labour Party. In one of the most interesting passages in his biography of Baldwin, G. M. Young compares the attitudes of Baldwin and Churchill to the Labour Party.

" Baldwin never troubled himself to study the intellectual groundwork (of the emergent Labour Party); neither did Churchill. But Baldwin was at all times sensitive to the moral challenge underlying the Socialist creed: Churchill was not; and on the understanding of Labour Baldwin founded his whole policy, in opposition or in office. If the distance between the two parties widened so far that mutual comprehension was impossible, then Parliamentary debate was impossible, and the way was open to actions and reactions, measures and counter-measures outside the scope of the Constitution framed by the experimental wisdom of the ages. Meanwhile, let Labour have its chance and learn its lesson."[1]

Baldwin's mildly sympathetic attitude to the first Labour Government greatly irked many of his more militant supporters. Indeed on the eve of the election of October, 1924, a group of Conservatives were so sceptical of its outcome that they made plans to oust him from the leadership of the party.[2] Baldwin publicly acknowledged the uneasiness of his followers about his attitude to Labour:

> " I know I have been criticized, and criticized widely, for being too gentle in my handling of the Labour Party, but I have done it deliberately, because I believe it has been a good thing for this country that that party, comprising as it does so many citizens of this country, should learn by experience what a great responsibility administering an Empire such as ours really is."[3]

Exasperation with Baldwin's attitude to Labour did not reach the stage of open rebellion; it was soon overshadowed by the results of the election of October, 1924, in which the Conservatives won what Baldwin described as " the greatest majority our party ever had ", but it was still an open question, as one observer suggested, whether Baldwin was the luckiest of incompetent politicians or the subtlest of competent statesmen. Baldwin himself took no credit for the party's success in the 1924 election. At a " victory demonstration " of the National Union at the Albert Hall on 4th December, 1924, he said, " since the battle of Alma there has been no such rank and file victory as we have just achieved. . . . I am under no temptation to believe that the victory was the result of leadership." [4]

But this very lack of leadership which Baldwin seemed here to cite as a virtue was to get him into continued difficulties during the life of the Conservative Government, 1924-9. The annual conference of the National Union which took place in October, 1925, a year after the party's return to power, reflected mounting anxiety

---

[1] Young, G. M., *Stanley Baldwin*, pp. 77-8.
[2] Steed, W., *The Real Stanley Baldwin*, p. 5.
[3] *Gleanings and Memoranda*, September, 1924, p. 373. However much these sentiments may have irked Baldwin's supporters, certain of his more perspicacious opponents have paid tribute to the importance of his attitude during the particularly delicate period in British politics when Labour first emerged as a contender for power. Prof. Laski in a private letter to Baldwin in 1930 wrote: " The spirit you represent has made the peaceful evolution of English politics much more certain than it would otherwise have been." Cited in Young, G. M., *Stanley Baldwin*, p. 151.
[4] *The Times*, 5th December, 1924.

within the party concerning the lethargy of Baldwin and his Government. Again and again during the conference debates delegates criticized what they considered to be the failure of the Government to grapple effectively with the problems facing the country.[1] The temper of the conference can be judged from the following incident. An emergency resolution on agriculture was presented, which read: " In the opinion of this conference the Government should without delay make a definite statement with regard to their agricultural policy, and carry the same into effect forthwith . . . " A supporter of this resolution warned, " heaven help the Government if they don't do something ", and another speaker who backed the resolution said:

> " Our loyalty to Mr. Baldwin and the Party is as strong as it was last year, but the fact still remains that throughout the length and breadth of Great Britain there is a strong feeling of impatience. I am going to ask the Government to produce their agricultural policy as quickly as they can, because it will be a stepping-stone towards re-establishing ourselves in the confidence of the people from whom we got our votes. *Our loyalty is the same as ever, but it has got to be ' On, Stanley, On.' "*

Significantly, this speech was greeted (according to the conference report) by loud applause and the resolution was carried unanimously.[2]

When Baldwin made his appearance before the mass meeting which customarily follows the National Union conference he had apparently decided that he could not ignore the evidence of dissatisfaction with his leadership and he gave what one press account describes as " a definite answer " to his " traducers ". Baldwin said that the purpose of his speech was " to render some account of the stewardship of my colleagues and myself since you returned us to power nearly twelve months ago ". But he concluded, in a remarkable passage, with a direct reference to his critics:

> " There are at the present moment a good many disgruntled people knocking about the country (laughter). I want to tell them that there is no originality in that. . . .
> " I don't mind criticism myself, although nearly all the criticism I get is just like that of the weary mother (who) said to the nurse, ' Just go upstairs and see what Tommy's doing and tell him not

---

[1] This 1925 conference provides one of the best illustrations of the rôle the Conservative annual conference can play in goading its own leaders into action. The 1925 conference debates are considered in greater detail in Chapter IV (pp. 226-7 below).

[2] *1925 Conservative Annual Conference Report,* folio 32. [Italics mine in quoted passage.]

to.' (Laughter.) Criticism from our own Party I welcome when it is criticism directed to the improvement of the Party (hear, hear) and of our prospects. I don't much care for criticism that comes from people with hot heads and cold feet (laughter).

" All the kind of criticisms that go on in the corners of clubs (laughter)—there is not a single leader we have had in my time of whom I have not heard the same things said that I know have been said about me. I remember when people got together and said with an air of mystery, ' Balfour is played out ', ' Bonar is not the man he was '.

" I have heard them all, and they always exist. When the Party wants to change its Leader I will step down, but not till then (loud and long continued applause). And remember this, that whether this country is going to get through the difficult years that lie immediately ahead of us depends more than anything else on the strength, the stability, and the loyalty of one to another and each to all." (Applause.)

In response to Baldwin's challenge the following resolution was moved:

> " That this meeting of representatives of the National Union of Conservative and Unionist Associations, assembled from all parts of the United Kingdom, thanks the Rt. Hon. Stanley Baldwin, M.P., for his address, expresses its unabated confidence in him as Prime Minister and as Leader of the Conservative and Unionist Party, and assures him of the most loyal support."

The mover of the resolution said: " The enthusiasm created by a great victory (has) died away, the dreamers who imagined the millennium had come were disappointed, candid friends were anxious to exercise their candour, and enemies, open or secret, had been practising their pernicious mischief." He was " quite sure that the speech of Mr. Baldwin (will) go like a breath of fresh air into a stuffy room.'" The official conference report notes that " the vote was carried with the greatest enthusiasm." Appended to the report (which is to be found in the Conservative Central Office) is a lyrical description of the scene by the political correspondent of a local newspaper (unidentified). He records that when Baldwin uttered his challenge (" when the Party wants to change its Leader I will step down but not till then "):

> " The vast audience gave their answer . . . in a manner that was not less than thrillingly emphatic. The instant these words were uttered, in a voice impassioned and indignant, another voice awoke, a voice like a mighty roar of thunder, and it was not stilled for some moments. People close to the writer were shouting, ' Bravo! Bravo! ' ' Stick to your guns! ' ' That's the way to defy them! '—and so on—but such exclamations were utterly lost

in the tremendous and prolonged torrent of enthusiasm. One has heard nothing like it in a long experience of political meetings. Then, for the second time—the first was when the Premier came on to the platform with Mr. Gerald W. E. Loder, the Chairman— the immense concourse sang, not to say roared, ' For He's a Jolly Good Fellow '. Nobody present will forget the rolling, volleying sounds at the vocal emphasis, ' And so say all of us ' . . . . He could not have hoped for or expected a more signal expression of approval of his policy and loyalty to himself personally. . . . "

The press account concludes by noting that Baldwin's reply to the vote of confidence was brief: " It has given me great pleasure, but I am afraid it will disappoint many people in the country." [1]

It seems obvious from the tone of the proceedings that Baldwin had been goaded into action by fairly clear evidence that his authority within the party had begun to crumble away,[2] despite the fact that just a year earlier under his leadership the Conservatives had won what he had called " the greatest majority that our party ever had ". This development is highly significant since it provides a further illustration of the fact that the exalted position nominally assigned to the Leader of the Party in no way guarantees him immunity from the critical scrutiny of his followers. In his speech to the mass meeting which followed the party conference, Baldwin appeared to imply that a conspiratorial clique inside the party was attempting to unseat him; in fact the conference report would suggest that there was widespread and genuine dissatisfaction with his slothful approach to the problems of the country. In a single, somewhat demagogic speech he managed to go a long way toward re-establishing his position, yet rumbling dissatisfaction with his leadership continued throughout the life of the Government.

The report of the Central Council of the National Union to the next year's annual conference (1926) made an earnest effort to convince the conference of Mr. Baldwin's sterling qualities as Leader.

---

[1] *1925 Conservative Annual Conference Report,* folios 48-57.

[2] Two years later, in a speech at the Conservative annual conference of 1927, Viscount Tredegar (then President of the National Union) reviewing Baldwin's career as Leader referred to " the curious reaction which followed on [the] victory [of 1924]. Only a brief time after the party had scored the most magnificent victory that any party had ever enjoyed the credulous carping critics were in full cry [although] there was nothing in the political situation to justify the faintest flicker of pessimism. The moment they got into office the Prime Minister and his colleagues began to carry out the programme with the same energy as they had prepared for victory. The majority in the House was untampered, and their supporters throughout the country were still on all material issues unanimously united." *1927 Conservative Annual Conference Report,* folio 50.

Sub-headed " The Prime Minister—Our Leader " a section of the report reads:

> " No man has done more than Mr. Baldwin to add to his reputation as a Statesman. He has shown immense courage. He has taken broad views. He has proved himself in critical times to be a man of character and purpose. He has earned, therefore, the affection of the Party and the respect of the Nation.
>
> " Your Council are convinced that the conference will take the earliest opportunity, not only of recording its complete confidence in the Prime Minister, but of expressing in emphatic terms its disgust with the malicious and slanderous attacks by the Socialists upon his character and honour."[1]

The conference was much less critical than that of the previous year but there was still a considerable undertow of impatience with Baldwin's leadership. A resolution was moved urging the Government to pass a law providing " that whilst it shall be perfectly legitimate to call attention to the advantages of a Trade Union, it shall be unlawful for anyone to make membership of a Trade Union a condition of employment ". In support of this resolution one delegate " urged the conference not to be content with pious resolutions, but to tell the Government: ' *we demand as delegates that these laws shall be altered* and that the industrial worker shall have his freedom. Get on with it or get out.' " The conference report notes that this speech was greeted by " loud applause " and that the resolution was carried by a small majority.[2]

A subsequent resolution went further. Moved by a Vice-President of the National Union, it read: " That this conference regrets the apparent inability of the Government to appreciate the necessity of amending the Laws governing Trade Unions." In supporting his resolution the mover said:

> " Resolutions like those concerning the unions that had already been carried had been passed year after year. . . . Last year three such resolutions were carried and this year eleven. Next year they would occupy the whole agenda, and he for one would not waste time on coming to listen to them any longer. . . . The conference should put a seal on the resolutions already passed by forcing the Government in the terms of his motion to act." (Cheers.)

The violent tone of the debate moved the Chairman of the Party Organization, Col. Jackson, to intervene. He said:

> " I have no fault to find with the forceful remarks on the motion, but I am sorry it was necessary to move it. I am satis-

---

[1] *1926 Conservative Annual Conference Report*, folio 14.
[2] *Ibid.*, folio 20. [Italics mine.]

fied myself, and you may be, that the Government do fully appreciate not only the necessity, but the urgency of dealing with Trade
Union legislation.

"I have done my best to convey to the Prime Minister and the
Cabinet the strong feeling there is not only in our party, but in
the minds of every man and woman in the country who cares for
its well-being. The Prime Minister and his colleagues share that
feeling. (Cheers.). . . . Fearless action, based on justice, will gain
support from every fair-minded man and woman, but it is a
serious question which cannot be dealt with except by the most
careful consideration of all its details. If you pass this resolution
the Government may regret your inability to trust them to deal
with a great national question with the care and wisdom it certainly requires."[1]

The mover of the motion accepted Col. Jackson's argument and
withdrew his resolution, saying he was prepared " to trust the
Government ". In his address to the mass meeting which followed
the conference, Baldwin in effect assured this delegate that his confidence was not misplaced. He took the occasion to promise that a
Government Bill on the subject would soon be introduced in the
House of Commons.

This debate on trade union legislation at the 1926 conference
provides an excellent illustration of the functioning of the party
conference at its most effective. It provided an opportunity for the
militants of the party to bring pressure to bear on the Leader and
his colleagues in the House. For those who shared their views such
pressure was obviously essential. G. M. Young records that after
the General Strike Baldwin's colleagues who wished to press on
with new trade union legislation found him indifferent and
languid, and he quotes Baldwin as saying to his colleagues, " leave
it alone . . . we are all so tired ".[2] It is probable, as Young argues,
that left to himself Baldwin would have been willing to let bygones
be bygones. His own inclination was to trust the trade unions, to
attempt to imbue them with his own contempt for the doctrinaires
and to keep the gap between constitutional and revolutionary socialism wedged open. The Trades Disputes Bill, Young argues, was
" a deviation under pressure ". Baldwin, he says, paradoxically,
was " the Leader of a Party, and ' Parties, like snakes, are moved
by the tail '." Whatever Baldwin's own inclinations, he gave in to
the powerful pressure of his own supporters both inside and outside
the House, and in G. M. Young's words " with the laying of the
Trades Disputes Bill the Disraelian make-believe rolled away like

---

[1] *1926 Conservative Annual Conference Report*, folio 21.
[2] Young, G. M., *Stanley Baldwin*, p. 120.

a morning mist and revealed the Conservative Party armed and accoutred to keep the Unions in their places and arrest the growth of the Parliamentary Labour Party. The Conservatives were, in fact, determined to make a party triumph out of what, rightly viewed, was a national victory, and Baldwin put himself in their hands."[1]

The National Union was not slow to express its gratitude following the passage of the Trades Disputes Act of 1927. Its Executive Committee passed the following resolution:

> " That the Executive Committee of the National Union expresses its emphatic approval of the Trades Disputes and Trade Unions Bill, and pledges itself to afford the Government its fullest support in its attempt, by means of this Bill, to protect the community against such acts of coercion as the General Strike, and individual Trade Unionists from intimidation and victimization.
>
> " It welcomes with special satisfaction the proposal to free non-Socialist Trade Unionists from the gross injustice of the political levy." [2]

The conference of the Women's Unionist Organization followed suit on 26th May, 1927.[3] Later in the year the annual conference of the National Union prided itself on its triumph. Speaking to the conference Sir Robert Sanders, the Chairman of the Council, said:

> " I am sure there are two measures on which this conference may be particularly anxious to congratulate the Government, and, if I may say so, to congratulate itself. The two matters on which the conference was most insistent were the expulsion of Arcos —(cheers)—and the amendment of the Trade Union law (cheers).
>
> " Those twins, begotten at (last year's conference) had seen the light at Westminster, and, in spite of most violent attempts at infanticide they are now strong, healthy children, likely to live a useful and popular life." [4]

The conference might well congratulate itself. They may not have been right in assuming that Baldwin was prepared to commit infanticide where their Trades Disputes Bill was concerned, but there is good reason to suspect that without their pressure he might have allowed their child to die of neglect. It is of considerable significance that one of the most important single pieces of legislation of the 1924-9 Government should have been so evidently the product of pressure from the party rank and file both inside and outside the House. The Leader of the Party may in theory have the

---

[1] Young, G. M., *Stanley Baldwin*, pp. 124-5.
[2] Cited in *Gleanings and Memoranda*, May, 1927, p. 542.
[3] Cited in *Gleanings and Memoranda*, July, 1927, p. 4.
[4] *1927 Conservative Annual Conference Report*, folio 3.

sole right to formulate policy but in this case an indifferent Leader seems to have abdicated this right.

The period 1927-9 has been properly labelled " the years of decay " as far as the Conservative Government was concerned. G. M. Young records that Baldwin by then appeared to be " little more than an amiable observer of events, at home and abroad, which, even if he had the power, he had no will to direct or control "; this despite the fact that his Government was " sliding into a slumberous exhaustion such as had overtaken (the Conservative Government of) 25 years before ".[1]

Impatience with Baldwin's lassitude became general throughout the party, and there was public discussion in the Conservative press and elsewhere of the expediency of a change in the leadership of the party. One Conservative newspaper published the names of no fewer than nine possible Prime Ministers, all of whom it appeared to assume would be preferable to Baldwin.[2] In the House Baldwin was in frequent trouble with his own supporters. A strange scheme for House of Lords reform introduced by the Lord Chancellor was badly received in the country and when the Labour Opposition tabled a motion of censure on the Government, no fewer than 70 " young Conservatives " signed an amendment to it which was the equivalent of a Conservative motion of censure upon the Government. Under this pressure Baldwin and his colleagues decided to drop the Lord Chancellor's scheme. The incident is described by one of Baldwin's biographers as a " manifestation of chaotic incompetence ".[3]

Baldwin tried fitfully to clear the air and to restore confidence in himself and his Government. On one occasion he chose the strange device of an open letter to his own Chief Whip. " My dear Eyres Monsell," it began, " you have told me that there has been some confusion of thought amongst Unionist Members arising from condensed reports of certain recent speeches and various tendentious articles in the unfriendly Press,"[4] and the letter continued

[1] Young, G. M., *Stanley Baldwin*, pp. 134-5. Young, incidentally, quotes Austen Chamberlain as saying that only once in fourteen years had he known Baldwin to influence a Cabinet decision.

[2] Steed, W., *The Real Stanley Baldwin*, p. 103. Steed adds, oddly enough: " Mr. Baldwin himself was understood to favour the choice of Mr. (now Lord) Bridgeman, the First Lord of the Admiralty, as his successor—an idea eminently calculated to defeat its object. Whether Mr. Baldwin knew it or not, Mr. Bridgeman enjoyed the reputation of being one of the least perspicacious Ministers in a Government devoid of perspicacity."

[3] *Ibid.*, p. 105.

[4] Cited in the Report of the Central Council, *1928 Conservative Annual Conference Report*, folio 14.

with an attempt to re-state the Government's position on certain major issues. But the grumbling continued and there were more critical resolutions at that year's annual conference of the National Union.[1] At the conclusion of the conference Baldwin made a remarkably complacent speech:

> " I believe our organization to-day is better than it has ever been at headquarters and in the country. . . . To-day I see a closer co-operation between the Central Office and the local organizations than I ever remember, and I see unlimited enthusiasm and ability.
>
> " I sprang from the rank and file and they have supported me through good times and through bad. They stood by me after the election of 1923, when many stout hearts wavered. They have stood by me since. *They have followed my strategy without asking too many questions. They have trusted me. (Cheers.) Once more in the coming fight I ask you to continue that trust in my Leadership.* I am convinced that if you will give me that same confidence that I have in you, once more we shall rout our foes, combined or separate, as we routed them four years ago, and continue again for a further period of ordered progress in the traditions of that greatest of our leaders whom we are all so proud to follow—Lord Beaconsfield." [2]

This plea for confidence seemed intended to take the place of a Conservative programme:

> " Mr. Snowden (Baldwin said), always cautious, and sometimes wise, says that the Conservative Party has never committed the folly of issuing a list of a few dozen items of reform which it proposes to carry out. Nor will it ever do so as long as I am Leader." [3]

It was apparently considered necessary to provide some sort of public demonstration on the eve of the election of 1929 that Baldwin still had the support of his party. The report of the Central Council for that year records, " there was a representative attendance of members of the Council at a meeting of the Party Organization held . . . at the Theatre Royal, Drury Lane, London, on 18th April last when a resolution of confidence in the Leader of the Party was passed." [4]

---

[1] *1928 Conservative Annual Conference Report,* folio 30 ff.

[2] *Ibid.,* folio 52. [Italics mine.]

[3] Cited in Young, G. M., *Stanley Baldwin,* p. 136. Keith Feiling (in *What is Conservatism?*) no doubt had Baldwin in mind when characterizing a typical sort of Conservative leader he wrote: " There are (in the party) men of good-will, who trust that bread cast on the waters, ' not of Gennezareth, but of Thames ', will return after not too many days, and hold that character in itself constitutes a programme."

[4] Report of the Central Council, *1929 Conservative Annual Conference Report,* folio 7.

But this confidence in Baldwin (such as it was) was shaken by the resounding defeat of the party in June, 1929. Baldwin had led his party to defeat twice within six years and again there were those who argued that the party must rid itself of him as Leader. Baldwin appears to have been saved as much as anything else by the fact that he had no powerful rival or obvious successor.[1] The party as a whole was slothful and dispirited in opposition. A prominent sympathizer described it at the time in these terms:

> " To all appearances the existing party is lax in its attendance, barely agreed on fundamentals, and pessimistic in outlook, the more cheerful hoping that Labour is in office for two years, the more gloomy feeling that it may be there for ten. Accustomed in the past to a definite lead from above, it has of late often had to do without it, and so, while one section waited for the spark from heaven to fall, another brandished a fiery cross kindled elsewhere. Taken as a whole it is still much too deferential to wealth, too patient of old men, too closed to the young and too unwelcoming of brain. Its worst offenders are the many local associations who ask little of their Member, except that he should pay. . . . Some of its leaders identify private with public virtue, others resent legitimate criticism and fail to distinguish a craving for leadership from a hunger for the loaves and fishes . . . " [2]

In an attempt to strengthen his position with the extra-parliamentary organization of the party, Baldwin addressed the Central Council on 2nd July, 1929. In the course of his review of the political situation he said:

> " We have been through many hard fights together; we have won, and we have lost, and we shall win again. But it is always natural in a moment of defeat that there should be, that there must be, a certain amount of heart-searching and of criticism. Nobody likes being beaten, and by the end of an election everyone is a little tired and a little strained, and nerves are a little on edge. Hence it is, human nature being what it is, that we think at the moment not of ourselves, but of the shortcomings of others. I have no objection to criticism of whatever kind. We expect it. . . .
> " We shall examine with the utmost care the weak places that

[1] Writing about this time Wickham Steed observed " the Conservative front-benchers are a scratch lot, with some ' duds ' and some ' talents ' among them; but not one of them would the Party unanimously prefer to Mr. Baldwin as its leader, nor would an outsider like Lord Beaverbrook be generally acceptable either on his own merits or as Lord Rothermere's nominee ". Steed, W., *The Real Stanley Baldwin*, p. 16.

[2] Feiling, K., *What is Conservatism?* pp. 6-7. One delegate to the party conference of 1929 put the matter more succinctly: the party " had been suffering (he said) from damp rot ". *1929 Conservative Annual Conference Report*, folio 25.

may have been revealed in the course of this recent struggle ; and that work and re-organization and evolution will proceed with renewed energy. But this is not a time to ask for the head of anyone on a charger ; and I for one am not going to cut off any head to put on it.

" With regard to myself I would only say one word, because only one word, I think, is necessary. I hold the position I hold entirely by your good will and your consent ; and the moment, the moment that is removed, the moment there is anyone else that you wish to take my place, I will surrender that place at that moment and go right out of politics. That, I think, is the only fair thing that a leader can say. . . . "[1]

There was no overt move at the Council meeting to take up Baldwin's offer; in fact a resolution was passed saying " that this meeting of the Central Council places on record its entire confidence in the Rt. Hon. Stanley Baldwin, M.P., and assures him, as Leader of the Conservative Party, of its loyalty and support in the future ".[2] It was decided however to set up an Emergency Sub-Committee which would supervise the circulation of a questionnaire to the constituency organizations inquiring into the reasons for the defeat of the party at the General Election. This Sub-Committee presented an interim report to the 1929 conference of the National Union. This report (which is examined on p. 268 below) contains several passages which reflect concern about the relationship between the Leader and the party organization. The relevant passages of the report read as follows:

" (1)   On the relationship between the Executive Committee and the Council of the National Union and the Leader of the Party, your Sub-Committee recommend that the present practice, under which the Resolutions of Conferences and Central Council Meetings are remitted to the Executive to be conveyed to the Leader of the Party, be continued, and that the Executive Committee should act as recommended in paragraph 3.

" (2)   With regard to the Executive Committee, your Sub-Committee are of opinion that a general feeling exists among the members of the National Union that a closer contact should be established with the Leader of the Party. Your Sub-Committee therefore suggest it is desirable that the Leader of the Party should attend the meetings of the Executive Committee and confer with the Committee when matters of special interest are under consideration.

" (3)   With regard to Resolutions passed by the Executive Committee which the Committee consider ought to be conveyed to the Leader of the Party, your Sub-Committee consider that such Reso-

---

[1] *The Times*, 3rd July, 1929.
[2] *Gleanings and Memoranda*, August, 1929, p. 90.

lutions, together with Resolutions remitted to the Executive from Conferences and Council Meetings, ought to be conveyed personally by members of the Executive to the Leader of the Party, and it is therefore recommended that a Sub-Committee of the Executive at once be set up for the purpose. It is further recommended that this Sub-Committee normally consist of five members of the Executive and two ex-officio members, but that for any special occasion the Executive Committee may nominate one or more extra members. It is considered that this Sub-Committee should be appointed annually at the first meeting of the newly elected Executive Committee in each year. Your Sub-Committee further consider that this Sub-Committee would also prove a useful channel for communications between the Leader of the Party and the Executive Committee."[1]

It is significant that the report concludes with the statement that " the above report has received the approval of the Leader of the Party."

When the report was presented to the 1929 conference of the National Union it was the basis of a lively and at times heated discussion.[2] One delegate spoke of the many resolutions passed at National Union conferences about which they never heard any more and he added pointedly that while members of the party did not want to " lead their Leader " he was quite sure that their present Leader would always appreciate any well-considered views put forward by the rank and file. There should be some machinery such as that now suggested to put their resolutions before their Leader, and those who had put forward resolutions should hear the result. In reply the Chairman of the Sub-Committee said that they proposed to set up what, in effect, was a panel which would approach the Leader of the Party and which he in turn would approach if necessary; all resolutions would be conveyed direct to the Leader through this panel, and the panel would also remit his replies to the people concerned. Another delegate deplored what he described as " the impression of soulless indifference " which pervaded the present relationship between the leadership and the rank and file. To help correct this situation another speaker urged that the party leaders should attend the conferences of the National Union and " breathe its atmosphere". In reply to this suggestion the Chairman of the Council promised " to use his influence in this direction."

---

[1] Report of the Central Council, *1929 Conservative Annual Conference Report*, folio 7.
[2] *1929 Conservative Annual Conference Report*, folios 3-5 and *passim*.

The sharpest criticisms came from Sir Charles Marston who moved to refer back certain sections of the report. He alleged that the party was " very democratic until it reached the top," that it was in fact " an autocracy masquerading as a democracy". He did not think that the Leader of the Party should be elected by the National Union but neither did he think that the Leader of the Party should " appoint the Chairman of the Party Organization without proper consultation with the Executive."[1]   (This aspect of the Leader's powers and the rôle of the Chairman of the Party Organization is considered p. 272 below.) In the course of the conference deliberations one delegate did, however, re-state with the apparent approval of the conference the traditional Conservative view of the rôle of the Leader. He said the one thing he prayed and hoped was that they would never modify their party organization on the lines adopted by the Socialists. There was only one way to run a party " *when they had once elected a leader they must back him or sack him.* (Cheers.) It would be impossible to work out a party programme in a huge conference like that. *The main function of the conference was to give the leaders a broad indication of the directions in which it was desirous the party should go.*"[2] The speaker concluded by urging the conference that there was far better work for them to do than attacking one another. Let them, he urged, " go bald-headed for the other side and stop sniping among themselves."

It is sad to note however that sniping did not cease and the Conservatives continued to " go bald-headed " for each other for almost their entire period in opposition until the fall of the second Labour Government. Addressing the concluding mass meeting of the 1929 conference of the National Union Baldwin had again told the party that they could get rid of him whenever they chose.

> " Let me remind you (he said) of some words that were uttered, when he was in Opposition, shortly before he won a glorious victory, by one of the greatest leaders we ever had—Benjamin Disraeli. Speaking in Glasgow in 1873 he said: 'The reason that I have been able to lead a party for so long a period and under some circumstances of difficulty and discouragement is that the party which I lead is the most generous party which ever existed.' (Cheers.) 'I cannot help,' he added, 'smiling sometimes when I hear the constant intimations that are given by those who know all the secrets of the political world of the extreme anxiety of the Conservative Party to get rid of my services. The fact is,' said Mr. Disraeli, not me (laughter) 'the Conservative Party can get

[1] *1929 Conservative Annual Conference Report*, folios 4–5.
[2] *Ibid.*, folio 16. [Italics mine.]

rid of my services whenever they give me the intimation that they so desire.' "

Certain of Baldwin's Conservative critics seemed determined during 1930 to seize the opportunity which he (quoting Disraeli) had appeared to offer them. Lord Beaverbrook spearheaded the attack[1] and chose as his issue Baldwin's alleged failure to adopt a sufficiently militant policy toward the Empire. At the party conference in November, 1929, Baldwin had said: " I think we owe a word of gratitude to one—not always a supporter of our party—Lord Beaverbrook, for bringing before the country the idea . . . of a united Empire." Lord Beaverbrook apparently took this as evidence that Baldwin was prepared to throw the weight of the party behind his " Empire Crusade " and there was an intricate exchange between the two men in which an attempt was made (with some success) to reach a common understanding. But no such reconciliation was achieved when another and even more critical peer, Lord Rothermere, renewed what had been a long-standing campaign against Baldwin's leadership. During the spring of 1930 the Rothermere press returned again and again to the attack, alleging that Baldwin was altogether too hesitant and indifferent in his attitude toward imperial policy. The campaign succeeded in winning considerable support within the party and Baldwin apparently became convinced that in order to consolidate his own position he would have to call a special party meeting and lay his case before them. He called such a meeting for 24th June, in London, and invitations were sent to all Conservative M.P.s, peers and candidates.

The meeting aroused enormous interest[2] since it was clear that Baldwin's position as Leader was at stake. In preparation for the meeting he addressed a series of public meetings in various parts of the country elaborating his imperial policy. Then before the assembly itself he said:

"We are told that there is a crisis in the party. . . . there will be a crisis if you cannot make up your minds what you are going to do. I have made up my mind, but you have got to make up yours.

---

[1] On Beaverbrook's relations with Baldwin see Driberg, T., *Beaverbrook*, London, 1956, Chapter VIII and *passim*.

[2] Even Prof. Laski wrote a personal letter to Baldwin on the eve of the meeting to wish him success. " There are many Socialists (wrote Laski) who, like myself, . . . feel grateful for the quality of the human directness you bring to our political life . . . We resent, not less than your own friends, the effort to usurp a leadership the distinction of which has been, if I may say so, an honoured feature of our time." Cited in Young, G. M., *Stanley Baldwin*, p. 151.

You have been told . . . that we have no policy. . . . We have a policy which I have been explaining up and down the country."

He referred with some bitterness to the fact that " even members of the Carlton Club have written for payment and worked and done all they can *to destroy my position, and, with me, the party* . . . " He bracketed Lord Rothermere and Lord Beaverbrook with William Randolph Hearst, adding " there is nothing more curious in modern evolution than the effect of an enormous fortune rapidly made and the control of newspapers of your own." Lord Rothermere and Lord Beaverbrook, he alleged, " desire to dictate the policy (of the) party, . . . to choose (the) leader, . . . to impose Ministers on the Crown: the only parallel to that was the action of the TUC in 1926. . . . We are told that unless we make peace with these noblemen, candidates are to be run all over the country. The Lloyd George candidates at the last election smelt; these will stink. The challenge has been issued. . . I accept the challenge as I accepted the challenge of the TUC. . . . when I fight I go on to the end, as I did in 1926." Then in a masterstroke Baldwin produced a letter from Lord Rothermere in which the latter said that he would not support Baldwin " unless I have complete guarantees that such policy will be carried out if his party achieves office and unless I am acquainted with the names of at least eight, or ten, of his most prominent colleagues in the next Ministry." Baldwin had no difficulty in showing that this proposition was both ludicrous and unconstitutional. " Now (he said) those are the terms that your leader would have to accept, and when sent for by the King he would have to say: ' Sire, these names are not necessarily my choice, but they have the support of Lord Rothermere.' A more preposterous and insolent demand was never made on the leader of any political party. I repudiate it with contempt and I will fight that attempt at domination to the end."[1]

The occasion was a tremendous personal triumph for Baldwin, who seemed with a single speech to have re-established his command of the party; but the issue was not yet settled. The Beaverbrook and Rothermere press renewed their campaign and it proved to have considerable attraction for certain elements within the party. As G. M. Young notes, " a referendum taken on personality would have given Baldwin 100 votes to Beaverbrook's 10; taken on policy, taken in the party—the numbers would be nearer even."[2] Baldwin found it necessary to continue an exchange of public correspondence on the issues of Empire policy with Lord Beaver-

[1] *The Times,* 25th June, 1930.
[2] Young, G. M., *Stanley Baldwin,* p. 154.

brook. The tone of the correspondence is in many ways surprising. On 21st October, 1930, Baldwin wrote, " I have read the offer which you made to me in your speech at South Paddington yesterday. . . . You will see from what I have said that I am asking the country to give me a completely free hand to discuss with the Dominions all the alternative methods, including taxes on foreign foodstuffs, by which our common object may be achieved, and I ask you whether you are prepared in these circumstances to stand by your declaration (of support) which you made a few months ago."[1] In a speech the next day Lord Beaverbrook rejected Mr. Baldwin's proposals and made it clear that he proposed to continue his " Crusade ".

There were demands within the Conservative Party for a special meeting to reconsider the question of party leadership. Such a meeting was held on 30th October, and was attended by Conservative peers, M.P.s and candidates. Baldwin opened with a statement of his conception of the fiscal policy of the party, and ended by saying, " will all those who support that policy hold up their hands? . . . And on the contrary? . . . Carried unanimously, no, not unanimously."[2] (Lord Beaverbrook, according to Gleanings and Memoranda, was the sole dissentient.)[3] A resolution was then moved by the famous old Die-Hard, Col. J. Gretton, M.P., and seconded by another M.P., declaring that a change in the leadership of the party was necessary in the national interest. After discussion it was rejected by 462 votes to 116.[4] Thereafter the following resolution was carried nem. con.: " That this meeting affirms its confidence in Mr. Baldwin as leader of the Conservative Party and pledges itself loyally to support his policy and leadership within Parliament and in the constituencies."

Again there was a flood of congratulations and a series of public declarations by prominent Conservatives affirming that the unity of the party had been re-established. " We have had our doubts, perplexities and divisions," said L. S. Amery, M.P. (Colonial Secretary in the previous Conservative Government), " but we have overcome those difficulties; we have surmounted our divisions. We are to-day united in support of one leader and united on the policy which we will put forward."[5] Baldwin, according to Sir Robert

[1] The Times, 22nd October, 1930
[2] The Times, 31st October, 1930
[3] Gleanings and Memoranda, December, 1930, pp. 467–8.
[4] The Times, 31st October, 1930. On these events see also Lord Winterton, Orders of the Day, p. 218; Amery, L. S., My Political Life, III, p. 22 ff., and Wrench, J. E., Geoffrey Dawson and our Times, p. 286.
[5] The Times, 6th November, 1930.

Horne, M.P., had "re-created their confidence in him and re-established his authority. . . . his wise guidance had brought the party to a point at which complete unity of aim became possible without creating those permanent splits which would have completely destroyed the influence and the usefulness of their great organization."[1] The Central Council meeting on 25th November heard an address by Baldwin and then passed a resolution which read in part: "That this Council expresses its implicit and unabated confidence in Mr. Stanley Baldwin as Leader . . . and its grateful appreciation of the eminent services he has rendered to the Party at all times."

But Baldwin's victory was in no sense decisive; it provided no more than a lull in his struggle to retain the leadership. A large section of the party had been unhappy for some time about his attitude to the future of India. The Round Table Conference on India, which assembled on 12th November, 1930, helped to bring into the open the deep cleavage within the party on the subject. There was also renewed dissatisfaction with Baldwin's stand on imperial economic affairs. On 25th February, 1931, the party's Chief Agent wrote to Neville Chamberlain, then Chairman of the Party Organization, saying, "it would be in the interests of the Party that the Leader should reconsider his position."[2] It seems clear from G. M. Young's analysis of Baldwin's reaction to this letter, that the Chief Agent intended that Baldwin should reconsider the advisability of his resigning the leadership of the party; Young reports that Baldwin's first reaction (even to the expurgated edition of the letter which Chamberlain forwarded to him) was that he should retire immediately from politics. His second impulse was to apply for the Chiltern Hundreds and offer himself as a candidate in a pending by-election in the St. George's Division of Westminster (the prospective Conservative candidate had withdrawn on the grounds that he could not defend his leader).[3] In the event Baldwin took neither step, but managed to retrieve his position to some extent by his performance in the Commons.

As early as January Baldwin had boldly pledged his support to

[1] *The Times,* 6th November, 1930.

[2] Cited in Young, G. M., *Stanley Baldwin,* p. 156. The memorandum to Chamberlain, a document of first importance, has now been published in full in Iain Macleod's *Neville Chamberlain,* Chapter VIII. As *The Times* has commented (4th December 1961), it shows how "delusory" the Conservative Party's theory of its own leadership really is.

[3] The prospective candidate's place was taken by Alfred Duff Cooper, who stood successfully as the official Conservative candidate against an anti-Baldwin Conservative. Duff Cooper later claimed, no doubt rightly, that Baldwin would have had to resign if this by-election had gone against him. See Duff Cooper, *Old Men Forget,* pp. 172 ff.

the Labour Government's attempt to work out an agreed policy for India with representative Indian leaders;[1] he had given this pledge despite the fact that Winston Churchill in protest had quit the Conservative Party's Shadow Cabinet. On 6th March at a public meeting Baldwin renewed his pledge; but then, strangely, three days later the India Committee of the Conservative Party published a resolution welcoming " the decision of Mr. Baldwin that the Conservative Party cannot be represented at any further Round Table Conference to be held in India . . . " It looked, one observer put it, as if Baldwin " had been driven by Churchill and the imperialists into eating his own words," but on 12th March in the Commons Baldwin clarified the situation in one of the most important speeches of his career.

The speech was primarily addressed to his own supporters. He warned them that the Empire of 1931 was not the Empire of 1887 and added. . . . " it cannot be supposed that in this world of evolution, India alone is static." The Round Table Conference had broken up and his party would not send a delegation to a renewal of the conference in India although they would co-operate if further meetings could be held in London. He explained the background of the (Conservative) India Committee resolution of 9th March. He had agreed with the party committee that delegates should not proceed to India but he had been reluctant to have the party give to the press an official statement to that effect. " . . . When I was asked (he said) if I had any objection to an authentic statement going out that that decision had been come to I was in a little bit of a difficulty for this reason. I would much rather, quite frankly, that no statement had been made. These conversations had been private communications between a leader and a committee of his followers and they ought to be private. I noticed that there was some communication between that committee of my party and that section of the press which had announced its intention to smash us. . . . I knew the results might be unfortunate, not to myself—I do not care twopence about that—but I was afraid of the reaction in India." He was fearful that the extremists here in Britain would help to create a revolutionary spirit in India and he staked his whole position as Leader of his Party on his right to tell them the truth as he saw it, adding:

> " I know the difficulties . . . in my party—difficulties of conviction and of old ties. I do not believe the bulk of our party either in the House or in the country, will take any different view. . .

[1] For a full account of the struggle over India see Templewood, Lord, *Nine Troubled Years*, p. 45 ff., and Amery, L. S., *My Political Life*, Vol. III, pp. 96 ff.

I shall carry out that policy with every desire to overcome the stupendous difficulties that face us. If there are those in our party . . . who would have to have forced out of their reluctant hands one concession after another, if they be a majority, in God's name let them choose a man to lead them. If they are in minority then let them at least refrain from throwing difficulties in the way of those who have undertaken an almost superhuman task, on the successful fulfilment of which depends the wellbeing, the prosperity and the duration of the whole British Empire." [1]

This speech was in many respects the climax of Baldwin's struggle to retain the mastery of his party. The struggle over the party's Indian policy was far from settled (cf. pp. 202-5 below) and there were a number of subsequent minor challenges to Baldwin's authority, but his speech on 12th March, 1931, unquestionably won him the enduring allegiance of a very large proportion of his followers in the House and in the country. G. M. Young quotes a remarkably interesting analysis of Baldwin's achievement written on 13th March by an (anonymous) friend of Baldwin:

" (Baldwin) has been having as bad a time as ever any man has been called on to bear, and yesterday he put his fortune to the touch in a way that makes everyone who loves him proud to see. His followers have been jockeying about in the most contemptible and treacherous way, making his position more insecure and eating into his reputation all the while because he didn't call them to heel or disassociate himself from them. It looked as if he might fall from the leadership through an accumulation of petty undefined issues and not go down, if he had to go down, with flying colours on some clearly defined big principle. . . .

" His colleagues all advised him not to take a strong line and not to speak out, whether through treachery or cowardice, I don't know ; but this advice would have been fatal to him if he had taken it. However, he took his own line and kept his soul even if he loses his party. I don't think he will lose the party now : the moment he spoke to them from the heights, the bulk of them looked to me to be rallying to him.

" Read his speech : though of course it can't give you the impression of what it was like in the tense human atmosphere of the House, charged with personality and passion. A most manful speech, so touching in its courage and simplicity : and one felt so happy for him because, after that, whether he stands or falls, he is all right, and none of the insinuating littleness of his political councillors or the clamour of the press has touched him at all." [2]

---

[1] *House of Commons Debates,* 12th March, 1931.
[2] Cited in Young, G. M., *Stanley Baldwin,* p. 161.

A few days later Baldwin proved the truth of the final phrase regarding " the clamour of the press ". In a public meeting he delivered a savage attack against the Beaverbrook and Rothermere press.

Despite the defeat of their attempt to unseat Baldwin at the October meeting, the hostile Press Barons had been far from repentant. Speaking at Islington on 30th January, 1931, Lord Beaverbrook had said: " It is my purpose to break up the Conservative Party if the Conservative Party does not adopt the policy (of Empire Free Trade)." [1] Lord Rothermere's papers too had renewed their bitter personal attacks on Baldwin.[2] The latter finally replied in one of the strongest statements ever made by a Conservative leader on the subject of the press. He gave instances of what he considered to be the distortions and hypocrisy practised by " the insolent plutocracy " represented by Lords Beaverbrook and Rothermere, and he added:

> " The papers conducted by Lord Rothermere and Lord Beaverbrook are not newspapers in the ordinary acceptance of the term. They are engines of propaganda, for the constantly changing policies, desires, personal wishes, personal likes and dislikes of two men. . . .
>
> " What are their methods? Their methods are direct falsehood, misrepresentation, half-truths, the alteration of the speaker's meaning by publishing a sentence apart from the context . . . suppression and editorial criticism of speeches which are not reported in the paper. These are methods hated alike by the public and by the whole of the rest of the Press.
>
> " What the proprietorship of these papers is aiming at is power, and power without responsibility—the prerogative of the harlot throughout the ages. . . . " [3]

[1] *The Times,* 31st January, 1931.

[2] As early as 18th November, 1927, the then Chairman of the Party Organization (J. C. C. Davidson) had issued an official statement in reply to an " open letter " from Viscount Rothermere to the Conservative Party. Mr. Davidson wrote: " Anyone who has taken the trouble closely to watch Lord Rothermere's publications will have noticed a systematic endeavour to irritate the Conservative rank and file against the Conservative Government by holding up the policy of Ministers for criticism and denunciation." *Gleanings and Memoranda,* November, 1927, p. 417. And Baldwin in addressing the mass meeting following the party conference in the same year said, " I am driven to ask him from this platform, openly, three questions. (Applause.) Is Lord Rothermere a supporter of the Unionist Party with me as the leader? (Shouts of ' No '.) Is Lord Rothermere a supporter of the Unionist Party with someone else as leader? (Shouts of ' No'.) Is Lord Rothermere a supporter of Mr. Lloyd George? (Shouts of ' Yes'.)" *1927 Conservative Annual Conference Report,* folio 54.

[3] *The Times,* 18th March, 1931.

Shortly thereafter, however, a truce was negotiated between Lord Beaverbrook and the leaders of the Conservative Party. On 29th March correspondence which had passed between Neville Chamberlain (then Chairman of the Party Organization) and Lord Beaverbrook was made public. Chamberlain had invited Lord Beaverbrook to state the terms on which he would be prepared to support the party's policy. Beaverbrook replied outlining his own views particularly with regard to agricultural policy and Chamberlain then wrote as follows: " I have discussed (the terms of your letter) with Mr. Baldwin and he authorizes me to say you have correctly stated the present Conservative policy in regard to agriculture." Chamberlain then reviewed Baldwin's intentions in this regard and ends his letter: " Accordingly I am glad to think that we shall have the co-operation of yourself and your friends in our task, and I welcome your support."[1]

The economic and political crisis later in the year (1931) put an end for the time being to internal party feuds. In the negotiations which preceded the formation of the National Government Baldwin appears at first to have acted independently of his party colleagues, but Young explains that " when Baldwin told his immediate friends, his Shadow Cabinet, that he had agreed in their name to join the (new) Administration not a voice was raised against him."[2] His action was formally endorsed at a meeting of Conservative peers, Members of Parliament and candidates on 28th August. The following resolution was moved by Lord Hailsham and seconded by Sir Henry Page-Croft, M.P.: " that this meeting of Conservative Members of both Houses of Parliament and candidates support their leader in his decision to take part in the formation of a National Government to deal with the present national emergency."[3]

Thereafter during his subsequent six years as Leader of the Party Baldwin's position was never challenged as forthrightly as it had been during 1930-31. He was frequently under pressure from his colleagues particularly with regard to his India policy. (These difficulties are examined in greater detail in Chapter IV since they provide an important illustration of the rôle of the party conference and of the Central Council in the functioning of the Conservative Party.) Here it is perhaps sufficient to note that the Die-Hards' struggle over India provoked Baldwin on one occasion to say to the Conservative annual conference that it was " interesting to remem-

---

[1] *The Times*, 30th March, 1931.
[2] Young, G. M., *Stanley Baldwin*, p. 167.
[3] *The Times*, 29th August, 1931.

ber that (Joseph) Chamberlain (had) found more sympathy, more willingness to go forward and less desire to stagnate among the Tory leaders than among some of the rank and file." Baldwin added with, one suspects, a touch of irony, that he was thankful to say that there was no such tendency to sag into the old negative habits, but he asked the conference to remember Joseph Chamberlain's words: " long after I have gone . . . remember that when the old tendency to sag comes, kick the party into some kind of life and don't let 'em do it."[1] As if in reply, the President of the National Union turned to Baldwin when introducing him to the conference mass meeting in the following year and said: " the annual conference was not called for uttering sweet nothings into Mr. Baldwin's ear but that we might tell him home truths."[2] But a year later, on the eve of the General Election of 1935, the Chairman of the conference could say: " last year at the conference and at the mass meeting . . . the then President (of the National Union) in his speech had to tell Mr. Baldwin that there were a certain number of complaints and differences on the matter of policy between members of our party. Thank God, I can assure the Prime Minister that every man, woman and child in the Conservative Party stands solidly behind him at the present moment. We have seen in that great conference which has just closed the unanimity of the Conservative Party and we can assure you, sir, that however difficult your task may be we are behind you to a man."[3] Subsequently there were occasional minor difficulties;[4] but Baldwin weathered them without much difficulty until he retired in 1937.

It can be argued that Baldwin's fourteen-year term as Leader of the Conservative Party is the most interesting and significant field of study in the history of the Conservative leadership since Disraeli. He was not driven from the office, as were Austen and Neville Chamberlain, nor did he, despite great provocation, retire in despair as did Balfour. Neither on the other hand did he enjoy the assured ascendancy over his followers of a Salisbury; nor, of course, did he achieve the sort of stature in the public mind which enabled Churchill largely to ignore the periodic rumbling of discontent within his party.[5] For fourteen years, in power and out, Baldwin

[1] *1933 Conservative Annual Conference Report*, folio 41.
[2] *1934 Conservative Annual Conference Report*, folio 45.
[3] *1935 Conservative Annual Conference Report*, folio 52.
[4] See for example Kim, " Revolt Against Baldwin ", *Saturday Review*, No. 162, 17th October, 1936.
[5] Churchill, like Bonar Law, has been to some extent protected from the more forthright criticism of his followers by the fact that party activity (during at least a part of the period of his leadership) was suspended due

managed to retain the leadership of the party. As has been suggested above, his followers were often cantankerous, almost continually impatient and, on at least one occasion, came fairly near (in Baldwin's own phrase) to " demanding (his) head on a charger ". Baldwin's experience underlines the argument advanced above that the Leader of the Conservative Party can never under normal circumstances play the aloof, almost Olympian rôle which the party constitution appears to assign to him. The phrase from *The Times* article quoted above (" the whole Constitution of the Conservative Party tends to exaggerate the isolation of the leader from the rank and file. . . . It is difficult to imagine how a revolt against the Leader of the Conservative Party would be conducted ") appears even more surprising the more one re-examines Baldwin's experience as Leader.

Baldwin himself, after eleven years as Leader, attempted to put into words a description of the real relationship between the Conservative Leader and his followers. Speaking to the Conservative annual conference of 1934 he said:

> " Disraeli laid our principles down at the Crystal Palace many years ago, and you cannot go wrong if you stick to them. They were: ' the maintenance of our institutions and of our religion ; the preservation of our Empire, and the improvement in the condition of our people.' That does not tell you how you are to adapt your policy in changed circumstances and changed ages. That is the duty of a leader. The responsibility—and it is a great responsibility—that rests with a leader is to try and adapt the policy according to the deep-laid foundations of the Party principles to meet whatever may come in this world.
> " Equally as it is the duty and the responsibility of the Leader to do that, it is the right of the Party, if they think fit, to challenge its interpretation. That is democratic. If in sufficient numbers they can challenge it so that it inevitably leads to the choice of a new leader, that is democratic, and that is the way we do things."

And he added (it had been a conference which had insisted on its rights to " tell him home truths "):

> " But I want to say that I am at present Leader of this Party, and so long as I lead I am going to lead it."[1]

Baldwin's statement recalls the concluding sentence of A. L. Lowell's chapter on " Party Organization in Parliament " (in his

to war conditions; it could be argued of course that the formation of the National Government in 1931 helped to minimize factional disputes within Baldwin's party in a somewhat similar way.

[1] *1934 Conservative Annual Conference Report,* folio 49.

The Government of England). He wrote: "When appointed, the Leader leads and the party follows." [1] But this statement requires amendment in light of the fate of Conservative Leaders since Lowell wrote in 1908. It should perhaps read . . . "when appointed, the Leader leads, and the party follows, except when the party decides not to follow; then the Leader ceases to be Leader."

[1] Lowell, A. L., *The Government of England*, Vol. I, p. 457.

CHAPTER IV

THE "HANDMAID" OF THE PARTY—THE NATIONAL UNION OF CONSERVATIVE AND UNIONIST ASSOCIATIONS

I

THE EARLY YEARS OF THE NATIONAL UNION

PERHAPS the most significant comment on the origins of the National Union was made in 1873 by one of its founders, H. C. Raikes, M.P., then Chairman of the Council: "The Union has been organized," he said, "rather as . . . a handmaid to the party, than to usurp the functions of party leadership."[1] It would be unfair to make too much of the master-servant relationship implied in the word "handmaid" (although it does anticipate in an amusing way the remark attributed to Balfour to the effect that he would as soon take advice from his valet as from the annual conference of the National Union). But it is important to underscore the fact that from its earliest beginning the popular organization of the Conservative Party *outside* Parliament was conceived as a servant of the party *in* Parliament. As has been argued above, the position in the Labour Party (in its early period) was precisely the reverse; the band of Labour M.P.s in Parliament were considered to be the servants of a Labour Movement which already existed outside Parliament. The National Union, however, was the creation and (especially in its early years) the creature of the Conservative Party in Parliament.

There were powerful reasons why the Conservative leaders of 1867 should have decided to create a mass party organization outside Parliament. Such an organization would help to minimize the dangers inherent in the Tory Party's "leap in the dark" in 1867. Their Reform Act of that year had roughly doubled the electorate (in round numbers from one to two million); and, of particular importance, the new electors were mainly members of the working and lower middle classes in the urban areas. They could hardly be relied upon automatically to recognize their identity of interest with

---

[1] *1873 Conservative Annual Conference Report*, p. 10.

the Conservative Party; it is not surprising therefore that the earliest efforts of the National Union were devoted to wooing the newly enfranchised urban voters. After a rather casual beginning these efforts grew in intensity since there was soon stiff competition from the Liberal Party inspired by Joseph Chamberlain and the Birmingham Caucus. Then, in the 'eighties, restrictions on campaign expenditures (which limited if they did not eliminate electoral bribery and corruption) made it increasingly necessary to rely on the assistance of voluntary party workers.[1] And finally, of course, the spread of public education and the increased literacy of the masses made it imperative that the party in Parliament should have facilities for the preparation and distribution of party literature.

The directness and urgency of the Conservative appeal to the working classes is the most striking feature of the early work of the National Union. The Conservative leaders of the day were vividly aware, as Lord Derby put it in an address to a meeting of Conservative working men in 1875, that " (the working man) is master of the situation. His class can, if it chooses, outvote all other classes put together."[2] The inspiration for the campaign to woo the working classes came, of course, from Disraeli himself. In a magnificent phrase written on the second anniversary of Disraeli's death, *The Times* recalled that: " In the inarticulate mass of the English populace which they held at arm's length (Disraeli) discerned the Conservative working man as the sculptor perceives the angel prisoned in a block of marble."[3] There are innumerable illustrations in the speeches and writings of Disraeli of " the sculptor " at work. Again and again he emphasized that there must be a grand alliance of *all* the classes in defence of the institutions of the country. In his famous speech to the National Union at the Crystal Palace in 1872, Disraeli said: " . . . The Tory Party, unless it is a national party, is nothing. It is not a confederacy of nobles, it is not a democratic multitude; it is a party formed from all the numerous classes in the realm—classes alike and equal before the law, but whose different conditions and different aims give vigour and variety to our national life."[4] And with respect to one of the

[1] See p. 164 below.
[2] *Speech by the Earl of Derby at Edinburgh, 17th December, 1875*, publications of the National Union, No. 27, p. 6.
[3] *The Times*, 18th April, 1883.
[4] *1872 Conservative Annual Conference Report*, p. 16. Disraeli's argument in favour of an alliance between the classes was, of course, pushed to its ultimate conclusion after his death by Lord Randolph Churchill, who claimed: " The Conservative Party will never gain power until it gains the confidence of the working classes. The latter will not be led by any class interest. Our interests are perfectly safe in their hands if we will trust

institutions to which Disraeli drew increasing attention, the working classes had a particular responsibility: " I look (he said) to the cultivation of public opinion, and *especially in the working classes* for the maintenance of the British Empire."[1] On one famous occasion Disraeli publicly deplored the grouping of working-class Conservatives into separate organizations within the party. Speaking to a deputation of Conservative working men he said, " I have never been myself at all favourable to a system which would induce Conservatives who are working men to form societies confined merely to their class. In the Church and in the polling booth all are equal —and all that concerns Conservative working men and interests them concerns and interests the great body of Conservatives of whom they form a portion. Therefore, it is to the Conservative Association I see before me, of whom a very considerable majority consists of working men, it is to that Association that I address myself." [2] But these separate working-men's organizations persisted within the party; they reflected, as it were, one of the institutions in society—the class system—which the Conservative Party of the day seems to have dedicated itself to preserve.

Some of Disraeli's less subtle colleagues used harsher terms than his in their analysis of the relations between the classes. Thus Lord Derby (described in a National Union pamphlet of the period as " (this) giant among the sympathizers with the poor ")[3] in a speech to Conservative working men in 1875 explained that *they* had most to lose if revolution were to threaten the established order of society. "Whatever troubles the waters of society, whatever frightens the timid and the rich—and money is always timid—the artisan and the labourer are the first sufferers. The shopkeepers or the manufacturers lose their profit, but he loses his daily bread." In any

them . . . You must invite them to a share and a real share in the party government." *1883 Conservative Annual Conference Report* (manuscript minutes) folio 13.
[1] *Presentation of Addresses from the Conservative Associations to the Earl of Beaconsfield, K.G., and the Marquess of Salisbury, K.G., at the Foreign Office, 6th August, 1878.* Publications of the National Union, No. 36 (1878), p. 21. [Italics mine.]
[2] *Speech of the Rt. Hon. B. Disraeli, M.P., to the Conservative Association of Glasgow, on Saturday 22nd November, 1873.* National Union Publication, No. 24, November, 1873, p. 4. Later (1878) Disraeli contradicted himself saying, " I favoured (Conservative Working-Men's Associations) from the beginning . . ." Cited in Ostrogorski, M., *Democracy and the Organization of Political Parties,* Vol. I, p. 259.
[3] *The Tory Reform Act,* National Union pamphlet, No. 4, 1868, p. 19. " Only think," the pamphlet adds, " what sacrifices of personal ease and comfort, Lord Derby, with the besetting assaults of his inexorable ' enemy ', the Gout, has made to his Sovereign and his country! "

case, he added that he could see no reason why the working man should be other than satisfied with his lot. Lord Derby was particularly scornful in his condemnation of those who tried to stir up resentment among the working classes against the existing distribution of property. For these trouble makers, the Master of Knowsley had a devastating reply: " No one (said Lord Derby) who reads the advertisements in the papers can venture to contend that there is not land enough for sale to meet all possible wants."[1]

Lord Derby's themes are echoed in other early publications of the National Union. " . . . Continued agitations destroy the confidence of the classes above us . . " and this (one pamphlet explains) may lead to a withdrawal of capital. A firm reminder follows: " capitalists can seek other spheres . . . "[2] If they did so, the result (explains another National Union pamphlet) would be almost too horrible to contemplate: " Only put a period to the accumulation of property in the hands of men and families of birth and high honour and intelligence, and nothing will remain of that social power which has made England's greatness . . . "[3] Other Conservative spokesmen insisted with Lord Derby that the working class had no grounds for self-pity. In an address to the Brighton Conservative Association a Mr. Douglas Straight conceded that it was unfortunate that " there must be distinctions of class ". But he reminded

---

[1] *The Conservative Working Man.* (Speech by the Earl of Derby at Edinburgh, 17th December, 1875); National Union Publication, No. 27, pp. 5-7. It is worth noting that in the period in which Derby spoke, " a landed aristocracy of about 2,250 persons owned together nearly half the enclosed land of England and Wales, or nearly 15 million acres out of 33 million, and 400 peers and peeresses owned nearly 6 million." Broderick, *English Land and Landlords,* (1881), p. 166; *Cf.* Clapham, *Economic History of Modern Britain,* Vol. II. p. 253, and Smellie, *One Hundred Years of English Government,* p. 40.

[2] *The Political Future of the Working Classes,* or *Who are the Real Friends of the People ?* Publications of the National Union, No. 7, 1873, p. 3.

[3] *The Tory Reform Act,* National Union Pamphlet, No. 4, 1868, p. 16. Lord Salisbury was later, of course, to provide classic warnings against the introduction of class issues into British politics. In the peroration of his address to an audience of 6,000 meeting under the auspices of the Working-Men's Conservative Association in Liverpool in 1882, he warned: " . . . if you wish to uphold the glory and strength of your country, in which we are all so deeply interested—if you wish to promote the interest of all classes, high or low alike—you will discourage the kind of . . . politics which sets against each other the classes who, after all, are members of a common country, and who have a far higher interest in the common growth and prosperity of all than they can have in any petty and sectional victory of one class over another." *Speech of the Marques of Salisbury, at Liverpool, 13 April, 1882,* Publications of the National Union, No. 67, p. 12.

his audience that the wealthy have their worries too, and added: " in his station the burden of one man is pretty nearly as heavy as another." For himself Mr. Straight was " sick and tired of hearing of these proposals of exceptional legislation in the interests of the working man . . . "[1]

Straight's observation may well have been a fairly typical reaction of a middle- or upper-class Conservative to the stream of literature pouring out from the offices of the National Union. *Conservative Legislation for the Working Classes* (Publication No. 6); *The Political Future of the Working Classes or Who are the Real Friends of the People?* (Publication No. 7); *Practical Suggestions to the Loyal Working Men of Great Britain; or, Points of Policy and Duty at the Present Crisis* (Publication No. 5). These were typical early titles. It seems clear that the founders of the National Union were operating on the principle put into words by one of the speakers (a Capt. Field, R.N.) at the ninth annual conference of the National Union: " It was essentially the duty of gentlemen to go amongst the working men, and not to fold their arms, sit idle at home, and leave the working men to fight alone." [2] That the working men *were* prepared to fight against the Radicals who threatened the existing order of society, the Conservative leaders appeared (publicly at least) to have not the slightest doubt.

Their confidence must have been considerably strengthened by the remarkable meeting in 1867 (the year, it should be remembered, of the publication of the first volume of Marx's *Capital*) at which the National Union was formed. The manuscript minutes of this meeting (to be found in the offices of the National Union) make fascinating reading.[3] "Among the gentlemen and delegates present " at the Freemasons Tavern, London, on 12th November, 1867, were representatives from 55 cities and towns (and the University of London Graduates). John Gorst, M.P. (who three

---

[1] *Conservative Policy*, an address delivered by Mr. Douglas Straight on 2nd May, 1877, to the Brighton Conservative Association. (Published by the National Union.)

[2] *1875 Conservative Annual Conference Report*, pp. 46-7. The Captain illustrated his principle by explaining that the Conservatives at Portsmouth had organized a scheme whereby " working men subscribed one penny each per week, and once a year sat down, to the number of over 400, to a grand dinner."

[3] *Minutes of the Proceedings at the First Conference of the National Union of Conservative and Constitutional Associations* held at the Freemasons Tavern, London, 12th November, 1867. This meeting is discussed in some detail here because none of the previous studies of the Conservative Party has quoted more than a brief passage from these Minutes.

years later was to be appointed by Disraeli to organize the Conservative Central Office—see p. 262 below) took the chair, explaining that he had had to do so because neither of the two noble lords who had been invited to serve as chairman had found it possible to attend. The explanation offered by one of the noble lords casts an interesting light on the degree of importance he must have attached to the meeting: " Lord Holmsdale . . . has been obliged *at the last moment* to send an excuse because it is perfectly impossible for him to disappoint some friends with whom he has another engagement."[1]

In his opening remarks the chairman left no doubt about the purpose of the meeting: " We are all, I believe, united in our loyalty and devotion to the Conservative cause; we all of us believe that we Conservatives are the natural leaders of the people." He explained further that the gathering was " not a meeting for the discussion of Conservative principles in which we are all agreed, *it is only a meeting to consider by what particular organization we may make these Conservative principles effective among the masses.*"[2]

The honorary secretary was then invited to speak; he read an important statement elaborating Gorst's opening remarks:

> " The working classes of England some time back commenced forming themselves into associations to support the present Government upon the question of reform, and to maintain the fundamental principles of our ancient constitution. It was felt that their position would be strengthened and their influence augmented by the formation of a Central Union. Conferences were convened in the early part of this year to consider the question, which were numerously attended by representatives from the northern districts, and it was therefore decided to establish a union for this purpose.[3] At the present occasion it is proposed to finally settle the name, rules. and constitution of this society, and to appoint the first officers.

[1] *1867 Conservative Annual Conference Report*, folio 3.   [Italics mine.]
[2] *Ibid.,* folios 3-4. [Italics mine.]
[3] This placid account of the origins of the National Union was rather oddly contradicted some years later by one of its founders. J. Ross of the London and Westminster Association speaking to the eighth annual conference of the National Union in 1874 said: " I remember the first meeting for the purpose of organizing this Union ... I remember how we used to meet week after week, and month after month, and it seemed on more than one occasion as if we should have to give the matter up in despair. . . . Violent hands were placed on working men who had the temerity to come forward and give utterance to their Conservative opinions." But Ross was able, incidentally, to report by 1874 that " every borough throughout the metropolis has its Association ". *1874 Conservative Annual Conference Report*, p. 17.

"This association will afford a centre of communication and action between local associations supporting constitutional views. There is of course no intention to interfere in any way with local action; the object of the union is to strengthen the hands of local associations where existing in their respective districts, and to encourage the establishment of associations in districts where they are wanting, and further, to organize associations by the holding of meetings for the general expression and diffusion of constitutional principles, and the dissemination of sound information upon topics of general political interest, and to ensure the combined action of all constitutional associations."[1]

It will be noted that this statement contains no hint that the new National Union might in any way influence, much less control, the actions of the Conservative Party in Parliament. Its sole purpose would be to propagate the Conservative message and to recruit and organize Conservative supporters as effectively as possible. Since there is no reference in the minutes to any discussion or criticism of the honorary secretary's statement it must be assumed that it met with the full approval of those present.

The meeting then proceeded to choose a name for the proposed organization. Various phrases were suggested, most of them naturally enough embodying the word " Conservative ". This moved a Mr. Eadie from Newcastle (he was, he explained, the son of a working man and " had mixed among working men for years ") to protest that in Radical areas " they would be unable to get men into their unions by using the word 'Conservative'. He was not a Conservative, he never pretended to be one, and he never should be."[2] (At this point, according to the minutes. Mr. Eadie's remarks were drowned in " hisses and confusion " and the chairman threatened to quit if the incident were repeated.) After further discussion it was unanimously agreed that Rule 1 of the constitution of the new organization should read: " The name of the Society shall be the National Union of Conservative and Constitutional Associations and its object to constitute a centre for such bodies." It was also decided (Rule 3) that " every such Association subscribing one guinea or more per annum to the funds may, by vote of the Committee, be admitted a member of the Union." Further, under Rule 4, " any Branch or Affiliated Association, consisting of not less than one hundred members, may, either in common with its Chief or Parent Association or alone, be admitted, on a separate subscription, as an individual member of the Union."

A lively discussion developed in connection with the finances of the

---

[1] *1867 Conservative Annual Conference Report,* folios 5-6.
[2] *Ibid.,* folio, 16.

new organization. A proposed rule (number 18) read: " The statement of accounts as audited shall be printed and be open for the inspection of all representatives and Honorary Members at the offices of the Union for two days at least before the Annual Meeting of the Conference, and a copy of the same shall be sent to each subscribing Association." One delegate, a Dr. Royle (anticipating a view which was later to be widely accepted within the party) observed that " in a Union like theirs it might not be proper and prudent to circulate the whole items of expenditure." Another delegate observed that since it was proposed to make everyone who subscribed a guinea to the funds of the National Union an Honorary Member it would be possible for anyone wishing to have a copy of their financial statement to obtain one merely by paying such a sum into the funds of the organization. But despite these protests Rule 18 was adopted.

The election of officers provoked a remarkable discussion. H. C. Raikes (one of the moving spirits in the organization of the National Union) explained that " it was desirable to confine their vice-presidents to persons of really very considerable position," and a proposed list of names for this office included 13 Peers, 6 Members of Parliament, 2 Knights and 6 others. It was explained that " letters had been sent out to all the Conservative peers asking them to become vice-presidents, but owing to the late period at which those letters were sent answers had not been received from more than (the thirteen) who were named." All the names proposed for vice-presidents were adopted by the meeting and, in addition, the Earl of Dartmouth was named President. A further list of " noblemen and gentlemen " was then nominated for election to the Council of the National Union. The list contained the names of certain working men who were present and several of them appear to have been overcome by the honour which was being offered to them. One of them, a Mr. Cotter, said that the National Union would not " wish to have second-rate names on the committee [sic]. His own name was there and he was very sorry to hear it read out. He had objected to it very strongly. The committee was not the place for a working man, but should be composed of the best men they could possibly obtain." Eadie (who had earlier opposed the use of the word " Conservative " as the name of the organization and had described himself as the son of a working man) said that in his view the Council should be " of a mixed character comprising both the upper and the working classes." But Mr. Smith of Rotherhithe remained unconvinced. He said, " Their leaders should make the Council heard. What could working men do there? They required men of influence and men of money. . . . He was a working man and would stick up for the working man.

but still he had no business at that board. His business was at his own locality." There could hardly be a better illustration of the mood of deference in which the Conservative working men of 1867 assembled to launch their National Union. The meeting showed not the slightest inclination to discuss any of the political issues of the day and, except for the truculent Mr. Eadie of Newcastle, none of the delegates showed any disposition to challenge the ideas of their betters.

After so dull and uninspiring a beginning it is not surprising to discover from the manuscript minutes of the second conference of the National Union in 1868 that the organization appeared almost to have foundered and collapsed. The previous year at the in-augural meeting a delegate had argued that the second conference should be held in Birmingham: " What could help them to build up the great cause of Conservatism better than to go into the very stronghold of the great enemy? Nothing would tell so strongly against John Bright as taking the conference to Birmingham."[1] Another delegate pointed out that Birmingham had the most power-ful Conservative Working-Men's Association in the country with a membership of nearly 3,000 men. The proposal to take the second conference to Birmingham was adopted; but the results seem to have been almost disastrous. The manuscript minutes of the con-ference held there on 29th December, 1868, record a total atten-dance of 7 (the Earl of Dartmouth, the President, in the chair; H. C. Raikes, Vice-Chairman of the Council, two representatives from the " Coventry Working-Men's Associations ", one from the " Birming-ham Working-Men's Liberal and Conservative Association ", another from the " West London Conservative Association " and the honorary secretary, L. Sedgwick). The meeting, which appears to have lasted only an hour or two, was much briefer and even duller than the inaugural conference of the year before.

At the annual conference in the following year (on 11th June, 1869, at Liverpool) one delegate proposed " that a deputation from the conference should wait upon some of the influential leaders in London and impress upon them the importance of developing and strengthening the National Union."[2] In closing the discussion on this subject H. C. Raikes stated that " the National Union possessed the confidence of the leaders of the party, but (he added) it wanted the assistance of their names in obtaining some funds for (its) pur-poses." This third conference had been attended by a total of 36 delegates and it was reported that some 50 associations had joined since the last conference. The only significant decision of the con-

[1] 1867 Conservative Annual Conference Report, folio 82.
[2] 1869 Conservative Annual Conference Report, folios 6-7.

ference was to create a new classification of honorary officers. Henceforth the National Union was to have a " patron " and not more than 10 " vice-patrons ". Raikes, now Chairman of the Council, explained: " It was felt when the Conservative Party were in office that it was undesirable that the names of noblemen and gentlemen in high Cabinet positions who had consented to join the Union should appear among the officers, as they might be connected by the Radical press with some pamphlet or publication, or some act of the Union which they might not endorse. The office of Vice-President carried with it the authority of being one of the governing body. The Council thought this (problem) might be met by creating the office of vice-patron, carrying with it no responsibility, and they might at the same time be able to pay a compliment and do honour to themselves. The list (Raikes assured the conference) would be confined to persons of the highest eminence ". In this spirit the Earl of Derby was duly nominated and elected patron of the National Union, and ten persons, presumably " of the highest eminence ", became vice-patrons.

It is not necessary to review in detail the proceedings of each of the annual conferences of the National Union in the early years after its formation. Until 1876 the conference made no attempt to pass policy resolutions which might have brought to the attention of the leaders the views of the rank-and-file members of the constituency associations; indeed such policy resolutions as were passed in the decade *after* 1876 did little more than express confidence in the leaders of the party. It was not until 1885 that the conference began to debate and to pass resolutions dealing with current political issues.[1] In the early years, the annual conferences were no more than a few hours in duration and the proceedings were so unspectacular as to be almost perfunctory. Occasionally conference reports reflect what must have been a fairly widespread sense of exasperation with the apparent indifference of many party leaders to the work of the National Union. Thus at the eighth annual conference in 1874, J. Ross (of the London and Westminster Associa-

---

[1] There is evidence however that local associations were given mild encouragement to pass resolutions on political issues as early as 1882. Thus in that year the National Union republished in pamphlet form a paper read at the conference of Conservative Associations of the Northern Counties at Durham on 10th October, 1882, by W. H. Rowe, entitled: " The Platform as a Conservative Agency ", in which the speaker warned that political demonstrations must not be an end in themselves (lest they become what Gorst had called " political dram-drinking "). " The occasion (said Rowe) should always be utilized to enrol new members, distribute Conservative literature, and, *if desirable, pass resolutions on the current political questions of the day.*" The Platform as a Conservative Agency, 1882, pp. 5-6. [Italics mine.]

tion) said: " I hope the members of the Government will not think of giving the cold shoulder to these Associations.... Our anxiety now is to enable the Conservative Government to maintain their place; and that will be done by their ascertaining what are the feelings of working men—honest, hardworking, loyal Conservative working men, who detest everything in the shape of tyranny and more especially that Radical tyranny which they have at last found insupportable."[1] But there is little evidence of any great eagerness on the part of the Conservative leaders in Parliament to " ascertain the feelings of working men " through the deliberations of the National Union. In the same year (1874) a statement of the principles and objects of the National Union read: " The National Union was established for the purpose of effecting a systematic organization of Conservative feeling and influence throughout the country, by helping in the formation and work of the Constitutional Associations which have so rapidly increased in numbers. It is notorious that the Constitutional cause has suffered much from the want of organization amongst its supporters."[2] Again it will be noted that it is not suggested that the Union has any responsibility to interpret and convey Conservative opinion to the leaders of the party. Rather, in the same pamphlet (p. 10) the emphasis is on loyalty and discipline. " . . . Besides trusted leaders and a united Parliamentary party, it is necessary to have that steady popular support upon which the success of any political combination must depend." Again and again prominent speakers at annual meetings of the National Union emphasized the importance of discipline and hard work. Thus the Earl of Shrewsbury speaking at the sixth annual conference in 1872 said: " The duty of a soldier is obedience, and discipline is the great characteristic of the army and the navy, and I may also say that in a like manner it is characteristic of the Conservative Union."[3] This was to be disciplined effort for a very clearly defined purpose; in the course of an inspirational talk at the dinner concluding the annual conference in the following year a Mr. Wheelhouse, M.P., said: " Work, not only at your dinner on this occasion, but at your register; work every single soul of you. Don't suppose you have finished your work when you go home to-night; pull up someone to the register, and when the day of election comes, every man of you take some half-dozen to the poll."[4]

But the classic statements on the need for party discipline were

[1] *1874 Conservative Annual Conference Report,* p. 18.
[2] *The Principles and Objects of the National Union,* (1874), p. 5.
[3] *1872 Conservative Annual Conference Report,* p. 14.
[4] *1873 Conservative Annual Conference Report,* pp. 35-6.

made a few years later, in 1878, by Salisbury and Disraeli addressing a deputation (representing the Conservative Associations) who
came to congratulate them on their triumph at the Congress of
Berlin . . . " It is only in this country (said Salisbury) where you
will find that affairs are maintained on the support of a thoroughly
organized majority, depending upon distinctive principles; and,
therefore, it is that the course of our State goes so firm and so easy,
and that we are not driven aside in one direction or another by the
revolutions of opinion which less favoured nations are liable to."
A Government, he concluded, must have an organization behind it
with " complete discipline".[1]

Disraeli on the same occasion was even more emphatic on the
subject: " . . . In the conduct of public affairs (he said) there is
nothing more precious than discipline, and it is a great mistake to
suppose that discipline is incompatible with the deepest convictions
and even with the most passionate sentiments. Whether we look
into military affairs in ancient or modern times, we see many illustrations of that principle." Then, after reviewing the course of
military history in support of his argument, Disraeli added, " nature
is herself organization ; and if there were not a great directing
force which controls and guides and manages everything, you would
have nothing but volcanoes, earthquakes, and deluges. In public
life without organization similar effects would be produced. . . . It is
for you now (he said, speaking to the Conservative delegates before
him) the assembled officers of the great constitutional army that
you have formed in England to feel convinced of these views. . . .
Act upon those views of organization. . . . It is only by encouraging
that spirit of discipline that you will be able to maintain yourself in
that power which you have now obtained and which is the most
perfect answer to those who once sneered at Constitutional Associations . . . "[2]

Perhaps to facilitate the maintenance of discipline within the
National Union its headquarters had been placed in 1872 under
the same roof with the Central Office [3] (which was then under the

[1] *Presentation of Addresses from the Conservative Associations to the
Earl of Beaconsfield, K.G., and the Marquess of Salisbury, K.G., at the
Foreign Office, 6th August, 1878, Report of Proceedings,* Publications of
the National Union, No. 36, 1878, p. 24.

[2] *Ibid.,* pp. 18-22. Disraeli added: " It is no light thing to belong to a
nation where liberty and order co-exist in the greatest degree. That must
benefit all classes and most particularly it must benefit the working men."
Therefore, Disraeli concluded, " . . . of all men, working men must be most
Conservative."

[3] For the origins of the Central Office see Chapter V

administration of the Whips' Office). The annual report of the Central Council for 1872 notes: " Since the last conference, an arrangement has been made by which the work of the Union has been more closely incorporated with that of the party generally, and its offices have been removed to the headquarters of the party in Parliament Street." The report provides a hint that the results of this arrangement may be mutually beneficial both to the National Union *and the leaders of the party* since, the report adds, the new arrangement has " brought the Union into more direct contact with the leaders of the party, . . . thereby enhancing the value of its operations . . . "[1] In moving the adoption of the report Lord John Hamilton stated that the intention was " not to restrict or fetter local action, but to endeavour to stimulate and assist country Associations, and *to promote the circulation of opinion between them and the leaders of the party.* Nobody could be in a healthy state who had not a free and rapid circulation; . . . rapidity of communication between the local Associations and the leaders of the party would be most effectually secured by the step which had been taken."[2] This, incidentally, is one of the earliest references in conference reports to the conception of a two-way system of communication between the leaders of the party in Parliament and their followers in the constituency associations.

In the following year this theme was developed by H. C. Raikes, the Chairman of the Council, when he argued that had it not been for the National Union and the local associations, " the leaders of the party would not have had the same, or any adequate means of knowing what were the sentiments of their followers . . . " In a highly perceptive analysis of the new function of the mass party, Raikes explained that " we had now outlived the time of great family influences and also that period which succeeded the first Reform Bill, which might be called the period of middle-class influence in boroughs. We were living in a day in which the people were to be applied to in a much more direct, clear, and positive manner than was the case under the older forms of the Constitution, and, therefore, *any party who wished to retain their hold upon the country must ascertain how far their proceedings were in harmony with the wishes of the people.*" This speech, the conference report notes, was greeted by cries of " hear, hear ". The enthusiasm of the response may conceivably have led Raikes to conclude that he was encouraging the National Union to aspire to a rôle for which it was never intended, and he proceeded to put it in its place with his famous statement of its functions referred to at the opening of this

[1] *1872 Conservative Annual Conference Report*, p. 7.
[2] *Ibid.*, p. 9.

chapter. The conference report continues: " Having observed what were the functions of the National Union, (Mr. Raikes) said sometimes complaints were made that it did not do all that it ought to do; but he pointed out that it was often suggested that it should do things which did not belong to its peculiar line of duty. The Union had been organized rather as what he might call a handmaid to the party, than to usurp the functions of party leadership."[1]

The conference reports for the early years contain much information about the expansion of the National Union and the nature of its work. Thus the report for 1875 reviews the steady increase in the number of associations affiliated to the National Union:

> 1871 — 289
> 1872 — 348
> 1873 — 407
> 1874 — 447
> 1875 — 472 (plus 228 branch or subordinate associations[2]).

Another National Union publication (in 1874) gives some indication of the extent of the publishing activities of the National Union. Since the formation of the Union seven years earlier some 500,000 pamphlets and 300,000 circulars were distributed; four-fifths of the former were made available without charge (the others presumably were sold). As was noted earlier, a large proportion of these pamphlets took the form of direct appeals to the working class for support, others contained more general statements of the Conservative view of current controversies.[3]

The 1875 conference report explains that the work of the National Union in that year " has been confined chiefly to affording assistance in the formation of new associations, and in giving information wherever it has been applied for, and on a great variety of subjects ".[4] At about this time the National Union had " appointed a gentleman as their travelling agent ", because, it is explained,

---

[1] *1873 Conservative Annual Conference Report*, pp. 9-10.

[2] The report notes further that " a very considerable number of (the) Associations (affiliated to the National Union) are composed almost entirely of the artisan class." *1875 Conservative Annual Conference Report*, p. 43.

[3] See list of publications on back page of National Union pamphlet No. 35 (1878), entitled *The Treaty of Berlin and the Convention of Constantinople*. The ninth annual conference report notes, incidentally, that no new pamphlets were published that year " in the absence of any exciting political question of importance." *1875 Conservative Annual Conference Report*, p. 8.

[4] *1875 Conservative Annual Conference Report*, p. 7. The report adds (p. 8) that " the Council desire to say that they will at all times be glad to receive suggestions from any quarter, which may have for their object the improvement of the organization of the party; and would especially impress upon all its members the importance of losing no opportunity

" it has always been one of the chief objects of the Union to collect the most complete information respecting the various constituencies in the country, information which is at all times most valuable, and without which it would be impossible to arrive at any reliable estimate of the progress of Conservative feeling." A travelling agent had been appointed " in order to do this more efficiently, and at the same time to bring the Union into closer and more intimate relations with the local associations . . . " During his first year's work the agent had visited 25 cities and towns. " In many instances he has been able to give material help and advice, while, on the other hand, the Union has received much valuable information from the local agents and associations, . . . " [1] It is sad to note, however, that two years later the local associations appeared to have become somewhat indifferent to the work of the travelling agent. At the 1875 conference the Chairman of the Council observed: " There was a gentleman connected with the Union who is always prepared to visit any association for the purpose of organization; but that of late few applications had been made for his services." Another member of the Council added: " if local associations show that they want lecturers the Council would supply the need, but there has lately been a slackening in the number of requests to the Union for lecturers." [2]

A further comment on this lethargy was provided by another speaker in the 1875 conference debate who said " even his limited experience pointed to the fact that, although we have Conservative associations in nearly every constituency, between contests there is a certain amount of apathy which told against organization. There are some that are merely associations in name, and never do anything in the way of maintaining organization." The speaker went

of increasing the efficiency of their local Associations, so as to render the position of the great Tory party secure and lasting."

[1] 1873 Conservative Annual Conference Report, p. 8.

[2] 1875 Conservative Annual Conference Report, p. 18. The same member of the Council (p. 18) urged local associations to pay particular attention to obtaining the support of the local press. He said: " The most powerful of all influences is the Press, and no Association should be content unless it has in close connection with it, some local organ of public opinion. The first question a man who has had any experience in political fighting asks on entering a town is, ' What is your newspaper? ' If it is favourable to your politics you have an organ for the publication of all your speeches and addresses. Let Associations look to that; it is a matter in which the Union cannot interfere. I think that if our friends in different parts of the country *will take care of* local newspapers, they will have no difficulty (in obtaining adequate publicity) when they ask the Union to send lecturers down to speak." [Italics mine] We are left to speculate as to what may be involved in " taking care of " local newspapers.

on to recommend that associations wherever possible should be converted into working-men's clubs to provide " a place where working men, after their day's toil is ended, might meet for the purpose of reading, affording information to each other and thus giving life to the cause."[1]   At the previous conference another speaker (R. Heath, M.P.) had explained:

> " the object of converting Associations into Clubs is to enable members to obtain recreation as well as knowledge. . . . All work and no play (added the speaker) makes Jack a dull boy. Merely meeting together to read newspapers has no attraction for many of the people whom we would wish to bring under the influence of Constitutionalism. In connection with (my own) Association (of Stoke-upon-Trent) we have reading rooms ; but although I have had the honour to be selected by the borough of Stoke-upon-Trent to represent them in the present Parliament, I have never made a really electioneering speech to them. My advice to them is to read the newspapers for themselves, and not to be led away by me or any stump orator. . . . We have billiard tables and every kind of amusement, together with refreshments. The great difficulty generally in connection with clubs is to prevent their being abused, but we have experienced no embarrassment of that sort. As a proof that there has not been any extravagance, I may mention that last year the average paid per member was 11s. 6d. for use of rooms and refreshments and that gambling has been strictly prohibited. The existence of the Club has brought to us a great acquisition of strength, and has had a most beneficial effect . . . " [2]

Again and again conference speakers emphasised the value of the establishment of working-men's clubs. At the 1875 conference one representative told of his local association's success " in returning a Conservative member for the first time in a Radical stronghold (Tower Hamlets) ". He explained that " finding a great deal of difficulty during the contest in discovering who were friends, the Conservatives immediately set to work and opened a Conservative Club. It has now been in operation for two years, and has worked very beneficially." He added that " he was sorry to see that there was a large amount of money standing idle in the hands of the Council." He thought that " if Conservative Clubs were to be instituted, it was a great pity to keep so much money idle." He understood that " there was not only a balance of £600 in hand, but £800 invested." He hoped the " National Union would consider whether

---

[1] *1875 Conservative Annual Conference Report*, p. 13.
[2] *1874 Conservative Annual Conference Report*, pp. 16–17. The speaker, who was president of the Constitutional Club of Stoke-upon-Trent, also explained that the borough included " six or seven small towns, each of which has its Constitutional Club."

some of it could not be distributed in order to encourage the movement for the establishment of Conservative Clubs throughout the
country."[1]

As far as one can tell from the Central Council reports and the
annual conference minutes the National Union did not show
particular enthusiasm in adopting this suggestion. It offered advice
and assistance when requested by local associations to do so, but
no very extensive organizational campaign was undertaken. The
manuscript minutes of the 1883 annual conference contain
a copy of the National Union budget for the year ending 1882.
It is incorporated here since it provides an indication of the modest
extent of the Union's activities [2] during this period:

National Union Budget for the year ending 1882

Receipts	£	s.	d.	Expenditure	£	s.	d.
To balance from 1881	172	16	9	Printing, advertising			
Subscriptions and				and stationery ...	444	10	2
Donations	926	10	6	Conference expenses			
				(Bristol)	17	8	0
				Lecturers' fees	125	0	0
				Postage	113	5	5
				Telegrams, messages,			
				parcels	27	1	11
				Housekeeper, furni-			
				ture	42	1	8
				Rent & office expenses	218	15	0
				Literary fees	7	7	0
				Travelling expenses	18	2	8
				Sundries	4	5	2
				Balance in hand ...	81	10	3
	£1099	7	3		£1099	7	3

The same report notes, incidentally, that during the year under
review (1882) 85 new Conservative associations and 25 clubs were
formed. The chairman added: " the only danger to be guarded
against is that the political aims of these institutions may in some
cases come to be regarded as secondary to the social objects, a

[1] *1875 Conservative Annual Conference Report*, pp. 13-14.
[2] This budget includes of course only the money spent at the centre and
gives no indication of the expenditure of the local associations nor of the
huge sums of money spent by the party for electoral purposes. For a valuable
account of electioneering costs in the nineteenth century, see Gwyn, W. B.,
Democracy and the Cost of Politics in Britain, Chapters I–IV.

course which the Council would strongly deprecate, although by no means implying that it had been followed to any great extent."[1]

Another function of the National Union is reflected in a speech by the chairman of the 1883 conference; he reported that on the recommendation of the previous year's conference the National Union had conducted an inquiry into the efficiency of the various associations affiliated to the Union. A number of confidential reports had been received and the chairman promised that " the Council will make a careful examination of these reports, and without travelling beyond the proper province of the National Union, and unduly interfering with the domestic concerns of the associations, will endeavour to point out to any special cases, the necessity for greater activity wherever it is needed."[2] Other conference reports refer from time to time to the function of the National Union as an arbiter in disputes within or between local associations. Thus the ninth annual conference report includes a speech by the delegate from Ipswich who drew attention to " the present condition of the Conservative Working-Men's Association at Ipswich, which, owing to divisions in the party, had lately decreased in influence. He urged that an inquiry should be made into the circumstances by the National Union with a view to the satisfactory settlement of the matters in dispute."[3]

There are numerous tributes in the Conservative literature of the 'seventies and 'eighties to the electoral impact of the recently organized Conservative associations. Thus at the 1874 conference Lord Hampton, President of the National Union in that year, praised " the working of this great machine",[4] and the Council's report to the same conference states that " the Council wish to direct especial attention to a remarkable fact connected with the signal victory gained by the Conservative cause at the General Election (of 1874), which appears to them to prove, in an unanswerable manner, the great value, *even for electoral purposes*, possessed by political associations. It has been found, on examining the election returns, that, among the 74 English and Welsh constituencies which were wholly or partially wrested from the Radical Party, in no less than 65 cases were associations of this nature in active operation, and their entire energies were employed in favour of the Con-

---

[1] *1883 Conservative Annual Conference Report*, folio 6. In the year under review the report notes that 520 lectures were given by gentlemen representing the National Union, nine new pamphlets were printed and 13 reprinted, and in all 356,000 pieces of literature were sent out.

[2] *Ibid.*, folio 8.

[3] *1875 Conservative Annual Conference Report*, p. 14.

[4] *1874 Conservative Annual Conference Report*, p. 10.

servative candidates." There are also numerous tributes by individual M.P.s to the effectiveness of their local associations. Thus J. Ashbury, M.P. for Brighton, speaking at the annual conference which met in that town in the year following the general election of 1874, said: " I have the honour of being in this present position as a consequence of the perfect system of organization which has been adopted in this town . . . " and he added " the fact of the Conservative Party being now in power is almost solely attributable to the energy and continuous exertions of the body of gentlemen (the National Union conference) whom we have before us."

" The energy and continuous exertions " of the members of the National Union were even more highly prized after the passage of the *Corrupt and Illegal Practices Prevention Act*, 1883.[1] It has not generally been noted that this Act provided a very important stimulant to the development of the mass party in this country. Evidence of this is provided by the manuscript notes of a talk given privately in 1883 (shortly after the passage of the Act) to party supporters on " The Condition of the Conservative Party in the Midlands " by a Mr. G. C. T. Bartley.[2] The speaker discussed the impact of the Corrupt Practices Act on the finances of the party in his area. He pointed out that the total cost of contesting 55 seats in his area in the election of 1880 was " about £100,000 ". Under the new Act of 1883, the maximum permitted expenditure would be approximately £37,000 (exclusive of the Returning Officer's expenses and the candidate's personal outlay). Narrowing his illustration to the " five Midland counties " he reports that the campaign of 1880 for 24 seats (two were uncontested) had cost the party £57,812; they would be permitted under the new Act to spend only £19,980. In the two-member constituency of Leicestershire North (population 109,250, with 6,849 electors) the Conservative campaign had cost £6,306;[3] they would be permitted under the new Act to spend only £1,425.

---

[1] There is now a considerable literature on electoral corruption and its elimination including O'Leary, C., *The Elimination of Corrupt Practices in British Elections 1868–1911* ; Gwyn, W. B., *Democracy and the Cost of Politics in Britain;* Jennings, Sir Ivor, *Party Politics*, Vol. I, Chapter IV; Hanham, H. J., *Elections and Party Management*, Chapter XIII.

[2] " The Condition of the Conservative Party in the Midlands ", manuscript notes of a talk by Mr. G. C. T. Bartley, 1883. (Offices of the National Union, London.)

[3] In return for the expenditure of £6,306, Bartley reports that the Conservatives at Leicestershire North won 3,369 votes (against 2,674 for their Liberal opponents). *The party appears therefore to have spent an average of over £1 17s. per vote*. The comparison with party expenditure in the 1951 election is striking. The average Conservative candidate on that occasion spent £773 and won 22,232 votes. Thus the expenditure per vote

Bartley explained that these drastic limitations on campaign expenditures would seriously curtail the electoral activities of the party; he therefore made a strong plea for a great increase in *voluntary* work by party supporters. ". . . the day has quite gone by (he said) when any success can be hoped for without the great mass of electors being organized and encouraged themselves to take an active part in the work of the party ". He warned that electors will not canvass nor undertake other voluntary electoral work " unless they have been taught to understand that they are part and parcel, and a most important part and parcel, of the organization of the party." He closed with a plea for party members to undertake " intensive work as well as large demonstrations ". A brief discussion which followed Bartley's address served to underline the importance of his plea. A Mr. Rowlands from Birmingham reported on the difficulty his party had experienced in obtaining voluntary assistance during elections: " . . . in borough elections (he said) we have had to depend to a very large extent on paid canvassers." But in future under the new Act they would be able to afford only one clerk and one messenger for every 500 electors. He emphasized that in his view volunteer workers were in any case more reliable than paid men. Bartley's address and the brief discussion that followed is striking evidence that the limitations on campaign expenditures introduced in 1883 provided one of the most powerful stimulants to the development of the mass party in this country.[1]

Even Lord Salisbury, hardly the most enthusiastic supporter of popular democracy, came to recognize the vital rôle of the National Union and its constituent Conservative associations and clubs;[2] but he saw also in the emergence of the mass party a potential threat to the free institutions of the country. In the year immediately preceding Lord Randolph Churchill's bold attempt to " democratize " the Conservative Party and to transfer effective control of its affairs to the National Union Lord Salisbury gave his party a dire warning:

for Conservative candidates in 1951 was less than 1s. 6d. (See Butler, D. E., *The British General Election of 1951*, pp. 139 and 251.) It is also of interest to read the chapter entitled " A Midland Borough Constituency " (in the 1951 campaign) in the same book in light of the comments by Bartley and Rowlands on the problems of campaigning in the Midlands in the 1880s.

[1] In September, 1883, the Conservative Central Office printed and circulated throughout the party an abstract of the Act. See Publications of the National Union, No. 79.

[2] See *The Conservative Demonstrations at Plymouth*. Speeches by the Marquess of Salisbury, on 4th and 5th June, 1884, Publications of the National Union, No. 104.

"The people are taking a more direct interest in political business and assuming a more direct control over their representatives . . . . (The two Houses of Parliament) are still, and they must necessarily remain, of the highest importance; but their importance has diminished . . . by the fact that the people throughout the country, meeting in meetings like this (he was addressing an audience of six thousand people assembled under the auspices of the Working-Men's Conservative Association in Liverpool) can give an impulse to the public policy of the nation which is, in some degree, independent of the action of its representatives at Westminster." He said he did not deplore this development but he warned of its potential dangers. The House of Commons (" a body for whom I have so sincere a reverence ") might become " a House enslaved by the caucus . . . . The competition of parties is so keen, the machinery of elections is so perfect, the power of applying pressure to individual members is so complete, that every year you will see our representatives, assumed to be independent, more and more exposed to the danger of being forced to fit their convictions into a single mould . . . "[1]

Salisbury had mainly in mind, no doubt, the influence of the Liberal caucus then approaching the zenith of its power. But there could be no doubt that there were similar currents within the Conservative Party.

Some years earlier, influential members of the National Union had begun to propose that it should be re-organized to make it more representative in character. Such a suggestion was made in 1876 by John Gorst (who had for a time combined the offices of both Principal Agent at the Central Office and Honorary Secretary of the National Union, although in 1876 he held only the latter post). Raikes took the lead in defeating Gorst's proposal and despite recurrent criticism of the structure of the National Union no basic changes were introduced until after the great Conservative defeat of 1880.[2] This event, coupled with the death of Lord Beaconsfield in 1881, threw the party into a state of great confusion which culminated in the strange struggle between Lord Randolph Churchill and Lord Salisbury over the relationship between the National Union and the Conservative Party in Parliament. It is not necessary here to recount the details of that struggle although some attention must be given to its causes and its net effect on the position of the National Union within the Conservative Party organization.

[1] *Speech of the Marquess of Salisbury*, 13th April, 1882. Publications of the National Union, No. 67, pp. 4–5.

[2] In that year a new set of rules was adopted by the annual conference which provided for the re-organization of the Council on a more representative basis.

Balfour was probably right in describing Lord Randolph's scheme to " democratize " the National Union and to give it effective control of policy and finance primarily as part of his personal campaign to win control of the party. " . . . the ingenious idea occurred to Lord Randolph (wrote Balfour) that if by judicious management he could dominate (the National Union) and endow it with new powers, it might effectually further his political ends . . . "[1] Balfour, it will be recalled, also concluded that Lord Randolph decided to drop his campaign when he became convinced that he was approaching the pinnacle of supreme power within the Conservative parliamentary party; it then became clear to him that any scheme which was intended to transfer control of the party's affairs to the National Union outside Parliament would be quite intolerable. " . . . If (Lord Randolph) was a potential leader (wrote Balfour) it behoved him to look at party problems from a leader's point of view; and how could any man do so, whatever his prejudices, without perceiving that if all executive powers and all financial control were transferred to an independent body, leadership in the ordinary sense would cease?. . . There was no ground whatever for supposing that, however fortunate, (the Council of the National Union) could run the Party executive with prudence, or successfully collect and wisely spend the Party funds. In my belief (added Balfour) Lord Randolph had for some time perceived these truths. He had recognized that, through no fault of his own and no remediable defects in its constitution, the National Union was essentially incapable of giving him the kind of assistance he needed; but by the time he made this discovery he had also recognized that he needed assistance no longer. . . . His own right arm had won for him a unique position in the party . . . "[2] On this analysis Lord Randolph's campaign to breathe new life into the National Union and to give it effective control of the party's affairs becomes merely an incident in his own hectic struggle for power.

There seems little doubt that self-interest was Lord Randolph Churchill's principal incentive; but neither can there be any doubt that there were strong forces within the party which were pressing in the same direction and for which he became, in effect, the spokesman. As Ostrogorski has argued, there was at the time a good deal of dissatisfaction both in the party in Parliament and in the National Union with the old aristocratic leadership of the Conservative Party. Disraeli's last Ministry had been composed almost entirely of *grands seigneurs*; some were members of the House of Lords, most of the remainder represented in the Commons the old-

---

[1] Balfour, A. J., *Chapters of Autobiography*, p. 159.
[2] *Ibid.*, pp. 169-70.

established landed interests in the country. Little or no representation had been given in the Government or the councils of the party to the representatives of the new urban constituencies which had been won from the Liberals in 1874 largely through the efforts of the recently organized Conservative associations. The most forceful statement of the resentment of this group appeared in 1882 in an anonymous article in the *Fortnightly Review*, which, as was widely known, had been written by Drummond Wolff and John Gorst. "Unfortunately for Conservatism (they wrote), its leaders belong solely to one class; they are a clique composed of members of the aristocracy, land owners and adherents whose chief merit is subserviency. The party chiefs live in an atmosphere in which a sense of their own importance and the importance of their class interests and privileges is exaggerated, and which the opinions of the common people can scarcely penetrate. . . . They half fear and half despise the common people. . . ." The Conservative associations, it was alleged, were largely ignored by the aristocratic clique which controlled the party, although these associations had contributed mightily to the victory of 1874. ". . . As soon as success was achieved the men who had stood aloof since 1868 rushed in to share the spoils. A Ministry was formed composed almost exclusively of peers and county members. Those by whom the campaign had been planned and fought were forgotten . . ." The Conservative associations languished; and now, argued Gorst and Wolff, "the entire organization of the Tory Party must undergo a radical revolution. . . . In its existing shape it is managed by a committee in London whose names are unknown to the people at large, and who act without mandate from the constituencies. The complaint of the individual associations prior to 1874 that they were not patronized by the privileged class can no longer be made. They are corrupted by patronage and few escape its baneful influence. The object for which a great number of the associations exist is to hold periodically demonstrations at which some member of the late Cabinet may exhibit his oratorical talents before the admiring crowd . . . (Thereafter) their zeal collapses and the association languishes until there is a fresh opportunity of catching a lion . . ."[1]

John Gorst, the co-author of this bitter attack, had served, it must be remembered, both as Principal Agent and Honorary Secretary of the National Union; however much the article may have reflected his own and Wolff's personal animosity towards the leaders of the party, it was bound to carry very great weight in-

---

[1] "Conservative Disorganization", *Fortnightly Review*, Vol. 32 (New Series), 1882.

deed. Inevitably the attack was received sympathetically by many of the new adherents to the Conservative cause who were being recruited into the local associations. The Conservative working men seem for the most part to have been satisfied with the subservient rôle assigned to them in the early days of the National Union. But the newer recruits to the party were hardly likely to prove so docile. They were being drawn increasingly in the 1870s from the rapidly expanding and intensely ambitious Victorian middle-class. As Ostrogorski put it: " In proportion as the political and commercial claims of the middle-class were satisfied and it had to defend its own position against new assailants, its Liberalism evaporated and it became Conservative . . . " As manufacturers, small business and professional men moved into the Tory Party they became intensely dissatisfied with the " hole-and-corner management of (its) affairs . . . "[1] The Liberal pace-setters had already created an extensive popular organization; the Conservatives had no alternative but to follow suit.

Alongside the older working-men's clubs the Conservatives set up representative associations which bore a striking resemblance to the Liberal caucus. These new associations were readily galvanized into action by Lord Randolph Churchill when he launched his attack on the " aristocratic clique which dominated the affairs of the party." It did not matter whether Churchill's motives were primarily or even exclusively personal; he became the spokesman for the widespread resentment within the National Union against the tight bureaucratic control and the benevolent indifference of the parliamentary leaders of the party. At the National Union conference in October, 1883, a Mr. Hudson moved a " rider " to the annual report of the Council to the effect " that the Conference of the National Union while thanking the Council for the past year for their services directs the Council for the ensuing year to take such steps as may be requisite for securing to the National Union its legitimate influence in the party organization."[2] Hudson spoke of the importance of thrashing out all questions at the annual conference and added that he thought the " Conservative working men should not be led by the nose," but that a representative body like the National Union should have the direction of its own policy. The association wished to be more *en rapport* with the Council and that the latter body should be strengthened.

Lord Randolph Churchill, then a vice-president of the National Union, rose to " loud cheers " to express his " cordial concur-

[1] Ostrogorski, M., *Democracy and the Organization of Political Parties*, Vol. I, pp. 267-8.

[2] *1883 Conservative Annual Conference Report*, folio 3.

rence."[1] He recounted how Lord Beaconsfield, in reviewing the cause of the Tory defeat in 1880, had placed " first in the list . . . our defective organization ". He had appointed a Central Committee to review the position of the party but this Committee had " passed by " the National Union. " They decided to centre in their hands all the powers and the available financial resources of the Tory Party. . . . It was necessary that all rival bodies be stifled. . . . Your Council (claimed Lord Randolph) has been kept in a state of tutelage. You have been called upon year after year to elect a council which does not advise and an executive which does not administer." Churchill then came to the hub of his proposal: " I should like to see the control of the party organization taken out of the hands of a self-elected body, and placed in the hands of an elected body. I should like to see the management of the party funds taken out of the hands of an irresponsible body. The Central Committee is a self-elected and irresponsible body, while the Council (of the National Union) is an elected and responsible body. . . .

" At the last election (he charged) the corrupt practices on our own side were so grave and flagrant that we were unable properly to expose in Parliament the far greater corruption of the Liberal Party. . . . Such practices must absolutely cease in the future, and you will have no guarantee for their cessation until your party funds are managed openly. Wherever you have secret expenditure you will have corrupt expenditure, Royal Commissions, party disgrace and public scandal. . . . The money that the Council (of the National Union) expends consists partly of doles from the Central Committee. I suggest that the secret disposal of money by the Central Committee is dangerous and ought to be altogether changed." Churchill turned then to a passionate defence of the right of working men to a share in the administration of the affairs of the party, and he concluded by proposing that the Council of the National Union should have the "chief control of the party organization". The Council should send out reports of its work four times a year to local associations who would thus be kept fully informed and would be in a position to debate the work of the Council at their annual conference. The local associations in turn " should constantly communicate to the Council the current of public opinion on passing events."

In the debate which followed Churchill was accused of threatening to wreck the unity of the party: he was urged to direct his energy " against our enemies and not against our friends." Another speaker asked, " Would the subscribers to the Central (Committee's)

[1] *Manuscript Minutes of the 1883 Conservative Annual Conference.* Lord Randolph Churchill's speech appears at folio 9 ff.

fund transfer their subscriptions to the National Union? . . . As practical men we know there are certain funds which must be delegated to a small committee. Whatever leaders we have we must place confidence in them. While this association is capable of doing great and good work it had not the power to ask the Central Committee to destroy themselves." A delegate from Bedford " had heard with surprise of the existence of the Central Committee," and he concluded sadly " that in electing (the National Union Council) they had been indulging in a solemn farce." Earl Percy, in challenging Lord Randolph, pointed out that Raikes and others were members of both the Central Committee and the Council of the National Union. (" They were," he said, " on the Central Committee as representing the National Union.") There was a constant interchange of ideas between the two bodies. Pointing to the subsidy which the Council received from the Central Committee, he added, " the Central Committee does not monopolize all the funds." The National Union therefore has " the advantage of getting money without the trouble of collecting it." As might be expected Lord Randolph's most influential support came from John Gorst, who maintained hopefully that there was no danger of a party split. There was indeed " never a time when the Party was more united. . . . When you read of Lord Randolph Churchill fomenting disunion do not believe it."

But there was disunion aplenty within the party in the winter of 1883-4. The " rider " moved by Hudson (calling on the Council to secure " to the National Union its legitimate influence in the party organization ") had been approved by the 1883 conference and, with the backing of the Council, Lord Randolph set about attempting to implement it. His negotiations with Lord Salisbury during the next six months were extraordinarily complicated; for the purposes of this account it is necessary only to note two or three passages in Lord Salisbury's exchanges with Lord Randolph since they provide a useful indication of the former's conception of the rôle of the National Union. (It should be remembered that this was the period of the " duumvirate," but within two years Lord Salisbury was to emerge as the unchallenged Leader of the Party.) Speaking for both himself and Sir Stafford Northcote (then Leader of the Party in the House of Commons), Lord Salisbury wrote to Lord Randolph: " It appears to us that that organization (the National Union) is, and must remain, in all its essential features local. But there is still much work which a central body like the Council of the National Union can perform with great advantage to the party. It is the representative of many Associations on whom, in their respective constituencies, the work of the party greatly depends It can superintend and stimulate their exertions; furnish them with advice, and in some measure with funds; provide them with lecturers; aid them in the improvement and the development of the local press; and help them in perfecting the machinery by which the registration is conducted and the arrangements for providing volunteer agency at election times. It will have special opportunity of pressing upon the local associations which it represents the paramount duty of selecting, in time, the candidates who are to come forward at the dissolution."[1]

Oddly enough, Churchill and his supporters claimed to perceive in Lord Salisbury's statement a " charter " for the National Union which opened up tremendous possibilities for the expansion of its work along lines similar to those upon which the National Liberal Federation operated. When Salisbury learnt of their proposals he tried immediately to disabuse their minds, writing to Lord Randolph: " I have been told on good authority that you had inferred, as the result of our recent communications, that in our contemplation the National Union was in some manner to take the place of the Central Committee and to do the work which the latter exclusively does now." He pointed out that his own previous letter had not mentioned the Central Committee and added, " I should blame myself severely if I had misled you. . . . The Central Committee are appointed by us and represent us: and we could not in any degree separate our position from theirs. *I hope, however, that there is no chance of the paths of the Central Committee and the National Union crossing*: for there is plenty of good work for both to do."[2] Churchill replied predicting that Salisbury's hope that the paths of the two organizations would not cross would be disappointed. He wrote: " In a struggle between a popular body and a close corporation, the latter, I am happy to say, in these days goes to the wall; for the popular body have this great advantage—that, having nothing to conceal, they can, at any moment they think proper, appeal fully (and in some measure recklessly) to a favourable and sympathizing public, and I am of opinion that in such a course as this the National Union will find that I may be of some little assistance to them." [3]

It is not surprising that shortly thereafter Lord Salisbury and Sir Stafford Northcote were provoked into what was no doubt a tactical mistake; they announced that they had decided to evict the National

---

[1] Lord Salisbury to Lord Randolph Churchill, 29th February, 1884, cited in Churchill, W. S., *Lord Randolph Churchill,* Vol. I, p. 314.

[2] Lord Salisbury to Lord Randolph Churchill, 6th March, 1884, cited *Ibid.,* p. 316. [Italics mine.]

[3] *Ibid.,* p. 317.

Union from the building which they had shared with the Central Committee in the Central Office of the party. But this threat apparently shocked both sides into realizing that the dispute was threatening to ensure their mutual ruin. In a long and highly complicated set of negotiations the conflict was resolved. But *throughout the negotiations Lord Salisbury never showed the slightest disposition to grant the National Union effective control over policy, finance or candidatures.* At one point he wrote: " To ensure complete unity of action, we think it desirable that the Whips of the party should sit, *ex officio*, on the Council (of the National Union), and should have a right to be present at the meetings of all (its) Committees. Such an arrangement would be a security against any unintentional divergences of policy, and would lend weight to the proceedings of the Union. Business relating to candidates should remain entirely with the Central Committee. On the assumption, which we are entitled now to make, that the action of the two bodies will be harmonious, a separation of establishments will not be necessary. . . . There is some advantage, undoubtedly, in their working under a common roof, for it is difficult to distinguish between their functions so accurately, but that the need of mutual assistance and communication will constantly be felt." [1]

Lord Randolph Churchill was at first furious at what he described as this attempt to reduce the National Union to " its former make-believe and impotent condition ", and he predicted that " under the present effete system of wire-pulling and secret organization " disaster would overtake the Conservative Party at the next general election.[2] But despite this trumpeting protest Churchill made peace with the party leaders not long afterwards. By his campaign he succeeded in obtaining nothing more than a few thousand pounds, increase in the annual subsidy paid by the Central Committee to the National Union. The latter organization's rôle as a " handmaid " to the party in Parliament remained unaltered. Subsequently, it is true, the Central Committee was formally abolished; there was never any question, however, of modifying the right of the Leader and those he chose as his immediate associates to control the affairs of the party. But, partly no doubt as a result of Lord Randolph Churchill's campaign, the National Union was re-organized. And as a consequence of this re-organization there emerged the broad outlines of the National Union as we know it to-day.

Until the annual conference of 1884 the Council of the Union had consisted of 24 elected members who had power to co-opt an additional 12. But at the conference of that year " co-optation "

---

[1] Cited in Churchill, W. S., *Lord Randolph Churchill*, Vol. I, p. 319.
[2] *Ibid.*, p. 322.

was abolished and provision made for the election by the conference of all 36 members of the Council.[1] In 1885 it was decided that every Conservative association " should be affiliated without the need of any formal action," and, as A. L. Lowell has commented, " the Union thus came to be a really national party organization in a way that it had never been before . . . "[2] A new set of rules were adopted at a special conference in May, 1886, and they included a list of the special functions of the Union which included the following: " To maintain such relations with the affiliated associations as will, at any time, enable them to give early and unanimous expression to the Conservative feeling of the country by petition or otherwise."

The parallel with the National Liberal Federation became increasingly evident and was to cause Ostrogorski gloomily to observe that the " Tory democrats " were destroying the older Conservatism and setting up " a new kind of plebiscitary Cæsarism exercised not by an individual but by a huge syndicate: by means of well-adjusted legislation the people will get its *panem* (the *circenses* will soon follow) and in return will allow the Tory Party to govern with its Lords, established Church and landed interest ; the Tory Party will not assume this mandate itself, the aristocratic leaders will not be allowed to invest themselves with it, but the people assembled in the gatherings of the party, in the caucuses, will confer it on the men of its choice."[3] As suggested earlier, Ostrogorski's lurid nightmare never became a reality. Elsewhere he himself concedes that the National Union had no dramatic influence on the course of events. Perhaps his most accurate estimate of its rôle is to be found in the passage in which he observes " . . . in spite of the retiring part played by the Union of Conservative Associations, and its slight official influence, the local Organizations, by their daily, hourly imperceptible action, indirectly affected the policy of the party and the attitude of its chiefs. In fact, the mainstay of the Ministry in the House was now the Tory members for the large towns, most of whom represented the middle-class and the workmen identified with the democratized associations." [4]

The 1886 revision had also provided for the setting up of ten provincial or divisional unions which were to include all the members of the National Union within the territorial division concerned.[5]

[1] *The Times*, 24th July, 1884.
[2] Lowell, A. L. *The Government of England*, Vol. I, p. 557.
[3] Ostrogorski, M., *Democracy and the Organization of Political Parties*, Vol. I, p. 282.
[4] *Ibid.*, p. 324.
[5] See p. 231 below.

The ostensible purpose of this re-organization was to provide for the more effective development of the party's work throughout the country; however, there was no doubt considerable justification for Lowell's claim that " (the provincial divisions) were expected to act like watertight compartments, as it was believed that all ten divisions would not go mad at once, and that any man would find it very hard to capture enough of them, one at a time, to control the Union." [1] An arrangement was also introduced whereby official representatives of the professional organization of the party were given *ex officio* seats on the provincial councils.

For the next twenty years (1886-1906) the Conservative Party was continuously in power except for one interval of three years. During most of this twenty-year period the party organization functioned with remarkable smoothness. This may have been in part the result of the fact that after Lord Randolph Churchill lost interest in the National Union no figure of national importance devoted serious attention to its affairs. Further, Lord Salisbury (who led the party during the years 1885-1902) obviously had very clear-cut views on the rôle of the National Union and was insistent that it must in no circumstances attempt to usurp the functions of leadership It will be remembered that in his correspondence with Lord Randolph Churchill he had observed, speaking for himself and Sir Stafford Northcote: " It appears to us that that organization (the National Union) is, and must remain, in all its essential features *local*." He frequently returned to this theme in his public speeches. Thus (speaking to an audience of five thousand persons meeting under the auspices of the Plymouth Conservative Association on 4th June, 1884) he said:

> " I have to move a resolution of success to the Conservative organizations. . . . A more important resolution it is impossible to imagine, for it is on the success of these associations . . . that the future triumph of the Conservative Party, and with it the triumph of sound principles in the government of this country, depend . . . " He conceded that it was necessary to have an " organization which shall have its centre in the metropolis ", but added : " do not let any consideration of central action divert your attention for a moment from *the supreme importance of having local organizations*—a local organization of personal influence of man with man—the effect of voluntary officers upon those who have not given their attention to politics or are lukewarm in the cause. . . It is upon the willingness with which men will devote themselves to that work that the future destinies of our great Empire hang." [2]

---

[1] Lowell, A. L., *The Government of England*, Vol. I, p. 559.
[2] *The Conservative Demonstrations at Plymouth*, speeches of the

But for the central organs of the National Union Salisbury had very little enthusiasm. He was convinced that they inevitably drifted into the control of the " militants and the wire-pullers who were not representative of the Conservative opinion in the country as a whole." More than that, after his experience with Lord Randolph Churchill he became convinced that the mass party organization might become the gravest possible threat to the survival of free institutions. Speaking to a mass meeting in Glasgow on 1st October, 1884, he gave a classic warning of the menace of the caucus:

> " I should have thought anyone who had studied the history of the world, and could read the signs of the times, would know that if freedom runs any dangers, it is certainly not from any possible revival of the power of the aristocracy. . . . freedom when it has been destroyed has always been destroyed by those who shelter themselves under the cover of its forms, and who speak its language with unparalleled eloquence and vigour. . .
> They have always begun in the scrupulous, and ostentatious, and obsequious observances of all the ceremony and language, and dialect of free institutions. And under the pretence of this there has grown up an organization and a power by which the reality of freedom was destroyed . . . . If you have any danger to fear to (sic) the free working of our institutions, it is from the growth of the power of the wire-puller, centred in the caucus, acting under the direction of a Prime Minister, master of the House of Commons, master of the House of Lords, paying nothing but an apparent and simulated obedience to the orders of the Sovereign, gathering into his own hands every power in the State, and using them so that, when the time of renewal of power comes his influence may be overwhelming, and that the powers may be renewed. . . . Do you expect that, under such a system, the people will have any real hold over the conduct of affairs ?"[1]

It is important to recall the circumstances in which Lord Salisbury uttered this warning. The competition for the title " Leader of the Party " (in succession to Lord Beaconsfield) had not yet finally been settled. This was still the period of the duumvirate between himself and Sir Stafford Northcote, and although a settlement had been reached during the previous July with Lord Randolph Churchill it was at the moment by no means certain that Churchill would not succeed in capturing both the leadership of the party and absolute

Marquess of Salisbury, 4th and 5th June, 1884, Publications of the National Union No. 104, pp. 3-4. [Italics mine.]

[1] *Conservative Demonstration at Glasgow*, speech of the Marquess of Salisbury, at St. Andrew's Hall, on Wednesday, 1st October, 1884, Publications of the National Union, No. 107, pp. 13-14.

control over the affairs of the National Union. One could only assume that this ominous possibility was uppermost in Lord Salisbury's mind when he delivered the speech quoted above. In the next year the issue of the leadership of the party was settled in Salisbury's favour and thereafter he seems to have been less concerned about the menace of the caucus. He was brilliantly served by Captain Middleton, a remarkably able party manager. Middleton, who was named principal agent of the party in 1885, became honorary secretary of the National Union in 1886, and continued to hold both offices until 1903. Under Middleton's skilful administration it did not appear to matter that the National Union was granted the right after 1885 to pass resolutions dealing with current political issues; its pronouncements appear to have carried very little weight; certainly during this period there was no question of a serious clash with the parliamentary leaders of the party. As Lowell put it, writing of the work of the annual conference of the National Union during this period: " The action of the conference (was) not fettered; it (was) ignored."[1]

Some of the National Union conferences in the Salisbury-Middleton era appear to have been so docile that they failed to fulfil their responsibility to keep the parliamentary leaders of the party informed of the mood of Conservative opinion in the country. Even the friends of the National Union were moved to exasperation. Thus *The Times* for 27th November, 1901, carried a critical account of the annual conference of the National Union for that year. The conference (consisting of 800 representatives meeting at Wolverhampton) was the scene of a series of rather innocuous debates. Subsequently Balfour, then Leader of the Party in the House of Commons, was to have addressed the evening meeting on 26th November, but he was prevented through illness from doing so. The Earl of Dartmouth, in the chair, said that they had expected " to hear from Mr. Balfour a clear explanation of the Government's policy but as that was impossible they must improve on the occasion by telling what they thought their policy ought to be. ' When the cat's away, the mice will play ' should (he said) be the keynote of the speakers that evening." But the speakers (most of whom were M.P.s) seemed mainly preoccupied with the issues involved in the South African war and the meeting confined itself to a unanimous vote of complete confidence in Her Majesty's Ministers; the National Union had told the Government nothing.

The Times leader the next day asked where the Government was to find warning against discontent that might be silently gathering unless from the delegates representing the local party organizations.

[1] Lowell, A. L., *The Government of England*, Vol. I, p. 563.

No person could imagine it possible or desirable to turn out the Government and bring in the " motley crew " who made up a " discredited opposition ". But Ministers should be told how grievously their shortcomings disappointed their adherents. *The Times* did not find that the delegates had " improved the occasion " as Lord Dartmouth had suggested they should. In a bitter phrase *The Times* adds: " It would seem that, in the view of the experts in the curiously technical art of party management, it is deemed inexpedient to encourage the slightest indications of criticism or dissent. . . . The party managers are doing no service to the Unionist cause or to the Unionist Government by promoting such a conspiracy of silence."[1] It would seem indeed that a strong case could be made for the view that the " experts in the curiously technical art of party management " (no doubt the leader writer had Captain Middleton primarily in mind) had by this time grown so used to " managing " the National Union and to ignoring its advice that they had failed to keep sufficiently in mind that the mass organization of the party had an indispensable function in keeping the parliamentary leaders informed of the mood and opinions of their followers outside Parliament. This oversight or neglect no doubt contributed to the disaster that overcame the Conservative Party in 1905.

Yet, strangely, ten years later (after the double defeat of the party in 1910), *The Times* was to recall the era of Captain Middleton as the golden age of the party organization. The explanation probably lies in the fact that in the early years of Middleton's administration the machinery of the party reached technical perfection, but that by 1901 it had begun to rust. Then too, although Lord Salisbury, the Party Leader, and Balfour, his nephew and deputy, believed in the work of the local associations as vote-getting agencies, neither of them showed more than a faint interest in the functions of the National Union in reporting on the state of opinion among their Conservative supporters; and they were hostile to any suggestion that it should advise the parliamentary leaders on the policies they should pursue.

But it is worth returning to *The Times*'s retrospective description of Captain Middleton's administration (which appeared in a series of three leader-page articles on the party organization in January, 1911). *The Times* noted that with the re-organization of the National Union in 1885-6, " it was made a really national party

---

[1] *The Times*, 27th November, 1901. The paper also notes that some of the debates on home policy appeared to excite very little interest and points to the fact that the resolution on " the imposition of countervailing duties " was carried by only 57 against 25. This despite the fact that there were 800 delegates nominally in attendance.

organization," and that Captain Middleton became the key figure in tying together the three principal sections of the party, the party in Parliament, the mass organization (the National Union) and the Central Office. He held the two positions of principal agent and honorary secretary of the National Union from 1886 to 1903. As principal agent he administered the affairs of the Central Office under the supervision of the Party Whips. He had the right of direct access to the Leader of the Party and as honorary secretary of the National Union he had a dominating influence in its affairs. As *The Times* put it: "The machine was linked up, the control was not dissipated, and the relations between the two chief bodies in the organization were placed on the friendliest footing." Although the arrangements for the provision of speakers, literature, posters and propaganda were nominally the province of the National Union, Captain Middleton "had no difficulty in superintending them. *It is not too much to say that the powers of the National Union were in Captain Middleton's hands.*" In each of the provincial divisions he had his own Central Office agent, who was also made an honorary secretary of the local committees of the National Union. These agents, as officers of the provincial divisions, sent their reports to the National Union, and as agents of the Central Office they also sent reports direct to the principal agent. Thus, concludes *The Times*, "The democratic character of the National Union was preserved and friendly relations tactfully maintained, while at the same time the principal agent, the Chief Whip and the leaders were always well informed as to the real state of the organization in the country."[1]

This, as has been suggested above, is no doubt a somewhat idealized description of the functioning of the Conservative Party organization under Captain Middleton's administration; certainly it fails to take into account what appears to have been the growing indifference of the parliamentary leaders to the functions of the National Union as a channel of communication between themselves and their followers outside Parliament. Yet, this one reservation apart, the striking fact remains that if one changes the phrase "Principal Agent" to "Chairman of the Party Organization" (an office created a few months after the articles of January, 1911, appeared in *The Times*), The Times's *description of the functioning of the Conservative Party organization in the period 1886 to 1903 comes very close to applying equally to the structure and working of the party in our own day.* There have been perhaps half-a-dozen major party re-organizations in the intervening period. Each re-organization has been intended either to make the organs of the

[1] *The Times*, 23rd January, 1911.

National Union more broadly representative of the party member-ship or to provide more effective channels of communication be-tween the party organization outside Parliament and the party leaders in Parliament. But none of these changes has in the slightest degree altered in principle the relationship which existed in Captain Middleton's day between the three main sections of the Conservative Party organization. The party in Parliament has pre-served its autonomy; the Central Office has continued to function in effect as the personal machine of the Leader and has fulfilled most of the executive responsibilities of the National Union; and the latter organization has, with varying degrees of docility, fulfilled its function as an electoral machine and a channel of communica-tion between the parliamentary leaders and their followers in the country. It is not too much to say that what *The Times* of 1911 describes as the " really national party organization " which emerged in 1885 from the ashes of Lord Randolph Churchill's attempt to " democratize " the Conservative Party has remained in principle unaltered. It is therefore unnecessary to trace in minute detail the evolution of the party organization during the half-century which has elapsed since Captain Middleton vacated the posts of honorary secretary of the National Union and principal agent in 1903. One can turn directly to an analysis of the contemporary structure of the National Union without recalling in detail the labyrinthine story of party re-organizations during that period.

Nevertheless it is worth recording a few general observations about the process—an extraordinarily cyclical process—by which party re-organizations have taken place. Defeat in a general election traditionally leads to more or less vociferous demands on the part of party supporters for a re-organization of its structure; the leaders in Parliament (or the National Union itself) appoint a committee of inquiry which recommends more or less extensive modifications in party structure without ever seriously suggesting a redistribution of power between the three main sections of the party organization. There may be grumbling protests that the re-organization has not gone far enough, but these are forgotten as the party begins the uphill struggle involved in attempting to win its way back to power.

In this century the Conservative Party has been defeated in 1906, 1910 (twice), 1923, 1929, 1945 and 1950; most of these defeats were followed by major re-organizations of the party.[1] This " cause and

[1] Minor modifications in the party organization have also been made in response to electoral changes. Thus, for example, the report of the Central Council for 1920 notes: " In accordance with resolutions passed at the Special Conference on 30th November, 1917, the Rules (of the Central

effect " relationship was noted by the earliest students of the mass party organizations. In 1878, one writer observed sagely: " The beaten side are (always) unwilling to recognize the fact that the verdict of the nation has gone against them . . . ; their inevitable inclination is to blame their defeat on some inadequacy of their party organization."[1] *The Times* remarked in January, 1911, for example (after the party had suffered two defeats in the previous year): " Since the General Election a good deal of abuse has been heaped by Unionists on the heads of the party organization; but although particular officials have been named and denounced, the denunciation has been of the vaguest description."[2] A few days after this *Times* comment, the party's Chief Whip (Sir Alexander Acland-Hood) added that he was in no way surprised that there should be criticisms of the party organization and attacks on himself. " It would, in fact, have shown a very poor spirit in the party (he said) if, after they had been beaten twice, they had not said there must be something wrong with their organization." He therefore " liked the idea of a committee to inquire into their organization, and he himself strongly advised Mr. Balfour to have such a committee." [3]

Sometimes in the recriminations which have followed defeat there have been the harshest criticisms of the party organization. For example after the defeat of 1906 the colourful L. J. Maxse, a vice-president of the National Union, said at a special party conference that " it was universally admitted that the machinery of their party was antiquated and out of date. They had been endeavouring to run a democracy on oligarchic lines with the inevitable result."[4] Exactly the same argument recurs in the debates which followed the defeat of 1929. It was on this occasion it will be recalled that Sir Charles Marston said: " The party was very democratic until it reached the top "; it was an " autocracy masquerading as a democracy."[5] At the same conference there was a spirited debate in which it was charged that the party organization was out of date; that the Chairman of the Party Organization " had more power vested in him

Council) have been adjusted to meet the altered conditions consequent upon the passing of the Representation of the People Act, giving votes to women. The altered Rules providing that one third of the representatives shall be women." *1920 Conservative Annual Conference Report* (Report of the Central Council), folio 4.

[1] Wilson, E. D. J., " The Caucus and its Consequences ", *Nineteenth Century*, Vol. IV, October, 1878, pp. 695-712.

[2] *The Times*, 16th January, 1911.

[3] *The Times*, 27th January, 1911. For recently published evidence on the state of the party organization in 1911, see Blake, R., *The Unknown Prime Minister*, pp. 99 ff.

[4] *The Times*, 28th July, 1906.

[5] *1929 Conservative Annual Conference Report*, folio 4.

than a Tammany Hall boss "; that the resolutions of the conference had been ignored by the party leaders; and that the Central Office was guilty of " bad staff work". [1] On other occasions, the Central Council had reflected the mood of exasperation which has followed defeat. Thus after the party's defeat in 1923, the Central Council passed the following resolution (12th February, 1924): " That in the opinion of this meeting, it is desirable that more democratic methods should prevail in the councils of the Party, and that a re-organization should take place both in the constituencies and in the Central Office wherever it is found to be desirable." [2]

The party leaders and Central Office officials have (wisely) never sought to evade the traditional demand for party re-organization following a defeat. Sometimes the leaders of the party have taken the initiative in reviewing the consequences of an electoral defeat. Thus in 1906 we find Joseph Chamberlain writing to Alderman Salvidge: " Personally I am anxious that the representative Associations of the party shall now be reviewed, especially with the object of popularizing them and of securing the cordial assistance of the working classes. . . . Having satisfactorily determined the basis of our policy we can proceed with confidence to secure a more efficient and democratic representation. A small committee is to be appointed by Mr. Balfour and myself and we shall take evidence from different parts of the country as to the lessons of the election. I shall take care that you are invited to attend and to give us the advantage of your large and successful experience." [3] Again, in 1911, Balfour appointed a special committee to review the party organization. [4] In 1929 the Central Council established a special sub-committee " to consider the replies to a *questionnaire* issued to the chairmen of constituencies in England and Wales inquiring into the reasons for the defeat of the Party at the General Election." Another sub-committee was appointed " to examine the rules and organization of the National Union, to inquire into the relationship between the National Union, the Central Office and the Leader of the Party, and to report with recommendations for alteration or improvement." [5] A somewhat similar procedure was followed

[1] *1929 Conservative Annual Conference Report,* folio 16. See also pp. 268 ff. below.

[2] *1924 Conservative Annual Conference Report,* folio 13.

[3] Joseph Chamberlain to A. T. Salvidge, 17th February, 1906, cited in Salvidge, S., *Salvidge of Liverpool,* p. 71.

[4] See references to its report in *The Times,* 17th November, 1911.

[5] *1929 Conservative Annual Conference Report,* folio 3. The chairman of the first sub-committee reported, incidentally, that " the sub-committee found very soon after starting its work that the volume of information coming in, the amount of advice given, and the recriminations of the constituencies, would cause the members a good deal of detailed work. They

(although on a more elaborate scale) following the defeat of 1945. By decision of the Executive Committee of the National Union a " Committee on Party Organization " was set up under the chairmanship of Sir David Maxwell Fyfe. Its terms of reference required that it " examine the Constitution of the National Union and the relationships between the Constituencies, the Provincial Areas, the National Union and the Party as a whole." It was further to " study the reports of (three additional committees set up to deal with) Party Finance, Financial Arrangements of Candidates and Employment of Agents, and to suggest how their proposals can best be implemented." The Maxwell Fyfe Committee was to " report on the above matters to the Chairman of the Party Organization and to the Executive Committee of the National Union as soon as possible."[1]

The Maxwell Fyfe Committee appears to have held approximately a score of meetings and its report explains, " We have consulted and heard evidence from a great many officers, officials and members of the party at all levels." It also sent a questionnaire to each constituency association requesting its views on a wide variety of issues regarding the local, area and national organization of the party. The questionnaire concluded by asking: " Has your Association any suggestions for improving the organization and arrangements of the Party in any other respects? "[2] The interim and final reports of the Maxwell Fyfe Committee run to some 72 pages and provide the most extensive review of the party organization which has been undertaken in this century.

Frequently (as for example in 1906[3] and 1930[4]) special conferences of the National Union were called to receive and to debate the revisions proposed in the party organization by the special committees of inquiry. An examination of the various revisions of the party organization reveals a fairly consistent pattern. First, the demand

therefore felt quite early that the work they had to do could not be done properly by question and answer alone, and decided to invite the chairmen of Provincial Divisions and those responsible for organization to come up to see them, and to discuss these questions in person."

[1] *The Maxwell Fyfe Report* (Interim and Final Reports of the Committee on Party Organization 1948 and 1949) p. 3. All the members of the Maxwell Fyfe Committee except the chairman himself and the secretary were members of the Executive Committee of the National Union.

[2] *Maxwell Fyfe Report*, p. 27. This questionnaire appears to have elicited a remarkably poor response from the associations since the report explains (same page) " we received replies from 209 Associations, including the Central Offices of a number of Divided Boroughs."

[3] See *The Times*, 28th July, 1906.

[4] See *Gleanings and Memoranda*, August, 1930, pp. 90-1.

that the National Union should be " more democratic " has led to a steady expansion in size of most of its principal organs. Thus the Central Council [1] has grown in size from 24 to a potential member-ship of 3,600, while the annual conference has expanded from an average size of less than one hundred to 5,600. A second tendency has been to shuffle responsibilities for various features of the work of the party from one section of the party organization to another. Thus, to meet impatience with Central Office control, it was decided in 1906 to emphasize the responsibility of the National Union for the superintendence of organization, the provision of literature and party speakers (other than M.P.s). But in 1911, in a new mood of reform and re-organization, it was decided that " all executive power as regards organization, literature and speakers should be vested entirely in the Central Office." [2] The third tendency in the periodic re-organizations has been to attempt to find some means of keeping the Leader of the Party more intimately in touch with the mood and opinion of his followers in the country. Various devices have been suggested, the most notable of which was the so-called Advisory Central Committee established in 1906. It consisted of three representatives of the National Union, the Chief Whip, and three others named by him. In the event, it proved to be in the words of *The Times* " a work of supererogation " since . . . " there (was) little or nothing for it to do." [3] However, this Advisory Central Committee (and other devices suggested during the period of Bald-win's leadership) reflected the perennial desire of the National Union to give itself an effective voice in the highest party council.

But as has already been suggested, the party leaders and principal officials have invariably resisted every suggestion that the National Union should be given effective *control* over either the party in Parliament or the Central Office. The most forthright re-jection of such proposals was given in 1906 by the Chief Whip, Sir Alexander Acland-Hood. When it had been suggested to him that the Advisory Central Committee set up in that year should have executive responsibilities for the determination of party policy, he said that he " could not imagine anything more disastrous to the party welfare than to have the party managed by a committee. The party could stand many things, but it would not, in his judgment, ever stand a caucus. (Cheers.) The policy of the party must be initiated by its leader, who would, without doubt, receive valuable advice and assistance from the Advisory Committee, but they could never submit to have the policy of the party dictated by a committee.

[1] See pp. 199 ff.
[2] *The Times*, 26th October, 1911.
[3] *The Times*, 23rd January, 1911.

No leader and no Whip would ever submit to it."[1] Few party leaders have spoken so bluntly as Acland-Hood, but none have retreated from the principle he here enunciated.

II

THE NATIONAL UNION: THE MODERN STRUCTURE

The Maxwell Fyfe Committee began its examination of the contemporary structure of the Conservative Party with the remark: " . . . we have recognized the need . . for an organization which is an educative political force and a machine for winning elections."[2] In deference to its real importance the second of these functions should probably be listed first; and in addition, two further functions should be added: the party organization also serves as a two-way channel of communication between the Leader of the Party and his colleagues in Parliament on the one hand and the rank and file members of the mass party organization on the other; and finally, the party organization provides an opportunity for the politically active section of the party's supporters to play some part (however small) in the selection of the party's leaders and in the formulation of its policies. But it is perhaps significant that neither of these two additional functions were emphasized by the Maxwell Fyfe Committee in the section of their report in which they introduced their discussion of the mass party organization. The Committee were of course reflecting the traditional reluctance of Conservative leaders to encourage the party organization outside Parliament to develop pretensions about its right to influence (much less to control) the policy or strategy of the party. But whatever the Maxwell Fyfe Report and other official party documents may concede, the party organization has been (and is) more than an " educative political force and a machine for winning elections," although, wisely no doubt, the party leaders eschew any very elaborate or formal description of its additional functions. In the remainder of this chapter it is intended to examine the present structure of the voluntary section of the party outside Parliament (the professional organization of the party, the Central Office and the secretariat generally is considered in Chapter V).

The Conservative Party organization outside Parliament[3] is a

---

[1] *The Times,* 28th July, 1906.

[2] *The Maxwell Fyfe Report,* p. 28.

[3] The principal party documents setting forth the structure of the party are: *The Rules and Standing Orders of the National Union,* London, 1951; *The Maxwell Fyfe Report,* London, 1948-9; Conservative Annual Con-

TABLE 2

THE CONSERVATIVE PARTY

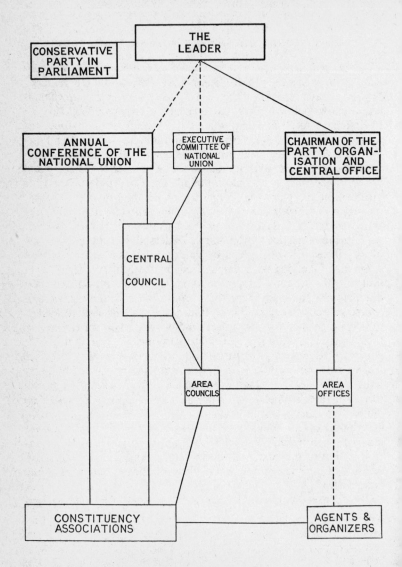

vast and complex structure and a description of it should be read in conjunction with the diagram opposite. The National Union is a federal organization to which are affiliated some 542 constituency associations throughout England and Wales, with a nominal membership of perhaps 2,250,000.[1] There is also a separate Scottish Unionist Association, and a separate organization for Northern Ireland. The nominal head of the National Union is its President,[2] but this is an honorific post involving for the most part only ceremonial duties, such as presiding at the annual mass meeting which the Leader of the Party normally addresses after the conclusion of the annual conference. The position of Chairman of the National Union[3] involves more onerous duties since its occupant normally presides over the annual party conference and meetings of the Central Council. The Chairman is assisted by three Vice-Chairmen, one of

ference 1952, *Official Report*, pp. 4–13. Recent non-official publications describing the party organization include: Birch, N., *The Conservative Party*, London, 1949; Bulmer-Thomas, I., *The Party System in Great Britain*, London, 1953; and a chapter by the same author entitled " The Organization of British Parties " in *Parliament; A Survey*, London, 1952; McKenzie, R. T., " Party Organization " in *The British Party System*, (ed. Bailey, S.), London, 1952; Beer, Samuel, " The Conservative Party of Great Britain, *Journal of Politics*, Vol. XIV, No. 1, February, 1952, pp. 41–71. For Lord Woolton's comment on the state of the party organization when he became Chairman see his *Memoirs* Ch. XX.

[1] The National Union has become very vague about its actual membership; its officials " estimate " that the membership may be the figure quoted. Allegedly, central records of actual membership are not kept. Yet the Central Office did not hesitate to claim a precise membership of 2,805,032 (*Press Release 4085*) on 19th March 1953, after a campaign launched the previous year had brought the membership to what was probably the highest total since the war. The membership figure for 31st December, 1946, had been 911,600; for 31st December, 1947—1,200,000; and for 30th June, 1948—2,249,031. See *1948 Conservative Annual Conference Report*, p. 45. Only a tiny fraction of this paper membership plays any regular part in the affairs of the party.

[2] At the inaugural meeting of the National Union, Mr. (later Sir) John Gorst took the chair. Subsequently no commoner held the office of President before 1914. The 34 who were elected President from 1868-1914 included 5 Dukes, 5 Marquesses, 15 Earls and 9 Barons. Since 1914 the office has been held by 1 Duke, 2 Marquesses, 2 Earls, 2 Viscounts, 10 Barons, 1 Baronet, 2 Knights, 5 without titles or knighthoods who were M.P.s and 3 who were not. See *1952 Conservative Annual Conference Report*, pp. 6-7.

[3] Between the foundation of the National Union in 1867 and 1914 the position of Chairman of the National Union was held by 1 Duke, 1 Marquess, 1 Earl, 2 Viscounts, 5 Barons, 5 Baronets, 7 Knights, 3 other commoners who were not M.P.s, and 9 who were. Since 1914 the position has been held by 2 Earls, 7 Baronets, 5 Knights, 6 other commoners who were not M.P.s and 5 who were, plus 8 women, of whom one was a Countess. See *1952 Conservative Annual Conference Report*, pp. 6-7.

whom is now usually a woman. All five officers are elected by the
Central Council. They are served by an honorary secretary (who in
recent years has been the General Director of the Central Office of
the party) and a secretary. These two officers, the honorary secretary
and the secretary, are appointed by the Executive Committee of the
National Union. The offices of the National Union have since 1872
been within the premises occupied by the Central Office. This and
other arrangements discussed below ensures a close link between the
popular organization of the party and the Central Office.

The functions of the National Union are defined in the official
party literature as follows:

> 1. To promote the formation and development of a Conserva-
> tive and Unionist Association in every constituency in England,
> Wales and Northern Ireland, and to foster thought and effort in
> furtherance of the principles and aims of the Party.
>
> 2. To form a centre of united action, and to act as a link
> between the Leader and all organizations of the Party in England,
> Wales and Northern Ireland.
>
> 3. To maintain close relationship with the Conservative and
> Unionist Central Office.
>
> 4. To work in close co-operation with the Scottish Unionist
> Association and the Ulster Unionist Council.[1]

The Maxwell Fyfe Report in its statement on the functions of the
National Union emphasized one aspect of its work: " The functions
of the National Union are primarily *deliberative* and *advisory*. Its
various representatives in the Areas and at the Centre enable the
collective opinion of the Party to find expression. Its views are
conveyed to the Leader of the Party or the Chairman of the Party
Organization *as may be necessary and convenient*. The opinions
of the Executive Committee are sought from time to time on matters
of policy connected with organization, political education and
propaganda."[2]

The Annual Conference

The annual conference of the National Union is the most important annual gathering of the party.[3] The composition of the conference is as follows: All members of the Central Council, who may

---

[1] *The Party Organization*, 1961, p. 7.
[2] *The Maxwell Fyfe Report*, p. 29. [Italics mine.]
[3] It should be noted that the Central Council (see p. 199 below) and not
the annual conference is " the governing body of the National Union."

number under present arrangements a maximum of approximately 3,600; three additional representatives appointed by each constituency association (one of each sex and a Young Conservative), including the honorary treasurer of the association (or a deputy), plus the certificated agent and certificated organizer of each constituency association and central association. Under these arrangements each constituency is entitled to be represented by a total of no less than seven men and women (two men, two women, two Young Conservatives and the Chairman of its Conservative Trade Union Council) in addition to its agent and organizer. The total potential membership of the annual conference under the present rules of the National Union is approximately 5,600. Since 1945 actual attendance has averaged well over three thousand; indeed, the Chairman of the 1948 conference at Llandudno boasted: " This is the largest political conference held in the world."[1]

Despite its size, the conference attempts to transact an enormous amount of business. In a two-and-a-half days' meeting it receives and discusses (as a rule very briefly) the report of the Central Council and of the Executive Committee of the National Union and it debates about a score of resolutions scattered across the whole range of party and public affairs. The size of the conference itself and of its agenda tends of course to preclude any very careful or thoughtful deliberation. As will be shown below, there have been many instances (particularly during the inter-war years) when the conference became an important forum for the debate of policy differences within the party or where the outcome of its deliberations was a major matter of concern to the leaders of the party. But since 1945 most of the resolutions before each conference have been carried unanimously or nearly so; and the conference has tended to serve primarily as a demonstration of party solidarity and of enthusiasm for its own leaders.[2]

---

[1] *1948 Conservative Annual Conference Report,* p. 32. The 3,600 representatives in attendance at this conference met in two halls approximately a mile apart. The representatives in the " overflow " hall could follow the proceedings in the main hall by means of a public address system, but they could not, of course, take part in the debates in any spontaneous way unless they had already made arrangements to be in attendance in the main hall. Nevertheless at the end of each debate the representatives in the overflow hall were polled and the results of their voting telephoned directly to the conference chairman in the main hall. At some conferences the overflow hall has been connected to the main hall on a closed television circuit.

[2] At the close of the 1948 conference at Llandudno Lord Woolton commented: " There has been no clash of opinion . . . here at Llandudno. Our ranks are closed. . . . The Press must have found us perhaps a little dull,

The Leader of the Party himself does not put in an appearance until he addresses the mass meeting which is held immediately after the conference has adjourned,[1] but other prominent figures in the party are in attendance and customarily they deliver set speeches which in recent years especially have almost invariably been the occasion for warm conference ovations. Conference resolutions are on some occasions not much more than invitations to one or other of the party leaders to give such speeches. At the 1948 conference, for example, the resolution on foreign policy read: " That this conference would welcome a clear restatement of Conservative Foreign Policy in light of the present grave tension in international affairs."[2] As might be expected, this resolution provoked only a brief, perfunctory debate which was followed by a major statement of Conservative foreign policy by Anthony Eden. Neville Chamberlain, when he was Minister of Health, explained to the Conservative conference that " there were two advantages from the point of view of a Minister coming to such a conference. In the first place it enabled him to gauge to some extent the feeling in the party about any proposal with which he was concerned and in the second place if any criticism was called forth by those proposals it might give him an opportunity to answer such criticism." He illustrated his observation by noting that several proposals involving his department had been brought before the conference, and he felt " it was very important that . . . (the conference) should know what it was they were driving at in these proposals and what were the pros and cons with regard to them before they went into the fight."[3]

In the inter-war years, particular Conservative Ministers had sometimes to grapple with the conference for several years running. Thus at the 1935 conference a resolution was moved stating " that this conference while acknowledging with grateful appreciation what

but in the face of the enemy it is wise that we should be united. This is a conference of people who know that they are going to govern the country, and therefore you have no time for frivolities." *1948 Conservative Annual Conference Report*, p. 145.

[1] The one exception occurred in 1922 when Bonar Law, then Leader of the Party and Prime Minister, addressed the conference and reviewed the position of the party and the principal domestic and foreign problems facing the country. " This (notes the Conference Report), was the first time a Prime Minister had addressed the Conference, although previous Prime Ministers have addressed public meetings held in connection therewith." *1922 Conservative Annual Conference Report*, folio 1.

[2] *1948 Conservative Annual Conference Report*, p. 86.

[3] *1928 Conservative Annual Conference Report*, folio 27. There are many illustrations in the inter-war years of brief conference debates followed by lengthy ministerial statements which were clearly designed to educate party members and explain Government policy.

the Government has already done for agriculture, desires to point out that the position in many branches is still critical, and urges the Government to use every endeavour to improve the condition of . . . those engaged in it." An amendment was moved " to delete all after the word critical " and to add a passage which urged " the application of tariffs preferential to the Empire on imported food-stuffs, and the curtailment of restriction on home production as essential factors in promoting agricultural and National prosperity." After a spirited debate Walter Elliot, the Minister of Agriculture, replied saying that " he welcomed the (original) resolution and took it as strengthening him in his work. (But) he thought the amendment went further in some respects than the facts justified." On this occasion the conference responded obediently and the report notes that " the amendment was lost and the resolution was carried unanimously."[1] A year later, however (1936), the Minister of Agriculture was defeated on the same issue. A resolution was introduced calling for a protective tariff for agriculture and the Minister advised the conference not to pass it. " We must employ tariffs where tariffs are the best (remedy) "; but, he added, " we must not go to the country and say that our policy is to disregard the struggle of the housewife in the industrial districts. . . . That is a strong statement, I would not myself support it. Let the conference think twice before pinning its faith so absolutely to one remedy." The mover of the resolution, replying to Elliot, said he did not feel disposed to withdraw his resolution, saying (amid laughter and applause) that " he would rather go down with his guns firing and his flag flying than surrender." A delegate moved from the body of the hall that the conference should proceed to the next business, but the chairman ruled that a vote must be taken. The resolution was " carried by a considerable majority ". [2]

In the course of some conference debates, the parliamentary leaders have had to resort to desperate appeals to party loyalty to forestall hostile conference resolutions. At the 1923 conference, for example, Viscount Curzon, M.P., moved a resolution on foreign affairs which had been labelled in *The Times* as " hostile to the Government ". Curzon denied the charge, but admitted that his resolution " was purposely drafted in vague terms so as to enable him, and those who agreed with his views, to give vent to their very sincere and profound anxiety as to our foreign relations, and as to the attitude of the Government towards the great problems of the day." The seconder called for a free vote of the conference on the

[1] *1935 Conservative Annual Conference Report*, folios 44–47.
[2] *1936 Conservative Annual Conference Report*, folio 31.

resolution; but in replying to the debate the Under-Secretary of State for Foreign Affairs appealed to the mover and seconder not to press their resolution. In reply to cries of " Why? " the Under-Secretary added:

> " The Conservative Party prided itself that it alone amongst political parties had the caution and the discretion to treat foreign affairs, especially in times of national crises, with a greater regard to the national interests than was to be perceived in their political opponents. It was also another tradition that until those whom it had placed in responsible positions had clearly and obviously betrayed their trust the party would take from those persons a declaration that the time for a particular discussion was inopportune. It would not further the national interest nor the party interest to pass this resolution. If they passed the resolution it would be contrary to the policy of His Majesty's Government."

The Foreign Under-Secretary closed with a remarkable appeal for loyalty to Baldwin, the Prime Minister and Leader of the Party :

> " The Prime Minister is speaking to-night, and *I have not the least idea what he is going to say,* but I do ask you not to let the Prime Minister, your own leader, who is coming here to make a most important speech, find that while he is travelling to Plymouth his hands have been tied by his followers. (Applause.) If you distrust him—(cries of ' No, No ')—I have not a word to say. Proceed with your resolution. If, on the other hand, you feel that he is the best man at this moment—(Applause)—at the head, not merely of the greatest party of the State but head of the British Empire, I do entreat this Conservative Party to put their trust in Mr. Stanley Baldwin, to hear what he says, and after he has declared what the policy of the Government is, if you are dissatisfied and distrust him, you will have plenty of opportunity of turning him out. But don't do it now." (Applause.)

The Chairman then reminded the conference that the speaker was Under-Secretary for Foreign Affairs, " so delegates would know what importance to place on what he said." The report of the debate ends: " There was no further discussion, and a motion from the hall that no resolution should be put to the meeting was carried unanimously."[1]

These illustrations of Ministers in trouble at the party conference should not be taken as representative of its normal procedure.

---

[1] *1923 Conservative Annual Conference Report,* folio 29.

Especially since 1945 spectacular debates have been rare (much rarer than at the Labour Party conference) and there can be no doubt that the conference in recent years has served primarily as a demonstration of party solidarity and as a source of stimulation to the constituency representatives who attend. The chairman of one recent conference defined its purpose in colloquial but apt terms: " In a way (he said) this is the power house for the next year's propaganda for the good old Tory Party." [1]

The huge size of the conference no doubt contributes to its value as a source of excitement and stimulation for the constituency representatives who attend. But the more thoughtful leaders of the party have nevertheless been concerned to reduce its size to more practical proportions. Speaking to the 1950 conference Sir David Maxwell Fyfe said: " Since the war the Conference has grown into a great and continuous Mass Meeting. . . . Enthusiasm runs among a great audience like a prairie fire. But on the other hand, there is the difficulty of giving a considered view and answer to a difficult question of policy, which may be of the utmost importance to the future of the Party." [2] Sir David's Committee had drawn attention to the fact that the conference at its present size could be accommodated within a single conference hall only in London and Blackpool. In all other centres the representatives would have to be distributed through two or more halls. The Committee had considered a proposal that the conference should be divided between different halls by subject, but " as each representative should have a complete view of affairs and such a proposal might have for example precluded a representative who was specially interested in Defence from participating in a debate on Housing this proposal was rejected." The Committee had therefore recommended instead a drastic reduction of constituency representation from seven to two in order to make it possible for the conference to move as it wished from year to year from one provincial centre to another.[3] This recommendation provoked a spirited debate followed by one of the few instances since the war of a recorded ballot. The voting resulted in a decisive defeat for the recommendation that the size of the conference should be reduced. (For the recommendation, 1,552; Against, 1,859.) The reason for this action was given most succinctly in the debate that preceded the vote. A Mrs. Joan Benton said: " This is my first Conference. It has been the most exciting

[1] *1948 Conservative Annual Conference Report*, p. 33.
[2] *1950 Conservative Annual Conference Report*, p. 72.
[3] This arrangement would have provided for a maximum attendance of 2,820 and a probable actual attendance averaging about 2,300. *Maxwell Fyfe Report*, p. 48.

thing that has ever happened to me; and Mrs. Benton wants to come again."[1]

Yet oddly enough, despite the belligerent refusal of the conference to reduce its potential size the attendance at conference sessions has usually fallen far short of the numbers who have indicated their intention of attending the conference. As early as 1924 a woman delegate moved that " an addition be made to the rule, in order to ensure effective representation in conference. She asked that prior to the selection of delegates an assurance should be given that it is the intention of the representative selected to attend all sessions of the conference." It was time, she said, " to end the nominal representation with which they had been cursed in the past and substitute live delegates. The old practice of selecting Sir Somebody or Other or Lord Thingammy, when neither had any intention to attend, should be ended." The speaker raised a round of laughter by saying that at one conference several delegates were absent, and it was found that they had spent the afternoon at the Zoo. In response to her appeal the conference decided " to add a recommendation to local Executives to the effect that delegates be selected who intimated their intention of attending the conference."[2] This recommendation appears, however, to have had little effect. The conference report for 1933 notes, for example, that while " the total number of acceptances was 1,834. . . . the largest attendance (at any conference session) represented only 65 per cent. of the number of acceptances." [3] And on the back page of the minutes of the 1933 conference (in lieu of the usual typed list of delegates) the following somewhat petulant note is appended: " A list of those who intimated their intention to be present at the conference is not placed here as it was obvious many of them were not present, and

---

[1] *1950 Conservative Annual Conference Report*, p. 75. A somewhat similar move to cut the size of the annual conference was defeated " by a large majority " at the conference of 1927. See *1927 Conservative Annual Conference Report*, folios 18-19. This issue was raised again at the annual meeting of the Central Council, 20th March, 1953, when a representative moved " that in order to overcome the unsatisfactory arrangement whereby many of the representatives to the Party Conference have to listen to the proceedings by loudspeaker relay, arrangements should be made at further conferences, when it is not possible for all the representatives to meet in one hall, for motions on different subjects to be discussed simultaneously in separate halls." (See *Agenda for the Annual Meeting of the Central Council*, 19th and 20th March, 1953, published by the National Union, London, 1953.) After discussion this motion was heavily rejected by the Council.

[2] *1924 Conservative Annual Conference Report*, folio 15.

[3] *1933 Conservative Annual Conference Report*, folio 38.

others were present about whom there was no official knowledge." [1]

The preparation of the agenda for the conference is the responsibility of the General Purposes Sub-Committee. [2] Motions intended for the consideration of the conference may be submitted in the names of either the Executive Committee, the General Purposes Sub-Committee, the National Advisory Committees of the Executive Committee, the Area Councils, or the constituency associations and central associations. The General Purposes Sub-Committee normally groups the resolutions under broad topic headings and in the preparation of the agenda marks one of the resolutions for the consideration of the conference. [3] No attempt is made to draft " composite resolutions " as in the case of the Labour Party annual conference. [4]

It is the responsibility of the Secretary of the National Union to send by post to every member of the conference a copy of the agenda (along with the report of the Executive Committee) " fourteen clear days " before the conference assembles. Those who plan to attend the conference may, if they wish, discuss the agenda with their local associations, but it is important to note that they are not " delegates " of their associations in the ordinary meaning of the term. They are not therefore *instructed* by their local associations as to how they should vote on the resolutions which are to be dis-

[1] *1933 Conservative Annual Conference Report*, folio 32. This situation appears to have remained unsatisfactory throughout the 1930s. Thus in 1935 " the total individual attendance was 1,510, which represents 73.3 per cent. of the number of acceptances." (*1935 Conservative Annual Conference Report*, folio 51.) Equivalent figures given in the 1936 Report (p. 43) are 68.2 per cent., and in the 1937 Report (p. 79) 67 per cent. Even at the 1953 conference, when a ballot was taken after a heated debate on the payment of post-war credits, the total of the votes cast was only 1,858, although it had been announced that " over 4,000 " delegates were attending the conference. *1953 Conservative Annual Conference Report*, p. 106.

[2] See p. 207 below.

[3] For example, an examination of the agenda of the 1948 conference shows that twelve resolutions were submitted on " Imperial Policy." One of the most comprehensive of these (p. 46) was marked with an asterisk and became the basis for the conference debate on imperial policy. A point was made, however, of calling (as speakers in the debate) the movers of a number of the resolutions on the same subject which were not marked for discussion. *Programme of Proceedings, 69th Annual Conference of the National Union*, 6th–9th October, London, 1948. However, as a result of a recommendation of the Executive Committee in 1948 it was decided at the conference of that year that one of the resolutions not marked by the Sub-Committee for consideration would be selected by ballot of the whole conference for debate at the final conference session. Annual Report of the Executive Committee, *Programme of Proceedings*, 1948 Conference, p. 81.

[4] See p. 495 below.

cussed at the conference, but are " free to speak and vote according to their consciences."[1] The Conservative Party claims this is a more democratic arrangement than a system under which delegates are " tied beforehand to vote this way or that." A case can be made for this claim, although it can also be argued that the system is workable only so long as the conference has no real power to determine policy and there are no vital debates or clashes of opinion. It is important to note that on the rare occasions in recent years when the conference has been forced to take a decision of major importance (as for example at the 1948 conference on the presentation of the Interim Report of the Maxwell Fyfe Committee embodying a major re-organization of party finance) many representatives were fearful of committing their constituency associations. In the debate on the Report one speaker protested: " I have no mandate to vote on this matter from my constituency ", and another added: " How can we know whether we can implement this Report until we have given those folks (in the constituency associations) a chance of expressing their opinion?" [2] The Report was finally received after the representatives were reassured that they were not thereby committing their organizations. (The Report merely recommended certain new financial arrangements but did not bind the associations to implement them.)

Another problem should be mentioned in connection with the reluctance of the party either to brief or mandate constituency representatives. No satisfactory study has been made of the opinions of the constituency representatives who attend the conferences, but to judge from the opinions expressed in the debates there are grounds for suspecting that they tend to be the most militant

[1] *The Party Organization*, 1961, p. 1. The report of the Council for 1926 notes that a sub-committee which had been set up " to consider various matters affecting the annual conference " had recommended that " there should be included in the preliminary notice of the conference, sent to Constituency Chairmen and Agents, a paragraph calling attention to the fact that the Agenda is issued fourteen days prior to the date of the Conference and pointing out that the Central Council of the National Union is of the opinion that, wherever possible, Constituency Executives might consider the desirability of holding a meeting for the purpose of reviewing the Resolutions included in the Agenda, so that the Constituency Representatives may be acquainted with the views of the Constituency Executive thereon before they proceed to the Conference." *1926 Conservative Annual Conference Report*, (Report of the Council), folio 6. Although this recommendation appears to have been adopted, it would not seem (from conversation with constituency representation at a number of annual conferences) that it is now normally acted upon. In any case, of course, the 1926 recommendation did not propose that the representatives should be bound to act in conformity with the views of their constituency executive.

[2] *1948 Conservative Annual Conference Report*, p. 39.

and energetic members of the constituency associations. (It should be remembered that in many instances representatives have to get time off from work to attend, or else they must devote part of their vacation to attending the conference.) There is reason to suspect therefore that the views of the constituency representatives tend to be more extremist than those of the rank-and-file members of the constituency associations. This theory might help to explain the persistence of strong Die-Hard opinion which has so frequently (during the inter-war years especially) proved a problem for the party leaders in conference discussions. If the conference representatives were required to review the agenda with a representative gathering of members of the constituency associations some of these difficulties might be precluded.

The basis of representation and the system of voting [1] at the conference is also of importance. Each constituency association *regardless of size* has the right to equal representation at the conference (seven plus the agent and/or organizer) and each representative has *equal voting rights*. In other words, there is no equivalent to the trade union " block vote " at the Labour Party conference [2] on which the Conservative Party leaders can rely to defeat a popular rebellion among the constituency representatives. One of the best recent examples of such a popular rebellion is provided by the housing debate at the 1950 party conference. The conference was discussing a rather colourless resolution condemning the Labour Government's housing record and demanding (without mentioning a specific figure) an increased housing programme. In the course of the debate one delegate mentioned the figure " 300,000 " as a desirable annual goal for a Conservative housing programme. Other speakers picked up the figure amidst mounting enthusiasm and Lord Woolton, the Chairman of the Party Organization, finally accepted on behalf of the party leaders the goal of 300,000 houses per year. [3]

It would seem reasonable to suspect that the party leaders were reluctant to commit themselves in advance to build a specific

[1] Standing Orders of the conference provide that " every motion shall be put to the vote by a show of hands. No division will be taken unless the vote is challenged and in the Chairman's opinion is supported by 100 members rising in their places, or the Chairman thinks a division desirable. In order to ascertain the vote on any division a ballot paper shall be given to each member present and entitled to vote. Scrutineers shall be appointed to cast up the votes and the Chairman shall announce the result as soon as practicable." *The Rules and Standing Orders of the National Union*, 1951, p. 16.

[2] See pp. 501-4 below.

[3] *1950 Conservative Annual Conference Report*, pp. 65 ff.

number of houses per year, and, in light of the economic position of the country, it would seem most improbable that they were eager to commit themselves to increase the rate of house building by so much as 50 per cent. But Lord Woolton apparently thought it wise to give way to the mood of the conference. Later the Chairman of the Young Conservatives boasted that the conference had, on this occasion, " educated the platform ".[1] Although the platform could not protect itself by any system of block votes the Leader of the Party was, of course, ultimately safeguarded by the fact that he cannot be bound by any conference decision. Nevertheless, had the subsequent Conservative Government decided (perhaps for the best of economic reasons) against attempting to raise the building rate to 300,000 houses per year, the conference rebellion in favour of the 300,000 figure would then have provided the opposition party with a very handy stick with which to beat the Conservative Government. In the event, the Conservative Government elected in 1951 exceeded its objective of building 300,000 houses per year. But this incident of the housing rebellion of 1950 highlights the somewhat precarious relationship between the Conservative leaders and their party conference. They cannot be bound by conference decisions; but it is conceivable that they may be mightily embarrassed by them, and in a huge assembly through which, in Sir David Maxwell Fyfe's phrase, " enthusiasm runs . . . like a prairie fire," an assembly composed of non-mandated constituency representatives and without any system of block votes, the leaders must rely on their personal authority and prestige (and on the traditionally deferential attitude of the rank and file) to win their way with the conference. They have usually (but not invariably) succeeded in doing so.

A further word should be added about the fate of conference resolutions. Sometimes the Leader in addressing the mass meeting which follows the annual conference makes a point of giving approval to particular conference resolutions. Thus, at the conference of 1929 Stanley Baldwin made special reference to a resolution passed by the conference on the subject of Empire trade; he said: " The only expanding markets in the world, the only markets in whose expansion we may take part without fighting to rob someone else of their share, lie in the Empire, and the Empire in the New World. (Cheers.) You have to-day at *your* great conference passed a resolution on that subject. (Cheers.) On behalf of my colleagues and myself I accept that resolution. (Loud cheers and ' Good Old Stanley.')" But, as was noted above, whether or not the

---

[1] *1950 Conservative Annual Conference Report*, p. 74. For Lord Woolton's own comment, see his *Memoirs*, p. 345 ff.

Leader refers to particular conference resolutions they are in any case " conveyed " to him for his information, and the succeeding annual report of the Central Council normally contains some general reference to the Leader's reaction to them. Thus the Central Council report for 1948 contains this reference to the fate of the resolutions of the previous conference in 1947:

> " The Resolutions passed at last year's Conference were presented to the Leader of the Party, who discussed them in detail with the Chairman of the National Union, the Chairman of the Executive Committee and the Chairman of the Party Organization. Mr. Churchill expressed his pleasure at the terms of the Resolutions and asked that they should be printed as a pamphlet to which he contributed a foreword."

Periodically in the history of the National Union there have been rebellious complaints from conference speakers who have alleged that resolutions have been passed year after year and consistently ignored by the parliamentary leadership. In recent years, however, the party conference has appeared to be satisfied that its work has been taken sufficiently seriously by the Leader and his associates in Parliament.[1]

The Central Council

The Central Council (which is the governing body of the National Union) normally meets once a year [2] in London. Its membership includes the Leader of the Party and other principal officers and officials (including, it is important to note, the Chairman of the

---

[1] There have, however, been illustrations of Conference exasperation with Government policy, for example, with respect to " Schedule A " tax on householders. See Biffen, W. J., " Party Conferences and Party Policy," *Political Quarterly*, July–Sept., 1961, pp. 257–66.

[2] The 1953 meeting of the Central Council was held on 19th and 20th March, at Church House, Westminster. The agenda of the meeting gives some indication of the scope of the Council's work. The first session opened with the presentation of the report of the Executive Committee, followed by a lengthy discussion on certain amendments to the rules of the National Union recommended by the Executive Committee. The meeting then discussed a series of motions which had been submitted by constituency associations on a wide variety of subjects, including defence and foreign policy, Western Germany, housing, home production, education, welfare of the aged, Communism, penalties for crime, and mutual aid. There was, in addition, a spirited discussion of certain of the party's internal affairs, including the arrangements for the annual conference and the supply of party speakers. See *Agenda for the Annual Meeting of the Central Council,* 19th and 20th March, 1953, published by the National Union, London, 1953.

Party Organization and the General Director and other principal officials of the Central Office); all Conservative M.P.s and Peers in receipt of the party Whip; prospective candidates; the members of the Executive Committee of the National Union; representatives of the National Advisory Committees of the National Union and *four* representatives from each constituency association plus representatives from central associations of boroughs and provincial area councils.[1]

As in the case of the annual conference of the National Union, the General Purposes Sub-Committee is responsible for determining the agenda of the annual meeting of the Council. The specific duties of the Council include the election of the President, Chairman [2] and three Vice-Chairmen of the National Union and the consideration of the report of the Executive Committee of the National Union. The Council also has power to amend the rules of the National Union. In addition, it considers motions on party or public affairs which have been submitted by area councils and other lower echelons of the party and like the party conference it " conveys " its decisions to the Leader of the Party for his consideration. The Press has been admitted to the meetings of the Central Council since 1933.[3]

Apart from the specific functions with which the Council is charged, it becomes in practice a smaller and briefer version of the annual conference of the National Union. It provides a half-yearly opportunity for the representatives of the constituency associations to ventilate their opinions on any matter which particularly concerns them and to hear reports from the Leader of the Party and his

[1] For a detailed description of the constitution of the Central Council see the *Rules and Standing Orders of the National Union*, 1951, pp. 5-7; see also the discussion of the provisions for representation of the Scottish Unionist Association and the Ulster Unionist Council, *The Maxwell Fyfe Report*, pp. 51-2.

[2] Except during the period of the two great wars a different person has held the office of Chairman each year since 1889, although up to that date it had been common to re-elect the incumbent Chairman. (H. C. Raikes, for example, held the office from 1869-1874 inclusive.) Lowell provides a likely explanation for the change after 1889: " As a further security against capture of the Union (by a single individual) the practice was established in 1889 of changing the Chairman of the Council every year, so that no one could acquire influence enough to be dangerous." Lowell, A. L., *Government of England*, Vol. I, p. 569.

[3] *1933 Conservative Annual Conference Report*, (Report of the Council), folio 6: " At this meeting [on 28th June last when 1,200 members were present] a recommendation of the Executive Committee that, with a view to the avoidance of unfair criticism and for the purposes of proper publicity and general record, the Press should be admitted to future meetings of the Council, was approved . . . "

colleagues. It should be emphasized of course that (as in the case of the annual conference) the Central Council tends to be representative of the more militant elements in the party, and as the leaders are bound to realize, it is unlikely to reflect a cross-section of Conservative voting support in the country. This was obliquely and perhaps unconsciously acknowledged at a Central Council meeting in February, 1921: " The Chairman pointed out that one of the chief objects of these Council meetings was *to enable those representing the live workers of our party in the constituencies* to meet to express the views *as they think they are held* in the various localities on the important questions of the day."[1]

The meetings of the Council in recent years have tended to be even less spectacular than those of the annual conference. But in the past the Council has on occasion played an important if not a decisive rôle in the affairs of the party. When the Conservatives have been in office the Council has not hesitated to advise the Government on legislation and policy. Thus, for example, in 1921 the Council passed resolutions as follows:

" (a) Urging upon the Cabinet the increasing necessity for the strictest economy in public expenditure, both Imperial and local.

" (b) That a definite and constructive Trade Policy based upon a national tariff, is indispensable to the continued welfare of the country, and urging upon the Government the adoption of such a policy.

" (c) Calling attention to the immense importance attached to the immediate reconstruction of the Second Chamber, and requesting the Cabinet Committee examining the subject to report in sufficient time to enable legislation to be passed this year.

" (d) Requesting the Government to remove at the earliest date the Liquor Control Board restrictions.

" (e) That it is the duty of the Government to take immediate action to prevent the spread of Communistic and Bolshevik propaganda." [2]

The Council has also on frequent occasions arranged for deputations to interview Conservative Ministers on specific items of policy. The report of the Council for 1937 notes: " The (Executive) Committee further reported on the outcome of a Deputation to the Chancellor of the Exchequer for the purpose of advocating that the Old Age Pension should be paid to wives of contributory Old Age Pensioners on the husband becoming qualified at 65 years of age,

[1] Central Council meeting, 22nd February, 1921, cited in *Gleanings and Memoranda*, April, 1921, p. 310. [Italics mine.]
[2] *1921 Conservative Annual Conference Report,* (Report of Council), folio 4.

provided the wife was between 60 and 65 and the couple had been married for at least five years." The report pointed out that the Chancellor was " unable to concede the demand made to him and that the Committee, whilst regretting that such was the case, but at the same time appreciating the difficulties in the way of so doing, felt that there was no alternative, at the present time, but to accept the Chancellor's decision." This statement illustrates the willingness of the Council to attempt to initiate policy; but it reflects also a recognition on the part of the Council that the extra-parliamentary organizations of the party have no ultimate power to force acceptance of their proposals.

With the party in opposition the Council has sometimes assumed the right to instruct the party in Parliament. Thus at a meeting of the Council on 4th March, 1930, the following resolutions were passed :

> " That this meeting of the Central Council urgently *demands* that the Conservative Party at the next General Election shall place a wider programme of Safeguarding as the principal and foremost item in the Party Programme, thereby continuing the beneficial results already recorded in safeguarded industries with consequent reduction of unemployment and taxation.
>
> " This meeting of the Central Council is profoundly disturbed by the slackness of the attendance of the Conservative Members in the House of Commons. It would remind the Conservative Members that they owe a duty to their leader, Mr. Stanley Baldwin, and to those who elected them. Any failure on their part to do so causes great discouragement amongst the rank and file of the Party. The meeting further urges that His Majesty's Government should be defeated on every possible occasion with a view to decreasing their prestige."[1]

The most spectacular meetings in the history of the Council took place in December, 1934, in the course of the great intra-party struggle on India.[2] The issue had arisen in dramatic fashion at the annual conference in 1933 when Viscount Wolmer, M.P., moved a resolution which Neville Chamberlain, Chancellor of the Exchequer, described (in replying to a heated debate) as a " direct challenge to the Government." He added that " while the resolution professes confidence in the Government it really amounts to this—a vote of want of confidence in the Government's Indian policy. (Cheers and

---

[1] *Gleanings and Memoranda*, April, 1930, p. 331. [Italics mine.]
[2] For a general account of the dispute over India see Templewood, Lord, *Nine Troubled Years*, pp. 42–103 and Amery, L. S., *My Political Life*, III, pp. 96–115.

renewed cries of ' No '.) . . . No one (said Mr. Chamberlain) denies the
right of the Conservative Party to express its opinion on anything,"
but he begged the conference to keep very clearly before them the
fact that the resolution was a vote of want of confidence in the
Government's Indian policy and he urged the conference to support
an amendment which was acceptable to the Government. On a
show of hands the amendment was declared carried and the result
was announced as follows:

For the amendment   737
Against   344 [1]

The critics of the National Government's Indian policy had returned to the attack at the conference of 1934. Again they moved
a resolution expressing their anxiety at the trend of the Government's Indian policy. In moving the resolution Brigadier-General
Sir Henry Page-Croft, M.P., had tried to anticipate the charge that
the critics were asking the conference to express lack of confidence
in the Government. This he strongly denied and told the conference
" you are completely free as men and women of honour to express
any fears you may possess on this occasion, which is your last
opportunity before these revolutionary proposals (with respect to
India) are decided upon." The Central Council, he alleged, had
been " persuaded to muzzle itself," and he told the conference
" you are the democratic parent of the Council. I ask you sincerely
to exercise complete frankness and freedom to-day. . . . It is positively
your last chance to influence the situation." The proposals for India
then before Parliament were, he said:

> " opposed to the instinct, tradition and faith of Conservatives. It
> is a reversion to the ideals of Cobden, whose one aim was to quit
> the Empire. Why should 460 Conservative (M.P.s) be asked to sur-
> render their principles at the behest of 30 Liberals and 10 Social-
> ists? . . . . It is proposed to . . . risk the fate of one fifth of the
> human race and, I say it deliberately, to risk the final ruin of
> Lancashire and the destruction of our greatest market. Why?
> Because a few agitators with goat and loin-cloth make a row in
> India and your representatives over there have not the will to
> rule. There is only one force which can now save India for the
> Empire—the Conservative Party—and the heart of that Party is
> this conference."

Again, as at the previous conference, an amendment acceptable
to the Government was moved and its seconder " invited the conference to have faith in their leader." At the conclusion of the debate the conference report states " on a show of hands and after

---

[1] *1933 Conservative Annual Conference Report,* folios 27-33.

the vote had been taken twice, the Chairman declared the (pro-Government) amendment carried, an announcement which was received with loud cheers and angry protests." It was at once moved that a ballot should be taken and this was agreed to. As the conference report notes: " The result was declared amid intense excitement . . . as follows:

For the amendment   543
Against   520 "[1]

Thus by the narrowest of majorities the conference had refrained from repudiating Baldwin's Indian policy.

A few weeks later, in December, 1934, the issue was carried to a meeting of the Central Council. The Joint Select Committee (of the House of Commons) on Indian constitutional reform had now reported and Baldwin addressed the Council explaining its provisions: " . . . With a full sense of responsibility as Leader of the Party," he declared his acceptance (of the report) " as a basis for legislation and strongly recommended the Council also to do so." The debate was then opened on a motion by L. S. Amery, M.P., which approved "the general principles embodied in this Report". An amendment (hostile to Baldwin's policy) was moved by the Marquess of Salisbury; the amendment hoped " that Parliament will not take the irrevocable step of establishing Central Responsible Government (in India) on the lines of the White Paper and the Report of the Joint Committee." A major debate ensued in which the following speakers took part in the order shown by the number against their names:

For the Motion:
  1.   The Lord Eustace Percy, M.P.
  3.   The Earl of Derby, K.G.
  5.   The Marquess of Linlithgow
  7.   The Viscountess Bridgeman
 10.   Sir Austen Chamberlain, K.G., M.P.

For the Amendment:
  2.   The Viscount FitzAlan, K.G.
  4.   Mr. Winston Churchill, M.P.
  6.   Sir Alfred Knox, M.P.
  8.   The Marquess of Hartington, M.P.
  9.   Sir Henry Page-Croft, M.P.

Clearly, on this occasion the meeting became a grand council of the party. Every participant in the Council debate was either an M.P. or a Peer; no member of the rank and file of the party appears

---

[1] *1934 Conservative Annual Conference Report,* folios 28–31.

to have attempted to speak, or at least none was called. But the constituency representatives attending this Central Council meeting were nevertheless called upon to decide between the two points of view put to the meeting by the eminent spokesmen of the two schools of thought within the party. The Report of the Council records: " on the amendment being put to the meeting, it was declared, on a show of hands, to have been lost, whereupon a ballot was demanded. The demand having been acceded to, a ballot was taken, the votes cast thereon being declared as follows:

> For the amendment 390
> Against 1,102
> Majority against 712 "

The original motion was thereupon put to the meeting and declared carried by " an overwhelming majority,". The Council report includes the following note: " It is worth recording that this decision, which may prove to be of historical importance, was taken at a meeting at which the attendance represented 67 per cent. of the total membership of the Council at that date; that the speeches delivered reached a very high level of excellence, and that the tone of the proceedings throughout, having regard to the strong feeling that prevailed, redounded to the credit of the speakers and all present."[1] A motion that a special conference should be summoned to further consider the question of India was subsequently submitted and defeated (on a show of hands) by an overwhelming majority.

This meeting in December, 1934, is unique in the history of the Central Council; it is in no way typical of the Council's normal proceedings. But it throws an important light on the function of the party organization outside Parliament in a major crisis in the affairs of the party. The parallel with the debate on the future of Ireland at the great National Union conference of 1921 is striking. In each case the Die-Hard wing of the Conservative Party in Parliament had attempted but failed to carry majority support among its parliamentary colleagues. The Die-Hards then turned to the National Union in an attempt to prove that the parliamentary leadership had lost the confidence and support of the popular organization of the party outside Parliament. One can only speculate as to what would have happened had Austen Chamberlain failed to carry the 1921 conference in support of his Irish policy, or if Baldwin had failed to carry the December 1934 meeting of the Central Council in support of his Indian policy. In theory neither

---

[1] *1935 Conservative Annual Conference Report*, (Report of the Council), folios 5-7.

Leader would have been forced either to reverse his policy or to resign, since as the Conservatives are never tired of insisting, the Leader alone has sole responsibility for policy; yet there is ample ground for arguing in both cases that the Leader, had he been defeated, would have found his position intolerable and might well have thrown in his hand. Certainly it would have been extremely difficult for him to have proceeded with his policy if it had been emphatically rejected by the National Union. These instances provide the two most important pieces of evidence in the proof of the proposition that the National Union cannot, in the last analysis, be dismissed in Ostrogorski's phrase as " a show body".

The Executive Committee

The Executive Committee of the National Union (which normally meets every other month) consists [1] mainly of representatives of the areas (who in turn of course represent the constituencies in the areas); the Leader and the other principal officers of the party (including again the Chairman of the Party Organization and the General Director of the Central Office) are also members. The Executive Committee handles the affairs of the Central Council in the intervals between the latter's meetings and annually it recommends to the Central Council for election the officers of the National Union; in addition it elects its own chairman and appoints an honorary secretary of the National Union (who is now usually the General Director of the Central Office) and a secretary. Resolutions and reports on party or public affairs submitted by the provincial areas or the constituencies are considered by the Executive Committee and forwarded to the appropriate quarters.

The Executive Committee also has important power with respect to membership of the constituency associations in the National Union. It must approve the admission of associations and it may withdraw such approval. In addition, the Executive Committee has power to settle disputes within or between constituency associations. The Executive Committee also elects representatives of the National Union to the various National Advisory Committees of the party.[2] It submits a report to the Central Council and an annual report to the conference.

Since the appointment of the General Purposes Sub-Committee in 1933, the Executive Committee has been able to rid itself of a

---

[1] The total membership of the Executive Committee is approximately 150. For full details of its composition see *The Rules and Standing Orders of the National Union*, (1951), pp. 8-9.

[2] See p. 208 below.

good deal of detailed work and to devote itself to broader issues of policy. The report of the Council for 1934 notes: " Under the scheme for making better provision for dealing with the ever-increasing work of the National Union, the business hitherto dealt with entirely by the (Executive) Committee (is now) shared between the Committee and the General Purposes Sub-Committee appointed for that purpose, all matters considered by the Sub-Committee being subsequently reported on to the Executive Committee. This arrangement has given the Committee itself more time to discuss other than routine business and to have the advantage of regular addresses from Ministers upon matters of Public interest, particularly concerning their respective Departments of the Government, and has been of considerable assistance to the Committee in arriving at a proper conclusion upon the subject matter of Resolutions submitted for its consideration, and in regard to which representation to the Leader of the Party was desired or considered to be necessary. . . . At the first meeting of the Committee as newly constituted for the current year, the Leader of the Party attended and spoke especially upon some of the more important points affecting the Principles and the Organization of the Party."[1] As this Report suggests, much of the detailed work of the Executive Committee is now done by the General Purposes Sub-Committee,[2] which normally meets monthly. Like each of the other organs of the party which have been examined above, the General Purposes Sub-Committee is a surprisingly large body in light of the tasks it is intended to perform. It consists of approximately 56 members and includes among these the principal officers of the National Union, the Chairman of the Party Organization, the General Director of the Central Office, the Chief Whip in both Houses of Parliament, the Chairman of each Area Council and 12 representatives of the Executive Committee. Its principal task is to " perform all ordinary and emergency acts on behalf of the National Union " with the exception of certain special duties reserved to the Executive Committee, such as the arbitration of disputes between constituency associations. In addition the Sub-Committee considers the reports of the National Advisory Committees and circulates them to the members of the Executive Committee for information; it also considers the resolutions passed by the area councils and the constituency associ-

[1] *1934 Conservative Annual Conference Report,* (Report of the Council), folios 6–7.
[2] There is some confusion in the party literature about the correct title of this organization. It is normally referred to as the " General Purposes Sub-Committee " but the *Rules and Standing Orders of the National Union,* 1951, p. 10, refer to it as the " General Purposes Committee ".

ations. Perhaps the most important duty of the Sub-Committee is the preparation of the agendas for the meetings of the Central Council and the annual conference. Specifically, of course, this means that the Sub-Committee determines which of the long list of resolutions sent in by the constituency associations shall be selected for debate.

The National Advisory Committees and other Central Committees and Boards

The Executive Committee is advised by a series of National Advisory Committees which include the following: the National Advisory Committee on Political Education; the Women's National Advisory Committee; the Young Conservative and Unionist National Advisory Committee; the Trade Unionist National Advisory Committee; the National Advisory Committee on Local Government; the National Advisory Committee on Publicity and Speakers; the Central Advisory Committee of the Conservative and Unionist Teachers' Association; the Central Committee of the Federation of University Conservative and Unionist Associations (undergraduates). Each of these advisory committees has power to make rules for its own composition and management provided that these rules are approved by the Executive Committee.

The membership of these committees (which averages approximately 50) consists mainly of representatives appointed at area level. A review of the work of the national advisory committees is incorporated into the annual report of the Executive Committee of the National Union.[1] One might take as an illustration the work of the Women's National Advisory Committee. This committee advises the Executive " on all questions affecting the organization of women supporters of the Party, and the subjects in which they are especially interested."[2] During the year 1953-4 the committee met on nine occasions. It was addressed on one occasion by a junior Minister and on another by an official of the Central Office. It also organized its own discussions on the work of the United Nations,

[1] See, for example, the Executive Committee's report to the annual meeting of the Central Council, 19th and 20th March, 1953, published by the National Union, London, 1953.

[2] *The Party Organization*, 1961, p. 9. The *1920 Conservative Annual Conference Report*, folio 1, notes that in that year " for the first time in the history of the party ladies had a substantial representation both on the platform and in the body of the hall." The Women's Advisory Committee was set up as a result of a decision of the 1928 Conservative annual conference and the original constitution of the Committee is to be found in the Report of the Executive Committee in the *1929 Conservative Annual Conference Report*, folio 7.

on the Government's housing programme, new towns and housing estates, the Government's agricultural policy, television, the Young Britons' organization and the publicity and propaganda work of the party. Members of the committee who had been delegates representing this country at the United Nations and at other international gatherings presented reports on their experiences. The committee also received and reviewed the resolutions received from area and constituency women's organizations and where their resolutions met with the approval of the committee they were forwarded for consideration of the National Union or conveyed directly to members of the Government. The report of the Women's Advisory Committee records that the resolutions received from the areas and constituencies " included many showing appreciation of the Government's achievements. The subjects dealt with (by the resolutions) have included Agriculture; Old People; Retired Workers; Widows' Pensions; Housing; Education, including the education of deaf children; Purchase of Meat; the Welfare State; Trade Unions; Electoral Reform; Propaganda and Publicity." [1] The committee also appointed a number of sub-committees including a Parliamentary Sub-Committee, which kept under review aspects of legislation which particularly affected the position of women. The sub-committee made recommendations to the full committee which were then conveyed to the Executive Committee of the National Union, and to members of the Government.

The highlight of the Women's Advisory Committee's activities is its annual one-day women's conference and mass meeting,[2] held usually in London and attended by women representatives of the constituency associations in England and Wales and by guests from Scotland and Northern Ireland. Members of the Government attend the conference by invitation and are usually invited to do so when debates affecting their own departments take place. The Leader of the Party or a senior deputy usually addresses the mass meeting held at the conclusion of the conference. It is clear that the Women's Advisory Committee along with the other advisory committees merely provides an extended opportunity for certain elements within the National Union to meet together to encourage and stimu-

---

[1] *Annual Report of the Women's National Advisory Committee, 1953-4*, p. 8.

[2] At the 1953 conference held on Tuesday, 28th April, in the Central Hall, Westminster, motions on the following subjects were discussed: food; housing; education; the Commonwealth; the United Nations; care of old people; juvenile delinquency; national savings; reform of the House of Lords. See *Agenda for the 26th Annual Conference, Women's National Advisory Committee*, published by the National Union, London, 1953.

late each other in fostering the work of the party, and to convey their views on particular problems to the party leaders in Parliament. They provide, in other words, a focal point for the activity of special interest groups within the party; they elaborate and expand the opportunities for an exchange of views between the party in Parliament and its active supporters in the country.

As is explained below, the departmental organization of the Central Office is arranged to conform very closely to the national advisory committee structure of the National Union. Thus, for example, the Trade Unionist National Advisory Committee is paralleled by the Industrial Department of the Central Office.[1] The national advisory committees are, of course, composed of non-professional volunteer party workers; inevitably, therefore, the day-to-day work of the party in the various fields covered by the National Advisory Committees is undertaken by the appropriate Central Office department. In addition, the head of the department serves as honorary secretary to the equivalent national advisory committee. These arrangements are intended to ensure that the voluntary and professional wings of the party work in close co-operation rather than at cross-purposes to each other.

In addition to the national advisory committees which are, of course, responsible to the Executive Committee of the National Union, there are six other central committees or boards of great importance *which do not report to the Executive Committee.* The official Central Office publication, *The Party Organization,* says of these central committees or boards, rather innocently, that they "occupy an important place within the framework of the Party Organization." [2] It becomes apparent that this is no exaggeration when one notes the official titles of the six committees or boards. They are as follows: 1. The Advisory Committee on Policy; 2. The Consultative Committee on Party Finance; 3. The Central Board of Finance; 4. The Standing Advisory Committee on Parliamentary Candidates; 5. The Examination Board (for agents and organizers); 6. The Superannuation Fund. *The first four of these are concerned with the most important features of the work of any party : the determination of policy, the raising of funds and the selection of candidates. Yet none of these committees or boards is responsible to any organ of the National Union.* This is perhaps the most significant evidence of the National Union's lack of authority in the really vital spheres of party activity.

The Advisory Committee on Policy is certainly one of the most

---

[1] See table p. 288 below.
[2] *The Party Organization,* 1961, p. 11.

important committees in the entire party organization. Yet its principal officers, the chairman and deputy chairman, are personal appointees of the Leader of the Party and the committee is responsible solely to him.[1] The fifteen other members of the committee (apart from the chairman and deputy chairman) are selected as follows: seven are members of one or other House of Parliament (five selected by the Conservative Members Committee—the " 1922 Committee," and two selected by Conservative Peers) ; the other eight are selected by the Executive Committee of the National Union from its own members. In addition the Committee has power to co-opt up to four members and to appoint sub-committees, and it has at its disposal the resources of the Conservative Research Department (which is discussed in Chapter V).

The Maxwell Fyfe Report traced the emergence and subsequent evolution of the Advisory Committee on Policy. In October, 1941, the Report recalled, the National Union established a Post-War Problems Committee which included a number of sub-committees which were instructed to examine the various aspects of policy and to prepare reports for submission to the Leader. The findings of these sub-committees were published as a comprehensive report which was issued in the name of the individuals who composed the Post-War Problems Committee; " it was intimated that it was a document on the basis of which Party policy might subsequently be framed. . . . " And the Maxwell Fyfe Report adds that " many of the suggestions put forward found a place in the Statement of Policy issued by Mr. Churchill on the eve of the General Election." The Central Council at a meeting on 28th November, 1945, reviewed the work of the Post-War Problems Committee and passed a resolution reconstituting it under the name of the Advisory Committee on Policy and Political Education. It was decided that the new committee would be " given the widest possible power to develop quickly a scheme to promote the study of suitable subjects for the benefit of the Party (and) the members were to be chosen, not as representing any particular section of the Party, but because

[1] The use of the word " advisory " in the title of this committee may easily lead to its being confused with the eight National *Advisory* Committees of the National Union. It is therefore important to underline the fact that its responsibility is to advise the *Leader of the Party*, whereas the eight National Advisory Committees are responsible for advising the Executive Committee of the National Union. For a recent assessment of the work of the Advisory Committee on Policy, see Hennessy, D., " The Communication of Conservative Policy, 1957–59," *Political Quarterly*, July–Sept., 1961, pp. 246–8 and a comment on the article by Sir Michael Fraser in the succeeding number of *The Political Quarterly*.

of their knowledge of the subjects to be considered." [1] It was also recommended that the Chairman of the new committee should be appointed head of the Conservative Research Department to help to ensure the closest possible co-operation between the two bodies. The members of the committee were also to be approved by the Executive Committee of the National Union. (R. A. Butler, M.P., was, of course, appointed to the chairmanship of this committee by the Leader and thereafter played a major rôle in the development of party policy.) When four years later the Maxwell Fyfe Committee reported on its examination of the structure of the party it noted that " a great deal of excellent work has undoubtedly been done by the Advisory Committee on Policy and Political Education," but a further comment in the Report appears to reflect a certain dissatisfaction within the party about some aspects of the work of the Committee. The report adds: " We do, however, regard it as vital that the powers of the Committee should be defined and that the Party should have absolute confidence in it. What is needed is a Committee so strong that the Executive of the National Union will have full confidence both in its examination and in its approval or disapproval of all policy documents submitted to it which are designed to be published under the authority of the Party." [2]

The Maxwell Fyfe Report therefore made a number of recommendations providing for the re-organization of the Advisory Committee. First, that it should cease to be concerned with political education; second, that the committee " should consist of a Chairman and Deputy Chairman, appointed by the Leader, and of at least fourteen others, half to consist of Peers and Members of Parliament, to be chosen by whatever means *other than his personal choice* the Leader considers appropriate, and half selected by the Executive Committee of the National Union from its own members." [3] Other recommendations were added providing for the co-

[1] *The Maxwell Fyfe Report*, pp. 36-7.

[2] *Maxwell Fyfe Report*, pp. 37-8. This is a strangely ambiguous passage to appear over the name of Sir David Maxwell Fyfe, but one can only assume that it is intended to acknowledge, but not to refer too specifically to, a widespread uneasiness within the Executive Committee of the National Union about the activities of Butler and his " back-room boys " who played so active a part in the immediate post-war years in the reform and modernization of the social and economic policies of the Conservative Party. (See p. 285 below.)

[3] *The Maxwell Fyfe Report*, p. 38. [Italics mine.] The phrase " other than his personal choice " reflects one of the rare occasions on which an official party document has formally proposed a specific limitation on the powers of the Leader (although, as has been repeatedly pointed out, there are a great many practical limitations on the Leader's authority). As will be gathered from the statement above outlining the present composition of

option of additional members of the committee and any sub-committees which it might choose to set up with the additional provision that the names of the members of such sub-committees " should be known to the Executive of the National Union." The Advisory Committee would, as one of its main functions, examine and either approve or disapprove documents submitted by these sub-committees.[1]

The Maxwell Fyfe Committee summarized the main purpose of this proposed re-organization by saying that it was intended to ensure that the re-organized Advisory Committee " would be in full liaison both with the Leader and the Executive of the National Union." The word " liaison " used in this connection is, in a sense, misleading, since the committee (as has already been emphasized) is in fact *responsible* to the Leader rather than to the National Union, although the latter does, of course, select seven of the sixteen members of the committee. The Maxwell Fyfe Report provided, however, that there would be some provision for these National Union representatives to ventilate their unhappiness (if such should develop) about the work of the Advisory Committee. The Maxwell Fyfe Committee recommended that the Advisory Committee " would submit regular reports to the Leader (but) if one or more of the members drawn from the Executive (of the National Union) were not content they could individually or collectively report their disagreement to the National Executive." There is no further indication in the Report as to what subsequent action would result, but it is fair to assume that the Executive Committee of the National Union could, if it chose, endorse the protest of its representatives on the Advisory Committee and forward their views to the Leader. The latter would not of course be bound to take action on the basis of the Executive Committee's observations; but here again the wise Leader would not in practice ignore any evidence of really serious dissatisfaction on the part of the Executive Committee of the National Union.

The second and third of the central committees and boards mentioned (p. 210) above, each have to do with party finance. The *Consultative Committee on Party Finance* was set up as a result of

the Advisory Committee on Policy the Leader chose to permit the Conservative Members Committee to " select " five of the parliamentary representatives on the committee and he authorized the Conservative Peers to " select " the two other members.

[1] The Maxwell Fyfe Committee had discovered, apparently to its surprise, that sub-committees of the old Advisory Committee on Policy and Political Education had " independently produced certain reports which (had) not, in fact, been examined by the main Advisory Committee." *Maxwell Fyfe Report*, p. 37.

a recommendation by the Maxwell Fyfe Committee, which had noted in its Report that if the rank and file of the party were to accept greater responsibility for the raising of funds then " they will expect to have a closer knowledge of the administration of Headquarters funds. The rank and file will also require to have a reasonable assurance that the money they raise is being wisely spent."[1] The composition of the Consultative Committee provides, therefore, for ample representation from the voluntary sections of the extra-parliamentary organization. The committee includes the chairman of the Executive Committee of the National Union and the treasurer of each Provincial Area. In addition, the party in Parliament is represented by one nominee of the Conservative Members Committee and one nominee of the Conservative Peers. Finally, the professional organization of the party is represented by the Chairman of the Party Organization and the Treasurers of the Party. The Consultative Committee can also co-opt not more than three additional persons.

The functions of the Consultative Committee are officially defined (rather vaguely) in party literature as follows: " to receive information and to assist the Treasurers of the Party by giving advice and information." [2] It is significant that the Chairman of the Party Organization is *ex officio* Chairman of the Consultative Committee and the two Treasurers are Deputy Chairmen. When it is recalled that all three of these individuals are the direct personal appointees of the Leader of the Party, the parallel with the administrative structure of the Advisory Committee on Policy becomes evident. The Maxwell Fyfe Report emphasized that the Consultative Committee was not intended to fulfil the functions of a " Budget or Accounts Committee ". It was intended however to ensure that " each Area . . . would be kept in touch (through the work of the Consultative Committee) with the financial position (of the Party and) would be aware in general of what was being done and what was required, and would have the opportunity of raising questions on any matters of Party expenditure in which the Area was interested or upon which it desired to make representations." [3] This observation is intended no doubt as justification for the Consultative Committee's lack of ultimate executive control of the financial affairs of the party. It was apparently intended, however, that the Chairman of the Party Organization and the Treasurers of the Party should keep the Consultative Committee thoroughly briefed concerning the financial position of the party and that the Consulta-

[1] *Maxwell Fyfe Report*, p. 34.
[2] *The Party Organization*, 1961, p. 11.
[3] *Maxwell Fyfe Report*, p. 35.

tive Committee should give " a confidential report " on this situation to the Executive Committee of the National Union. But, adds
the Maxwell Fyfe Committee firmly, " such a report could not be
published." [1] It was further recommended that " the confidential
channel for the communication of necessary facts should be . . .
through the Area Treasurers to the Chairmen and Treasurers of
Constituency Associations."

A second central organization concerned with finance, *The
Central Board of Finance*, is responsible for raising " for the Party
money which would not normally be obtained by or go to the
constituencies."[2] The composition of the Board is almost identical
with that of the Consultative Committee on Party Finance. It consists of the Party Treasurers, the Area Treasurers and up to a maximum of five co-opted members. The Board has power to elect its
own chairman from among its members, *but it is responsible to
the Chairman of the Party Organization.* Since there is no public
statement of party accounts there is no way of knowing what proportion of the party funds are raised by the Central Board of
Finance. But it is important to note that the Board is officially said
to carry out its work throughout England and Wales " by means of
representatives in each of the Provincial Areas." [3] There appears to
be ground for believing that its principal function is to approach
well-to-do party members and sympathizers throughout the Provincial Areas who can be prevailed upon to make a somewhat larger
contribution to the finances of the central organization and the
Provincial Areas than they would perhaps be willing to make as
members of their local constituency association. It would appear
further that the Party Treasurers themselves (perhaps in co-operation with leading officials of the Central Office and the party in
Parliament) are responsible for obtaining the even larger contributions from sympathetic national organizations and well-to-do
individuals. If this analysis, which at best can be no more than
reasonably well-informed speculation, is correct it would then
follow that the Central Board of Finance is in fact mainly responsible for what might be termed the " middle-sized " contributions
to the party funds and, along with the Consultative Committee on
Party Finance, it serves the useful purpose of bringing those who
are actually concerned with the financial affairs of the party in the
Provincial Areas part way into the inner sanctum of the keepers
of the coffers of the Conservative Party.

It should be re-emphasized yet again that while the National

[1] *Maxwell Fyfe Report*, p. 35.
[2] *The Party Organization*, 1961, p. 11.
[3] *Ibid.*

Union is well represented in the composition of both the committees concerned with party finance, *it in no way controls the work of these committees*. The Chairman of the Party Organization is in effective control of each and he in turn, of course, is responsible solely to the Leader. Again, in theory at least, the reins of authority are in the Leader's hands alone.

The fourth of the central committees or boards is the *Standing Advisory Committee on Parliamentary Candidates*. Technically it is a committee of the National Union and came into being as a result of a recommendation by the Executive Committee of the National Union in 1935. The Executive Committee in its report to the Central Council that year had stated, " the unquestioned right of a Constituency to select its own Candidate is recognized, but it is suggested that before the final selection of any Candidate, not previously approved of by the Party Organization, is completed, the Chairman of the Constituency Association should get into touch with the Standing Advisory Committee in order to ensure that the proposed Candidate shall receive the full support of the Party, which otherwise it might be necessary to withhold."[1] On the strength of this advice the National Union decided in 1935 that " if a Constituency Association adopted a Candidate who had not been approved by the Standing Advisory Committee, it would not be possible to give support to such a Candidate by procuring a letter of commendation from the Leader of the Party, by the supply of Parliamentary speakers, by a financial grant towards the election expenses or by Central Office assistance."[2]

The Maxwell Fyfe Report noted (p. 53) that the " purpose of the (Standing Advisory Committee on Parliamentary Candidates) is to assess on broadest grounds the suitability of men and women who are desirous of becoming approved Candidates. . . . (In order) to protect the good name of the Party . . . no Candidate is adopted unless the Committee is previously satisfied as to: (i) personal character; (ii) Party loyalty; (iii) past record and experience; (iv) political knowledge; (v) speaking ability; (vi) financial arrangements." The Committee maintains a list of " approved candidates " and this list, which includes brief biographical data, is sent *on request* to constituency associations which are selecting a prospective candidate.[3] The Maxwell Fyfe Committee had noted with concern the situation which had developed after the 1945 general election. Some 373 candidates were required for English and Welsh

---

[1] *1935 Conservative Annual Conference Report*, folio 8.
[2] *Maxwell Fyfe Report*, p. 54.
[3] See p. 250 ff. below for a description of the procedure by which the constituency associations select and adopt their candidates.

constituencies but "instead of drawing their Candidates from the list of names already approved by the Standing Advisory Committee, Associations were frequently adopting Candidates and subsequently seeking endorsement of their candidatures." The Maxwell Fyfe Report therefore recommended (p. 54) that "Candidates should be approved by the Standing Advisory Committee before their names are submitted to Constituency Association Selection Committees." It acknowledged that "a Constituency Selection Committee may, of course, recommend someone not already on the list, but in that case, the Association should see that the Candidate receives the approval of the Standing Advisory Committee and so is recognized as an official Conservative Prospective Candidate before adoption as Prospective Candidate takes place." In other words, the Maxwell Fyfe Committee was anxious to ensure that prospective candidates should be screened *before* adoption by the Constituency Associations rather than that they should be adopted first and their names then submitted to the Standing Advisory Committee for approval.

The Standing Advisory Committee is charged with the duty of maintaining "a wide range of Candidates on its list, completely representative in every possible way."[1] The Maxwell Fyfe Report further notes (p. 55) that "no member of the Conservative Party is debarred from submitting his or her name to the Advisory Committee (but) there is no onus on the Standing Advisory Committee to produce evidence to prove that a Candidate is unsuitable. It is entitled to withhold approval if it is not satisfied that he or she is in every way suitable."

Clearly the Standing Advisory Committee would appear to have great potential influence on the determination of the quality and calibre of those who may eventually become the members (and, indeed, the leaders) of the parliamentary party. Therefore the composition and powers of the committee are of very considerable importance. It is composed as follows: the chairman of the Central Council of the National Union; the chairman of the Executive Committee of the National Union; the chairman of the Women's National Advisory Committee; the chairman of the Young Conservative National Advisory Committee; the chairman of the Trade Unionist National Advisory Committee; the Chairman of the Party Organization; the Chief Whip of the Party in the House of Commons and the Honorary Secretary of the National Union.[2] (The occupant of the last-named post is, as has already been noted, the General Director of the Central Office.) The eight-member

[1] *Maxwell Fyfe Report*, p. 54.
[2] *The Party Organization*, 1961, p. 12.

committee consists therefore of five who represent the voluntary, non-professional organs of the party, two professionals from the Central Office and one representative of the party in parliament. On the face of it, this would appear to suggest that in this vital matter of preparing lists of potential candidates for the party, representatives of the National Union play a decisive rôle. But in practice this hardly seems to be the case. As is explained in the official publication, *The Party Organization* (1950), one of the two Vice-Chairmen of the Party Organization (who is, of course, a personal appointee of the Leader) " is responsible for all questions of Parliamentary candidature."[1] In addition it is significant that the Standing Advisory Committee on Candidates unlike the eight national advisory committees (see p. 208 ff. above) *does not report on its work to either the Central Council or the annual conference.*[2]

Indeed it is difficult to understand in what respect the Standing Advisory Committee on Candidates is an advisory body, or whom or what it advises. And surprisingly, the Vice-Chairman of the Party Organization, who is " responsible for all questions of Parliamentary candidature," is not even a member of the Standing Advisory Committee. J. P. L. Thomas, who then occupied the position, explained to the 1948 conference: " Although I am not a member of the Standing Advisory Committee of the Party on Candidates, I do report to them very fully on every candidate."[3] It is to be noted that he was speaking in reply to the conference debate on a motion which read in part: " this conference urges the Party's Standing Advisory Committee on Candidates to take all possible steps to ensure that candidates are drawn from men and women of character, ability, and sound political knowledge and from all walks of life, and that the financial rules imposed by the Party to limit candidates' expenses are rigidly enforced without exception." It is not clear why Thomas, who, as he was careful to explain, was *not* a member of the Standing Advisory Committee, should have replied to the debate. It would have seemed appropriate for the chairman of the Standing Advisory Committee or some other member of the committee to have done so; but no speaker in the debate identified himself as a member of the committee. Thomas, on the other hand, took up almost as much time as all other speakers in the debate combined; it seems perfectly clear that

[1] *The Party Organization*, 1961, p. 13.

[2] See the annual report of the Central Council and Executive Committee in the *1952 Conservative Annual Conference Report*, pp. 14-20. The reports of the other advisory committees of the National Union are included, but there is no report from the Standing Advisory Committee on Candidates.

[3] *1948 Conservative Annual Conference Report*, p. 119. For Lord Woolton's comment, see his *Memoirs*, p. 332.

his was a definitive exposition of party policy with respect to candidates. One is led to conclude that the Standing Advisory Committee on Parliamentary Candidates is a body of comparatively minor importance. The fact therefore that a majority of its members are representatives of the National Union in no way ensures popular or non-professional control over policy with respect to candidates. Here again final authority lies with an official of the Central Office who is a direct personal nominee of the Leader.

In addition to the Central Committees which have been described above there is a very important *ad hoc* Liaison Committee (first established when the Conservatives returned to power in 1951) which is nowhere described in the Party's official literature. Its primary job as described by David Hennessy, a former member of the Executive of the National Union, is " to identify what is likely to be controversial in the reception of Government policy, to advise on timing in the execution of policy, and to consider what forms of Party propaganda could be used to ease its communication."[1] It normally meets under the chairmanship of the Cabinet minister responsible for Government Information Services and its membership includes the Party Chairman, both Vice-Chairmen of the Party, a junior minister from the Foreign Office, the Deputy Chief Whip, the Directors of the Conservative Research Department and Conservative Political Centre, and the Chief Publicity Officer. Undoubtedly this Committee, meeting weekly, has played a vital rôle particularly during the period leading up to the Conservative victory in the election of 1959. But again it is significant that all its members were, through one channel or another, responsible to the Prime Minister, as Leader of the Party.

This chapter has been devoted so far to a description of the principal *national* organs, boards and committees of the Conservative Party outside Parliament, with the exception of the party Central Office or secretariat, which is considered in Chapter V. There has emerged a picture of a vast sprawling unwieldy organization, a clumsy giant; all of the principal organs of the National Union have expanded and burgeoned in a most remarkable fashion. Each demand for greater internal party democracy seems to have been met by broadening the representation accorded to every section of the party—the regions, women, youth, trade unionists, all are given every opportunity for representation at every level of the party organization. In one sense it is hard to imagine a more completely democratic organization. Certainly the National Union is

---

[1] Hennessy, D., " The Communication of Conservative Policy, 1957–59," *Political Quarterly*, July–Sept., 1961, pp. 245–6.

well equipped to function as a vast sounding board of Conservative opinion; but manifestly it would prove hopelessly cumbersome if it were intended to control and manage the affairs of the Conservative Party in any serious sense. But this, as we have seen, it is not intended to do. The National Union is intended in effect only to manage its own affairs and this it succeeds in doing with the paternal assistance of the Central Office. The key functions of the party are without exception controlled by officials and committees who are responsible to the Leader or to his personal appointee, the Chairman of the Party Organization. The National Union can and does debate policy resolutions which are conveyed to the Leader for his information; but the really effective work in the preparation of policy documents is undertaken by the Advisory Committee on Policy presided over by a chairman and deputy chairman appointed by the Leader. The National Union is generously represented on this committee but it in no way controls its work. Prominent officials of the National Union and of the area organizations appear also on the Consultative Committee on Party Finance and the Central Board of Finance. But the former committee is presided over by the Chairman of the Party Organization and the Central Board of Finance is responsible to him. Officials of the National Union compose more than half of the Standing Advisory Committee on Parliamentary Candidates but this committee does not report to the National Union and it appears to play a much less important rôle in the determination of policy with respect to candidature than does the Leader's appointee, the Vice-Chairman of the Party Organization, who is " responsible for all questions of Parliamentary candidature." *Thus all serious responsibility for, or control of, policy, finance and candidatures is clearly removed from the control of the National Union.*

But again it must be emphasized that it is both inaccurate and dangerous to assume with Lowell that the National Union is a " sham " or with Ostrogorski that it is " a show body ". The party constitution does make every effort to protect the Leader and his colleagues from any attempt by the National Union to exert over them any form of arbitrary control. In practice, however, (as has been shown in Chapter III) the Leader's powers are in no sense those of an autocrat; it can further be shown that he ignores the moods and opinions of the National Union at his peril.

III

THE INFLUENCE OF THE NATIONAL UNION

IN the formulation of party policy, the rôle of the National Union is, to borrow a word from the Maxwell Fyfe Report, "advisory". The various organs of the National Union have often enough acknowledged their own limited rôle. Thus the report of the Council for 1927 stated: "The Government, having already carried out the greater part of their pledges at the last General Election, will no doubt shortly address themselves to the future policy and programme of the Party. Resolutions passed by the Conference and by the Central Council have been of great service in the past in informing the Government of matters in which the rank and file of the Party are interested. *Suggestions* of policy in future will no doubt be equally welcome."[1]

There have been remarkably few occasions in the history of the National Union when one can state with confidence that the Union had a decisive influence in the adoption of a particular policy by the party whether it was in power or opposition. Indeed, the incident of the "three hundred thousand houses" (discussed above) has no exact parallel in the whole history of the organization. On the other hand there can be no doubt that on certain issues the National Union's pressure to adopt a certain policy was so powerful as to be very nearly decisive. It will be recalled that the Chairman of the Council addressing the 1927 conference and referring to the Trades Disputes Act which had just been put on the statute book, said: " . . . this conference may be particularly anxious to congratulate the Government and, if I may say so, *to congratulate itself.*"[2] An examination of conference reports in the preceding years shows a continued and insistent demand for some such legislation.[3] It will be recalled that this demand reached its climax at the 1926 conference when a powerfully worded resolution was moved by a vice-president of the Union stating: "That this conference regrets the apparent inability of the Government to appreciate the necessity of amending the Laws governing Trade Unions." The heat with which this motion was pressed moved the Chairman of the Party Organization to intervene: the mover of the resolution agreed to withdraw his resolution and "to trust the Government," but there must have remained echoing in the ears of the party leaders the phrase uttered by one of the speakers in the debate, "Get on with it or get out."[4] It could, of

[1] *1927 Conservative Annual Conference Report,* (Report of the Council), folio 14. [Italics mine.]
[2] *Ibid.,* folio 3. [Italics mine.]
[3] See *1921 Conservative Annual Conference Report,* folio 27; *1922 Conservative Annual Conference Report,* folio 18; *1923 Conservative Annual Conference Report,* folio 31; Report of the Central Council meeting, 22nd June, 1926, (*Gleanings and Memoranda,* July, 1926, p. 6).
[4] *1926 Conservative Annual Conference Report,* folios 20-1. For further discussion of this debate, see p. 126 above.

course, be argued that it took a general strike to produce the sort of legislation which the conference had been urging since 1921. On the other hand, as G. M. Young has shown,[1] once the strike was broken Baldwin had been reluctant to introduce legislation which was bound to be considered harsh and retaliatory by the trade unionists it affected. There can be little doubt that pressure of the conference was a significant (and perhaps almost a decisive) factor in forcing him to do so.

It has also been shown that the National Union played an important rôle in bringing about the downfall of the Coalition (and of Austen Chamberlain personally) in 1922. These events need not be recalled in detail, but it is worth noting that as early as the conference of 1920 the proposal to return to independent Conservative action had been openly pressed. In that year a resolution had been proposed calling for " closer co-operation of all supporters of the Coalition in order to continue the work of reconstruction . . . " An amendment had been moved, however, calling for " the formation of a Conservative Government which alone can apply the financial, economic and industrial principles necessary to stabilize the position of Great Britain." In support of this amendment, the mover said: " Let the great Conservative Party which holds [a majority] in the House of Commons come out into the light of day, declare its principles, and summon together its supporters, and the response would astound its most sanguine members." A supporting speaker (who claimed " an intimate acquaintance with working class opinion in Wales ") insisted that " if the Unionist Party did not cut itself away from the Coalition, Unionist working men would drift off to the ranks of the Socialists. . . . Unless something was done to rehabilitate the Party, in three years' time there would be no Conservative working men left. Thousands of Conservative working men in South Wales expected the conference to sound either a clarion call to action or the Last Post." Lord Salisbury led a strong counter-attack, calling for unity of all parties " to fight Bolshevism and Nationalization. . . . There should be cordial co-operation between all those who were opposed to the extreme Labour people— Bolsheviks—in their midst but he did not see that was any reason why the old organization of the Unionist Party in all parts of the country should be scrapped." Eventually a compromise was reached urging unity of all parties " to combat the evils of socialism, always provided that the organizations of the Unionist Party in each constituency be kept up in full efficiency." [2]

But the pressure for the break-up of the Coalition grew steadily

[1] See p. 127 above.
[2] *1920 Conservative Annual Conference Report*, folios 15 ff.

during the next year, and it will be recalled that Younger (the Chairman of the Party Organization) warned Chamberlain as early as December 1921 of the rising tide of opposition to the Coalition " not so much in the House of Commons (he said) as in the Constituencies." When in September 1922 Younger learnt that Chamberlain intended to go to the country under Lloyd George's leadership he had added: " from my knowledge of the constituencies which I get every morning . . . I knew the constituencies were dead against this policy. I knew that if a special conference of our Party was called they would say to our Ministers that that was the view of the country." The Executive Committee of the National Union decided on 18th October (*the day before* the Carlton Club meeting) to call just such an emergency conference. The proposed conference was cancelled after the fall of Chamberlain and the Coalition on 19th October because it became clear that a general election was imminent. Sir Alexander Leith (then Chairman of the National Union) testified later that he had joined Sir George Younger in warning Chamberlain that " the majority of the Unionist Party would not agree to another Coalition Government." There can be no doubt that popular pressure through the National Union was a major factor in bringing about the downfall of the Coalition; certainly it enormously strengthened the hand of those within the parliamentary party who sought this end.

On some issues, however, pressure from the National Union (however strong and insistent) appears to have been almost completely ignored by the parliamentary leadership of the party. The most striking illustration is the very nearly complete failure of the National Union's campaign for the reform of the House of Lords. Resolutions calling for such reform appeared on the agenda of almost all of the party conferences in the inter-war years and on the agenda of a great many meetings of the Central Council and other organs of the party. These resolutions were almost invariably passed either unanimously or by an overwhelming majority. At first they were almost amiable in tone; thus early in 1921 the Executive Committee passed a resolution " to assure the Government of our hearty co-operation with it in establishing a strong representative Second Chamber based upon direct contact with the people, and endowed with adequate powers." [1] When the Central Council learnt that the Government felt it might not be able " in this Session to enact the necessary legislation for the reconstruction of the Second Chamber," the Chairman of the Council expressed " great misgivings " and a motion was passed urging " that every

[1] *1921 Conservative Annual Conference Report,* (Report of the Council), folio 10.

Constituency, Association and club, and every Provincial Division, should be asked to pass . . . resolutions (calling for the reform of the House of Lords) and send them to the leaders of our Party . . . " [1] The Executive Committee appointed a deputation " to wait on the Prime Minister and Mr. Bonar Law (then Leader of the Party in the Commons) to urge that the Bill providing for the Reform of the Second Chamber should be introduced without delay, and that the necessary facilities for its passing into law this Session should be given." [2] The Council reported later in the year that " the outcome of these representations was that the Prime Minister promised a Bill and stated it to be the intention of the Cabinet to make it the principal measure of the next Session." [3]

When, two years later (with a Conservative Government in power), no action had been taken, a member of the Central Council moved a resolution (at the 1923 annual conference) stating in part, " . . . this conference calls upon the Government to proceed *at once* with the reform of the House of Lords or the repeal of the Parliament Act." The speaker who seconded the resolution reminded the conference that in the past similar resolutions had been carried at conferences but not put into effect. " What are we? (he cried). Is our word something or is it not? Are we to pass these idle resolutions and let off steam, or are the powers that be to pay attention to our demands ? " With the passage of the Parliament Act in 1911, he claimed, " (the British) Constitution (had been) wrecked—that Constitution which they had learned to love and respect at school and which civilization throughout the world had learned to respect . . . it was on the scrapheap. . . . We are absolutely in a worse condition than Russia or any other civilized country." And he added, " I must finish on a note of reprobation. I think our leaders have betrayed us on this matter; I think our Conservative Press have betrayed us . . . " But most of all he blamed the members of the party since they elected their leaders and Members of Parliament. " Do not let us waste time in talking (he said). Let us do deeds. We love our country and we will not let the Constitution of our country be wrecked."[4] The resolution was carried unanimously; but still no action was forthcoming.

On his return to power in 1924, Baldwin pledged that it was the intention of the Government " to deal with this question in the lifetime of the present Parliament."[5] The conference of 1926

[1] Cited in *Gleanings and Memoranda*, March, 1921, p. 310.
[2] *Ibid.*, p. 311.
[3] *1921 Conservative Annual Conference Report*, (Report of the Council), folio 5.
[4] *1923 Conservative Annual Conference Report*, folios 21–22.
[5] Cited in *Gleanings and Memoranda*, September, 1926, p. 323.

"welcomed" his assurances and passed a resolution stating "that this conference . . . respectfully urges that it would be advisable that a Measure on the subject should be introduced next Session."[1] In 1927 Viscount Cave, the Lord Chancellor, indicated in the House of Lords "the general lines upon which the Government has been considering the very difficult problem of Second Chamber reform." But when a storm of criticism of the scheme broke in the Commons and in the country Baldwin made it clear that the scheme was a tentative one "offered for criticism and for ventilation." [2] Nevertheless the conference of 1927 offered the Government "its hearty congratulations". When Lord Londonderry and R. S. Hudson, M.P., tried by means of an amendment to explain to the conference that any such fundamental change in the constitution must be by agreement between the parties (which was proving very difficult to obtain) the conference decisively rejected their argument.[3]

Again, however, the Government appeared to falter in its intention to proceed with its scheme for House of Lords reform, and the conference in 1928 debated a resolution (moved by a young newcomer, Anthony Eden) "that in view of the repeated resolutions passed by the National Union on the subject of the Second Chamber, this conference trusts that the Government will, during the lifetime of the present Parliament, pass such legislation as will ensure . . . . etc." [4] But the reforms were not forthcoming either then or in the years that followed. The resolutions continued to be passed with monotonous regularity. Said a Mrs. Wood (of the Handsworth Division) in supporting the traditional resolution at the conference of 1933, " . . . all delegates (are) sick and tired of seeing the resolution on their agendas year after year without anything being done."

Their impatience is reflected in the phrases of mounting exasperation which appear in subsequent resolutions. Thus in 1934: "That this conference calls on the Government *at once* to submit to Parliament such proposals for the reform of the House of Lords . . . as may rescue the constitution from its present dangerous position before a dissolution takes place." [6] And in 1936 the mover of the second chamber resolution (Lord Lloyd) said: "Twelve Conservative conferences (have) passed resolutions in favour of House of Lords reform. It was a matter for regret that their leaders had so

---

[1] *1926 Conservative Annual Conference Report,* folio 22.
[2] Cited in *Gleanings and Memoranda,* August, 1927, p. 75.
[3] *1927 Conservative Annual Conference Report,* folios 20-5.
[4] *1928 Conservative Annual Conference Report,* folio 20.
[5] *1933 Conservative Annual Conference Report,* folio 24.
[6] *1934 Conservative Annual Conference Report,* folio 22. [Italics mine.]

far found it impossible to give effect to the party's repeatedly declared wishes. . . . What then could they do about this persistent
neglect of a question so vital to the whole future of Parliamentary
Government in this country in face of the party's declared desires
and of so many pledges? " [1]

The answer was, of course, " precisely nothing ". The seconder of
the resolution claimed: " If they demanded that the Government
must take this matter in hand they would have to do so." But this,
again, was nonsense. The demand for House of Lords reform has
echoed again through several of the post-1945 conferences but it
has produced no significant result. This story of endless frustration
provides conclusive proof that the Conservative organization outside Parliament cannot force its party to take action *inside* Parliament which the Leader and his colleagues consider to be inappropriate or impolitic.

During the very years of their most exasperating failure in this
matter of second chamber reform, the National Union proved again
and again that it insists on its right to function as a goad and stimulant to the party in Parliament. The report of the annual conference for the year 1925 shows that the National Union (at its most
forthright) is anything but a passive apologist for its own Government. An illustration has already been given (p. 123 above) of the
temper of the conference debates in that year. The trouble began
early in the conference when the chairman moved the adoption of
the annual report of the Central Council. It contained a somewhat
defensive passage :

> " A review of the work of the first Session of a Government
> which is supported by a loyal majority, and has every expectation
> of a normal Parliamentary life must be an interim report.
> "Intact and unassailable, such a Government can plan for
> several years ahead. Free from the constant fear of defeat by
> temporary hostile combinations in Parliament, it is not obliged to
> indulge in superficially brilliant policy in order to obtain support.
> It is not continuously forced into ignominious surrenders, against
> its better judgment, under pressure from nominal adherents." [2]

[1] *1936 Conservative Annual Conference Report,* folio 33. His seconder,
an M.P., maintained that the situation was even more intolerable than the
mover had suggested. " The resolution had been passed 15 times, and only
twice since the war had the conference not dealt with matters of this kind. . . .
Mr. Baldwin (the speaker said) had called attention again and again to this
danger and his words were not those of a panic-monger; he was one of the
slowest-acting men in existence. The Conference should demand from their
leaders that this matter should be dealt with at once." The resolution was
carried by an overwhelming majority.

[2] *1925 Conservative Annual Conference Report,* folio 5.

A bitter controversy ensued when a delegate moved an amendment to refer the report back for further consideration. He said it was with extreme regret that he felt compelled to bring forward his motion and that his object was " not to produce any disruption of the party . . . (but) to bring before the Government how grave and serious was the discontent throughout the country (caused) by their inaction. (Cries of ' No! ')." Unemployment, he warned, was increasing by leaps and bounds and " it (was) a terrible state of things . . . surely after ten months the Government might have found some palliative." He added, " it is well to discuss these matters among ourselves rather than have them thrashed out in the public Press. We want to assist the Government not to hinder it . . . (but they must) give us some hope that we are going to better our condition instead of allowing us to drift worse and worse (sic). . . . If the Government doesn't do that the Government will fall." After venting his feelings the mover offered to withdraw his amendment but it was seconded from the body of the hall and put to the conference. The motion was overwhelmingly rejected,[1] but the deep undercurrent of uneasiness was reflected in subsequent debates at the same conference.

One resolution called on the Government in somewhat imperious tones to reduce the estimates in the next budget. And another (passed unanimously) said " that this conference while appreciating as an ideal the Prime Minister's appeal for peace in industry once more demands the amendment of the Trade Union Act of 1913, realizing that peace cannot be attained so long as the workers of this country have not got complete freedom of political thought." [2] And it will be remembered that the speaker who seconded the resolution calling for urgent action to meet the agricultural problems of the country ended his peroration with the sentence: " Our loyalty is the same as ever, but it has got to be ' On Stanley, On '."

In many respects that sentence summarizes the attitude of each of the Conservative conferences during the life of the Baldwin Government of 1924-9. Again and again the conference recorded its exasperation with the Government. Thus a resolution at the 1928 conference read: " This conference reaffirms the unanimous resolutions of the last three conferences calling for the widest possible extension of the safeguarding of industries consistent with the Prime Minister's election pledge; *regrets the slow progress made;* and, in view of the grave and continued unemployment over large areas of the country, urges that the earliest possible steps should be taken to safeguard additional industries." The mover

[1] *1925 Conservative Annual Conference Report*, folios 5-6.
[2] *Ibid.,* folio 37.

" repudiated the idea that his resolution was hostile to the Government. Such an idea was grotesque." But it is significant that when an amendment was moved to delete the phrase " regrets the slow progress made " only about 200 supported it; the amendment was thus lost and the full resolution was carried.[1]

Despite the earnest efforts of the conference during the years 1925-9 to goad the Baldwin Government into taking the sort of action the National Union wanted, very little was achieved; apart from the Trades Disputes Act hardly any of the Government's legislation can be traced to the inspiration of the National Union. It is not surprising that when the party went into opposition in 1929, a number of resolutions appeared on the conference agenda in this vein: " That this conference, whilst appreciating the efforts of our Party Leaders during the very difficult period 1924-9, would welcome an assurance from them that in future the opinions of the Party will be sought to a greater extent than in the past."[2] No such assurances were given, but this did not dampen the spirits of the National Union. In the years immediately after the crisis of 1931 the conference of the National Union was more docile. On some issues, however, it was both forthright and insistent in pressing its views on Baldwin and the party in Parliament. The principal preoccupation of the conference (apart from House of Lords reform) was the problem of defence. Foreign policy was rarely debated, despite the fact that in the years immediately before the Second World War the party was committed to the highly controversial policy of appeasement from which some prominent Conservatives dissented. But in the matter of defence the conference spoke with a clear and consistent voice. The 1933 conference unanimously passed a resolution (" amid scenes of great enthusiasm ") stating " that this conference desires to record its grave anxiety in regard to the inadequacy of the provisions made for Imperial defence." In support of the resolution Winston Churchill said " the moment (has) come when it (is) indispensable for the conference to give a strong indication to the Government that a change must now be made, and we must not continue longer upon the course on which we alone are getting weaker, while every other nation is growing stronger. . . . One would have expected (he said) that one of the three Ministers of the Fighting Service would have come here to reassure (us). . . . " The fact that not one of them was there proved to Mr. Churchill's

---

[1] *1928 Conservative Annual Conference Report*, folios 30–31. [Italics mine.]
[2] *1929 Conservative Annual Conference Report*, folio 18. This particular resolution was not reached but the issues it raised were debated in the discussion on party re-organization at the same conference (pp. 13 ff).

mind that they shared the conference's misgivings and he believed that they would "welcome a feeling that the party as a whole wished to see the defences put into better order in the dangerous times of to-day."[1]

In the following year (1934) the conference underlined its anxiety by passing a resolution *identical in wording* to that of the previous year. On this occasion Neville Chamberlain, then Chancellor of the Exchequer, took part in the debate and conceded that "it had been stated with truth that Imperial defence had reached a dangerously low level." But, he added, "that is not due to the action of the present Government. It is due to the deliberate policy of successive Governments for the last eight and a half years. That includes the last Conservative Government when the Chancellor of the Exchequer was Mr. Churchill." Chamberlain then invited the mover of the resolution to add to his resolution the following words which he said had been uttered by Churchill: "and assures the Chancellor of the Exchequer that heavy as are its burdens it prefers the safety and security of our native land above all other benefits." By accepting this amendment, Chamberlain added, the mover could "pay a compliment to his absent colleague, Mr. Churchill." The amendment was accepted and the motion carried "with only two or three dissentients."[2] In 1935 Churchill secured the passage of a resolution which stated in part that it was "the duty of His Majesty's Government forthwith to repair the serious deficiencies in the defence forces of the Crown. . . . (and that) this conference pledges itself to accept and support any financial measures which may be necessary for the national safety, no matter how great the sacrifices may be." For the Government, Neville Chamberlain welcomed the resolution, saying, "it is not necessary, I can assure you, to remind the Government of their duty to the nation in this matter of defence."[3] At the 1937 conference Churchill intervened to say "our slowness in beginning to rearm hampered us now (but) the National Union of Conservative Associations was certainly not to blame. The resolutions were upon record . . . four or five years ago the alarm was sounded. But all that was in the past. At present the Government was making a great effort for rearmament."[4] In retrospect, not everyone would concur with Churchill's apparent

---

[1] *1933 Conservative Annual Conference Report*, folio 24.

[2] *1934 Conservative Annual Conference Report*, folios 24–26.

[3] *1935 Conservative Annual Conference Report*, folio 26.

[4] *1937 Conservative Annual Conference Report*, folio 31. Churchill added (somewhat surprisingly) that he "urged support for the foreign policy of the Government which commanded the trust, comprehension and comradeship of peace-loving and law-respecting nations in all parts of the world."

approval of the National Government's rearmament effort in 1937; but there can be little doubt about the fairness of his claim regarding the record of the National Union. In the matter of defence successive conferences spoke with a clear voice in urging upon their Government a substantial increase in its armament programme. There is ample room for debate as to whether the Government responded adequately to the challenge of the conference; but it is evident that on this issue the National Union endeavoured, with at least some success, to play the part of goad and stimulant to the party in Parliament.

In summarizing the influence of the National Union on the affairs of the Conservative Party, one must emphasize again that the National Union does not make policy, and, of course, that it does not in any sense direct the work of the party in Parliament. Nor does the National Union exert executive control over the working of the party machine on the national level, which is the responsibility of the Central Office. But this is not to say that the National Union is totally devoid of influence in the affairs of the party. Lord Woolton has said: " The strength of any Government in the last resort is the knowledge of the strength it commands in the country. Those undertaking the strain of Government need the sense of a powerful and dominant membership behind them."[1] As Lord Woolton here implies, the success of a party in Parliament is dependent, to a considerable degree, on the support it receives from its mass organization outside Parliament.

The party in Parliament must have the support of what Winston Churchill has described as a band of " ardent partisans "[2]; and they inevitably must be organized into a national association. Because they are so "ardent". the views of these partisans often tend to be more extremist than the views of the leaders of the party or of the many millions of their supporters in the country who do not belong to the party. The ardent partisans are likely to be impatient with the compromises which both Parliament and the two-party system make inevitable. On very rare occasions (as has been shown above), the ardent partisans may succeed in exerting a decisive influence on the actions or policies of their leaders. But in ordinary circumstances the attempts of the mass organization to influence or control the actions of the party in Parliament constitute no more than *one* of the pressures (and usually not the most important) which the party leaders must take into account. The wise Conservative

---

[1] Lord Woolton, speaking at Rottingdean, Sussex, 22nd August, 1953, *Conservative Central Office Press Release 4278*. This observation applies with very nearly equal force, of course, when the party is in opposition.

[2] See p. 257 below.

Leader has done all in his power to carry the National Union with him and at all times he takes its views into account. When powerful colleagues within the parliamentary party disagree with the Leader's policies, they may on occasion succeed in forcing him to allow the National Union to become a forum in which some great issue (such as the future of Ireland or India) is fought out. But this has happened rarely in the history of the National Union, and on each occasion on which it has happened the Leader of the Party has succeeded in carrying the day. We are therefore left to speculate as to what would have happened to a Leader who had succeeded in defeating his opponents in the party in Parliament, but had subsequently been defeated on the same issue at the Central Council or the annual conference of the National Union[1]. These speculations apart, however, the normal rôle of the National Union is clear: though it may sometimes endeavour to rise above its station or, in a mood of forgetfulness, may even attempt to instruct its betters, the National Union remains what it has always been: a " handmaid " to the party in Parliament.

IV

THE REGIONAL ORGANIZATION OF THE CONSERVATIVE PARTY

[This study is concerned primarily with the distribution of power in the Conservative and Labour Parties at the *national* level ; the regional and local organizations of the parties are therefore dealt with more briefly. The intention is merely to provide an outline of the party organization at these levels and a brief comment on its rôle within the national party organization.]

IN 1886, nineteen years after the formation of the National Union, it was decided to set up a system of regional organization. "Provincial Unions " (as they were then called) were established and certain of the functions of the Central Council were delegated to them. The structure of these Provincial Unions was subsequently altered in the course of the re-organizations which have taken place periodically in the history of the National Union. The broad outlines of the present-day provincial organization of the party took shape as the result of the re-organization which followed the defeat of 1929. In that year, it will be recalled, a sub-committee of the Central Council was appointed to inquire into " the reasons for the defeat of the Party at the General Election . . . to examine the rules

---

[1] For Gaitskell's experience as a Labour Leader finding himself in such circumstances, see pp. 608 ff. below.

and organization of the National Union, to inquire into the relationship between the National Union, the Central Office and the Leader
of the Party, and to report with recommendations for alteration or
improvement." [1] This sub-committee in the course of its work interviewed the chairmen of the Provincial Divisions (as they were then
called) in an attempt, as the chairman of the sub-committee put it,
to devise means whereby " the constituencies could work together
a little better than they had in the past on questions of common
political interest, without attempting to destroy their individual
personalities."   The sub-committee submitted its report to the
Central Council on 4th March, 1930. [2] Its recommendations were
accepted (after amendment) by the Central Council and subsequently by a special one-day conference of the National Union held
in London on 1st July, 1930. In so far as it affected the regional
structure of the party, the 1930 re-organization was based on the
sub-committee's view that " while preserving full individuality to
the constituency as a unit, it (is) to the greater activity of the Provincial Areas that (we) must look in future for a revival of local
interest and a more extended means of spreading our political principles." [3] Subsequently there have been a number of minor changes
in the structure of the Provincial Areas but the pattern has not been
basically altered since it was established in 1930.

England and Wales are divided into 12 areas and each Provincial
Area organization consists of a voluntary federation of constituencies. [4] These Provincial Area organizations have both advisory
and executive responsibilities. Under the former head they are expected " to express the collective views of the Party in the Area ";
their executive responsibilities require that they " utilize the financial and other resources of the Area in the best interests of the Con-

[1] *1929 Conservative Annual Conference Report*, folio 3.
[2] *The Times*, 5th March, 1930.
[3] *The Party Organization*, 1961, p. 4.
[4] The following is a list of the Provincial Areas with an indication of
the number of constituencies in each: LONDON (City of London and London
Boroughs) 43; NORTHERN (Cumberland, Durham, Northumberland and
Middlesbrough) 34 ; NORTH WESTERN (Lancashire, Cheshire, Westmorland)
80 ; YORKSHIRE (excluding Middlesbrough) 56 ; EAST MIDLANDS (Derbyshire,
Leicestershire, Lincolnshire and Rutland, Nottinghamshire, Northamptonshire) 42; WEST MIDLANDS (Gloucestershire excluding Bristol, Herefordshire, Shropshire Staffordshire, Warwickshire, Worcestershire) 58;
EASTERN (Bedfordshire, Cambridgeshire, Hertfordshire, Huntingdon-
shire, Norfolk, Suffolk) 28; HOME COUNTIES NORTH (Essex and
Middlesex) 52; HOME COUNTIES SOUTH-EAST (Kent, Surrey and Sussex)
48; WESSEX (Berkshire, Buckinghamshire, Dorsetshire, Hampshire, Isle
of Wight, Oxfordshire, Wiltshire) 37; WESTERN (Cornwall, Devonshire,
Somersetshire, Bristol) 28; WALES AND MONMOUTHSHIRE 36. *Rules and
Standing Orders of the National Union*, p. 17.

stituencies," and that they should " organize on an area level such activities as will assist the constituencies to improve their organization." [1] It is evident that the functions of the area organizations are closely parallel to those of the central organs of the National Union; they are intended to serve as a sounding board of Conservative opinion and a source of advice and information for the party leaders; in addition they co-ordinate and administer their own affairs within their own area.

This parallel between the central and regional organs of the National Union is even more striking when one examines the structure of the area organization and its relationship to the professional or Central Office personnel of the party. The principal voluntary officials and organs of the Area include the chairman, the Area Council, the Area Executive Committee and a range of advisory committees similar to the national advisory committees. The Central Office is represented in each area by an area office, which is under its direct control. The senior official of the area office, the Central Office Agent, serves as honorary secretary to the Area Council, thus providing an exact parallel to the situation at the national level where the General Director of the Central Office serves as honorary secretary to the National Union. The Maxwell Fyfe Committee noted that " theoretically any member (of the Conservative Party) in the Area can hold the office of Honorary Secretary," and added, " the question therefore at once arises: Is the Central Office Agent under the orders of Central Office or of the Area Chairman?" The Report set all such doubts at rest with the emphatic statement, " the Central Office Agent is directly under the orders of the General Director "; but the Report adds, perhaps somewhat optimistically, " in practice the Area Chairman and the Central Office Agent both work together harmoniously in the pursuance of a common task." The Maxwell Fyfe Committee had discovered some dissatisfaction with current arrangements; its Report observes, " it has been suggested that Area Agents should be appointed by the Area from a panel approved by the Executive Committee of the National Union. We do not (says the Report) concur with this suggestion, but the Area Chairman should always be consulted before the appointment of any new Area Agent." [2]

The area chairman, the Maxwell Fyfe Committee further observed, should be " a man of outstanding energy, distinction and tact." [3] When one examines the list of his duties [4] it becomes clear

[1] *Maxwell Fyfe Report*, p. 42.
[2] *Ibid.*, pp. 42-3.
[3] *Ibid.*, p. 44.
[4] *The Party Organization*, 1961, pp. 19–20.

that this is no exaggeration. He is, of course, both the leader of the voluntary federation of constituencies in his area and its spokesman in the councils of the party. He presides at meetings of the provincial area council and executive committee and "endeavours to ensure that their conclusions are representative of the views of the Party as a whole throughout the Area." He is further charged with the responsibility of "interpreting" the views of his area to the Executive Committee of the National Union and to the Chairman of the Party Organization. He is expected to be personally acquainted with as many as possible of the constituency officers and agents within the area and to help with arbitration of difficulties which may arise. He is responsible for ensuring that the national campaigns of the party (for example, membership drives) are fulfilled within his area, and he must try to ensure that the recommendations of the party headquarters in respect of organization are put into effect in the constituencies. He advises the Standing Advisory Committee on Parliamentary Candidates "when requested in particularly difficult cases," and, in consultation with the area honorary treasurer, he advises the Central Board of Finance on the collection and administration of party funds within the area and "keeps the treasurers of the Party in touch with the Area's financial needs."

The Maxwell Fyfe Report considered (not surprisingly) that it is a serious problem " to find to-day at least twelve such men or women—outstanding personalities who are able and willing to devote to the activities of the office of Area Chairman a large portion of their time."[1] But the Report concluded that " the advantages which *would* follow the appointment of individuals of this type would amply repay the great effort which may be necessary to find them." The use of the conditional in this Report is a tacit admission that the party has by no means always succeeded in obtaining men or women of the calibre required. This conclusion is borne out by first-hand observation of the work of the party in the areas. The job of Area Chairman if undertaken conscientiously is extremely onerous and the rewards (all of them non-material) are slight. It would take a considerable stretch of the imagination for an Area Chairman to convince himself that he had any significant influence on either the policy or tactics of the Conservative Party. He has only a very limited share of the very limited influence of the National Union itself. However, for those of lesser social or political eminence among the Area Chairmen there is this compensation: they have an opportunity to see with their own eyes and even to rub shoulders with the great ones of their party when the latter make their appearances at the meetings of the national organs of

[1] *Maxwell Fyfe Report*, p. 45.

the National Union. And this (combined with the satisfaction of serving the party's cause) is no doubt sufficient reward for many of the conscientious party stalwarts who devote so much of their spare time to the exacting duties of Area Chairman.[1] On the other hand some of the chairmen have already had long records of public or political service in other capacities and there is reason to believe that they have collected this particular office as merely one of a long list of honorary appointments which help to enhance their social prestige. Those area chairmen who accept the appointment in this spirit rarely invest in the work the time or energy which the office requires. The other officers (who like the chairman are elected annually by the Council of the provincial area) include the president (an honorific post), the vice-chairmen, the honorary treasurer and the honorary secretary.

The provincial area council includes in its membership in addition to the area officers, representation of every constituency and of every unit of the party organization within the area. Like every other organ of the National Union the area council has certain advisory responsibilities which require that it should sift, debate and forward to the National Union resolutions with respect to policy which may be originated either in the constituencies or in the council itself.[2] Its executive responsibilities include the organization of propaganda and educational activities on the area level, and in addition the council disposes of certain funds provided for the assistance of needy constituency associations within the area.[3]

[1] The 12 area chairmen for 1953-4, for example, included one woman and 11 men. Their assorted distinctions include the following : three were Members of Parliament; two were Knights; five were Justices of the Peace; four were Deputy Lieutenants of their counties; three had military ranks (retired) of Lt.-Col. or better, and five had civilian or military decorations. A review of the lists of those who have held office since 1945 shows that on the average they have been re-elected to the post for three consecutive years.

[2] The Central Council Report for 1934 noted " that numerous resolutions on various matters of Policy received from Provincial Areas and Chief Constituency and Central Associations had been passed to the Leader of the Party after having received the consideration of the (Executive) Committee. Reference was made to the fact that the Committee gave regular and careful attention to all Resolutions submitted for its consideration; that they were looked upon as of additional importance if they had first received endorsement by the Executive Committee or Council of a Provincial Area, and that it was of material help if, when considering these Resolutions, the Committee knew the numbers present at Meetings and voting upon them." *1934 Conservative Annual Conference Report* (Report of the Council), folio 6.

[3] Official party literature notes " during recent years there has been a tendency to devolve more and more financial responsibility upon the Areas.

The area councils normally meet from two to four times per year, and in the interim the administrative work of the area organization is supervised by the Area Executive Committee.[1] The executive committee also sets up a series of advisory committees which exactly parallel (in the subjects with which they are concerned) the national advisory committees of the National Union which were discussed above. The work of the area advisory committees may be illustrated by reference to the work of the area women's advisory committee. Its function is to advise the Area Executive Committee on all questions affecting the organization of the women supporters of the party in the area and on all subjects in which women are particularly interested. The area women's advisory committee often sponsors special educational courses and conferences for women; it may undertake research projects into women's problems and make recommendations to the Area Executive Committee based on its findings.

Any examination of the area activity of the party reveals a wide disparity in efficiency between one area and another. The Maxwell Fyfe Committee attributed this in part to a lack of a standard by which efficiency could be judged, and also to the fact that " on matters relating to organization there (was) little systematic interchange of information between one area and another." To meet this situation the committee suggested (among other recommendations) that there should be quarterly meetings between the Chairman of the Party Organization and the 12 area chairmen,[2] and these meetings now take place. The work of the Area Office is considered in Chapter V, which deals with the professional organization of the party.

In 1932, area reports were included for the first time in the Central Council reports to the annual conference[3]; a reading of the reports subsequently presented and a fairly extensive investigation of the area activities shows that the life of the party on the area level has been on the whole singularly unspectacular. The areas have continued to fulfil their executive responsibilities with varying degrees of efficiency and enthusiasm and they have served

The Central Office no longer makes grants direct to Constituencies. All Areas have funds at their disposal and a majority of them have linked their finances with those of the Centre under budgetary arrangements which guarantee that the agreed financial requirements of the Area shall be forthcoming." *The Party Organization* (1950), p. 20.

[1] For composition, see *The Rules and Standing Orders of the National Union* (1951), p. 4, and for a list of some duties of the executive committee, see *The Party Organization*, 1961, p. 21.

[2] *Maxwell Fyfe Report*, p. 45.

[3] *1932 Conservative Annual Conference Report*, folios 7-13.

as a useful channel through which party opinion has percolated to the top. But Ostrogorski's comment of more than half a century ago (written only ten years after the formation of the provincial unions) remains to a large extent valid. They had not succeeded, he wrote, in developing " an autonomous life ". He added that the headquarters of the party " were not anxious for them to take a high flight " and he described what he called the " clever contrivance (used by the Central Office) to get them into its toils."

> " Over this provincial organization (the Central Office) has placed agencies of its own, the territorial jurisdiction of which exactly coincides with that of the Provincial Unions. By offering them the gratuitous use of their offices and staff, the agencies soon managed to get a footing in the (Provincial) Unions, and they rapidly became the mainspring of the Conservative organization down to the electoral Divisions. Without possessing any formal power in them, the provincial agent of the Central Office nevertheless controls all the local Associations in the Union, thanks to the fact that he represents the Central Office not only with its prestige as organ of the great leaders, but also with its resources of which the Associations so often stand in need—speakers for the meetings, political literature, and last, but not least, money ; an Association which does not try to conciliate the agent of the Central Office would not obtain any assistance. To this material power it adds the seduction of civility to the secretaries of the local Associations. Thus, (concludes Ostrogorski, in sardonic mood) without even resorting to much wire-pulling, the Central Office ensures the organization of the party a complete unity of management which makes all the threads converge in the London office and utilizes the popular Associations for its own ends, so as to get hold of the voters all the more easily."[1]

A. L. Lowell, writing ten years later, took a very similar view; he too decided that the divisional unions had not developed " any vigorous life of their own. . . . (they) were designed as a safeguard against popular caprice and personal ambition."[2] It would be unfair to apply Ostrogorski's or Lowell's comments without modification to the present relationship between the Central Office representative and the provincial organizations. There is no reason to suspect a sinister conspiracy to frustrate the popular will in the provincial areas; and yet the relationship has not changed significantly since Ostrogorski wrote. The Area Office, representing the Central Office, is in effective control of the work of the provincial area and

---

[1] Ostrogorski, M., *Democracy and the Organization of Political Parties*, Vol. I, pp. 526-7.

[2] Lowell, A. L., *The Government of England*, Vol. I, p. 559.

is almost invariably successful in canalizing the energies of the area into channels which are acceptable to the Central Office.

In the history of the National Union there is only one important example of the outbreak of militant area activity which had an important bearing on the life of the party. This was the famous " Lancashire Plot "[1] which followed as a result of the defeat of the party in the election of 1923. This incident has been mentioned in Chapter III as one illustration of the many troubles Baldwin had with his followers, but it is worth re-examination in rather more detail since it provides the most interesting illustration of the way in which the regional organization of the party could spring into life if the national leaders were to commit themselves to a policy which in the view of the regional party workers might have a severely adverse effect on their interests.

After the defeat of the party in the 1923 election, Alderman Salvidge recorded in his diary: " The election results were appalling everywhere but nowhere worse than in Lancashire. . . . Interviewed by London papers a few days after the disaster, I said that those who were responsible for this rushed election might just as well have rolled tons of dynamite into Liverpool to uproot the Conservative Party. . . . " Lord Derby shared Alderman Salvidge's sense of outrage: " I have never known (Lord Derby) so infuriated as he was when we met to discuss the returns (wrote Salvidge). He said, ' It is an overwhelming disaster, and you and I know whom we have to thank for it. It maddens me to think that the Prime Minister should within six months of taking office bring us to this ' . . . "[2]

Lord Derby and Salvidge proceeded to mobilize and register the resentment of their local associations against Baldwin's handling of the election of 1923. A special meeting of the Council of the Lancashire and Cheshire Division of the National Union was called at Manchester on 9th February " to discuss the political situation." The attendance, which at such gatherings usually numbered two or three hundred, was on this occasion nearly a thousand. Colonel Jackson (the Chairman of the Party Organization) and Admiral Hall (the Principal Agent) came up from London to put the case for the Central Office. The chair was taken by Lord Derby who, according to Alderman Salvidge, was " eager for Lancashire to make its voice heard but anxious that the party managers should not be unduly embarrassed." To the latter end the Press was ex-

---

[1] See Chapters 18 (" The Lancashire Plot ") and 19 (" The Great Recovery ") of Salvidge, S., *Salvidge of Liverpool*, also *Gleanings and Memoranda*, March, 1924, pp. 242 ff.; and Churchill, R., *Lord Derby*, Ch. XXIV.

[2] Cited in Salvidge, S., *Salvidge of Liverpool*, p. 255.

cluded. But after the meeting Lord Derby made an official statement in which he described the proceedings.[1] Colonel Buckley, a Conservative Free Trader, had moved a resolution which would have placed on record " the dissatisfaction (of the meeting) with the policy of the Conservative Party in forcing an election on the issue of Protection," and urging that " Protection should be definitely abandoned as a plank in the policy of the party." This resolution was seconded by one M.P. and supported by another. Then Alderman Salvidge moved an amendment:

> " That this meeting . . . believing that the verdict of the country at the recent election was against a change in the fiscal system, respectfully represents to the leaders of the party that it is undesirable that Protection should be included in the programme of the Conservative policy at this juncture. Further, it respectfully protests against the methods adopted previous to the recent General Election when an appeal was made to the electors on the issue of Protection without affording the party organizations throughout the country an opportunity of expressing their opinions thereon ; and urges that, with a view to securing in the future greater harmony and better to obtain the representative opinion of the party, a satisfactory method of *liaison* be established between the leaders of the party, the Central Office, and the local organizations."

After several speeches on this amendment the original motion was withdrawn and Alderman Salvidge's amendment became the substantive motion. An attempt was then made to soften the Salvidge motion when two M.P.'s proposed the following amendment:

> " That this . . . meeting . . . considers it undesirable in the interests of the country and of the party to abandon any portion of the Unionist programme, but is of opinion that the order of precedence of the items forming the programme, and the time and method of presenting the same for the approval of the electorate, should be left to the leaders of the party to determine after full inquiry and as circumstances may require."

After some debate this amendment was defeated " by a large majority." Col. Jackson intervened for the Central Office and apparently tried to " head the delegates off from expressing a definite opinion on policy." [2] But his advice was ignored ; Salvidge's

---

[1] The excerpts from the report of the meeting which follow are taken from a verbatim account of Lord Derby's statement in *Gleanings and Memoranda*, March, 1924, pp. 242-3.

[2] Salvidge, S., *Salvidge of Liverpool*, p. 266.

motion was carried and, according to Lord Derby's statement, " by an overwhelming majority."

The next day in an interview in the *Morning Post*, Lord Derby added:

> " I wish to emphasize the fact that before the Salvidge resolu-
> tion was put to the meeting everybody understood, indeed, it was
> so stated, that it should on no account be looked upon as a vote
> of censure on the leaders of the party." He particularly desired it to
> be understood that " there was no thought of disloyalty to the Head
> Office . . . and that the main thought pervading the meeting was to
> restore the feeling of mutual confidence and to arrive at the best
> methods of giving expression to the principles for which they stood
> and from which they had never wavered."[1]

Clearly the Lancashire rebels were no more willing to challenge the authority of the Leader or of the Central Office than were any of the other dissidents. Two days after the Lancashire meeting (11th February), it will be remembered, Baldwin won a vote of confidence from a meeting of Conservative peers, M.P.s and defeated candidates, and subsequently (12th February) from a meeting of the Central Council. But at both meetings he made it clear that he would not favour submitting the proposal for a general tariff to the electorate again until there was clear evidence that public opinion was disposed to reconsider its judgment. No doubt the Lancashire revolt helped to convince Baldwin of the necessity of making this statement. There is little reason to doubt that if the national leadership of the Conservative Party were again to adopt policies which threatened to betray the interests of a particular region of the country the provincial area concerned would not hesitate to make its voice heard.[2]

The Regional Councils of the Labour Party might well serve a similar function in like circumstances. But as is shown below in Chapter VIII, the regional organs of the Labour Party are precluded from discussing national and international issues unless they have a particular bearing on the region concerned. The other functions of the Labour area organization are almost identical with those of the Conservatives; both are primarily concerned with advancing the fortunes of the party in their area. Neither regional organization is of any real importance to an analysis of the distribu-

---

[1] The *Morning Post*, 11th February, 1924.

[2] It should be kept in mind that such developments are likely to be rare in a country so homogeneous as this. Tariff policy apart, there are comparatively few issues on which one can identify a clear-cut regional interest or viewpoint.

tion of power within the party concerned. It must be recognized, however, that the Conservative provincial areas have a certain scope for action which is denied to their Labour counterpart; they can and do discuss any issue about which they are concerned and they can submit resolutions for the consideration of the annual conference of the National Union. It is also important to recall that the Executive Committee of the National Union includes a strong representation from the provincial area organization of the party. Each area is represented on the Executive by its chairman, treasurer, chairman of the Women's Advisory Committee, one Young Conservative from the area, one trade unionist and (depending on the number of constituencies in the area) one or more additional representatives. There are, in contrast, very few national organs of the Labour Party which are composed of representatives from the regions. Limited though the influence of the Conservative provincial areas may be, it is probable that the work of the Conservative Party at this level has greater meaning for members of the party than is the case with Labour.

V

THE CONSERVATIVE CONSTITUENCY ASSOCIATIONS; THE SELECTION OF CANDIDATES

THE constituency association is the basic unit in the structure of the Conservative Party outside Parliament. Since the party has no affiliated organizations (equivalent to the trade unions and socialist societies, in the case of the Labour Party) all of its approximately 2,250,000 members in England and Wales belong to the party by virtue of their membership in one or other of the constituency Conservative Associations.[1] The whole vast pyramid of the National Union is built upwards from the constituency associations, and the representatives named by the associations constitute by far the largest element in the provincial Area Councils, in the Central Council, and in the annual conference of the party.

Great emphasis is placed in Conservative literature on the fact that the constituency associations have complete autonomy in the

---

[1] There is a fairly wide variation in the official titles of the local units of the Conservative Party. In England and Wales they are mostly known as "Conservative and Unionist Associations," although some call themselves merely "Conservative Associations." In Scotland they call themselves "Unionist Associations" and in Northern Ireland "Ulster Unionist Associations." For additional material on constituency associations see Potter, A. M., "The English Conservative Constituency Association," *The Western Political Quarterly*, Vol. IX, No. 2, June 1956 and Blondel, J., "The Conservative Association and the Labour Party in Reading," *Political Studies*, Vol. VI, No. 2, June 1958, pp. 101 ff.

management of their own affairs. They elect their own officers, select and appoint their own agents, adopt their own candidates for parliamentary and local government elections, raise and administer their own funds, undertake their own programme of publicity and propaganda and conduct the election campaign in the constituency on behalf of the party. The weaker constituencies receive assistance either from the area or from the central organizations of the party, but even the weakest of constituencies is intensely jealous of its own right to full independence. The National Union does of course exert an ultimate disciplinary control over all constituency associations. The associations are admitted to membership of the National Union in the first instance subject to the approval of the Executive Committee. The latter reserves the right to withdraw that approval, an action which is of course equivalent to expulsion from the National Union.[1] But local associations have rarely been expelled and then usually only for some flagrant violation of party principles or practice. It is therefore fair to acknowledge that the right of the Executive Committee of the National Union to expel associations in no sense modifies the claim of the party that its constituency associations are autonomous bodies.

Neither, on the other hand, should the claim to autonomy be taken to imply that the constituency associations are in effective control of the affairs of the Conservative Party. They do of course administer their own affairs; but they do not control in any direct sense the day-to-day activities of their Members of Parliament and they play a very minor rôle in influencing the formulation of Conservative policy. It will be recalled that the National Union itself merely " conveys " its views on policy matters to the Leader for his consideration and in theory he has every right to ignore its views. Representatives of the constituencies do of course play the major rôle in the formulation of the views of the National Union at the meetings of the Central Council and the annual conference; but these constituency representatives are not for the most part man-

---

[1] *Rules and Standing Orders of the National Union* (1951), p. 1. An association which has been expelled is at liberty, of course, to continue in existence and to run candidates for office, but in the present state of British party politics expulsion from either great party consigns a rebel association effectively to oblivion. At Newcastle-upon-Tyne North the constituency association split in two as a result of an internal feud and in the 1951 election rival candidates were nominated, each claiming to be the true party standard bearer. It is significant that the nominee who secured the official endorsement of the party leaders won the election and the " Independent Conservative " barely saved his deposit. See Butler, D. E., *The British General Election of 1951*, pp. 93-4.

dated by their local associations. The representatives are selected by their associations and thereafter they are free to vote as they see fit at the meetings of the central organs of the National Union. Official party literature, as was noted above, treats this as a great virtue. (" The Conservative Party is opposed to the system of delegates, tied beforehand to vote this way or that. All members and representatives of the Conservative Party are free to speak and vote according to their consciences and each person's vote counts one and only one.") But the arrangement also has the effect of reducing almost to zero the influence of the average member of a local association on the ultimate determination of party policy. He plays some part in the selection of the representatives who will attend meetings of the provincial area councils, the Central Council and the annual conference, but those representatives thereafter may speak and vote as they see fit. And in any case their deliberations and decisions with respect to policy have no binding authority on the leadership of the party. Yet it would be wrong to ignore the fact that the Leader and his colleagues in Parliament must win at least the acquiescence and, if at all possible, the willing support of the constituency associations. When the associations are in open revolt against their leaders on a major matter of policy, as they were for example over the issue of the Coalition in 1922, they can help (if their views are reflected in any important way within the parliamentary party) to unseat the Leader and his colleagues. The rôle of the local associations in helping to bring about the downfall of Austen Chamberlain in 1922 is a reminder that they are by no means so impotent as a purely formal reading of the party constitution might suggest.

There is a fairly wide variation in the structure of constituency associations but most of them conform fairly closely to the Model Rules which associations are encouraged by the Central Office to adopt.[1] These model rules contain (p. 3) a useful summary of the objects of a constituency association:

(a) To provide an efficient organization of the Conservative and Unionist Party in the Constituency.
(b) To spread the knowledge of Conservative and Unionist principles and policy and generally to promote the interests of the Party in the Constituency.
(c) To secure the return of a Conservative and Unionist Member of Parliament for the Constituency.
(d) To secure the return at Local Government Elections of such Councillors as are chosen for support by the Party.

[1] Conservative and Unionist Central Office Organization Series, No. 3, *Model Rules* (1949).

(e) To watch the revision of the Constituency Register of Electors in the interests of the Party.

(f) To keep in touch with the Conservative and Unionist Associations in neighbouring constituencies, and to afford mutual assistance whenever possible.

(g) To co-operate with the Area Council and with Party Headquarters in the common aim of establishing in power a Conservative and Unionist Government, and to contribute to the Central Funds of the Party.

(h) To raise adequate funds for the achievement of the foregoing objects, including Fighting Funds for Parliamentary and Local Government Elections.

It is clear that the primary purpose of the local associations is to conduct propaganda and to raise funds with a view to securing the election of Conservatives to public bodies. It will be noted that the list of objects contains no reference whatever to the discussion of policy; there is no hint that the constituency associations are expected to formulate their views on national and international issues and forward them to the National Union. In practice they sometimes do so, not only in connection with the annual conference and the meetings of the Central Council, but also on rare occasions when members of the association become particularly concerned about some important public issue. There can be no doubt, however, that the discussion of policy questions occupies an even smaller part of the time of local associations than it does of the constituency Labour Parties.

Membership in a local association is open to all men and women resident in " or connected with " the constituency who declare their support of the objects of the association and subscribe annually to its funds. The explanatory notes which accompany the *Model Rules* observe that " the words ' or connected with ' are inserted to enable persons who have business interests in or personal links with the Constituency, but who do not actually reside in it, to be members of and support the Association." The size of the constituency associations varies enormously. The largest association (South Kensington) boasts a membership of over 11,000; the membership figures for most other associations are not available but the average membership must be just over 4,000, since the total membership of 2,250,000 is divided between 542 constituency associations. A large proportion of members appear to have joined merely to express their sympathies with the Conservative cause, since only a small fraction take any subsequent part in the work of the association. Even at an election the average association cannot rely on the active support of more than three or four hundred of its members and the turn-out of such numbers at an annual general meeting would be considered very large indeed.

The principal officers of an association are the president, the chairman, three vice-chairmen (one man, one woman, one Young Conservative) and the honorary treasurer.[1] The presidency of the association is described in party literature as "a post of honour" given to one "who has rendered distinguished service to the district and to the Party." The president is not expected to take an active part in the detailed work of the organization but Central Office emphasizes that "he should command general respect throughout the neighbourhood, be above local differences, and be ready to help or advise in the event of any dispute." As befits his rôle of elder statesman the president "may be invited to take the Chair at the Annual General Meeting or at any special public demonstration." But he is not to escape certain vital responsibilities with respect to the money raising activities of the party: "The president by his *example* and *influence* can often play an important part in securing financial support for the association."[2]

The effective head of the local association is its chairman. He must see that the party is continually in efficient fighting trim and he must "at all times be prepared to advise the Area on the feeling in the constituency on questions of policy." It is his particular duty also "to take the initiative in securing the best possible Parliamentary Candidate for the constituency." He must take a prominent part in the fund-raising activities and by working closely with all sections of the association endeavour to ensure that "an atmosphere of vigour and keenness is present everywhere." The somewhat paternal rôle which the party wishes the chairman to fulfil is reflected in the recommendation that while he "should not press his own views" at a meeting, "he is entitled to exercise a moderating influence ... if he thinks a meeting is going to take unwise or ill-considered action." The vice-chairmen are, in effect, deputies to the chairman and one of them is elected to act in his place if he is unable to carry out his duties for a prolonged period.

---

[1] The officers other than the woman vice-chairman and the Young Conservative vice-chairman are elected annually at the annual general meeting. The woman vice-chairman holds office by virtue of her office of chairman of the Women's Divisional Advisory Committee and the Young Conservative vice-chairman by virtue of his chairmanship of the Young Conservative and Unionist Divisional Committee. It is sometimes provided in the rules of the Association that none of the officers shall hold the same office for more than three consecutive years.

[2] Conservative and Unionist Central Office Organization Series, No. 2. *Duties of Officers and Committee Members* (1958), p. 3. [Italics mine.]

The Central Office warns that the honorary treasurer must " never be a mere figurehead (since) . . . on the result of his activities the financial strength of the Association and its ability to carry out its work efficiently may largely depend." The agent, it is acknowledged, will advise and help in the execution of the financial plans of the association but the treasurer (working in co-operation with the chairman and the finance committee) has full responsibility for raising the funds of the association. It is clearly preferable that the honorary treasurer should be a man of considerable personal standing in the community since he " must be prepared to make individual appeals for financial support himself, since a personal letter or a visit can very often secure a considerably larger subscription or donation than a circular letter. As an honorary Officer, giving his services voluntarily, he can persuade his neighbours to give money if they cannot give service." It is important to note that in the official descriptions of the principal officers of the association, the president, chairman and honorary treasurer, there is a consistent emphasis on the desirability of obtaining men or women of considerable social eminence who through their prestige and example should be able to inspire the association and Conservative sympathizers throughout the constituency to make a maximum contribution to the success of the party cause. A detailed study undertaken of the constituency organization of both the Conservative and Labour parties in Greenwich[1] showed that the socio-economic status of the officers of the Conservative association in the Greenwich constituency was well above that of the members of the association and of the population of the constituency as a whole. This finding is borne out by first-hand observation of the Conservative organization in many other constituencies.

The constituency agent is the only member of the professional " civil service " of the party who is directly responsible to the voluntary side of the organization.[2] The Central Office recommends that associations should employ only those who have received the certificate of the Central Office Examination Board; they usually do so, although in theory the constituency executive council (unlike the Constituency Labour Party; see Chapter VIII) may appoint whomever it wishes. The agent is " the chief official of the Party in the constituency. . . . He should act as Secretary of the Association,

---

[1] Benney, M., Gray, A. P. and Pear, R. H., *How People Vote: A Study of Electoral Behaviour in Greenwich*, London, 1956, p. 50.

[2] As was shown above, the Area Agent is of course responsible to the Central Office and the Central Office through the Chairman of the Party Organization is responsible to the Leader; although it should be remembered that the National Union has a paid secretary and a small professional staff which is housed jointly with the Central Office.

and should be invited to all meetings held in the constituency."[1] He is expected to work closely with all the elected officers of the association to ensure the smooth functioning of the organization. But " if he meets with difficulties which he cannot himself overcome, he should seek guidance from the Chairman of the Association." He should, adds the party literature, counselling perfection, " be on friendly terms with everybody, and avoid taking sides in any disagreements."[2] As secretary of the association he must carry out the decisions of the executive council, attend to correspondence, records, arrangements for meetings, etc. In addition to his responsibilities to the association, the agent has a particular obligation to serve the Member of Parliament or prospective candidate. The description of these obligations throws an important light on the working of party politics at the constituency level:

> " He is responsible for seeing that the Member is well known, and must keep him informed of all political activities in the Constituency, and of other local events of interest. He should arrange for him to be present at the principal gatherings whenever possible, and should take all possible steps to see that his speeches and activities are recorded in the local Press. Such local matters or developments as may require the personal and special attention of the Member or prospective Candidate should be reported to him at once and, when possible, arrangements should be made for fixed times at which the Member or prospective Candidate can interview any electors who wish to consult him. The Agent should aim at helping the Member or prospective Candidate to use his time to the best advantage on those constituency matters which none but he can deal with, while relieving him of petty duties and inquiries which the Agent himself can equally well handle."[3]

It is clearly the intention that the agent should, in addition to his other duties, serve as an executive assistant to the member or candidate and also, in a sense, as his eyes and ears in the constituency. The very best of the agents do fulfil these functions; but, as is the case in the Labour Party, there is a very wide range of ability amongst the party's agents. After discussions with a great many of them, one is left with the impression that the post has attracted men and women of a reasonable standard of competence and often with a very considerable devotion to the party cause; but the ideal agent

---

[1] *Duties of Officers and Committee Members* (1958), p. 6. For a general discussion of the work of the Conservative party agent see Comfort, G. O., *Professional Politicians, a Study of the British Party Agents*, Washington, D.C. (Public Affairs Press), 1958, Chapters II–VI.
[2] *Duties of Officers and Committee Members* (1958), pp. 6–7.
[3] *Ibid.*, p. 7.

must have a combination of talents which is rare indeed. It is not surprising that constituency associations rarely succeed in attracting the services of people of this calibre.

There is a considerable variation in the structure of Conservative associations throughout the country but usually the governing body of the association is its executive council,[1] which is presided over by the chairman of the association and served by the agent in the capacity of secretary. The executive council deals with all matters affecting the association (subject to any resolution of the association in general meeting) and it elects the representatives required by the rules of the National Union and of the provincial areas to their councils and committees. The council meets at least quarterly and more frequently if called by the chairman. The council appoints annually a number of committees including a finance and general purposes committee [2] and such other committees as it may consider desirable. These normally deal with political education, trade union affairs, local government, publicity, etc. The finance and general purposes committee "forms an inner executive (which normally meets monthly) and has responsibility for most of the essential routine work of the association between meetings of the executive council. . . . With the Honorary Treasurer it is particularly responsible for the maintenance of a sound financial position and the raising of sufficient money to maintain an efficient organization." [3] The association as a whole meets in annual general meeting where it receives, discusses and adopts reports from the executive council and its committees, and reviews the financial position of the association. The meeting is usually addressed by the Member of Parliament or prospective candidate for the constituency.

The special interests of women are provided for either by the formation of a " Women's Divisional Branch " or (where the con-

---

[1] The executive council is composed as follows: the officers of the association (see above); the chairman of each committee (finance and general purposes and other committees which may be established by the executive council); two elected representatives (one man and one woman) from each ward or polling district branch of the association and additional representatives for each two thousand members of the electorate covered by the branch; one representative from each ward or polling district branch of the Young Conservative and Unionist organization; one representative from each subscribing Conservative club; co-opted members (not exceeding six); the Central Office Agent for the Area who may attend in " an advisory capacity." *Model Rules*, 1956, pp. 6-7.

[2] Its membership consists of the association officers, in addition to three men, three women and three Young Conservatives elected by the executive council. The committee has power to co-opt up to three additional members. *Model Rules*, p. 7.

[3] *The Party Organization*, p. 24.

stituency is organized on what is known as a "fused basis") by
the appointment by the executive council of a Women's Divisional
Advisory Committee. In addition each constituency association is
expected to encourage the formation of Young Conservative
branches,[1] and "to provide them with the necessary facilities to
ensure their efficiency." These branches are open to all young men
and women between the ages of 15 and 30; the even younger Conservative supporters are organized in Young Britons branches
which are intended for children between the ages of 9 and 15.[2]

To deal with the problems of political heresy and of intra-party
disputes the Central Office recommends to the associations the inclusion in their rules of the following paragraphs:

"19. The Executive Council (of the Association) may strike off
the membership roll any member whose declared opinions or
conduct shall, in its judgment, be inconsistent with the objects
of the Association, but before such power is exercised, seven
days' notice shall be given to the person concerned, and an
opportunity afforded him (or her) of showing cause before the
Executive Council why he (or she) should not be so dealt with.

20. (1) The Executive Council may (and shall if so requested by
any Branch of the Association) submit any dispute or difference
arising in connection with the Association or any of its Branches
to the Officers of the Provincial Area of the National Union
with a view to their bringing about a settlement of such dispute
or difference.

(2) If the Officers of the Provincial Area shall fail to bring
about a settlement acceptable to all parties to the dispute or
difference the Executive Council may (and shall if so requested
by any Branch of the Association) submit such dispute or difference to the Executive Committee of the National Union which
may give a decision upon or take such steps as it thinks fit to
bring about a settlement. . . ."[3]

[1] Conservative and Unionist Central Office Organization Series, No. 5,
The Young Conservative and Unionist Organization, 1956. The party claims to
have the largest youth movement of any democratic political party in the world.
But membership figures are not regularly published.

[2] Conservative and Unionist Central Office Organization Series, No. 11,
The Young Britons Organization. At present the organization has 132 branches,
but the total membership is not available. The organization was formed in
1925 "primarily to counteract the blasphemous and seditious doctrine of the
Communists . . . the objects of the Organization are to teach patriotism, knowledge of the Commonwealth, good citizenship and the basic principles of the
Conservative way of life to the children of this country and to instil into them
the need for Young Britons to set a good example in matters of self-discipline
and behaviour." *The Young Britons Organization*, p. 2.

[3] *Model Rules*, p. 14.

The first of these recommended rules provides a further evidence of the autonomy of the local association. It has exclusive right to expel its own members and the latter have no right of appeal to any higher echelons of the party. The second of the recommended rules represents a fairly recent development; until April 1951, constituency associations were invited to call on the Central Office to arbitrate such disputes.

One feature of the work of the local association is of particular importance: the selection of a parliamentary candidate. There is some variation in procedure from one association to another but the method described here is customarily adopted.[1] When a constituency finds it necessary to adopt a new candidate the executive council of the association appoints a selection committee. The chairman of the association may meanwhile make a personal visit to the Central Office for an informal discussion of the position with the Vice-Chairman in charge of candidatures. The association chairman is likely to give some general indication of the type of candidate whom he feels would be suitable for his constituency; and he will in turn learn something of the current views of the Central Office with respect to candidatures; he will also be told informally the names of individuals considered to be particularly promising. The chairman of the association is also likely to have a talk with the area agent, who may play a very active part in helping the Constituency to find a candidate they consider suitable.

A meeting of the selection committee will also be called for a general discussion of the procedure to be followed and also for an exchange of views on the type of candidate which the selection committee feels would be most suitable for their constituency (in working-class constituencies or in a rural area, for example, there may be a discussion as to whether the committee should seek a candidate who is identified by social class or type of occupation with the majority of voters in the constituency). The selection committee will also be informed of the views of the Vice-Chairman; he may have told the chairman of the association that the party is particularly anxious to secure increased representation for women or trade unionists in the House of Commons. And it is possible that the Vice-Chairman may have indicated that Central Office is anxious to secure a nomination for some distinguished figure in the party who was perhaps defeated at a previous election. Apart from

---

[1] The Central Office has published an excellent guide to the constituencies in this matter, entitled *Notes on Procedure for the Adoption of Conservative Candidates in England and Wales* (1953). For Lord Woolton's explanation of the reforms in candidate selection after 1945, see his *Memoirs*, pp. 345 ff. See also Hare, John, " M.P. After Your Name," *Onward*, March, 1955, p. 9.

these general considerations the constituency chairman will have formally requested Central Office to provide a list of people who would, in its view, prove suitable candidates. This list is provided by the Vice-Chairman of the Party himself from among the list of those who have been approved as potential candidates by the Standing Advisory Committee on Candidates. In addition to this list the selection committee may decide to include other names of local party members (some of whom indeed may have raised their own name for consideration); these local names must be submitted for approval to the Standing Advisory Committee if they have not hitherto been considered by that Committee. By this process the selection committee will have compiled a list of perhaps seven or eight persons whom they invite to appear before them for interview. Often the chairman also arranges to see these potential nominees for private interview in case he wishes to raise matters connected with their private lives which may prove a source of embarrassment if discussed before the full committee.

The selection committee then usually recommends three or four names to the executive council of the association, which invites the persons concerned to appear before a special meeting of the council. They are asked to address the meeting (usually for about twenty minutes) and to answer questions. A series of ballots will then be taken until one person obtains a clear majority of the votes. The executive council's choice is submitted to a general meeting of the association and, except on the rarest occasions, the general meeting proceeds to adopt the individual concerned as its prospective parliamentary candidate. When Parliament is dissolved or a writ is issued for a by-election another general meeting is held at which the candidate is formally adopted.

The right of veto of the Standing Advisory Committee on Candidates is the only limitation on the otherwise complete autonomy of the local association in selecting its prospective candidate. But it is important to note that this veto is applied only on those very rare occasions when the proposed candidate is in the view of the Advisory Committee totally unsuited to represent the party. Apart from this one formal limitation on the autonomy of the association, there may on some occasions be some informal pressure brought to bear on an association to adopt an ex-Cabinet Minister or some other leading party stalwart who has been mentioned by the Vice-Chairman. Officials of Central Office may negotiate with prominent members of a local association to try to ensure that they will co-operate to secure his adoption as candidate. This process is sometimes cited as evidence that local associations are no more than puppets which move on the behest of the " party bosses " in the Central Office. But this is an unfair interpretation since there is no reason to doubt that local associations are often more than willing to accept as their candidate someone of considerable political eminence who has had the misfortune to lose his seat in Parliament. Certainly if the local association refuses to co-operate there is no method by which they can be forced to do so.

Particular reference must also be made to the financial relationship between candidates or M.P.s and their constituency associations. Central Office admits frankly that " just over a quarter of a century ago it was a fairly common practice for candidates to defray the whole of their election expenses. Many were expected to pay in addition a large annual subscription to the Association."[1] This is an honest enough admission and needs to be modified in only one respect: these practices were current as late as 1948 when the Maxwell Fyfe Committee presented its interim report. Indeed it was as a result of their report that rigorous restrictions have now been placed on the amount of money candidates or M.P.s may expend on electoral or other political activities in their constituencies. They must make no contribution towards their election expenses other than what is known as their " personal expenses " (which under electoral law must not exceed £100), and constituency associations are encouraged (where their candidates' limited resources make this necessary) to defray these expenses too. In addition a prospective candidate may contribute up to a maximum of £25 a year to the funds of his association and, if he is elected to Parliament, he may contribute no more than £50 a year. If the candidate cannot afford the personal expenses involved in " nursing " a constituency, the local association is encouraged to help him with hospitality and transport. Central Office insists that there must be no discussion of the candidate's financial resources or of his ability to contribute within the prescribed limits to the funds of the party.[2] There is no way of knowing whether any of these arrangements are secretly violated, but from extensive discussions with active party workers it seems very doubtful that they are. It seems evident that questions of finance now play a less important rôle in the adoption of Conservative candidates than they do in the case of Labour candidates.[3]

The commendable effort which the Conservative Party has made to eliminate financial considerations in the selection of candidates has raised another problem which has caused some concern to the Central Office and the party leaders. The party has always sub-

---

[1] *Notes on Procedure for the Adoption of Conservative Candidates*, p. 3.

[2] Lord Woolton has argued (*Memoirs*, p. 346) that their financial changes "did more than any single factor to save the Conservative Party."

[3] Cf. pp. 555 ff. below.

scribed to Burke's conception of the relationship between an M.P.
and his constituents. Indeed the official party pamphlet on the
adoption of candidates quotes Burke's words:

> "Your representative owes you not his industry only, but his
> judgment; and he betrays instead of serving you if he sacrifices
> it to your opinion . . . authoritative instructions, which the Mem-
> ber is bound blindly and implicitly to obey, though contrary to
> the dearest convictions of his judgment and conscience, are
> utterly unknown to the laws of the land, and against the tenor
> of our constitution."

The Central Office admits that it was comparatively easy for the
M.P. to protect himself against unwarranted pressures from his
constituents when he was paying most of the costs both of the election and of running the association between elections. But the
relationship is a different one when the M.P. is paying only a small
proportion of these costs. The members of the association may find
themselves irresistibly tempted to try to convert their M.P. into a
spokesman for the association. The Central Office gives the sternest
warning against yielding to this temptation. From conversations
with Conservative M.P.s and members of constituency associations it seems plain that for the most part these warnings are
heeded; constituency associations do not normally attempt to
press their member to speak or vote against his better judgment.
As Burke insisted, this is as it should be according to British
parliamentary practice; but it must also be emphasized that it
eliminates almost completely the possibility that members of
Conservative associations should have any really important influence on the policies pursued by their parliamentary party. Pressure
from the constituency associations on behalf of a particular policy
can be only one factor, and normally not a major one, to be taken
into account by Members of Parliament.[1]

VI

THE CONSERVATIVE BRANCH ASSOCIATIONS

In constituencies in which the Conservative Party is highly organized, branches of the constituency association have been set up in
each ward or polling district. It is the party's aim that such
branches should ultimately be organized in every ward and polling
district in the country for the purpose of keeping " in close touch
with all the electors in the district and . . . keeping the activities
of the Party and the name of the Conservative M.P. or prospective

[1] For important developments since this was written, see pp. 631–4 below.
A recent party Chairman, Lord Hailsham, discussed "problems in choosing
parliamentary candidates " in the *Sunday Times*, 25th January, 1959.

candidate before them."[1] The basis of membership in a branch is
the same as that of a constituency association and indeed membership of a branch automatically entitles the subscriber to membership of the association. The officers of the branch normally include
a chairman, one or more vice-chairmen, an honorary treasurer
and an honorary secretary.[2] These officers are elected by a branch
annual meeting and together with such other persons as the meeting
may decide to name they constitute a committee which manages
the affairs of the branch. Party literature warns emphatically
against allowing a branch to be " a one-man show " or allowing
its affairs to be controlled by a tiny self-perpetuating clique.[3] The
warnings are stern, and from first-hand observation, one must add,
justified; there has been a persistent tendency towards autocratic
control of branch organizations. The duties of committee members
as listed in official party literature are roughly what one would expect, but there are in addition one or two of particular interest. The
committee member " should collect and pass on to the Branch
Secretary all information obtainable regarding Opposition activity
or propaganda." In addition " he should find out in what subjects
the electors are particularly interested, and should keep the Branch
Secretary informed so that suitable action may be planned. There
are usually several burning topics in people's minds, and it is important to get clear information on matters of local as well as of
national interest." [4] Here is an important indication of the rôle
assigned to the local party militant. He is to spy out the land on
behalf of his party, to report on enemy movements and to help
gather information on the basis of which the strategy and tactics
of his own party may be determined.

A number of local branch members are normally named as
representatives from the branch to the executive council of the
constituency association. They act in effect as a two-way channel
of communication between the branch and the association as a
whole. Again there is a warning against allowing this important
function to drift into the permanent control of a small clique:
" great care should be exercised in electing the best representatives
and the same people should not be automatically re-elected year

---

[1] *The Party Organization*, 1961, p. 27. For a more detailed list of the
objects of the branches, see *Model Rules*, p. 18.

[2] In addition a president is sometimes (but not usually) chosen; he
does not take an active part in the detailed work of the organization. He is
usually an eminent local citizen who is expected to " use his influence to
promote the general progress of the Branch." *Duties of Officers*, p. 8.

[3] *The Party Organization*, 1961, p. 28.

[4] *Ibid.*, p. 28.

after year."[1] At this level (oddly enough) the party at one time entertained the possibility that members of the branch might wish to exert direct control over their representatives. " If (representatives) have express instruction from their branch to speak and vote in a certain way," then, said *The Party Organization* (1950 ed.), " they should follow these instructions." But an interesting explanation follows: " This course is taken, however, only when the branch is in full possession of all particulars concerning the subject to be decided. The usual, and preferable, course is to allow the representatives to consider the arguments placed before them, and to arrive at a decision after hearing the discussion, bearing in mind the views of their own branch, so far as these are known." This is the only occasion in party literature in which reference is made to the possibility that representatives may be required to follow the specific instructions of the members of the organization they represent. However, this passage was subsequently dropped from later editions of *The Party Organization*.

Two very important features of the organization and work of the branch are the " block system " and the " canvassers corps ".[2] The former provides for the division of each ward or polling district into " blocks " or groups of households, each in charge of one (or at most two) voluntary workers, known as canvassers. In heavily populated districts a block will consist of a number of houses or flats along one or more streets. In country districts a block will include all the houses or hamlets within a certain area. In either case the total number of households will not be more than can be visited regularly by one or two canvassers.[3] Ideally the block should be looked after by the same party workers both between and during elections. Their functions are to distribute party literature; to spread verbal propaganda; to deliver invitations to meetings and social functions; to collect information for the association's " Marked Register "; to enrol members in the Association; to recruit active workers and helpers of all kinds; to act as " intelligence officers "; and to undertake election work during campaigns for both parliamentary and local government elections.[4] All of the

[1] *The Party Organization*, 1950, p. 29.

[2] Conservative and Unionist Central Office Organization Series, No. 9, *The Voluntary Worker and the Party Organization*, 1961.

[3] The party recommends that where sufficient workers are available two may share the responsibility of a block between them, e.g. a man and a woman canvasser, or a senior member of the association and a Young Conservative. *The Voluntary Worker and the Party Organization*, p. 4.

[4] *The Voluntary Worker and the Party Organization*, p. 3.

canvassers in a given ward or polling district are under the supervision of a " district warden". If the ward or polling district is very
large several district wardens may be appointed and they will work
under the direction of a " group warden". The whole body of
voluntary canvassers in the constituency association is described
as the " canvassers corps". The party has prepared elaborate instructions for the use of the members of the canvassers corps (see
Chapters 3 and 4 of *The Voluntary Worker and the Party Organization*) and it is not necessary to review these instructions in detail
here. But there can be no doubt that the work of these canvassers
is of enormous importance to the life of the party both between and
during election campaigns.

It may be that the electoral activities of the voluntary party
workers is now less important than hitherto ; yet their doorstep canvassing provides the only face-to-face contact which a large
majority of the electors have with the party organization. Most voters
see and hear a number of television and radio addresses by the party
leaders during an election campaign,[1] and read newspaper accounts
of the speeches made at political meetings; they may or may not
read, in addition, the candidate's election address and other party
literature which is pushed through their letter-boxes. But even
during elections very few voters (perhaps somewhere between five
and ten per cent.)[2] bother to attend the political meetings addressed
by the candidates, and even fewer of course meet the candidates or
their principal supporters in person. The canvasser who appears on
the elector's doorstep is therefore likely to be the only official
spokesman of the party whom he meets in person. The canvasser
is recommended by the party to spend an average of ten minutes

[1] For a discussion of the rôle of radio and television in the 1959 Election, see
Butler, D. E., and Rose, R., *The British General Election of 1959*, Chapter VII
and Trenamen, J. and McQuail, D., *Television and the Political Image*, London,
1961.

[2] In a study conducted in the course of the 1951 campaign the author
discovered in a fairly typical London constituency that the total attendance
at Labour and Conservative meetings during the campaign was approximately 5,000. Since a large number of enthusiasts appeared to attend more
than one meeting it would seem probable that not more than five per cent.
of the electorate attended one or more meetings. McKenzie, R. T., " A
London Constituencey," in Butler, D. E., *The British General Election of
1951*, p. 166. The British Institute of Public Opinion found that 30 per
cent. of the electorate claimed to have attended a political meeting during
the 1951 campaign. Butler concludes (p. 142), and there seems to be little
doubt that he is right, that these claims are greatly exaggerated.

with each voter or perhaps as long as twenty minutes[1] if the voter appears a likely prospect as a recruit to the working force of the party. These brief interviews are the only certain moments of contact between the active party workers and the great mass of the public.

The revival of the Conservative Party which followed their great defeat in 1945 has been due in considerable part to the recruitment and organization of effective teams of local workers in constituencies throughout the country. Winston Churchill himself pressed home the importance of the local party worker in his address to the first National Union conference after the election of 1945. He said:

> "The prime thing I have to say this afternoon about Party Organization is this, it must begin from the bottom. In every ward, in every village, in every street, we must have a stalwart band of men and women who are convinced and active workers for our Party, and who know what to say and how to bring their influence to bear upon all the issues, which are pouring out upon us, in this time of depression and this class warfare at home. Once you have an organization which has its ardent partisans in every locality, it will be easy to build up a structure which will give these leading local men and women an ever more effective share in inspiring the policy of the Party as a whole and help them to make a lively and vigorous resounding contribution to the guidance which they will receive from the summit of the Party." [2]

The final oddly phrased sentence in this quotation provides an interesting reflection of Churchill's conception of the rôle of these party militants in relation to the formulation of party policy. The "ardent partisans" are to have "an ever more effective share in *inspiring* the policy of the Party"; and they are to make "a lively and vigorous resounding contribution to the guidance which *they will receive from the summit of the Party.*" Churchill is very careful to avoid suggesting that his "ardent partisans" will in any way *control* the affairs of the party, but they are to provide inspiration and to contribute in some strange way to the "guidance" which they will receive from their leaders. His comment assigns these local party workers to their true rôle in the party organization. Either because they believe with sufficient depth of feeling in their cause or because they enjoy the game of politics they provide

[1] *The Voluntary Worker and the Party Organization*, p. 11. This is of course in the more leisurely period of canvassing between elections. During the actual campaign the doorstep interviews are likely to be very much briefer.

[2] Cited in Riley, E. S., *Our Cause: A Handbook of Conservatism*, second edition 1948, p. 58. See also *The Times*, 7th October, 1946.

a vast reservoir of largely unpaid labour for election purposes. Between elections they keep their organizations intact by arranging a varied social programme and by holding occasional propaganda meetings on behalf of the Conservative cause. They only rarely take it upon themselves to discuss questions of public policy or to pass resolutions in an effort to influence the parliamentary leaders of their party. A few times each year (at the annual conference and at meetings of the Central Council) representatives named by the constituencies do meet for an exchange of views, to hear their leaders and to convey their own views to them. But for the most part the members of the constituency associations and the branches are content to be the voluntary servants of the parliamentary party. In an analysis of the distribution of power within the party they are of little importance; but by giving loyal service without expecting in return either material rewards or a controlling voice in policy they make a vital contribution to the successful operation of parliamentary democracy.

This chapter has been devoted to an examination of the extra-parliamentary organization of the Conservative Party, the National Union of Conservative and Unionist Associations. This organization, it will be seen, is as cumbersome and unwieldy as its name. Its basic unit, the constituency association, is a reasonably tight-knit and efficient organization; but above the constituency level the National Union appears bloated, top-heavy and ill-suited to manage the affairs of a great political party. The explanation, as has been shown, lies in the fact that the National Union has no such function. It manages only its own affairs and has no direct control over either the party in Parliament or the Central Office. It is represented on the bodies which advise the Leader on the formulation of policy, which assist in raising party funds and which determine policy with respect to candidates and agents; but it has no executive responsibility in regard to any of these matters. The fact that the National Union is so cumbersome and unwieldy is in large part a result of the elaborate efforts which have been made to ensure that it is fully representative of every region and section of the party. And this no doubt helps the National Union to fulfil its only other function (apart from the management of its own affairs): serving as a two-way channel of communication which keeps the Leader and his colleagues in Parliament informed of the mood of their followers in the country and which enables the leaders, in turn, to explain their policies to their supporters in the country.

In sum, the National Union appears to serve its limited purposes very well and it is significant that the Maxwell Fyfe Committee, after a thorough review of its structure, recommended few fundamental changes. As the Committee observed, " we have recognized the need, not so much for a Constitution which seems tidy to the student of political history or logical in all respects, as for an organization which is an educative political force and a machine for winning elections."[1]

[1] *Maxwell Fyfe Report,* p. 28.

CHAPTER V

THE CONSERVATIVE CENTRAL OFFICE

I

THE EARLY YEARS

THE formation of the Conservative Central Office in 1870 followed logically from the organization of the National Union three years earlier; as has been suggested above, both were the direct consequence of the expansion of the electorate. The existence of a mass electorate made it necessary that the more enthusiastic supporters of the party should be organized into a voluntary national association; the efficient operation of this national association required the establishment of a cadre of full-time professional party workers. This party " civil service " in the Central Office was in its beginning an emanation of the Whips' Office; it remains to-day responsible to the Leader of the Party rather than to the popular organization of the party over which (in the words of one Conservative publication) it exerts " an almost paternal influence".[1]

Until the first Reform Act the Conservative Party neither had (nor felt the need of) anything resembling a central party organization apart from the Whips' Office. Outside Parliament the party leaders met somewhat casually and informally in the great semi-political clubs such as White's, Brooks's and Boodle's; rather more formal party meetings took place in premises in Charles Street, St. James's Square. At the height of the reform agitation the Carlton Club was formed (in 1831) and it became, in effect, the first central organization of the Conservative Party outside Parliament. Within a few years of its foundation the club was being referred to as

---

[1] Riley, E. S., *Our Cause; a Handbook of Conservatism*, 1948, p. 70. On the history of central party organizations in the 19th century, see also Hanham, H. J., *Elections and Party Management*, London, 1959, Chapter 16.

" the headquarters of the party organization ".[1] By modern standards the Carlton Club was a rather casual, amorphous sort of headquarters organization; but a party bureaucracy—largely at first an amateur bureaucracy—took shape within the club and made itself responsible for the co-ordination of the work of the party. The officials who met in the Carlton Club were primarily concerned with the party in Parliament; they had little to do with the work of the party in the constituencies where patronage and local influence were still dominant factors.[2] But during election periods the party officials in the Carlton Club took the initiative in scrutinizing the electoral rolls.[3] And between elections they kept in contact with local associations and party agents and stimulated them to keep up with the work of electoral registration. In addition, the Carlton Club provided the opportunity for continuous informal contact between prominent provincial party workers and the leaders of the party in both Houses of Parliament. These provincial notables were in no sense under the direction or control of the party leaders, but they inevitably came much under their influence as a result of their periodic social contacts and informal discussions with them at the Carlton Club.

The central party organization which emerged after 1832 owed much, of course, to the inspiration of Sir Robert Peel; when he broke with the party in 1846 the organization fell into a sad state of disrepair. The great schism was reflected within the Carlton Club itself and for some years the party lacked any effective central direction. The task of re-organization was undertaken by Disraeli; he was to provide the modern Conservative Party not only with its ideological foundations but also with the broad outlines of a party structure which has endured until the present day. Disraeli

[1] Letter from Londonderry to Buckingham, 9th March, 1836, The Duke of Buckingham and Chandos, *Memoirs of the Courts and Cabinets of William IV and Victoria*, 1861, Vol. I, p. 228; cf. Hill, R., *Toryism and the People*, p. 38. See also, Gash, N., *Politics in the Age of Peel*, Chap. 15 (" Club Government ") and *passim*.

[2] Hill discusses a prevalent contemporary opinion that the Carlton Club undertook responsibility for subsidizing local Conservative working men's associations. He decides that there is no conclusive evidence one way or the other and adds " there are no grounds for supposing that the Carlton Club, in its collective capacity, was in the habit of contributing to the maintenance of any particular local association . . . . Any systematic payment by the Carlton Club would have been regarded as an unwarrantable arrogation of authority by a London political organization, and would have been bitterly resented by local Tories who still almost universally held the view that local patronage begins at home." Hill, R. L., *Toryism and the People*, pp. 56-7.

[3] Rae, W. F., " Political Clubs and Party Organization," *Nineteenth Century*, Vol. III, No. 15, May, 1878.

was first stimulated to undertake his work of re-organization by the Conservative defeat of 1852. A colleague wrote to him at the time: " Had you twice the talent and eloquence you possess, you could do nothing with the incapacity which prevents our details from being properly managed . . . . we lost the election (of 1852) by bad management."[1] Disraeli appears to have been in full agreement with these observations and took the initiative in arranging for a clean sweep of those in charge of the Whips' Office and of the party organization outside Parliament. Beresford, the Chief Whip, who had been censured by a Committee of the House for " reckless indifference to bribery," was replaced by Sir William Jolliffe, afterwards Lord Hylton. The responsibility for the management of the party outside Parliament, Disraeli placed in the hands of his friend and confidential agent, Rose.

Rose and a member of his law firm, Spofforth (who succeeded him), attempted in turn to bring some sort of order out of the chaos within the party organization in the years before Disraeli's formal accession to the leadership in 1868. Since the party suffered a series of electoral defeats in this period, it seems clear that these efforts were insufficient to meet the needs of the time. In 1861 the Liberal Whip established a central party organization called the Liberal Registration Association, which became in effect a central office for the Liberal Party. The principal concern of this new national organization was to encourage the formation of registration societies and to help them in their work on behalf of Liberal candidates. The first Conservative response to this challenge was to organize the National Union in 1867 to co-ordinate the work of the Conservative associations throughout the country. But the Conservatives suffered a further defeat in 1868 and two years later Disraeli proceeded to organize the Conservative Central Office. His biographers record that he became convinced that the old forms of the party organization " were wholly insufficient . . . for an age of household suffrage and large popular constituencies. An entirely new system must be set up; and Disraeli looked about for a young and ambitious Conservative who would be ready to devote the best years of his life to working out a scheme." [2]

Disraeli chose for this task J. E. Gorst, a young barrister who had served briefly in Parliament and who, it will be recalled, had presided at the first conference of the National Union in 1867. Gorst was appointed Principal Agent of the party with the respon-

[1] Cited in Monypenny and Buckle, *The Life of Benjamin Disraeli, Earl of Beaconsfield*, Vol. III, p. 482.
[2] *Ibid.*, Vol. V, p. 184.

sibility for organizing the new Central Office. As a first task he was told by Disraeli to ensure that every constituency should have a suitable candidate ready for the next election. To ensure a close link with the voluntary organization of the party, Gorst was in the following year (1871) made Honorary Secretary of the National Union. In 1872 the head offices of the two organizations were brought under the same roof.[1] Under Gorst's leadership the Central Office stimulated and encouraged the organization of local associations and kept in regular touch with those already in existence. The Central Office also kept a register of approved candidates which it made available to the constituencies.

Although he gave Gorst a comparatively free hand Disraeli paid constant personal attention to the work of his Central Office. He wrote to a friend in 1873: " . . . after every borough election, an expert visits the scene of action, and prepares a confidential despatch for me, that, so far as is possible, I may be thoroughly acquainted with the facts."[2] The Central Office could claim some credit for the improved fortunes of the party, which were reflected in a series of by-election victories from 1871 onwards. And in 1874 the Conservatives won their first general election victory in more than two decades.

With the party in power the Central Office appears to have become somewhat slothful and inefficient (a development which found its parallel in a temporary waning of interest in the National Union). Gorst resigned as Principal Agent and became an outspoken critic of certain features of the party organization. It will be recalled that he proposed in 1876 that the Council of the National Union should be re-organized to make it more representative in character and, writing to Disraeli in the following year, he urged the imperative need to renovate the party organization: " You must put a stop (he wrote) to that which has been the chief cause of all the mischief that has occurred—the system . . . of managing elections at the Treasury." He pointed out that " the established principle of non-interference with the local leaders has in many instances been neglected; and those leaders have been constantly offended and alienated both in the distribution of patronage and in other matters. . . . Unless some energetic measures are speedily adopted our organization, whenever the election does take place, will be as

[1] See *1872 Conservative Annual Conference Report*, p. 7, and see p. 157 above. Indeed the two organizations worked so closely together for a time that their identity seems almost to have become confused. Thus one notes, for example, in the *1875 Conservative Annual Conference Report* (p. 7), reference to " the Central Office of the National Union ".

[2] Cited in Monypenny and Buckle, *The Life of Benjamin Disraeli, Earl of Beaconsfield*, Vol. V, pp. 185-6.

inferior to that of our opponents as it was superior in 1874."[1] No
serious attempt seems to have been made to act upon Gorst's advice
and (whether through the inefficiency of the Central Office or for
some other reason) the Conservative Party went down to defeat in
1880.[2]

Three years later in 1883-4 the decisive battle took place to
determine where the effective control of the affairs of the party
should lie. As was shown above (p. 169) the struggle was fought
out between the National Union, galvanized and led by Lord
Randolph Churchill, and the leaders of the party in Parliament.
The Central Office did not figure largely in the conflict but there
can be little doubt that if victory had gone to the National Union
the Central Office would have become in effect its servant. As we
have seen, however, Lord Salisbury and the Central Committee were
victorious; Lord Randolph Churchill became preoccupied with
other matters and the National Union became again the more or less
docile servant of the party in Parliament.

With the appointment of Captain Middleton the party organization outside Parliament entered upon what has been described in
Chapter IV as its Golden Age. It was argued that the working of
the party during the period in which Captain Middleton served
both as Principal Agent and Honorary Secretary of the National
Union (1886-1903) established a pattern which has not since been
modified in any fundamental respect. As *The Times* pointed out,
Captain Middleton became the key figure in tying together the
three principal sections of the party, the party in Parliament, the
mass organization (the National Union) and the Central Office.
He had direct access to the Leader of the Party, he administered
the affairs of the Central Office as Principal Agent, and he had
effective control of the work of the National Union in his capacity
of Honorary Secretary. As *The Times* put it: " The machine was
linked up, the control was not dissipated, and the relations between

[1] Cited in Monypenny and Buckle, *The Life of Benjamin Disraeli,
Earl of Beaconsfield,* Vol. VI, pp. 519-20.

[2] In a rather harsh judgment Disraeli's biographers claim (pp. 520-2)
that the defeat of 1880 proves that " the Central Office was quite ignorant
of the mind of the electorate (since) its representative advised the dissolution in March, and calculated that the party would lose six or seven seats in
Scotland, five or six in Ireland, and five on balance in England, but would
return with a working majority for the Government." In fact the Conservatives lost 108 seats, but the authors concede that it is only fair to
note that the Liberal managers were as surprised at the result as were their
Conservative opposite numbers. In light of the primitive state of the
" science " of public opinion measurement at the time, it would seem unfair to use the result of the election of 1880 as a stick with which to beat the
Central Office.

the two chief bodies in the organization (of the party outside Parliament) were placed on the friendliest footing."[1] As the Conservative Party organization grew in size and complexity some slight devolution of responsibility subsequently became necessary. The office of Chairman of the Party Organization (which is discussed below) was created in 1911, but it was clearly intended that the holder of this office should link together the various parties of the Conservative organization just as Captain Middleton had done in his capacity of Principal Agent. Subsequently in 1931 the post of General Director of the Central Office was created, but this official has remained responsible to the Chairman of the Party Organization and has served in effect as deputy to him, managing the affairs of the Central Office. These changes apart, the rôle of the Central Office and of its principal official has not been fundamentally altered since Captain Middleton's day.

It is important to emphasize the extent to which the Central Office was then (and is now) the personal machine of the Leader. He appoints all his principal officials, and they remain responsible solely to him. In addition the Leader can if he wishes establish close personal links with the Central Office organization. This Lord Salisbury did with great success during the Middleton era. In her biography of Lord Salisbury, his daughter provides a useful account of Salisbury's relationship with the officials of the Central Office. She states that the working of the party machine took its quota (" though a limited one ") of Salisbury's time and attention and she adds:

> " there was no need for interference with its methods. That was the classic period in Conservative electioneering. Under Mr. Akers-Douglas as Whip, and Captain Middleton as Chief Agent, the organization attained a completeness which could hardly have been improved upon. The accuracy with which Captain Middleton, whether by intuition or from experience, could calculate the ' co-efficient of error ' in the returns of his local workers, became proverbial. He would send forecasts to Lord Salisbury on the eve of a by-election which would be almost exactly reproduced in the numbers polled the following day. Apart from their efficiency, both party officials had a straightness, loyalty, and simplicity of outlook which made them very pleasant to work with, and their chief's relations with them were intimately easy. A then junior member of the staff recalls how often, after the close of a House of Lords sitting, his brougham would draw up at St. Stephen's Chambers and, seating himself at Captain Middleton's table, while subordinates withdrew to a discreet distance, he would

[1] *The Times,* 23rd January, 1911.

go through the last reports from the constituencies, weigh the qualifications of proposed candidates, or discuss with Whip and Agent
the latest teacup-storm among some section of his supporters."[1]

The extent to which Salisbury and Middleton were able to control the activities not only of the National Union but even, when it
became necessary, of the local associations, was demonstrated in
the election of 1886. Early in the campaign Salisbury had pledged
his word that " so far as his influence and that of his central organization could prevail, no man who voted against (the Irish Home
Rule Bill of 1886) should be opposed by a Conservative at the ensuing elections." His intention was, of course, to protect Chamberlain and the Liberal Unionists who had broken with their party on
this issue. As Lady Gwendoline Cecil points out, there were obvious
difficulties in implementing this pledge. Until recently the dissident
Liberals had each in his own constituency embodied " the enemy "
to the uncompromising provincial Tories; and especially if these
Liberal Unionists were followers of Chamberlain, they had been
identified with attacks upon the principles and institutions which
the Tories most cherished. There was the further consideration
that Gladstone had pledged to run his own candidates against each
of the Liberal Unionists; in many instances therefore a straight
Conservative victory in these three-cornered contests seemed almost
inevitable. Lady Gwendoline concludes that the fact " that, under
such circumstances, out of 93 Liberals who voted against the Bill
there were only six who were either opposed by Conservatives or
forced to retire in their favour, witnessed to a substantial achievement in patriotic self-suppression." It also " witnessed to a substantial achievement " in Central Office control of the constituencies. As Lady Gwendoline notes: " Mr. Douglas (Chief Whip)
and Captain Middleton worked hard for this result, and their
chief (Salisbury) assisted by appeals in his public speeches and
through a copious private correspondence when difficulties arose."

From the election of 1886 throughout the Middleton era, the
party organization remained a model of technical efficiency even if
(as was shown above) it was " managed " so skilfully that by
the turn of the century the National Union had almost ceased to
fulfil its function as a channel of communication conveying to the
party leaders the moods and opinions of their supporters in the

---

[1] Cecil, Lady Gwendoline, *The Life of Robert, Marquis of Salisbury*,
Vol. III, p. 197. An invaluable contribution has now been made to an under-
standing of the working of the Party in this period with the publication of *Chief
Whip: The Political Life and Times of Aretas Akers-Douglas, 1st Viscount
Chilston*, London, 1961, by the 3rd Viscount Chilston.

country. The difficulties increased when Captain Middleton began to lose interest in his organization; two or three years before he resigned in 1903 he accepted an outside business appointment and it soon became vividly evident that the successful working of this elaborately interlocked Conservative organization was greatly dependent on the personality, skill and devotion of the Principal Agent. A Captain Wells succeeded to the office of Principal Agent in 1903 and under his administration the organization deteriorated rapidly. He decided not to take on the second post of Honorary Secretary of the National Union and other innovations were introduced which widened the gulf between the professional and popular organizations of the party. As *The Times* remarked sadly some years later: " Although (Captain Wells) was successful in pulverizing Captain Middleton's organization, he left no trace of his constructive ability at the Central Office . . . . He retired in 1905 and was succeeded for a short time by Colonel Haig, who did nothing to remedy the parlous state of the organization . . . it will be seen (concludes *The Times*) that the dissensions in the Unionist Party on policy before 1906 synchronized with a disintegration of the organization."[1]

As was noted above, there was a considerable shuffling and reshuffling of responsibilities between the Central Office and the National Union in the course of the re-organization which took place in 1906 and 1911; but none of these changes significantly modified the rôle of either organization. During the administration of J. P. Hughes as Principal Agent (1906-12) a harmonious relationship between the two organizations was successfully re-established. The 1911 re-organization (which had been undertaken by a committee nominated by Balfour) provided for the establishment of a new post carrying the title " Chairman of the Party " (this officer has subsequently come to be called " the Chairman of the Party Organization "). It was decided that the Chairman of the Party should supersede the Principal Agent as head of the Central Office and that he should be " an officer of cabinet rank . . . (that) he should be a member of one of the Houses of Parliament, but otherwise have no special Parliamentary functions." No doubt was left about the fact that " under the Leader of the Party he should be responsible for the management of the affairs of the Party." It was further decided that the Chairman of the Party should be assisted at headquarters and in the districts by " a competent and well-paid staff " and it was " strongly recommend(ed) as essential that the new Chairman of the Party, being responsible for the effici-

---

[1] *The Times*, 23rd January, 1911. On the condition of the Central Office in 1911, see Blake, R., *The Unknown Prime Minister*, pp. 99 ff.

ency of the work, should select his own staff."[1] The 1911 revision
also provided for the establishment of an Advisory Board " for the
purpose of considering and discussing the political situation and its
developments as affecting the party." This Board was to be composed of the heads of the committees of the National Union and it
was to meet monthly " under the presidency of the Chairman of the
Party." This Advisory Board ultimately became the Executive
Committee of the National Union and from 1911 until 1930 it continued to be presided over by the Chairman of the Party Organization.

This arrangement obviously gave the Chairman of the Party
Organization (hereinafter referred to as the Chairman) great influence over the day-to-day operations of the National Union, and
it is in many ways surprising that it persisted as long as it did. A
defence of the arrangement is to be found in the Report of the
Council for 1924. It will be recalled that there had been a good
deal of dissatisfaction at that time with the way in which Baldwin
had precipitated the election of 1923 and it was urged in some
quarters that efforts should be made to keep the Leader of the
Party in closer touch with the moods and opinions of his followers
in the National Union. The specific suggestion had been made that
a special " Central Committee " should be set up " to keep the
leader in more direct touch with the constituencies." But the Report of the Council for 1924 records that " The (Executive Committee) came to the conclusion that another central committee was
not required so long as the Chairman of the Party Organization
remained Chairman of the Executive Committee, and decided to
take no further action on that point." [2]

The arrangement broke down completely however after the defeat of the party in 1929. It will be recalled that a Sub-Committee
of the Central Council had been set up " to examine the rules and
organization of the National Union, to inquire into the relationship
between the National Union, the Central Office and the Leader of
the Party, and to report with recommendations for alteration or
improvement." The Sub-Committee reported that " with regard to
the chairmanship of the Executive Committee the majority of your
Sub-Committee feel, having regard to the close and almost daily
connection which must exist between the Party Organization and
the National Union Council and Executive and their officers,

[1] *The Times*, 26th October, 1911. (The passages quoted above are
from the official party document outlining the duties and responsibilities
of the Chairman of the Party Organization.)

[2] *1924 Conservative Annual Conference Report*, (Report of the Council),
folio 6.

it is desirable that the Chairman of the Party Organization should remain Chairman of the Executive Committee. This conclusion has been reached without reference to any personal considerations, and the recommendation is made as a matter of principle on the ground of practical convenience in essential questions of organization and policy."[1] The Sub-Committee added that its report had " received the approval of the Leader of the Party." But this did not prevent the 1929 conference of the National Union from dealing with the report in a very rough fashion. In the course of the stormy debate which ensued Sir Charles Marston, a member of the Executive Committee, moved to refer back " that part of the report dealing with the appointment of the Chairman of the Party as Chairman of the Executive Committee." It was in this connection that Marston claimed that the Conservative Party " was very democratic until it reached the top . . . (that it was) an autocracy masquerading as a democracy. He did not think the Leader of the Party should be elected by that organization but he also did not think the Leader of the Party should appoint the Chairman of the Party Organization without proper consultation with the Executive. (Cheers.) The Sub-Committee now proposed that that should continue." Marston argued that " to make the Chairman of the Party Organization Chairman of the Executive was to create a bottleneck, and this had been responsible before Mr. Davidson's day (he was then Chairman of the Party) for a great deal of the trouble from which they were now suffering. (Hear, hear.) It created a feeling of irresponsibility in the Executive. They felt that all the time at the top they were being controlled and directed, whereas they ought to have a perfectly free hand. (Cheers.) The result of the General Election was brought about by causes started years ago, and among those causes was the fact that the Chairman of the Party was also Chairman of the Executive." The Chairman of the Sub-Committee which had made the recommendation said in reply:

> " So far as the present Executive was concerned, it would have elected the present Chairman whether it had been obliged to do so or not. (Cheers.) They had to preserve in the National Union a close contact with the party organization. If they cut out the Chairman of the Party Organization in the way suggested they would have to elect a chairman who must give his whole time to the work (cries of ' Why not? '). It was impossible to find each year (cries of ' No ') anyone who could give the amount of work that to-day was required to keep up a proper liaison between the party organization and the Executive.

[1] *1929 Conservative Annual Conference Report*, (Report of the Council), folio 7.

"The party organization Chairman to-day was able, sitting where he did, to answer the countless questions put to him from the Executive. If he was to be left practically on one side in the future there would inevitably be a tendency for the party organization to slide away from the National Union (cries of ' No '). . . . He asked the conference to vote against the amendment, because after full discussion the Executive Committee had decided by 30 votes to 8 that, having regard to the best interests of the party and the National Union, it was advisable to keep things as they were."[1]

The then Chairman (J. C. C. Davidson, M.P.) intervened to explain that he did not propose to speak either for or against the amendment but " he thought it right the conference should know that when this matter was being discussed, both by the Sub-Committee and by the Executive, he left himself entirely in the hands of both those Committees. He expressed no view one way or the other, because he considered that the chairmanship of the Executive Committee was a matter entirely for the Executive, and the decision come to was completely uninfluenced by anything said by him."[2] Sir Charles Marston's amendment when put to a vote was, according to the conference report, " carried by a substantial majority."

During a subsequent conference debate a resolution was moved which (in part) deplored that adequate steps had not yet been taken to investigate the remedy and causes of the Conservative failure in the recent General Election. Its mover, an M.P., charged that " the Chairman of the Party, responsible to no one but the leader, had more power vested in him than a Tammany Hall ' boss '. If there had been another system which did not place them in the hands of two men—practically of one man—many resolutions passed by the conference would have been honoured." [3]

Six months later Davidson resigned his office. In a public exchange of correspondence with Baldwin he wrote: " I cannot but be aware of the criticism levelled against the central organization, especially during the last few months, and although I have no doubt that time will show much of that criticism to be ill-founded, I am convinced that in the interests of the party a change is necessary." Davidson then added: " I have often mentioned to you that the duties which the Chairman of the Party is required to discharge in existing circumstances are too much for any one man, and no doubt you will consider this before making a new appointment." In reply Baldwin wrote: " I can only regret

[1] *1929 Conservative Annual Conference Report,* folio 5.
[2] *Ibid.,* folios 3-5.
[3] *Ibid.,* folio 16.

very deeply that the overwhelming nature of the task compels you to lay down the post, but I deeply appreciate the disinterested motives which have led to your present decision." He added that he would take into account the advice Davidson had given: " Nobody who has been in intimate contact with the work of the organization can fail to have observed the tremendous growth in the responsibilities attaching to the post of Chairman of the Party, and I agree with you that the time has come when the whole question must be thoroughly examined."[1] Baldwin added that he proposed " to review the position immediately " and a few weeks later it was announced that Neville Chamberlain had agreed, evidently with some reluctance, to take over the post of Chairman for a brief period. In a letter to Baldwin on 23rd June Chamberlain wrote: " I have given much anxious thought to your present request that I should, for a time at least, undertake the chairmanship of the party. In ordinary circumstances I should never have considered the acceptance of a post which is at best a thankless one, involves much additional work, and must inevitably necessitate frequent absence from the House of Commons." Chamberlain added that he would, however, accept the post since Baldwin had convinced him that by this means he could " best help the cause".[2]

One of Chamberlain's earliest actions was to fulfil the wish of the 1929 conference that the Chairman of the Party should cease to serve as Chairman of the Executive Committee. At the Executive meeting on 14th October, Kingsley Wood, M.P., was unanimously elected Chairman of the Executive for the remainder of the year ending February, 1931. Subsequently it was announced in March, 1931, that " as a result of a Committee of Investigation set up by the Chairman of the Conservative Party Organization, the Rt. Hon. Neville Chamberlain, M.P., it has been decided that the Chairman of the Party shall be empowered to appoint a deputy to act for him should he, for any reason, find it temporarily impossible to give the whole of his time to the duties of his office." It was further announced that " the title of Principal Agent becomes absorbed in that of General Director. The General Director, Mr. H. R. Topping, will be in control of every branch of the Central Office."[3] The following year the new General Director was appointed Honorary Secretary to the National Union.

---

[1] *The Times*, 30th May, 1930.
[2] *The Times*, 24th June, 1930. For an account of Chamberlain's work at Central Office, see Macleod, Iain, *Neville Chamberlain*, Chapter 8.
[3] *Gleanings and Memoranda*, April, 1931, p. 251.

Chamberlain resigned as Chairman in April, 1931. He wrote to Baldwin : " I now find myself in a position to ask for the fulfilment of our agreement (that I should be allowed to resign when I had carried out any measures of re-organization which I might consider to be necessary). While the work of re-organization at the Central Office is by no means complete, the lines have been firmly laid down; the key positions are allocated; and such detailed arrangements as are still necessary can be quite well carried out by my successor."[1] Chamberlain's successors (there have been nine including Lord Woolton) have introduced a number of modifications in the structure of the Central Office but in broad outline the arrangements in respect to principal officers have remained unchanged, as has the general structure and function of the Central Office.

II

THE CENTRAL OFFICE: THE MODERN STRUCTURE

" The rôle of the Central Office," according to the Maxwell Fyfe Report, " is to guide, inspire and co-ordinate the work of the Party throughout the country, to advise and assist Constituency Associations and Area Councils and to provide such services as can best be organized centrally." [2] Clearly it is the purpose of the Central Office to provide a cadre of full-time professional party workers who operate the machinery of the party organization. The Central Office staff do not so much duplicate the functions of the voluntary section of the party organization as see that its job gets done. The Central and Area Offices are in a sense the steel skeleton on which the rather flabby flesh of the National Union hangs. And the brain which directs the movements of this skeleton is the Leader of the Party acting through his personal appointee, the Chairman of the Party Organization.

The Chairman of the Party Organization

In justifying the arrangement whereby the Chairman is a direct personal appointee of the Leader of the Party the Maxwell Fyfe Report stated (p. 33): " This arrangement is necessary because (the Chairman) must enjoy the full confidence of the Leader; it also gives the Leader an opportunity of recruiting to this office an outstanding personality, not necessarily already related to the party

---

[1] Cited in *Gleanings and Memoranda*, April, 1931, p. 339.
[2] *Maxwell Fyfe Report*, p. 31.

organization." If one accepts the proposition that the professional organization of the party should be responsible to the Leader of the Party in Parliament rather than to the mass organization outside Parliament then this argument is, of course, unanswerable. If the views of the National Union (or considerations of seniority within the Central Office) had to be taken into account then the Leader might well find himself saddled with a Chairman with whom he had great difficulty in working.

Winston Churchill's appointment of Lord Woolton[1] provides a useful illustration of the process by which the Chairman is selected. Lord Woolton's predecessor, Ralph Assheton, had had the misfortune to be in command of the party organization on the occasion of its worst defeat since 1906 (he had been appointed in October, 1944, so presumably he could hardly be considered primarily responsible for the disaster that overcame the party in July, 1945). There were many demands during 1945 and 1946 that the party machine should be streamlined and modernized and the Leader of the Party apparently decided to call upon the services of one of his most successful war-time Ministers, Lord Woolton, despite the fact that the latter had had only the briefest contact with the Conservative Party organization. Speaking to the 1946 Conservative conference three months after his appointment (in July, 1946) as Chairman, Lord Woolton confessed that this was the first time he had attended a political conference. He had, he said, " joined the (Conservative) Party at 12 o'clock on the day of the defeat of the National Government." There was certainly, however, no public indication that the members of the party thought the fact that he had been converted so recently had in any way disqualified him for the appointment; and in the event, of course, Lord Woolton proved to be one of the most successful and popular Chairmen in the party's history.

In speaking of the function of the Chairman, the President of the National Union for 1925 said, " the mechanism of the Party may not inaptly, I think, be compared with the mechanism of a watch. It calls for very delicate treatment, and the smooth working depends entirely upon the efficiency of the mainspring—(the Chairman of the Party Organization)." The analogy is in many respects

[1] Lord Woolton has now provided his own account of these events and his rôle as Chairman in his *Memoirs*, London, 1959, and in a series of six articles in *The New York Herald Tribune*, April 23–29, 1956. For an account of the work of one of the most successful of Lord Woolton's successors, Lord Hailsham, (Chairman of the Party 1957–9) see Hennessy, D., " The Communication of Conservative Policy 1957–59," *Political Quarterly*, July–Sept., 1961, pp. 238 ff.

appropriate. Since the formation of the Conservative Central Office in 1870, 20 men have headed the party organization;[1] there is ample evidence to show that their personalities and abilities have had a direct and vital bearing on the well-being of the party. It becomes evident why this is so if one examines the range and complexity of the responsibilities which fall to the Chairman.

His primary task is to supervise the work of the Central and Area Offices, although of course the immediate and detailed management of these affairs is the responsibility of the General Director. In addition, the Chairman must by tact and persuasion " manage " the National Union or at least ensure that any efforts it may make to goad or stimulate the party in Parliament or the Central Office are kept within reasonable bounds. His ideal must be to ensure that the National Union functions as an effective propaganda organization and electoral machine, high-spirited in its work on behalf of the party yet comparatively docile in its willingness to allow the parliamentary leaders to control the affairs of the party. Whenever there are signs of unrest or dissatisfaction the Chairman must, of course, keep the Leader fully informed and at the same time do all in his power to eliminate the sources of trouble.

The best public demonstration of the rôle of the Chairman is to be seen at the Conservative annual conference. Traditionally the Chairmen have made comparatively few interventions in the conference debates. Most of them appear to have operated on the principle enunciated by Lord Woolton at the 1947 conference when he said: " I consider that I can serve the best interests of this Party at the Annual Conference by being a silent observer, listening to the views of Delegates and subsequently advising the Leader of the Party as to the trend of opinion among us." [2]   The Chairmen have

[1] The first seven until 1911 as Principal Agent, thirteen as Chairman since then. See *1952 Conservative Annual Conference Report*, p. 8.

[2] *1947 Conservative Annual Conference Report*, p. 109. A contemporary journalistic account of Lord Woolton's rôle at a Conservative Party conference (1950) notes: " Lord Woolton's value to the party should not be underestimated. Though he has seldom intervened in this conference, he has, in indirect and subtle ways, done a great deal to make it a success. A gathering of 4,000 people is apt to become cold and inhuman . . . It is Lord Woolton who has largely generated the warmth. Radiating ceaseless benevolence, he has given the delegates the feeling that they were sitting round the fire at home, having a nice cosy chat about their difficulties. Perhaps the secret of Lord Woolton's gift is that he never lets up . . . (he) is always on the job. When anybody made a playful joke about him at this conference, he was to be observed, thrown far back on his chair, shaking with great sobs of laughter. If an unknown delegate was at the rostrum, he would prop up his great head on his hand and remain absorbed until

normally tended to intervene in conference discussions either to explain and defend the policy of the parliamentary leaders or of the Central Office, or alternatively to pledge to the conference to convey their feelings to the Leader of the Party. As an illustration of the former type of intervention, an incident may be cited from the conference of 1926. A delegate had moved that the conference should express itself as favouring the use of corporal punishment against " sinister revolutionary extremists " where " actual victimization by assault takes place." Colonel Jackson, the Chairman, said at the conclusion of the debate that the speeches they had listened to would convince any audience of the necessity of strengthening the law with respect to the handling of these extremists, but " before the conference voted on the question he would like to give the delegates the views of the Home Secretary, whom he thought it desirable to consult with reference to the latter portion of the resolution having reference to corporal punishment." After giving the Home Secretary's view he asked the mover and seconder of the resolution " to consider for one moment as to whether it was really desirable to pass a resolution which, in his opinion, suggested rather too general an application of corporal punishment." He felt it was quite enough to say in the resolution that " stronger repressive measures are necessary to deal with the situation " and he assured the conference that the Home Secretary would welcome such support. The resolution as amended on the lines suggested by Colonel Jackson was adopted. The same Chairman, it will be recalled, had found it necessary to defend the party leaders against the charge that they had been too slow in introducing new trade union legislation.[1]

Sometimes a Chairman has intervened to commend and to urge the passage of a particular resolution under discussion. This occurred for example at the 1936 conference when a resolution was proposed which apparently echoed the Hoare-Laval controversy of the year before. The resolution (a rather remarkable one) read: " That this conference notes with alarm the tendency of our Foreign Secretaries to usurp the duties of trained Ambassadors, and, in the interest of World Peace, strongly urges the Government to reverse this policy." The mover said that he earnestly hoped the resolu-

---

the end. There was a triumphant moment when Mrs. Poynter, a genuine housewife, spoke in the cost-of-living debate. Lord Woolton, who, of course, invented the housewife, could scarcely contain his joy, and turned a radiant and fatherly face towards the hall as if this were the proudest day of his life." Our Political Correspondent (Hugh Massingham) " Blackpool Diary," *The Observer*, 15th October, 1950. For a further assessment see " Party Manager " (by R. T. McKenzie), *The Observer*, 9th October, 1955.

[1] See p. 126 above.

tion would not be construed as an attack on the National Government, and added that it was not intended as a reflection on the present Foreign Secretary, who was doing a heroic task nobly. Referring apparently to the negotiations of the former Foreign Secretary, Sir Samuel Hoare, with Laval, the mover added: " There. had grown up, largely owing to the function of the League of Nations, the practice of Ministers in high positions having discussions on the Continent and sometimes reaching conclusions, and there was sometimes real difficulty in maintaining touch with the Cabinet at home." The mover was convinced that " by passing the resolution they would be strengthening Mr. Baldwin's determination that such a position would not occur again." Somewhat surprisingly, Lord Stonehaven, the Chairman of the Party, commended this remarkable intervention by the conference into what was surely a matter for domestic arrangement within the Cabinet. Lord Stonehaven said that the resolution amounted to an endorsement of Baldwin's statement in the House after the Hoare-Laval incident. " By expressing their opinion in favour of Mr. Baldwin they would be strengthening his hand. Having spent twelve years in the diplomatic service (Lord Stonehaven continued) it seemed to him the views expressed in the resolution carried weight." With this endorsement the resolution was carried " with only one or two dissentients."[1] Lord Stonehaven's contribution to this debate appears to have been stimulated by his own Foreign Office experience. There have been very few other occasions where a Chairman has intervened in a discussion which touched upon such a delicate matter.

A more typical occasion on which the Chairman is likely to intervene is a debate which involves the affairs of the Central Office. At the 1921 conference, for example, a resolution was moved which in part urged the Central Office to see to it that the Conservative Party organization should be maintained in existence in each constituency. In support of his resolution the mover said: " In a lot of constituencies the associations had been closed down and furniture sold because (he was told) of the Coalition. That was nothing more nor less than the assassination of the Conservative Party." The seconder added that " he had heard it said that the Central Office would not assist in the formation of any Conservative Association in a place represented by a Coalition Liberal." And he proposed that the National Union itself should undertake such work if the Central Office declined to do so. In reply to the debate Sir George Younger, the Chairman of the Party, defended

---

[1] *1936 Conservative Annual Conference Report,* folio 42.

the Central Office, remarking that he " had not the funds to maintain associations all over the country by advancing sums of money to keep them going. It was no part of the business of the Central Office to finance local associations, though it was their duty to see that such associations were formed and remained constituted during the Coalition. It was unfair to say that (the Central Office) objected in any way to the formation of Unionist associations where a (Coalition) Liberal represented a seat.   They were doing their best to keep them all in active working order, because they never knew when they would need them."[1]

In another characteristic intervention at the same conference, the Chairman reported on his efforts to encourage the adoption of certain types of candidates. A resolution was moved stating: " that in view of the fact that the Liberal and Labour associations are preparing and putting forward women candidates for the next General Election, it is extremely desirable that the Unionist associations should not be behindhand in this respect." In support of the resolution Lady Astor said: " I have to try to represent the whole of the women in the country (a voice from the floor of the conference, ' Why? ') because there is a woman's point of view to everything, and I must have more women to help me to put that point of view forward. Don't be frightened of us (a voice, ' We are '). I know you are. There is something wrong and your conscience hurts you, that is why you are frightened." Sir George Younger spoke in support of the motion and said he agreed with Lady Astor. He added: " I have tried my very best to get certain constituencies to accept a lady candidate, and one chairman wrote back saying I had given him the shock of his life." With the Chairman of the Party's endorsement the resolution was carried.[2] Sir George Younger's statement reflects, of course, one of the important functions for which the Chairman is indirectly but ultimately responsible, namely the determination of policy with respect to candidatures. As was noted in Chapter IV, the Central Office, while accepting advice in this matter from the voluntary organization of the party, ultimately reserves exclusive responsibility for policy with respect to candidatures. It would be reasonable to assume that in this, as in most other matters, the Chairman implements the views of the Leader and his colleagues, but there can be no doubt that the Chairman can, if his views are respected by the constituency associations, wield considerable personal influence in the matter.

The Chairman often explains and defends the leaders of the party

[1] *1921 Conservative Annual Conference Report*, folios 12–13.
[2] *Ibid.*, folios 31-2.

(and the work of the Central Office) on the public platform and in the national press as well as at the annual conference of the party. He is particularly likely to do so if the Leader or one of his colleagues has been the subject of an attack which they would prefer to have replied to by the party organization in order to avoid becoming engaged in a personal exchange with their critics. This frequently happened in the course of Baldwin's struggle with the Press Barons (see p. 135 ff. above). An example is to be found in the exchange between Viscount Rothermere and J. C. C. Davidson, the Chairman of the Party Organization, in November 1927. In the *Daily Mail* for 18th November of that year Viscount Rothermere addressed an open letter to the Prime Minister on the subject of what he called the " Votes for Flappers Bill ". Rothermere accused Baldwin of proposing " to continue (his) policy of promoting legis-lation of a Socialist character by using his majority to give votes to ' flappers.' " He added: " I possess abundant means for ascertain-ing the political tendencies prevailing among the Conservative rank and file, and I emphatically assure you (Baldwin) that predominant among them is a very strong feeling against votes for ' flappers '. ... The most clear-sighted of your followers realize that persistence with the measure will simply mean the annihilation of the Con-servative Party at the next Election. ... " Baldwin himself made no reply but the Chairman issued a statement saying in part: "Any-one who has taken the trouble closely to watch Lord Rothermere's publications will have noticed a systematic endeavour to irritate the Conservative rank and file against the Conservative Govern-ment by holding up the policy of Ministers for criticism and denunci-ation."[1] Neville Chamberlain, when he took over briefly as Chair-man, was even more active as a spokesman for Baldwin in his controversies with the Press Barons.

On rare occasions Chairmen of the Party Organization have got themselves into serious difficulties when they have ventured to expound policy. Not long after the formation of the National Government, Lord Stonehaven, then Chairman, said in a public speech: " We have a National Government with a mandate to carry out a Tory policy." As might be expected this provoked an immediate uproar which caused Lord Stonehaven to say in his own defence a few days later: " My speech at (the) United Club dealt especially with policy of Imperial Development and was made on my sole responsibility." This statement by no means quietened his critics and the Chairman found it necessary to write further in *The Times* on 17th December, 1931: " When I said that we had a National Government in office with a mandate to carry out a

---

[1] Cited in *Gleanings and Memoranda*, November, 1927, p. 417.

Tory policy, I meant neither more nor less than that the electors, in giving the National Government the free hand for which it had asked, had thereby authorized it to carry into effect, if it thought desirable, the policies which the Conservative Party had unanimously advocated for months past."[1] It is possible that Lord Stonehaven was excused his indiscretion by the Leader of the Party since he had only very recently taken over the office of Chairman. But Lord Stonehaven must soon have realized that the Chairman is not expected to offer independent and original interpretations of the policy of his leaders in Parliament; he is expected rather to defend them against their critics both within the party and outside.

It is difficult to attempt a definitive assessment of the power and authority of the Chairman in the councils of the party since obviously most of his influence is exerted behind the scenes.[2] One of the few well-documented illustrations of the Chairman's rôle during a crisis in the affairs of the party was reviewed above in the discussions on the break-up of the Coalition in 1922. On that occasion, it will be recalled, Younger, the Chairman, interpreted it as his duty to warn Austen Chamberlain that he was failing completely to carry the party with him in his attempt to continue the Coalition. Younger later recalled: "I made up my mind that if there was going to be a split it should split from the top and not from the bottom, and that the leaders who were responsible for pushing such a disastrous policy were the men to go, and not the tail. I (therefore) took care to see that the party should not be wrecked." Younger then added the hint that he had been responsible for encouraging Bonar Law to " come forward and re-establish unity." The scornful Lord Birkenhead had already described Younger's activities in the course of the 1922 crisis as the insubordination of " the cabin-boy". Younger, it will be remembered, replied to the charge by saying in the speech quoted above: " When a skipper was driving the ship on the rocks it was not a bad idea to have a cabin boy there to see that a new skipper and crew were provided for the barque."

---

[1] *The Times*, 17th December, 1931.

[2] As in the case of Lord Woolton, the Chairman can normally expect to be called into the inner circles of the parliamentary party when the Conservatives are in opposition, and to serve as a Minister when the party is in power. A new departure occurred after R. A. Butler became Chairman in 1959; he continued to carry heavy parliamentary responsibilities as Home Secretary and Leader of the House. His successor as Chairman, Iain Macleod, also served as Leader of the House. It is very doubtful if it is in the party's best interests that the Chairman should carry such heavy additional burdens.

In assessing the rôle of the Chairman in the crisis of 1922 some allowance should be made for the fact that Younger probably exaggerated his own influence on the course of events. On the other hand it seems evident that the Chairman (whether Younger or anyone else) was bound in a crisis of this sort to play a highly influential part. It was obvious that Austen Chamberlain was attempting to lead the party in a direction in which it did not want to go. It therefore became the proper function of the Chairman to report the attitude of the party to him in an attempt to save both the Leader and the party from disaster. It may be argued that Younger went beyond the boundaries of his responsibilities in working for the replacement of Austen Chamberlain when he realized that Chamberlain was determined to persist in his Coalition policy. But Younger subsequently argued, as we have seen, that he felt his first duty was to ensure the survival of the party rather than to give priority to his obligation to support and defend his Leader.[1] Perhaps the most important fact to note in connection with this crisis is that the Chairman's main contribution was to throw the weight of the National Union into the scales against Austen Chamberlain. Younger decided to do this not (as far as can be discovered) through motives of personal gain or for any desire merely to exercise his own power, but rather because he decided, apparently quite objectively, that he was implementing the will of the members of the National Union and salvaging the fortunes of the Conservative Party.

This raises a further point which must be made about the rôle of the Chairman. It will be recalled that a critic in the party once described the Chairman as having " more power vested in him than a Tammany Hall ' boss.' " There is indeed a certain superficial parallel between the rôle of a Chairman and that of a " boss " within the American political system. Neither is subject to effective popular control by the members of the party with which he is associated. But there the parallel ends, since the Chairman, unlike most American party bosses, does not exert power over the elected representatives of the party. With the one possible exception of the incident in 1922 which has just been discussed, each Chairman appears loyally to have served the Leader of the Party, and to have

---

[1] It is worth recalling, of course, that Younger had been appointed in the first instance by Bonar Law (see *Gleanings and Memoranda,* January, 1917, p. 66) and further that Austen Chamberlain was merely Leader of the Party in the House of Commons rather than Leader of the Party as a whole. Chamberlain, it should also be remembered, was a somewhat arrogant and remote figure who clearly did not readily inspire deep personal loyalties. These factors may have helped to contribute to Younger's readiness to place his loyalty to the party above his loyalty to the Leader.

attempted to interpret to him the moods and opinions of the popular organization of the party. There can be no suggestion that any Conservative Leader has ever been forced to serve the interests of his Chairman. Perhaps the nearest parallel in a foreign political system is to be found in the rôle of the Chairman of the National Committee of either of the great American political parties. Following the adoption of a presidential candidate, the party normally accords the candidate the right to choose the person he wishes to serve him as Chairman of the National Committee. The Chairman then manages the affairs of the party along lines broadly determined by the presidential candidate. Subsequently, if the candidate is successful, the Chairman of the National Committee is often rewarded with Cabinet office (traditionally as Postmaster General) and continues as principal party manager. This parallel cannot of course be pushed too far since patronage plays an enormously greater part in the management of the affairs of an American political party than it does in this country. But there are interesting points of similarity between the rôle of the Chairman in the Conservative Party and the Chairman of the National Committee in either of the Democratic or Republican parties in the United States.

The other Senior Officers[1] and the Departmental Organization of the Central Office

The Chairman is assisted by two Vice-Chairmen, both of whom are (like the Chairman himself) personal appointees of the Leader of the Party. Their duty is to " assist the Chairman generally in interviews and supervision of the various party activities." One Vice-Chairman is normally a woman and she is expected to take particular responsibility for women's activities in the party. The other Vice-Chairman is " responsible for all questions of Parliamentary candidature". Other senior officials appointed by the Leader include the two Honorary Treasurers, who are " responsible for the finances of the Party". The Central Offices (and the Area Offices) are administered by the General Director who is responsible to the Chairman. The total staff of the Central Office, both administrative and clerical, numbers approximately 200.[2]

---

[1] In special circumstances during the period 1957–9 a special post of Deputy Chairman was created. See Hennessy, D. " The Communication of Conservative Policy, 1957–59," Political Quarterly, July–Sept., 1961, p. 248.

[2] David Butler estimated that the Central Office employed a total of 220 during the election of 1951 (of whom he estimated one-third were salaried and might be considered in the administrative class) compared with approximately 100 persons employed at Transport House. See Butler, D. E., The British General Election of 1951, pp. 25 and 27.

The range of activities of the Central Office is as follows:[1]

1. *The Organization Department* (which is under the direction of the Chief Organization Officer) maintains close contact with constituency officers and agents and provides them with advice on all matters of organization and finance and electoral procedure. The department is also responsible for the training of constituency agents and organizers.

2. A group of departments under the *Chief Publicity Officer* is responsible for most types of party literature and all aspects of the party's publicity, press, radio, television and public relations. Area publicity officers responsible to the Chief Publicity Officer assist with this aspect of the party's work in the Areas.[2]

3. *The Speakers Department* arranges speaking engagements for Members of Parliament and for other lecturers both voluntary and paid who undertake the propaganda work of the party. The Department is also responsible for the briefing and training of speakers.

4. *The Industrial Department* is responsible for the organization of Conservative Trade Union Councils and Labour Advisory Committees as well as for undertaking such studies of industrial and social problems on matters of particular interest to trade unions and co-operative societies.

5. *The Local Government Department* is responsible for co-ordinating the working of the party in local government elections and for assisting Conservative members of local councils.

6. *The Young Conservative Department* is responsible for the stimulation and co-ordination of the work of the Young Conservatives, Young Britons, and the Federation of University Conservative and Unionist Associations.

---

[1] See Chapter 5, in *The Party Organization*, pp. 13 ff.

[2] *The Report of the Council for 1929* gives an indication of the extent of the party's activities in this field at that time: " Since the last annual conference the production and circulation of literature has exceeded all previous records. During the period October to December 1928 inclusive 4,016,571 leaflets and pamphlets were taken by the constituencies. Between 1st January and the date of the dissolution (10th May) 16,495,719 were distributed, and during the General Election period itself the total reached 85,159,776 exclusive of posters to the number of 464,614 and the special election address cover, 8,360,800 of which were ordered. The General Election figure of 85,159,776 leaflets and pamphlets compares with a similar figure for the 1924 election of 36 million." *1929 Conservative Annual Conference Report,* (Report of the Council), p. 9. Mr. David Butler estimated that the Conservative Party printed and distributed some 18 million leaflets during the campaign of 1951. Butler, D. E., *The British General Election of 1951,* p. 26. The decline in the number of leaflets distributed may be accounted for by the impact of the regulations regarding campaign expenditure since all literature distributed to the constituencies must be charged to the expenditure of the individual candidate.

As is shown in Chapter IV these Central Office departments correspond closely to the pattern of the national advisory committees of the National Union.

There are two additional organizations of major importance at party headquarters. The first, the Conservative Political Centre, is a semi-autonomous part of the Central Office; the second, the Conservative Research Department, is not a department of the Central Office although " it comes within the framework of Party Headquarters."[1] *The Conservative Political Centre* grew out of what was originally the educational department of the Central Office. An official party statement in January, 1928, reported " the work which, up to the present, has been initiated and administered by the Educational Department of the Conservative Central Office has now, by a decision of Mr. J. C. C. Davidson, M.P., Chairman of the Party, been entrusted to a new organization, which will be known as the Conservative and Unionist Educational Institute. . . . The work hitherto carried on by the Educational Department will be considerably extended, particularly in the direction of the formation and encouragement of Study Circles, Lecture Courses and Correspondence Courses in constituencies throughout the country." The next major advance in this field took place at the end of the Second World War in the course of the re-organization of the party. The stimulus which led to the setting up of the Conservative Political Centre was provided by R. A. Butler in February, 1946,[2] and subsequently *The Times* reported (2nd May, 1946): " The Conservative Party's political education movement is gathering impetus and a Conservative Political Centre—of which a bookshop will be a prominent feature—has now been established in London." Subsequently the Conservative Political Centre has appointed representatives in each of the provincial areas.

The Conservative Political Centre is not primarily concerned with providing party members and speakers with ammunition for use in immediate political controversy. Its purpose is rather to provide background information and to encourage the study of long-term problems. For these purposes it publishes a wide range of pamphlets and study courses and provides a system of postal tutorials either for individual or group study. Under the latter head, its most important experiment has been the so-called " Two-

---

[1] *The Party Organization*, 1961, p. 16. For further comments on the work of the Conservative Political Centre see *Political Quarterly*, July–September, 1961 (Special Number on the Conservative Party) pp. 253–4, 267–8.

[2] See Butler, R. A., *Fundamental Issues*, a reprint (by the Conservative Central Office) of a speech in February, 1946.

Way Movement of Ideas" programme, which was designed to
establish " a continuing partnership between the Party leaders and
its rank and file in the formation of Party policy on political issues."[1]
In connection with this programme, the Conservative Political
Centre publishes a series of pamphlets, each one devoted to providing background factual material on national or international
problems. These are distributed to voluntary discussion groups
organized throughout the party and members of the groups are
invited to answer a set of questions appended to each pamphlet. In
the first phase of the Two-Way Movement of Ideas (January to
June, 1947) some 150 groups contributed 212 reports and in 1958,
525 groups submitted 1,241 reports. A cumulative summary of the
findings of these discussion groups is prepared and sent to the
Research Department, the Chairman of the Advisory Committee
on Policy and the Chairman of the Party for their consideration.

The Conservative Research Department

Until the nineteen-thirties the work of research undertaken
by the Conservative Central Office appears to have been on
a comparatively casual basis. Thus, for example, one finds Austen
Chamberlain writing to his brother Neville regarding the campaign
for Protection in 1923: "Cannot you . . . get the Central Office
to give a handsome fee to Professor Ashley and any other suitable
men of whom you can think to prepare material for our campaign? " A few years later it was recognized that this sort of *ad
hoc* arrangement was far from satisfactory and an official statement
issued by the Conservative Central Office in November, 1929,
reported:

> "In view of the growing complexity of the political aspect of
> modern industrial, Imperial and social problems, Mr. Stanley
> Baldwin has decided to set up a special department charged with
> the task of organizing and conducting research into these matters.
> The department will be under the direct control of the Leader of
> the Party, who has entrusted the task of organizing it to Lord
> Eustace Percy and to Mr. Joseph Ball, who has been appointed
> director of the new department. It is understood that it is Mr.
> Neville Chamberlain's intention, on his return from South Africa,
> to associate himself actively with the work of the department.
> In the conduct of its operations the department will be indepen-
> dent of, but will work in close liaison with, party headquarters."[2]

---

[1] *1947 Conservative Annual Conference Report*, p. 16.
[2] *Gleanings and Memoranda*, December, 1929, p. 461.

In the re-organization of the party after the 1945 defeat the present Conservative Research Department was set up (in 1948) incorporating the organization which had served as a Parliamentary Secretariat, and the Library and Information Department of the Central Office. The basic pattern of the present organization is very similar to that established in 1929 by Baldwin. The Chairman of the Department is a personal appointee of the Leader and is directly responsible to him. The chief executive is the Director, who also acts as Secretary to the Advisory Committee on Policy with which the Department works in close association. The functions of the Research Department are as follows:

(a) to undertake long-term research and to assist in the formulation of party policy.

(b) to provide official secretaries for the parliamentary committees of the party (see p. 62 above) and to prepare briefs on issues coming before Parliament.

(c) to provide Members, candidates, speakers and all party workers with information and guidance on current political affairs.

(d) to assist all departments of the Central Office with factual information.[1]

Of these functions the first two have obviously been the most important, especially during the period 1945-51. The party during these years undertook a wholesale re-examination of its policies and produced as a result a series of " charters " dealing with several major aspects of public policy. As a result of the initiative of R. A. Butler,[2] an extremely able group of young men was assembled in the Research Department; they undertook most of the preliminary research and prepared draft papers which became the basis for the discussions of the Advisory Committee on Policy and they played a prominent part in preparing the charters themselves.

The work of the Research Department in servicing parliamentary committees of the party and preparing briefs for Conservative front-bench speakers was also of great importance while the party was in opposition. The prominent spokesmen of the party were without ministerial briefs for the first time since 1931 and they undoubtedly leaned heavily on the assistance first of the Parliamentary Secretariat and subsequently of the Research Department when the former became merged into it. There can be little doubt that the Research Department played an important part in shaping the thinking of the Conservative Party during the years in opposi-

[1] *The Party Organization*, 1961, p. 16.
[2] See Boyd, F., *Richard Austen Butler*, pp. 92–103.

tion. It would probably not be unfair to suggest that in normal circumstances the party spends less time thinking (or at least arguing) than does its Labour opponent; controversy over policy and ideological splits in the Conservative Party are comparatively rare. Therefore, during a period when by common agreement the party had suddenly to do a great deal of thinking, the personnel assigned to undertake research and to prepare draft statements for the Advisory Committee on Policy undoubtedly wielded a good deal of influence. It would be wrong to suggest, however, that they *controlled* the development of Conservative policy during this period. The initiative in this matter lay with the chairman of the Advisory Committee on Policy, and he, like the head of the Research Department, is a personal appointee of the Leader. There could be no question therefore of the Leader being pressed to move in a direction in which he did not want to go; he could readily dismiss either of the principal officials concerned if he became dissatisfied with their work. But apart from this safeguard there can be no doubt that the personnel of the Research Department were able to bring very considerable influence to bear on the development of Conservative policy during the period in opposition. With the return of the party to office in 1951 their influence diminished sharply. A number of their more prominent members entered Parliament and indeed several achieved Ministerial rank. Initiative in the formulation of Conservative policy inevitably passed to the Prime Minister and his Cabinet. It is doubtful whether the Research Department will play a really major rôle in the development policy until the party again finds itself in the wilderness,[1] although even with the party in office it has an important rôle in undertaking " thinking " and research on the longer-range goals of party policy.

III

THE RELATIONSHIP BETWEEN THE CENTRAL OFFICE AND THE NATIONAL UNION

Again and again it is emphasized in official party literature that the principal function of the various departments of Central Office is to provide advice and assistance to the constituency associations. Elaborate efforts are made to avoid any suggestion that the affairs of the party are *managed* by the Central Office. The reason for this concern no doubt relates to the fact that the Central Office is responsible only to the Leader of the Party and not to the National

[1] See also Hennessy, D., " The Communication of Conservative Policy 1957–59," *Political Quarterly*, July–Sept., 1961, pp. 252–3.

Union. As has already been shown there have been periodic protests against what many party members have considered to be the undemocratic nature of this arrangement, since it provides in effect that the civil service of the party is in no way controlled by the mass organization. Prominent officials of the party have often sought to justify this arrangement, usually by emphasizing the ultimate autonomy of the constituency associations. Thus, for example, at the 1923 annual conference the Principal Agent spoke in a debate on a resolution which proposed " that at the next General Election every constituency in the Kingdom should be contested : that a central fund should be set aside by the Central Office to help necessitous constituencies; and in those constituencies where the initiative is not taken by the local Unionists that the Central Office should take steps to see that a candidate is available; all bye-elections to be similarly contested." The Principal Agent said that the resolution " implied a jurisdiction of the Central Office over the constituencies which it neither desired nor, he was sure, did the constituencies desire. *The whole basis of their organization was that the constituency was autonomous. The Central Office existed to help when asked, to give advice when asked, and generally to keep the whole party together in a common policy.* If this motion be passed (said the Principal Agent) it would mean that it expects the Central Office to give orders. As long as I am at the Central Office, and I am imbued with the spirit of the Conservative Party as deeply as anybody, I am not going to give orders."[1]

Despite such insistence on the modest rôle of the Central Office, delegates have continued to protest periodically against what they consider to be excessive Central Office control of the affairs of the party; but, almost as frequently, other delegates have spoken in its defence. Thus for example at the 1935 conference one speaker said that he " would like to refer to a factor which tended to discourage very materially the enlistment of helpers and workers. That was the loose, irresponsible, and unjust criticism frequently directed against the Central Office Organization." The speaker said that he had had nothing whatever to do personally with that organization beyond the fact that he had worked as a voluntary speaker, but he had had " exceptional opportunities to study the methods, procedure and work of the Central Office. I have been amazed (he added) at its extent, its colossal ramifications, and the efficiency of its performance . . . . Here we have an organization which pro-

---

[1] *1923 Conservative Annual Conference Report,* folio 17. [Italics mine.] The mover of the resolution, an M.P., said in reply to the Principal Agent : " If the conference wishes it, after that excellent explanation, I will withdraw," and this was agreed.

vides us with the strategy and education, and the lines of communication, the most efficient weapons, and the most effective propaganda and ammunition. Let us recommend these critics to make use of the facilities at their disposal."[1]

There are still flickering evidences of dissatisfaction with the relationship between the Central Office and the voluntary organizations of the party. The Maxwell Fyfe Report noted: "Some answers to the Questionnaire (distributed to local associations inviting them to express their opinions on the subject of party reorganization) have shown us that suspicions which formerly prevailed are being dispelled by experience. *Nevertheless we regret the attitude which still survives in a few quarters, where Central Office is still regarded as a remote body which exercises an unsympathetic control over the Party.* The purpose of Central Office and the Area Offices . . . is to provide all possible help." [2] In order to integrate the work of the Central Office and the National Union even further the Maxwell Fyfe Report proceeded to recommend the establishment of two additional National Union Advisory Committees to parallel existing departments of the Central Office. The chapter of the Maxwell Fyfe Report in which this recommendation is made deserves close examination because it includes several quite remarkable inaccuracies which tend to veil significant features of the relationship between the Central Office and the National Union. The first paragraph of this chapter (called "The Link between the National Union and the Central Office") reads as follows:

"Various Departments of the Central Office are linked with the National Union through Advisory Committees of the Executive Committee of the National Union. If our recommendations in Chapters IV and V are accepted the resultant relationship could be set out in the following form:

National Union	*Central Office*
1. Consultative Committee on Party Finance	Chairman of Party Organization and Treasurers of Party
2. Advisory Committee on Policy	Conservative Research Dept.
3.*	Conservative Political Centre (Education Department of Central Office)

* Hitherto the Advisory Committee on Policy and Political Education.

---

[1] *1935 Conservative Annual Conference Report*, folio 43.
[2] *Maxwell Fyfe Report*, p. 31. [Italics mine.]

National Union—continued	*Central Office—continued*
4. Central Women's Advisory Committee	Woman Vice-Chairman of the Party Organization
5. Young Conservative and Unionist Central Committee	Young Conservative Department
6. Central Trade Union Advisory Committee	Labour Department
7. Local Government Advisory Committee	Local Government Department
8. Standing Advisory Committee on Parliamentary Candidates	Candidates' Department

In comment on this paragraph the Report noted that the Maxwell Fyfe Committee's recommendation that " the present Advisory Committee on Policy *and Political Education* should be reconstituted as an Advisory Committee on Policy leaves the education movement of the Party without a direct link with the National Union." The Committee therefore recommended that " an Advisory Committee on Political Education should be established, consisting of the Chairman of the Area Education Committees and nominees of the Executive Committee of the National Union, with power to co-opt." This Committee would then take its place at item 3 above. There would then be only two Central Office departments not linked in the manner set out in the above table: the Organization Department and the Publicity and Speakers' Departments. The Maxwell Fyfe Committee decided that " the functions of the Organization Department are mainly technical and administrative and we do not consider that there is need for a standing Advisory Committee to be specially set up in association with it." They recommended however the establishment of a (National Union) Advisory Committee on Publicity and Speakers emphasizing that it " *should be of an advisory and not an executive character,*" and that it would provide " a valued means of bringing up for discussion constructive suggestions and criticisms for improving the helpfulness of the work of these Departments in Central Office." But lest there should be any misunderstanding the Report adds: " The responsibility for the direction and conduct of (the work of the Publicity and Speakers Departments) will remain with the General Director acting on behalf of the Chairman of the Party Organization."[1] To complete its tidy diagrammatic illustration of the link between the Central Office and the National Union the report recommended that a 9th item should be added to the list as follows:

[1] It should be noted that this relationship exists between each Advisory Committee of the National Union and its Central Office equivalent. *Executive responsibility is not shared in any way with the popular organization of the party.*

National Union	*Central Office*
' 9. Advisory Committee on Publicity and Speakers	Publicity Department, Speakers' Department."[1]

It has been suggested that there are several errors in the table quoted above from the Maxwell Fyfe Report. In the first place it seems almost inconceivable that the members of the Committee should have listed the Consultative Committee on Party Finance and the Advisory Committee on Policy as if they were committees of the National Union. As was shown in Chapter IV, they are of course nothing of the sort. The National Union is represented on each committee, but it has no ultimate control of their work. It was perhaps forgivable to include item 8, the Standing Advisory Committee on Parliamentary Candidates, since it was set up originally by the National Union, although the committee does not report to its parent body. It must be assumed that these were errors in good faith since all members of the Maxwell Fyfe Committee except the Chairman and Secretary were members of the Executive Committee of the National Union, and as such they would presumably have no reason to give a misleading impression of the influence and authority of the National Union in the affairs of the party. But the fact remains that nowhere in the Maxwell Fyfe Report, nor for that matter anywhere else in official party literature, is there a forthright acknowledgment of the fact that the really vital functions of the party (regarding policy, finance and candidatures) are controlled exclusively either by the Leader himself, or by the Chairman of the Party or another of the Leader's nominees.

In the formulation of policy the Leader, as we have seen, bears sole ultimate responsibility, and the committee which has been set up to advise the Leader is presided over by a Chairman and Deputy Chairman appointed by him and responsible to him. This Advisory Committee on Policy is served by the Conservative Research Department whose Chairman again is a personal appointee of the Leader. The finances of the party are the responsibility of the two honorary treasurers both of whom are appointed by and responsible to the Leader. They are assisted by the Central Board of Finance (which is responsible to the Chairman) and the Consultative Committee on Party Finance (over which the Chairman of the Party presides as *ex officio* chairman, assisted by the two honorary treasurers themselves who are deputy chairmen). " All questions of Parliamentary candidature " are the responsibility of one of the two Vice-Chairmen, who again is a personal appointee of the

---

[1] *Maxwell Fyfe Report*, pp. 40-1.

Leader. This Vice-Chairman is assisted by the Standing Advisory Committee on Parliamentary Candidates but this committee does not report to the National Union. *It would be difficult to envisage a more tight-knit system of oligarchical control of the affairs of a political party.* The three most vital functions of the work of the party are not in any way controlled by the mass organization; each is controlled by one or another of a small band of people all of whom are personal appointees of the Leader of the Party. Even in other less important fields such as " publicity and speakers " and " political education," the functions of the various national advisory committees of the National Union involve no executive responsibilities. In every instance such responsibilities are retained by the Central Office. The party bureaucracy, responsible only to the Leader of the Party, is just as fully in control of the affairs of the party as it was in the heyday of Captain Middleton sixty years ago. The " evils " (if they were evils) which Lord Randolph Churchill thought he saw in the control of the affairs of the party by a parliamentary clique are as real as they were in the 1880s.

No serious attempt to transform the situation has been made since Lord Randolph Churchill's day. The members of the National Union may have grumbled from time to time but they have made no concerted effort to win control of the management of the affairs of the party. A half-hearted attempt to raise the issue was last made at the annual conference of 1948. One representative moved a resolution which stated in part that " the (establishment of) control of Central Office by the National Union is overdue, and should take place without further delay." The National Union, he argued, " in structure and constitution . . . is essentially democratic, because it has its roots in the individual member of the Party, who in his Local Association appoints his officers, and from his officers makes his appointments to the Areas, and the Areas in turn make their appointments to the Executive of the National Union. So there is built up from the individual member a complete structure, a democratic structure. . . . On the other hand you find that (the Central Office) originated as an organ at the top, and its principal object (when it was founded) was to secure a candidate in every Constituency. But as the National Union came to cover the whole country, you will see that very largely that original object of the Central Office came to an end, and undoubtedly as time went on there inevitably must be overlapping and some lack of co-ordination."

To meet the situation he described, the speaker urged that the Central Office should be placed under the direction and control of the National Union. He found an additional argument in support of this proposition in the fact that the National Union had recently been challenged by Lord Woolton to undertake considerable responsibility for raising the finances of the party. " When Lord Woolton came to the body corporate of the Party for £1 million, the National Union (the speaker suggested) for the first time took on its proper work." As long as the finances of the party were raised by the Central Office, the National Union was " bound to be out of the picture, because although it may not have been democratic it was at least logical that the person who paid the piper—that is Central Office—should call the tune." But now the National Union was " taking up (its) rightful position in the Party and assuming (its) rightful duties and responsibilities " (with respect to finance) the speaker urged that Central Office " should be the servant, the proud servant, of the Party, responsible to you and reporting to your democratic National Executive."

The seconder of the resolution reminded the conference that " the principle of ' no taxation without representation ' is not new; it is deep-rooted in our history, and . . . the violation of that principle cost us an Empire in America." Perhaps not altogether wisely the seconder added: " This Resolution was first proposed at the annual Party Conference in 1884 when Lord Randolph Churchill was in the Chair. Neither my proposer nor myself can be accused of indecent haste in again bringing the matter to your notice." He concluded by saying: " I believe that if you support this Resolution, you will be making certain that our Party is not only democratic in aim, but truly democratic in structure."

But the proposal that the Central Office should be made responsible to the National Union was not discussed at all since an amendment was moved which proposed that no action should be taken until the final report of the Maxwell Fyfe Committee had been received. The mover of the amendment explained that he hoped " this Conference is not going to spring to a sudden decision as to what are to be the future relations between the National Union and the Central Office." His proposition was " not to reject the ideas which have been put forward," but to urge the conference to await the findings of the Maxwell Fyfe Committee. The amendment was carried with only 11 votes cast against it and the amended motion (to the effect that the conference would "await with interest " the report of the Maxwell Fyfe Committee) was carried with five dissentients.[1]

[1] *1948 Conservative Annual Conference Report*, pp. 121-3. Remarkably enough, not a single constituency representative apart from the mover and seconder spoke for the original motion nor did any speaker oppose the amendment.

The Maxwell Fyfe Report at no point either referred to, or dealt with, the issue raised in the original motion. It merely reproved those members of the party who " still regarded (the Central Office) as a remote body which exercises an unsympathetic control over the Party," and the report insisted again and again that the sole function of the Central Office is to " advise . . . to assist . . . to provide all possible help." Wittingly or unwittingly the Maxwell Fyfe Report entirely evaded the argument that in a democratic political party the Central Office machine should be responsible to the mass organization of the party rather than to the Leader. The Maxwell Fyfe Committee appeared to assume that it had dealt with all possible objections to the existing arrangements by reiterating the argument that " . . . no orders can be given to Constituency Associations either by the Central Office or by the Area offices."[1]

IV

THE AREA OFFICES

The work of the area offices need not be dealt with in detail because their relationship to the provincial area organization of the party is identical in principle to the relationship between the Central Office and the National Union. It should be underlined however that the area offices, which are to be found in each of the 12 areas of England and Wales, are in effect branch offices of the Central Office. They function under the supervision of an official known as the Central Office Agent in the Area, who is responsible to the General Director; the Central Office Agent serves as honorary secretary of the Area Council, thus providing the customary link between the professional and voluntary organizations of the party. The other officials of the area office usually include the Deputy Central Office Agent (" normally a woman where a man is Central Office Agent, and vice versa "); the Area Political Officer; the Labour Department (which usually includes a Trade Union Organizer); and the Young Conservative Department (with a Young Conservative Organizer). The Maxwell Fyfe Report noted that: " There has been a certain amount of criticism of the usefulness of various appointments on the Provincial Area staff." But the Report balanced against this the claim by others that the same officers were quite indispensable. The Report concluded by recommending that: " The filling of these offices should remain permissive and not mandatory, and that in doubtful cases a decision should be reached by consultation between the Area Chairman and the General Director."[2]

[1] *Maxwell Fyfe Report*, pp. 30–1.
[2] *Ibid.*, p. 43.

PART II

POWER IN THE LABOUR PARTY

CHAPTER VI

THE LEADER OF THE LABOUR PARTY

"Though politics is, of necessity, a highly competitive profession, not least in the Labour Party, we have a strong sense of social security near the top. To do a man out of his job, at that eminence, is against good followership."—Hugh Dalton.[1]

THE Labour Party has traditionally been as hesitant as the Conservatives have been forthright in publicly acknowledging the power and the authority they accord the Leader of their party. As was shown in Chapters II and III, the formal description of the powers of the Conservative Leader would suggest that, once elected, he can play the autocrat with impunity; in contrast, the Labour Leader appears to be hemmed round with restrictions which ensure his subservience both to the party in Parliament and to the mass party organization outside. The Conservative Leader is not required to submit himself for periodic re-election; but the Labour Leader (except when he is Prime Minister) is subject to annual re-election by the Parliamentary Labour Party (hereinafter PLP). The Conservative Leader, whether his party is in power or in opposition, does not normally attend the meetings of his back-bench followers nor is he bound by their decisions. The Labour Leader is expected to attend the meetings of the PLP; indeed when Labour is in opposition he presides at party meetings and in theory serves primarily as spokesman for the policies which his colleagues decide to adopt. The Leaders of both parties are, of course, free to choose their Cabinet colleagues when they hold the office of Prime Minister; but the Conservative Leader retains a similar right in the selection of his Shadow Cabinet, while the Labour Leader must work with a shadow cabinet (the Parliamentary Committee) chosen for him by the PLP. The Conservative Leader has sole ultimate responsibility for the formulation of policy and is not formally bound by the decisions of any organ of his party either inside or outside Parliament. The Leader of the Labour Party is bound to attempt to implement the programme determined jointly by the PLP and the mass party organization. The Conservative Leader does not normally attend the annual conference of his party; he need do no more than address the mass rally which is traditionally held after

[1] Dalton, H., *Call Back Yesterday*, p. 191.

the conference has ended. The Labour Leader on the other hand usually presents to his conference the report on the work of the PLP during the previous year. And finally, the Conservative Leader is in complete charge of the party bureaucracy and appoints all of its principal officers (who remain responsible solely to him). The Labour Leader in contrast has no personal control over the affairs of his party's head office. He is merely an *ex officio* member of the 28-man National Executive Committee (hereinafter NEC) which controls its affairs.

The contrast in the rôles assigned by the two parties to their respective Leaders would appear to be complete; yet in practice the contrast is nothing like as great as the formal statement of their respective rôles would suggest. Certainly this is the case when the two parties are in office. Each party Leader then normally becomes Prime Minister; as such he is overwhelmingly the most powerful political personage in his party, or for that matter in the country. Attempts have been made at intervals in the history of the Labour Party to devise party mechanisms which would control or restrict the authority which the Labour Leader otherwise automatically acquires on assuming the office of Prime Minister. But, as will be shown below, these attempts have come to nothing. There are of course variations in the degree of authority assumed by particular individuals on becoming Prime Minister, but there is no significant difference in this respect between *Labour* Prime Ministers and *Conservative* Prime Ministers as such; the variations depend on the personality, temperament and ability of the individual concerned rather than on his party affiliation.

When the Conservative and Labour Parties are in opposition the *apparent* gulf between the power and authority accorded by the parties to their respective Leaders is striking. This arises largely from the fact that the Conservative Party when in opposition has traditionally been much more conscious than Labour of the fact that its Leader is a *potential* Prime Minister. The Conservatives therefore leave their Leader free to choose his Shadow Cabinet and to direct the affairs of the party in much the same way as a Prime Minister is free to choose his Cabinet and to assume full executive authority. And, again like a Prime Minister, the Conservative Party Leader in opposition need not submit himself to annual re-election by his supporters; he retains his great authority so long as (*but only so long as*) he retains the confidence of his followers in Parliament.

The Labour Party on the other hand came only gradually to recognize that the Chairman (as he was at first called) of their parliamentary party was in fact a potential Prime Minister. This was understandable enough since in the early years of the party the prospect of Labour forming a government seemed very distant indeed. The Chairman was treated therefore as the party's " spokesman " rather than as its " Leader," in the sense that that term was used by the older parties;[1] and when the party is in opposition this attitude still persists. But since 1922 the Labour Party has had to reconcile itself to the fact that the Chairman (or Leader) of the PLP is also a potential Prime Minister, and as such he has inevitably come to acquire a degree of authority that is nowhere acknowledged in the constitution of the party. To take but one illustration: although the Labour Party requires its Leader to subject himself to annual re-election, no Leader, once elected, had to submit himself for re-election between 1922 and 1960[2] (for the special circumstances in the latter year see pp. 620–22 below). Nor can it be argued that Labour Leaders have had less security of tenure in office. As was shown in Chapter III, three Conservative Leaders in this century have, in effect, been driven from office by their own followers; and a fourth, Baldwin, retained his office only with the greatest of difficulty. On the Labour side, Lansbury might be said to have been driven from office in 1935, although it is important to recall that he became Leader almost by accident and that he never considered himself to be more than the temporary " spokesman " of his party. The downfall of Clynes in 1922, also a special case, is examined below. Neither Conservative nor Labour Leaders are likely to be destroyed by a popular uprising amongst the mass of their supporters in the party *outside* Parliament, but it is worth recalling that of all the Leaders of the Conservative and Labour Parties in this century, a Conservative, Austen Chamberlain, probably came nearest to being destroyed by a revolt against his leadership in the party outside Parliament. It will be recalled that it appeared likely that Chamberlain would have been repudiated by the National Union if he had not been broken by his parliamentary colleagues at the Carlton Club meeting. MacDonald, on the other hand, had no difficulty in retaining office as Leader (despite the deep gulf which opened between him and his followers) until he broke with his party in 1931. And Clement Attlee, it should be noted, never had to face

[1] Indeed, not until Labour became the second party in the state in 1922 was its Chairman formally accorded the title of Leader. See p. 306 below.

[2] Unless it is argued that the case of Attlee's re-election to the leadership after the election of 1935 is an exception (see p. 361 below). It should be noted, however, that he was elected (unopposed) "for the remainder of the session " following Lansbury's resignation immediately before the election. The PLP appeared to wish to postpone the election of a new Leader until after the election when a wider choice would be available.

an overt challenge to his authority, despite the fact that he led his party for a longer period than any other British politician has led a political party in this century.

Clearly it would be wrong to conclude from the apparent contrast in the rôles assigned by the two parties to their respective Leader, that the Conservative Leader is the all-powerful master of his party's destinies, while the Labour Leader is the weakest of vessels through which the party for the moment chooses to work its will. It cannot be stressed too strongly that the Leader of each of the great parties is either Prime Minister or a potential Prime Minister. And it is this fact, not the internal mechanisms of the party, which is the governing influence in determining the rôle the Leader plays in the affairs of his party. The internal arrangements of the Conservative Party appear indeed to be based on this realization; those of the Labour Party (at least while the party is in opposition) hardly appear to take it into account at all. And of course the wholly different " style " of Labour politics, and the recurrent and bitter public quarrels over policy questions, tends to suggest that the party is perpetually on the verge of anarchy. But by accepting the conventions of Cabinet and Parliamentary government the party has ensured that in practice its Leader acquires influence and authority nowhere laid down in the party constitution.

It is intended in the course of this chapter to examine first, the changing attitude of the party to its leader; then, the procedure by which the party has selected each of its Chairmen and Leaders from Keir Hardie to Attlee will be reviewed; and finally, the exodus of MacDonald and Lansbury from the leadership will be discussed.

I

FROM SPOKESMAN TO LEADER: THE EVOLUTION OF THE CONCEPT OF THE LEADER IN THE LABOUR PARTY

The problem of selecting someone to serve as Leader of the Labour Party in Parliament (whatever title he might be accorded) did not arise until after the election of 1906. Before that date Labour had only four Members of Parliament; of this first quartet of Labour M.P.s, Keir Hardie obviously ranked first in seniority in the House and in the magnitude of his contribution to the building of the party. But the party was in no sense the creation of a single individual [1] and there was therefore no question of granting auto-

---

[1] As Attlee has commented, the emergence of Labour as an independent party " . . . was not (the result of) the inspiration of a great leader

matic primacy to any particular person in the early years after 1900. The tiny Labour group was in any case very loosely organized and it was apparently not thought necessary to designate any one of its members as a presiding officer.[1] But when Labour was returned 29 strong after the election of 1906 it became imperative to place in the hands of some member of the group responsibility for co-ordinating the work of Labour M.P.s and speaking on their behalf. It is significant, as is suggested above, that the person chosen for this task was accorded the title of " Chairman " rather than " Leader "; it is also important to note that the PLP decided that, in contrast to the Conservative practice, elections for the office of Chairman should be held annually. As Snowden later recalled, writing of the early years of the PLP, " The Labour Party had always set its face against a permanent Chairman, and had insisted that the Sessional Chairman should not be regarded as the ' Leader'. It was considered to be undemocratic. The Party must not permit one man to dictate the policy of the Party. The Chairman was simply the mouthpiece of the Party, stating its decisions to the House of Commons. The Party in its turn was expected to take its directions from resolutions of the Party Conferences."[2] As Snowden adds: " Fortunately it never quite worked out like that in practice." Nevertheless, the most earnest efforts were made in the early years of the PLP to ensure that no one individual should be allowed to develop the illusion that he had a prescriptive right to lead and speak for the party.[3] Consideration is given below to the process by which the early Chairmen were chosen but it is sufficient here to note that three men held the office in turn during the years 1906–11 (Keir Hardie 1906–8; Arthur Henderson 1908–10; G. N. Barnes 1910–11).

It should not be assumed, either from Snowden's comment

. . . but (rather of) a judgment of the House of Lords (the Taff Vale judgment) which deprived the Trade Unions of the legal status which they had enjoyed for many years." Attlee, C. R., *The Labour Party in Perspective and Twelve Years Later*, p. 45.

[1] Although strangely enough, as Henry Pelling recalls (*The Origins of the Labour Party*, p. 240) Keir Hardie wrote an open letter to John Morley in April, 1900, asking him to act as Leader of the emergent Labour Party.

[2] Snowden, *An Autobiography*, Vol. I, p. 218.

[3] John Parker, M.P. (in *Labour Marches On*, p. 48) claims " The status of the Chairmen of the National Executive and of the Parliamentary Party was originally on a par, when both held office for only a year at a time." But even from the earliest years it is clear that the Chairman of the PLP was a more important person than the Chairman of the NEC. Parker's comment also overlooks the fact that the first two PLP Chairmen were re-elected (without opposition) for a second year while the office of the Chairman of the NEC was from the earliest beginnings held by a different person each year.

quoted above or from the fact that the first three Chairmen held the
post for such short periods of time, that a definite two-year maximum
had been laid down by the parliamentary party. As far as can be
determined, Hardie could have retained the chairmanship for more
than two years had he proven himself sufficiently competent and
had he wished to do so. His successor, Henderson, was competent
enough and could almost certainly have held office for a longer
period had he wished; but his primary interests lay elsewhere, in
the organizational work of the party outside Parliament. Barnes,
who followed, was both ill and unhappy in the post. So, for a
combination of reasons (of which perhaps the most important
was that given by Snowden), the office of Chairman was held for
short periods of time by several persons in turn during the early
years of the party.

It is important further to note that during these years the Chairmen
enjoyed nothing like the privileged position of ascendancy in the
councils of the party which the Liberals and Conservatives accorded
to their Leaders. The PLP of these years was deeply divided on
many major issues and the Chairman often found himself in an
impossible position when he tried to act as spokesman for his party.
Barnes's difficulties provide an apt illustration. At one stage in the
battle over the House of Lords, Barnes condemned Asquith's
procedure and was thought by many to have won the initiative
for the Labour Party. As Keir Hardie explained to the ILP conference: " . . . when it became evident that the Government was
funking the issue with the Peers, Mr. Barnes issued a manifesto
which riveted the attention of the country on the (Labour) Party
and made it a factor of prime importance in the situation. All the
good effects of this were more than lost, first by the disclaimers in
the Press, and then by the Party throwing over the policy of the
Chairman." [1]

On other occasions the Chairmen appear to have missed notable
opportunities to speak on behalf of their colleagues in the PLP.
This may be illustrated by reference to an incident which occurred
at the conference of 1909. A resolution was moved urging " that
the time has now arrived when the Labour Party should formulate
a definite Parliamentary programme . . ." In opposing the motion,
Bernard Shaw, speaking as a delegate from the Fabian Society,
said:

> " . . . that his first duty in rising to oppose the resolution was to
> explain to the Conference why he took upon himself a duty that
> properly belonged to the Leader of the Parliamentary Party. The
> reason was that during the previous day's proceedings when the

[1] *1910 I.L.P. Conference Report,* p. 58.

question of the Parliamentary Report came on, when the great moment of the Conference had apparently arrived at last, when the delegates were waiting for Mr Henderson (then Chairman of the Parliamentary Party) to deliver an address that would have been delivered at a Liberal Conference by Mr. Asquith, or at a Unionist Conference by Mr. Balfour, and while the delegates were waiting for that speech in dead silence, no one venturing to intervene, to his utter astonishment the President [of the conference] passed on to the next business."[1]

But it is doubtful whether many delegates shared Bernard Shaw's disappointment at the failure of their Chairman to play the classic rôle of Leader as it was conceived in the two older parties. Most of the delegates were no doubt perfectly happy that the Chairman should serve primarily as the mouthpiece for the party in Parliament.

But Henderson, according to his biographer, gradually became convinced that the parliamentary party's lack of a recognized Leader, in the sense that the older parties had such Leaders, was in fact a liability; and he was further convinced that Ramsay MacDonald (until then Secretary of the Party) was by far and away best suited to fill this rôle.[2] MacDonald was elected Chairman for the first time in 1911 (see p. 339 below). He appears to have been somewhat reluctant to accept the post since it meant giving up the (paid) post of Secretary of the Party. Further, there seemed some doubt in MacDonald's mind as to whether he could expect to retain the chairmanship for more than a two-year period. As he wrote to Bruce Glasier at the time: " So the proposition is not ' Be Chairman also ' (in addition to Secretary of the Party), but ' Leave the Secretaryship and be the Chairman instead '—some adding ' for two years only, mind '."[3] MacDonald nevertheless accepted the chairmanship and soon settled into the post in a way that none of his predecessors had done. He was (as Balfour had put it) " A born Parliamentarian". He did a first-class job of mobilizing the slender

[1] *1909 Labour Annual Conference Report*, pp. 84-5.

[2] Hamilton, M. A., *Arthur Henderson*, p. 72. Others had begun to share Henderson's conviction. When MacDonald retired as Secretary of the Party (in 1912) after he had succeeded to the chairmanship, Keir Hardie in the course of an eulogistic speech remarked: " Many were the influences which went to the building up of a great Movement, but without the man to rally round no Movement recorded in history had ever found its way to success . . . " *1912 Labour Annual Conference Report*, p. 67.

[3] Letter of J. R. MacDonald to J. Bruce Glasier (undated late in 1910) cited in Lord Elton, *The Life of James Ramsay MacDonald*, p. 191. In the same letter MacDonald gives some indication of the importance then attached to the office of Chairman. He said he was being asked to " give up £150 a year (as Secretary of the Party) for the honour of being our *figurehead*." [Italics mine.]

and ill-assorted resources of the Parliamentary Labour Party [1]; under his leadership the party came near to achieving its maximum impact (such as it was). From one point of view MacDonald's position was stronger than any possible rival. He had entered Parliament as one of the small band of ILP Members and at first he had been viewed with suspicion by the stolid trade unionists who composed the majority of the parliamentary party; but he had soon come into conflict with the left wing of the party and came to be trusted by the trade unionists as a bulwark against extremism. Impatient and exasperated by dissensions within the party Mac-Donald apparently contemplated resigning the chairmanship after he had held the office for two years. But Lord Elton records that he was " persuaded to continue " and adds that even the *Labour Leader*, the mouthpiece of the left, considered that MacDonald could " best maintain the unity of the party as it is now constituted ".[2]

It must be remembered that at this time there seemed to be hardly even the remotest prospect that Labour would form a government in the foreseeable future. The spectacular initial gains of 1906 had been succeeded by the disappointing results of the two elections of 1910; the party won not a single by-election between December 1910 and August 1914; it suffered, indeed, several losses. Even to the far-seeing MacDonald it must have been doubtful whether the office of Chairman of the Parliamentary Labour Party opened up any very promising avenue to the Premiership. It was a tiresome, tedious and exasperating job. As Clynes recalled later, writing of his own experience in the office, the Chairman had " to give the closest attention to Parliamentary duties for five days each week, frequently till a late hour, and sometimes all night. He must exert himself as propagandist and spokesman of his side. He is in demand at innumerable conferences and

---

[1] One must acknowledge Mrs. Webb's prophetic reservations. After a meeting with MacDonald in late 1912 she referred in her diary to " . . . MacDonald's astute but over-cautious and sceptical leadership — sceptical of all the reforms which he is supposed to believe in. If we could see into MacDonald's mind I don't believe it differs materially from John Burn's mentality." (*Beatrice Webb's Diaries 1912–24*, p. 10.)

[2] Cited in Elton, *The Life of James Ramsay MacDonald*, p. 219. Elsewhere (p. 136) Elton records an incident which occurred at one of the meetings of the parliamentary party at which MacDonald was re-elected (it may well have been that of 1913): " I have been told by one who was present, that on one occasion when the Parliamentary group was about to re-elect MacDonald as its Chairman—the election was a foregone conclusion and there were no rival candidates—Snowden unexpectedly delivered a bitter tirade against MacDonald's chairmanship. When he had finished, he was asked whom, then, he wished to propose. He replied that he proposed nobody."

demonstrations. He must work in the closest touch with executives and committees, and toil ceaselessly behind the scenes in discharge of routine duties." [1] And in the period of MacDonald's first chairmanship it must be remembered that the position carried neither promise of high governmental office in the immediate future nor even at that time any special emolument in addition to his parliamentary salary. One need hardly doubt the sincerity of MacDonald and other early Chairmen when they spoke and wrote from time to time of their strong inclination to resign the post.

If it had not been for MacDonald's resignation from the chairmanship in August 1914, there is little reason to doubt that he would have become Leader of the Party in the fullest sense of the term. By 1914 he had established an ascendancy over his followers certainly greater than that of Balfour in the years immediately before 1911 and as great as (or greater than) that enjoyed by Bonar Law during 1911-14. Mrs. Webb described MacDonald's performance at the 1914 Labour Party conference as " a personal triumph . . . . with his romantic figure, charming voice and clever dialectics (he) is more than a match for all those underbred and under-trained workmen who surround him on the platform and face him in the audience. . . ." And after a conversation with one of MacDonald's colleagues on the NEC Mrs. Webb wrote of MacDonald's relationship with those around him: " (He) rules absolutely and the other Labour Members stick to him as their only salvation from confusion. Whenever anyone like poor little Jowett wants to strike out in the constructive Socialist direction, MacDonald quietly proves that his proposed action is ' out of order.' MacDonald, himself, does not want anything done in particular; he honestly disapproves of nearly all the planks in the ostensible party programme." But after reviewing MacDonald's possible rivals Mrs. Webb concludes, " So long as he chooses to remain leader of the Labour Party he will do so." [2]

Clearly, under MacDonald's dominant leadership the pre-war Labour Party was well on the way to accepting a relationship to their " Chairman " almost indistinguishable from the traditional relationship between the older parties and their respective Leaders. But this process was abruptly halted when MacDonald resigned in disagreement over the party's war policy. Henderson returned to the chairmanship, obviously impelled, as he was to be again in 1931, to take up the burden which his more colourful and less reliable colleague had thrown down. [3] It was subsequently decided

---

[1] Clynes, J. R., *Memoirs*, Vol. I, p. 323-4.
[2] *Beatrice Webb's Diaries 1912-24*, pp. 17-18.
[3] The Parliamentary Report of the PLP presented to the 1916 con-

that Henderson should serve as " Chairman for the war period,"[1] but when Henderson served in the Cabinet (May 1915–August 1917), two acting Chairmen in turn took his place (John Hodge and George Wardle). On leaving the Cabinet Henderson resumed the chairmanship; but shortly after he resigned (to devote his full attention to the re-organization of the party outside Parliament) and he was succeeded as Chairman by another stop-gap appointment, William Adamson. Throughout this period the old concept of the Chairman as spokesman for the party was largely operative; none of those who held the office during the war years could be equated with the Leaders of either of the two older parties (nor with MacDonald during the period 1911–14). Clynes later wrote of his own experience in the office (he was acting-Chairman during Adamson's illness in 1920 and Chairman, February 1921 to November 1922) that the Chairman of the PLP ". . . must, above all, be more approachable than the leader of any other Party. He is not free to go where he chooses with the confidence that he will be loyally followed. He has often to defer to the views of his colleagues of all shades of opinion, and decide with them collectively, day by day, what their action is to be on Parliamentary and public questions." [2]

MacDonald was returned to the House in the election of 1922 and under rather remarkable circumstances, which are discussed below, he unseated Clynes as Chairman of the PLP. Labour had emerged from the election the second largest party in Parliament and its Chairman became therefore Leader of the Opposition. This may account for a striking variation in terminology which appears in the Parliamentary Report of the PLP for 1923. The report presented to the previous year's conference (1922) had recorded: " The Officers for Session 1922 were . . . elected . . . as follows: *Chairman:* J. R. Clynes; Vice-Chairmen: S. Walsh and J. C. Wedgwood, etc." [3] But the 1923 Report records that " At the beginning of the new Parliament on 23rd November, 1922 . . . Mr. J. Ramsay MacDonald was elected Chairman *and Leader*; Mr. J. R. Clynes, Deputy Leader; Messrs. Stephen Walsh

ference recalled these events: " . . . . In a few days (after the outbreak of war) the Prime Minister (Asquith) brought forward a Motion for a War Credit . . . . The (PLP) held a special meeting and after full consideration, it was decided that no statement be made on this Motion, and as a consequence the Chairman (MacDonald) felt compelled to resign his office. For the remainder of the Session, Mr. Arthur Henderson, the Chief Whip, was requested to look after the work of the Party." (*1916 Labour Annual Conference Report,* (*Parliamentary Report*), p. 51.)

    [1] See a retrospective review of the war years in the *1918 Labour Annual Conference Report* (*Parliamentary Report*), p. 52.

    [2] Clynes, J. R., *Memoirs,* Vol. I, p. 324.

    [3] *1922 Labour Annual Conference Report,* p. 101. [Italics mine.]

and J. C. Wedgwood, Vice-Chairmen, etc." [1] This is the first occasion on which the words " Leader " and " Chairman " are bracketed together. This may merely reflect the fact that the Chairman had now won formal recognition as Leader of the Opposition; but there is a good deal of other evidence to suggest that as the party captured control first of the Opposition, and just over a year later, of the Government, the rôle of the Chairman again came more and more to resemble the rôle of Leader in the other two great parties. After the election of 1923 and before the downfall of the Baldwin Government a joint meeting of the NEC and the General Council of the TUC on 13th December, 1923, registered its "complete confidence in Mr. J. Ramsay MacDonald, M.P. as *Leader of the Parliamentary Labour Party*, being assured that should he be called upon to assume high office he will in all his actions consider the well-being of the nation in seeking to apply the principles of the Labour Movement." Later the same day the Executive Committee of the Parliamentary Labour Party " unanimously endorsed the resolution of confidence in Mr. MacDonald passed by the joint meeting." [2] It seems clear that an attempt was being made to elevate MacDonald to the status of national Leader of the Party. It must be remembered that the group which had met in the morning—the NEC and the General Council—had played no part whatever in MacDonald's election as " Chairman and Leader "; yet they took this opportunity to demonstrate that he had every right to claim to be the Leader of the Labour movement as a whole. Later on the same day the Executive Committee of the PLP merely endorsed the action of the NEC and the General Council. The Chairman of the PLP, soon to be Prime Minister, now for the first time could claim to be Leader of the Labour Party in the fullest sense of the term.

And as was to be expected, MacDonald responded immediately to the opportunities offered by this new development. The mantle of party Leader and of Prime Minister fitted gracefully around his shoulders; he went about the task of forming his Government in 1924 (as he did again in 1929) exactly as a Leader of any of the older parties would have done in the same circumstances. MacDonald never appears to have doubted that a Labour Prime Minister would be as free from restraint or direction as his Conservative or Liberal equivalent. Writing in 1920 about the formation of a possible Labour Cabinet he had said: ". . . in assigning offices, a (Labour) Prime Minister *whose hands are free* will fit his colleagues into the Departments where their interests and experience will be most

[1] *1923 Labour Annual Conference Report*, p. 101. [Italics mine.]
[2] *The Times*, 14th December, 1923. [Italics mine.]

valuable and have the greatest driving force." [1] Certainly in 1924 there was no question of MacDonald sharing formal responsibility for Cabinet-making with any of the organs of the Labour movement either inside or outside Parliament. Snowden recalls that when it became evident (during December 1923) that Labour would be called upon to form a Government MacDonald, Henderson, Webb, Clynes, Thomas and Snowden met to discuss the strategy which should be followed. " Nothing was said (Snowden writes) about the allocation of Ministerial offices beyond that *this should be left to the Prime Minister, Webb urging that we should follow in this respect the usual constitutional practice.*" After the meeting Henderson " expressed some misgiving about leaving the appointment of Ministers wholly to MacDonald, and hoped that he would consult us freely upon this important matter before finally coming to a decision." But MacDonald retired to Lossiemouth and proceeded to prepare a number of drafts of his Ministerial appointments in a very secretive fashion. Henderson and Snowden were soon expressing resentment at MacDonald's secrecy and arguing that " he ought to be in London in regular consultation with his colleagues. Henderson (adds Snowden) thought that we ought to have sought from MacDonald . . . some indication (in advance of the announcement of his final Cabinet list) of how he proposed to fill the particular offices." [2]

But there appears to have been no attempt by any of the executive bodies of the Labour movement (either inside or outside Parliament) to intervene. Beatrice Webb wrote in her diary: " The meetings of the various Executives—Labour Party, Trades Union Congress, Parliamentary Labour Party—have all shown the most exemplary unity of front and atmosphere of mutual congratulations. ' Mac has forty offices in his pocket and there are about forty people present,' whispered the somewhat cynical Gillies to Sidney (Webb) at the first meeting of the Labour Party Executive and General Council." Henderson, she wrote on 15th January, 1924 (after her husband had seen Henderson privately), " was also doubtful whether such appointments as were likely to be made by (MacDonald) were wise: ' the Trade Unions were being too much ignored,' he said." Yet, oddly, it appears from Mrs. Webb's account that MacDonald's only extensive consultations during his Cabinet-making were with the two " outsiders ", Haldane and

[1] MacDonald, J. R., *A Policy for the Labour Party,* London, 1920, p. 122. [Italics mine.]

[2] Snowden, *An Autobiography,* Vol. II, pp. 596–8. [Italics mine.] Webb's own account has now been published in the *Political Quarterly,* Jan.–March, 1961, pp. 6 ff. See also Lyman, R. W., *The First Labour Government, 1924,* p. 99 ff., and Shinwell, E., *Conflict Without Malice,* pp. 90–1.

Parmoor.[1] He apparently did not take serious counsel with any of his party colleagues; certainly he made no effort to secure the formal approval either of his senior colleagues or of the parliamentary party for his list of Ministers.

This was surely a decisive moment in the evolution of the Labour Party's conception of the rôle of the Leader. The term " Leader " had been formally adopted when it became clear that the Chairman of the PLP would be designated Leader of the Opposition immediately after the election of 1922; and thereafter when the party achieved office MacDonald acted (and *was permitted to act*) exactly like any other party Leader in the formation of his Government. It may well be argued that this was by far the wisest procedure that either MacDonald or the Labour Party could have followed. But it was by no means inevitable that events should have taken this course; it would have been quite possible for the PLP to have evolved a totally different system of Cabinet-building modelled perhaps on that adopted by the Australian Labour Party which provides for the election of M.P.s to the Cabinet by the parliamentary party.[2] But MacDonald conformed to the usual British parliamentary practice and as far as is publicly known no attempt was made by his immediate colleagues or by the PLP to impose any other system on him. By accepting all of the customary parliamentary practices with regard to both the Prime Minister and the Cabinet, the Labour Party moved in one great stride towards the full acceptance of the leadership principle which has been operative throughout the modern history of the Conservative and Liberal Parties. Thereafter, even when the Labour Party returned to opposition, it could not seriously be pretended that the Chairman of the PLP was merely an ordinary member of the parliamentary party who happened to be chosen to serve for a year as spokesman for his colleagues.

The more perceptive of the Conservative leaders were well aware of the significance of the developments within the Labour Party when it took office in January 1924. It will be recalled [3] that a

---

[1] There would seem to be some grounds for questioning Haldane's suitability as an intimate consultant in the formation of a Labour Cabinet. Mrs. Webb reports a conversation with Haldane in 1927 and quotes him as saying that he joined the Labour Party " . . . because (it) is the most idealist of the three parties . . . But (Mrs. Webb adds) he is always contemptuous of the way they express their idealism and even of the ideals themselves, and he abhors all the Labour Party's specific proposals—alike in home and foreign affairs." *Beatrice Webb's Diaries,* October, 1927, folio 13.

[2] Overacker, Louise, *The Australian Party System,* p. 109.

[3] See p. 115 above.

special meeting of Conservative Peers, M.P.s and candidates was held on 11th February, 1924, at which Baldwin presented himself for a renewal of his mandate after he had led his party to defeat in the election of the previous December. Austen Chamberlain took a leading part at that meeting in rebuffing all suggestions that the Leader should be subject to stricter control by his followers. He said in part: " Do not weaken the hand of the man whom you choose for your leader, and do not ask of him or of any of us that we should remit executive decisions to be debated in public meetings. That way confusion and disaster lie. That has been the practice of the Labour Party, and *unless their arrival in power leads to a direct breach with their past traditions*, leads to their giving to their leaders a confidence, a responsibility, and a power that they have never been entrusted with so far, they will come to an early and speedy disaster. . . . Do not let us at this hour, with all our traditions, with all our experience behind us, fall into the error which that new party has committed, and of which it is trying to shake itself free."

As events were soon to show, the Labour Party did succeed in " shaking itself free "; the party's arrival in power did lead to " a direct breach with their past traditions." During the nine months in which Labour held office, MacDonald became an overwhelmingly dominant figure in the party. This was partly a result of the multiplicity of offices which he held. In the Government MacDonald was Prime Minister and Foreign Secretary; and in the party outside Parliament he was both Treasurer (as he had been since 1912) and, as it happened, Chairman of the NEC for the year 1923–4. Few Prime Ministers enjoyed more obvious ascendancy over their Cabinet colleagues. Mrs. Webb wrote, six months after the Government had taken office, that her husband (President of the Board of Trade under MacDonald) " . . . still reports that J.R.M. is head and shoulders above the rest of the Cabinet."[1] But MacDonald's intellectual ascendancy was coupled with a strange aloofness which amounted almost to high-handedness. A few weeks after she had written the above entry in her diary, Mrs. Webb added that MacDonald " . . . seems . . . to have become even more aloof and autocratic towards his Ministers. For instance, Sidney saw announced the other day the appointment by MacDonald of a Committee to advise the (Foreign Office) as to the effect of the Dawes Scheme of reparations *on British Trade*— without a word of consultation with the President of the Board of Trade! " When enquiries were made at the Foreign Office Sidney Webb learned " . . . that the P.M. had not consulted the (Foreign

---

[1] *Beatrice Webb's Diaries*, 21st July, 1924, folio 80. See also Lyman, R. W., *The First Labour Government, 1924, passim.*

Office) officials, they know nothing about it. It appeared that MacDonald just fired off letters to certain representatives of the ' interests ' (concerned) . . . asking them to serve." [1]

This sort of behaviour inevitably stirred much uneasiness among MacDonald's colleagues in the House and, to some extent, among his followers in the party outside Parliament. But when he appeared before the party conference in early October (as Chairman of the NEC he presided over its opening session) he was rapturously received. C. T. Cramp (of the National Union of Railwaymen), vice-chairman of the NEC, moved a resolution which read in part: " That this Annual Conference of the Labour Party takes this, the first, opportunity of congratulating J. Ramsay MacDonald upon the success achieved in the political organization of the Labour Movement, the task to which he set his hand twenty-five years ago, and upon his attainment to office as Prime Minister at the head of the first Labour Government; we place on record our appreciation of the service he has devoted to the Party, and express our hearty confidence in his leadership." The motion was seconded by Herbert Smith of the Miners' Federation; there was no discussion and it was " carried unanimously amidst cheers". When MacDonald, at the close of the conference, rose to announce that the Government, having sustained a defeat in the Commons, would go to the country he received what the conference report describes as " a tumultuous ovation". [2] No Conservative Leader ever received more fulsome praise or more ecstatic approbation.

While the first Labour Government was in office, the PLP adopted the practice (which has been maintained during each subsequent Labour Government) of electing a back-bencher as Chairman of the PLP; during the lifetime of the Government therefore the offices of Chairman and Leader were divorced. Thus when the Labour Party went to the country in 1924, its electoral appeal was signed by MacDonald as " *Leader of the Labour Party*," Clynes " Deputy Leader," Robert Smillie " *Chairman of the Parliamentary Labour Party Executive* " and George Lansbury " Vice Chairman". But with the fall of the Government in 1924 the title " Leader " was linked again with that of " Chairman".

At the annual conference of 1925 MacDonald was frequently referred to as the " Leader ". Thus the conference report records: " Mr. J. Maxton, M.P. (ILP) said he wished to ask the Chairman

---

[1] *Beatrice Webb's Diaries*, 2nd September, 1924, folio 85. But Webb, it now appears, thought MacDonald's behaviour in Cabinet was " perfect". Webb, S., " The First Labour Government," *Political Quarterly*, Jan.–March, 1961, p. 19.

[2] *1924 Labour Annual Conference Report*, pp. 113-16 and p. 182.

(of the conference) a somewhat extended question, but he understood from the leader of the Parliamentary Labour Party that, in order to do that, it was necessary that he should move the reference back and in obedience to the request of his leader, he was prepared to do so." [1] MacDonald spoke indeed on three of the four days on which the 1925 conference took place and subsequently there were protests from the left wing of the party about the dominant rôle which he had now assumed in the affairs of the annual conference. George Lansbury wrote of the 1925 conference: " It is quite impossible to escape from the conviction that as a conference the gathering from first to last was a complete failure. The proceedings were managed and controlled from above. Individual delegates had very little chance. . . . From start to finish MacDonald and Henderson dominated the delegates . . . ." [2]

At the 1926 conference MacDonald again played a more prominent rôle than any PLP Chairman ever had before; he spoke on no less than twenty occasions.[3] And by 1928 he was indicating in most emphatic fashion that the PLP under his leadership would not be subject to outside domination or control. In the discussion at the conference of that year on the report of the parliamentary party, Fenner Brockway (on behalf of the ILP) moved the reference back of the paragraph dealing with the PLP's decision to sit on the Statutory Inquiry on the Government of India (the Simon Commission). Brockway criticized the PLP for taking part, in view of the fact that there was much opposition to the Commission from Indian organizations. Speaking in reply to the debate, MacDonald said in part: " There was one thing he would like to say, and he thought it was about time they said it. As long as he held any position in the Parliamentary Party—and he knew he could speak for his colleagues also—they were not going to take their instructions from any outside body unless they agreed with them." [4] MacDonald's comment is dealt with below in a discussion of the autonomy of the PLP, but it is significant also in another

[1] *1925 Labour Annual Conference Report*, p. 216.

[2] George Lansbury, writing in *Lansbury's Weekly,* 10th October, 1925.

[3] See *1926 Labour Annual Conference Report.* MacDonald's interventions in the conference proceedings can be classified as follows: Replying to resolutions or winding-up debates or moving adoption of policy resolutions, 8 times; answering points raised on PLP report, 9 times (including a reply to a heated debate on M.P.s' attendances); a personal explanation (of his attitude to the Miners' Relief Fund); a speech of thanks for a gift of sixty roses and £60 on his sixtieth birthday; moving a final omnibus vote of thanks. It should be noted that Henderson, the Party Secretary, was absent from the conference which placed a heavier burden on MacDonald.

[4] *1928 Labour Annual Conference Report,* p. 174. On a card vote Brockway's motion was lost 150,000 to 2,959,000.

context. MacDonald's prime purpose in making this remark was no doubt to indicate that the PLP had no intention of bowing to pressure from Indian political organizations; but neither, MacDonald made it clear, had the PLP any intention of accepting domination or direction from the party conference. The words MacDonald used in insisting on the autonomy of the parliamentary party would have been just as appropriate in the mouth of a Conservative Leader.

Later, at the same conference (after MacDonald had departed) one delegate, in moving the reference back of a section of the Parliamentary Report, said in part: ". . . He hoped the Leader of the Parliamentary Party would be good enough to help them by reporting on (a particular) point." Clynes (in the absence of MacDonald) said " he would report that view to the Leader of the Parliamentary Labour Party." And when, on another issue, questions were put to Lansbury, the Chairman of the conference, he said: " he was not the Leader of the Parliamentary Party . . . . the question was put to the Leader, and the Leader, unhappily, could not stay there all the time." [1] These remarks were not particularly important in themselves but they suggest an attitude of deference to the Party Leader which was new to the Labour conference and strikingly reminiscent of the atmosphere of the Conservative conference.

Within the PLP itself, MacDonald was re-elected annually without opposition throughout the period 1924-9. There had been undertones of opposition on the occasion of the first PLP elections after the return to opposition. The Lobby Correspondent of the *Daily Herald* wrote of the meeting (which took place on 3rd December, 1924): " I understand that . . . When the motion to elect Mr. MacDonald (Chairman and Leader), which was moved by Mr. Henderson, was put there were five dissentients. During the preliminary discussion Mr. Maxton reviewed the record of the Labour Government, some aspects of which he criticized severely. He nominated Mr. George Lansbury for the leadership . . . . (but) Mr. Lansbury, who said he was unaware of the intention to nominate him until just before the meeting, declined to allow his name to be put forward. *He urged that a change of leadership would be most inopportune in the present circumstances.* A further suggestion was made by Mr. Ben Smith that the election of a leader should be postponed until there had been further and adequate inquiry into the circumstances of the alleged Zinoviev letter. . . . After Mr. Henderson had emphasized the intention to pursue the Zinoviev inquiry Mr. Ben Smith withdrew his motion." [2] With even George

---

[1] *1928 Labour Annual Conference Report*, pp. 177-8.
[2] *Daily Herald*, 4th December, 1924.

Lansbury agreeing that a change of Leader would be " inopportune", MacDonald's position was secure. There could no longer
be any doubt that he had become Leader of the Party in almost
exactly the sense that the term was used in the Conservative Party;
and ironically his ascendancy over his followers was greater during
1924-31 than was that of Stanley Baldwin during the same period.[1]

Until 1930 MacDonald continued to hold his position on the
NEC by virtue of his election by the annual conference as Treasurer
of the party, but in the constitutional revisions of 1929 it was provided that: " The Leader of the Parliamentary Labour Party shall
be *ex officio* a member of the National Executive Committee."
The background of this constitutional change is of importance.
Since 1912 MacDonald had each year been nominated by the ILP
for the office of party Treasurer and re-elected to that post unopposed, except on one occasion during the Great War when a candidate
stood unsuccessfully against him. By 1927, however, MacDonald's
relations with the ILP had become very strained and the National
Administrative Council (hereinafter NAC) of the organization
decided not to nominate him for the treasurership of the party.
This decision was confirmed by the annual conference of the ILP
when an attempt to move the reference back of the report of the
Council's decision was defeated by 312 votes to 118.[2] On the last
day of the conference an effort was made to soften the effect of the
decision. The NAC submitted through its chairman, James
Maxton, M.P., an explanation that the ILP delegation to the Labour
Party annual conference " would be free . . . to vote for Mr.
MacDonald's retention of the position of Treasurer if the nomination came from another quarter." Maxton added: " We retain
personal friendliness towards Mr. MacDonald and recognize him
as leader of the Parliamentary Party which includes members of all
sections of the Labour Party. In that capacity, while retaining our
recognized right to express our distinctive point of view on occasions,
we shall faithfully give him the support which our loyalty to the
wider movement requires."[3]

At the following Labour Party conference MacDonald was
re-elected without opposition to the position of Treasurer. But
clearly the action of the ILP in withdrawing its nomination of Mac-

[1] See p. 113 ff. above. For an account of the currents of opposition to Mac-
Donald after 1924, see Lyman, R. W., *The First Labour Government, 1924*,
p. 272 ff.

[2] MacDonald, who was at the time visiting the United States, said when
interviewed in New York (18th April): "The ILP did not make up the
bulk of the Labour Party. They are a ' cave ' within the party. They are
angry with me because I do not go out on the house tops and shout socialism." *Daily News*, 19th April, 1927.

[3] *The Times*, 18th and 20th April, 1927.

Donald had raised the further ugly possibility that they (or some other constituent element of the Labour Party) might eventually nominate a rival candidate for the office of Treasurer. MacDonald would then be faced with the embarrassing necessity of testing his popularity in the mass party outside Parliament, a test which the Leader of any parliamentary party would be most reluctant to face. Arrangements were therefore made to provide for the Leader's *ex officio* membership of the Executive. Here then is another indication of the process by which the Leader of the parliamentary party came to resemble the Leader of the other parties in Parliament. It represented a further step in eliminating the possibility of direct control of the Leader by the mass organization.[1]

Meanwhile on the eve of the formation of the second Labour Government there were spirited discussions in certain sections of the Labour movement on the subject of Cabinet-making. At the annual conference of the ILP in April 1929, James Maxton, M.P., opened a discussion on " the selection of a Socialist Cabinet". He said he knew that " when Mr. Ramsay MacDonald's Government came into office (in 1924) there was no consultation with the responsible Labour officials." A resolution was moved on behalf of the Scottish branches of the ILP stating that " in view of the possibility of the Socialist Government being returned to power at the next general election the conference declare against the past procedure of a Prime Minister selecting the Cabinet, and pledging itself to support the proposal that the Prime Minister and the Cabinet should be selected by the Parliamentary (Labour) Party." Another branch moved an amendment in favour of the Prime Minister submitting his suggested Cabinet to the parliamentary party for approval. This amendment was defeated, as was another which proposed that the Prime Minister should select the Cabinet in conjunction with the NEC. A third amendment deleting the proposal in the original motion that the Prime Minister himself should be selected by the parliamentary party was, however, accepted and the amended resolution therefore proposed merely that the Cabinet should be selected by the PLP. Emanuel Shinwell, M.P., opposed the resolution, claiming that it would be " very perplexing to select a Cabinet by ballot". He hoped that until they had some years of experience in government they would not tamper with the undoubted right of the Prime Minister to select the men who were, in his judgment, best fitted to undertake Cabinet responsibility. In reply, James Maxton urged that *after* the general election the parliamentary

---

[1] Subsequently MacDonald resigned as Treasurer of the Party on 25th June, 1930, and thereafter until his break with the party he served on the NEC in an *ex officio* capacity. *Daily Herald,* 26th June, 1930.

party should elect its Leader, and that in selecting his Cabinet he should be required to consult with the " most responsible officials of the Labour Party." He added: " I know from Lord Haldane's autobiography that there were consultations with him (during the formation of the 1924 Government) but what was Lord Haldane's responsible official relationship to the Labour Party at the time? He was taken into the Cabinet. I want responsible consultations with the PLP. *I want the last word in control.* . . . it is absolutely necessary that the ultimate real power should be in the hands of the rank and file of the working class movement." After Maxton had spoken the resolution (as amended) was carried.[1]

It was to be expected that the ILP would reflect the most deep-seated suspicion of the tremendous authority accorded a Prime Minister in the formation of his Cabinet. As early as 1914 the annual conference of the ILP had passed by a large majority a resolution which read in part: " That Cabinet rule, which involves the suppression of the rights of the private member to any adequate voice in the policy of his Party . . . is inimical to the good government of the country; (and) that with a view to the ultimate break-up of this system, the Parliamentary Labour Party be asked to take no account of any such considerations . . ." The resolution won wide favour in the conference and even one of the speakers who opposed it (William C. Anderson, who argued that it was too negative and proposed no alternative system) had added: " He was not persuaded that the present method of making a Cabinet was the only possible method; he was not persuaded that if the Labour Party came into power they would form a Cabinet on the present absurd system. That was not the way the Labour Party went to work in Australia. There was room for infinite development and a great sweeping away of anomalies . . ."[2] But in 1929, as in 1924, none of the " anomalies " were swept away and MacDonald followed the customary parliamentary practices in the formation of his Government. In contrast to 1924 he conferred, however, more closely with his senior colleagues in the PLP, in particular with Snowden, Thomas, Clynes and Henderson.[3]

---

[1] *Morning Post,* 3rd April, 1929. [Italics mine.] Cf. Haldane, *An Autobiography,* pp. 319-25.

[2] *1914 I.L.P. Annual Conference Report,* pp. 111 ff.

[3] See Snowden, *An Autobiography,* Vol. II, Chapter LXI, for a description of the rather acrimonious discussions between MacDonald and his colleagues on the subject of Cabinet-making. See also Dalton, H., *Call Back Yesterday,* p. 210. Dalton reports a conversation with Henderson in which the latter told him of a meeting he had attended with MacDonald, Snowden, Clynes and Thomas (approximately seven weeks before the 1929 election): " J. R. M. said he hoped they would all put themselves in his hands, ' or rather in your own hands '. He seemed to regard the other four

Again, as in 1924, the party outside Parliament made no effort to intervene. Snowden described in his autobiography a meeting of the NEC and of the Parliamentary Executive held on 5th June while the Cabinet was in process of formation: " We expected (he wrote) that there would be questions about the way in which the Government was being formed, and that the dissatisfaction which had been felt in 1924 at the large share of the appointments which had then been given to the non-Trade Unionist element in the Party would find expression. However, MacDonald made a brief and tactful opening statement. He revealed nothing, and there was not a word of enquiry as to the construction of the new Government. Everybody there who was an M.P. evidently hoped that he would be in the new Government, and was afraid to speak. The meeting showed a desire to leave MacDonald free in the appointment of his Ministers."[1] Indeed, both in Cabinet-making and in his work as Prime Minister in both Governments, MacDonald exercised the usual prerogatives of the office of Prime Minister and was no more subject to external controls than the Leader of any other party.

Had MacDonald's second Government proved a success, or alternatively had he resigned the office of Prime Minister in August 1931 and continued as Leader of the Labour Party, he would in all probability have won and retained an authority as secure and untrammelled as that ever accorded any Liberal or Conservative Leader. But MacDonald's " betrayal " of the Labour movement in 1931 came as a traumatic shock from which the party has by no means yet fully recovered. In the short run it stimulated a widespread demand within the party that safeguards should be devised to preclude the possibility of any one individual achieving such a dominant position in the affairs of the party. There were demands from all sections of the party that the Leader must henceforth be brought under more effective control. Walter Citrine, secretary of the Trades Union Congress, said on October 14th, 1931: " The Labour movement could reasonably complain of dictation. It resented the attempted dictatorship of Mr. MacDonald. Never again would a Labour Prime Minister or a Labour

as an informal committee to discuss and advise on appointments, without any formal departure from the constitutional practice by which the Prime Minister alone selects Ministers." At pp. 213 ff. Dalton has a further discussion on Cabinet-making in 1929.

[1] Snowden, *An Autobiography*, Vol. II, p. 762. Fenner Brockway writes that at a PLP meeting shortly after the 1929 Government took office, both he and John Wheatley (for the ILP groups) condemned the decision to take office while Labour was in a minority. But when MacDonald replied " most of the Labour M.P.s rose to greet him, clapping their hands rapturously and . . . cheering . . . " Brockway, F., *Inside the Left*, pp. 197-9.

Chancellor of the Exchequer be permitted to exercise such auto-cratic power."[1]   The left-wing section of the party was even more insistent.   At the 1931 conference Fenner Brockway (speaking on behalf of the ILP) said in part: ". . . when you come to apply the principles of democracy to the Parliamentary Labour Party this is the fact you have to face, that the policy of the Labour Party when you have a Labour Government is not in the hands of the Parlia-mentary Labour Party at all.   The policy is determined by a Prime Minister who has selected his own Government, and again and again the Parliamentary Party is faced with proposals brought forward in such a way that it is impossible in a democratic way for the Parliamentary Party to reverse those proposals."   He gave several instances of actions by the second Labour Government which he claimed were overwhelmingly opposed by the Parlia-mentary Party and added that the PLP was nevertheless forced " under duress and under threat " to endorse the Government's action.

A special committee representing both the NEC and the Executive of the PLP was set up to examine " various matters relating to the Labour Party again taking office as a Government " and the problem of party discipline generally.   The 1932 conference report notes that this committee ". . . has had the opportunity of hearing the views of members of the late Labour Cabinet.   Owing to the neces-sity for the fullest consultation . . . the Committee has not yet com-pleted its report: but proposes to continue its work immediately after the (adjournment of this conference)." A number of speakers insisted, however, on raising the matter at the 1932 conference.   Sir Charles Trevelyan (who had served as Minister of Education in the second Labour Government) noted that there were a large number of resolutions on the agenda relating to the formation of the next Labour Government and " those resolutions express considerable dissatisfaction at the present system under which a single man or a single man with one or two other people helping him is able to form a Government and carry out the policy of the Government at his own sweet will."   Trevelyan then asked: ". . . whether the plat-form can give us a definite promise that at the next Conference a report will be brought up which will deal with the question of what is to happen when the King has next to send for a Labour Prime Minister, how that Prime Minister is to be selected and how he is to select his colleagues."   The speaker added that " most of us " feel that there must be " great evolutionary developments in the direction of giving the mass of the movement a chance of saying

[1] *The Times*, 15th October, 1931. For Herbert Morrison's comment on the Party's almost neurotic fears of leadership after 1931, see his *Autobiography*, Chapter XII.

how it shall be ruled. The events of last year were a great shock to
this party in its confidence in men, but there is no shock to its
confidence in itself, and we have got to evolve a system for the
future."

Henderson (then Leader of the PLP, as well as Secretary and
Treasurer of the NEC) replied that all these matters " are being
very, very carefully considered." And the conference chairman
added: " There will be a report; you may take that for granted."
A delegate then moved a resolution instructing the NEC to confer
with the General Council of the TUC and the PLP to formulate a
scheme for submission and approval by the next annual conference:
" (a) to determine whether the Labour Party shall form a government when an invitation has been extended, (b) to provide a more
satisfactory method for the selection of members of any future
Labour Cabinet, (c) to ensure that the administration and proposed
legislation of a Labour Cabinet should not depart from the principles embodied in conference decisions, etc." The seconder of the
resolution warned that if there was a swing of the pendulum,
" you may have (another Labour) Prime Minister who will turn
round, as MacDonald did, and say, ' I take no notice of you and
your conferences.' " Henderson in reply again reminded the
conference that these matters were already being considered; but
he gave a specific pledge (which is discussed below) on behalf of the
Executive that " we will undertake the formation of no Government until we have called this conference together again . . . . to
consider on what lines we should proceed and what our policy
should be." After this assurance from Henderson the resolution
was withdrawn.[1]

But there were other evidences at the 1932 conference that the
members of the party were determined not to allow the Leader of
the Party and his colleagues freedom of action to decide the nature
of the programme which would be followed by a future Labour
Government. Sir Charles Trevelyan moved a resolution: " That
the leaders of the next Labour Government and the Parliamentary
Labour Party be instructed by the national conference that, on
assuming office, either with or without power, definite Socialist
legislation must be immediately promulgated and that the Party
shall stand or fall in the House of Commons on the principles in
which it has faith." In support of this resolution Trevelyan said:
" Let us make no mistake when our chance comes again. We do
not know who our leaders may be, but let there be no mistake as to
what they have got to do, whoever they may be. . . . Let us lay
down in some such resolution as this the unshakable mandate that

[1] *1932 Labour Annual Conference Report*, pp. 168-71.

they are to introduce at once, before attempting remedial measures of any other kind, great Socialist measures . . . " There was strong support for the resolution (from among others, C. R. Attlee, M.P., see p. 364 below). Arthur Henderson spoke against the resolution, warning the conference " . . . if you accept this resolution you are tying your hands. . . . I think if you do it you will regret it." But he met with the most hostile reception he had ever received from the party conference.

There was no mistaking the mood of the conference; they were convinced they had been betrayed by their Leader and his associates and were determined that it should never happen again. Against Henderson's advice Trevelyan's resolution was carried. But the conference was still not satisfied that it had eliminated every possibility that the leaders of the next Labour Government might escape the direction and control of their followers. Another resolution was moved that stated in part: " Labour M.P.s taking Ministerial office shall be subject . . . to decisions of the Parliamentary Labour Party." Again supporting speakers recalled that certain Ministers in the second Labour Government had refused to make decisions of the PLP operative. One delegate added: " I may be told by the platform that the worst offenders in this respect have left us. That may be true but we have been caught once, and that, perhaps, was not our fault, but if we are caught a second time it will be our fault." Another supporting speaker added: ". . . I say we should control the Cabinet, so that the policy laid down by this Conference shall not be, ' we hope to do this or that,' but that when we put these people in office they will carry out the will of the Movement, they will obey the mandates of this Conference, failing which this Party shall have power to remove them. All that we are seeking is the control of the machine which we have built up . . ." George Lansbury (then Chairman of the PLP) replied for the Executive and succeeded in getting part of the resolution defeated; but the section quoted above (that Ministers should be subject to the decisions of the PLP) was carried.[1]

At the following year's conference (1933) the NEC presented an elaborate report (based on its consultations with the parliamentary party) dealing with most of the issues which had been raised during the previous conference about relations between a Labour Prime Minister, his Cabinet, the PLP and the party outside Parliament. This report is examined below, but reference must be made here to the sections which dealt with the rôle of the Party Leader. The NEC began by noting that it was the practice of the parliamentary

[1] *1932 Labour Annual Conference Report*, pp. 204–9. On the mood of the Party during this period, see Miliband, R., *Parliamentary Socialism*, Chapter VII.

party prior to the close of each session to elect its Executive for the following session, and the NEC recommended: " That when a Dissolution takes place, the election of the Executive of the Parliamentary Party should be deferred until after the General Election . . ."[1] The NEC then proceeded to outline a detailed set of recommendations regarding the procedure to be followed in the event that Labour was in a position to form a Government (either on a majority or minority basis). And several further suggestions were made regarding the rôle of a Labour Prime Minister. In the choice of Ministers, the NEC stated that " it is realised that final responsibility . . . must rest with the Prime Minister." But it proposed that three members of the PLP should be elected to *advise* the Party Leader, and that the Secretary of the Party should be associated with them in this task. The NEC further proposed that " the Prime Minister should be subject to majority decisions of the Cabinet, and that he should only recommend the Dissolution of Parliament on the decision of the Cabinet confirmed by a Parliamentary Party meeting." Other recommendations were made designed to " put an end to the practice by which excessive authority (in the field of financial policy) has in the past been exercised by the Chancellor of the Exchequer," and to ensure closer liaison between members of the Government, the parliamentary party and the Labour movement outside Parliament.[2]

In speaking to this report on behalf of the NEC Clynes said: ". . . we propose that never again should any one leader of the Party be empowered singly to use his personal authority, and himself alone choose his Cabinet or appoint his Ministers. We say he should only act in that regard after consultation with other leaders of the Party in close touch with the members, who are perhaps as fitted as any Prime Minister can be to suggest appoint-

[1] The circumstances in which this recommendation was made must be kept in mind. The party had been reduced to a representation of 46 in the House of Commons and Lansbury, as the only former Cabinet Minister returned, had been elected Chairman of the PLP, with Henderson continuing for a time as Leader although he was not in the House of Commons. Subsequently, on Henderson's resignation, Lansbury had been elected Chairman and Leader at the opening of the parliamentary session 1932-3. *1933 Labour Annual Conference Report*, p. 73. The clear intention of the above recommendation was that the party wanted to leave itself free to choose someone other than Lansbury as Chairman and Leader from among the much larger number of M.P.s they expected would be returned following a general election. It was apparently assumed that in the event of the Labour Party being returned with a majority the sovereign would await the meeting of the PLP at which a new Chairman and Leader would be elected and that he would then call whoever had been selected and invite him to form a ministry.

[2] *1933 Labour Annual Conference Report*, pp. 8-10.

ments . . ." But Clynes added: "To select by election, or to choose by election, to appoint by a show of hands, or by a majority action, would, in our judgment, be a fatal blunder and give rise to even greater discontent than this process might allay . . ." He concluded: ". . . *our view is that actual power must be vested in a leader who, by his past work, has been placed in that position, but he must act only in consultation and conjunction with others of his colleagues.*" [1]

One wonders whether the members of the conference realized that Clynes was here describing exactly the procedure which MacDonald had followed in the selection of his 1929 Cabinet. All available evidence suggests that he had indeed consulted " other leaders of the party in close touch with the members " and pro- minent among them, of course, had been Clynes himself. Yet Clynes appeared in this statement almost to imply that MacDonald had consulted no one (and presumably that this accounted for the ineptitude of the Cabinet which he had selected). It is important to note that Clynes, on behalf of the NEC, firmly rejected every suggestion that a future Labour Prime Minister should be required to share formal responsibility for Cabinet-making either with the PLP or with any other organ of the Labour Party. The Leader would be required to do no more than consult with three of his parliamentary colleagues named by the PLP and with the Secretary of the Party. After he had heard their advice he would presumably be free to consult anyone else he wished; he could then set about the formation of his Government (like the Leader of any other party) with no external interference or control.

Some members of the conference were clearly dissatisfied with Clynes's observation on the subject of the Labour Leader's rôle in Cabinet-making. An amendment was moved: " That this Con- ference condemns the principle of granting to any one man the right to nominate members to form the Cabinet, as being entirely un- democratic, and herewith declares that, in the event of Labour once again securing the right to form the Government of the country, the selection of men and women to hold Cabinet rank, or other Govern- mental posts, shall be made by a Joint Committee of the National Joint Council (representing the Trades Union Congress and the Labour Party) and the Co-operative Party." This amendment was lost by 519,000 to 1,579,000 [2] and the NEC report was adopted. Whether the conference realized it or not the matter was left almost exactly where it had been before. There was no reason at all to expect that the method of Cabinet-building pursued by a Labour

[1] *1933 Labour Annual Conference Report,* p. 167. [Italics mine.]
[2] *Ibid.,* p. 168.

Leader would differ in any significant respect from the procedure followed by a Conservative Leader. And in the event, Clement Attlee ignored completely the 1933 conference resolution when he came to form his Cabinet in 1945.[1]

Clynes had also commented on the NEC recommendation that " the Prime Minister should be subject to majority decisions of the Cabinet, and that he should only recommend the Dissolution of Parliament on the decision of the Cabinet, confirmed by a Parliamentary Party meeting." Clynes observed: " There is nothing devastating in that. It is merely applying to Cabinet work the same democratic rule by which the House of Commons does its work, and by which every Trade Union works . . ." In fact, of course, there *was* something devastating about this, as Clynes must certainly have known. The Cabinet had never operated on the narrow principle of majority decision, nor has it since. The writer has discussed this matter with members of the Attlee Cabinets and is satisfied that their method of operation differed in no significant respect from the standard practice of previous Liberal and Conservative Cabinets.[2] There was no question that " the Prime Minister should be subject to majority decisions of the Cabinet." Nor, incidentally, did Attlee implement the NEC recommendation that a Labour Prime Minister " should only recommend the Dissolution of Parliament on the decision of the Cabinet confirmed by a Parliamentary Party meeting." In the dissolution of 1951, there is good reason to doubt that Attlee consulted the Cabinet; certainly he did not consult the PLP.[3] In retrospect it is clear that the debates which took place at the party conferences of 1932 and 1933, and the recommendations of the NEC with regard to a Labour Prime Minister and his Cabinet, merely reflected a quite understandable revulsion against what the party considered to be the arrogant aloofness of MacDonald and his intolerable betrayal of the party. But the safeguards they hoped to devise appear to have been ignored or forgotten when Labour came to power again in 1945.

Meanwhile it was perhaps fortunate that from the downfall of MacDonald throughout the 1930s the party was served by a series of three Leaders none of whom roused serious apprehension in the minds of their followers. Henderson succeeded MacDonald and carried on as Leader (although he was outside Parliament) from the election of 1931 until October 1932,[4] while Lansbury served as

[1] See p. 332 below.

[2] See also Morrison, H., *Government and Parliament,* Chapter I.

[3] See also Attlee's own comment on these events in *As It Happened,* p. 207 and Dalton, H., *High Tide and After*, p. 377.

[4] Henderson became convinced that his early return to Parliament (by way of a by-election) was unlikely and that the party was at a disadvantage

Chairman of the PLP. After Henderson's resignation Lansbury combined the posts of Leader and Chairman until his own resignation in 1935, when he was succeeded by Attlee.   Henderson's election to the leadership had obviously been a stop-gap arrangement and so in a sense was that of George Lansbury. Lansbury was elected solely because he was the only Labour ex-Cabinet Minister returned to the House of Commons in the debacle of 1931, and he readily recognized that the mood of the party and his own almost accidental elevation to the leadership made it necessary that he should tread carefully. He confessed to the 1934 Labour annual conference: " I never dreamed in my wildest imagining that I would ever be called upon to act as the spokesman—*I have never considered myself Leader*—but as the spokesman of my colleagues in the House of Commons. . . . It was an accident that put me there—the accident of the last General Election—and I am only there so long as my colleagues think it wise for me to be there." [1]

But if Lansbury denied that he considered himself Leader he nevertheless recognized that even as spokesman for his party he could not submit himself to day-to-day direction by any section of the Labour movement. Thus when Ernest Bevin wrote condemning him for agreeing to speak at a meeting called by the Socialist League without first getting permission of the National Joint Council of the Labour Party and the Trades Union Congress, Lansbury replied defiantly: " Whenever I feel it is impossible to state the Party's own view I shall of course resign, not merely from leadership but from membership; but I do maintain my right to put the Party's case . . . wherever an opportunity occurs, and I do not think I am called upon to ask permission from anybody to do this—and certainly have no intention of doing so." [2] But as the gulf widened between Lansbury's personal views on the issue of peace and war and those of the party as a whole his position as " spokesman " of the party became increasingly difficult. As he explained to the party conference of 1935:

in having a Leader who was outside Parliament. He wrote a letter to the PLP which read in part: " I have reached the conclusion that the interests of the party, both in Parliament and in the country, would best be served if we reverted to the former practice of regarding the Chairman of the Parliamentary Party as the actual leader." *The Times*, 19th October, 1932. See also Dalton, H., *The Fateful Years*, p. 24.

[1] *1934 Labour Annual Conference Report*, p. 146. The parenthetical observation ("I have never considered myself leader ") was no doubt warmly welcomed by a party still suffering from the shock of what Attlee has called (*As It Happened*, p. 74), " the greatest betrayal in the political history of this country."

[2] Cited in Postgate, R., *The Life of George Lansbury*, p. 288.

" Often—and only the Executive and my colleagues know how often—I have disagreed with their policy, and because I was a member of the Executive, and lately because of my other position (Leader), I have remained silent during the whole of the Conference. . . . During the last six years—first in the Labour Government, and secondly as Leader of the Party—I have been in a kind of Dr. Jekyll and Mr. Hyde position. I have had to speak for the Party . . . and on each occasion when I have spoken for the Party . . . I tried honestly and straightforwardly to state the Party's position. . . . but my position personally has never shifted." [1]

There could be no better indication of the extent to which Lansbury had attempted to fulfil the rôle of spokesman and had renounced the rôle of Leader as it is normally conceived. Ultimately, however, his position became intolerable and he resigned immediately after the annual conference of 1935.

Attlee, who succeeded Lansbury, also appeared at first to be a stop-gap choice.[2] It was assumed by most observers (and by many members of the party) that Labour must somewhere discover a more dynamic Leader if they were ever to win office again; even Attlee himself has half conceded that he shared the same assumption. As he puts it in the concluding sentence of his autobiography, ". . . I have been a very happy and fortunate man . . . in having been given the opportunity of serving in a state of life to which I had never expected to be called." [3] But Attlee's apparent modesty and lack of dynamism was to help him to win acceptance as Leader; and these same qualities made it easier for his followers to tolerate the abrupt transformation in their relationship to their Leader when they assumed office in 1945 and he became Prime Minister. As Roy Jenkins has put it, " Attlee, as a Labour leader, is partly a product of the reaction to MacDonald. . . . . Better a pedestrian speaker who meant what he said than a spell-binder who bemused himself with his own words; better a middle-class man with no social ambitions than a worker who was trying to rise; better a self-effacing modesty than a self-destroying vanity." [4]

In the immediate pre-war years Attlee tended, like Lansbury, to act more as chairman and spokesman than as Leader. There was frequent public criticism of his work, even in Labour quarters,[5] and

---

[1] *1935 Labour Annual Conference Report*, pp. 175-6.

[2] See pp. 357-61 below for a discussion of Attlee's emergence as Leader.

[3] Attlee, C. R., *As It Happened*, p. 217.

[4] Jenkins, R., *Mr. Attlee*, pp. 102-3.

[5] The following quotation from the *Labour Organizer* is fairly typical: " One of the misfortunes of the Labour Party in recent years is that since 1931 it has been minus the wealth of leadership which it had before the split. . . . (this) has afforded some opportunity to back-seat drivers to make their presence felt . . . *A strong leader would have put these people in their places.*"

Attlee himself has recalled that while he was ill in the summer of 1939 ". . . it occurred to a few people that this would be a good opportunity to change the leadership of the Party." But, as Attlee adds laconically ". . . this move got little support." [1]

Attlee's careful handling of the negotiations which led to Labour's entry into the Churchill coalition and his quiet competence as Deputy Prime Minister undoubtedly greatly increased his stature both in the party and in the country. During the negotiations with Chamberlain and Churchill in May 1940, he was extremely careful to work in close consultation with the party organization both within and outside Parliament. He has provided his own account of the events which followed immediately after the Commons debate of 8th May during which it had become clear that the downfall of Chamberlain's Government was inevitable.

> " On Thursday, May 9th, (he wrote), the day after the debate, Chamberlain asked Arthur Greenwood and me to call at Downing Street. We found him with Lord Halifax and Churchill. I told him that I knew the views of our party in the House and in the country and I was perfectly certain that they would not consent to come into a Government of which, in effect, he was the head. It was not a pleasant task to tell a Prime Minister that he ought to go, but I had no option but to tell him the truth. I was then asked whether Labour would take part in a Coalition of which someone else was the head. I said that I thought they would but that as the Party was holding its Annual Conference at Bournemouth I would go down and ask the delegates. It was accordingly agreed that I should put to them two questions:
>   (1) Would they enter a Government under the present Prime Minister? (2) Would they come in under someone else?" [2]

The next day, Friday, 10th May (the day in which German troops invaded Holland and Belgium), Attlee met the NEC at Bournemouth and placed the two questions before them. The NEC unanimously answered " No " to the first and " Yes " to the second. Chamberlain resigned during the afternoon to be succeeded by Churchill. Later the same evening Attlee discussed with the new Prime Minister the allocation of the key offices in the new Coalition Ministry. Earlier he had apparently discussed with Greenwood, the Vice-Chairman of the PLP, the names of those he

---

Quoted in *Politics in Review*, January–March, 1936, p. 101. [Italics mine.] The same article warned, incidentally, against the " tendency " of the Labour Party in this period to become a very humble servant of the TUC.

[1] Attlee, C. R., *As It Happened*, p. 105. See also Dalton, H. *The Fateful Years*, Chapter XVI, and Shinwell, E., *Conflict without Malice*, p. 132 ff.

[2] *Ibid.*, pp. 112–13.

intended to recommend for office. Two days later Attlee returned to Bournemouth and reported on his actions to a joint meeting of the NEC and the General Council of the TUC: they gave their unanimous approval. On the following morning Attlee moved an emergency resolution at the opening session of the full party conference. It read in part: " That this Conference endorses the unanimous decision of the NEC that the Labour Party should take its share of responsibility as a full partner in a new Government, which, under a new Prime Minister, commands the confidence of the nation," and that " this Conference further pledges its full support to the new Government in its efforts to secure a swift victory and a just peace." [1] The resolution was carried by 2,413,000 for, 170,000 against.

During 1940–45 Attlee continued to serve as Leader while Lees-Smith and Pethick-Lawrence in turn were elected " Acting-Chairman " during 1940–42. After Arthur Greenwood (who had been Deputy-Leader since 1935) left the Government in 1942 he was elected Acting-Chairman and in that capacity presided over the meetings of the PLP. The members of the PLP who were not in the Government sat on the opposition side of the House and this may have helped on occasion to widen the gulf between the Labour Ministers and their followers. But there were few occasions on which any considerable proportion of Labour M.P.s voted against the Coalition Government. Perhaps the most important was on the presentation of the Beveridge Report in February 1943. The PLP became dissatisfied with what it considered the lukewarm attitude of the Government spokesman and put down an amendment expressing disappointment. Ninety-seven Labour M.P.s, including Greenwood, supported the amendment and while there was no suggestion that they intended to force the Labour Party to leave the Coalition, Attlee and his Labour colleagues in the Government apparently made it clear at a private meeting of the PLP that a repetition of such an incident would almost certainly force their resignation from the Government.[2]

At each of the wartime Labour Party conferences Attlee presented a resolution of support for the prosecution of the war and for the Coalition Government. These resolutions were invariably carried by overwhelming majorities although on specific resolutions criticizing various features of Government policy the NEC was sometimes defeated. There was evidence in voting for constituency representatives on the NEC that the popularity of some of the Labour Ministers declined steadily, presumably largely as a result

[1] *1940 Labour Annual Conference Report*, p. 123.
[2] Jenkins, R., *Mr. Attlee*, pp. 234-5.

of their blanket defence of Government policy.[1] But the provision made in 1929 that the Leader should be granted *ex officio* membership of the NEC made it unnecessary for Attlee himself to test his popularity with the party outside Parliament. On balance, however, Jenkins is no doubt justified in claiming that Attlee's complete identification with the administration did not seriously endanger his position as Leader of the Party.[2]

Certainly there was no frontal challenge to Attlee's leadership throughout the war period. This may have reflected a confidence that Attlee still conceived himself primarily as a spokesman for the Labour Party and that there was not the slightest danger that, like MacDonald, he would betray them to the enemy. Harold Laski appears to have been one of the few prominent members of the party who had the temerity to tell Attlee that he should make way for someone else. According to Kingsley Martin's account, Laski told Attlee to his face in 1944 that he ought to give up the leadership " in deference to someone with more of the essential gifts." Laski also appears to have used the dreaded word " MacDonaldism," for Attlee replied (1st May, 1944) in a personal letter to Laski: ". . . I am sorry that you suggest I am verging towards MacDonaldism. As you have so well pointed out I have neither the personality nor the distinction to tempt me to think that I should have any value apart from the Party which I serve. I hope you will also believe that because I am face to face every day with the practical problems of Government I am none the less firm in my Socialist faith and that I have not the slightest desire to depart from it. . . ." [3]

Attlee's rôle in the break-up of the Coalition throws further light on his relationship as Leader of the Party with his followers both within and outside Parliament. He and his other senior colleagues apparently hoped that the Coalition would survive at least until the autumn of 1945 since an autumn election would have provided a more complete electoral register. But Churchill made it clear that the Labour Party must either continue in the Coalition until the end of the war against Japan or else face an immediate election. He showed Attlee privately a letter which he proposed to send him offering the two alternatives. And according to Churchill, Attlee proposed the inclusion of a sentence in Churchill's letter pledging that " we (the Parties of the Coalition) would together do our utmost to implement the proposals for social security and for full employment contained in the White Paper

---

[1] Herbert Morrison, for example, was defeated in the elections to the NEC in 1943.

[2] Jenkins, R., *Mr. Attlee*, p. 239.

[3] Cited in Martin, K., *Harold Laski*, p. 162.

which we have laid before Parliament." Churchill apparently
assumed that in asking for the inclusion of this sentence Attlee
was giving evidence of his intention to accept the proposal that the
Coalition should continue until the end of the war against Japan.
But it seems evident that Attlee had no intention of committing
his party to such a proposal without taking advantage of an
opportunity which happened to be available to consult his followers.
The annual party conference was due to be held in Blackpool a
few days after the publication of Churchill's letter and, according
to Roy Jenkins, Attlee " considered himself the servant as well as the
Leader of the Labour party and he was going to Blackpool to discover the feeling of the delegates and not merely to tell them what to
do."[1] It is an open question, however, whether Attlee would have
insisted that a special conference of the party should be called if it
had not happened that, quite by chance, the conference was in
session when this issue arose. On balance, it seems doubtful that he
would have done so.[2]

Churchill's letter was considered by the NEC on the weekend
19-20th May, 1945, and at a private session of the party conference
on the following day, 21st May, Attlee read the Prime Minister's
letter, reported on the NEC's discussion, and then read to the
conference the text of the letter he proposed to send to Churchill
in reply. The conference report notes that several delegates took
part in the subsequent discussion which was concluded with a
speech by Herbert Morrison on behalf of the NEC. When the
chairman then asked the conference to vote on the question of
Labour Ministers remaining in the Government until the end of the

[1] Jenkins, R., *Mr. Attlee*, p. 245. Jenkins pauses at this point to contrast the attitudes of a Labour and Conservative Leader to their respective
conferences. It is almost inconceivable, as he implies, that a Conservative
Leader would deliberately seek the advice of his party conference on an
issue of this magnitude. But it is worth remembering that the question
of continued participation in the Coalition in 1922 was settled by a full
meeting of the Conservative parliamentary party: and there can be little
doubt that had that meeting at the Carlton Club not decided in favour of
withdrawal from the Coalition the conference of the National Union
(meeting a few days later) would certainly have demanded such action in
such emphatic language as to make Austen Chamberlain's position intolerably difficult. It can hardly be maintained therefore that there is inevitably
a black and white contrast between the way in which an issue of this sort is
likely to be settled in the Conservative and Labour Parties.
[2] In his autobiography he writes: " It will be remembered that the
formation of the wartime Government (in 1940) coincided with the Labour
Party Conference at Bournemouth which enabled me to get the full backing
of the Party for entering Churchill's government. *Fortunately* the same
thing happened in 1945." Attlee, C. R., *As It Happened*, p. 135. [Italics
mine.]

Japanese war, " two hands were held up in favour of this course, which was negatived by an overwhelming majority. The Executive Committee's resolution was then put to the conference and carried with the same two dissentients." [1] Two days after the conference decision Churchill resigned and then returned to office as head of a Caretaker Government.

One incident in the subsequent electoral campaign which was mentioned in Chapter I must be recalled here, since it provides a further illustration of the development of Attlee's conception of his rôle as Leader. Churchill, it will be remembered, invited Attlee and Ernest Bevin to the Potsdam Conference which was to take place after polling day but before the announcement of the results three weeks later. Harold Laski, then Chairman of the NEC, issued a statement which said in part: " It is, of course, essential that if Mr. Attlee attends this gathering he shall do so in the rôle of an observer only." Laski then revealed a really extraordinary misconception of the working of the Labour Party when it is in office by adding:

> " . . . the Labour Party cannot be committed to any decisions arrived at, for the Three-Power Conference will be discussing matters which have not been debated either in the Party Executive or at meetings of the Parliamentary Labour Party."[2]

The next day Churchill formally invited Attlee to attend the conference but drew his attention to Laski's statement, expressing surprise and querying the advisability of Attlee attending the conference under such conditions. Attlee replied, accepting the invitation, and saying that he had consulted his principal colleagues in the House of Commons; he denied any suggestion that he proposed to go as a mere observer. Subsequently, there was a vigorous exchange on the issue between the two party Leaders, in the course of which Churchill commented:

> " . . . the constitution (of the Labour Party) would apparently enable the Executive Committee to call upon a Labour Prime Minister to appear before them and criticize his conduct of the peace negotiations." (And he added) " . . . personally I do not

---

[1] *1945 Labour Annual Conference Report,* p. 87.

[2] Cited in Martin, K., *Harold Laski,* pp. 169-70. Martin cites Laski's memorandum to the NEC defending his action. It goes some way to extenuate Laski's intervention but the incident leaves one with the impression that he assumed that a Labour Prime Minister and Cabinet would be subject to the direction of the NEC and PLP. Attlee himself comments tartly: " [Laski] . . . had no authority to [make this statement]. The Chairman of the Executive does not make authoritative pronouncements of this kind." Attlee, C. R., *As It Happened,* p. 145.

believe that the controversy on these very important issues can be satisfactorily cleared up until the public has a statement signed jointly by yourself and the Chairman of the Executive Committee regarding the use of these powers in future."

Attlee, in reply, conceded that the NEC had " a right to be consulted " but he vigorously denied that it had " power to challenge [the] actions and conduct [of a Labour Prime Minister]."[1] This was more than the exposition of sound constitutional doctrine regarding the rôle of the Prime Minister; it was a clear indication of Attlee's own conception of what was to be his relationship to the NEC once he had become Prime Minister.

There is no evidence that Attlee formally consulted anyone before assuming office as Prime Minister on 26th July, 1945. He has given a characteristically pedestrian account of the events which took place during the course of the day on which the ballots were counted. He wrote that after a visit to his own constituency:

"We drove through the City and picked up my daughter Alison, who was returning from school, and went on to Transport House . . . . We were greeted with great enthusiasm . . . . By the middle of the afternoon it was clear that we had won a great victory.

"Wyndham Portal (later—Attlee adds—Viscount Portal of Portal pre-fab houses fame: he became Chairman of the Great Western Railway) gave us all tea at the Great Western Hotel and presently I was told by the Prime Minister that he was resigning and I had a summons to the Palace.

"My wife drove me round and waited outside for me. The King gave me his Commission to form a Government. He always used to say that I looked very surprised as indeed I certainly was at the extent of our success.

"We went to a victory rally at Westminster Central Hall where I announced that I had been charged with the task of forming a Government, looked in at a Fabian Society gathering and then returned to Stanmore after an exciting day." [2]

The " victory rally " to which Attlee refers was chaired by Professor Laski, then Chairman of the NEC, who introduced Attlee to the meeting as Leader of the Labour Party and made no reference to his having been called to the Palace. It appeared evident that Laski was as surprised as everyone else when Attlee told the meeting that he had been invited by the King to form a Government.[3]

---

[1] See *1946 Labour Annual Conference Report*, p. 5, for a summary of these exchanges. See also Williams, F., *A Prime Minister Remembers*, Chapter VII.

[2] Attlee, C. R., " The Drama of 1945—I Become Premier," *The Star*, 4th June, 1952.

[3] The writer was present as an observer at this meeting.

Laski immediately leapt to his feet to congratulate " the Prime Minister " on his assumption of office. There can hardly be any doubt that Attlee had not consulted the NEC; nor was there any evidence then, or in the article quoted above, that he had sought formal approval of the PLP before he accepted the King's commission to form a Government.[1]

Two days later, after Attlee had made his initial Cabinet appointments, he was unanimously confirmed as Leader at a special meeting of the PLP. But meanwhile he had set about the formation of his Government exactly as the Leader of any other party would have done in the circumstances. He did not invite the PLP to nominate three " advisers "; nor did the PLP reprove him for failing to do so. It may be assumed that he had informal conversations with certain of his colleagues and with the party Whips (there is no indication one way or another on this point in his autobiography); but it is virtually certain that the procedure Attlee followed was in no significant respect different from that followed by MacDonald in the formation of his second administration. From the tone of the passages referring to the formation of the Government in Attlee's autobiography [2] (and from other remarks he has made) one gathers that because of the pressure of international events (the Potsdam conference was still in session) Attlee felt compelled to make his principal appointments with particular speed and therefore with a minimum of preliminary consultations. But clearly this is by no means the whole explanation of why Attlee ignored the 1933 conference decision since elsewhere in his autobiography he remarks blandly:

> " It is not without interest to recall that, after the 1931 Election débâcle, with the very strong feeling that had naturally arisen against MacDonald, proposals were made to restrict the powers of any future Labour Prime Minister. He was to have colleagues selected by the Party to act with him in choosing members of the Government. *The passage of time and further experience has led to these proposals being tacitly dropped.* In my view, the responsibility of choosing the members of the Government must rest solely with the Prime Minister though, in practice, he will consult with his colleagues. If he cannot be trusted to exercise this power in the best interests of the nation and the Party without fear, favour or affection, he is not fit to be Prime Minister. I am quite sure that the method of the Australian Labour Party, whereby a

---

[1] It is now clear that Morrison urged Attlee to delay going to the Palace until the new PLP could meet to elect its Leader and that Morrison would probably have challenged Attlee for the Leadership. See Williams, F., *A Prime Minister Remembers*, p. 3; Morrison, H., *An Autobiography*, p. 245; Dalton, H., *The Fateful Years*, p. 473.

[2] Attlee, C. R., *As It Happened*, pp. 148 ff.

number of members are elected by the Caucus and all that is left to the Prime Minister is to fit the pieces into a jig-saw puzzle as best he may, is quite wrong."[1]

In this comment Attlee does not make it entirely clear that it was he who " tacitly dropped " the decision of the 1933 conference respecting Cabinet-making. This was a development of considerable importance. By this first action after becoming Prime Minister, Attlee gave the clearest possible indication that he intended to exercise all the power and authority which accompanies that office. He made no concessions to the party's former sensitivity on the issue of Cabinet-making.

Throughout Attlee's six years of office there was to be regular and frequent consultation between the Government and the NEC, but there is not the slightest indication that the NEC controlled the affairs of either of Attlee's Governments.[2] The members of the Labour Party were left in no doubt about the fact that the Prime Minister and Cabinet could not share responsibility with the party organization outside Parliament. As Attlee told the 1948 party conference: ". . . the collective responsibility both in home and foreign policy is with the Cabinet. We share the blame or the credit for every action of the Government." Within the PLP an elaborate liaison arrangement was again set up (it varied somewhat from the 1924 and 1929 arrangements) to keep the back-benchers of the party in touch with the activities of Ministers. And, in addition, as the reports of the PLP note: " The Prime Minister, members of the Cabinet and other Ministers (frequently attended the fortnightly meetings of the PLP) to answer points raised in discussions affecting the policy of the Government and administration." But the policies of the Government were not in any sense determined by a majority decision of the PLP any more than they were governed by the decisions of the NEC or the conference. Common sense dictated that he should take into account their views.

---

[1] Attlee, C. R., *As It Happened,* p. 156. [Italics mine.] It is not surprising that again in 1950 Attlee did not invite the PLP to name " advisers " to assist him in Cabinet-making. It can now be assumed therefore that this issue is dead.

[2] Attlee appears to have been particularly irked by the speeches and writings of Harold Laski while he was Chairman of the NEC. Attlee apparently feared that Laski's views might be interpreted abroad as reflecting Government policy. He wrote to Laski privately in the summer of 1946 warning him: " You have no right whatever to speak on behalf of the Government " and added, in a harsh phrase: " I can assure you there is widespread resentment in the Party at your activities and a period of silence on your part would be welcome." Cited in Martin, K., *Harold Laski,* p. 182.

If he outraged his followers in the House, his Government would fall; if he- outraged his followers in the country, he might find himself left without an electoral machine. These two considerations govern any Prime Minister's relations with his followers. But the illusion harboured by some in 1932 and 1933, that a Labour Leader when he became Prime Minister would be primarily a mouthpiece for the PLP and for the movement outside Parliament came to nothing.[1]

Nevertheless Attlee when Prime Minister still thought it wise to say to the party conference: " I have always felt that the right course is to put my views before my colleagues, discuss with them, and then accept their decision. They may not convince me that they are right, but I believe that the foundation of democratic liberty is a willingness to believe that other people may perhaps be wiser than oneself."[2] Comments such as this no doubt helped to reassure Attlee's followers; in addition, his modest manner and apparent lack of conceit helped to smooth the transition from the deep suspicions of the 1930s to the calm acceptance after 1945 of the enormous concentration of authority in the hands of the Prime Minister which the British constitution provides.[3]

After 1951 Attlee appeared to adjust himself with remarkable ease to the more restricted rôle assigned to the Leader of the Party when Labour is in opposition. His colleagues in the Parliamentary Committee were again chosen for him by election of the parliamentary party and he appeared again to emphasize his rôle as spokesman rather than as Leader. But in fact, even with the party in opposition again, Attlee was much more than a mere " spokesman". He was still a potential Prime Minister with a strong prospect of again being able by his own decision to determine the political fate of every one of his colleagues. Attlee was scrupulously careful, however, not to play upon his colleagues' sensitivities in this regard. By his performance both as Prime Minister and as ex-Prime Minister Attlee did more than any other individual to help the Labour Party to adjust itself to the realities of political power as it operates at the highest level in the British system of Cabinet government. Under his leadership, the Labour Party, almost without realizing it, came to accept a principle of party leadership fundamentally similar in its essentials to that which operates in the Conservative Party.

[1] For Attlee's considered view on this issue given ten years after he left office see Williams, F., *A Prime Minister Remembers*, p. 91. His rôle as Prime Minister is assessed by J. P. Mackintosh in his *The British Cabinet*, 1962, pp. 429 ff.

[2] *1948 Labour Annual Conference Report*, p. 160.

[3] For a description of an abortive attempt to remove Attlee in 1947, see Dalton, H., *High Tide and After*, Chapter XXIX, and Williams, F., *A Prime Minister Remembers*, p. 223 ff.

II

THE EMERGENCE OF LABOUR LEADERS: KEIR HARDIE TO ATTLEE

Since 1922 the Labour Party appears to have taken for granted that the Leader of the PLP is in fact " the Leader of the Labour Party "; it seems surprising therefore that no demand ever appears to have been made that the party outside Parliament should play any part in his election, despite the fact that the Conservatives have (since 1937) granted the right of the Executive Committee of the National Union to vote in the elections of the Leader of the Party. In the Labour Party the position remains to-day that while the party is in opposition the PLP elects a " Chairman and Leader "; when the party wins an election he can expect to be called to the office of Prime Minister, and, as long as he holds that office, he is not subject to annual re-election by the PLP. During the life of a Labour Government, a back-bench M.P. is elected each year to serve as Chairman of the PLP; but when the party returns to opposition the offices of Chairman and Leader are combined again and held by one person.

It is worth examining the process by which each of the principal figures who have held the office of Leader have emerged to that position. Since the Labour Party has, in effect, had only three Leaders, MacDonald, Attlee and Gaitskell, their emergence obviously provides the most important illustrations of the process by which Leaders are selected.[1] But some reference must also be made to the early elections to the chairmanship of the PLP before the emergence of MacDonald.

After the election in January 1906 of 29 candidates sponsored by the Labour Representation Committee, Ramsay MacDonald, as Secretary of the LRC, wrote to the members of the Executive Committee of the LRC to notify them that a joint meeting of the Executive and of the newly elected Labour M.P.s was to be convened. He noted that the following questions would be on the agenda: " upon which side of the House should our Party sit?; arrangement for Whips' Office and right of entry to Inner Lobby; attitude of our party to other Labour Members "; and he added: " I propose to put the following points upon the Agenda *which will be discussed by the M.P.s themselves:* (i) Chairman of the group, (ii) Whips, (iii) Meetings of the Party . . ."[2] There

---

[1] The emergence of Gaitskell as Leader is discussed on p. 601, and that of Harold Wilson on p. 630 below.

[2] [Italics mine.] A carbon copy of this letter appears as Folio 370, in Part I

is no indication as to why the LRC so readily and so wisely recognized the wisdom of allowing the M.P.s themselves to select their own Chairman rather than attempting to obtain for themselves some part in the process of his election.   No doubt the main explanation lies in the fact that at that stage the Chairman was in no sense considered to be the Leader of the Party as a whole. His duties, as Snowden emphasized, were primarily to serve as spokesman for his fellow M.P.s and to organize the work of the party in the House.

At their meeting in January 1906, the M.P.s chose as their first Chairman Keir Hardie. It has occasionally been suggested that their choice was an inevitable one [1] but in fact this was far from being the case. Certainly Hardie had contributed more than any one other individual to the building of the party,[2] and in addition he had longer service in Parliament, having first been elected in 1892. But of the 29 members of the LRC elected in 1906, Hardie was one of only seven who had been sponsored by the ILP (although 11 others were members of the ILP). Many of the trade union M.P.s were suspicious of the avowedly-socialist ILP nominees. One of the trade union M.P.s, Shackleton, stood against Hardie in the election for Chairman and, as Snowden recalls, it was generally expected that Shackleton would easily be elected. Snowden concluded that " a number of trade union Members must have voted for Hardie, and they had done so, no doubt, because they felt that his great services in building up the political Labour Party deserved recognition." [3] Certainly there can be little doubt that none of the other socialist M.P.s would at that stage have stood a chance of defeating Shackleton; Keir Hardie himself managed to win by a margin of only one vote.[4] In

of the collection of manuscript documents relating to the early years of the Labour Party, in the British Library of Political and Economic Science. They will be referred to hereinafter as *Labour Party Documents*.

[1] Thus, for example, Raymond Postgate has written, " Hardie had been selected as first chairman of the Parliamentary Labour Party, in 1906, because no other choice was conceivable;" but in fact, as is shown above, Hardie was elected by the slimmest of majorities. Postgate, R., *The Life of George Lansbury*, p. 98.

[2] See Stewart, W., *J. Keir Hardie*, introduction by Ramsay MacDonald and Chapters I to X. Also Williams, Francis, *Fifty Years' March; the Rise of the Labour Party*. Williams notes (pp. 84-5): " Without (Keir Hardie) there might have been an independent Socialist Party or an independent trade-union party—but certainly not a Labour Party." But Williams adds, " . . . in a sense his true life work came to an end when the Labour Party was born." See also Hughes, Emrys, *Keir Hardie*.

[3] Snowden, *An Autobiography*, Vol. I, p. 125.

[4] Lord Elton has provided an interesting (although perhaps apocryphal)

the election for other offices in the PLP Shackleton was named deputy chairman, MacDonald secretary and Henderson chief whip.

It was soon recognized by both Hardie and his colleagues that he would not make a success as Chairman. He was temperamentally unsuited for the post; as he later confessed: " Nature never intended me to occupy an official position . . . I am not guided so much by a consideration of policy, or by thinking out a long sequence of events as by intuition and inspiration." [1] He was alternately bored and exasperated by the tiresome parliamentary work required of the Chairman. Most of the business arrangements he left to Henderson, and often he refused to enter into the usual negotiations with the officials of other parties even about the time-table of business to come before the House. " You bring your proposals to the House publicly," he used to say, " and we'll tell you quick enough whether we like them or not."[2] Hardie agreed, apparently with considerable reluctance, to stand for the chairmanship again and with the energetic support of Henderson he was re-elected for a second term. Before the 1908 session he let it be known that he did not wish to be nominated a third time; indeed he went further and argued that the office of Chairman ought not to be held continuously by any one individual.

Hardie gave a further explanation of his refusal to stand for a third term in a letter to Snowden:

> " My strongest reason for desiring to get out of the Chair is that I may be free to speak out occasionally. In the last Session the Party has practically dropped out of public notice. The comic papers and the cartoonists are ignoring us. A fatal sign! The tendency is evidently to work in close and cordial harmony with the Government, and if this policy be persisted in we shall lose our identity and be wiped out along with the Liberals, and we should richly deserve our fate. By another Session, those of us in the Party who are Socialists and who believe in fighting will have to get together occasionally on our own account, and if we cannot drag the Party with us we will ' gang oor ain gait '." [3]

For two months before the opening of the session of 1908 there

account of the election. " I am told, by one who was present (Elton wrote), that the first vote, by show of hands, resulted in a tie. MacDonald had not voted. ' MacDonald, you must vote,' they said. The next vote was by ballot, but again the voting was equal. ' MacDonald, you *must* vote this time.' At the next trial Hardie was elected by one vote. Afterwards he privately told my informant that MacDonald must have voted for Shackleton, for at the last ballot he, Hardie, had for the first time, voted for himself." Cited in Elton, *The Life of James Ramsay MacDonald*, p. 132.

[1] *1914 ILP Report*, p. 131. See also Bealey and Pelling, *Labour and Politics*, p. 190.

[2] Cited in Brockway, F., *Socialism Over Sixty Years*, p. 74.

[3] Cited in Snowden, *An Autobiography*, Vol. I., pp. 174–5.

were protracted negotiations behind the scenes in an effort to reach agreement on a successor to Hardie.[1] Shackleton seemed the obvious choice and would no doubt have been elected had he been willing to stand. But as MacDonald wrote to Bruce Glasier (late in 1907): ". . . I was told the other day that Shackleton is so angry with criticisms passed upon him in the *Labour Leader* that he is to decline to stand for the Chairmanship of the Party in Parliament . . . (it) looks as though the cause of division was TU *v.* Socialism. . . . What are we to do? . . . As Chairman of the ILP I shall have to say something, and as far as I can see it must be that the Press must be free to criticize personal achievements . . ."[2] MacDonald himself was a possible candidate although he was as yet reluctant to stand for the office.

When Shackleton formally declined to accept nomination Henderson was prevailed upon to allow his name to go forward and he was elected without opposition. He held office for two sessions and as Snowden put it, ". . . without being brilliant he discharged his difficult task with efficiency."[3] He made no effort to " dig himself in," although Mrs. Hamilton claims (no doubt with justification) that he could have done so.[4] At the end of his second term in office Henderson declined to stand again and was succeeded by G. N. Barnes, who had served as Vice-Chairman under Henderson. Snowden's account of the election of Barnes casts interesting light on the way these matters were decided.

> "When Mr. Henderson vacated the Chairmanship (Snowden writes) . . . the usual intrigues and soundings went on about a successor. Keir Hardie was strongly opposed to MacDonald offering himself for the position. Hardie wrote to me to this effect. From conversations I had with him I think his reason was this. He was at the time much dissatisfied with the absence of a more militant policy by the Parliamentary Labour Party, and he regarded Mr. MacDonald as being largely responsible for this. Hardie wrote to MacDonald saying he ought not to stand for the Chair. MacDonald replied to him in a letter which gave Hardie great offence. . . . Hardie was in favour of George Barnes, who was willing to accept if MacDonald was not, but he would not stand against MacDonald. Mr. Shackleton pressed Mr. MacDonald to allow himself to be nominated. Mr. MacDonald replied to both Barnes and Shackleton that he was in the hands of the Party. After this ' queer things' happened and when the Party met for

[1] It is interesting to note that as early as 1908 efforts were being made to avoid the necessity of balloting for the chairmanship.

[2] Cited in Elton, *The Life of James Ramsay MacDonald*, pp. 159-60.

[3] Snowden, *An Autobiography*, Vol. I, p. 176.

[4] Hamilton, M. A., *Arthur Henderson*, p. 72.

the election of the Chairman only the name of Mr. Barnes was submitted."[1]

It is evident that the process of election to the chairmanship had begun to resemble the process by which Conservative Leaders have always been chosen. Intense behind-the-scenes discussion, negotiation and bargaining resulted in the unopposed election of the Chairman.

Barnes spent one unhappy year in the office and declined to be renominated.[2] Again there were intense private discussions which culminated in January 1911 in the unopposed election to the chairmanship of Ramsay MacDonald. MacDonald's correspondence with Bruce Glasier and Snowden immediately before his election casts an interesting light on his attitude to the position. Late in 1910 he wrote to Glasier that the fact that Barnes was ill and reluctant to accept renomination " changes the whole situation— unfortunately against my desires and intentions. I do not want the chairmanship." He gave as his principal reason the lack of unity in the party and what he considered to be the irresponsibility of Keir Hardie. MacDonald added:

> "I see in it nothing but vexation of spirit and barrenness of effort. . . . (Some of my colleagues) come to me and say, ' . . . Settle it like a good fellow. It's worrying us and we want to continue our studies on how to smash up things and go on voting in whatever damned lobby we jolly well like.' That's the temper of the Party to-day. The coercion of the position . . . lies in ' there's nobody else,' and I see that driving me into a fix."

Then, oddly, although he had begun his letter by protesting that he did not want the chairmanship, MacDonald continued as if it were a foregone conclusion that he would be elected: " I shall not lead as a great many people want, because I shall say what I mean, whereas so many of our folks want declamation, stage dressing, paint and daggers in the belt." [3]

Snowden also records that MacDonald wrote to him late in 1910 to say that, in case Snowden should be approached to support him for the chair, on no account would he (MacDonald) accept the position. MacDonald added: " In view of the disloyal action of

[1] Snowden, *An Autobiography*, Vol. I, p. 219.

[2] For a discussion of some of the difficulties he faced see Brockway, F., *Socialism Over Sixty Years*, p. 105; speeches by Keir Hardie and G. N. Barnes at the 1910 ILP conference (*1910 ILP Conference Report*, pp. 57-60); Manuscript Minutes of the Executive Committee of the Labour Party, 30th January, 1911, (*Labour Party Documents*, Part II, Folio 177); report by G. N. Barnes on the work of the PLP to the 1911 party conference and debate on the report (*1911 Labour Annual Conference Report*, pp. 31-2 and 72).

[3] Cited in Elton, *The Life of James Ramsay MacDonald*, pp. 189-90.

certain of our colleagues I see no prospect of the chairman being of the least use." But a few days later MacDonald had apparently changed his mind and Snowden records that MacDonald wrote asking him to make inquiries as to how the land lay: " I could not do this myself (MacDonald wrote) as I should be open to the charge that I am working for my own hand. Such accusation could not be made against you! " Snowden explains that he refused MacDonald's request since he had always made a point of keeping clear of party intrigues. Snowden adds:

> "I had just retired from the Executive of the Labour Party, of which I had been a member for some years, and was not in the private conversations which took place during the (annual party) Conference (which was held a few days before the opening of the new Parliament) on the matter of the Chairmanship of the Parliamentary Labour Party. However, the way was cleared there for Mr. MacDonald . . . . It was understood that a bargain was made that Mr. MacDonald would resign his office as Secretary of the outside Labour Party at the end of the year, and that the position would go to Mr. Arthur Henderson, who had long hankered after the post."[1]

As a result of these negotiations MacDonald was elected Chairman without opposition and at the next annual party conference Henderson succeeded him as Secretary of the party; at the same conference MacDonald was elected Treasurer, a post he was to hold until 1930.

Lord Elton comments that " There was remarkably little personal ambition in MacDonald's attitude to the Chairmanship. Seldom can a more reluctant leader have been elected." [2] In an immediate and short-range view the remark is obviously justified. The lack of discipline in the PLP and the unrewarding nature of the Chairman's duties undoubtedly diminished MacDonald's enthusiasm at the prospect of election. In a sense he appears quite genuinely to have accepted the position because, as he puts it, " there's nobody else." But again and again, as has been shown in the review of the emergence of the Conservative Leaders (Chapter II), the same situation has obtained on the eve of their election. Several of them protested in retrospect that they found themselves thrust into a post which they never sought. The Labour Party appears to have chosen MacDonald, its first real Leader, by a process not unlike that of the older parties. And certainly in the closing stages of the negotiations which preceded MacDonald's election it is evident (if we accept Snowden's testimony) that MacDonald was no more unwilling than any of his Conservative opposite numbers to take up the burden of leadership.

[1] Snowden, An Autobiography, Vol. I, pp. 219-20.
[2] Elton, The Life of James Ramsay MacDonald, p. 188.

It is important to recall the process by which MacDonald emerged as the " inevitable " Leader of the Party. He was born at Lossiemouth in 1866 in what has been described as " grinding but not hopeless poverty " and from his early years showed quite outstanding talent in various minor organizational rôles. Even his least friendly biographer concedes that MacDonald " no sooner joined any organization than he was lifted almost at once into an executive position." [1] He first came into contact with the emergent socialist movement when, at 18, he came south to work in Bristol for a newly organized Boys' and Young Men's Guild. He became a member of a tiny sectarian socialist group connected at that time with the Social Democratic Federation.[2] Subsequently in 1886 he came to London, was unemployed for a time, and even when he eventually got ill-paid employment he lived in dire poverty. In 1888 he began a four-year period of work as private secretary to Thomas Lough, a Liberal of comfortable means who was candidate for West Islington. This experience gave MacDonald an invaluable insight into the mechanics of party organization; it also gave him his first experience of a higher stratum of society which he was subsequently to find increasingly attractive.

During the same period MacDonald became honorary secretary of the Scottish Home Rule Association and in this capacity first came into contact with Keir Hardie. When Hardie stood as a Labour parliamentary candidate MacDonald wrote (in his capacity as secretary of the Scottish Home Rule Association) to wish him success. MacDonald had joined the Fabian Society in 1886 (and was to serve as a member of its Executive from 1894 to 1900 [3]), although like many other Fabians he still looked to the Liberal Party as a possible vehicle for the sort of fundamental social change in which he believed. Two events in 1894 disillusioned him: he hoped to be adopted as a Liberal-Labour candidate at Southampton, but the negotiations broke down; later in the same year in an important by-election a local Liberal Party refused to adopt a trade union candidate and the ILP (which had been formed the year before) ran their own independent candidate in the by-election. MacDonald then decided to throw in his lot with the ILP. He wrote to Hardie: " I have stuck to the Liberals up to now, hoping that they might do something to justify the trust that we had put in them." But the Liberal hostility to a trade union candidate in the by-election

[1] Weir, L. MacNeill, *The Tragedy of Ramsay MacDonald*, p. 16.

[2] Bryher, S., *An Account of the Labour and Socialist Movement in Bristol;* see Elton, *The Life of James Ramsay MacDonald*, Foreword and Chapter II.

[3] See Pease, E. R., *History of the Fabian Society*, London, 1925, pp. 127 and 133.

referred to above convinced MacDonald, as he explained to Hardie, that

> " it was quite impossible for me to maintain my position as a Liberal any longer. . . . So I must accept the facts of the situation and candidly admit that the prophecies of the ILP relating to Liberalism have been amply justified. The time for conciliation has gone by, and those of us who are earnest in our professions must definitely declare ourselves. I may say that in the event of elections, I shall place part of my spare time at the disposal of the Party, to do what work may seem good to you."[1]

In the next year MacDonald stood as an ILP candidate at Southampton in the general election, but polled no more than 867 votes. In 1896 he was elected to the National Administrative Council of the ILP and soon became, with Keir Hardie, Philip Snowden and a few others, one of its most prominent spokesmen. He broke with the Fabians over their failure to denounce the South African War and resigned from their Executive in 1900. He took an active part in a " National Stop The War Committee " and unhesitatingly ran the risks involved in a forthright denunciation of the South African campaign.

MacDonald played a prominent part in the negotiations that led to the formation of the Labour Representation Committee in 1900. It seems almost certain that he, jointly with Hardie, drafted the resolution of 1899 which proposed that the Parliamentary Committee of the Trades Union Congress should take the initiative " in convening a special Congress . . . to devise ways and means for securing the return of an increased number of Labour members to the next Parliament." He served on the joint committee which laid plans for the Memorial Hall meeting of February 1900 and at the meeting itself he helped to ensure the adoption of the " middle course," which provided that the new party was to be neither a mere trade union pressure group nor, in any explicit sense, socialist. And—a decisive development—MacDonald was chosen as the first Secretary of the LRC. The report of the first conference records that it was at first suggested that the LRC should have two secretaries, but this met with no favour. F. Brocklehurst was then proposed, but he declined to stand and nominated MacDonald instead; the latter was elected unanimously.[2] A remarkably persistent legend has survived to the effect that MacDonald was chosen by accident and that the conference thought it was electing a James MacDonald of the SDF and the London Trades Council.

---

[1] Cited in Stewart, W., *J. Keir Hardie*, pp. 96-7. MacDonald later observed to Herbert Samuel, " We didn't leave the Liberals. They kicked us out and slammed the door in our faces." Lord Samuel, *Memoirs*, p. 26.

[2] *Report of the Conference on Labour Representation*, 1900, p. 16.

It is to be found as early as 1912 in Hyndman's *Further Reminiscences*,[1] and as recently as 1953 in Hugh Dalton's *Call Back Yesterday*.[2] But there seems little doubt that the story is without foundation. Mary Agnes Hamilton says that Henderson never allowed the legend to pass without refuting it.[3] And Elton points to the fact that on the occasion of MacDonald's election to the chairmanship of the parliamentary party Keir Hardie recalled:

"I remember the anxious hours spent before the first Conference was called, trying to find someone who had the necessary qualities and abilities to undertake the most responsible of all tasks at that period—to act as Secretary to the Party. Those who had known MacDonald's work in the ILP felt that he was the one man above all others who, if he could be induced to take the position, would give our then nascent movement its best chance of coming to fruition."[4]

The subsequent career of the other James MacDonald would make it seem highly unlikely that he could seriously have been considered for the position. He was elected a member of the Executive of the LRC as a representative of the SDF at the first conference, but the manuscript minutes of the Executive for 8th June, 1900 (four months after the formation of the LRC), record that: "A letter from James MacDonald was read, resigning his membership of the Committee as representative of the Social Democratic Federation."[5] It seems highly doubtful that one who showed such an impatient and transitory interest in the LRC would seriously have been considered for appointment as its first Secretary.

MacDonald threw himself with enormous energy into his work as Secretary.[6] The post was at first unpaid, but this did not deter him from devoting by far the largest part of his time to speaking, organizing, and preparing party literature. There can be no doubt that a resolution which was carried by acclamation at the conference of 1905 expressed the feeling of those who had the opportunity to judge the quality of MacDonald's work. The resolution (which was moved by two trade unionists) read:

"That this Congress hereby places on record its hearty appreciation of the valuable services rendered to our movement by J. R

[1] Hyndman, H. M., *Further Reminiscences*, 1912, p. 269.
[2] Dalton, H., *Call Back Yesterday*, p. 188.
[3] Hamilton, M. A., *Arthur Henderson*, pp. 37-8. She adds "MacDonald's was not a personality, then or at any time, subject to confusion with that of others. He had done an enormous amount of preliminary work, and was chosen, of set purpose, by those who wanted the new committee to be a success. There were others who did not; they diffused the legend."
[4] Cited in Elton, *The Life of James Ramsay MacDonald*, p. 104.
[5] *Labour Party Documents*, Part I, folio 4.
[6] See Chapter IX for a discussion of the early work of the Secretary.

MacDonald, Secretary of the LRC, and assures him that the success of our educational work in the country is in no small measure due to the tireless energy he has displayed not merely in the general organizing work in the several districts, but also to the literature issued dealing with the various social problems."[1]

Although none of his biographers seem to have been aware of the fact, MacDonald appears to have seriously considered resigning the office of Secretary in February 1903. He sent a duplicated letter marked " private and confidential " to the members of the LRC discussing the future work of the Committee in which he said in part:

> " I think we have reached a point when we may allow the movement to grow of itself and direct our energies to unifying it . . . . I now consider that the preliminary work of launching this movement has now been completed . . . . I should like to say that my own feeling is to slip out of the position which I now hold. I have a great deal of work on hand, and for some years I have been hoping to do certain things which I see with much regret slipping further and further away beyond my reach. My inclination is to try and get some leisure time for myself, and I do not see how that is to be secured whilst I remain your responsible official."[2]

There is no record of what means the Committee used to persuade MacDonald to carry on as Secretary, but it is perhaps significant that in the following year he was granted a considerable increase in the paltry funds allowed to him to pay for his own and other office salaries.[3] Members of the LRC already appreciated the qualities of their Secretary. The President (as he was then called) of the 1902 conference, in speaking to a vote of thanks to MacDonald, had said: " Before this conference he had not the pleasure of knowing Mr. MacDonald as he did now, and he was sure that he will conduct the movement in a gentlemanly manner, and to a successful issue." [4]

MacDonald meanwhile was acquiring further first-hand electoral experience. He stood as a candidate at Leicester in the Khaki Election of 1900 and was roundly defeated. He had also stood unsuccessfully for the LCC in 1898, but was returned in 1901 for Central Finsbury which he represented until 1904. At the 1906

---

[1] *1905 LRC Annual Conference Report,* p. 57. See also tributes by Snowden in his autobiography, pp. 220-2 of Vol. I; and Clynes, J. R., *Memoirs,* Vol. I, p. 91.

[2] Letter from J. R. MacDonald to members of the Executive of the LRC, 24th February, 1903, *Labour Party Documents,* Part I, folios 173-4.

[3] See p. 561 below.

[4] *1902 LRC Annual Conference Report,* p. 26.

election he was elected (along with a Liberal) for the two-member constituency of Leicester. In the same year he became Chairman of the ILP, a post he held until 1909. On MacDonald's retirement from the ILP chairmanship Keir Hardie described him at the 1909 conference as " the biggest intellectual asset which the Socialist movement had in this country to-day." [1] On these grounds alone (as a left-wing intellectual) there was no question of his being selected as Chairman of the PLP in its early years. It is clear, however, that as early as 1907 MacDonald was seriously considering his own prospects as a potential Chairman of the PLP. In a letter to Bruce Glasier written late in 1907, he wrote:

" . . . . It would be a little awkward at present to put a ' mere ' Socialist in the chair because it might hinder the process of consolidation . . . . Barnes tells me he is willing to propose me . . . . If I took it, I would have a troublesome time until I beat down opposition, and then Hardie's declaration that the honours should go the rounds would mean that when the storm was blowing itself out my chances of doing effective work would be about ended. I am not in the least afraid of facing the leadership. But to take the job on for a period of two years, at the maximum, is a bit discouraging for a start . . . . The chief question we shall have to settle is: Would it be better to give an old gang leader a chance after Hardie and get a Socialist in two years from now (if we could), or take just as much as a majority vote will give us at present? "[2]

In the event, both Henderson and Barnes were to serve before the party elected MacDonald without opposition in 1911. On the eve of his election when MacDonald had resigned himself (apparently with reluctance) to accept the post he wrote to Bruce Glasier: ". . . I see nothing but storms and heartaches ahead." [3] The storms came thick and fast and reached their first climax with MacDonald's resignation from the chairmanship in 1914; the heartaches came later, in 1931.

It is unnecessary to review in detail either the reasons for MacDonald's resignation in August 1914 or his activities during the course of the war. It is important to note, however, that he continued to hold the office of Treasurer (to which he had been elected at the 1912 party conference) [4] throughout the war years, and only

---

[1] *1909 ILP Annual Conference Report,* p. 49.

[2] Cited in Elton, *The Life of James Ramsey Macdonald,* pp. 160-1.

[3] *Ibid.,* p. 190.

[4] *1912 Labour Annual Conference Report,* p. 86. Apparently largely as the result of the influence of Henderson it was decided at that time that henceforth the office of Treasurer should be filled by election by the whole conference; hitherto the NEC itself had appointed one of its own members to fill the post.

once during that period did a candidate run against him. Fortunately for MacDonald, no attempt was made to drive him into the wilderness. Despite the deep divergence within the party on the issue of the war the two factions worked together in surprising harmony.[1] MacDonald ceased to speak from official Labour platforms but no attempt was made by the party to restrain his right to explain his views to the country. Inevitably MacDonald drifted into close association with the ILP, an association which was to prove an enormously important factor in ensuring his return to the chairmanship in 1922.

MacDonald was defeated at Leicester in the election of 1918, spent some time abroad, and on his return devoted himself to the work of the ILP. Meanwhile his prospects were enhanced by the ineffectiveness of the Parliamentary Labour Party which was returned to the House as a result of the election of 1918.[2] A very large proportion of the 59 members were trade unionists, most of whom had been strongly pro-war and were little trained in the technique of opposition. They chose as their Chairman William Adamson ; even the semi-official *Book of the Labour Party* conceded: " It is generally agreed now that the first (post-war) choice of a Parliamentary leader was not a wise one." The choice of Adamson is explained (in this account) by the fact that a large proportion of the PLP were miners as was Adamson himself, and the further comment is added: " The belief is held in many quarters . . . that the choice of Mr. Adamson was a compromise between the followers of Mr. Clynes and Mr. J. H. Thomas." [3] Clynes was chosen Vice-Chairman and subsequently succeeded Adamson in 1920.

The PLP of those years sadly lacked the parliamentary skills which MacDonald had demonstrated so convincingly during his own years in the House. Snowden relates that it was suggested while MacDonald was out of Parliament that he

" should be invited to accept a position of General Adviser to the Party on the best method of making itself more efficient. Mr. MacDonald, on certain terms, agreed to accept that onerous position. A Committee of members of the Parliament Group was

[1] Mrs. Hamilton no doubt justifiably gives great credit in this connection to Arthur Henderson. Again, as in 1908, he could probably have entrenched himself as Chairman and Leader but appears to have made no effort to do so. Hamilton, M. A., *Arthur Henderson*, p. 98.

[2] The work of the PLP was severely criticized at the early post-war conferences of the party. See *1919 Labour Annual Conference Report*, pp. 127-32, and *1920 Labour Annual Conference Report*, pp. 147-53. See also pp. 409-11 below.

[3] Tracey, H., (ed.), *The Book of the Labour Party*, Vol. I, p. 236.

appointed to consider this suggestion, and to consult with Mr. MacDonald. They reported their conclusions to the full Parliamentary Party, which was divided on the question ; and, after what one of the members told me was a most violent discussion, a majority decided they would not enter into any arrangement which involved having an outsider to advise them how to do their own business."[1]

MacDonald meanwhile attracted great public attention when he contested a by-election at Woolwich in 1921. He was opposed in one of the bitterest campaigns on record by a Unionist candidate (who was a holder of the Victoria Cross) and narrowly defeated. MacDonald's powerful campaign greatly enhanced his reputation both in the country and, above all, within the PLP. He was tireless too as a propagandist on behalf of the party in the press and on the platform. It was during this period that he produced one of his most effective expositions of his party's case entitled *A Policy For The Labour Party*.[2]

At the close of the 1921 session it was decided to revise the longstanding practice of electing the officers of the PLP at the first meeting of each parliamentary session. As the PLP Report records, it was decided that " it would be in the interests of the Party and of the Officers appointed if, towards the *close* of each Session, the election of the Officers for the ensuing Session were taken so that those elected might be in a position to make arrangements during the Recess to enable them to give constant attention to their official duties in the House." [3] Clynes was duly re-elected Chairman at the close of the 1922 summer session. After the fall of the Coalition Government, the general election was called for 15th November, 1922. As a result of the election, the PLP increased in strength from 57 to 142 and its composition was transformed. Only eight of the M.P.s elected in 1918 had been representatives of the ILP or of the Divisional Labour Parties; but in 1922 the ILP returned 32 candidates and the divisional parties 19. The trade union nominees had risen to 85, but clearly the influence of the more militant socialist element in the PLP was enormously strengthened; and what was particularly important, the PLP was reinforced by a whole group of younger men who were to become leaders of the party during the next three decades. In addition, a number of the most colourful pre-war leaders were returned including Snowden, Lansbury, Jowett and Ramsay MacDonald.

The new PLP met for the first time on 22nd November, 1922,

[1] Snowden, *An Autobiography*, Vol. II, p. 532.
[2] MacDonald, J. R., *A Policy for the Labour Party*, London, 1920.
[3] *1922 Labour Annual Conference Report* (Parliamentary Report), p. 101. [Italics mine.]

eight days after the election. No records of the meeting are available but several of those who were present have given their accounts of what took place; these accounts are in substantial agreement and are worth examining since the meeting was in some respects the most important in the history of the PLP. MacNeill Weir recalls that the new M.P.s assembled in an atmosphere of excitement and expectancy.[1] Twenty-two of the 142 were, however, absent; most of them, as Snowden recalls, " were unable to reach the party meeting in time on account of some Trade Union work which detained them." [2] Clynes, then Chairman of the PLP, presided and he opened the meeting by welcoming the newly-elected M.P.s.[3] The first item on the agenda was the question of the allocation of seating space in the House of Commons and some observers have attached great importance to the nature of this discussion. The point at issue was which party should occupy the front opposition bench. The Speaker had apparently agreed that the leaders of the PLP should be given precedence over the Liberals in all important debates and three out of four supply days would be allocated to the PLP. The Speaker was not prepared to agree, however, that the PLP should occupy the major portion of the opposition front bench. Clynes explained to the meeting that as Chairman of the PLP he had expressed strong disapproval of the proposed arrangement, but (according to MacNeill Weir)

> " It was plain that Clynes did not regard the matter as of much importance ; he was evidently convinced that the Speaker had definitely made up his mind that the Liberals should have this concession, and that nothing that he (Clynes) could do would make him change. The demeanour of Clynes disappointed the meeting. In this first meeting of the Parliamentary Party, reporting the first encounter of the Session with the Speaker, he seemed to have been too easily put off and to be advising them to accept defeat." [4]

MacDonald seized the occasion to intervene strongly in protest against the Speaker's ruling. MacNeill Weir is convinced that the protest represented a calculated move on MacDonald's part designed to demonstrate his own militancy and thus to win the support of the newly elected members of the PLP. Largely as a result of

---

[1] See Weir, L. MacNeill, *The Tragedy of Ramsay MacDonald*, p. 104.

[2] Snowden, *An Autobiography*, Vol. II, p. 574.

[3] Mary Agnes Hamilton claims (*Arthur Henderson*, p. 229) : " Henderson was, by acclamation, voted into the chair and conducted the proceedings." In fact Clynes appears to have opened the meeting and to have vacated the chair only when the voting for the Leader took place. Weir L. MacNeill, *The Tragedy of Ramsay MacDonald*, p. 108.

[4] Weir, L. MacNeill, *The Tragedy of Ramsay MacDonald*, pp. 105-6.

MacDonald's intervention, apparently, it was resolved that a letter be sent to the Speaker insisting on the Labour Party's right to the exclusive use of the front bench and of the benches immediately behind.

It was then moved that the PLP officers who had been elected at the close of the previous session should continue in office; in other words, it was proposed that the system of balloting for officers *at the end of the session* (which had been adopted in the previous year) should continue in operation. MacDonald's supporters moved an amendment that all officers should be elected then and there for the current session and for the session beginning in the following year. The amendment was carried by a show of hands. For the first time since 1906 there was to be a contest for the chairmanship of the Parliamentary Labour Party. And for the first time much more was at stake; the new Chairman would be Leader of the Opposition and therefore a potential Prime Minister.

According to Clynes's own account, he had made no effort to organize support for himself (nor, he claims, was in any way disturbed by his subsequent defeat). He wrote:

> "Among a large number of my colleagues there was now the feeling that I ought to continue the leadership, and I therefore accepted nomination at the Party meeting to choose a leader .... I was told that many who had intended to support me had been so sure of my election that they were not present at the meeting .... Since that time Ramsay MacDonald has struck such a blow at British Labour as will never be forgotten, though it will be survived. It is possible that, had I been able to see into the future, I might have taken another line of action in 1922 which would have deprived him of the power to strike that blow. I was not in the least troubled by my defeat at the time, but when, later, I learned of the complicated plans and schemes made for my defeat, I confess feeling that some of my colleagues had been ungrateful as well as disloyal, in face of the previous two years of work which had been so successful in securing Labour's return as the Official Opposition."[1]

That "complicated plans and schemes" were made for Clynes's defeat there seems no doubt. Snowden records: "It had come to my knowledge that Mr. MacDonald had been actively canvassing among his friends for support, and he had been especially concerned to get the support of the new Scottish members."[2] The extent to which he had in fact won their allegiance was demonstrated at a special meeting of the ILP members of the PLP which was held before the full party meeting. That meeting was by no means

[1] Clynes, J. R., *Memoirs,* Vol. I, pp. 330-1.
[2] Snowden, *An Autobiography,* Vol. II, pp. 573-4.

unanimous in its support for MacDonald, but his most ardent backing came from the Clyde group of ILP men. David Kirkwood, a member of the group at the time, has since described the attitude of his colleagues and the atmosphere of the occasion: " No sooner had we arrived in London than we were plunged into the atmosphere of intrigue. We did not know that atmosphere. . . . Now we breathed a new air, the air of intrigue, of personal vanity, of desire for position and power, of suggestion or shrugged shoulders that often conveyed more than words." Kirkwood adds that the Clyde group had no doubt whatever as to who should lead the party. " We were Ramsay MacDonald's men. It was the Clyde group of Labour members who made Ramsay MacDonald leader of the Party, and so opened the path to all his future greatness—and failure." He records that his group were greatly surprised to discover that even the ILP meeting itself was sharply divided in its attitude to Mac-Donald. But the Clyde group proposed that ILP should nominate MacDonald and " the proposal was carried by our votes." Arthur Henderson (according to Kirkwood) told them: " You Clyde men are determined to put MacDonald in. Well: if you do, it will only be a few years before you are trying to put him out."[1] Kirk-wood adds, " so all-pervading was this feeling that even John Wheatley, whose admiration of MacDonald was unbounded, began to grow uneasy as to what was behind all the head-shaking and shoulder shrugging. ' What does it mean? ' he asked. ' Is it jealousy? . . . . The man seems to have no friends.' "

But the Clyde group remained firm in its support. They had apparently been convinced by MacDonald's stand during the war that he was a man of the left; they pointed to the fact that unlike Clynes and Henderson he had not contaminated himself by par-ticipation in the War Coalition.[2] As Roy Jenkins has put it: " They believed that a man who had refused to compromise with imperialism would be equally unbending toward capitalism. They confused pacifism with revolutionary fervour." [3] It seems fair to

[1] This remark may have been intended by Henderson as a comment on the Clyde group rather than an indication of his own opposition to MacDonald.

[2] MacDonald himself had been at pains to disassociate himself from certain of the actions of those Labour M.P.s who entered the wartime coalition. He wrote in 1920, for example, " It is hard to forgive the Labour members of the (Coalition) Government who accepted for themselves and foisted upon Parliament the miserable apology for a Labour Department which was created in 1917. It was one of those niggardly things which not only show how Labour is regarded by all Governments, but how Labour too often regards itself." MacDonald, J. R., *A Policy for the Labour Party.* pp. 140-1.

[3] Jenkins, R., *Mr. Attlee,* p. 102.

assume that MacDonald was aware that the race would be close, and in an attempt no doubt to rally support for himself as the " indispensable leader," he sought to give the impression that he did not, after all, seek the post. Kirkwood claims (although the other principal accounts of these events make no reference to the fact) that MacDonald " let it be known that he was not going forward to election as leader. There was rumour that he did not feel well enough." But Kirkwood adds, " We dismissed that easily . . . he was always tired. But we knew that he was a terrific worker."[1]

Most of the important figures in the party appear to have favoured Clynes. Snowden certainly did. He explains in his autobiography that he felt it would have been wise to allow Clynes to continue in the office of Chairman in view of the work he had done in the immediately preceding years: " My other objection to Mr. MacDonald taking the chair at this time was that I did not think it likely he would give the Party a vigorous lead. I had seen a good deal of him in such a position when he was Chairman before the War, and his passion for intrigue and compromise and his desire to be regarded as a ' gentleman ' by the other parties, disqualified him to lead a party which contained so many members who had come into the House of Commons filled with enthusiasm for a fight." Snowden also resented what he considered to be Mac-Donald's deliberate and essentially hypocritical appeal to the party's left wing. He recalls that MacDonald had contributed a weekly article to the Glasgow socialist paper *Forward* " in which he had played up to the Left Wing, an attitude strikingly different from that he had pursued when in the House of Commons in previous Parliaments." [2] Henderson, according to Mary Agnes Hamilton, still retained what she describes as his " often-stated view that MacDonald was the indispensable leader." But it seems agreed that J. H. Thomas was opposed to MacDonald's election on the grounds that " Clynes had borne the heat and burden of the day " and that under the revised party rules he should have retained the office at least throughout the current session. All accounts agree also that Clynes had the support of a majority, although by no means all, of the trade union M.P.s, some of whom were absent.

But MacDonald had preponderant support among the newly elected members of the PLP; he was nominated by one of the most vigorous of these, Emanuel Shinwell[3] (who, ironically, was

[1] Kirkwood, D., *My Life of Revolt*, pp. 194-7.
[2] Snowden, *An Autobiography*, Vol. II, pp. 573-4.
[3] For Shinwell's account, see his *Conflict without Malice*, pp. 83-4.

later to administer to MacDonald his worst electoral defeat, at
Seaham Harbour in 1935). MacDonald had a further enormous
advantage : as no one else in the Labour Party did, he exemplified
the qualities of Max Weber's "charismatic leader". Kirkwood
has recalled: "Nature had dealt unevenly with (the two con-
testants). She had endowed MacDonald with a magnificent presence,
a full resonant voice, and a splendid dignity. Clynes was small,
unassuming, of uneven features, and voice without colour. There
they sat: Clynes at ease and indifferent; MacDonald with his head
in his hands, looking drawn, anxious, and ill."[1] During the voting
Clynes vacated the chair and Arthur Henderson, the Chief Whip,
took his place (although he was not then an M.P.). MacNeill Weir
claims that ". . . the Members of Parliament on that day did not
realize what tremendous consequences their decisions would imply.
They thought that they were merely electing a Party Chairman;
they were really choosing the future Prime Minister of the British
Empire."[2] It certainly seems fair to assume from Clynes's own
account that he was only dimly aware of the significance of the
vote. But MacDonald, it would seem, was in no doubt.

The accounts vary as to the majority MacDonald received but
he clearly won by less than half a dozen votes. MacNeill Weir
gives the result, "Clynes 56, MacDonald 61, majority for Mac-
Donald 5." And he adds, "the election of MacDonald was then
put as a substantive motion and carried *nemine contradicente*."[3]
As Kirkwood points out, MacDonald's majority was less than the
number of the votes of the Clyde men. And he adds: "The result
acted like magic on MacDonald. He sat up at once. All the
lassitude and illness disappeared. He was as vigorous as any man
in the room. John Wheatley looked at me and shrugged his
shoulders. His uneasiness was growing. Clynes turned never a
hair." [4] MacDonald, amid loud cheers, thanked the party for the
honour it had done him and urged the election of Clynes as Deputy
Leader; he was unanimously so elected. After his own election
MacDonald received a telegram of congratulations from the Glasgow ILP which declared: "Labour can have no truck with tran-
quillity."[5]

---

[1] Kirkwood, D., *My Life of Revolt*, p. 197.

[2] Weir, L. MacNeill, *The Tragedy of Ramsay MacDonald*, p. 108.

[3] *Ibid.*, p. 109. Snowden (*An Autobiography*, Vol. II, p. 574) says Mac-
Donald was elected by a majority of two votes. Dalton (*Call Back Yesterday*, p. 191) gives his majority as four.

[4] Kirkwood, D., *My Life of Revolt*, p. 197.

[5] Cited in *Gleanings and Memoranda*, February, 1927, p. 218. The day
after the election of the new Chairman, Mrs. Webb wrote in her diary one

MacDonald served as Leader of the Labour Party for nine years —years that were anything but " tranquil "—and was succeeded on 24th August, 1931 (four days after the formation of the National Government) by Arthur Henderson. " Now," said Henderson in the House on 8th September, 1931, " I find myself in a position I never sought." [1] Such disavowals of ambition are common enough amongst those who have won the highest party offices; but in Henderson's case the remark cannot be dismissed as coy mock-modesty. Mrs. Hamilton argues convincingly that Henderson made no attempt to consolidate his position on either of the two previous occasions when he had been elected to the chairmanship of the PLP. He performed the duties of Chairman competently enough during the period 1908–10 but made no attempt to dig himself in, nor did he try to do so when MacDonald resigned at the outbreak of war: " Had (Henderson) been merely ambitious (wrote Mrs. Hamilton), 1914 was his opportunity. Quite easily he could have entrenched himself in the leadership; quite easily, in 1915, he could have driven MacDonald out into the wilderness of fractional opposition. He did nothing of the kind. He did the precise opposite. And it took some doing." [2]

All accounts agree that again in 1931 Henderson showed no eagerness to secure for himself the leadership of the party. Hugh Dalton quotes from his own diary [3] a passage written between the announcement of the formation of the National Government and the meeting of the PLP which was to name Henderson as MacDonald's successor: " There is a feeling in all our minds that (Henderson) is now the only possible leader. But he is very unwilling." Then follows a summary by Dalton of the reasons given by Henderson to explain his reluctance. Most of these are understandable enough: " (Henderson) says (wrote Dalton) that he is now 68; . . . that he must look after the party organization, in view of an early election; that we must not drive (MacDonald) and the others out; that this is only an interlude in the life of the Party, like the war; that Clynes is Deputy Leader and must not be pushed aside; and much more." There is only one other phrase in Dalton's diary which appears to conflict with the otherwise consistent accounts of Henderson's lifelong reluctance to strive for the office of Leader. " (Henderson) says . . . they wouldn't have him 15 years ago." There is no ready explanation of this phrase, since

of her less perceptive observations: " If (MacDonald) is not the best man for the post, he is at any rate the worst and most dangerous man out of it." *Beatrice Webb's Diaries 1912–24*, p. 231.

[1] *House of Commons Debates,* 8th September, 1231.

[2] Hamilton, M. A., *Arthur Henderson*, p. 98.

[3] Dalton, H., *Call Back Yesterday*, p. 274.

" 15 years ago " (in 1916) Henderson was in fact Chairman of the PLP and, as Mrs. Hamilton claims, there seems no reason to doubt that he could have consolidated his position had he sought to do so. But otherwise Dalton's account is consistent enough and certainly there could be no doubt that in 1931 Henderson took no active steps to secure the leadership for himself. Rather (as Dalton puts it), " he gradually yield(ed) to pressure from all sides."

On 27th August, Dalton wrote in his diary: " at a meeting of ex-Cabinet Ministers this morning, (Henderson) apparently agreed to accept the leadership, and Clynes, magnanimous as usual, will propose this himself tomorrow at the Party Meeting."[1] Clynes's own account varies slightly in that he appears to imply that there was a considerable demand that he (Clynes) should take the leadership. His terse summary of these events reads: " MacDonald was degraded from his high place as leader of the Labour Party and I was asked to succeed him. I did not wish to do so, as others deserved the position; I persuaded Arthur Henderson to accept the post." [2] The party's almost pathetic sense of loyalty to its leaders might have ensured Clynes's election had he, as Deputy Leader, allowed his name to be placed in nomination at the meeting called to choose MacDonald's successor. But there can be little doubt that the consensus of opinion in the party favoured Henderson.

The PLP assembled on 28th August under the chairmanship of James Barr, who was at the time Chairman of the Consultative Committee which had been re-established following the election of the second Labour Government (see p. 432 below). The members of the General Council of the TUC had also been invited to be present (" this—wrote Dalton—is an innovation, suggested by [Henderson], to mark unity "). Barr reported on the work of the Consultative Committee during the days immediately preceding the downfall of the Labour Government and then, on behalf of the Committee, he moved a resolution approving their action and recommending that the party go into opposition to MacDonald's new Government. There were messages from MacDonald and Snowden [3] and a speech by Lord Sankey, the only prominent

---

[1] Dalton, H., *Call Back Yesterday*, p. 276.

[2] Clynes, J. R., *Memoirs*, Vol. II, p. 198.

[3] Hugh Dalton writes in his autobiography (*Call Back Yesterday*, pp. 277-8): " (MacDonald) had sent a querulous letter saying that he had had no notice of the meeting, but had read of it only in the Press, that he had already arranged to go to Lossiemouth, and that, if he *had* attended the meeting, he could not have told them anything, as confidences were always betrayed ' by one or two,' and then a postscript saying that he had just received an invitation, dated August 25th, which must have been delayed in the post. (Snowden) sent a shorter and much more dignified letter, saying

member of the MacDonald group who attended the meeting. In a speech given later at the meeting Sankey said he believed that MacDonald had saved the country, but, putting his hand on Henderson's shoulder, he added: " Mr. Henderson has saved the soul of the Labour Party." [1] Henderson himself was given an ovation when he rose to make a long statement narrating the events of recent weeks which culminated in the downfall of the Labour Government. After a brief debate the resolution approving the action of the Consultative Committee was accepted. [2]

Then Clynes moved that Henderson be elected Leader. He recalled his own loyal acceptance of defeat by MacDonald for the leadership in 1922 and added, according to Dalton's diary, that " (Henderson) has strongly urged *him* (Clynes) to be the leader, but he realizes, in view of all that has happened, that (Henderson) is the only possible choice. For himself, he has been so long in the Movement that he has no longer any undue personal ambition. But he has not lost the love of service. He will serve willingly as No. 2, No. 3, No. 4 or in any other position which his colleagues may decide." [3] There were no other nominations and the motion to elect Henderson was carried with five ILP dissentients. When Henderson took the chair, Dalton records that he expressed regret at the lack of unanimity in the vote which had just taken place, but added that since it was generally felt that he should accept the office he would " give it a trial," in spite of his other work as Secretary and Treasurer of the Party. He then moved that Clynes and William Graham should be made Deputy Chairmen and this was agreed. [4]

Henderson was defeated in the general election that followed

that he did not think it would serve any good purpose for him to attend, as he saw from the Press that a financial policy had already been decided on." Dalton adds a footnote: " These two letters were both read aloud, and I made these notes in my diary at that time. Snowden in his *Autobiography*, p. 953, states that (MacDonald) sent no message to this meeting and that he himself was not aware of it till after it had been held. His memory was clearly at fault."

[1] Cited in Hamilton, M. A., *Arthur Henderson*, p. 389.

[2] None of the available accounts record the vote on this resolution.

[3] Dalton, H., *Call Back Yesterday*, p. 279.

[4] In a statement to the Press after the meeting Henderson said he was strongly of the opinion that Clynes should have advanced to be Leader of the Party, but forces were too strong for him (Henderson) and it was Clynes himself who proposed that he should be Chairman and therefore Leader of the Party. Henderson also explained that it was in order to ease his own burden, while Leader of the Party and Secretary and Treasurer of the national organization, that he suggested the appointment of a second deputy. See *The Times* and *Daily Herald*, 29th August, 1931.

but at the first meeting of the PLP after the election of 3rd November, 1931, a resolution was carried expressing " unabated confidence in Mr. Arthur Henderson, and requesting him to continue in the position of Leader." [1]   At the same meeting George Lansbury was elected Chairman of the PLP with C. R. Attlee as Vice-Chairman.[2] A week later the NEC passed a resolution expressing " its unabated confidence in Mr. Henderson as Leader of the party." [3]   In 1924 and 1929 the offices of Leader and Chairman had been dissociated; now for the first time the same action had been taken with the party in opposition. The explanation was simple. Lansbury was the only former Cabinet Minister to be returned in the election of 1931. As Raymond Postgate has put it: " The Nabobs had vanished, never to return. For almost twenty years now a group of men had shared among themselves, and allotted to others, positions of power in the Labour movement and later in the government. . . . Now they were swept away for ever. . . . It was as though a huge tide had smashed through a breakwater, sweeping it away and carrying the timber far out into the sea, leaving standing only one tall, stout and solitary stanchion." [4]   It might have been expected that Lansbury, the " solitary stanchion," might have had a prior claim to be elected both Leader and Chairman. He was very probably the most beloved figure in the Labour movement. But it must have seemed inconceivable to many that the 72-year-old Lansbury with his long record as a highly independent (and often troublesome) member of the PLP should have seriously been considered as Leader of the Party.[5]   Henderson, wise, cautious and infinitely knowledgeable where party and parliamentary affairs were concerned, was clearly

---

[1] *1932 Labour Annual Conference Report* (Parliamentary Report), p. 87.

[2] *Ibid.* The actual phrase in the report of the PLP elections of 3rd November, 1931, reads: " Mr. George Lansbury was *re*-elected Chairman." This appears, however, to be an error since until that meeting Henderson had been both Chairman and Leader and Lansbury was elected on this occasion for the first time. See *The Times,* 4th November, 1931.

[3] *The Times,* 11th November, 1931.

[4] Postgate, R., *George Lansbury,* p. 276.

[5] Dalton lists the former Labour Ministers (including himself) defeated in the election of 1931 and comments somewhat wistfully, although no doubt quite accurately: " It is safe to say that almost any one of this list, had he been re-elected, would either have been chosen leader in the next Parliament in preference to Lansbury, or deputy leader in preference to Attlee—particularly as both of these were London M.P.s and the latter not a member of either the National or the late Parliamentary Executive." Dalton, H., *Call Back Yesterday,* p. 297. This seems a valid comment, with one reservation: the PLP has certainly shown no hesitation in electing two London M.P.s to the offices of Leader and Deputy Leader; Attlee and Morrison, both " London M.P.s " served as Leader and Deputy Leader respectively for some years.

much to be preferred over Lansbury as Leader of the Party; further, it was assumed that Henderson would soon be returned to the House at a by-election. He was therefore re-elected Leader while Lansbury was elected Chairman (and, in effect, " spokesman ") for the PLP within the House of Commons.

A year later, in October 1932, Henderson had become convinced that the arrangement was proving a liability to the party and that his own return to Parliament could no longer be considered imminent (see p. 323 n. 4 above). He therefore resigned the leadership and Lansbury was elected Chairman and Leader at the close of the parliamentary session 1931–2.[1] Lansbury held the dual appointments for three years until his resignation in October 1935.

The emergence of C. R. Attlee, Lansbury's successor as Leader of the Labour Party, has few parallels in the history of party leadership in this country. His period of office as Leader of the Labour Party was to be longer than that achieved by the Leader of any party in this century. Yet Attlee is popularly considered to have emerged as Leader almost by accident or at least by a combination of fortuitous circumstances rather than through evidence of qualities which particularly fitted him for leadership. This interpretation is obviously inadequate. Attlee's success after he won the leadership in 1935, and the authority he wielded without overt challenge, can hardly be dismissed as the record of a misfit who stumbled into the leadership by accident.

Clement Attlee was the first Leader of the Labour Party of comparatively prosperous middle-class origins.[2] A son of the senior partner in an old-established firm of City solicitors, he was educated at preparatory school, Haileybury and University College, Oxford. After qualifying at the Bar in 1905 he became interested in, and later manager of, Haileybury House, a settlement in Limehouse supported by his old school. Originally of Conservative persuasion, Attlee became convinced of the validity of the socialist case as a result of his experience in the East End of London. He joined the Fabian Society in 1907 and, a year later, the Stepney Branch of the ILP which he served for a time as secretary.[3] He stood unsuccessfully for the local Council and in 1912 was appointed to the staff

[1] *1933 Labour Annual Conference Report* (Parliamentary Report), p. 73.
[2] An account of Mr. Attlee's early life is to be found in his autobiography, *As It Happened,* and in Jenkins, R., *Mr. Attlee : An Interim Biography,* London, 1948; this passage is based mainly on these two sources.
[3] One finds him as early as 1914 intervening along with MacDonald, Snowden and others in an important debate at the ILP conference in April of that year. His contribution, while not spectacular, does not suggest the shy young man that many would be inclined to assume Attlee must have been at 31 years of age. See *1914 ILP Annual Conference Report*, p. 81.

of the London School of Economics. After his return from the war (in which he had risen to the rank of major) he contested Limehouse for the LCC unsuccessfully in 1919 and was subsequently adopted as parliamentary candidate for the division. He was co-opted as an alderman for the Stepney Borough Council and subsequently served as mayor; he also had valuable experience on various London local government committees.

Attlee was first elected to Parliament in 1922 (at age of 39) and —an important development— was selected by MacDonald as one of his two Parliamentary Private Secretaries in the same year. In the first Labour Government he was appointed Under-Secretary of State for War.[1] His brief Ministerial experience qualified him for a seat on the front opposition bench when the party went into opposition. Thereafter Attlee took an increasingly active part in parliamentary debate and, on at least one occasion, was appointed to lead for the party in a debate of some importance. From November 1927 to April 1930 he was much preoccupied with his work as member of the Indian Statutory Commission, an experience which broadened his horizon beyond the spheres of local government and the domestic concerns of Parliament. Attlee was not included in the 1929 Government nor was he given any explanation by MacDonald for his exclusion. Attlee, says his biographer, " was not thirsting for office, but he was irritated by the manner in which he was passed over . . ." [2] Attlee himself recalls " MacDonald (had) assured Hartshorn and myself that membership of the Indian Statutory Commission would not in any way militate against our inclusion in the next Labour Government should the next General Election result in Labour taking office. However, neither of us was included, and it was characteristic of MacDonald that he did not take the trouble to inform us of his decision." [3] On 24th May, 1930, however, Attlee succeeded Mosley on the latter's resignation as Chancellor of the Duchy of Lancaster; he was to serve in this capacity as " a sort of economic assistant to the Prime Minister . . . . (Attlee) dealt with big issues, but in an advisory capacity, and without the power, himself, to take important decisions." In a minor Government reshuffle in March 1931 Attlee succeeded Lees-Smith as Postmaster-General. " We had a great time at the Post Office (wrote Attlee) having first to master the

[1] His work in office provoked few comments, although *Time and Tide* did observe (18th April, 1924): " At some future date, if public confidence in the Labour party continues to grow, Attlee should make an excellent Home Secretary." Cited in Jenkins, R., *Mr. Attlee*, p. 110.

[2] Jenkins, R., *Mr. Attlee*, p. 127.

[3] Attlee, C. R., *As It Happened*, p. 66.

organization of this enormous business and then to endeavour to introduce reforms." [1]

The near annihilation of the Parliamentary Labour Party in 1931 is, of course, the key to Attlee's phenomenal emergence from the comparative obscurity of his rôle in the second Labour Government to the office of Leader of the Party in 1935. None of the speculative comments on the personalities in British politics written in the late 1920s or during the lifetime of the second Labour Government even mentioned Attlee as a possible party Leader.[2] Even the admiring Jenkins concedes that " had all the Labour leaders survived their contests (in the 1931 election) and been available for selection by the Parliamentary party, Attlee would hardly have been among the first ten candidates." But in fact Attlee and Cripps were the only Ministers apart from Lansbury to be returned to Parliament. Since Cripps had served for only one year in the House and was a recent recruit to the Labour Party, Attlee's election as Deputy Chairman of the PLP in 1931 was, Jenkins admits, " almost automatic."

In the Parliamentary Labour Party returned after the election of 1931, even one of Attlee's modest manner and comparatively limited Ministerial experience was almost certain to shine. Of the 46 members of the Parliamentary Labour Party, no less than 32 had been sponsored by trade unions (23—half the total strength of the PLP—by the Miners alone); 13 were sponsored by Divisional Labour Parties and one by the Co-operative Party. " We have worked as a band of brothers (says the Report of the PLP for 1933, somewhat pathetically) united together by our faith in Socialism . . ."[3] But the debating strength of the band of brothers was sadly limited. Most of its members were conscientious, but somewhat inarticulate, middle-aged trade unionists, sure enough of their first principles but of limited use in parliamentary debate. They fought with tenacity under Lansbury's painstaking leadership, but they were no doubt happier marching through the lobbies

---

[1] Cited in Jenkins, R., *Mr. Attlee*, p. 134. As Jenkins points out, Attlee's five months' experience at the Post Office was his first, and almost his only, experience as head of a Government department. His next experience in such a capacity came during the war when he was responsible for the Dominions Office, but he was soon taken up with other duties as Deputy Prime Minister. As Jenkins adds, MacDonald apart, no other Prime Minister in this century, with the possible exception of Bonar Law, came to office with so limited an experience of departmental ministries.

[2] To take but one example, a book entitled *The Feet of the Young Men; Some Candid Comments on the Rising Generation* (by " Janitor," London, 1928), contains no reference whatever to Attlee, although others such as Morrison and Dalton are discussed at length.

[3] *1933 Labour Annual Conference Report* (Parliamentary Report), p. 90.

singing the " Red Flag " (as they did on more than one occasion) than in examining the intricacies of the Finance Bill.

Postgate writes warmly of the support Lansbury received from his two principal lieutenants, Attlee and Cripps: " In Attlee (Lansbury) found a very clear brain, an immense capacity for work, an invaluable assiduity in absorbing and classifying the vast amount of material that descended upon any leader of the Opposition, and an unassuming willingness, as his deputy, to carry out all the work that was laid upon him." But Lansbury, according to his biographer, ". . . no more than anyone else . . . (foresaw) a great future for this rather diffident committee-man; his successor, as party leader and in due course Premier, he expected to be Cripps . . ." [1] Arthur Greenwood was returned to Parliament in 1932 and Henderson in September 1933; but when George Lansbury met with a serious accident in December 1933 and was confined to hospital until the following summer, Attlee took his place as Acting Leader. This development was of decisive importance in ensuring Attlee's ultimate accession to the leadership. By general agreement he discharged the duties that fell on him in Lansbury's absence with a high degree of competence. The report of the NEC to the 1934 conference went out of its way to state: " The Committee . . . desire to associate themselves with the Parliamentary Party in congratulating Major Attlee upon the efficient and untiring manner in which he has served the party during Mr. Lansbury's enforced absence." [2] Significantly, at the same conference Attlee was elected for the first time to the NEC, coming third after Morrison and Dalton.[3] Thus, by deputising successfully for Lansbury, Attlee had an invaluable opportunity to demonstrate his parliamentary skills; and he thereby won for himself both the commendation of the party outside Parliament and election to its National Executive.[4]

A year later (on 8th October, 1935) Lansbury resigned the leadership. Although asked to reconsider his decision he refused to do so, and Attlee was thereupon elected (in the rather restrained words of the PLP report) " to *act* as Leader for the remainder of the Session." Many had expected that Arthur Greenwood, who had

---

[1] Postgate, R., *George Lansbury*, p. 279. Postgate adds that when Lansbury incautiously told Henderson that he hoped Cripps would succeed him, Henderson answered: " If that happened, I would feel that all I have worked for had gone for nothing."

[2] *1934 Labour Annual Conference Report* (Report of NEC), p. 59.

[3] *1934 Labour Annual Conference Report*, p. 190. Attlee was re-elected to the NEC at the 1935 conference (immediately before his election to the chairmanship); he again came third after Dalton and Morrison.

[4] For Dalton's account of the emergence of Attlee, see his *The Fateful Years*, pp. 64–83.

been a member of the second Labour Cabinet and a much more prominent figure in the party than Attlee, would be named as Lansbury's successor. But Jenkins argues, no doubt with justification, that " . . . the desire for some degree of continuity in the leadership, combined with an appreciation of Attlee's proved ability in the House, were more weighty factors. There was a feeling that while the Labour members of the new House should be left to make their own choice for the future (as was indeed their customary right) the existing parliamentary party could not do better than ask Attlee to lead them through the General Election campaign." [1] Attlee led the party creditably but without particular distinction during the 1935 campaign. But when the PLP, now increased in numbers to 154, reassembled for its first meeting of the new Parliament, it was generally assumed that the question of the future leadership of the party was wide open.

Attlee and Greenwood had been returned, and, in addition, Herbert Morrison and Clynes re-entered Parliament for the first time since 1931. It was expected that these four would prove the strongest contenders, although others such as Hugh Dalton and A. V. Alexander could not be ruled out. Clynes withdrew from the race. As he wrote in his memoirs: " When Parliament reassembled I was asked once again to accept nomination as Leader of the Opposition, but I refused to do so. Others have done much in recent years to entitle them to lead the Party, and there are many important things that I must do which would have to be abandoned if I took the Leadership a second time."[2] Morrison, however, was a very strong contender; he had already won distinction both as Minister of Transport in the second Labour Government and more recently as leader of the Labour majority on the London County Council. Arthur Greenwood had close links with the party headquarters and was something of a protégé of Arthur Henderson. The names of the three (Greenwood, Morrison and Attlee) were placed in nomination and on the first ballot the results were Attlee, 58; Morrison, 44; Greenwood, 32. Greenwood withdrew and on the second ballot Attlee defeated Morrison by 88 votes to 44. Morrison and Greenwood moved that Attlee's election be made

[1] Jenkins, R., *Mr. Attlee,* p. 162. Jenkins quotes a comment by a political journalist in the *Daily Mail* of 14th October, 1935, which was not untypical of the general public reaction: " So the leader of the Socialist Opposition is to be Major Attlee. I am afraid that he will not be so for long but he deserves the success that is his momentarily." The *Annual Register* for the same year speaks of " . . . the Labour Party, of which the head *for the time being* was Mr. Attlee." *Annual Register for 1935,* p. 87. [Italics mine.]

[2] Clynes, J. R., *Memoirs,* Vol. II, p. 228.

unanimous and Greenwood was subsequently elected Deputy Leader without opposition.[1] Jenkins's interpretation of the voting figures would seem to be justified. He writes:

> "The figures in the first ballot strongly support the view that Attlee's principal support came from his colleagues of the previous four years. His vote coincided almost exactly with the number of Labour members in the previous House. They were the men who knew him best and whose support, for this reason, he had every cause to value most. Arthur Greenwood's support probably came largely from northern trade unionists, and these, it is clear, voted solidly for Attlee as their second choice."[2]

J. T. Murphy has argued that had the leadership depended upon the mass vote of a Labour Party conference, " It would then have been a struggle between Morrison and Greenwood on the basis of their greater platform qualifications and personal acquaintance with the mass membership of the party." [3] But the supporting evidence for this view is not very strong. Greenwood had not stood in any recent contest for the Executive while Attlee, it should be remembered, had run a good third to Morrison and Dalton in the 1934 and 1935 contests for the NEC. (In those years, of course, even the candidates for the constituency sections of the NEC were voted upon by the whole conference.) But in any event the question of the popularity within the mass party outside Parliament of the various candidates for the leadership of the PLP was probably of only limited interest to the members of the PLP when it came to choosing a parliamentary Leader.[4] For them, the decisive factor would appear to have been Attlee's painstaking competence as Lansbury's Deputy (and subsequently for a time as Acting-Leader of the Party) during the lean years 1931–5. In addition, of course, Morrison was handicapped by the fact that he had not yet won the confidence of certain powerful sections of the trade union movement. In particular, Ernest Bevin was deeply distrustful. One of his biographers goes so far as to claim that this factor alone

---

[1] Morrison has now given his account of these events in his *Autobiography*, p. 162 ff.; see also Dalton, H., *The Fateful Years*, Chapter III.

[2] Jenkins, R., *Mr. Attlee*, p. 167.

[3] Murphy, J. T., *Labour's Big Three: a Biographical Study of Clement Attlee, Herbert Morrison and Ernest Bevin*, p. 189.

[4] One might cite as supporting evidence for this view the fate of Aneurin Bevan in the PLP elections of 1952 and 1953. He had in every year since the war headed the poll in the elections for the constituency section of the NEC. Yet he was easily defeated by Herbert Morrison in the contest for Deputy Leader in 1952 and 1953. In 1952 he came last in the list of 12 successful candidates for the Parliamentary Committee and improved his position only slightly in the elections for the Committee in 1953.

" effectively prevented Morrison from attaining the leadership for which his Parliamentary talents, no less than his own ambitions, seemed likely at that time to mark him out." [1]

It is sometimes forgotten that Attlee, even by 1935, was fairly clearly established as a middle of the road or even moderately left figure among the leaders of the party; he was by no means identified with the hyper-cautious and conservative elements in the party. Neither, of course, was he linked with the militant left wing; but a re-examination of his intervention in conference discussions (and such evidence as is available of his rôle during the 1931 crisis) shows that on a number of issues he was somewhere left of centre. He had been active, for example, in the early post-war years in the advocacy of the principle of workers' control in industry; at the 1922 ILP conference, in the discussion on a new policy statement, he succeeded in securing the adoption of an amendment which committed the ILP to the support of a conception of " Industrial Democracy " based on workers' control. He was associated also with the strong anti-military sentiment in the Labour Party in those years. At the 1923 Labour Party annual conference he spoke in support of a resolution which read: " This conference is of opinion that it should be the policy of the Labour Party in Parliament to vote against all Military and Naval Estimates." The report of Attlee's speech on this resolution reads in part: " At any rate, (Attlee) maintained that so long as they had capitalist governments they could not trust them with armaments, even though they might say that those armaments were not intended to be used . . . " Attlee himself has recalled that he was an uneasy and sometimes critical member of MacDonald's second Government. " Hartshorn and I, like many others in the Party (Attlee writes), were disturbed at the failure of the Government to take any drastic steps to deal with unemployment. Several times the Cabinet asked us to wind up debates on Unemployment, but we both replied that until we saw signs of a more vigorous policy we would not speak."[2]

Hugh Dalton's diary of the events of August 1931 casts further light on Attlee's attitude towards MacDonald. Dalton recorded that he had lunch with Attlee on the day on which MacDonald formed his National Government: " (Attlee) is hot against JRM (wrote Dalton), for his indecision and his inferiority complex, especially in all economic questions, and hotter still against Snowden who, he says, has blocked every positive proposal for the past two years." Later the same day MacDonald met the Ministers

---

[1] Williams, F., *Ernest Bevin*, p. 187. See also Bullock, A., *The Life and Times of Ernest Bevin*, Vol. I, p. 571 ff.

[2] Attlee, C. R., *As It Happened*, p. 69.

and junior Ministers who had not been members of the Cabinet to explain his action. The meeting appears to have been surprisingly docile and Dalton (who was present) recorded in his diary that " only a question or two " were put to MacDonald. But significantly: " Attlee ask[ed] what would be done to the rentiers."[1]

It would seem evident from Dalton's comments written at the time that Attlee must have emerged in the minds of many of his parliamentary colleagues as a forthright (though hardly flamboyant) critic of MacDonald and his friends; this must certainly have strengthened the respect with which Attlee was held in the PLP. After the great " betrayal " he intervened in one of the important debates (see p. 320 above) at the 1932 annual party conference which reflected the deep disillusion of a great many party members with the weakness and equivocation of the second Labour Government. Trevelyan, it will be recalled, had moved: " That the leaders of the next Labour Government and the Parliamentary Labour Party be instructed by the national conference that, on assuming office, either with or without power, definite Socialist legislation must be immediately promulgated, and that the Party shall stand or fall in the House of Commons on the principles in which it has faith." Arthur Henderson (although he was then Leader of the Party) was continually heckled and interrupted during a speech in which he advised the defeat of the resolution. But amongst the strongest supporting speeches was one by the Vice-Chairman of the PLP, Clement R. Attlee:

> " I hope (he said) we are going to support this resolution . . . .
> For years this Party has been fighting as a minority trying to get various changes in the interests of the workers. I think the events of last year have shown that *no further progress can be made in seeking to get crumbs from the rich man's table.* . . . I think we have got to face the fact that, even if we are returned with a majority, . . . we shall have another crisis at once, and that we have got to have a thought-out plan to deal with that crisis ; . . . we have not got to wait until our mandate has been exhausted and frittered away, but, as Sir Charles Trevelyan says, we have got to strike whilst the iron is hot . . . " [2]

Here surely is a vivid contradiction of the widespread conception of Attlee as a meek and somewhat timorous political figure. In this debate he had joined Trevelyan in an attempt to pledge the next Labour Government (against the advice of the Leader of the Party) to introduce a full-blooded socialist programme. It is readily understandable that the PLP should have felt in 1935 that it was

[1] Dalton, H., *Call Back Yesterday*, p. 273.
[2] *1932 Labour Annual Conference Report*, pp. 204-6 [Italics mine.]

choosing as its Leader not only a competent parliamentarian but also a sincere and comparatively militant exponent of socialism.

But undoubtedly the main factor in ensuring Attlee's accession to the leadership was his success in winning the confidence of his fellow-members of the PLP by his demonstration of skill and diligence as a parliamentarian. Similar skills (much more colourfully demonstrated) had been the main factor in securing the leadership for MacDonald on two earlier occasions. They were also shown in Chapter II to be a prerequisite for those who have sought and won the leadership of the Conservative Party.

III

THE EXODUS OF LABOUR LEADERS: MACDONALD AND LANSBURY

The position of the Labour Leader appears to be much less secure than that of his Conservative counterpart, if for no other reason, because he is subject to annual election at least when the party is in opposition. Yet the striking fact is that in this century there have been fewer Labour Leaders deposed than there have been Conservative. The only two Labour Leaders who might be said to have been driven from office were J. R. Clynes in 1922 and George Lansbury who resigned the leadership in 1935 because of a sharp disagreement with his party over foreign policy. But it must be remembered that neither Clynes nor Lansbury could be considered Leaders of the Party in the full meaning of the term. Clynes in a sense was the last of the Chairmen; and Lansbury repeatedly insisted that he conceived of himself as spokesman for the parliamentary party rather than as Leader; his differences of opinion with his followers forced him, as he put it, to lead a kind of Jekyll and Hyde existence. Until Gaitskell became Leader only two men, MacDonald and Attlee, had achieved the full stature of Leader of the Party in the sense that this office has been conceived in the other great parties, and one is immediately struck by the unchallenged authority which these two Leaders enjoyed for a total of 29 years (MacDonald 1922–31, Attlee 1935–55).[1]

More or less furtive and half-hearted attempts were made on

---

[1] One can eliminate for these purposes MacDonald's first period as Chairman (1911–14) since he was not at that time Leader in quite the same sense as he was after 1922.

various occasions to remove both Attlee and MacDonald; but
none of these attempts culminated in a special party meeting to
debate a vote of confidence in the Leader of the sort Baldwin had
to face. It seems particularly strange that no serious effort was made
to unseat MacDonald during 1924-9, and that no one should ever
have stood against him at the annual elections for the chairmanship
of the PLP. In retrospect even MacDonald's colleagues were
baffled to account for their failure to challenge his authority over
so long a period. In December 1932 Lansbury, as Leader of the
Labour Opposition, went to see MacDonald as Prime Minister and
leader of the National Government, to appeal to him on a civil
liberties issue regarding the Home Secretary's action with respect
to Tom Mann. Afterwards Lansbury wrote to Cripps: " (Mac-
Donald) is a terrible mixture of vanity, cowardice, and utter lack of
principle. He is like a rudderless vessel, just drifts. . . . *I came
away terribly distressed that a man with his mentality should have
led us all for so many years.* He never could have believed in civil
liberty or Socialism."[1]

As early as 1912, Mrs. Webb had had no doubt about Mac-
Donald's insincerity. She wrote in her diary in October of that
year: " J. R. MacDonald has ceased to be a Socialist." [2] And in
the years that followed there is ample evidence that she and others
had the deepest reservations about MacDonald's suitability as
Leader and the sincerity of his support for the Labour Party. Thus,
for example, she records a conversation with MacDonald at the
Labour annual conference at Scarborough, 4th June, 1920;
MacDonald, according to Mrs. Webb, discussed the Labour Party
with " angry contempt—he thought it might be better to make a
new combination and ' smash ' the present Labour Party."[3] He
appears, indeed, to have toyed with the idea as early as 1910–11.
Mrs. Webb quotes a conversation she had in October 1921 with
Henderson and Egerton Wake in which, she says,

> "Henderson told us that MacDonald (about 1910-11) pro-
> posed to enter a coalition Cabinet with Lloyd George and Balfour
> (to oust Asquith) and offered him (Henderson) an Under-Secre-
> taryship! Henderson refused decisively and declared that any
> such action would destroy the Labour Party and that he would

[1] George Lansbury to Sir Stafford Cripps, 31st December, 1932, cited
in Postgate, R., *George Lansbury*, p. 286. [Italics mine.]
 [2] *Beatrice Webb's Diaries 1912–24*, p. 6. She added: " . . . The Trade
Union M.P.s never were Socialists; Snowden is embittered and Lansbury
is wild . . . ", and she concluded fatalistically: " All one can do is to go
steadily forward without considering the likelihood of results " (p. 7).
 [3] *Ibid.*, p. 181.

not consent to it. J. R. M. tried to get George Roberts, who also refused. No more was heard of it."[1]

After MacDonald's first term as Prime Minister there was widespread dissatisfaction with his leadership at the highest levels in the party.[2] As important a colleague as Snowden let it be known that he considered MacDonald had revealed the gravest incompetence as Prime Minister. After the defeat of the party in the elections of 1924, Snowden wrote to Jowett, " I get no satisfaction from contemplating the increased Labour poll. That only makes it more painful. It is a proof of the great opportunities we have wantonly and recklessly thrown away by the most incompetent leadership which ever brought a Government to ruin." And he wrote to Jowett again (a few weeks later): " You know that I never trusted J. R. (MacDonald) but he has added to the attributes I knew, during the last nine months, an incapacity I never thought him capable of. He has thrown away the greatest opportunity which ever came to a party, and has landed us with five years of Tory Government. And his colossal conceit prevents him from being in the remotest measure conscious of what he has done. He is absolutely self-centred."[3]

There was dissatisfaction too on the trade union side. Francis Williams, one of Ernest Bevin's biographers, states:

> " Immediately following the Labour Government's fall (Bevin) began to pull every string he could to get MacDonald dismissed from the leadership. In this he found a good deal of support in the Parliamentary Party itself—particularly among many trade union M.P.s . . . and also—although they were curious allies for him to associate with—from Philip Snowden and others of the ILP group whom, in the normal way of things, (Bevin) disliked almost as much as he did MacDonald."[4]

[1] *Beatrice Webb's Diaries 1912–24*, p. 218. Lord Elton stoutly denies that MacDonald ever entered into such discussions with the Liberals. Elton, *The Life of James Ramsay MacDonald*, pp. 183–6. But it is difficult to believe that Henderson, who so faithfully refused to join in any move to unseat MacDonald, should have invented so damaging a story against MacDonald and passed it on to Mrs. Webb in 1921.

[2] See Lyman, R. W., *The First Labour Government, 1924*, p. 272 ff.

[3] Cited in Brockway, F., *Socialism Over Sixty Years*, pp. 222–3. Two months later, Snowden's wife (speaking at a public meeting in Montreal) said: " Undoubtedly we were the victims of the worst political leadership of modern times—our own leader (MacDonald), the man who took too much upon himself." Cited in *Gleanings and Memoranda*, February, 1925, p. 194. The comment created a minor sensation at the time and there was much speculation in the Press as to whether Snowden agreed with his wife's comment. Significantly he made no attempt to dissociate himself from it.

[4] Williams, Francis, *Ernest Bevin*, p. 122. See also, Bullock, A., *Ernest Bevin*, I, p. 255 ff.

Nor was Bevin the only trade unionist who was dissatisfied with
MacDonald's leadership. Mrs. Webb records in her diary (22nd
June, 1925) a comment on the situation by her husband (who was
then a member of the NEC): " Sidney reports that the joint meeting
of the (General Council) of the TUC and the LP Executive was most
disheartening—Robert Smillie with his little bodyguard of pseudo-
Communists is trying his level best to damage the PLP and cut off
trade union support from MacDonald, and the General Council,
which has always been restive, is now openly and defiantly so. For
the first time for some years they have summoned a TU Congress
on unemployment without any kind of consultation with or participation of the Labour Party Leaders. . . . The plain truth is that
JRM has lost all his moral (authority) with the PLP as well as with
the inner councils of the TU movement and his growing alienation
from the ILP is only symbolic of a general 'rotting' of his influence."[1]

In the columns of the ILP *New Leader*, H. N. Brailsford attacked
MacDonald bitterly and openly advised the party to get rid of him
as Leader. Others joined the attack. At the annual meeting of the
Scottish Council of the Labour Party in Glasgow on 1st March,
1925, J. B. Figgins of the National Union of Railwaymen said that
MacDonald was to blame for " not putting up a real fight (at the
last election). By allowing the (Zinoviev) letter to be published and
by his other actions, he did a most disastrous thing so far as Labour
was concerned. Before that Mr. MacDonald had created bewilderment in the minds of the electors by his weak speeches." It seemed
to Figgins that " if blame should be attached to anyone, it was not
to the Conservative Party but to Mr. MacDonald." And at the
same meeting James Maxton, M.P., added that he thought " it
would be a very bad thing if the Labour movement got into the frame
of mind that there was only one person who could lead them at any
time, and that he should not be the subject of criticism when he
was so doing." [2]

Both Snowden and Bevin approached Henderson in the hope
that he would be willing to allow himself to be proposed as successor
to MacDonald. Mrs. Hamilton records: " They came to see
(Henderson); they argued with him, forcibly, in the interests of
the Party. They assured him that, if he were prepared to run, he
could be elected leader. He listened to them; what they said did
not move him an inch. They were, in his judgment, entirely
wrong." [3] Francis Williams writes that Henderson told Bevin that
" to talk of swapping horses on the very morrow of defeat was

[1] *Beatrice Webb's Diaries*, 22nd June, 1925, folios 52-3.
[2] *The Times*, 2nd March, 1925.
[3] Hamilton, M. A., *Arthur Henderson*, p. 256.

disloyal and that he intended to stand firmly by MacDonald who in any event he regarded, despite all his faults, as the only man with the Parliamentary skill and public prestige to lead the Party back to recovery."[1] Sidney Webb's attitude was very similar to that of Henderson. Mrs. Webb wrote in her diary in September 1925, " (Sidney) is not going to join in the hue and cry against J. R. M. for the good reason that he sees no one to take his place and dislikes throwing over leaders."

The turning point for MacDonald appears to have come at the annual party conference in the autumn of 1925. As was noted above, he spoke more frequently and played a more prominent part in the conference than any Leader ever had before. Mrs. Webb, summarizing press reports and her husband's letters, conceded ungrudgingly that J. R. M. had done " brilliantly " and had " reasserted his dominance". On Webb's return from the conference he confirmed this; he told his wife: " MacDonald has completely re-established his ascendancy."[2] But there were lingering doubts in the minds of many of MacDonald's supporters. One incident, in particular, which had come to light during MacDonald's term as Prime Minister was bound to have caused uneasiness amongst his followers. On 11th September, 1924, the *Daily Mail* announced that it had discovered that on 12th March of the same year, according to a document registered at Edinburgh, " James Ramsay MacDonald, 10, Downing Street, London, S.W.1, Member of H.M. Privy Council," was allotted £30,000 preference shares by a Scottish biscuit company, the amount of cash paid or payable to the company on each share being £1. On 3rd June, 1924, Sir Alexander Grant, the controlling member of the company, received a baronetcy " for public services". In an interview at Lossiemouth on 12th September MacDonald, then still Prime Minister, said that the shares represented the endowment of a Daimler motor-car

---

[1] Cited in Williams, Francis, *Ernest Bevin*, p. 123. One wonders whether Bevin recalled Henderson's remark when he (Bevin) was approached in September, 1947, to join a move to unseat Attlee as Leader of the PLP and Prime Minister. Francis Williams writes of this incident: " When Bevin was approached . . . he replied shortly, sharply and, I am told by those privileged to see his anger, with impressive contempt, that it was not his habit to intrigue against a man he trusted and who trusted him or to swap leaders in times of temporary difficulty. Who, he asked, did they think he was? Lloyd George? He added that Attlee was the best Prime Minister any Labour Government could have . . . " Williams, Francis, *Ernest Bevin*, p. 240. See also Dalton, H., *High Tide and After*, Chapter XXIX.

[2] Cited in *Beatrice Webb's Diaries*, 2nd October, 1925, folio 85, and 5th October, 1925, folio 88.

with which Sir Alexander had presented him, and at his (Mac-
Donald's) death they would revert to the Grant family. The
allotment of the shares, the Prime Minister explained, really represented an incident in a very old friendship, although the two were
at opposite poles in politics.[1] Two days later Sir Alexander Grant
made a statement which substantiated that of MacDonald; and
he explained that the figure of £30,000 was arrived at after considering what sum would be necessary to clear the car of all
expenses including income tax and super tax.[2]

The opposition, naturally enough, pounced on this incident.
Speaking at Birmingham on 17th September, Neville Chamberlain
said that the Prime Minister, whose moral sense was revolted by
capitalism, nevertheless saw nothing inconsistent in accepting
from a capitalist provision in the shape of the income of £30,000 in
order that he might ride in a lordly motor-car for the rest of his
days. It must, Chamberlain thought, have given rise to no little
surprise amongst some of Mr. MacDonald's supporters. Some of
these indeed had already written to the *Daily Herald* which confessed on 17th September that it had received " several letters "
about the Prime Minister's motor-car, but it did not think " any
useful purpose would be served by publishing them." [3] Less
inhibited journalists among the left-wing press were scathing in
their comment on MacDonald's action. But strangely, most of his
immediate colleagues seemed unconcerned. Even in retrospect,
Clynes (13 years later) was satisfied that the honour awarded to
Sir Alexander Grant had been given in acknowledgment of his
generosity in endowing public libraries and in making " other
similar contributions toward the welfare of the very classes whose
benefit the Labour Government had at heart." Grant, explained
Clynes, had been convinced that it was undignified that " Britain's
Premier often had to ' strap-hang ' on his way between his house in
north London and his official residence in Downing Street."[4] But
among the more militant socialists the incident stirred a deeper
uneasiness about MacDonald's devotion to the Socialist Cause.

During the years between the two Labour Governments there
was much evidence of MacDonald's growing impatience with the
mood and manners of many of his followers. Relations with the
ILP became increasingly bitter. It is unnecessary to document in

---

[1] *The Times,* 13th September, 1924.
[2] *The Times,* 15th September, 1924.
[3] *Daily Herald,* 17th September, 1924.
[4] Clynes, J. R., *Memoirs,* Vol. II, pp. 48–9. For contrasting views of this
incident see Weir, L. MacNeill, *The Tragedy of Ramsay MacDonald,* Chapter XX
(" Biscuits ") and Bassett, R., *Nineteen Thirty-One: Political Crisis,* p. 436.

detail MacDonald's struggle with the ILP, but the atmosphere can be recreated from incidents such as the following: At a Yorkshire divisional conference of the ILP at Leeds on 14th February, 1925, a resolution was carried " congratulating the late Government on its work in office." An amendment to delete the congratulation on the ground that the Labour Cabinet " had members who already had a sufficiently big idea of themselves since they began to wear silk hats was defeated. (But) a personal complimentary reference to Ramsay MacDonald was withdrawn." [1] Later in the same year an ILP branch had sent a resolution reproving MacDonald for a letter he had sent to a Bulgarian socialist indicating that three British socialists who were recently in Bulgaria were not an official delegation. In reply to the ILP branch protest MacDonald wrote: " Perhaps (the branch) would mind its own business and regard Socialism, not as a creed of a lot of blethering easie-oozie asses who are prepared to pass any resolution without knowing its meaning, and on any subject without understanding it, but as something which requires rectitude of thought and consideration of action." [2]

By the next year MacDonald's impatience with the ILP and with other extremist elements in the party led him to write: " . . . The movement is being headed straight for destruction." [3] But many in the ILP were equally convinced that MacDonald himself was leading the movement " straight to destruction." At the annual conference of the Scottish ILP in January 1927, a resolution was moved by the Govan Branch which expressed disapproval of MacDonald's recent utterances and urged that " the time was opportune for a change in the party leadership." The mover of the resolution said that " as a practical leader of the working class Mr. MacDonald was a complete failure," and he asked conference " to show the whole movement that they did not approve of this fawning and contemptuous temporizing of leaders." [4] The resolution was defeated by the narrow majority of 61 votes to 57. A few days later MacDonald replied in *Forward:* " What we have been troubled with is not big men who were bossing but little men with swollen heads who were criticizing. . . . We are not to allow, if we can prevent it, the Labour Party dissolving into a disorganized mass of passionate but fatuous fighters." [5] In an attempt to preclude this appalling prospect MacDonald, speaking to a Labour Party meeting, warned his followers in February 1928: " I want to remind my Parliamentary colleagues that during the coming months they

[1] *The Times,* 16th February, 1925.
[2] *Daily Herald,* 19th June, 1925.
[3] *Socialist Review,* March, 1926.
[4] Cited in *Gleanings and Memoranda,* February, 1927, pp. 217-8.
[5] *Forward,* 22nd January, 1927.

will have to mind their p's and q's and do what they are told, I being the interpreter of your views to them. . . . In the House of Commons during the coming Session we will do our level best to maintain the dignity, honour, efficiency and power of the Labour Party." [1]   MacDonald marked his complete lack of sympathy with the ILP by resigning from it after his return to office. In explanation of his action he said: " It is not only what has happened just recently in the House, but there has been an accumulation of happenings—an evidence of a spirit that made one despair." [2]

It is easy to understand MacDonald's exasperation with the ILP during these years; however sincere they may have been, there can be no doubt that their factiousness and irresponsibility was tending to undermine the effectiveness of the Labour Party in the House of Commons. But there can be little doubt that MacDonald was increasingly exasperated with others in addition to the ILP. He had long since expressed his impatience with what he called the " whirlpool " of " class-conscious trade unionists " around him;[3] indeed the doubt seems to have grown steadily in his mind whether the Labour Party was in fact fit to govern the country.[4]

Simultaneously he found increasing common ground with his Conservative opponents. It was partly his similarity of viewpoint with Baldwin; they were more alike, Winston Churchill has claimed, than any other two men who had held the office of Prime Minister.[5] In addition, however, MacDonald found much to admire among many of Baldwin's supporters. As early as 1925 he said: " There is a large section of the Tory Party, especially the young Tories, who are men of very great promise. . . . (Sooner or later, he insisted), the partition between us and them will be so thin that they might as well break it down and come over to the Socialists' camp." [6] Baldwin saw this evident identity of viewpoint between MacDonald and many of the Conservative leaders in a different light: " In my view (he said) the leaders of the Labour Party have passed through that stage in which their followers still have their being, and I have been under the impression that since the disastrous year of 1926 they have been trying to wean their own followers from what they have taught them for a quarter of a century." [7]   This was no doubt

---

[1] *The Times,* 7th February, 1928.

[2] *Forward,* 22nd February, 1930.

[3] Cited in Snowden, *An Autobiography,* Vol. I, p. 175. MacDonald appears to have made this comment about his trades union colleagues in the PLP in 1908.

[4] Dalton, H., *Call Back Yesterday,* pp. 286-9, reviews the evidence of MacDonald's growing doubts on this issue after 1924.

[5] Churchill, W., *History of the Second World War,* Vol. I, p. 18.

[6] *The Times,* 20th April, 1925.

[7] *The Times,* 2nd August, 1929.

close to the truth. And when MacDonald found that he could not
wean his followers from " the teachings of a quarter of a century "
he did not hesitate to break with them and to establish the National
Government.

It is unnecessary to attempt to assess the sincerity of MacDonald
and the action he took in 1931. The important question for the
purposes of this study is rather to decide why, despite the enormous
accumulation of doubts about his sincerity, no serious effort was
made to unseat him as Leader after the furtive moves initiated by
Bevin and Snowden in 1924–5. Many must have agreed with
Snowden's judgment that MacDonald had manifested obvious
incompetence as Prime Minister of the first Labour Government;
MacDonald himself made little effort to hide his growing exasperation with an increasing number of his followers in the parliamentary
party. Yet in the end (as Dalton puts it) MacDonald " expelled
himself". At no time did he face anything like the difficulties
Baldwin faced in retaining the Conservative leadership. MacNeill
Weir, although he is a prejudiced witness, gives a convincing
summary of the reasons why the Labour Party failed to make a
serious effort to depose MacDonald:

> " (MacDonald) had earned the admiration and devotion of the
> great body of the Labour Party by his oratorical ability, by his
> intellectual ascendancy, by his personal attractiveness, by his
> specialized aptitude for his job, by his debating skill, and by his
> knowledge of Parliamentary technique. Moreover, he had assisted
> at the birth of the Party, rendered it a hundred services and
> suffered with it in its many reverses. Above all, MacDonald's
> prestige had been built up by years of hard work, and the grati-
> tude of the masses to their leaders (is) proverbial."[1]

But in the same passage MacNeill Weir adds this totally inaccurate
comment: ". . . in a democratic body like the Labour Party, the
only method of dismissal would be at an Annual Conference by
vote of the delegates." It would no doubt be accurate to argue that
MacDonald's resignation would have become inevitable had the
annual conference of the party either passed a vote of want of
confidence in him, or defeated a resolution on a major matter of
policy with which he had identified himself.[2] But MacNeill Weir
appears completely to ignore the fact that the Leader of the Labour
Party is chosen not by the party outside Parliament but by the PLP,
and that he is subject to annual re-election when the PLP is in
opposition. In theory it would have been perfectly possible for
any of MacDonald's colleagues to stand against him during the

[1] Weir, L. MacNeill, *The Tragedy of Ramsay MacDonald*, p. ix.
[2] Cf. Lansbury's resignation, discussed below.

annual elections for the office of Chairman and Leader. It would appear indeed to have been the hope of Snowden and Bevin that Henderson would agree to do so after 1924. But as Mrs. Hamilton put it, the scheme broke on the rock of Henderson's loyalty—this despite the fact that, according to both Snowden and Kirkwood, Henderson had favoured the election of Clynes rather than MacDonald in 1922. The Deputy Leader of the Party, Clynes, was equally unwilling to contest the leadership and the only other likely candidate, Snowden, never showed the slightest inclination to do so. Even Lansbury, it will be recalled, refused to allow his name to be put in nomination against MacDonald in December 1924 on the grounds that " a change of leadership would be most inopportune in the present circumstances."

No doubt Lansbury felt that to reject MacDonald immediately after the fall of the Government would be to repudiate Labour's record in office. But this consideration alone could hardly account for the failure of anybody to challenge MacDonald throughout the period 1925–9. Undoubtedly the party felt itself peculiarly dependent on him since he was so obviously superior in parliamentary skills to any possible rival. Mrs. Webb, who had long been disillusioned with MacDonald, combed again and again during these years through possible alternative leaders; but none, she decided, was remotely acceptable. Of Clynes, the Deputy Leader in this period, she wrote in 1926:

> " A silent refined little man . . . has more wisdom than all of them . . . . But he lacks vitality—and like Sidney, he has no desire to control his fellow men . . . . He is still a convinced Socialist ; he always says what he thinks and no more than he thinks, and he knows exactly what he does think . . . . but alas! although he is an admirable councillor he is not a leader of men—he is too modest and silent to be a force, whether on platform or in committee ; he is what he looks, a small man . . . "

Henderson, she felt, had important qualities that Clynes lacked:

> " He is, in fact, a first-rate *manager of men*—the only one in the front rank of the Labour Movement. Without Arthur Henderson, Heaven help the Labour Party! But *he* also is no leader of men— he has no personal magnetism."[1]

And, again, three years later she wrote:

> " Arthur Henderson is a magnificent moral stalwart and a sound party manager—but has no intellectual or artistic gifts—no imagination, he is dull and slightly commonplace ; within the Party he is trusted and even loved ; but outside the Party he is nobody."[2]

---

[1] *Beatrice Webb's Diaries,* 10th September, 1926, folios 15-16.
[2] *Ibid.,* 25th March, 1929, folio 163.

Lansbury, despite certain admirable qualities, was inconceivable as Leader. If he " had led or dominated (the Labour Party)," she wrote in 1928, " it would have been to-day in ruins." [1] Again and again, Mrs. Webb quotes the judgment of others in the inner circle of the Labour Party that if MacDonald went Snowden would have to be his successor. After Henderson had visited the Webbs in 1928, Mrs. Webb wrote that he and Sidney had " agreed that if J. R. M. disappeared Snowden was the best man for the Party leadership—better than good little Clynes, who seems the only alternative." [2] But neither Mrs. Webb nor anyone she quotes seems to have been able to generate any positive enthusiasm for the bitter, misanthropic Snowden: certainly no one seemed prepared to destroy MacDonald to make Snowden king.

" The worst of it is," Mrs. Webb concluded, "(MacDonald) is the best man we've got to put in our shop window . . ." [3] Yet the arguments against MacDonald which flooded into her mind now seem, in retrospect, almost overwhelming. In 1926 she wrote:

> " He is no longer intent on social reform—whatever indignation he ever had at the present distribution of wealth he has lost; his real and intimate life is associating with non-political aristocratic society . . . surrounded with the beauty and dignity which wealth can buy and social experience can direct." Nevertheless, she conceded: " He has great gifts as a political leader, he has personal charm, he has vitality, he is assiduous, self-controlled and skilful. In all these respects he is unique in the inner circle of the Labour Party made up, as it is, of fanatics, faddists, refined and self-effacing intellectuals and the dull mediocrities of the Trade Union Movement . . . "

As Mrs. Webb saw it, the plain fact was that the Labour Party had not yet found an adequate Leader. In the circumstances she decided: " Ramsay MacDonald is a magnificent substitute for a leader. He has the ideal appearance. . . . But he is shoddy in character and intellect." [4]

It is important to emphasize that disillusionment with the " magnificent substitute " (of the sort that is reflected in Mrs. Webb's

---

[1] *Beatrice Webb's Diaries,* 11th October, 1928, folio 131. Although in the same passage Mrs. Webb added that had Lansbury been a member of the inner circle of the party in those years he might have " added warmth and emotional grit to the Henderson-Snowden-Clynes-Webb combination, finished off as it has been in the thin, glittering façade provided by (MacDonald)."

[2] *Ibid.,* Whit-Sunday, 1928, folio 70. A cryptic passage follows in the diary—" 'Why not Uncle Arthur?' " said I (meaning Henderson). A conclusive *No* was the answer."

[3] *Ibid.,* 14th February, 1928, folio 38.

[4] *Ibid.,* 2nd August, 1926, folios 73-4.

diaries) appears to have been confined largely to the inner circle of the party; it was prevalent mainly among those (and not even all of them) who had an opportunity to judge MacDonald's work and character at first hand; his hold on the party outside Parliament was overwhelmingly strong. A palace revolution *might* have been possible if Henderson had allowed himself to become the spearhead of anti-MacDonald feeling in the councils of the party. Henderson might have succeeded in unseating MacDonald had he sought to do so in order to " save the Movement "; but his concept of loyalty prevented him.[1] It should not be assumed, however, that it would have been an easy matter even for Henderson (had he been willing to try to do so) to have destroyed MacDonald. In the elections for the Parliamentary Executive Committee after the fall of the first Labour Government, Henderson stood tenth in the list of 12 successful candidates for the Committee, securing only 38 votes against the 67 for Lansbury who headed the list. In the years that followed, Henderson's position on the list fluctuated remarkably; he was as low as twelfth in 1926 and rose to second in 1927. But certainly these election results do not suggest that Henderson was the overwhelming favourite of the back-benchers, nor that they would necessarily have voted him into office had he stood for the leadership against MacDonald. Loyalty, as MacNeill Weir suggests in the passage quoted above, runs strong and deep in the Labour movement. And it is important to keep in mind that MacDonald had had a spectacular record of unopposed re-elections to most of the principal offices of the party. He had been annually elected Secretary of the Party, unopposed, for the years 1900–11 inclusive; he was annually elected Treasurer 1912–30 (and opposed on only one occasion); he was elected Chairman of the PLP without opposition from 1911 to 1914 and, with the exception of the 1922 contest, he was re-elected unopposed from that year to 1931. Dalton's phrase quoted at the beginning of this chapter is distinctly relevant: ". . . We (in the Labour Party) have a strong sense of social security near the top. To do a man out of his job, at that eminence, is against good followership."

David Kirkwood goes so far as to claim that MacDonald could

---

[1] He later appears to have deeply regretted his failure to act. Mrs. Webb describes in her diary a visit to Passfield by Arthur Henderson's son William (later Lord Henderson), some months after the fall of the second Labour Government. She quotes William Henderson as saying that his father " was broken-hearted over the catastrophe of last autumn; (he) felt that his policy of putting up with and maintaining J.R.M. in the leadership since 1922, in spite of personal distrust, had been a big mistake and has temporarily, at any rate, ruined the Party." *Beatrice Webb's Diaries*, 22nd February, 1932, folio 33.

have carried the PLP with him had he bothered to attend and address the party meeting on 28th August, 1931:

> " Of one thing . . . (Kirkwood writes) I feel certain. If Ramsay MacDonald had come to a meeting of his Party and told them his views and invited them to join him in creating a National Government, most of them would have agreed. We all knew that national affairs were not going well. We had seen nations crash into chaos and had seen dictators rise to autocracy on the ruins. We were familiar with the idea of a non-party administration. Ramsay MacDonald had said on more than one occasion that he was willing to work along with any Party or any men, if by their combined efforts they could redeem the nation. So strong was the hold that Ramsay MacDonald had on the Party in the House that, if he had come to the meeting, anyone who challenged him would probably have been howled down. The Clyde group were definitely antagonistic. They had lost faith in their leader. Others were opposed to coalition on principle. But they would have been swamped."

MacDonald did not go to the meeting; he sent Lord Sankey, who, in Kirkwood's phrase, " talked to (the PLP) like a benevolent old gentleman who carried peppermints in his jacket pocket to give to the poor workers." [1] MacDonald's case therefore went largely by default.

Most of the survivors of this meeting strongly dissent from Kirkwood's judgment. In retrospect they deny that there was the slightest chance that MacDonald could have carried any considerable part of the PLP with him. Perhaps *at that late date* he could not have done so. But what if MacDonald had been less aloof from his followers during the preceding months? He might have set about attempting to carry them with him rather than so obviously seeking to rid himself of them. It is worth remembering that a considerable part of the Cabinet stood with MacDonald in the final critical vote on the proposal to cut the unemployment benefit.[2] He might have set about much earlier convincing them and the members of the PLP that only a coalition government could deal with what was widely considered to be the nation's desperate economic dilemma. It is at least an open question whether he might not have succeeded in such a campaign. There were few of the signs of revolt against MacDonald personally at the highest levels of the party of the sort that preceded the resignation of Balfour and Austen Chamberlain. Only the ILP waged open warfare against him and they were much less powerful than, for example,

---

[1] Kirkwood, D., *My Life of Revolt*, p. 248.
[2] Nicolson, Sir H., *King George the Fifth*, p. 464.

the section of Baldwin's party that sought to oust him. MacDonald, it must be remembered, was the first " Leader of the Party "; he was the first Prime Minister Labour had produced; he was obviously superior in personal accomplishments to all possible rivals. It is at least conceivable that he might have carried a considerable part of the PLP with him had he not, one strongly suspects, preferred to be rid of them.[1]

The only clear-cut instance of a Labour Leader being driven from office is the downfall of Lansbury in 1935. The circumstances in which he resigned the leadership need not be recounted in detail [2]; but certain aspects of the affair must be examined for the light they throw on the process by which a Labour Leader may, in certain circumstances, be driven from office. Lansbury, it will be remembered, had formally inherited the title of Leader following the resignation of Arthur Henderson in October 1932. On many

[1] The late Professor R. Bassett devoted a long and deeply emotional section of his book (*Nineteen Thirty-One: Political Crisis*, London, 1958, p. 422 ff.) to disputing my interpretation of MacDonald's rôle in 1931. His comments are based on an apparent misunderstanding of what I have tried to say in these pages. It was not my purpose to attempt a full-scale assessment of MacDonald's career nor even his rôle in the 1931 negotiations, and I certainly nowhere intended to suggest that the formation of the National Government represented the fulfilment of a long-standing plot on his part to form an anti-Labour alliance. But that he was largely out of sympathy with the party by 1931, seems to me incontestable.

When I wrote (p. 373) " it is unnecessary to attempt to assess the sincerity of MacDonald and the action he took in 1931 " (a phrase that particularly upset Bassett) I meant simply that whether in fact MacDonald parted company with the Labour Party with regret or relief, he did so, *in effect*, of his own volition. Despite the extensive evidence of uneasiness about his leadership and the recurrent hostility toward him by many of his colleagues, his position was at no time effectively challenged. Until the events of August 1931 his authority within the party was complete. Bassett is quite right in insisting that MacDonald was *formally* expelled from the Labour Party on September 28th, 1931 (more than a month after he accepted the commission to form a National Government). But I think that Dalton's remark, that " MacDonald expelled himself," is fully justified.

Incidentally, although Bassett makes a strong case for the argument that MacDonald in 1931 was inspired solely by a desire to serve the national interest in solving the immediate economic crisis of the summer of that year, he fails, curiously enough, to explain why MacDonald remained a member of the National Government until May 1937 and continued to support it until his death in November of that year.

[2] For a full account, see Postgate, R., *George Lansbury*, Chapter 22; Williams, F., *Ernest Bevin*, Chapter 17; Dalton, H., *The Fateful Years* pp. 62 ff.; Bullock, A., *The Life and Times of Ernest Bevin*, pp. 564 ff.; Cooke, Colin, *The Life of Richard Stafford Cripps*, pp. 144–177.

issues Lansbury's views were not typical of the majority of his colleagues in the PLP of 1931–5, but he managed nevertheless to speak effectively on their behalf, whatever private reservations he may have had about some of the views he was called upon to express. The arrangement became intolerable only when a deep gulf developed between the Leader and a majority of his party on the issue of peace and war. As the threat of Fascist aggression grew steadily after 1933, the Labour Party slowly, reluctantly, and amidst considerable confusion, came to accept the full implications of the policy of collective security, including the possibility that it might involve collective military resistance against aggression. But to Lansbury, the Christian pacifist, " collective security " remained an euphemistic description of war; he could not envisage the possibility that he might be expected to lead the party in support of a war however worthy the cause for which it might be fought.

During the annual party conference of October 1934 Lansbury had made it clear that he was prepared to resign the leadership whenever it was considered that his own pacifism had become an obstacle to the political effectiveness of the party; this offer was peremptorily refused and Lansbury agreed (apparently with mixed feelings) to carry on as Leader. But during the succeeding year his position became increasingly difficult. He was under considerable pressure from Arthur Henderson to carry on as Leader through the next election which was bound to come during late 1935 or sometime in 1936 [1]; but he found himself passionately opposed to the majority opinion of both the Labour Party and of the trade union movement on the subject of sanctions. The Trades Union Congress met in conference on 2nd–6th September, 1935, at Margate, and Lansbury was expected to carry fraternal greetings to the Congress from the Labour Party. He sought to avoid the assignment and urged that Attlee, the Deputy Leader, be sent in his stead. The NEC insisted, however, that Lansbury should attend in order to refute the rumours that there were deep divisions within the party.

At the Congress Lansbury heard Walter Citrine, the Secretary, urge the delegates to support a declaration prepared by the General Council calling upon the British Government, along with other nations belonging to the League, " to use all the necessary measures provided by the Covenant to prevent Italy's unjust and rapacious

[1] Mrs. Hamilton records that Henderson's correspondence includes " a long and intimate " exchange of letters with George Lansbury in which Henderson, though disagreeing with Lansbury's attitude to sanctions, nevertheless puts to him the argument that he alone could carry the party through an election. Hamilton, M. A., *Arthur Henderson*, p. 452.

attack upon the territory of (Abyssinia)." [1]   If the Congress rejected this declaration, " it will mean (said Citrine, with a touch of cruel irony, one would have thought,) turning down our Leader, George Lansbury." [2]   Citrine no doubt intended this remark as a further demonstration of the unity of the party, but Lansbury (according to his biographer) was appalled by the ambiguity of the position in which he had been placed by Citrine's statement. In private discussion with the Congress leaders Lansbury apparently let it be known that he felt that when he spoke to the Congress he must make it clear that he personally would have opposed the General Council's resolution. Citrine insisted, however, that Lansbury must do no more than state the official position of the Labour Party. Again Lansbury consulted his colleagues, and " with three exceptions they told him that his resignation would be a disaster to the Party. Everyone knew, they added, that if war came he could not be their leader; but that might be far away, and he had a duty to the Party whose revival was to a high degree his own work." [3]

Lansbury appears to have accepted the argument and in his address to the Congress he confined himself mainly to a denunciation of war in general terms; but with respect to the resolution passed by the Congress he said:

> " . . . speaking on behalf of the Labour Party, and as their spokesman here to-day, all I can say is that over and over again in Parliament and outside they have said that they stand resolutely by the decision arrived at at their last Conference, which is really on all fours with the resolution that was passed here yesterday." [4]

But now Lansbury was more than ever troubled by the ambiguity of his position. At a joint meeting of the NEC and the General Council of the TUC he explained his deep concern, only to be told again that " his position was understood, and that his work as leader was indispensable." [5]   On 17th September the leader of the party in the House of Lords, Lord Ponsonby, resigned on the ground that no honest pacifist could " hold a position as leader "

---

[1] *1935 TUC Annual Report*, p. 346.

[2] *Ibid.*, p. 371. The declaration was approved by the Congress by a vote of 2,962,000, to 177,000.

[3] Postgate, R., *George Lansbury*, p. 300.

[4] *1935 TUC Annual Report*, p. 407. In the same speech Lansbury reaffirmed his conception of his rôle as " spokesman " of the party. " Whatever views any of us may hold in the long run, when we speak on behalf of the Movement we can only state what the opinion and decision of that Movement is."

[5] Postgate, R., *George Lansbury*, p. 300.

in the party.[1] Yet again, Lansbury proposed privately to the NEC that he should resign; yet again he was told that such action would be " inexcusable".

But by the time the Labour Party conference assembled on 30th September Lansbury had decided that he must quit the leadership. Italian troops had now invaded Ethiopia and a resolution would, he knew, be moved at the party conference which read in part:

> " United and determined in its opposition to the policy of imperialist aggression, this Conference calls upon the British Government, in co-operation with other nations represented at the Council and Assembly of the League, to use all the necessary measures provided by the Covenant to prevent Italy's unjust and rapacious attack upon the territory of a fellow member of the League. The Conference pledges its firm support of any action consistent with the principles and statutes of the League to restrain the Italian Government and to uphold the authority of the League in enforcing Peace." [2]

This resolution was put before the conference by Hugh Dalton on behalf of the Executive on 1st October. The issue was debated in a long and vitally important discussion during which it was evident that the tide was running strongly in the direction of those who supported the policy of sanctions. Lansbury received a tremendous welcome when he rose to intervene in the debate, but in his opening remarks he explained: ". . . I agree with the position of those of my friends who think that it is quite intolerable that you should have a man speaking as Leader who disagrees fundamentally on an issue of this kind . . ." He explained that he proposed to offer his resignation at a meeting of the PLP to take place in one week's time and added that he would consider it " natural and perfectly friendly " if the conference should decide to recommend to the PLP that his resignation should be accepted. There were cries of " No, no," and Lansbury, deeply moved, proceeded to re-state his own pacifist view.

In the closing passages of Lansbury's speech it would almost appear that he was leaving open the possibility that he might still revoke his decision to resign if the resolution was defeated. The phraseology certainly does not suggest that his decision was irrevocable: " *It may be* that I shall not meet you on this platform any more. (Cries of ' No.') There are things that come into life that make changes inevitable. *It may very well be* that in the carrying out of your policy I shall be in your way." Then a reference to his very serious illness of the year before: " When I was sick

---

[1] *The Times,* 14th September, 1935.
[2] *1935 Labour Annual Conference Report,* p. 153.

and on my back ideas came into my head, and one was that the only thing worth while for old men to do is to at least say the thing they believe, and to at least try to warn the young of the dangers of force and compulsion." He turned then to the charge that he had been irresponsible, a view (as he must have been well aware) that Ernest Bevin held strongly and was soon to put before the conference. " I am no more irresponsible a leader (said Lansbury) than the greatest Trade Union leader in the country." And then a final peroration which ended: ". . . I am ready to stand as the early Christians did, and say, ' This is our faith, this is where we stand, and, if necessary, this is where we will die.' "

The speech set off another great demonstration of affection for Lansbury; but while the cheers still echoed through the hall Ernest Bevin lumbered to the rostrum to deliver a powerful and ruthless reply.[1] He had long been convinced that Lansbury should resign; he had sat unmoved through Lansbury's emotional " farewell " to the conference as Party Leader. He could not have failed to notice that Lansbury had left open the possibility that he might still be prevailed upon to carry on. In the moment of the old man's personal triumph, Bevin seemed determined to exclude that possibility once and for all. " Let me remind the delegates (he began) that, when George Lansbury says what he has said to-day in the Conference, it is rather late to say it, and I hope this Conference will not be influenced by either sentiment or personal attachment. I hope you will carry no resolution . . . telling a man with a conscience like Lansbury what he ought to do. If he finds that he ought to take a certain course, then his conscience should direct him . . ." And then to Lansbury personally he directed one of the bitterest remarks in the history of Labour Party polemics. " (You are) placing the Executive and the Movement in an absolutely wrong position to be taking [2] your conscience round from body to body asking to be told what you ought to do with it." Amidst uproar and interjections, Bevin continued: ". . . I feel we have been betrayed."

---

[1] See Bullock, Alan, *Ernest Bevin*, Vol. I, p. 567 ff.

[2] The wording of the extracts from Bevin's speech given here is that of the official report of the conference. It is interesting to note, however, that Bevin's biographer twice quotes Bevin as accusing Lansbury of " *trailing* your conscience," while J. T. Murphy (who was present) is convinced that Bevin used the phrase, " *hawking* your conscience." Neither phrase is as bitter, however, as Bevin's reported answer to criticisms that his speech had been unnecessarily harsh: " Lansbury has been going about dressed in saint's clothes for years waiting for martyrdom. I set fire to the faggots." See Williams, F., *Ernest Bevin*, pp. 193-6, and Murphy, J. T., *Labour's Big Three*, p. 184.

Bevin then recalled the extent to which Lansbury had allowed himself to continue as spokesman for a policy with which he was in complete disagreement. Yet, on the very eve of the conference, Bevin said, Lansbury had made a personal statement to the press reaffirming his own personal position. " I think the TUC and all of us representing responsible Unions (said Bevin) have a very serious ground of complaint." [1] There was no acknowledgment in Bevin's speech of the efforts Lansbury had already made to resign, nor was there any reference to the fact that Lansbury had consistently distinguished on every occasion between the party position which he was required to state as Leader and his own personal viewpoint. When Bevin sat down, Lansbury understandably demanded the right of reply, although by the rules of the conference he would not normally have been granted the opportunity to intervene in the debate a second time. When he tried to speak the microphones were switched off. But he persisted, saying that he would shout loud enough for the delegates to hear. Lansbury tried to reply to Bevin point by point but now his hold on the conference was lost. Undoubtedly (as Postgate suggests) Lansbury's bitterest disillusionment sprang from the fact that not a single member of the Executive had risen to explain or to defend his position. The debate was adjourned and on the following day the Executive resolution in support of sanctions was carried by 2,168,000 to 102,000. Lansbury (says Postgate) returned to his home in Bow Road in a state of great distress.

On the following Tuesday Lansbury met the PLP and submitted his resignation. Incredibly enough, the PLP at first refused to accept it; by a vote of 38 to seven (with five abstentions) they urged Lansbury to reconsider. In retrospect there seems no possible justification for such a request. The conference had just demonstrated by a vote of 20 to one that Lansbury's views on the most vital issue of the day were totally unacceptable. He had been repudiated—and bullied—in public and in what can only be described as a degrading fashion; understandably, Lansbury refused to reconsider his resignation and the PLP proceeded (it will be recalled) to elect Attlee as Leader " for the remainder of the Session."

In reviewing the rôle of the Leader in the Labour Party it is important to emphasize that until 1955 only two men, MacDonald and Attlee, have led the PLP when it held more than 10 per cent. of

---

[1] *1935 Labour Annual Conference Report,* pp. 177-80.

the seats in the Commons.[1] Each of these Leaders formed two governments and the procedure they followed on both occasions differed
in no significant respect from the procedure followed by the Leaders
of other parties in similar circumstances.   Nor were MacDonald
and Attlee as Prime Ministers subject to greater measures of control
either by their followers in Parliament or by the mass organizations
of the party outside Parliament.   This is the basis for the argument
set forth at the beginning of this chapter that despite the profound
differences in the " style " and atmosphere of Labour Party politics
and the party's infinitely more complex constitution, it has in practice
accepted a principle of leadership which is not fundamentally
different from that which operates in the older parties.

When MacDonald and Attlee returned to opposition the former
certainly remained as dominant a figure in his party as any Conservative Leader in opposition.   Attlee (after 1951) was less so;
and therefore the party's devices to ensure " internal party democracy " have loomed larger than they did under MacDonald.   But
it can be argued that this is largely a consequence of Attlee's temperament and personality and also of his conception of the rôle
of Leader.   No doubt if he had chosen to be a more forceful and
dynamic Prime Minister he would also have been a more dominant
Leader in opposition after 1951.   This might have reawakened
the old fears of 1931-3, but there is no reason to assume that it
would necessarily have resulted in a successful revolt against his
leadership.

The Labour Leader's formal powers appear to be much more
limited than those of the Conservative Leader, but like the latter,
he becomes from the moment of his election as Leader a potential
Prime Minister.   It must be emphasized again that *this above all
else is the principal source of his influence and authority*.   Like his
Conservative counterpart, the Labour Leader wields this influence on
sufferance. If his followers in Parliament withdraw their consent to his
continued leadership, his authority collapses immediately. The PLP
provides an annual opportunity (while the party is in opposition)
for the Leader's parliamentary supporters to challenge his authority,
but it is not surprising that no one seized this opportunity during the
33 years from the election of MacDonald in 1922 to the retirement
of Attlee in 1955.   If a Labour Leader *were* again to be driven from

---

[1] Each of the others who held the office of Chairman or Leader did so
during periods (1906-22 and 1931-5) when the strength of Labour in the Commons ranged from 29 to 57 seats. Since Labour seemed so remote from office or
power the Chairmen in those periods inevitably appeared more in the rôle of
spokesman than of Leader. Certainly none of them appeared to be a potential
Prime Minister.

office the process would probably be much the same as that which has operated on such occasions within the Conservative Party. Like Balfour, the Labour Leader might find his views frequently and more or less overtly challenged. Or like Austen Chamberlain, he might find his advice on a single major issue rejected by a meeting of his parliamentary supporters. Or, of course, like Lansbury he might feel himself compelled to resign after a public demonstration at the party conference that his views on a major policy issue were overwhelmingly rejected by his followers.[1] But this, again, is the process of " withdrawal of consent " and it operates in both major parties in a strikingly similar way.

[1] Hugh Gaitskell's defiance of the 1960 Labour conference decision on unilateral disarmament and the 1961 conference decisions on " Polaris " bases and other matters is discussed on pp. 615 ff. below.

CHAPTER VII

THE PARLIAMENTARY LABOUR PARTY

I

LABOUR IN PARLIAMENT 1900-22

FORMALLY the Parliamentary Labour Party would appear to play a vastly different rôle within the Labour Party to that played by the Conservative Parliamentary Party within its party organization; and in day-to-day practice the two bodies clearly conduct their affairs in very different ways. Yet in certain important respects the two great parliamentary parties are fundamentally alike, despite the strongly contrasting circumstances of their origin. Each is an autonomous entity which throws up its own leaders and acknowledges its ultimate responsibility only to the electorate. Each maintains close relations with the mass organization of its active supporters outside Parliament and allows them to play some part in the determination of its policies and programme. But neither party in Parliament allows itself to be directed or controlled by its mass organization. As has been shown in Chapter IV, the Conservative Party has had little difficulty in establishing and maintaining this relationship with its supporters. But it is more surprising (in the light of its origins) that the PLP has succeeded, despite great and recurrent difficulties, in establishing its autonomy with so large a measure of success.

It is unnecessary to examine in detail the history of the party in Parliament since its emergence at the turn of the century.[1] But as a prelude to a discussion of the contemporary structure of the PLP it is necessary to recall that the party in Parliament from its earliest years was plagued by two problems; these might be described as the problems of independence and of coherence. As was noted in Chapter I, the PLP was in a sense *thrust into* Parliament by the Labour and Socialist movements outside. This raised from the beginning the problem of extra-parliamentary control, and it is important to trace the process by which the PLP established its right to independence of such control. The second problem, the problem of " coherence," is of less concern to this study since it involves ideological issues which are to a large extent outside the scope of this book. But it should be noted that this problem of coherence was also a by-product of the circumstances in which the

---

[1] For bibliography on the origins of the Labour Party see p. 457 below. Two recent publications are indispensable: Bealey, F. and Pelling, H., *Labour and Politics 1900–06*, and Poirier, P. P., *The Advent of the Labour Party.*

party was founded. The Labour Party began as a loose alliance or federation in which a number of trade unions had combined with several socialist organizations for the purpose of increasing working-class representation in Parliament. The PLP in its earliest days was committed neither to the conception of the class struggle[1] nor to any coherent socialist philosophy or programme. It was a trade union and social reform movement without doctrinal foundations, attempting (often with the aid of the Liberal Party) to improve the lot of the working classes. Most of the Labour M.P.s were trade unionists who did not claim to be socialists, although the PLP did include a small heterogeneous group of avowed socialists. With so diverse a composition it was not easy for the party to function in Parliament as an integrated political force which could lay claim to the status of a national party.

In recalling the origins of the Labour Representation Committee (hereinafter LRC), MacDonald remarked that " discretion moved the conference in the Memorial Hall (of 1900) to adopt the title, ' The Labour Representation Committee,' rather than one more definitely Party. Organized Labour was by no means ready to plunge into the task of Party making . . ." [2] The LRC itself confessed that it had been *propelled* into politics: " Menaced on every hand in workshop, court of law, and press, Trade Unionism has no refuge except the ballot box and Labour Representation." [3] In the elections of 1900 the LRC elected two members, Keir Hardie and Richard Bell, and during the life of that Parliament three others who had been endorsed by the LRC were returned at by-elections. But significantly, one of the two members elected in 1900, Richard Bell, deserted to the Liberals in 1904 despite the fact that he had been the first Treasurer of the LRC and its Chairman in 1902–3. Indeed, the tiny LRC group in the Parliament of 1900 was so far from thinking of itself as a parliamentary party that MacDonald later recalled they " did not even meet to consult each other on Parliamentary business. Each was a Party in himself."[4]

[1] The Second International had hopefully described the Labour Party as an unconscious instrument of the class struggle. On the occasion of the admission of the Labour Party it had declared (in a formula devised by Karl Kautsky): " The English Labour Party is to be admitted to the International Socialist Congress because, although it does not avowedly recognize the class struggle, it actually carries it on; and because the organization of the Labour Party being independent of the bourgeois parties is based upon the class struggle." Cited in Tracey, H., (editor), *The Book of the Labour Party*, Vol. I, p. 133.

[2] MacDonald, J. R., *A Policy for the Labour Party*, p. 24.

[3] *1902 LRC Annual Conference Report*, p. 12.

[4] MacDonald, J. R., *A Policy for the Labour Party*, pp. 24-5. See also Pease, E. R., *History of the Fabian Society*, p. 151.

Significantly, the pressure to end this state of affairs and to convert the band of LRC representatives into something resembling a party, came from the movement outside Parliament. The 1903 LRC conference adopted a revised statement of its objects which included the following:

> "To secure, by united action, the election to Parliament of candidates promoted, in the first instance, by an Affiliated Society or Societies in the constituency, who undertake to form or join a *distinct group in Parliament, with its own whips and its own policy on Labour questions,* to abstain strictly from identifying themselves with or promoting the interests of any section of the Liberal or Conservative Parties, and not to oppose any other candidate recognized by this Committee. All such candidates shall pledge themselves to accept this Constitution, *to abide by the decisions of the Group in carrying out the aims of this Constitution or resign,* and to appear before their constituencies under the title Labour candidates only."[1]

It is important to note that the phrase insisting that M.P.s should resign if they were unwilling to abide by the decisions of the group was included in the statement of objects at the insistence of the conference which passed an amendment to this effect by a majority of 501,000 to 194,000.[2] At the same conference, Philip Snowden (on behalf of the ILP) moved:

> "That inasmuch as there are now three representatives of the (LRC) in the House of Commons, and in order that a rallying centre may be created for the Trade Unions and Socialist organizations represented at this Conference, *we hereby press upon the three members aforesaid the necessity of at once forming a Labour Group in the House,* in accordance with the constitution of the Labour Representation Committee."

In support of the motion, Snowden emphasized that it was a corollary to the earlier decisions taken at the same conference. " If it passed," (he said), " it would enable the Executive (of the LRC) to instruct the members already returned under the auspices of this Committee to meet in the House and to adopt a joint and systematic policy." [3] Snowden's resolution was passed unanimously. Somewhat surprisingly the LRC was even prepared to undertake responsibility for " whipping " on behalf of the parliamentary group. The minutes of the Executive of the LRC meeting 12th May, 1904, record that: " Discussion took place upon the question of the Committee sending out ' Whips ' when the Labour

---

[1] *1903 LRC Annual Conference Report,* p. 40. [Italics mine.]
[2] *Ibid.,* pp. 32-3.
[3] *Ibid.,* pp. 36-7. [Italics mine.]

Group had Bills or Motions before Parliament." The following resolution was passed: " That when the Labour Group think that a ' Whip ' or ' lobbying ' is necessary that they are entitled to call upon this Committee to act in the matter." [1]

In an attempt to enforce loyalty and discipline on the part of its members in Parliament the LRC had a powerful sanction: in a period when Members of Parliament received no salary the LRC established a parliamentary fund from which grants were made to its own M.P.s.[2] The 1902 conference had carried the following resolution unanimously:

> " That this conference instructs the Committee to consider ways and means of raising funds to meet the expenses of those candidates who are run on our programme, and also for providing a Maintenance Fund for those who may be returned to Parliament. And that the Committee send out its scheme to all Trade Unionists, asking for their support."

In the following year a parliamentary fund scheme put forward by the Executive was also accepted unanimously and by 1904 the scheme was in full operation. The minutes of the Executive of the LRC for 30th June, 1904, reported that over £3,000 was in the parliamentary fund. It was therefore agreed to pay £200 a year maintenance to members of the parliamentary group from 1st July, 1904.

It is therefore evident that even before the sudden expansion of Labour representation in Parliament which occurred in 1906, the foundations of the Parliamentary Labour Party had been laid. The LRC members in the House had been instructed to form themselves into " a distinct group "; they were individually to receive payment from the parliamentary funds of the LRC on condition that they agreed to abide by the decisions of the group; and provision had been made for a system of whipping. It should be noted further that the LRC had in effect set its face against all proposals that its group or party in Parliament should limit its objectives to that of a pressure group which would throw its weight behind now one, now the other, of the two great parties. At the 1903 conference a resolution had been proposed insisting on the independence of the LRC from all other parties. In opposing this resolution, John Ward had urged that the Labour Group should follow the lead of the Irish Nationalist Party under Parnell. " Everybody knows (he said) that (Parnell) always . . . kept himself absolutely clear of any such resolution as this. Parnell supported

---

[1] *Labour Party Documents,* Part I, folio 248.

[2] For the history of the financing of working-class representatives, see Gwyn, L. B., *Democracy and the Cost of Politics in Britain,* London, 1962.

Liberals or supported Tories as the occasion demanded. . . . This resolution, if carried, would not allow them to take such action as Parnell did so successfully in his time. They would strangle themselves if they passed such a resolution as this, and they must be mad if they could not see that they were absolutely choking the movement in its inception." In reply, Keir Hardie had made a strong case for independent *Labour* action in the House of Commons. He conceded that in the LRC conference itself, there were Liberals, Conservatives, and of course, Socialists: and he conceded further that if his own group (the Socialists) insisted that all should adopt their principles, there could be no such gathering. But he argued that a common denominator could be found among all supporters of the LRC: " when acting in the House of Commons, they should be neither Socialists, Liberals, nor Tories, but a Labour Party." [1] In retrospect it can be argued that the PLP was forced by the circumstances of the parliamentary struggle during the period 1906–14 to conform fairly closely to the rôle of the Irish Nationalist Party, but it is nevertheless significant that as early as 1903 the LRC conference was prepared to adopt so rigorous a definition of its independent rôle.

It is clear that the emergent PLP achieved a measure of coherence and discipline largely as a result of the pressure of its mass organization outside Parliament. But this inevitably carried with it the danger that the parliamentary group would have no independent existence of its own and would become no more than a mouthpiece for its sponsoring body. At the LRC conference of 1905 Ben Tillett moved:

> " That it be an instruction to the Executive of the LRC to enforce the hearty adoption by LRC Candidates of all legislative proposals emanating from the Trade Union Congress. In view of the refusal of candidates, that it be the peremptory duty of the Executive to refuse or discontinue support financially and morally to said candidate or candidates."

The resolution was also intended of course to bind successful candidates who became Members of Parliament to the " hearty " adoption of all TUC proposals. It therefore raised in the clearest form the right of the emergent PLP to any sort of existence of its own. A. Gould (of the Hull Trades Council) in opposing the motion argued that " the formation of a programme should be left to their Members in Parliament." The previous question was moved and carried by 148 to 84. The supporters of Tillett's resolution felt strongly enough about the matter to insist on a card vote; but when it was taken the previous question was affirmed by 537

[1] *1903 LRC Annual Conference Report*, pp. 30-1.

to 245.[1] The wording of several other resolutions passed by the conference of the same year reflected a sounder appreciation of the rights and responsibilities of the conference with respect to its Members of Parliament. One resolution read, for example, " that this Conference *requests* the Labour M.P.s to promote legislation in the next session of Parliament, for the extension of the Outdoor Relief Friendly Societies Act . . . etc." [2] The word " requests " implies a recognition that the final authority to determine the policies to be advanced by the members of the parliamentary group lay with the M.P.s themselves, although (as will be shown below) the relationship between the mass party and the party in Parliament was by no means definitively clarified.

In the general election of January 1906 the Labour Representation Committee endorsed 50 candidates, of whom 29 were returned to Parliament. The " Labour Group " of 1900-5 had suddenly become a sizeable parliamentary party and—a significant step—it immediately began to act like a party, and to be treated like one by the Labour Representation Committee. It will be recalled that MacDonald, as secretary of the LRC, wrote a letter on 18th January, 1906, calling a joint meeting of its Executive and the newly elected Labour M.P.s which was to decide certain basic questions about the rôle of the newly elected Labour representatives in Parliament.[3] But MacDonald's letter added that he proposed that the M.P.s themselves should determine who should serve as " Chairman of the Group". As was suggested in Chapter VI, this was a development of decisive importance in the emergence of the PLP. It would not have been surprising if some of the members of the Executive of the LRC had tried to insist that their Executive should take part either in the elections of the Chairman or in the determination of the arrangements for its parliamentary work. There is no indication as to whether such suggestions were made and from the phrasing of MacDonald's letter (" I propose . . .") it would appear that he (as one of the newly elected M.P.s) appreciated the fact that some measure of autonomy for the emergent parliamentary party was essential.

The Executive also decided at this time to recommend to the conference that " in future the title ' The Labour Party ' should be adopted instead of ' The Labour Representation Committee.' " [4] Meanwhile the Parliamentary Labour Party at its first meeting on

---

1 *1905 LRC Annual Conference Report*, p. 52.
2 *Ibid.*, p. 44. [Italics mine.]
3 See pp. 335-6 above.
4 *1906 Labour Annual Conference Report* (Report of the NEC), p. 14. See also Brockway, F., *Socialism Over Sixty Years*, p. 69.

12th February, 1906 proceeded to elect its first slate of officers and when the annual party conference assembled three days later, Arthur Henderson reported: " We can congratulate ourselves to-day that a real live independent Labour Party, having its own chairman, its own deputy-chairman, and its own whips, is now an accomplished fact in British politics." [1]

In organizing the work of the PLP in Parliament, it was decided that the officers of the party should meet daily and the whole party once each week. The party meetings were called (as Clynes wrote) " to discuss plans of campaign, select speakers for Parliamentary debates and set up committees to deal with outstanding questions." [2] In addition, the party adopted the principle of selecting one speaker to speak for it in important debates. Keir Hardie, always impatient of the tedium of parliamentary debate, explained to the 1907 conference that this arrangement " were it generally followed, would relieve the House of the weary reiteration which marks so many of the debates and makes the proceedings so irksome." [3]   The Executive Committee (hereinafter, the NEC), also arranged to provide funds to hire a parliamentary clerk to assist with the detailed work of the PLP.[4]

The PLP was to have difficulty enough in welding itself into an integrated and effective force in the years that immediately followed, but, wisely no doubt, the very rigorous statement of the Members' responsibility to toe the party line adopted in 1903 (see p. 388 above) was modified by the 1906 conference. Candidates and Members of Parliament, it was decided, would henceforth be required to sign a pledge accepting the constitution of the party; in addition they must " agree to abide by the decisions of the Parliamentary Party in carrying out the aims of this Constitution; appear before their constituencies under the title of Labour Candidates only; abstain strictly from identifying themselves with or promoting the interests of any Party not eligible for affiliation; and they must not oppose any Candidate recognized by the Executive Committee of the Party." [5]   But it will be noted that it was no longer demanded that the candidate or Member should pledge himself to resign when he found himself in opposition to the majority of the PLP.   The PLP

---

[1] *1906 Labour Annual Conference Report*, p. 41.

[2] Clynes, J. R., *Memoirs*, Vol. I, pp. 111-12.

[3] *1907 Labour Annual Conference Report*, p. 37.

[4] *Labour Party Documents*, Part II, folio 12. The duties of the clerk are described in some detail in the *1907 Labour Annual Conference Report* (Report of the NEC), p. 9.

[5] It was also decided that " Candidates must undertake to join the Parliamentary Labour Party, if elected." *1906 Labour Annual Conference Report*, p. 72.

itself adopted a " conscience clause " giving freedom to members
of the party who felt a difficulty in accepting a majority decision
either to abstain from voting, or even to go to the length of voting
against the majority of the party. This led Snowden to comment
in retrospect: " There was a good deal more liberty given to
Members than might have been assumed from the rigid conditions
laid down in the constitution of the Party." [1] In his address to the
1907 conference Keir Hardie reported: " On great questions of
public policy a reasonable amount of freedom of action has been
allowed Members. Unity in things essential and in all things liberty,
fairly expresses the disciplinary rule of the Party . . ." And Hardie
added with more optimism than subsequent events were to justify,
". . . not only has harmony been maintained in the ranks but a
genuine feeling of comradeship and *esprit de corps* has grown with
the progress of the Session." [2]

At the 1907 conference a debate of fundamental importance
took place on the relationship between the PLP and the mass
organization of the party outside Parliament. As was noted above,
prior to 1906 the annual conference of the party had on occasion
passed resolutions " requesting " specific actions on the part of its
Members of Parliament. But at the 1906 conference stronger
language had been used. One resolution read, for example:
". . . this conference hereby *instructs* its Labour M.P.s to draft and
introduce into the House of Commons, as early as possible, a Trade
Union Amendment and Consolidation Bill, defining the position
of Trade Unions in the clearest possible terms." [3] And at the
conference of 1907, as Keir Hardie (the Chairman of the PLP)
pointed out, there were no less than 17 resolutions on the agenda
" giving the Parliamentary Party definite instructions to introduce
this and that." [4]

The NEC itself was clearly disturbed by this evidence that the
party conference appeared determined to direct the activities of
the PLP in so specific a fashion.[5] In their report to the conference
circulated some weeks in advance, the NEC indicated their intention
to recommend the adoption of the following statement: " That
Resolutions on the Agenda, which seek to instruct the Parliamentary
Party as to their action in the House of Commons, be so amended

[1] Snowden, *An Autobiography*, Vol. I, p. 135.
[2] *1907 Labour Annual Conference Report*, p. 40.
[3] *1906 Labour Annual Conference Report*, p. 55. [Italics mine.]
[4] *1907 Labour Annual Conference Report*, p. 49.
[5] The sympathetic concern of the NEC for the dilemma of the PLP is
better understood if one recalls that approximately half its members as well
as its Secretary (MacDonald) were Members of Parliament. For a discussion
of the overlapping membership of the PLP and the NEC see p. 421 below.

by the Standing Orders Committee as to register the opinions of the Conference without prejudice to any future course of action that may be considered advisable by the Party in Parliament." [1] This declaration, if adopted in this form, *would have established almost exactly the same relationship between the party in Parliament and its mass organization outside as that which has always existed in the Conservative Party*. It would have been most surprising if the conference had agreed so completely to abdicate its control of the PLP. Arthur Henderson confessed during the conference discussions that " the Executive acknowledged that the first wording of the resolution was unsatisfactory." It had therefore been reworded by the Executive itself and appeared before the conference in the following form: "That resolutions instructing the Parliamentary Party as to their action in the House of Commons be taken as the opinions of the Conference, on the understanding that the time and method of giving effect to these instructions be left to the Party in the House, in conjunction with the National Executive." [2]

The resolution, even in its modified form, aroused a fair amount of opposition. R. Morley (of the Workers Union) said that he " thought the Executive were trying to test the feeling of the Conference without there being any need for it at all. . . . The Conference and not the Parliamentary Party should decide the Parliamentary business." And J. Baker (of the Enginemen) said that they found members going to the House of Commons and " not only disregarding the instructions given them, but absolutely voting against the registered wish of the Conference. He thought they had a right to be suspicious of actions like those. The Executive Committee would be exceedingly wise to withdraw this resolution and not challenge the conference to give it a slap on the face." Significantly, neither of these speakers were Members of Parliament; and equally significantly, the case for the resolution was made by P. Curran (of the Gasworkers), a member of the Executive Committee who was returned to Parliament in a by-election in 1907. Curran believed that the resolution went as far as the Conference would desire to go in instructing " the Parliamentary Group". If the Conference passed a number of resolutions containing definite instructions to the parliamentary group then they were bound to entrust those resolutions to the National Executive; he thought that " if the Executive they elected deserved the confidence of the delegates, then it ought to be able to keep the Parliamentary Group

---

[1] *1907 NEC Report and Balance Sheet*, p. 15.

[2] *1907 Labour Annual Conference Report*, p. 49. The debate follows in subsequent pages.

up to its duty, and to co-operate with them as to the best measures to be taken up in Parliament. . . . The power of deciding which measures should be taken up would have to be delegated to the Executive and the Parliamentary Group."

Arthur Henderson also spoke for the resolution and explained that " it was not the Conference that caused them (the PLP) trouble; it was the affiliated organizations who, after getting their resolutions carried, if they did not get them put into the shape of a Bill, were constantly sending letters of protest." He could not see how any delegate could raise any objection to the resolution. Keir Hardie then explained why the PLP wanted " to safeguard themselves". They did not want at the next conference to have it said that they had displayed favouritism in their choice of conference resolutions which they pressed in Parliament. They asked therefore to have the right to decide in co-operation with the Executive which issues should have priority. " There had been a fuss about the Party wanting to be boss, to play the part of dictator and all that kind of nonsense, which was most ridiculous. The recommendation lent itself to no such interpretation. The Party in Parliament was a composite Party. It was composed of the Socialist movement and of the Trade Union movement. There must be some freedom of action, some free play between these two sections. . . . It should be understood that the Party in Parliament desired to be nothing but the servant of the movement as a whole." In a card vote taken at the conclusion of the debate the amended resolution was carried: in favour, 642,000; against, 252,000.

It is important to emphasize that the first impulse of the NEC (with its heavy representation of M.P.s) was to attempt to secure for the PLP the same freedom of action which the Conservative and Liberal Parties enjoyed in the House of Commons. When it became clear that such an arrangement would probably prove unacceptable to the conference, the Executive retreated to a statement which appeared to acknowledge the right of the conference to determine the objectives toward which the PLP must work, but which left the PLP free (in consultation with the NEC) to determine the priorities to be granted to the various instructions of the conference. Even this arrangement did not prove acceptable to the whole conference, as the voting on the revised resolution shows. Those who harboured suspicion of the freedom of action sought by the PLP returned to the attack later at the same conference. Ben Tillett (of the Dockers) moved that:

> " The Executive is instructed to secure united and consistent action on the part of its representatives in Parliament. For the aforesaid object the Committee should be sole authority granting

the right to back Bills, or support measures, directly or indirectly affecting Labour. The Executive shall organize a Committee within the House of Commons, of Labour Party Members, to instruct and advise its fellow Members in all Parliamentary work . . . . "

The conference defeated Tillett's resolution by a majority very similar to that by which it had adopted the amended recommendation of the NEC (in favour, 590,000; against, 229,000).[1] In 1907 there was (and has been ever since) a considerable minority of the mass membership of the party which resented its lack of effective control of the activities of the PLP. But the resolution adopted by the 1907 conference has remained nevertheless as the standard definition of the relationship between the party organizations inside and outside Parliament.

Before the 1907 conference adjourned, the issue of control of its parliamentary representatives was raised yet again in even sharper form, when Hardie (the Chairman of the PLP) found himself in basic disagreement with a resolution passed by the conference on the subject of women's suffrage. At the close of the conference when he moved a vote of thanks to the press, Hardie had startled the delegates by saying: ". . . if the motion they had carried that morning was intended to limit the action of the Party in the House of Commons he should have seriously to consider whether he could remain a member of the Parliamentary Party." [2] The situation was subsequently saved by Henderson's action in convincing both the PLP and the NEC that Labour Members of Parliament should be free, as individuals, to take whatever stand they wished with respect to any bill enfranchising women that might be introduced. Hardie did not fulfil his threat to resign; but his speech must have come as a warning to those who still believed that the conference could direct the activities of its parliamentarians.

There was widespread evidence of suspicion and hostility toward the PLP during 1908. The irrepressible Ben Tillett, the hero of the dock strike of 1889, published a bitter attack, a pamphlet entitled *Is the Parliamentary Labour Party a Failure?* He described Henderson, Snowden and others as " sheer hypocrites", " who for ten and five guineas a time will lie with the best", " softly feline in their purring to Ministers and their patronage", " repaying with gross betrayal the class that willingly supports them", and " Press flunkeys to Asquith".[3]   Tillett found little support for his ill-

---

[1] *1907 Labour Annual Conference Report,* p. 58.

[2] *Ibid.,* p. 63. See also Hughes, E., *Keir Hardie,* London, 1956, for an elaboration of Hardie's views on this issue, and p. 627 below.

[3] Tillett, Ben, *Is the Parliamentary Labour Party a Failure?* London, 1908, pp. 10–15.

tempered attack on the parliamentary party but at the annual
conference of the same year there were several attempts to restrict
PLP control of the mass party outside Parliament. It was moved
that " not more than one-third of the Executive Committee of the
Labour Party shall be Members of Parliament." And the Rochdale
Trades Council wanted to go even further, proposing " that Members
of Parliament be not eligible to sit on the Executive Committee of
the National Labour Party." Both resolutions were defeated (the
former by a vote of 402,000 to 312,000; no figures were given for
the latter) although the support received by the first of these resolutions appeared to indicate a considerable uneasiness about the
extent to which the political Labour movement was now controlled
by the leaders of the PLP.[1]

Repeated attempts were also made during this period to impose
a political programme on the parliamentary party. In reply to one
such effort at the 1909 conference, Ramsay MacDonald insisted, in
the spirit of the 1907 conference decision, that these matters should
be left to the parliamentary party. He agreed that

> " . . . they would never be able to have a Party in the House
> of Commons without a programme; but it was the Party in the
> House of Commons that ought to lay down in the shape of a pro-
> gramme the sentiments and the principles expressed from year to
> year at the Conferences. What they had got to do at an Annual
> Conference was to indicate their point of view—indicate to the
> Party in the House of Commons the large questions in which
> they were interested; and for the next twelve months that Party ought
> to busy itself in carrying out the decisions of the Conference . . . . "

The resolution which had urged the NEC to draft a programme for
the PLP was put to the conference and declared lost.[2] It seems
fair to conclude from the result of this debate that a majority of the
conference were reasonably satisfied with the formula laid down
at the 1907 conference governing its relationship to the parliamentary party.

The " 1907 formula " can be seen in operation in the conference
reports and in the minutes of the NEC for this period. Thus, for
example, at the 1908 conference at Hull a number of resolutions
had been passed of which the following is fairly typical: " That the
Labour Party *be instructed* to draft a Bill, and submit the same to

---

[1] *1908 Labour Annual Conference Report*, pp. 60-2. In the course of
the same debate it was decided by a vote of 608,000 to 202,000 " that no
Member of the Parliamentary Committee of the Trade Union Congress or
of the Management Committee of the General Federation of Trades Unions
shall be eligible for the Executive Committee of the Labour Party." The
significance of this decision is discussed on p. 519 below.

[2] *1909 Labour Annual Conference Report*, pp. 84-5.

the House of Commons, for the nationalization of railways." The manuscript minutes of the NEC meeting on the morning of 28th January, 1908, record that the following resolution was passed: " That a list of the resolutions passed at the Hull Conference be submitted to the (joint conference with the) Parliamentary Party in the afternoon."[1]

But significantly, the summary of the parliamentary activity of the PLP for the year 1908 contains no reference to the introduction of a Bill for the nationalization of railways; such time as the party had at its disposal was devoted to presenting other measures which presumably were accorded a higher priority by the joint meeting of the NEC and the PLP.

It also became the custom during this period, however, for the NEC to prepare a list of Bills and motions which it wished the PLP to support in Parliament. The NEC reviewed the various resolutions of the Labour Party conferences and compiled from them its list of Bills and subjects for motions. These were then discussed with the PLP at a joint meeting at the opening of each session and normally adopted with only slight modification. Members of Parliament were then expected (if successful in the ballot for Bills) to put forward the party Bills in order of priority decided by the joint committee. If they had an opportunity to move motions it was apparently agreed that they would be left free to select the subject of any motion on the party list which they might prefer.[2]

It also became an established practice for the PLP to report on its work to the annual party conference. In the years immediately after 1906 this report had taken the form of a personal statement by the Chairman of the PLP which was not subject to debate by conference. Keir Hardie had given the first of these Chairman's reports at the 1907 conference. He began his remarks by saying: " *At the request of the Executive Committee* I herewith submit a brief report of the work done by the Party in the House of Commons during the session."[3] This practice had continued until the 1911 annual conference when a considerable dispute broke out over one passage in the report of the Chairman of the PLP (G. N. Barnes), in which he criticized " the irregularity of attendance . . . of some of the Members [of Parliament] " and named, as particular offenders, the trade union M.P.s. This led to a lively controversy about the right of

---

[1] *Labour Party Documents,* Part II, folio 68.

[2] The procedure is reviewed in rather more detail (p. 318) in the official party publication, *The Labour Year Book,* in its first edition (London, 1916); this *Year Book* was issued under the auspices of the Parliamentary Committee of the TUC, the NEC of the Labour Party and the Fabian Research Department.

[3] *1907 Labour Annual Conference Report,* p. 37. [Italics mine.]

the PLP Chairman to criticize some of his colleagues in the course of his report which (according to the ruling of the conference chairman) was not debatable by the conference.[1] There were further protests at the next annual conference when the PLP Chairman (MacDonald) warned in the course of his report that the efficiency of the PLP was in danger because of the openly expressed differences of opinion among its members.[2] In reply to these protests, the conference chairman promised that the Executive would consider the demands which had come from the floor of the conference that delegates should be permitted to debate the report of the Chairman of the PLP. Subsequently a joint committee of the PLP and the NEC recommended to the NEC in October 1912 " that henceforth there should be no Chairman's Report as in previous years, but that a Report on the work of the Parliamentary Party should be submitted for inclusion in the Executive's Report to Conference." This recommendation was endorsed by the NEC.[3] The decision was reported to the 1913 annual conference; the Executive noted in its report that the record of the work of the PLP was attached as an appendix to their own report and that it would be " open for discussion by the delegates." [4] In subsequent years, the Parliamentary Report was taken paragraph by paragraph (in the same way as the NEC Report); questions were asked on certain paragraphs and the report was then adopted. On occasion these interrogations became somewhat gruelling, particularly since there was widespread disappointment in the party with the performance of the PLP during the years immediately before 1914. The PLP Report for 1913–14 (signed by MacDonald as Chairman and Charles Duncan as Secretary) concluded defensively:

> " The Parliamentary Party makes but one claim upon the Party outside. It asks that criticisms of its work should come from knowledge. Its greatest fault is its weakness in number, but for that the constituencies and not itself is responsible."[5]

During the first World War the PLP suffered from sharp internal divisions. After MacDonald's resignation in August 1914, there

---

[1] *1911 Labour Annual Conference Report*, pp. 28-32 and p. 72.

[2] *1912 Labour Annual Conference Report*, pp. 29 and 75.

[3] Manuscript Minutes of the NEC, 16th October, 1912, *Labour Party Documents*, Part II, folio 326.

[4] *1913 Labour Annual Conference Report* (Report of the NEC), pp. 29-30. The Parliamentary Report appears at pp. 35-41 and it is "signed on behalf of the Parliamentary Party " by James Parker, Acting Chairman (in the absence of MacDonald) and Charles Duncan, Secretary. Hitherto the Parliamentary Report had appeared over the signature of the current Chairman of the PLP only.

[5] *1914 Labour Annual Conference Report*, p. 45.

was (as was seen in Chapter VI) a sad lack of continuity in the leadership as Henderson and several others in turn held the office of Chairman of the PLP. After some early uncertainty, a majority of the PLP was soon won over to support of the war effort; but of the seven M.P.s who sat in the Commons under ILP auspices, five (MacDonald, Snowden, Hardie, Jowett and Thomas Richardson) were either against the war or in favour of the earliest possible peace. It was only with considerable difficulty, therefore, that the PLP succeeded in functioning as a coherent political force. As a result the extra-parliamentary organization of the party came to have a decisive influence in determining the rôle the PLP should play.

Strangely enough, the decisions both to *enter* the Asquith Coalition (in May 1915) and to *leave* the Lloyd George Coalition (in November 1918) were taken against the wishes of the majority of the PLP. The circumstances which surrounded these two decisions throw an important light on the relations between the NEC and the PLP in this period. On 19th May, 1915, Henderson, as Secretary of the Party, reported to the NEC that he had received an invitation from Asquith for the Labour Party to co-operate in forming a Coalition Government; he personally had been invited to join the Cabinet. The report of the NEC records that " the circumstances under which the Coalition had been determined upon were very carefully considered and the Executive agreed that the Prime Minister's invitation should be accepted." [1] Later the same day Henderson, in his capacity as Chairman of the PLP, raised the matter at a meeting of the parliamentary party. They rejected the invitation (according to Snowden) by a vote of 9 to 8. [2] The NEC report accounts for this negative decision by attributing it to a doubt on the part of the PLP " as to whether the Party was within its powers in accepting the invitation without the sanction of a Party Conference." [3] But this appears to have been only part of the explanation. Clynes, for example, opposed Labour's entry into the Coalition, even though he had been an ardent supporter of the war.

> " I did not consider (he later wrote) that our assistance would give Britain increased ability in the Cabinet, and I followed the traditional Labour view that we were in danger of being engulfed in the new Tory-Liberal whirlpool that was forming, and that we should then cease to perform the peculiar function in Parliament for which our working-class voters had sent us there. Our inde-

---

[1] *1916 Labour Annual Conference Report* (Report of the NEC), p. 5.

[2] Snowden, *An Autobiography*, Vol. I, p. 388. There is no explanation offered of the smallness of the vote. The membership of the PLP at the time was 35. *Labour Year Book* (1916), pp. 320-1.

[3] *1916 Labour Annual Conference Report* (Report of the NEC), p. 5.

pendence, in the long run, was our life. I said, and the event proved me right, that we should not have access to the inner councils of war, nor be discussed [sic] when grave decisions had to be made."[1]

A joint meeting of the NEC with the PLP was then held and after a full discussion the joint meeting decided to accept the Prime Minister's invitation by a vote of 17 to 11. Again, according to Snowden, a majority of members of the PLP opposed the acceptance of the offer; they did so primarily on the grounds that " such a step as joining in a Coalition Government was so opposed to the constitution of the Labour Party that it was felt a decision ought not to be taken without the sanction of a Party Conference." [2] Henderson acted upon the majority decision of the joint meeting and entered the Coalition Cabinet as President of the Board of Education; two other Labour M.P.s were appointed to minor offices. In September 1915 the party's action in joining the Coalition was endorsed by the Trade Union Congress, but subsequently the TUC found itself in bitter dispute with the Asquith Government on the issue of conscription. The TUC met in special conference on January 6th, 1916, and passed a resolution condemning compulsory military service. In light of this decision, a joint meeting of the NEC and the parliamentary party agreed that the Labour Ministers should withdraw from the Coalition Government and thus leave themselves free to oppose Asquith's Military Service Bill. When notified of this decision, the Prime Minister asked permission to meet with the PLP and the NEC and at a joint meeting on 12th January he gave certain assurances regarding exemptions to be granted under his Bill. After he had left the meeting it was decided that the resignations of the three Labour Ministers should be withdrawn pending a decision on the issue which would take place at the annual conference of the party to be held later in January. The conference endorsed the decision (of the previous May) to enter the Coalition, although it proceeded to vote (1,716,000 to 360,000) against Asquith's Military Service Bill. Henderson was thus left in a somewhat anomalous position; he had been instructed to remain in the Government although his party was opposed to a major item of Cabinet policy.

[1] Clynes, J. R., *Memoirs*, Vol. I, p. 188.
[2] Snowden, *An Autobiography*, Vol. I, pp. 388-9. It was presumably not thought feasible to hold a special party conference to consider the issue. The conference which should have been held in January, 1915, had been postponed after a postal ballot of the member organizations. *1916 Labour Annual Conference Report*, (Report of the NEC), p. 9. Subsequently, however, several special party conferences were convened during 1917 and 1918.

When Lloyd George formed his Coalition in late 1916, the PLP was offered (and accepted) considerably larger representation. Lloyd George conveyed his invitation to the Labour Party to join the new ministry through Arthur Henderson. A joint meeting of the NEC and the PLP met on the morning of 7th December, 1916, to discuss the invitation.[1] The meeting was unable to reach a decision, but it was decided to hear Lloyd George in order that he might outline the policies which his new Government would pursue. Mrs. Webb records her husband's account of this strange occasion: " Lloyd George was at his worst—evasive in his statement of policy and cynical in his offer of places in the Government. The pro-war Labour members drank in his sweet words; the pacifists maintained a stony silence whilst . . . the waverers asked questions to which Lloyd George gave non-committal answers. All he definitely promised was a Ministry of Labour and a Food Controller—whilst he clearly intimated compulsory mobilization of labour." Later in the day the joint meeting re-assembled to discuss the proposal in a debate which (according to the official Labour Party report) was " remarkable for its frank facing of the issues involved and the general straightforward and unimpassioned declarations of a large number of the Members present." [2]

Snowden's account of the joint meeting suggests that there was strong opposition to accepting Lloyd George's invitation. The first resolution before the meeting proposed that the invitation be *not* accepted and a number of speeches followed, every one of which was opposed to accepting the invitation. Henderson was the first speaker to favour entering the Coalition; he stressed the fact that at the last annual conference of the party a resolution had been passed to the effect that the best interests of the nation would be served by the Labour Party representatives remaining in the Coalition, and he asked how circumstances had changed since that time. Parenthetically Snowden notes that they had " changed materially through the methods by which the break-up of the Asquith Coalition Government had been secured. To support Mr. Lloyd George's Government would be condoning the circumstances under which it had been formed." But Henderson had been unmoved by this argument: " If Labour were to take no part in the new Government (he said) it would give to the Allies the impression that the country was divided and was not behind the new Government." After a long discussion in which (Snowden insists) the weight of the argument was on the side of those who were against accepting the

---

[1] The fullest account of these negotiations is to be found in *Beatrice Webb's Diaries 1912–24*, pp. 72 ff.

[2] *1917 Labour Annual Conference Report* (Report of the NEC), pp. 3-4.

invitation the resolution (opposing entry into the Coalition) was put and defeated by 17 votes to 12.[1] Sidney Webb's account (as recorded by his wife) is in substantial agreement. He reported the voting in favour of accepting office as 18–12 and adds: " There was no display of temper—the most fervent objectors voting silently (against joining the Coalition)—not really wishing to prevent it." [2]

In accounting for the decision of the joint meeting to enter the Coalition, Snowden has a characteristic comment: " The announcement by Mr. Lloyd George that six or eight more Labour members were to be given posts in the Government had considerably reduced the opposition to accepting the invitation." Mrs. Webb also felt that an eagerness for the rewards of office had been a factor in their decision. " The prospect of six offices with an aggregate income of some £16,000 a year, to be distributed among 18 persons (presumably the 18 who voted to join the Coalition) is a big temptation. To enjoy an income of £4,000 a year, or even of £1,600, for a year or two means to any Trade Union official personal independence for the rest of his life." But Mrs. Webb felt that other factors were probably more important. Most important of all, she decided, was " the illusion that the mere presence of Labour men in the Government, apart from anything they may do or prevent being done, is in itself a sign of democratic progress. . . . Neither as individuals nor as a class do Labour men realize that they are mere office-mongers when they serve with men of trained intelligence or even with experienced middle-class administrators." She refers to Clynes's " illusion " that the participation of Labour men in the Government would ensure that they would have some say in the terms of peace as evidence of a characteristically naïve confidence in the potential value of Labour representation in the War Coalition.[3] Finally, added Mrs. Webb, " cementing pecuniary interest and class illusion there is a maddening muddle-headedness which makes them quite incapable of asking for terms for their own class before they consent to take office, and wholly blind to the distinction between supporting the Government on conditions and accepting the responsibility in advance for every plan which a majority of reactionaries may

---

[1] Snowden, *An Autobiography*, Vol. I, pp. 466-7.

[2] *Beatrice Webb's Diaries 1912-24*, p. 73. Mrs. Webb adds: " Sidney came back glad that he has done his best to prevent a decision disastrous to the Labour Party but inclined to be philosophical. He has long ceased to care about getting his own way, and he is always interested, as a student, in watching these breakdowns in Labour Democracy." The latter phrase reflects Mrs. Webb's own conviction that the joint meeting had betrayed the interests of the British working class by accepting membership in the Coalition.

[3] Cf. Clynes, J. R., *Memoirs*, Vol. I, pp. 203-4.

adopt." [1]   Whatever the justification for Mrs. Webb's impatient
reflections on the decision of the joint meeting of the NEC and the
PLP to enter the Lloyd George Coalition, her conclusions in one
respect seem hardly justified. She describes the decision as "a
breakdown in Labour Democracy." (See note 2, p. 403.) The
decision may have been taken for discreditable motives; it may
have reflected naïvety and muddle-headedness; but it was clearly
arrived at after a frank and thorough discussion by the elected
representatives of the party both inside and outside the House.
Thereafter Henderson entered the War Cabinet and a number of
his colleagues were named to other Ministries. The annual party
conference in January 1917 endorsed the PLP's action in joining
the Lloyd George Coalition by a vote of 1,849,000 to 307,000.[2]

The decision to withdraw from the Lloyd George Coalition was
taken at an "Emergency Conference on the General Election"
which assembled in London on 14th November, 1918. At an NEC
meeting on 7th November there had been what Sidney Webb
described as a "vehement discussion" of the attitude the party
ought to adopt towards the future of the Coalition. The PLP
"under pressure from the Labour Ministers" (as Webb put it)
wanted to continue in the Coalition until the peace was signed.[3]
Clynes warned that all candidates who did not get the "Lloyd
George letter" would be swept into oblivion and that the Labour
Party would be "finally smashed". According to Webb, "even
Henderson wavered"; but the Executive voted by twelve to four
to place a resolution before the conference declaring: "that a
General Election held for the purpose of choosing a Parliament to
carry on the business of the country after the war, terminates the
conditions under which the Party entered the Coalition . . ."
The resolution therefore proposed "that the Party shall resume its
independence and withdraw its members from the Government at
the close of the present Parliament."[4]   The opposition to this
proposal was led ironically enough (cf. p. 400 above) by Clynes on
behalf of the PLP. His view was "that Labour was now the only
moderating influence in Britain, and that it was our bounden duty

---

[1] *Beatrice Webb's Diaries 1912-24*, pp. 73-4.

[2] *1917 Labour Annual Conference Report*, p. 98.

[3] In comment on the attitude of the PLP Beatrice Webb wrote: "The
Labour Members have no nerve: or perhaps they lack personal disinterested-
ness; they hate being out of Parliament, still more (the prospect) of losing
office. What with placemen on the one hand, the professional rebels on the
other, the Labour Party goes into the electoral battle (the 1918 election) a
distracted, divided and depressed rabble of some three hundred nondescript
candidates." *Beatrice Webb's Diaries 1912–24*, pp. 134–6.

[4] *1919 Labour Annual Conference Report*, Appendix IV, p. 184.

to remain within the Government, no matter at what cost to ourselves politically, so that we might exercise a restraint on the more
vengeful elements when the Peace terms came to be drafted." [1]
But the majority of the conference, whose view was most effectively
presented by Bernard Shaw, decisively rejected Clynes's argument.
The Executive recommendation to quit the Coalition was carried by
a vote of 2,117,000 to 810,000. Clynes and most members of the
PLP loyally abided by the conference decision and withdrew their
support from the Government, but four Labour M.P.s fought the
election as Coalition candidates (G. J. Wardle, G. N. Barnes,
James Parker and G. H. Roberts).[2]

Henderson had resigned from the War Cabinet on 11th August,
1917; shortly after, he also resigned the chairmanship of the PLP
in order to devote the succeeding months to preparing the re-
organization of the Labour Party which took place in early 1918.
The details of that re-organization are discussed in Chapter VIII,
but reference must be made here to its effect on the relationship of
the PLP to the party outside Parliament. It should perhaps first be
noted that the energetic activities of Henderson and Webb in preparing the new constitution of the party and in drafting its new
programme had stirred considerable uneasiness among the leaders
of the parliamentary party. Mrs. Webb's diary contains a description of a conversation between Adamson, the Chairman of the PLP,
and Sidney Webb in January 1919. Webb had asked Adamson
whether the NEC and its advisory committees and staff might
supply the PLP with information " on foreign affairs, finance and
other technical questions not connected with trade unionism."
Adamson replied (dubiously, according to Mrs. Webb who was
present) that the PLP wanted " ' concise notes, statistics, facts.'
. . . But he would be frank with us, he added with some energy.
At (the PLP) meeting yesterday they had discussed their relation
with the Labour Party at Eccleston Square (the NEC and the party
head office)—in the past it had not been satisfactory. *The Labour
Party Executive, he complained, had during the last two years taken
the initiative in deciding policy without consulting the Labour M.P.s*—
the Labour members had found themselves committed to pro-

---

[1] Clynes, J. R., *Memoirs,* Vol. I, pp. 273-4.

[2] It should be noted that each of these M.P.s had held important offices
in the PLP or in the Lloyd George Coalition. Both Wardle and Barnes
had served as Chairmen of the PLP; James Parker had been Vice-Chairman
of the PLP and later Chief Whip; Roberts had succeeded Clynes as Food
Controller. One Labour candidate in the 1918 election, Stephen Walsh,
temporarily supported the post-war Coalition although he withdrew his
support under pressure from his own union; subsequently he served in the
1924 Labour Government.

grammes . . . with which they might not agree." Adamson's solution to the situation was simple enough: " This must be remedied by joint meetings . . . of the M.P.s and the Labour Party Executive—a sort of joint committee. (The PLP) were willing to co-opt experts from the Executive to sit on their standing committees." [1]

Adamson's comment seems to imply that there had been less consultation than in fact the record shows. His observation is perhaps more significant as an indication of the uneasiness of the PLP at the extent to which the affairs of the party had been dominated since the beginning of the war by the party organization outside Parliament. The PLP had been pushed into the Asquith Coalition in 1915 against their will ; they had been dragged out of the Lloyd George Coalition in 1918 with equal reluctance. Further, with MacDonald, Snowden and the ablest parliamentarians in the PLP precluded from leadership because of their attitude to the war, the second-string leaders who were in command of the PLP were little more than bystanders during a period (1917–18) in which Henderson and Webb had given the Labour Party a new constitution and a new declaration of policy.

The new constitution adopted in January and February 1918 [2] appeared in some of its passages to declare the ascendancy of the extra-parliamentary organs of the party over the PLP. It was firmly stated that " the work of the Party shall be under the direction and control of the Party Conference. . . ." [3] while " the National Executive shall, subject to the control and directions of the Party Conference, be the Administrative Authority of the Party . . . . (and) shall be responsible for the conduct of the general work of the Party," [4] although it was intended that there should be close liaison between the NEC and the PLP.[5] It seems clear that in preparing this revision Henderson and others must have been to some extent influenced by the weak and ineffective rôle the PLP had played in wartime. As was shown above, the PLP had succeeded in winning a measure of independence from extra-parliamentary control during the period 1906–14; yet, on one reading of the new constitution, the PLP might seem to have been reduced to a status of subservience.

One incident in the drafting of the new constitution showed the

---

[1] *Beatrice Webb's Diaries 1912–24*, p. 143. [Italics mine.]
[2] The text of the constitution is to be found at Appendix I, pp. 140-2, of *1918 Labour Annual Conference Report*.
[3] Clause 5 (1).
[4] Clause 6 (a) and (b).
[5] Clause 6 (c).

reality of this threat. It had been proposed in the draft constitution presented to the party conference of January 1918 that it should be " the duty of the National Executive, prior to every General Election, to define the principal issues for that Election." It was apparently intended that (within the limits defined by the general policy statements adopted by the conference) the NEC should have exclusive authority to determine the party's election programme; amazingly enough, the *PLP was to play no part whatever* although it would obviously have the ultimate responsibility for implementing the election programme if the party were to win the election. Naturally the PLP spokesmen resented their exclusion and an amendment was adopted which provided that " it shall be the duty of the National Executive *and the Parliamentary Labour Party*, prior to every General Election, to define the principal issues for that Election." [1] There is no indication as to what arrangements would be made to break the deadlock if the NEC and the PLP should find themselves in basic disagreement over the election programme; it seems fair to assume, however, that it was intended that in such circumstances the final arbiter should be the annual conference.[2] If, however, a sudden election were called it might be physically impossible to provide for a special party conference to arbitrate a dispute between the NEC and the PLP.

Despite the rather slighting attitude toward the PLP which seems implicit in certain passages of the 1918 constitution, the position of the parliamentary party was not, in fact, seriously weakened. There were loopholes in the constitution which clearly limited the extent to which the PLP could be subject to direction from the party outside Parliament. Although clause 5 (1) stated that " the work of the Party shall be under the direction and control of the Party Conference . . .", the statement of " Party Objects " included this passage (clause 3 (c)) ". . . to give effect *as far as may be practicable* to the principles from time to time approved by the Party Conference . . ." There is no indication as to which organ of the party should be responsible for determining the " practicability " of conference decisions. But it would seem reasonable to assume that this passage was intended to hark back to the " 1907 formula " which provided that the PLP should be allowed full authority to determine its own parliamentary timetable and that it should not be subject to specific direction in this regard from either the party conference or the NEC.

In certain other respects the 1918 constitution was ultimately to strengthen rather than to weaken the position of the PLP. As is

[1] Section 4 (b).
[2] Cole, G. D. H., *A History of the Labour Party from 1914*, p. 52.

shown in Chapter VIII, the new constitution provided for what amounted to trade union domination of the entire NEC in that all Executive members were to be voted upon by the whole conference; the Socialist Societies and the local Labour Parties would no longer vote separately for their representatives on the Executive as they had done prior to the 1918 revision of the constitution. The new provision did not guarantee the elimination from the Executive of "troublesome" left-wing elements. But it helped to ensure in the years after 1918 that the leaders of the PLP were unlikely to face an Executive which might be goaded or stimulated by a militant block into attempting to play a determining rôle in controlling the affairs of the PLP. In addition, the provision in the new constitution for the setting up of constituency Labour Parties ultimately proved the undoing of the ILP.[1] The constituency Labour Parties became the focal point for militant socialist opinion in the constituencies, and they were in their turn to prove on occasion a thorn in the flesh of the leaders of the PLP; but they never became anything like so tightly integrated nor so militant a minority faction as was the ILP at its moment of maximum influence. It should be further noted that the new Standing Orders of the party incorporated for the first time the decision of the 1908 annual conference that no member of the Parliamentary Committee of the Trade Union Congress should be eligible for nomination for the National Executive. This arrangement offered a further assurance that the trade union controlled NEC would be unlikely to include very many of the powerful personalities of the trade union movement; again this helped to minimize the prospect of friction between the NEC and the PLP.

Finally, there can be little doubt that the formal conversion of the party to socialism which took place in 1918 helped to give the PLP a measure of coherence which it had heretofore lacked. Under the new constitution the party was henceforth committed to work for "the common ownership of the means of production";[2] in addition, at the June 1918 conference, the party endorsed *Labour and the New Social Order* and a set of 27 resolutions based upon it. Thus the PLP emerged from the experience of the war and of the post-war re-organization committed to explicit socialist objectives; and despite some superficial evidence that the PLP might be subject to extra-parliamentary control, it remained essentially free to function as an autonomous parliamentary party.

Nevertheless, in the immediate post-war years, the PLP came under frequent and heavy fire from the party outside Parliament.

[1] See p. 481 below.

[2] At the 1929 Conference this Clause (IV) was amended without debate to provide, in addition, for the common ownership of the means of "distribution and exchange". *1929 Labour Party Annual Conference Report*, p. 206.

This was perhaps inevitable. As was noted in Chapter VI, the PLP Chairman of the day (Adamson) was as weak and ineffective as any man who ever held the post; most of Labour's able parliamentarians were outside Parliament and the PLP of 57 members was composed mainly of loyal but dull trade unionists who were no match for the overwhelming strength of the Coalition forces. Some efforts were made to improve the effectiveness of the work of the PLP. The 1919 conference report records that " a joint committee was appointed to consider questions of organization and working arrangements between the (NEC) and the (PLP) " [1]; this committee continued in operation and was described in 1920 by MacDonald (then outside Parliament) as " by far and away the best (machinery) that is adopted by any Party to keep itself in touch with the vital concerns of the community." [2] In 1919 the staff of the parliamentary party was increased to five persons, and in the following year a sub-committee of the PLP proposed that MacDonald should be invited to attend the House every day to consult with the PLP and to advise them on matters of parliamentary strategy. However, as was noted in Chapter VI, this proposal was rejected by the full meeting of the PLP.

None of these efforts to improve the work of the PLP saved it from scathing criticism at the annual party conference. At the 1919 conference a delegate of the London Labour Party (Herbert Morrison) supported the reference back of the Parliamentary Report on the grounds that it was " an insult to the energy, the intelligence, and the vigour of the whole Labour Movement of the country." When every allowance was made " they had got to admit that the Party had been a failure in the present Parliament." He therefore urged the conference to vote for the reference back " in order that the Parliamentary Party might know that (the conference) demanded vigorous, straightforward, and energetic politics . . ." Another speaker supporting the reference back condemned the lassitude of the PLP which was reflected, he claimed, in the fact that the average number of questions per M.P. put to the Government was only $1\frac{1}{2}$ per week. Adamson defended the record of the PLP in Parliament

[1] *1919 Labour Annual Conference Report* (Parliamentary Report), p. 57.

[2] MacDonald, J. R., *A Policy for the Labour Party*, pp. 32-3. MacDonald also pointed out that at this time the PLP Chairman regularly attended the meetings of the NEC although he was neither a member of the Executive in his own right nor was there then any provision in the party constitution for the PLP Chairman's *ex officio* membership of the NEC. It was also the custom for the Chairman of the NEC to attend the meetings of the PLP. MacDonald, with his strong parliamentary sense, emphasized, however, that " the Parliamentary Party . . . is free to pursue its own policy within the general limits of principle and programme defined by annual conferences . . . "

and the motion to refer back its report was defeated without a recorded vote.[1]

The critics of the PLP returned to the attack at the conference of the following year, and not surprisingly the demand was revived that the parliamentary party should be subject to the direction of the party outside Parliament. Again the reference back of the Parliamentary Report was proposed; the mover deplored the fact that the PLP acted as if " they were a law unto themselves." The Labour Party appeared to have " little or nothing to say to (the PLP) by way of control or supervision. . . . What control (he demanded to know) had the Executive Committee over the Parliamentary Party? Had they any control whatever? Did they exercise any supervision, and, if so, did the Parliamentary Party accept the suggestions made by the Executive? . . . . It appeared to him that the Party in the House resented outside interference. They objected to any advice being tendered to them. . . . He understood that the Party actually agreed to accept the services of Mr. Ramsay Mac-Donald in an advisory capacity, and then at the meeting which took place the following day they for some reason or other announced to the Movement outside they had suddenly rejected the decision of the previous day. It was of the utmost importance to the Labour Movement that the closest possible relationship should exist between the Parliamentary Party and the Executive. *The Parliamentary Party was the property of the Labour Movement.* . . . He therefore submitted that they (the party conference) must determine their policy and their advice to the Parliamentary Party that day in accordance with that view. . . ." [2] There could hardly be a more forthright reiteration of the old conception of the PLP as a creature of the movement outside Parliament. It is of interest to note that the speaker was himself to become a pillar of the PLP ; he appeared at this conference as " Councillor Emanuel Shinwell (ILP)".

In the debate that followed, Herbert Morrison returned to his

---

[1] *1919 Labour Annual Conference Report,* pp. 127-32. Outside the conference, in the extreme left-wing sections of the Labour movement, criticism was even more virulent. Jack Tanner, subsequently to become a leader of the Amalgamated Engineering Union and Chairman of the TUC General Council (1953-4), wrote in *Solidarity* (the " official organ of the Shop Stewards and Workers' Committee Movements ") of 25th March, 1921: " Imagine a Labour majority, a Labour Government composed of the present crowd of reactionaries, swindlers, and traitors. Imagine the patronage that will be in the possession of this evil crew—the number of jobs they will be able to give to their friends—the bribery and corruption that will be brought into the Labour Movement."

[2] This debate appears at pp. 147-53 of the *1920 Labour Annual Conference Report.* [Italics mine.]

attack of the previous year on the failures of the PLP. He denounced
in particular the shortcomings of Clynes (then Acting-Chairman of
the PLP in Adamson's absence) who, he charged, had failed in
Parliament to make the sort of " fighting speech against capitalism
that they expected." Morrison concluded sadly that " Mr. Clynes,
at the Labour Party Conference, was a very different Mr. Clynes
from the Right Honourable Gentleman who sits on the front bench
in Parliament." A number of critical speeches followed in which
specific evidences of alleged inaction on the part of the PLP were
listed. Several M.P.s rose to defend their work in the House. J.
Sexton, M.P., (of the Dock Labourers) appears to have been much
exasperated; he singled out the criticisms which had been made
by a representative of an affiliated organization (the British Socialist
Party) and replied: " There were some of (that party) who wanted
J. H. Thomas's head on a charger, and a bloody revolution, and all
that the British Socialist Party contributed to the (Labour) Party
funds was £50, so they didn't want much." William Brace, M.P.,
said " the fault was not with the personnel of the (PLP), but with
the organization. They had a better staff for doing the work at the
office of the smallest Trade Union in the land than they had in the
House of Commons, and yet they expected great deeds. . . . They
must have a staff and they must have money."

But by far the most important speech in the debate was made by
Clynes. He replied in some detail to the specific criticisms that
had been made of the work of the PLP and concluded with a blunt
affirmation of its ultimate autonomy. Shinwell, he said, " did not
know as much as he thought he knew about the things he criticized.
He would like to see sixty Shinwells in the House of Commons, who,
in the performance of their Parliamentary work, would be subject
to any outside body." The plain fact was that " *the Executive
Committee had no authority over the Parliamentary Party.*" He
readily recognized, however, that " it was highly desirable to have
the closest touch between these two bodies " and he proceeded to
review the arrangements (described on p. 409 above and n. 2) for
maintaining the closest possible liaison between the PLP and the
party organization outside Parliament. " All they could do to work
in the closest harmony had been done . . ." Significantly, Clynes
made no concession whatever to Shinwell's demand that the parliamentary party should acknowledge that it was " the property of
the Labour Movement " and submit itself to the direction of the
NEC.

Thus even in its moment of greatest weakness, when the standing
of the PLP in the Labour movement had reached what may well
have been its nadir and when almost all the most powerful figures

in the movement were outside Parliament, the leaders of the PLP
insisted that they could not allow themselves to be subjected to the
control and direction of any extra-parliamentary body. Two years
later, at the election of 1922, the party was to supersede the Liberals
as the second great party in the state; most of the powerful figures
in the party were to take their places in Parliament. Thereafter the
PLP increasingly demonstrated its autonomy from outside direction
and control.

II

THE PARLIAMENTARY LABOUR PARTY AFTER 1922:
IN OPPOSITION AND IN OFFICE

Since 1922, the Parliamentary Labour Party has held office for
14 years (with a majority for six years, in coalition for five, and
as a minority government for three); in addition it has constituted the principal opposition party for a total of 26 years. A review
of this extremely varied parliamentary experience suggests this
conclusion: while in opposition the PLP has clung to certain
" democratic " practices in its internal organization which distinguish it from the Conservative Party (including, for example, the
provision that the Leader and the Parliamentary Committee
should be subject to annual re-election); but in office the PLP has
conformed to the traditional practices of the other great parliamentary parties to a striking degree; so much so that the PLP in
power is essentially similar in its structure and functioning to the
Conservatives when they are the ruling party.

It would appear that the PLP's " democratic " practices are
jettisoned when Labour assumes office because the party considers
them to be incompatible with the cabinet system as it has evolved
in this country; they are revived only when the party returns to
opposition. The Conservative Party on the other hand carries over
into opposition certain aspects of cabinet practice. The Conservative leaders are not subject to annual election nor are they required
to submit themselves to any formal system of day-to-day control
by their back benches; but broadly speaking their position is not
dissimilar to that of the Labour leaders; they can move only in the
direction in which their supporters are prepared to follow. The
practices of the Conservative Party in opposition are no more
" undemocratic " than are the practices of *either* party in power.

(a) *The Parliamentary Labour Party in Opposition*[1]

While the PLP is in opposition it elects its " Leader and Chair-

[1] For a general discussion of the work of the PLP see Morrison, H.,
Government and Parliament, Chapter VII.

man " annually at the beginning of each new session of Parliament ;[1] elections are also held for a Deputy Chairman,[2] who as early as 1937 is also referred to as the " Deputy Leader ". During the periods of opposition in the years 1922–55, the position of Deputy Chairman was held in turn by Clynes (who had been runner-up to MacDonald in PLP elections for Chairman in 1922), by Attlee (who was second in ministerial seniority to Lansbury among the survivors of the 1931 debacle), by Arthur Greenwood (who ran third to Attlee in the 1935 elections for the leadership) and, after 1951, by Herbert Morrison (who had served as Deputy Prime Minister under Attlee during 1945–51). Each of these Deputy Chairmen was elected without opposition until Herbert Morrison was challenged by Aneurin Bevan in the elections for the Parliamentary Committee for 1952–3. Unlike the Conservative Party, the PLP also elects its Chief Whip (again, he is usually elected by acclamation). It was formerly the practice to elect junior whips also, but they are now appointed by the Chief Whip.

The work of the Parliamentary Labour Party is under the direction of a body now known as the Parliamentary Committee[3]. It consists of the following *ex officio* members: the Chairman of the PLP, the Deputy Chairman, the Chief Whip, the Chairman of the Labour Group in the House of Lords, the Chief Whip of the Labour Peers, plus 12 elected representatives of the Labour M.P.s and one elected representative of the Labour Peers.[4] The method of voting now used in the elections for the Parliamentary Committee is of some importance. All members voting must record votes for as many members as there are seats to be filled, a device intended to prevent minority groups from concentrating their votes in support of particular candidates. Originally the Parliamentary Executive

[1] All Labour members of the House of Commons are entitled to vote; Labour Peers are not. Nor are the members of any of the organs of the party outside Parliament.

[2] The terms " Deputy Chairman " and " Vice-Chairman " seem to be used interchangeably; on occasion within a single Labour Party report reference is made to the election of a " Deputy Chairman " who subsequently signs the Parliamentary Report as " Vice-Chairman."

[3] In 1955 Attlee also introduced a scheme bearing some similarities to the Conservative Shadow Cabinet system; he named 39 M.P.s to cover special subjects, of whom 12 were elected members of the Parliamentary Committee (*Daily Telegraph*, 15th July, 1955 and *Manchester Guardian*, 11th January, 1956). See also p. 604, n. 1 below.

[4] Originally no provision was made for the inclusion of Labour Peers in the Parliamentary Executive Committee, but in February, 1925, it was decided that the Labour Whip in the Lords would attend future meetings of the Executive (*Daily Herald*, 12th February, 1925) and subsequently it was provided (*The Times*, 21st February, 1925) that a second member of the House of Lords was to be selected by the Labour Peers to represent the Upper House on the Executive of the Parliamentary Labour Party.

Committee (as it was then called) met every parliamentary day except Friday " to discuss business coming before the House, and to settle Party policy, subject to the decisions of the weekly Party meetings."[1] But it has since become the custom of the Parliamentary Committee

TABLE 3

MEMBERSHIP ANALYSIS OF PLP EXECUTIVE 1935–53

Name	Number of Years on PLP Executive 1935–45; 1951–53 (max. 13)	Number of Years on NEC 1935–1953 (max. 19)
C. R. Attlee	13	19
H. Morrison	13	17
P. Noel-Baker	12	11
H. Dalton	11	17
E. Shinwell	10	11
Arthur Greenwood . . .	10	11
T. Williams	10	—
F. Pethick-Lawrence* . .	10	—
D. R. Grenfell . . .	10	—
J. Griffiths	8	14
A. V. Alexander* . . .	8	—
C. Edwards†	7	—
W. Whiteley	7	—
H. B. Lees-Smith† . . .	7	—
J. J. Lawson*	6	—
W. Wedgwood Benn* . .	5	—
T. Johnston	5	—

36 others (excluding representatives of Labour Peers) have served on PLP (Executive) Committee for 4 years or less.

Note:
* Subsequently elevated to the peerage.
† Deceased or retired.

to meet regularly once a week and to hold such other *ad hoc* meetings as may be necessary in the light of the parliamentary situation.

In the period 1935–53, chosen for analysis (See Appendix D, and Table 3 above and Table 4, p. 415)[2], the Parliamentary Committee

---

[1] *1925 Labour Annual Conference Report* (Parliamentary Report), p. 90.

[2] A major shift in membership occurred after the wholesale retirement of the party's " Old Guard ". (See Dalton, H., *High Tide and After*, Chapter XLIV). But a very similar continuity of membership can be traced in the composition of the Parliamentary Committee after 1956.

showed striking continuity of membership. During 13 of those years
the PLP annually elected a Parliamentary Committee of a dozen or
more members (while the party was in office, 1945–51, a small Liaison
Committee of five and later six was named of which two were *ex
officio* and the remainder elected by Labour M.P.s and Peers).

TABLE 4

PARLIAMENTARY COMMITTEE (1951–54)

Name	1951–2	1952–3	1953–4
C. R. Attlee . . .	X	X	X
H. Morrison . . .	X	x	X
P. Noel-Baker . . .	x	x	x
H. Dalton	X	x	x
E. Shinwell	x	x	x
J. Griffiths	X	X	X
W. Whiteley . . .	x	x	x
J. Callaghan . . .	x	x	x
Chuter Ede	x	x	x
H. Gaitskell . . .	x	x	x
A. Robens	x	x	x
E. Summerskill . . .	X	X	X
Glenvil Hall . . .	x	x	x
R. R. Stokes . . .	x	—	—
Anthony Greenwood . .	x	—	—
Sir F. Soskice . . .	—	x	x
Aneurin Bevan . . .	—	X	X*

x = *Member of Parliamentary Committee only.*
X = *Member of both Parliamentary Committee and NEC.*
 * *Resigned during term of office.*

Column 2 of Table 3 indicates the number of years (of a possible
maximum of 13) served on the Parliamentary Committee by certain
leading figures in the party. It will be noted that 11 persons served
for 8 or more of the 13 years in which a full Committee has been
elected. Of these 11, one (Arthur Greenwood) did not offer himself for re-election and two others (Tom Williams and D. R.
Grenfell) tried but failed to secure election after the party returned
to opposition in 1951; two others (Pethick-Lawrence and A. V.
Alexander) were elevated to the peerage and were thus no longer
eligible for re-election. But the remaining group of six (Attlee,
Morrison, Dalton, Noel-Baker, Shinwell and Griffiths) served
almost unbroken terms of office on the Parliamentary Committee.

When the party returned to opposition in 1951 they were joined by six others (all former Ministers), James Callaghan, Chuter Ede, Hugh Gaitskell, Alfred Robens, Edith Summerskill and Glenvil Hall, each of whom was subsequently elected for the following two years. R. R. Stokes and Anthony Greenwood, elected in 1951, were replaced in 1952 by Sir Frank Soskice and Aneurin Bevan, who retained their places in 1953. In that year, indeed, all of the previous year's committee of 12 were re-elected.

It will be noted (in column 3 of Table 3) that Attlee, Morrison, Dalton, Noel-Baker, Shinwell and Griffiths also enjoyed long periods of service on the NEC, as did Edith Summerskill and Bevan. As is suggested below, this overlapping membership is of vital importance in accounting for the lack of friction during much of the period between the PLP and NEC. In addition, the strong tendency of the PLP to re-elect its leaders has helped to ensure a high degree of continuity in policy and leadership. Indeed the continuity could hardly have been greater had the party left its Leader free (as is the Conservative Leader) to surround himself with those of his colleagues whom he finds congenial and competent associates.

The meetings of the PLP may be attended by all M.P.s and Peers accepting the Labour Whip [1]; since 1951, the PLP has been meeting on the average about three times a fortnight. A regular Thursday evening meeting is held to consider the business for the following week; in addition, a morning meeting is held at least every other week and sometimes more frequently if the business before the House makes this necessary. The PLP has also set up a number of parliamentary " Subject Groups " [2] similar to the functional committees of the 1922 Committee discussed in Chapter III. While the party is in opposition any member of the PLP may join any number of groups and is then accorded voting rights within the group. M.P.s may visit particular meetings of the party groups to which they do not normally belong and may take part in their discussions, although they are not expected to vote. Special groups are also set up to consider particular pieces of legislation of

---

[1] The decision to permit Peers to attend was taken 3rd December, 1924. (*Daily Herald*, 4th December, 1924. See also *1925 Labour Annual Conference Report* [Parliamentary Report], p. 90). They do not vote on issues which are of exclusive concern to the House of Commons.

[2] During the session 1952–3, for example, there were the following " Subject Groups ": Agriculture, Fisheries and Food, Arts and Amenities, Commonwealth and Colonies; Defence and Services, Education, Financial and Economic, Foreign Affairs, Health and Social Insurance, Legal and Judicial, Local Government, Nationalized Industries, Public Information. Ten of these groups were chaired by members of the PLP who held Ministerial rank at some time during 1945–51. *1953 Report of the NEC* (Parliamentary Report), p. 55.

major importance which may be coming before the House.[1] The PLP has also established a number of " Area Groups " to consider particular matters affecting the geographical areas represented by the members in the Groups. Members of the PLP sponsored by trades unions also meet regularly to consider matters of concern to the trades unions.[2] If a particular issue is coming before the House the PLP usually determines its policy by the following method: the issue will be considered by the relevant parliamentary group and, after debate, the group may produce a draft resolution which it proposes for adoption by the PLP. This resolution is then placed before the Parliamentary Committee which recommends either that the draft resolution or an alternative version of it should be adopted by the full meeting of the PLP. The recommendation of the Parliamentary Committee in turn may be adopted, modified or referred back to the Committee by the party meeting. But the policy which is finally adopted by the party meeting is binding on the Parliamentary Committee which then becomes responsible for ensuring that the policy is effectively expressed in the course of the subsequent parliamentary debate. In the normal course of events the PLP usually adopts the policy recommendations of the Parliamentary Committee although on certain occasions after the party returned to opposition in 1951 the views of the Parliamentary Committee were overridden.

At one time there appears to have been a possibility that the PLP (in opposition) might have adopted an organizational structure almost identical with that of the Conservative Party. After the fall of the 1924 Government and immediately before the elections for the Parliamentary Executive Committee, Mrs. Webb wrote (21st November, 1924): ". . . there being no Standing Orders (of the PLP) no one knows on what plan the Party Executive will be elected. There may be an attempt to exclude ex-Cabinet Ministers on the part of the rank and file with the result that these will fall

---

[1] Ian Mikardo, M.P., writing in *Tribune,* 5th June, 1953, stated: " I am not giving away any secrets by disclosing that, on a major measure like the Steel Bill, the main burden of opposition is carried by a working party of Labour M.P.s set up for the purpose under the authority of the Parliamentary Committee. This body decides on its " line " and drafts amendments designed to further party policy. In all appropriate cases there is consultation between the working party and the Trade Union movement. In the case of the Iron and Steel Bill . . . . the consultation with the representatives of the TUC General Council was close and constant."

[2] The *Daily Herald* for 12th December, 1924, reported that " The Trade Union Group of M.P.s decided, 11th December, to restrict its membership to persons whose candidatures were promoted and financed by Trades Unions." This regulation has applied ever since.

back on the shadow Cabinet—so that there will be two bodies. All of which is the reaction from an autocratic Prime Minister standing above and aloof from his party." [1]

Had this happened, the PLP would have become an exclusively back-bench organization like the 1922 Committee. The Leader of the Labour Party and the former members of his Cabinet would have become a semi-autonomous body very like the Conservative Shadow Cabinet; they would presumably have retained the primary responsibility for conducting the work of the party in opposition, although, like the Conservative Shadow Cabinet, they would have been faced with the necessity of retaining the confidence of the back-benchers' organization. In the event this did not happen. The Parliamentary Executive Committee was reconstituted on exactly the same basis as it had been when it was first set up in February 1923. The method of election adopted in November 1924 (which has subsequently been changed; see p. 414 above) was a strange one. Mrs. Webb records (12th December, 1924): " The Executive was selected by sending out to every member the whole list of M.P.s so that votes must have been considerably scattered if the result is scanned . . ." She gives the results as follows (there had been 151 M.P.s returned at the election of 1924 and eligible to vote): G. Lansbury 67; R. Smillie 65; P. Snowden 62; J. H. Thomas 53; J. Wheatley 52; J. Maxton 51; C. P. Trevelyan 45; W. Graham 43; J. C. Wedgwood 40; A. Henderson 38; H. B. Lees-Smith 38; F. O. Roberts 34. (MacDonald, Clynes and Spoor were elected Chairman, Vice-Chairman and Chief Whip respectively and thus became *ex officio* members of the Executive.) In comment on the PLP election results, Mrs. Webb adds: " The Parliamentary Executive is going to be *the dominating force in the life of the Labour Party* during its term of Opposition and though it is not predominantly left in composition, it is not pro-MacDonald . . ." [2] And some days later she wrote: " The twelve

---

[1] *Beatrice Webb's Diaries,* 21st November, 1924, folios 18-19. Mrs. Webb adds: " It is, however, curiously characteristic of the Labour Party that we none of us know *what is happening in the Labour Party.*" And she continues in a revealing passage, " The leaders so seldom see each other and are so reticent when they do meet. The ILP has a life of its own; the Clyde (group) is self-contained, the TU officials are dispersed in their homes all over the country and live within their own occupational circle—or at least within the trade union official world. Always friendly and polite, they are never intimate, and they seldom consult except on immediate questions that must be settled one way or another. Otherwise any casual change might happen in the leadership or the constitution of the party without the majority intending it . . . "

[2] *Beatrice Webb's Diaries,* 12th December, 1924, folios 22-3.

will form a close body and no one outside the select circle will be in the running or have much influence in deciding policy. And the twelve will end by deposing MacDonald from the Leadership of the party—probably by making his position intolerable." [1] Mrs. Webb appears here to anticipate that the PLP Executive Committee might attempt to halter MacDonald, and in this, of course, she was proved wrong. As was shown in Chapter VI, they acquiesced in his leadership despite the fact that some of them had grave doubts about both his character and his ability. But the earlier part of her comment was to prove amply justified. Certainly during the period 1924-9 the PLP Executive Committee did become " the dominant force in the life of the Labour Party."

It could well be argued that the Parliamentary Committee has continued ever since to be the most potent single organ of the party while Labour is in opposition. " Dominant force " is perhaps too strong a term. The PLP Committee does not enjoy anything like the power or authority of a Labour (or a Conservative) Cabinet or even of a Conservative *Shadow* Cabinet. Unlike the latter, it must evolve its policies by a process of close consultation with the parliamentary groups and especially with the full party meeting.[2] But a variety of factors combine to ensure that the Parliamentary Committee wields a powerful influence in determining the rôle the Labour Party plays in Parliament. It is presided over by the Leader, who is normally a former or a future Prime Minister (or both); it includes a number of the most powerful ex-Ministers and other influential figures in the party; and it should be remembered that the members of the Parliamentary Committee have traditionally played a dominant rôle in the party organization outside Parliament.

As was suggested above, there has been much confusion within the Labour Party about the real relationship between the PLP (including the Parliamentary Committee) and the mass organization. Attlee's traditional version of this relationship was quoted in Chapter I. It will be recalled that he wrote (in 1937): " . . . the Labour Party Conference lays down the policy of the Party and *issues instructions which must be carried out* by the Executive, the

---

[1] *Beatrice Webb's Diaries,* 19th December, 1924, folio 25.
[2] The difference between the Labour Parliamentary Committee and the Conservative Shadow Cabinet in this regard should not, however, be exaggerated. The Conservative Shadow Cabinet must also take strong currents of feeling in its parliamentary party into account. The events of 1922 provided a vivid reminder that the Conservative Leader and his colleagues can be destroyed by their followers even when they are in government. The same *could* happen when the party is in opposition if the Leader and his Shadow Cabinet persistently ignored the wishes of their followers.

affiliated organizations and *its representatives in Parliament* and on local authorities. . . ." [Italics mine.] But as has already been shown, as early as 1907 the leaders of the PLP insisted that they would find it intolerable to be forced to accept instructions from the party conference. And even when the prestige of the PLP had sunk to a low ebb during the 1918–22 Parliament, Clynes argued emphatically that the NEC had no constitutional right to control the affairs of the PLP. In the years since 1922, whatever the ups and downs of its fortunes, the PLP has never been forced to sacrifice its autonomy.

Indeed, it is difficult to find a single instance of major importance since 1922 in which it can be shown conclusively that the PLP was forced by the party conference or by the NEC to move in a direction in which it did not wish to go. On rare occasions the conference has passed resolutions which did not appear to meet with the approval of the leaders of the PLP. But often these resolutions were either ignored or sidetracked by the PLP.[1] There has rarely been any difficulty about this since the PLP has invariably insisted that it must " determine priorities". (If a low enough priority is assigned to a particular conference decision then it can be passed over indefinitely.) But in any case differences of opinion between the party outside and the party inside Parliament have been infrequent. Normally majority opinion in both the NEC and the party conference is in substantial agreement with the views of the majority in the Parliamentary Labour Party. There are many good reasons why this should tend to be so. One factor is the authority and personal ascendancy of the Leader of the Party. As an *ex officio* member of the NEC and the most important figure at the annual party conference he usually plays a highly influential and sometimes dominant rôle in the affairs of the party outside Parliament. Perhaps the best illustration is provided by MacDonald's ascendancy over the party conference, notably in 1925 and in succeeding years. Admittedly the conference has on occasion rejected the views of the Leader of the Party. Henderson's advice, it will be recalled, was rejected on a matter of major importance at the 1932 party conference (discussed in Chapter VI); and the outstanding instance

---

[1] For example, the 1931 conference passed a resolution demanding that " the banking and credit system " should be " brought under public ownership." In the following year, *against the advice of Hugh Dalton speaking for the NEC*, the conference carried an amendment calling specifically for the nationalization of the Joint Stock Banks. But this proposal was not included either in the party's 1935 electoral programme or in *Labour's Immediate Programme* (March, 1937). For the even more important instance of the 1960 Conference resolution on unilateralism, see p. 612 ff. below.

was the rejection of George Lansbury's views on foreign policy at the 1935 conference. But 1931–5 was an unusual period in the modern history of the party, since the PLP was pitifully weak and most of the leading personalities of the party were outside Parliament. The occasional rejections of the views of the Leader during 1931–5 do not therefore modify the proposition that the personal influence of the Leader of the PLP in the councils of the mass organization of the party are an important factor in minimizing the danger of extra-parliamentary control.

But even more important is the fact that the Leader has usually had with him on the NEC enough other members of the PLP to constitute a majority of the committee. Table 5 below shows the percentage of M.P.s on the NEC during the period 1900–53. It will be noted that as early as 1906–10, seven of the fourteen members of the NEC were M.P.s. If one includes the Secretary (MacDonald) among the M.P.s, then members of the PLP constituted a clear majority on the Committee. They lost this majority during the period 1910–22, and it is more than a coincidence that during part of this period (as was shown above) the PLP was subject to more specific direction from the party outside Parliament than at any other time in its history. Members of Parliament again constituted a majority of the Committee (if the Secretary is included) in 1923; and in every year since (except for the period 1931–5) they have retained either a bare majority of the places, as they did in 1924–9, or else a comfortable majority as in the periods 1929–31 and after 1945. And it should be noted that even in the period 1931–5 when the number of M.P.s on the NEC fell to three, there were in addition no less than eleven ex-M.P.s (including ex-Ministers) on the NEC; it is clear that most of them tended to reflect an essentially " parliamentary " point of view. Perhaps the best illustration is provided by Clynes's rôle at the 1933 conference during the debate on " a future Labour Government". Clynes during this period was outside Parliament. Yet again and again when he replied for the NEC to the conference debate, he reflected a parliamentary view.[1] The conference, he argued, must not commit itself to a declaration that the Labour Party would *never* enter another minority Labour Government. The Leader, he agreed, should be required to consult " other leaders of the Party in close touch with the members," but " to select (a Cabinet) by election . . . or by a majority action . . . would in our judgment be a fatal blunder . . . our view is that actual power must be vested in a leader who, by his past work, has been placed in that position . . ." It

[1] *1933 Labour Annual Conference Report*, pp. 166 ff.

TABLE 5

M.P. MEMBERSHIP OF NEC.

Parliament	Average Membership of NEC	Average Number of M.P.s	Average Number of Ministers
1900–06	12+	2+	
1906–10	14−	7	
1910	15	6	
1910–18	16−	6+	
1918–22	23	5+	
1922–23	23	11	
1923–24	23	14	9
1924–29	23	11+	
1929–31	24	16+	10
1931–35	25−	3*	
1935–45	27−	14−	
1945–50	27	16	9+
1950–51	27	18	9
1951–53	27+	17	

NOTES: With the exception of 1931, members of the NEC are counted as members of the PLP in the above chart if at any time during their one-year term of office they served in Parliament. It should be noted, incidentally, that the membership lists of the NEC included in the annual reports of the party are an unreliable guide to the numbers of M.P.s on the NEC; it has been found that for no apparent reason the reports fail to indicate that certain members of the NEC were M.P.s when in fact they were.

The Secretary of the party has not been included as a member of the NEC because he normally does not vote. However, it should be noted that during 1906–34 the Secretaries (MacDonald and Henderson) were both prominent members of the NEC and in addition, of course, MacDonald was an M.P. throughout his period as Secretary as was Henderson, except for short intervals when he was outside the House.

* In addition, during 1931–35 there was an average of 11 ex-M.P.s on the NEC.

was abundantly clear that Clynes was reflecting the view of his former parliamentary colleagues. He took a leading part in the debate in rebuffing attempts from the floor of the conference to devise tighter conference controls over the PLP and its leaders.

The rôle of PLP members on the important sub-committees of the NEC is also of great significance. Table 6 below shows the proportion of Ministers and other Members of Parliament on each of the NEC committees 1945–53. The composition of the Policy and International Sub-Committees is of particular interest. It will be noted that in every year there was invariably a majority of members of the PLP on both of these committees (with a very strong representation of Ministers or ex-Ministers). Indeed so much is this the case that *the sub-committees of the NEC during this period might almost be described as committees of the PLP to which have been added a minority of Trade Union leaders.* There could be no better guarantee that the policy statements in domestic and international affairs issued by the NEC were invariably acceptable to, if not the creation of, the parliamentary leaders of the party. *This is an essential clue to an understanding of why the Labour Party was able to claim that the " Movement " outside Parliament had a major share in the formulation of the policies which the PLP must implement in Parliament.*[1]

Admittedly, the M.P.s on the NEC do not always vote *en bloc* on policy issues, but at least they are likely to insist on the ultimate autonomy of the PLP and to have a comparatively realistic understanding of the limitations imposed by the parliamentary situation.[2] Even during periods when the parliamentarians on the NEC have been sharply split, as during the so-called " Bevanite " controversy after 1951, most of the non-M.P. section of the NEC tended to support the parliamentary leaders of the party rather than the dissident minority of the M.P.s who were supporting Bevan. The non-M.P. section of the NEC is composed for the most part of trade unionists of the second (or third) rank; they tend to be men and women of limited political experience and sometimes of limited ability. Their attitude to the parliamentary leaders tends to be one of mingled awe and respect; their attitude is strikingly similar indeed to that of the non-M.P.s on the Executive Committee of the Conservative National Union toward their party's leading parliamentarians. The non-M.P. sections of both Executives have rarely shown any tendency to develop delusions of grandeur or to attempt to dominate their parliamentary party. With some exceptions (of which perhaps the late Harold Laski is the most notable example), the non-M.P. section of the NEC has been inclined to support parliamentary leaders of the party against disaffected minorities in the PLP.

This raises another factor which has helped to minimize the danger of conflict between the mass organization of the Labour Party and the parliamentary party. This is the bond of confidence

[1] It should also be recalled that the leaders of the PLP, in effect, confer with themselves again when, in the process of drafting the party's election statements, the joint NEC-PLP consultation takes place.

[2] The attitude of Aneurin Bevan on this point is significant. Even though he was long one of the most militant representatives of the constituency parties on the NEC, on more than one occasion he warned the conference that it must not attempt to determine the parliamentary timetable nor to insist that the PLP should do its bidding (see p. 515 below).

TABLE 6

COMPOSITION OF NEC AND ITS SUB-COMMITTEES 1945–1953

(The figures in brackets indicate the number of Ministers who served from 1945 to 1951, and the number of ex-Ministers from 1951 to 1953.)

Committee		1945–6	1946–7	1947–8	1948–9	1949–50	1950–1	1951–2	1952–3	1953–4
NEC	Total membership	27	27	27	27	27	27	27	27	28
	Total M.P.s	16 (10)	16 (10)	16 (10)	16 (8)	17 (8)	18 (9)	17 (8)	17 (7)	17 (8)
	Others	11	11	11	11	10	9	10	10	11
ORGANIZATION SUB-COMMITTEE	Total membership	14	16	16	16	16	16	16	16	20
	Total M.P.s	9 (5)	9 (5)	10 (5)	8 (4)	7 (4)	8 (4)	9 (5)	9 (4)	14 (6)
	Others	5	7	6	8	9	8	7	7	6
INTERNATIONAL SUB-COMMITTEE	Total membership	16	16	17	16	16	16	18	17	20
	Total M.P.s	12 (9)	12 (9)	12 (8)	12 (5)	11 (6)	13 (6)	12 (5)	12 (5)	13 (8)
	Others	4	4	5	4	5	3	6	5	7
COMMONWEALTH SUB-COMMITTEE	Total membership	9	16	15	14	11	12	11	11	13
	Total M.P.s	4 (2)	7 (5)	7 (5)	10 (4)	8 (2)	9 (3)	9 (3)	9 (4)	10 (5)
	Others	5	9	8	4	3	3	2	2	3
POLICY SUB-COMMITTEE	Total membership	18*	19†	19†	18*	20*	20*	18*	19*	22*
	Total M.P.s	11 (8)	12 (8)	12 (8)	10 (8)	13 (8)	13 (9)	12 (8)	13 (7)	15 (8)
	Others	7	7	7	8	7	7	6	6	7
FINANCE AND GENERAL PURPOSES SUB-COMMITTEE	Total membership	13	12	12	12	13	14	14	14	16
	Total M.P.s	7 (5)	6 (4)	7 (7)	5 (3)	7 (3)	7 (3)	6 (3)	6 (3)	6 (4)
	Others	6	6	5	7	6	7	8	8	10

* Total includes 2 TUC representatives.   † Total includes 3 TUC representatives.

which has usually existed in the modern history of the party between most of the leaders of the biggest trade unions affiliated to the party and the leaders of the PLP. This factor is examined in greater detail in Chapter VIII, but it is sufficient here to note that a majority of the great trade unions have, on most important occasions, cast their block votes in the direction favoured by the parliamentary leaders on the NEC. This is not to say that the NEC has never been defeated at the party conference; but it has very rarely been rebuffed on a major matter of policy. To summarize (and to put the matter bluntly), the parliamentary party for the most part receives the advice it wants to hear from the NEC and the party conference, first, because the PLP normally dominates the NEC by a system of overlapping membership, and second, because the PLP leaders are usually in effective control of the conference since the block votes of a majority of the big trade unions are usually cast on the side of the parliamentary leaders of the party. And on those rare occasions when the NEC or the conference (despite these safeguards) tells the PLP what it does not want to hear, it is by no means inevitable that the PLP will accept the advice or " instructions " tendered to it.[1]

The debates on foreign policy at the 1935 and 1936 Labour conferences throw an important light on the relations between the PLP and the party outside parliament. At the 1935 conference (in the vital debate on sanctions) the NEC presented a resolution based on a statement by the National Council of Labour which had already been endorsed in substance by the Trade Union Congress a few weeks earlier. A number of the leading parliamentarians on the NEC (including Attlee, Dalton and Morrison) [2] spoke in favour of the NEC resolution. They were strongly backed by Ernest Bevin and the leaders of a number of the biggest trade unions. As a result, Cripps, Lansbury and the dissident minority of the PLP were overwhelmingly defeated (by a vote of 2,160,000 to 102,000). The rôle of the 1935 conference in this dispute was in some respects strikingly similar to that of the Conservative Central Council in its great debate on India in 1934 (discussed in Chapter III). On that occasion, it will be remembered, Baldwin succeeded in rebuffing a strong attack on his India policy led by Churchill and a dissident minority of Conservative parliamentarians. In each case, the mass organization of the party served in a sense as the

[1] See pp. 612 ff. below, for the events of 1960-61.
[2] Dalton and Morrison had been defeated at the 1931 election but they held ministerial office in the 1929-31 Government and throughout their careers on the NEC they always tended to reflect the majority view of the PLP.

final court of appeal in settling a dispute between warring factions
within its parliamentary party. The Conservatives sustained
their Leader while the Labour Party rejected theirs; but in each
case, the conference supported the majority view of their parliamentary leaders.

The debate on foreign affairs at the 1936 Labour conference
was as inconclusive as the previous year's foreign affairs debate
had been decisive.[1] The reason is simple enough. By 1936 the
logic of the PLP's position (in support of collective action against
aggression) demanded that it should cease its opposition to the
National Government's re-armament programme; but most of
the leaders of the PLP who spoke in the 1936 debate could not bring
themselves to admit as much in so many words. On this occasion
there had been no preliminary agreed statement issued by the
National Council of Labour; the Trade Union Congress had made
no pronouncement on the issue. The NEC resolution presented
to the 1936 conference gave no clear indication as to whether the
PLP intended to support or oppose the Government's arms estimates. The conference speeches by the parliamentary leaders
were for the most part evasive and to some extent they were contradictory. Ernest Bevin charged, in the course of the debate,
that the NEC resolution did no more than " pass the buck " to
the PLP. The resolution proposed by the NEC was endorsed by
the conference, but no one knew whether or not it committed the
PLP to support rearmament. G. D. H. Cole has summarized the
debate in a cruel comment: ". . . (The PLP) had in Parliament
to vote either for increased armaments or against them; and the
Conference wanted to know which it was supposed to be instructing
the Parliamentary Party to do. That, however, was what it was
never told, by any of the official speakers." [2] This comment lays
bare the essential relationship between the PLP and the mass
organization of the party. The Leaders of the PLP (through the NEC)
advise the party conference as to what the conference should
advise the PLP to do. *When the leaders are in substantial agreement*
they can be reasonably sure that they can (with the aid of a majority
of the trade unions) get the conference to advise them to do what
they want to do anyway. (But see note[3] below.)

And in any case, the conference has been reminded often enough
that it can offer no more than *advice* to the PLP; like the Conserva-

---

[1] *1936 Labour Annual Conference Report*, pp. 181 ff.

[2] Cole, G. D. H., *A History of the Labour Party from 1914*, p. 325.

[3] When there is a sharp division between the parliamentary leaders (as for
example on the issue of German rearmament in 1954) then the conference may
play, in effect, the rôle or arbiter. See p. 506, n. 2.

tive conference, it cannot *instruct* its parliamentary party as to what it must do, even when the party is in opposition. At the 1937 Labour conference Sidney Silverman, M.P., moved a resolution which read in part: " (This conference) instructs the Parliamentary Labour Party to vote against the Arms Estimates of the National Government." In replying for the NEC, J. Walker, M.P., said:

> I want to point out why the Executive cannot accept the resolution moved by Mr. Silverman. It contains an instruction to the Parliamentary Party. I think I will get the full and unqualified support of my friend Mr. Aneurin Bevan in this: that the Parliamentary Party reserves to itself the right to determine questions of procedure, so that the Conference in discussing a thing like this and in putting it into a resolution would be doing something contrary to the constitutional procedure not only of Parliament but of the Party itself."[1]

It is strange to recall that it was *in the same year* that Attlee, the Leader of the Party, wrote: ". . . the Labour Party Conference . . . issues instructions which must be carried out by . . . its representatives in Parliament . . ."

(b) The Parliamentary Labour Party in Office

As has been suggested at the beginning of this chapter, the relations of a Labour Government to the PLP and to the party outside Parliament is in important respects similar to the relations of a Conservative Ministry to its supporters. The decision to accept office in the first instance (if it is offered by the Sovereign) rests with the Labour Leader who consults whom he wishes in reaching his decision. As was shown above, MacDonald clearly had the approval of the NEC and the General Council of the TUC in deciding to form a Government in 1924,[2] although he appears to have taken the actual decision in light of his consultations with the inner core of the parliamentary leadership (Snowden, Thomas, Henderson, Clynes and Webb). Then (as the 1924 Parliamentary Report puts it), " prior to the opening of Parliament, when it was seen that the Conservative Government would probably be defeated on the Address " the NEC and the PLP Executive Committee finally decided in favour of the party taking office should the opportunity offer. The PLP as such does not appear to have been consulted.

After the sad experience of Labour's first minority Government, Ernest Bevin moved a resolution at the 1925 conference which

---

[1] *1937 Labour Annual Conference Report*, pp. 209–10.
[2] And in the autumn of 1924 the Labour Party annual conference gave retrospective approval to the decision (of the previous January) to form a government. See *1924 Labour Annual Conference Report*, pp. 113 ff.

stated: " This Conference is of opinion that in view of the experience of the recent Labour Government, it is inadvisable that the Labour Party should again accept office whilst having a minority of Members in the House of Commons." Several parliamentarians spoke against the resolution and MacDonald himself asked the conference to reject the resolution, " because if they tied their Candidates and their Party with a Resolution like that they would be putting them in a very silly position. . . . No leader could fight if he was tied in that way, and no body of Candidates could win if that decision were recorded." Bevin, in reply, denounced " the dictatorial attitude " of MacDonald; but the conference responded by defeating the resolution by a vote of 2,587,000 to 512,000.[1] Beatrice Webb was convinced nevertheless that MacDonald's parliamentary colleagues would ensure that he would be allowed nothing like the same authority to determine the affairs of the party that he enjoyed in the formation of the first Labour Government. She wrote in her diary, 19th December, 1924:

> " What is abundantly clear is that the British constitution is going to be altered in the next few years. The Parliamentary Labour Party—or rather the *Parliamentary Executive is going to take over the formation of the next Labour Ministry. Never again will the leader be allowed to determine who shall be in the Cabinet* and who shall speak for the party in opposition."[2]

This prognostication was falsified by events; as was shown in Chapter VI, the procedure followed in the formation of the second Labour Government appears to have been similar to that of 1924. Five days after the 1929 election, Beatrice Webb wrote in her diary (on 4th June, 1929): ". . . I gather that (MacDonald), Henderson, Snowden, Clynes and Thomas settled to take office and hold on for two years bringing in just as much reform as the present House will accept." [3]

Eleven years later, when the party entered the Churchill Coalition

---

[1] *1925 Labour Annual Conference Report*, pp. 244–52. When the same issue had been raised at the ILP conference in April, 1925, MacDonald had been even more forthright in denouncing the proposal: " . . . I decline absolutely to lay down the general principle that we will never take office again on a minority backing. *I am not going to have ropes round my neck for other people to pull when they like.*" [Italics mine.] See also Bullock, A., *The Life and Times of Ernest Bevin*, Vol. I, p. 258 ff.

[2] *Beatrice Webb's Diaries*, 19th December, 1924, folio 25. [Italics mine.]

[3] *Beatrice Webb's Diaries*, 4th June, 1929. A few days later (20th June, manuscript folio 24) Mrs. Webb wrote: " How comforting must be the sheet anchor of an anti-socialist majority to the political soul of (MacDonald). I wonder whether there are half a dozen of the Labour Cabinet who do not agree with the Prime Minister."

in 1940, Attlee conferred with his parliamentary colleagues (as MacDonald had done) and with the NEC; and, as was shown above, he also laid the issue before the annual party conference which happened then to be in session. But in 1945 there was no evidence that Attlee formally sought the approval of anyone before assuming office as Prime Minister and undertaking to form a Labour Government.

When the Labour Party has taken office a variety of organizational devices have been used to attempt to ensure close liaison between the Government and the PLP.[1] As has already been noted, the Labour Cabinet on each occasion has assumed full executive responsibility and in effect, therefore, it has superseded the Parliamentary (Executive) Committee. As the 1924 conference report put it: " With the Party in Office, a new situation, from the point of view of Parliamentary internal organization, arose. All the officers of the Party, and many of those who served on the Executive in the previous Session, had become Ministers, and it was decided therefore that, instead of an Executive composed mainly of the officers of the Party, there should be an Executive composed of 12 Members not in the Government plus three Ministers, to act as a liaison committee between the Party and the Government." The report explained the intended purpose of this new arrangement: " It is convenient to the Government to be able to consult a representative committee of the Party at short notice, and it is convenient to the Party as a whole to have a committee to make representations to the Government when it is considered necessary."[2] Robert Smillie was elected Chairman of the Consultative Committee,[3] George Lansbury Vice-Chairman and the three Ministers named to meet with the Consultative Committee were Clynes, the Deputy Leader, Arthur Henderson, the Home Secretary, and Ben Spoor, the Chief Whip.[4]

The Conservatives challenged these new PLP consultative arrangements. The official Central Office publication *Gleanings and Memoranda* noted in April 1924: " This executive committee appeared to be a constitutional body; but a fact has come to light

---

[1] For a review of the PLP's problems in 1924, see Lyman, R. W., *The First Labour Government 1924*, Chapter XIII and Webb, S., " The First Labour Government," *Political Quarterly*, January–March, 1961, pp. 6–34.

[2] *1924 Labour Annual Conference Report*, (Parliamentary Report), p. 98.

[3] Smillie, R., *My Life for Labour*, London, 1924, p. 303. Smillie explains, " When the Labour Party came into office I was invited to accept a position, but I did not feel inclined to do so."

[4] *The Times*, 19th February, 1924.

which demonstrates that in Socialist politics things are not always what they seem to be. The March issue of the *Monthly Circular* of the Labour Research Department reveals the fact that: ' It was agreed that this Committee should be informed of important decisions of policy before they were announced to the House.' This means (observed *Gleanings and Memoranda*) that a quite unconstitutional body has been placed between Parliament and Cabinet." [1] But the apprehensions of the Conservative Central Office were to prove groundless; there appears to have been no question of the Cabinet informing the Consultative Committee in advance of its specific intentions. For the dissident elements in the party this was a source of bitter complaint. MacNeill Weir (then an M.P.) wrote in retrospect: ". . . This means of communication (through the Consultative Committee) should have been adequate to meet the zealously democratic ideals of the Party, but in practice it did not work out so well. As it turned out, the Cabinet system was not only unsuited to a Socialist Party but contained elements that could not be tolerated in a Party founded on a democratic basis. In spite of theoretical checks, the Cabinet remained a body apart and quite uncontrolled." [2] The militant spirits on the back benches (and especially the ILP) were soon deeply disturbed by what they considered the remoteness of the Prime Minister and his colleagues.

Beatrice Webb wrote in her diary in March 1924 [3]: " The Parliamentary Labour Party is drifting badly in the House of Commons." She attributed this in part to failures of leadership. " Clynes (she wrote) is proving an incompetent and careless leader (of the House of Commons)—curiously so. . . . The relations between the leading Ministers on the Treasury Bench either do not exist or are far from cordial. The (Prime Minister) is unapproachable by Henderson who is responsible for the Labour Party organization in the country; and apparently by Clynes. . . . ' No. 10 and No. 11 (Downing Street) see no more of each other,' said Henderson to me, ' than if they slept and ate a hundred miles apart.' " The Whips appeared also to be falling down badly in their job. The Chief Whip, Ben Spoor (" never a forceful personality ") was absent through illness for most of the session, and " the dull-headed miners (the senior Fred Hall a notorious old slacker) who are subordinate to him, receive, but do not earn, over £1,000 a year as Household Officers. These Senior Whips—with the exception of Tom Kennedy who is admirable, either do not attend to the business or fumble it badly . . ."

---

[1] *Gleanings and Memoranda*, April, 1924, p. 362.
[2] Weir, L. MacNeill, *The Tragedy of Ramsay MacDonald*, p. 260.
[3] *Beatrice Webb's Diaries*, 15th March, 1924, folios 25-6.

In the circumstances, it was not surprising that the Consultative Committee arrangements were unable to compensate for the failures of leadership and the breakdown in the whipping arrangements. Mrs. Webb was convinced that serious back-bench revolt was inevitable. " How long the ILPers and the Clyde men will stand the strain of this aloofness of one whom they have created Prime Minister, we await to see." In the circumstances it would seem likely that the parliamentary party would sooner or later have burst at the seams had it not been defeated in the House. The first Labour Government may not have been as bad as some of its more savage critics insisted (Winston Churchill denounced it in May 1924 as " one vast monument of sham and humbug. . . . The leaders don't believe the doctrines with which they gull the crowd. They do not let them worry them for a moment in comparison with the opportunities of obtaining or retaining office ").[1] But Neville Chamberlain's observation on the eve of the formation of the Government was to prove prophetic; he favoured Labour taking office, he said, because they " would be too weak to do much harm but not too weak to get discredited." [2]

It is not surprising to find that there was also intense uneasiness in certain sections of the party outside Parliament. The annual conference which assembled on 7th October, 1924, was to be disrupted by the Prime Minister's announcement that the Government, having been defeated in the Commons, would go to the country. The conference adjourned precipitately and a long list of resolutions which had been submitted by constituency parties was abandoned. No less than 18 constituency parties and trades councils had introduced resolutions which are grouped under the heading " Control of the Labour Government and the Parliamentary Labour Party." One of these (which had been endorsed by eight local parties) read in part: ". . . this Conference decides that the Parliamentary Labour Party and Members of the Labour Government shall be directly responsible to the Annual Conference of the Party, and that between Conferences the activities and policy both of the Parliamentary Labour Party and the Labour Government as such, shall also be subject to the fullest control of the Executive Committee of the Labour Party." Other resolutions were even more specific in their demands. Most forthright of all, George Lansbury's own party (Bow and Bromley LP) proposed " that in view of Mr. J. H. Thomas's general behaviour it be asked that

---

[1] Winston Churchill addressing the Liverpool Workingmen's Conservative Association, cited in *Gleanings and Memoranda*, June, 1924, p. 720.
[2] Cited in Feiling, K., *Neville Chamberlain*, p. 111.

he be excluded from the Cabinet."[1]   These naïve exhortations reflected a pathetic failure to understand the nature of the parliamentary system; the parliamentary leaders would certainly have ensured their resounding defeat had they come before the conference.   But they also indicate the extent to which the 1924 Government had roused the apprehension of its supporters both inside and outside the House.

The problems faced by the 1929 Government in its relations with its parliamentary supporters are of vital importance in understanding the development of the modern PLP; they must therefore be examined in some detail.   Despite the shortcomings of the Consultative Committee established in 1924, an identical arrangement was adopted when Labour returned to office in 1929.   Again a Consultative Committee of 12 back-benchers was appointed to meet with three Ministers (Henderson, the Foreign Secretary, Clynes, the Home Secretary, and Spoor, the Chief Whip).   " It was felt " (said the 1929 Parliamentary Report) " that it would be of immense benefit to the Government to be kept informed of Party views on particular questions, and that it would be helpful and encouraging to the Members generally to know that their own elected Committee was consulted on proper occasions by responsible Ministers." [2]   Significantly, however, it was decided that meetings of the PLP should be held less frequently; they were to take place monthly rather than once or twice a week, which had been the arrangement while the party was in opposition.   An official Conservative publication noted with satisfaction: " Apparently Mr. MacDonald had little or no difficulty in persuading the Government's supporters that matters of policy must now be left to the judgment of the Cabinet." [3]   But there were storm signals to indicate that trouble lay ahead.   Maxton, Wheatley and Kirkwood of the ILP declined to offer themselves for election to the Consultative Committee because they preferred to maintain a position of complete independence.[4]

[1] *Resolutions for the 24th Annual Conference of the Labour Party,* October, 1924, pp. 12-13.

[2] *1929 Labour Annual Conference Report* (Parliamentary Report), p. 83.

[3] *Gleanings and Memoranda,* August, 1929, p. 173.

[4] Hugh Dalton has noted that membership of the PLP Executive inevitably has a somewhat hamstringing effect and in his autobiography he suggests, somewhat wistfully, that he himself may have become a member of the Parliamentary Executive Committee at rather too early a stage in his parliamentary career. Dalton, H., *Call Back Yesterday,* p. 160. During the lifetime of the second Labour Government several members of the Consultative Committee resigned in order to regain their freedom of action. J. Scurr, for example who had been elected Vice-Chairman, resigned after voting against the Government on its Education Bill. *Daily Herald,* 5th February, 1931.

In the early period of the life of the second Labour Government greater efforts appear to have been made by Ministers to maintain cordial relations with their back-benchers. In November 1929 Mrs. Webb wrote:

" Significant of the internal life of the Parliamentary Labour Party is the continuous contact of the Cabinet Ministers with the rank and file of the PLP and even with members of the party in the country. This takes place, not only in the frequent meetings of the whole of the PLP but in the smaller meetings of the Departmental Ministers with the little groups of enthusiasts and experts—mostly enthusiasts—interested in particular aspects of the Governmental policy. Sometimes these are convened by the Minister himself—(Sidney has asked his critics to tea here on one or two occasions) ; more often on the initiative of the Consultative Committee on special questions revolving round the Eccleston Square office of the [National Labour Party]."

Mrs. Webb then gives a useful illustration of the system of back-bench consultation in operation at the time.

" Last night . . . Sidney was summoned by the P.M. to come to his room at the House of Commons (at nine o'clock) . . . A (deputation), consisting of C. R. Buxton, Wedgwood and Scurr wanted to press their policy regarding Kenya on the P.M. . . . . The P.M. listened to their plea and asked Sidney to answer—while continuing to read his correspondence. Sidney and the deputation retired to (another) room to continue the conversation which lasted for over two hours."[1]

Mrs. Webb appears to imply that there was something distinctive about this process of Ministerial – back-bench consultation although in fact other parties when in government have adopted similar, if not identical, practices. Perhaps she attached particular significance to the incidents she describes because they stood out in contrast to what appears to have been the almost complete lack of contact between Ministers and back-benchers during the life of the first Labour Government.

But the 1929 Government was soon in the midst of fantastic difficulties with its own supporters. No doubt a socialist government in office but without effective power could not fail to disillusion its parliamentary followers whatever system of consultation had been adopted. But in 1929–31 the difficulties were particularly acute because of the peculiar position of the ILP. At its annual conference of 1930 it was decided on the advice of Maxton and

[1] *Beatrice Webb's Diaries,* 9th November, 1929, folio 112.

several of his colleagues to organize a tight-knit parliamentary group which would be responsible for implementing the decisions of the ILP even if this meant voting against the Labour Government (see p. 437 below). Fenner Brockway, then a prominent member of the group, has recounted that the ILP conference resolution embodying this decision " was circulated to the 140 M.P.s (who were nominally members of the ILP)—and only 17 accepted it! We reorganized ourselves as a compact body with regular meetings, a small executive committee and two secretaries who acted when necessary as ' unofficial whips.' " [1]

The mood of the ILP leaders of these years can be recaptured from the records of their speeches. As early as 1924 James Maxton had said: " It is not a bit of use my talking revolution in Parliament, being called the ' Wild Man,' leading wild and determined workers, unless there is evidence that these workers are wild and determined. If I could only hear that one revolutionary in Glasgow had broken one window at the Labour Exchange I would feel wildly elated." [2]   And in the earliest days of the second Labour Government Maxton was denouncing the shortcomings of the MacDonald Government: " The ILP was not prepared to wait for centuries for Socialism, nor to wade through blood to a better social order, but if they examined the Labour policy, they would be depressed about the realization of their hopes. Has any human being benefited (he asked) by the fact that there has been a Labour Government in office during the past two months? I can think of nobody except two murderers who were reprieved." [3]   Some weeks earlier, one of Maxton's Clydeside comrades, David Kirkwood, had warned: ". . . They (the ILP) were going to fight, no matter who was in power, if they did not deliver the goods. . . . A Labour Government was no use to them unless it was going to act in an opposite direction to any Government that ever was in control before." [4]

---

[1] Brockway, F., *Inside the Left*, p. 208. Brockway adds, " when in later years Maxton was sometimes criticized for unwillingness to impose discipline, he would retort that he had been responsible for the severest ' purge ' any party had ever undergone—the exclusion of 123 members from its Parliamentary Group."

[2] Cited in *Gleanings and Memoranda*, August, 1924, p. 253.

[3] *The Times*, 5th August, 1929.

[4] *The Times*, 24th June, 1929. The temper of the Clydesiders could hardly have been improved by the current taunts from the other side of the House. Said Winston Churchill in the Commons on 3rd July: " There is also that little band of representatives from the Clyde, including the hon. Member for Dumbarton Burghs (Kirkwood) and the hon. Member for the Bridgeton Division of Glasgow (Maxton) who have played such an important part (in the building up of the Labour Party) that their lot appears to require our sympathy . . . . They dreamed that they were clearing a path-

The extremist element of the ILP were soon to be repudiated by their more moderate colleagues. On 19th November, 1929, 66 M.P.s signed the following memorial, the terms of which were communicated to the Prime Minister and to the *New Leader*, the organ of the ILP: " We, the undersigned members of the ILP in the House of Commons, desire to make clear that recent pronouncements hostile to, or critical of, the Government, and purporting to be made in the name of the ILP Members of Parliament do not represent our views. We refuse to embarrass (the) Ministers in their work." [1] By December the question of expelling the Clydesiders was being freely canvassed. On 1st December at Glasgow, Maxton said publicly that there had been a proposal to expel five of them from the Labour Party. It had been officially denied by the Parliamentary Executive of the PLP, but, Maxton said, " there was no doubt that at the meeting, at which only Mr. Kirkwood of the five M.P.s was present, a motion was moved by a responsible member of the party, who was also a member of the National Executive of the Labour Party and the Parliamentary Secretary of one of the Ministers, to take disciplinary action against those five M.P.s." Maxton demanded that the responsible leaders of the party should " put a stop to any further attack of that description (and) see that a public apology was offered to the group." [2] Three weeks later Maxton, at a meeting at Bridgeton, was boasting that since he had last spoken three weeks earlier he had voted six times against decisions of a Labour Cabinet. " He was chairman of the ILP, and . . . . he was a member of the Labour Party which boldly stated in its constitution that social ownership and distribution were alone the solution. Therefore, as chairman of a Socialist organization and member of a Socialist party, he refused to accept blindly every decision arrived at by the Cabinet." [3]

Again there were counter-attacks from more moderate elements within the ILP. P. J. Dollan (Chairman of the Scottish ILP) wrote in *Forward*:

> " I am not prepared to allow even the chairman of the ILP to do as he thinks fit . . . . Mr. Maxton must be as amenable to party discipline and decision as Mr. Ramsay MacDonald . . . . The ILP

way along which the toiling millions were to advance towards Utopia, but they wake to find that all they have been doing was to set up a ladder by which the hon. Baronet the Member for Smethwick (Sir Oswald Mosley) could climb into place and power." *House of Commons Debates,* 3rd July, 1929.

[1] *Daily Herald,* 20th November, 1929.
[2] *The Times,* 2nd December, 1929.
[3] *The Times,* 23rd December, 1929.

at no time authorized anybody to defy the Labour Party or vote against the Labour Government . . . . The ILP is affiliated to the Labour Party, works for socialism through the Labour Party, and is loyal to the Labour Party. If Mr. Maxton and his friends disagree with that policy, then they should advocate disaffiliation of the ILP . . . "[1]

And from the leaders of the parliamentary party there was equally stern disapproval. In February, Clynes (the Home Secretary and Leader of the House) said:

" A few members of our own party are indulging in pharisaical protests to show that they are not as other men . . . . (but) in the sphere of constructive statesmanship and helpfulness they have shown themselves to be completely barren and unserviceable. If they have any ideas the party meeting is open to receive them at any time they wish and a consultative committee elected by the Parliamentary members is ever ready to hear from them what alternative they have in mind, apart from vague and unsubstantial complaints expressed upon public platforms."[2]

This brought derisive reply from the ILP militants. At a meeting of the London and Southern Counties Division of the ILP on 16th February, J. Beckett, M.P., (who said that he had acted as unofficial whip of " the rebel group ") declared that " party meetings are a farce," and cited as an illustration the proceedings at a recent meeting of the PLP called to consider the Unemployment Insurance Bill. " The meeting was unanimous (he said) with the exception of the Member for West Leyton (the Rev. Reginald Sorensen), in rejecting the Government proposals. The result was that Mr. Snowden and Miss Bondfield came to address them. He (Mr. Beckett), the eleventh speaker opposing the Government proposals, moved that the proposals should be sent back as unsatisfactory and redrafted by the Government. The chairman, Mr. John Scurr, asked him to withdraw the motion, because of the damage it would cause the Government if the news leaked out. Two days later the bill was printed." [3]

It is not surprising to find that a subsequent meeting of the PLP (on 19th March, 1930) was devoted to a consideration of party discipline. According to the *Daily Herald*, at this meeting, " the Foreign Secretary, Mr. Arthur Henderson, said the Government

[1] *Forward,* 14th December, 1929.
[2] Cited in *Gleanings and Memoranda,* March, 1930, p. 320.
[3] *The Times,* 17th February, 1930. Beckett added: " In view of the secret conferences which take place with the Liberals practically every week, whenever I want to know what the Government are going to do I go to the Liberals."

was doing its best in the face of obstacles, but its work was obstructed by criticism from minority groups and from M.P.s who wrote to the newspapers." Criticism, he urged, should be confined to the meetings of the PLP. He flatly denied that the Government was getting away from its 1929 programme, *Labour and the Nation*. The PLP meeting then decided that each M.P. should be supplied with a copy of the regulations with respect to party discipline drawn up in 1929 and that the matter should be discussed at a future meeting.[1] Totally unrepentant, the ILP militants re-asserted their own position at the ILP conference on 19th–22nd April, 1930. Maxton read a statement on behalf of the National Administrative Council of the ILP which reaffirmed that

> " the ILP has always been an independent Socialist organization, making its distinctive contribution to Labour Party policy, and having its distinctive function within the party. Whilst the ILP has worked with loyalty to Labour Party principles, its liberty of action, when fundamental Socialist issues are involved, has not been questioned . . . . The suggestion is now made that all Labour Members of Parliament and all Labour candidates should undertake never to vote against the Government. It is unreasonable to ask members of the party to accept without question all the proposals of the Government when those proposals are not themselves subject to the decisions of the Parliamentary Party and in many instances do not comply with the programme authorized by the Labour Party Conference."

The statement proceeded to justify the actions of the ILP members in opposing the Government on certain specific issues and concluded:

> " The National Council of the ILP hopes that the Labour Party Executive will not seek to enforce rigid discipline preventing liberty of action on matters of deep conviction. The ILP considers it desirable to make clear that it cannot accept new limitations of its rights and of the obligations of Members of Parliament to their constituents and to Socialism." [2]

The conference then proceeded to instruct the National Administrative Council " to reconstruct the ILP Parliamentary Group on the basis of acceptance of the policy of the ILP as laid down by the decisions of (the) annual (ILP) conference, and as interpreted by the NAC, and to limit endorsement of future candidates to nominees who accept this basis." W. J. Brown, M.P., in seconding the resolution, triumphantly observed that it " would give them a much smaller Parliamentary (ILP) Group five times as effective as they had at present." And Maxton added: " What I hope will happen in future will be that we will get a group who are anxious to press

[1] *Daily Herald*, 20th March, 1930.
[2] *The Times*, 21st April, 1930.

Socialism in our time. Normally the majority view (presumably of the PLP) will be the accepted view. But the majority view may be hostile to what this conference may have decided. In that case the NAC will be bound to see to it that the declared intention of the (ILP) conference must be the policy of the group."

The PLP returned to its discussion of party discipline in early June and decided to adopt a series of rules recommended by its Consultative Committee. They provided that any Labour M.P. who had any scruples on any matter of party policy should be free to abstain from voting but must not vote against the party. In the case of private members' bills or motions which did not raise any question of policy or on which the Government or the Consultative Committee or a party meeting had not come to a decision, members were to be allowed an entirely free hand. According to *The Times* account of the meeting, "members (were) urged to take the fullest advantage of the opportunity at party meetings of raising questions of party policy concerning which they may have doubts." Divisions henceforth must not be called except where the Whips have been informed and the leaders in charge have given their approval. Members were further urged to take care to refrain from attacking other members of the party.[1] In comment the following day, the *New Leader* remarked ominously: "Enforcement of such a rule would be to invite disruption." [2]

But disruption was now well under way. It came first of all not from the ILP but from dissident elements in the Government itself. Sir Oswald Mosley (who as Chancellor of the Duchy of Lancaster had been J. H. Thomas's second-in-command in dealing with unemployment) had resigned in May and at a subsequent meeting of the PLP on 22nd May he had moved (as a back-bench M.P.): "That this Party is dissatisfied with the present unemployment policy of the Government and calls for the formulation of an alternative policy more in accordance with the programme and pledges of the Party at the last election." During the discussion which ensued Mosley was asked to withdraw his motion. He refused to do so; the motion was put to the vote and rejected by 210 to 29 votes.[3]

---

[1] *The Times*, 5th June, 1930.
[2] *New Leader*, 6th June, 1930.
[3] *Daily Herald*, 23rd May, 1930. A week later Mrs. Webb wrote in her Diary (31st May, 1933, folio 61): " . . . Sidney (Webb) reported an interview with MacDonald who is struggling out of the depths of difficulties with the Party . . . . (Sidney) reports MacDonald as disgusted with the party and professing indifference to continued office and very angry with Mosley." And there was trouble over others in addition to Mosley. " Sixty members, (Mrs. Webb added, quoting her husband) had signed a demand for the

Meanwhile, the ILP revolt soon reached its culminating absurdity. In the House of Commons on 17th July, Fenner Brockway defied a ruling of the Speaker by way of protest against a decision of the Prime Minister not to have a debate on Indian affairs before the summer recess. Consequently Brockway was " named " by the Speaker and the Prime Minister moved that he be suspended from the service of the House. The suspension was carried by 260 to 26. When the tellers appeared at the table of the House, J. Beckett cried, " Mr. Speaker, it is a damned disgrace." He seized the mace and proceeded with it to the Bar of the House where he was stopped by the Serjeant at Arms, who took the mace and replaced it upon the table.[1] The Consultative Committee on 22nd July passed a resolution expressing its " strong disapproval " of Beckett's action which " had brought discredit upon the PLP." And the PLP the following day endorsed this resolution by 90 votes to 28 and approved the Consultative Committee's decision to report Beckett to the National Executive Committee for his action.[2] Beckett managed to escape excommunication, only to desert the PLP with Mosley in February 1931.[3]

In comment on Beckett's action, one of his ILP colleagues, S. Sandham, M.P., told a divisional meeting of the ILP at Manchester that it was absurd for the PLP to condemn Beckett when so many of its own members had transgressed in much graver fashion: " The sheer stupidity of this ghost house (Parliament) has got most of the members in its deadly grip. Labour Members can receive bribes to help to pass doubtful Bills in the interests of private individuals, Labour Members can get stupidly drunk in this place; but none of these things are against the sacred traditions of the House—in fact, they are in keeping with them. It is known that Labour Members accepted money from money-lenders and other interests, and it is known that Labour M.P.s get drunk in the House. Our Leaders see nothing wrong in that, or at any rate such conduct is not bad enough to create a demand for their expulsion." [4] Not

---

dismissal of Thomas and the P.M. was considering how to find a way out for his old friend and colleague." Subsequently it was decided to split the Dominions and Colonies; Thomas became Secretary of State for the Dominions, while Webb continued as Colonial Secretary.

[1] *House of Commons Debates,* 17th July, 1930. See also *Daily Herald,* 18th July and Brockway, F., *Inside the Left,* pp. 205-6.

[2] *Daily Herald,* 24th July, 1930. Characteristically Beckett's own local party (the Peckham Labour Party) passed an unanimous vote of confidence in their Member. *The Times,* 24th July, 1930.

[3] Subsequently he became for a time a prominent member of the British Union of Fascists.

[4] *Manchester Guardian,* 28th July, 1930.

surprisingly, the Prime Minister moved that Sandham's charges be referred to the Committee of Privileges. As a consequence of its report Sandham was admonished by the Speaker but he appears, however, to have remained unrepentant.

On July 25th, 1930, there began the protracted and ultimately unsuccessful negotiations between the leaders of the Labour Party and the ILP in an attempt to reconcile the differences between them. But almost immediately after these preliminary discussions began, the NAC of the ILP took action which was to make its final break with the Labour Party inevitable. A document was sent to the 36 M.P.s whose candidatures were assisted financially by the ILP at the previous general election asking that they should give an undertaking that they would accept the programme of the ILP (as determined by its annual conference) and give effect to that programme in the House of Commons. This was a move of decisive importance; it was clearly intended to ensure that henceforth the first loyalty of the ILP group must be to its own party conference rather than to the Labour Government or the PLP. It raised, in sharpest form, the issue of extra-parliamentary control and it proposed a relationship between M.P.s and their extra-parliamentary organization which could not be reconciled with the practice of the Labour Party or indeed with the parliamentary system as it has operated in this country.

Dissatisfaction within the PLP during the winter of 1930–31 spread far beyond the boundaries of the tight-knit ILP group. Fenner Brockway, writing early in 1931, claimed that in three important instances the Government disregarded decisions reached in party meetings and acted contrarily. He also listed 122 Labour Members of Parliament who, he claimed, had voted against the Government on various occasions.[1] In the Commons on 31st October, 1930, F. W. Jowett, who had been First Commissioner of Works in the 1924 Government, moved an amendment to the King's Speech regretting that it " contains no proposals making for Socialist reorganization of industry, agriculture, banking and the import and export trades, and for the fairer distribution of the national income." [2] The amendment was rejected by 156 to 11 but it gave a fair indication that a considerable section of the party was now in open revolt. On 12th November, *The Times* reported that the Consultative Committee of the PLP had sent a letter to all Labour M.P.s " urging them to avoid hostile action in public." The letter pointed out that domestic troubles were bound to arise in

[1] Cited in McHenry, D. E., *The Labour Party in Transition, 1931–8*, pp. 241-2.

[2] *House of Commons Debates*, 31st October, 1930.

such a democratic party, but it added that the committee was trying to avoid hostile speeches being made in public or unfriendly motions or amendments being brought forward against the Government. Members were asked when they had a grievance " to bring it before the Consultative Committee instead of before the House of Commons." But six days later the Consultative Committee found it necessary to call before it seven M.P.s who had committed a variety of offences. Two (W. J. Brown and J. Kinley), it was decided, should be reported to the NEC " for appropriate action to be taken " and the remaining five were to have their attention called " to the need for adhering to the procedure which the Parliamentary Party has laid down." [1] On 20th November Arthur Henderson announced that the NEC was unable to endorse the candidature of Baillie T. Urwin in a forthcoming by-election; the ILP announced on the same day that " in view of the refusal as many M.P.s as possible should proceed at once " to assist Urwin in the by-election. [2]

In desperation, the leaders of the PLP sought new methods of re-establishing party coherence. On 2nd December, Snell, Chairman of the Consultative Committee, reported to a PLP meeting that his committee had had a joint session with the NEC " to consider the general question of party discipline " and it had been decided to set up a joint committee to devise a new procedure in dealing with cases of indiscipline. [3] But meanwhile the ILP was pushing its attempt to control its M.P.s even further. At a meeting on 12th December the NAC of the ILP had agreed that " ILP members having Government posts and desiring admission to the reconstituted ILP Parliamentary Group, should be asked for an assurance that, if an occasion arose on which the NAC considered that circumstances had developed of such a nature as to make it necessary that they should be requested to resign office, they should be prepared to do so; and, further, that such members should give assurances that they were advocating the policies of the ILP within the Labour Party." The NAC was also determined to take a hand in future Cabinet-building. They decided " that on the appointment of Labour Governments in future it should be the duty of members of the ILP Parliamentary Group to consult the NAC before taking office." [4]

Early in 1931 Maxton was forced to report that the new ILP campaign had achieved only very limited success. One hundred and fifty-six Labour M.P.s were nominally members of the ILP and 36

[1] *The Times*, 19th November, 1930.
[2] *Daily Herald*, 21st November, 1930.
[3] *The Times*, 3rd December, 1930.
[4] *New Leader*, 19th December, 1930.

had received official support at the previous election. But to date only 17 had signed the document circulated by the National Council. Under heavy fire from the orthodox leaders of the party, the *New Leader* did its best to defend its own rigorous disciplinary rules. " The ILP recognizes (said the *New Leader* on 16th January) the general authority of the annual conference of the Labour Party. It accepts the Constitution of the Labour Party. But it cannot accept the imposition of a hard and fast rule that its members must never vote against the Government. . . . This rule is made more inequitable by the fact that the PLP does not control the policy of the Government. On more than one occasion the party meeting has reached decisions which the Government has ignored." [1] Maxton himself had a terser and more colourful defence. People, he said, had questioned his dual allegiance (to the ILP and the PLP); he had been told that a man could not ride two horses. " All I can say is that if you cannot ride two horses you have no right to be in the bloody circus."

Maxton's " bloody circus " soon became a disordered spectacle far beyond the control of any ringmaster. On 28th February, Sir Oswald Mosley announced the formation of his " New Party," and a few days later he issued an appeal for voluntary workers in every constituency and for financial support. [2] At a meeting of the PLP on 10th March it was reported that W. J. Brown, Oliver Baldwin, and Lady Cynthia Mosley had resigned from the party along with Mosley himself. The NEC on the same day resolved that " adhesion to the proposed new party is incompatible with membership of the Labour Party and instructs the secretary to communicate accordingly to the affiliated organizations and to the members of the Parliamentary Party." [3]

The ranks of the Government itself were broken by resignation when Sir Charles Trevelyan resigned his office of President of the Board of Education. He appeared at a meeting of the parliamentary party on 3rd March to justify his action and (according to the Parliamentary Correspondent of the *Manchester Guardian*) he warned the party that they " would never get what they actually wanted done until they changed their Leaders." One might have expected that by now some such attack on MacDonald and his colleagues might have won a sympathetic response from a considerable section of the PLP. But according to the *Guardian* account, Trevelyan's speech was received in " stony silence . . . a silence maintained throughout." And when MacDonald rose to reply he was received

---

[1] *New Leader,* 16th January, 1931.
[2] *The Times,* 2nd March, 1931.
[3] *The Times,* 11th March, 1931.

with " cheers which lasted a full two minutes." MacDonald said that " There had been some resignations and it was likely there would be more. The sooner these came the better, for it would be well to know who was for and who was against. He wanted to have a loyal team." [1] MacDonald resorted also to public appeals for party loyalty. On 13th March he said, " We have now reached the time when there must be some team spirit, when no member of the party, however able or however rich, is in a position where he can discard the decisions of his colleagues in the House of Commons. . . . I appeal to the Labour constituencies in this country to see that their members play fair (and) . . . to see to it that when the party as a whole comes to a decision at one of its meetings in the House of Commons, when the party policy is declared by those elected to declare it, that the members in commonsense and ordinary loyalty stand by that decision . . ." [2]

The joint committee on party discipline appointed in December had reported to the PLP on 23rd April. It recommended the appointment of a Standing Joint Committee of the PLP and the NEC to examine all alleged serious breaches of discipline. The Joint Committee would, " if in their opinion the circumstances warrant such a course, recommend to the Parliamentary Party that the Whip be withdrawn, and on receipt of such recommendation the Parliamentary Party shall have the power to decide. Provided that before such decision is taken the National Executive shall be informed of all the circumstances." The report was adopted with seven members of the PLP voting against it. [3] But by early summer the second Labour Government was in its death agonies. The discipline problem became worse rather than better and even the annual Parliamentary Report of the party (published after the downfall of the Government) found the story too complicated and too tragic to relate. It was decided, the 1931 Report remarks sadly, " to start with a clean sheet in the hope that the appointment of this Joint Committee (on party discipline) would have a salutary effect." The situation continued, however, to deteriorate, and reached a climax with an Amendment, which was moved by Labour M.P.s, to the Unemployment Insurance Bill, " which was a direct challenge to the Government." These facts and other individual

[1] *Manchester Guardian*, 4th March, 1931. See also Weir, L. MacNeill, *The Tragedy of Ramsay MacDonald*, p. 267.

[2] *The Times*, 14th March, 1931.

[3] *The Times*, 24th April, 1931. In a derisory comment the *New Leader* reminded the newly established Joint Committee that " of the 283 Labour M.P.s, 126 have on one occasion or more voted against the Government." *New Leader*, 1st May, 1931.

cases (the Report adds) were reported to the Joint Committee which came to the conclusion that " in view of the early rising of Parliament and the fact that the Annual Conference would be held before resumption in the Autumn, rather than take action at once, it would be better in the interests of the whole Movement to refer the matter to the conference with a request that some definite decision to guide the Party should be taken." [1]

The final phrase in this Report was clearly a counsel of despair. The party outside Parliament had already shown that it could not provide the effective leadership which MacDonald and his Cabinet colleagues had failed to provide, nor could it establish unity and coherence in a PLP which was broken and demoralized. Two party conferences (in 1929 and 1930) had taken place during the lifetime of the second Labour Government and at both Ministers had played a dominant rôle. There were several spirited debates which reflected widespread anxiety about the Government's record, especially in regard to the unemployment problem. But throughout both conferences the NEC acted primarily as a watchdog for the Government; in no instance involving an important matter of policy did the conference reject the advice of the NEC. Throughout 1929–31, as has already been shown, the NEC itself was heavily weighted with members of the PLP and Ministers (the latter including of course the Prime Minister, Foreign Secretary and Home Secretary); and there is no evidence that the non-M.P. section of the NEC made any attempt to control the affairs of the Government or of the PLP. Indeed, during the final crisis when MacDonald, Snowden, and Thomas were preparing to " go over to the enemy," the NEC appeared to have become little more than a baffled and horrified spectator. Certainly it played a much less significant rôle than did the General Council of the TUC. The impotence of the mass organization of the party during the dying hours of the second Labour Government is demonstrated in Hugh Dalton's account of these events. He describes a meeting of the NEC on 20th August. It first met in joint session with the TUC General Council to hear MacDonald and Snowden. Then the two bodies met separately " the General Council (Dalton recorded in his diary) sit late, and then send a deputation, in highly critical mood, to the Prime Minister. The NE(C), on the other hand, get through the rest of (their) business quickly, *after deciding to leave the main question, for the moment, in the hands of those of (their) members who are in the Cabinet, i.e. (Henderson) and Clynes.*" Then, as throughout the lifetime of the Government, there was not the slightest question

---

[1] *1931 Labour Annual Conference Report* (Parliamentary Report), pp. 93-4.

of extra-parliamentary control of the Government or of the PLP by the mass organization outside. (But see note[1] below.)

As will have been evident from this account of the events of 1929–31, the most serious breakdown in Labour Party machinery was within the PLP itself. The Consultative Committee failed completely in the purpose for which it was established; it did not manage to evolve any effective system of liaison between the Government and its own back-benchers. But again, as in 1924, it is doubtful whether *any* machinery could in the circumstances have achieved this purpose. Certainly the experience of the PLP during the second Labour Government showed conclusively that no parliamentary party could tolerate a fully organized " party within a party " particularly when, like the ILP, it insisted upon acknowledging its own annual conference as its governing body.

Indeed it was on this last issue that the ILP may be said to have broken finally and completely with the Labour Party. The differences between the two groups were not merely ideological; nor was it solely a question of the ILP's refusal to accept the discipline of the PLP, although it was on this immediate issue that the ILP broke away. The real problem was that *the ILP refused to conform to British parliamentary practice in the way the Labour Party itself had already done*. The ILP refused to acknowledge the autonomy of its parliamentary party and insisted that its parliamentarians should be subject to the direction of the party organization outside Parliament. This was the basic issue involved and it was more fundamental than either party to the dispute appeared to recognize in the course of the controversy. The PLP, although it did not say so in so many words, had accepted all the conventions of Cabinet Government; and, further, it had broken completely with the old, naïve view that a parliamentary party should be the servant of the mass movement. But unfortunately for the PLP, the situation was bedevilled first by the fact that the Cabinet could not (and in any case, probably would not) attempt to introduce a socialist pro-

---

[1] It is certainly the case, however, that the T.U.C., which as such has never been affiliated to the Labour Party, played a major rôle in influencing the line taken by those members of the PLP who did not follow MacDonald. As Alan Bullock remarks however " The T.U.C. . . . did not force its views upon the Cabinet: it was the Cabinet which called it into consultation . . . there was no constitutional impropriety . . . in sounding opinion on the General Council. As Bevin remarked later, if the General Council had supported the Prime Minister, they would have been hailed as " statesmen "; when they disagreed, they were accused of dictation and minding the privileges of the Cabinet." Bullock concludes: " There is no ground in the evidence for the accusation that the General Council ' dictated ' to the Labour Government." (*The Life and Times of Ernest Bevin*, Vol. I, pp. 476 ff. and, in particular, p. 489. This passage effectively refutes Bassett's comment (*Nineteen Thirty-One: Political Crisis*, p. 428).

gramme, and secondly, its leaders "betrayed the party to the enemy." All of this was too much for the ILP, which took refuge in seeking more and more rigorous control by the mass organization over its parliamentary leaders. Indeed, as was shown above, even the PLP was so shocked by the events of 1931 that it sought in a fumbling and ultimately unsuccessful way (during 1931–3) to devise more effective control over a future Labour Government. But these schemes came to nothing; the Labour Party never adopted the tight system of extra-parliamentary control favoured by the ILP.

After the excitements of 1929–31, the history of the inner life of the PLP during 1945–51 seems remarkably placid. There were problems of disaffection (particularly following the resignation from the Government of Aneurin Bevan and two other Ministers in the spring of 1951), but for the most part these were no more than the customary difficulties faced by any party in power. There was fairly continual grumbling from minority groups in the party who were dissatisfied with the extent to which the back-benchers were able to influence the formulation of government policy, but again it is easy to cite similar evidence of discontent in the experience of the Conservative Party when it is in office. To some extent the Cabinet system, reserving as it does full executive responsibility and initiative to the Prime Minister and those he has chosen to work with him, makes this inevitable; and it becomes the task of any parliamentary party organization to minimize these inevitable frictions and to maintain as high a degree of morale as is possible among the rank and file of the party. This was accomplished on the whole with surprising success during 1945–51.

The explanation may be found in part in the new system of organization devised by the PLP after 1945. But undoubtedly a much more important factor was that, in contrast to 1924 and 1929, the PLP took office in 1945 with a clear working majority. Further, the Attlee Government proceeded to implement the overwhelming part of the electoral programme (*Let Us Face the Future*) on which the party had gone to the country in the 1945 elections. Where there was disillusionment and disappointment it was not primarily caused by the Government's failure to implement its programme; it was rather because of the harsh external economic circumstances in which the programme had to be introduced. Or, as the Labour Party's critics would no doubt wish to add, because of the short-comings and lack of realism of the programme itself.

As the 1946 Parliamentary Report notes: " As soon as the new

Parliament assembled, the whole organization of the Parliamentary Party was brought under review." [1] A very different liaison arrangement from that which had been set up on previous occasions when Labour had taken office was established. The 12-man Consultative Committee which had been appointed to meet with three members of the Government during the lifetime of the 1924 and 1929 Governments was replaced by a small Liaison Committee whose primary job, according to the Parliamentary Report, was " (to maintain) a close contact between the Government and the back-benchers." The Liaison Committee as set up in 1945 was composed of a Chairman and Vice-Chairman elected by the PLP,[2] a Labour Peer (elected by his colleagues), the Leader of the House of Commons, the Chief Whip and the Secretary of the PLP (who is not a Member of Parliament). The Committee met at least weekly and served principally as a channel of communication between the Government and its parliamentary supporters. It kept the Government informed of current opinion within the party and evidences of incipient revolt; it arranged for special meetings of Ministers with groups of back-benchers who were particularly concerned about aspects of the Government's policy. The two elected representatives of the Liaison Committee appear to have considered themselves primarily as representatives of the PLP who were obligated to convey the views of the party to the Government; but they also attempted to interpret the Government and its problems to back-bench critics of the party leaders. Votes were not taken within the Liaison Committee; an attempt was made to resolve its problems by a free exchange of views. In this respect the contrast with the Consultative Committee of 1924 and 1929 is striking; on the earlier occasions, the 12-man Consultative Committee elected by the PLP tended to function to some extent as a back-benchers' " Cabinet " in which the 12 elected members (meeting with the three Ministerial nominees) often provided an all too vivid demonstration of the preponderance of back-bench opposition to certain items of Ministerial policy.

Full meetings of the PLP were held fortnightly (as against an average of three meetings a fortnight when the party returned to opposition) although special meetings were occasionally called at

[1] *1946 Labour Annual Conference Report*, (Parliamentary Report), p. 56. The purpose of these changes, according to the rather glowing phrases of the Report, was " to allow initiative and individuality to have full scope . . . so that the widely representative character of the Party might bring new life to our Parliamentary institutions." See also, Morrison, H., *Government and Parliament*, pp. 123 ff.

[2] A second vice-chairman was later added. See *1950 Labour Annual Conference Report*, (Parliamentary Report), p. 70.

the request either of the Government or of a particular party group (see below). The Prime Minister and all members of the Government were eligible to attend these party meetings and usually did so when their duties permitted; but again, as in 1924 and 1929, there was no question of the Government revealing in detail its parliamentary proposals or seeking formal approval for them in advance of their presentation to Parliament. The broad outlines of policy were of course discussed at the PLP meetings and back-benchers were given an opportunity to ventilate their views.[1] Ballots were rarely taken, although formal motions requiring a vote could be moved either by members of the Government or by back-benchers. The Government normally kept itself well informed about the moods and opinions of its supporters through the usual whips' channels; and Ministers tended to take party feeling into account before attempting to make a case for a particular line of policy at the party meeting. When an issue *was* forced to a vote the Government could rely on a solid block composed of approximately 70 members of the Ministry. In addition, of course, those who hoped to win promotion into the Government tended to take care not to carry any misgivings they might have concerning the Government's policies to the point of voting against them. And in any case the party's strong sense of loyalty to its leaders and its internal cohesion almost invariably sustained the Government.

It was also decided in 1945 to set up a number of party groups (or standing committees of the PLP) which between them covered the whole field of government activity.[2] These groups were chaired by back-benchers, most of whom appear to have been the " perpetual back-bencher " type since only one of the M.P.s elected to chair a party group in 1945 (Ernest Davies) and one Acting Chairman (James Callaghan) achieved ministerial rank during the subsequent six years. The relationship between these party groups and

[1] The 1946-7 Parliamentary Report explained that " The Prime Minister and other Ministers have frequently attended (PLP meetings) in order to reply to discussions affecting the general policy of the Government and of the administration of particular Departments." *1947 Labour Annual Conference Report* (Parliamentary Report), p. 64. There is no suggestion here that the Government sought formal advance approval of its legislation by a party meeting.

[2] *1946 Labour Annual Conference Report* (Parliamentary Report), p. 56. The 20 groups established in 1945 were as follows: Agriculture and Food; Arts and Amenities; Civil Aviation; Blitzed Areas; Defence and Services; Education and Recreation; Electoral Reform; External Affairs; Finance; Fisheries; Fuel and Power; Housing and Town Planning; Labour Questions; Legal and Judicial; Local Government; Health; Shipping; Social Insurance; Trade and Industry; Transport. Subsequently this list varied somewhat from year to year.

the Ministers in charge of relevant departments was subtle and complex. The Parliamentary Report for 1945–6 (p. 56) explained the relationship in careful language. " Ministers *without prejudice to their responsibilities to Parliament* have been meeting these Groups for the interchange of views on matters affecting their Departments." (Italics mine.) Some Ministers kept in close touch with the party group concerned with the affairs of their department (for example, Hugh Dalton, the Chancellor of the Exchequer, maintained cordial relations with the party group on finance); but other Ministers appear to have been exasperated by what they considered to be the intolerable inclination of the groups to meddle in the affairs of their Ministry (Ernest Bevin made little effort to conceal his disdain for the activities of the External Affairs Group).

To the great regret of some of the more active back-benchers, the groups appear to have had little influence on the formulation of the Government's policy. Ministers without exception considered it constitutionally improper to reveal the details of proposed policy to the groups in advance of its presentation to Parliament; and in any case many of the Ministers felt that the groups tended to be composed of militants and extremists in the PLP whose views were not necessarily representative of the PLP as a whole. This led to bitter dissatisfaction in some quarters and undoubtedly stimulated the development of unofficial pressure groups within the PLP such as the " Keep Left " group, which is discussed below. It would be inaccurate to suggest, however, that none of the party groups succeeded in influencing the development of government policy. There is no doubt that the Civil Aviation Group played an important part in influencing the nature of the Government's plans for bringing civil aviation into public ownership.[1]

In 1947 it was decided that some reorganization of the group system was necessary and, as the Parliamentary Report for 1947–8 noted, " The Parliamentary Party approved the recommendations of the Liaison Committee that a number of changes in machinery be made. These included proposals for giving wider scope to the area groups, and linking them more closely with the Regional Councils of the Party in the country." [2] It had apparently been decided that the subject groups, appealing as they did to the enthusiasts within the PLP who were specially interested in a par-

---

[1] *The Times,* 22nd May, 1946, reviewing the Government's Civil Aviation Bill, noted: " The Government have already made concessions to back-bench opinion in their shaping of the Bill and they are likely to be asked for more."

[2] *1948 Labour Annual Conference Report* (Parliamentary Report), p. 73. For a discussion of the Regional Councils, see Chapter VIII.

ticular subject, tended to be unrepresentative of PLP opinion. The area groups on the other hand brought together M.P.s solely on the basis of the propinquity of their constituencies; these groups had heretofore been concerned solely with the discussion of local and regional problems, but as a result of the new arrangements established in 1947 they were encouraged to consider national and international issues as well. It was assumed that each of them would provide a microcosm of the PLP and they would be able to make their views known to the Government through the appropriate junior Whip responsible for M.P.s from their particular area.

The Parliamentary Report for the following year (1948-9) claimed jubilantly that, with the widening of the scope of the area groups, " there (could) be no doubt that . . . immeasurable success (had) attended upon the changes made in the organization of the Parliamentary Party." [1]   This appears to have been a gross exaggeration. There is no real evidence to suggest that the area groups played any significant part in the development of Government policy; nor did they in any way minimize the dissatisfaction of the back-bench militants at what they felt to be their intolerable exclusion from the councils of the party. But again it must be acknowledged that the existence of this perpetual unhappiness and sense of grievance among the back-bench militants is the normal condition of every parliamentary party. Without a drastic change in the Cabinet system of government it would appear to be impossible to devise any party mechanism which can obviate these dissatisfactions. A government which implements the programme on which it was elected, which has a sensitive and skilled leadership and corps of whips, can minimize the frictions which are inseparable from the Cabinet system. This Attlee and his colleagues succeeded in doing. But it is no criticism of their work that they were not totally successful in eliminating back-bench discontent.

Throughout the life of both Attlee Governments a number of informal party groups which were not organized by the PLP functioned within the parliamentary party. The most important of these was the Trade Union Group which has been in existence throughout the lifetime of the PLP; it consists of M.P.s whose candidature was sponsored and financed by trade unions affiliated to the party. Major matters of concern to the trade union movement were of course discussed in direct consultation between the General Council of the TUC and members of the Government; the Trade Union Group in Parliament was concerned mainly with holding a watching brief for trade union interests where these interests were affected by legislation or by Government policy. In addition,

[1] *1949 Labour Annual Conference Report* (Parliamentary Report), p. 77.

within the PLP there were several " ideological " groups of shifting composition which met informally for the discussion of various matters of government policy. The best known of these was the so-called " Keep Left " Group. In the immediate post-war years it maintained a running fire of criticism in the press, on the platform, at party meetings (and to a lesser extent in the House of Commons) of the foreign policy of Ernest Bevin. The Keep Left Group, which at one time met weekly, made little effort to conceal its activities.[1] A number of the more prominent members of this group subsequently became leaders of the so-called " Bevanite " group which gathered around Aneurin Bevan following his resignation from the Government in 1951. On rare occasions leaders of the Keep Left Group led open revolt on the floor of the House of Commons. But their most important channel of influence was in the PLP meetings where less inhibited attacks could be made on items in the Government's policy.

One back-bench revolt in which Keep Left leaders played a prominent part, provides an important illustration of the potential influence of back-bench opinion on government policy. This was the controversy surrounding the Conscription Bill in 1946–7.[2] Because of a shortage of military manpower the Government decided to introduce a bill to provide for an eighteen-month period of conscription. The Prime Minister gave a general indication of the Government's intention at a meeting of the PLP on 6th November, 1946. After a lively discussion the issue was taken to a vote and the Government's proposal was sustained in a vote which was divided in the Government's favour by about 5 to 2. When the Bill was laid before the House in March 1947, 80 Labour back-benchers signed an amendment asking the House to reject it. The Prime Minister again defended the Bill at a meeting of the PLP, but subsequently in the House of Commons, 72 Labour M.P.s voted against it and as many more either abstained or were absent. Two days later the Government appeared to relent under pressure from its supporters and the proposed period of National Service was reduced from 18 to 12 months. Thereafter the measure was adopted by a vote of 368 to 17. With the deterioration of the international situation the period of national service was subsequently lengthened to two years without serious opposition from the PLP. But the original revolt on the national service issue is perhaps the most striking single

---

[1] It produced several pamphlets signed by their authors, including for example, *Keep Left* (London, 1947).

[2] For a detailed discussion of this incident see Burns, J. M., " The Parliamentary Labor Party of Great Britain," *American Political Science Review*, December, 1950, p. 865.

illustration of the effectiveness of back-bench opposition to Government policy during the lifetime of the 1945 and 1950 Governments.

A bold experiment in party discipline was attempted on the formation of the Labour Government in 1945. As the 1945–6 Parliamentary Report recorded: ". . . the operation of the Standing Orders has been suspended (subject to review if circumstances require) until the end of the Parliamentary Session of 1946–47, though this is not to prejudice the right of the Party to withdraw the Whip from Members, should occasion require." The motive behind the experiment (the Report added hopefully) " is the belief that the building of a tradition of free discussion, combined with a true spirit of good fellowship, co-operation and comradeship in a great cause is to be preferred to written Standing Orders." [1] This experiment was judged a success and the suspension was subsequently renewed for the lifetime of the Labour Governments of 1945 and 1950. There were several notable instances of party insubordination which resulted in the expulsion of several M.P.s from the PLP, and a number of other less drastic disciplinary actions.[2]

The relations between the Attlee Governments and the PLP on the one hand and the mass organization outside Parliament need not be examined in detail here since they are discussed at some length in Chapter VIII. It need only be noted that the NEC tended throughout the lifetime of both Governments to function again, as in 1929–31, primarily as a guardian of the Government at the party conference. As has already been noted, the essential explanation is probably to be found in the fact that a considerable majority of the NEC was composed of Members of Parliament. During the period 1945–51 (inclusive) there were never fewer than 16 M.P.s on the 27-man NEC and the number rose as high as 18; the number of Ministers on the NEC varied from year to year but ranged from eight to ten. (See Table 6 at p. 424.) In addition, Ministers and other M.P.s constituted a majority of most of the principal sub-

---

[1] *1946 Labour Annual Conference Report* (Parliamentary Report), p. 57. See Appendix C for standing orders in operation at the time and also those which were imposed again in 1952.

[2] The principal cases including the " Nenni telegram " incident, the Ireland Bill (in which 60 members of the PLP voted against the Government in May, 1949) and the case of Konni Zilliacus, are reviewed in some detail in Burns, J. M., " The Parliamentary Labor Party in Great Britain," *American Political Science Review*, December, 1950, pp. 867-9. See also *1948 Labour Annual Conference Report* (Report of the NEC), p. 17, for a discussion of the expulsion of Messrs. John Platts-Mills, M.P., and Alfred Edwards, M.P., and the NEC action over the Nenni telegram; and *1949 Labour Annual Conference Report*, pp. 18, 112 and 119 for a further discussion of the case of Konni Zilliacus.

committees of the NEC. Again, it can be argued that the NEC and its committees became in effect a set of sub-committees of the PLP on which Cabinet Ministers played a dominant part and to which a number of trade union leaders (mostly of the second rank) had been added. As a result it is no surprise to find that the NEC never advocated at party conferences or elsewhere any item of policy which was at variance with the policy of the Government. And further, the NEC invariably recommended the rejection of policies proposed at the conference which might prove in any way embarrassing to the Government. In the overwhelming proportion of instances the conference acted on the advice of the NEC. And on the very few occasions on which the NEC advice was rejected [1] the Government ignored the conference decision.

The Labour Party head office was clearly aware of the need to re-educate the mass organization of the party on its relationship to the Parliamentary Labour Party and the Labour Government. After 1945 a new and firmer note began to creep into official comments on the subject. Thus, for example, the 1951 edition of *Handbook: Facts and Figures for Socialists* (prepared by the Labour Party Research Department) stated firmly: " The Parliamentary Labour Party is an *autonomous* body, with its own Standing Orders, and electing its own leaders. . . . Provision is made in the Party Constitution for periodical consultation between the Parliamentary Labour Party and the National Executive Committee, but *the latter has no authority over the actions in Parliament of Labour Ministers or Labour Members*."[2] An even stronger passage appeared in another official party publication entitled *The British Labour Party* (" prepared for the guidance of foreign visitors desiring to know more about the structure of our Movement "). After explaining the provision for liaison between the NEC and the Labour Government then in power, the publication added: " In this way, at least, Parliament and Government are not *unaware of* the decisions and deliberations of the Party's governing body."[3] The phrase " not unaware of " would no doubt have startled some of the founding fathers of the party, just as it must have seemed outrageously arrogant to many of the militant spirits in the constituency parties of to-day. But it does reflect a realistic recognition of where the real centres of power in the party lie.

[1] See p. 512 below.

[2] *Handbook: Facts and Figures for Socialists*, 1951, pp. 301-2. [Italics mine.] Although this passage makes no reference to the party conference it could equally have been added that it has no authority over the actions in Parliament of Labour Ministers or Labour Members, despite the statement that appeared in another head office publication quoted p. 11 above.

[3] *The British Labour Party* (duplicated, 1950), p. 12. [Italics mine.]

The dominant and all-persuasive influence of the Cabinet extended to the preparation of the electoral programmes on which the party went to the country in 1950 and 1951. The process by which these programmes were formulated is considered in more detail in Chapter VIII. But it is important to note here that the principal official of the party head office who served the NEC Policy Committee during this period (Wilfred Fienburgh, then Research Secretary at the party head office, subsequently elected a Member of Parliament in the 1951 general election) has written: ". . . Ministers, heavily immersed in day-to-day governmental responsibilities, assumed what amounted to a power of veto in the framing of election manifestos. This, plus ministerial caution, ministerial fatigue, and ministerial remoteness resulted in the strangled and emasculated manifestos of 1950 and 1951." [1] One need not debate the virtues or the shortcomings of the manifestos to which Fienburgh refers. But it is important to note that one who was in a strategic position to observe the process of policy-making should have testified so forthrightly on the extent to which the control of the affairs of the party had become dominated by the leaders of the Government. It is doubtful whether the situation was very different from that which has prevailed at comparable moments in the history of the Conservative Party. Labour makes more elaborate efforts to give the mass membership of its party a sense of participation in determining policy; and the vastly complex machinery of the party provides far more numerous opportunities for public disputes over policy. But when the Parliamentary Party has been in office its leaders, who then constitute the government, have been just as effectively in control of their party as have Conservative leaders in office. In opposition the position of the Labour parliamentary leadership is more complex and, in a sense, more precarious. But they normally play the leading rôle in the formulation of policy and, so long as they maintain the working alliance with a majority of the leading figures in the trade union world, which is the key to an understanding of the Labour Party (as is shown in Ch. VIII), they are most unlikely to be over-ridden by the extra-parliamentary elements of the party.

[1] Fienburgh, W., "Put Policy on the Agenda," *Fabian Journal,* February, 1952, No. 6, p. 25. Fienburgh adds: "When Labour was in government initiative and authority in policy-making fell almost entirely into the hands of those members of the Labour Party who were at the same time members of the Government . . . . In affairs of state this was constitutionally desirable. In evolving the long term policies of the Labour movement it was politically most undesirable . . . . I have no complaint about ministerial attitudes. They were natural and inevitable. And it was essential that the advice of Ministers should be considered. But although Ministers should govern the nation's affairs in the light of party policies, the party as a whole should decide those policies."

CHAPTER VIII

THE LABOUR PARTY OUTSIDE PARLIAMENT: THE RÔLE OF THE TRADE UNIONS AND THE CONSTITUENCY PARTIES

IT follows from the argument of the two previous chapters regarding the authority of the Leader and the autonomy of the PLP that the mass organization of the Labour Party outside Parliament cannot and does not play the rôle so often assigned to it in party literature. The acceptance by the party of the conventions of Cabinet and Parliamentary government ensure that while Labour is in office the annual conference of the mass organization cannot function as a " parliament of the movement " issuing instructions to its elected representatives. And even when Labour is in opposition it has been amply demonstrated that the parliamentary party and its Leaders have not been prepared to accept direction and control from the conference. With the party in opposition the mass organization does tend to have considerably greater influence. Indeed, a re-examination of the history of the Labour Party would suggest that it can be taken almost as axiomatic that the influence of the mass organization varies inversely with the strength of the PLP.[1] But it is important to emphasize again that even when the PLP has been at its weakest it has stubbornly refused to abdicate control over its own affairs.

It has already been noted that the mass organization of the Labour Party is *formally* accorded a much more important rôle in the affairs of the party than is the case on the Conservative side; the annual conference of the Labour Party has in theory the deciding voice in determining the goals which shall be pursued by the party in Parliament. This makes it inevitable that the parliamentary leaders should be involved in a far more elaborate (and sometimes highly damaging) procedure in securing formal approval of the policies which they normally take the initiative in proposing. But as was shown in Chapter VII, a number of factors have combined to ensure that the PLP has hardly ever found itself seriously out of step with the mass organization of the party. The leaders of the PLP have there-fore rarely found it necessary to provoke their followers outside Parliament by reminding them that the PLP is an autonomous

[1] See pp. 399 ff. and 317 ff. above for a discussion of the rôle of the mass organization during the periods 1914-22 and 1931-5.

political entity; they need not borrow the somewhat brutal language of the Conservative Party and tell the members of their mass organization that they have no more than advisory functions. The political machinery and the " ethos " of the two parties are in many respects in sharp contrast, as is evident from the analysis in this book. It is inevitable, none the less, that if any political party accepts the fundamental assumptions of the British constitution effective power and authority will come to be concentrated in the hands of its parliamentary party and its leaders.

It may be argued, of course, that the Labour leaders are allowed to wield authority on sufferance. It would be quite possible in theory for the Labour Party to repudiate its parliamentary leaders either by passing one or more resolutions condemning the policies they were pursuing or by formally expressing their lack of confidence in the leaders themselves. In either case, the leaders might well find themselves so discredited that they would be forced to resign and they would be supplanted by other members of the PLP who enjoyed the confidence of the mass organization. But it should not be forgotten that in theory this is also possible in the Conservative Party. As was shown in Chapter III, had Austen Chamberlain not been defeated at the Carlton Club meeting in 1922 (and in effect destroyed by his parliamentary followers), he would have faced a hostile conference of the National Union which would probably have passed a resolution demanding a withdrawal from the Lloyd George Coalition. In both parties the members of the mass organization have a certain ultimate sanction: if they are sufficiently dissatisfied with the work of their parliamentary leaders they can, in effect, refuse to perform their primary function as a vote-getting agency. Aware of this possibility, the parliamentary leaders of both parties must always do all in their power to retain the confidence of their mass organization. But this is normally in both parties a comparatively simple matter. Except on rare occasions the Conservatives can rely upon the deferential and almost docile attitude of their followers; while the Labour leaders, as long as they retain the confidence of a small group of leading figures in the trade union world, can be reasonably confident that no hostile majority will form against them within their mass organization.

I

THE EVOLUTION OF THE CONSTITUTION OF THE LABOUR PARTY TO 1918

As was noted in Chapter VII, the meeting at the Memorial Hall in February 1900 decided to undertake what appeared at first to be no more than a very limited political experiment.[1] It set up a committee representing a number of trade unions and three tiny socialist societies for the purpose of ensuring that ". . . working class opinion (should be) represented in the House of Commons by men sympathetic with the aims and demands of the Labour movements, and whose candidatures are promoted by one or other of the organized movements " (which it was hoped would affiliate to the Labour Representation Committee).[2] It was intended (resolution 2) that these representatives of working-class opinion should establish " a distinct Labour Group in Parliament, who shall have their own Whips, and agree upon their policy . . ." But the definition here implied of political independence in Parliament was modified in the same resolution which added ". . . their policy . . . must embrace a readiness to co-operate with any party which for the time being may be engaged in promoting legislation in the direct interest of labour, and be equally ready to associate themselves with any party in opposing measures having an opposite tendency . . ." [3]

Two attempts were made at the 1900 conference to commit the new Labour group either to a clearly defined programme or to a specific social philosophy. One amendment to the first resolution (quoted above) would have converted the group into little more than a mouthpiece for the trade union movement; another, sponsored by the Social Democratic Federation (hereinafter SDF), would have converted the group into a specifically socialist party committed to an acceptance of the Marxist theory of social change. Both proposals were rejected and the conference adopted instead the somewhat ambiguous resolution which committed its parliamentary representatives to what remained an undefined " Labour "

[1] For detailed accounts of the origins of the Labour Party, see Pelling, H., *The Origins of the Labour Party*, London, 1954; Crowley, D. W., *The Origins of the Revolt of the British Labour Movement from Liberalism* (an unpublished thesis presented for the degree of Ph.D. in the University of London, 1952); Cole, G. D. H., *British Working Class Politics 1832-1914*, London, 1941; Cole, G. D. H., *A History of the Labour Party from 1914*, London, 1948; Williams, Francis, *Fifty Years' March: The Rise of the Labour Party*, London, 1949; Beer, Max, *The History of British Socialism*, London, 1948; Tracey, H., (ed.), *The Book of the Labour Party*, Vol. I, London, 1925; Shepherd, Lord, *Labour's Early Days*, Tillicoultry, Scotland, (n.d.). Two recent valuable additions to the literature of the early years of the Labour Party are Bealey, F. and Pelling, H., *Labour and Politics 1900-1906*, London, 1958,[1] and Porrier, P. P., *The Advent of the Labour Party*, London, 1958. For a highly critical history of the Party, see Miliband, R., *Parliamentary Socialism*, London, 1961.

[2] Resolution 1 adopted by the Conference on Labour Representation, Memorial Hall, London, 27th February, 1900. See *1900 LRC Annual Conference Report*, p. 11.

[3] Resolution 2, *1900 LRC Annual Conference Report*, p. 12.

policy.[1]   Keir Hardie had been the principal architect of the compromise resolution and the wisdom of his strategy was to be amply
demonstrated in the years that lay immediately ahead. A more
specifically socialist policy, if adopted at that time, would almost
certainly have alienated large sections of the trade union movement
which were still under predominantly Lib-Lab leadership. An
acceptance of the " trade union pressure group " conception would
hardly have stimulated the socialist elements in the LRC to devote
their energies to the work of propaganda and organization which
was essential if the LRC was to become an effective political force.
Hardie's compromise resolution was of course much too flabby in
the eyes of the SDF and they were to quit the LRC in 1901. But
their allegiance could hardly have been retained short of a full
acceptance by the conference of their " class war " doctrine, and
this was a price that no one outside their own ranks was prepared
to pay.

The organization set up by the 1900 conference consisted of a
committee of 12 members served by an unpaid secretary. It had at
first been proposed that the Executive Committee should consist
of 18 representatives (12 from trade unions, two from the Fabian
Society, two from the ILP and two from the SDF) with provision
that " such members shall be elected by their respective organizations." The mover of this resolution, Ben Cooper (of the Cigar
Makers), commented that " as the overwhelming number of
persons represented at the Congress were the Trade Unionists,
who would have to find the bulk of the money, a proportionately
large share of the members of the Committee ought to be Trade
Unionists." This seemed a reasonable argument, but J. Burgess
(of the ILP) nevertheless moved an amendment which proposed
that the LRC should be reduced in number to a total of 12, composed
as follows: seven representatives of the trade unions, one of the
Fabian Society, two of the ILP, two of the SDF. He proposed in other
words that the trade union representation should be cut by five
and the socialist representation by one. His argument, which
seems a little disingenuous, was that as " a matter of efficiency and
economy " the committee should be smaller than the 18 proposed
by Ben Cooper. Keir Hardie rallied to Burgess's support; in

[1] Hyndman of the SDF wrote derisively of the failure of the ILP to
back the SDF demand for a specifically socialist policy, " . . . the Independent Labour Party, then a declared Socialist body, instructed its delegates at the first important 'Labour' Conference held in 1900 to throw
Socialism overboard, and voted for a Labourism that nobody could define." Hyndman, H. M., *Further Reminiscences*, p. 259. See *1900 ILP Conference Report*, pp. 6-7, for the ILP reply to the SDF attack on their rôle
at the 1900 meeting.

seconding the amendment he argued: "... the smaller the Committee the more efficient would be its work." This moved A. Wilkie (of the Shipwrights) to warn the conference that "The Socialists were having an undue proportion on the Committee. ... They were at the starting of a new movement, and he urged them to move carefully if they wished to secure the support of the Trade Unionists." The issue was put to the conference and the amendment reducing the members of the Executive to 12 was adopted by a vote of 331,000 to 161,000.[1]

In retrospect it is difficult to account for the docile acceptance by the trade union delegates to the 1900 conference of the disproportionate representation accorded to the socialist societies on the new Executive. The trade unionists were in an overwhelming majority in the conference itself. They had 129 delegates (representing 568,177 trade union members) against 12 delegates representing the three socialist societies (seven ILP delegates for 13,000 members, four SDF delegates for 9,000 members and one Fabian Society delegate for 861 members).[2] Clearly the trade unions could have assured themselves any sort of majority they had wanted on the Executive. Shaw, who had been one of the two Fabian representatives on the original committee which had planned the 1900 meeting, subsequently gave his own account of the rather strange proceedings involved in the setting up of the LRC Executive. The LRC, he wrote, "was formed by the Socialist societies and their leaders, with its doors open to the trade unions as such, no matter what their opinions of Socialism (mostly contemptuously hostile) might be. As their voting numbers were overwhelming and their money indispensable, they would have swept out all the Socialists and replaced them with old Conservative or Lib-Lab trade union secretaries if the LRC had been democratically constituted; so we fell back on the good old Tory device of *ex officio* members." Shaw illustrates the operation of this "device" by noting that in the original recommendation regarding the composition of the Executive "the Fabian Society, with less than 2,000 members, all middle class to the marrow of their bones, was actually allowed

---

[1] *1900 LRC Annual Conference Report*, pp. 13–14.
[2] *List of Delegates to Conference on Labour Representation, Memorial Hall, 27th February, 1900*, London, TUC Parliamentary Committee, 1900. The 129 trade union delegates represented, incidentally, rather less than half the strength of the Trades Union Congress. But there was nevertheless some justification for Ernest Bevin's boast many years later: "Our predecessors [in the TUC] formed [the Labour] Party. It was not Keir Hardie. The Labour Party grew out of the bowels of the TUC." Cited in Williams, F., *Ernest Bevin*, p. 195.

two members *ex officio*."[1] But Shaw's comment leaves the basic
question unanswered. He uses the phrase, " *we* fell back on the
old Tory device of *ex officio* members." But why did the trade
union delegates accept this arrangement? Admittedly it had been
decided to set up a kind of federal organization, but this did not
make it inevitable that the socialist societies should be granted
positions on the Executive as of right. One would have expected
the conference to have adopted the system of election subsequently
embodied in the 1918 constitution whereby all nominees for the
NEC were voted upon by the whole conference.[2]

The explanation of the surprising readiness of the trade union
delegates to acquiesce in the remarkably generous representation
of the socialist societies may perhaps be found in the rather casual
attitude to the whole proceeding adopted by a great many of the
trade unionists present. MacDonald later wrote, in recalling the
circumstances of the meeting, that some of the delegates intended
" to bury the attempt (to set up a new political organization) in
good-humoured tolerance " and that others were firmly determined
" that burial would be its fate." A majority of the delegates, he
wrote, were sympathetic with the experiment and eager to " give
it a chance." [3] But it seems clear from MacDonald's comment
and from other contemporary accounts that, for the most part,
the trade union attitude was one of casual benevolence; there was
little disposition to haggle with the strong-willed Keir Hardie and
his ILP friends. The latter in turn had shown a willingness to
compromise by forswearing any demand that the LRC should
commit itself to a specifically socialist programme. It may be that

---

[1] Subsequently, of course, the Fabian Society representation was cut to
one. Shaw explained that " Keir Hardie was determined to get rid of this
clever bourgeois element and more especially of me . . . . " Accordingly,
Shaw claims, Keir Hardie secured the reduction of the Fabian Society
representation to one, " and thus got rid of me (with my cordial consent),
leaving Pease, as the Fabian secretary, in possession. Pease liked being on
the LRC and could see nothing wrong in any of its proceedings: an attitude which suited Hardie and MacDonald exactly . . . . " Cited in Elton,
Lord, *Life of James Ramsay MacDonald*, pp. 102-3.

[2] At the 1905 conference an attempt was made by a trade union delegate to change the LRC constitution to provide that the Executive should
be " elected by a ballot of the whole of the delegates (to the LRC Conference) " on the grounds that this would eliminate " dual representation".
This move was defeated by a vote of 510,000 to 391,000. But it was
" unanimously agreed " that the socialist societies should be jointly rather
than separately represented; the Executive would henceforth include " three
(representatives) for the Socialist Societies " rather than " one for the
Fabian Society and two for the Independent Labour Party." *1905 LRC
Annual Conference Report*, pp. 49-50.

[3] MacDonald, J. R., *The Socialist Movement*, p. 235.

the socialists won their reward by the recognition granted to their societies on the LRC Executive.

After the adoption of the resolution constituting the new Executive the conference adjourned into separate sections to elect the members of the new committee.[1] When the conference reassembled it proceeded to adopt a series of resolutions which defined the work of the LRC. Its principal function was described in resolution 4: ". . . the Committee appointed by this Conference shall prepare a list of candidates run in accordance with resolution 1 (see p. 457 above), shall publish this list as the official candidates of the United Labour Party, and shall recommend those candidates for the support of the working-class electors." And it was further decided that the committee should " keep in touch with Trade Unions and other organizations, local and national, which are running Labour candidates and shall convene a Labour Representation Conference in the month of February each year."

There was an important discussion on the question whether the LRC should be held responsible to its constituent organizations. It was moved (resolution 7) " that (the Executive) shall also report annually to the Trades Union Congress and the annual meeting of the National Societies represented on the Committee, and take any steps deemed advisable to elicit opinions from the members of the organizations to which the Committee is ultimately responsible." The clear intention of this resolution was to ensure that the Executive should be primarily responsible not to the LRC annual meeting but to the national organizations which composed it. G. N. Barnes (of the Engineers) warned that this would prove a most unsatisfactory arrangement. If the LRC Executive was " going to undertake the work in a practical and serious manner " it was far preferable they should report to its own annual meeting. But J. Ward (of the Navvies), who had proposed the resolution, argued that " if the movement was entirely separated from the Trades Union Congress, his own society would object to sending delegates, and he believed that would be found to be the attitude of the Trade Unions generally. (The work of the LRC, he claimed) was

[1] *1900 LRC Annual Conference Report*, p. 15. The *Fabian News* subsequently reported that "Edward R. Pease provisionally appointed himself, as the only Fabian delegate, to be on the Executive Committee," and the (Fabian) Executive Committee subsequently confirmed his appointment. As Pease himself later recalled, "this little comedy was carried on for some years. The Fabian Society was only entitled to send one delegate to the annual conference, but that delegate had the right of electing one member to the Executive Committee, and I was appointed by my Committee to serve in both capacities." Pease, E. R. *History of the Fabian Society*, p. 149.

absolutely useless apart from the Trade Union movement." The resolution was endorsed by a vote of 360,000 to 124,000.

The final act of the conference was to adopt a resolution which urged that the Executive Committee " be instructed in calling the next conference to issue invitations to Trades Councils . . ." They should be accorded one representative on the Executive Committee and one delegate to the annual meeting for every 25,000 members affiliated. An amendment was moved to extend the invitation on the same basis to Co-operative Societies. The chairman warned that these proposals " entirely altered the constitution of the Conference," but it was carried on a card vote: 218,000 for; 191,000 against. The limited ambitions of many of those prominently associated with the Memorial Hall meeting is reflected in the concluding remarks of the chairman, W. C. Steadman, himself a Lib-Lab M.P. He hoped, he said, that " in the near future labour would be better represented in the House of Commons than it was to-day." The expectations of *The Clarion*, one of the few newspapers that paid serious attention to the meeting, were not very much greater: " At last (its correspondent wrote) there is a United Labour Party, or perhaps it would be safer to say, a little cloud, no bigger than a man's hand, which may grow into a United Labour Party . . ." [1]

At the first annual conference of the LRC on 1st February, 1901, the Executive was able to report a total affiliated membership of 375,931, composed as follows: 41 trade unions affiliated on the basis of 353,070 members; ILP 13,000; SDF 9,000; Fabian Society 861. In addition, trades councils in seven urban areas with a membership of 101,000 were associated with the work of the LRC, and five of the councils were represented at the 1901 conference. The 1901 Report also recorded the rather unspectacular performance of the LRC in the 1900 election. The dissolution had taken place in September 1900, only seven months after the formation of the LRC, and as a result no more than 15 candidates were run by affiliated organizations and supported by the Committee. The Committee's revenue for the first year had been £243, and of this sum £33 had been spent on the printing and distribution of election literature. Two members endorsed by the Committee (Richard Bell and Keir Hardie) had been returned, and the LRC's 15 nominees had polled 62,000 votes in all. The record was not discreditable; but clearly, after its first year's operation, the " little cloud " was still not much larger than a man's hand.

As MacDonald later wrote: ". . . for six years the Party was

[1] Cited in Pelling, H., *The Origins of the Labour Party*, p. 223.

allowed to grow in obscurity . . ." [1] The activities of the LRC attracted little public attention, but during the years 1900–06 the Committee laid the groundwork for the Labour Party which was to emerge in Parliament 29-strong in January 1906. Detailed consideration was given in Chapter VII to the process by which the mass organization outside Parliament goaded and aided its tiny parliamentary team to organize itself into the nucleus of a parliamentary party. Meanwhile, the mass membership of the party grew spectacularly. The first *Labour Year Book* later recalled: "The years 1903, 1904, and 1905 witnessed the most carefully planned and enthusiastic period of political organization in the history of the British Labour Movement . . ." [2] At the end of the year 1905 the Executive reported the affiliation of 158 trade unions comprising 904,496 members; this was very nearly a threefold increase over 1900, an increase which was largely attributable, of course, to the trade union reaction to the Taff Vale decision.[3] The socialist society membership remained small. It sagged in 1901 when the SDF withdrew from the LRC, but recovered (on paper at least) to something approximating to its 1900 strength as a result of an increased membership reported by the ILP. By 1905 there were also 73 trades councils affiliated to the LRC. An amendment to the party constitution adopted in 1905 provided for the admission of local LRCs under certain circumstances and it was reported to the 1906 conference that two had applied for affiliation.[4]

In addition, during this period the LRC had established its claim to represent a fully independent political force. The original intention of resolution 7 of the 1900 conference appears to have been to ensure that the LRC should be little more than a liaison committee co-ordinating the political activities of its constituent elements; the resolution required, it will be recalled, that the committee should " report annually to the Trades Union Congress and the annual meeting of the National Societies represented on the Committee." But in practice the LRC does not appear to have done so; there is no indication in the 1901 annual reports of the TUC, the ILP or the LRC itself that the LRC made formal reports in the manner apparently required by the resolution.[5] And it is

[1] MacDonald, J. R., *The Socialist Movement*, p. 235.
[2] *The Labour Year Book* (1916), p. 307.
[3] See Tracey, H. (ed.), *The Book of the Labour Party*, Vol. I, p. 129.
[4] *1906 Labour Annual Conference Report*, p. 7.
[5] However, a resolution was passed at the 1901 Trades Union Congress which read: " That this Congress expresses its gratifications with the success of the Labour Representation Committee, and further appeals to all Trade Unions to become affiliated with the government." *1901 TUC Report*, p. 74.

significant that the constitution of the LRC published in the *1902 Annual Conference Report* merely states: " That the Committee shall keep in touch with Trade Unions and other organizations, local and national, which are running Labour candidates . . ." The Trades Union Congress for its part seems to have been perfectly willing to wean the LRC. When an attempt was made at the 1904 Trades Union Congress to debate certain aspects of LRC organization it was decided that such discussion would be out of order because the LRC was " an independent and outside body " over which the Congress had no control.[1]

Thereafter, however intimate the fraternal relations may have been between the TUC and the LRC (or, subsequently, the Labour Party), they were nevertheless the relations between *autonomous* organizations. The independence of the LRC was underlined by the action of the 1905 conference in rejecting Ben Tillett's resolution: " That it be an instruction to the Executive of the LRC to enforce the hearty adoption by LRC candidates of all legislative proposals emanating from the Trades Union Congress." [2] This new relationship was reflected in the course of preparations for the 1906 elections. A joint conference was held in February 1905 between the Parliamentary Committee of the TUC, the LRC and the General Federation of Trade Unions " to discuss points of common action for the coming General Election." At this meeting it was agreed that " all Candidates adopted by the LRC under its Constitution shall receive the loyal and hearty support of all sections of the Labour Party." And reciprocally: " all Labour and Trade Union Candidates approved by the Parliamentary Committee in accordance with the Standing Orders of the TUC shall receive the support of the LRC in so far as its Constitution allows . . ." [3]

Co-operation between the LRC and the trade union movement was facilitated by the fact that during the 1900–06 period little was done to clarify the LRC's long-range objectives; it remained committed to an indefinite " Labourism " which appeared to imply more than pressure for fulfilment of trade union demands but less than a clearly defined socialist programme. Officially the LRC had no platform at all. Thus the minutes of a meeting of the Executive Committee for 6th September, 1902, record that " letters proposing a deputation from the National Union of Women's Suffrage Societies were read." The Executive " agreed to write asking what they wanted and to point out that the Committee has no political platform and therefore cannot make use of their

---

[1] *1904 TUC Report*, p. 91.
[2] See p. 390 above.
[3] *Labour Party Documents*, Part I, folios 299–300.

plank." [1] The more militant socialist element within the LRC made persistent efforts to convert the organization to a statement of socialist objectives. Bruce Glasier (on behalf of the ILP) moved at the 1901 conference a resolution which would have described the goal of the LRC as " the creation of an Industrial Commonwealth founded upon the common ownership and control of land and capital and the substitution of co-operative production for use in place of the present method of competitive production for profit." In support of the resolution he said: " The Independent Labour Party desired to co-operate with Trade Unions in a fair and wholehearted way. But it was advisable to declare the political ideal of this movement." He conceded that there were a great many trade unionists in the LRC " who did not agree with him on this point," but he and his friends were convinced that a resolution of this sort should " be adopted by the Labour Movement as a guiding idea in politics." Inevitably, the SDF, which at the time had not yet quit the LRC, complicated the situation by moving an amendment " that no candidate for Parliament should receive the support of the (LRC) who is not pledged to the above principles and to the recognition of the class war as the basis of working-class political action." Quelch, who moved the amendment, asked rhetorically: " If there was no class war, why was there a Trade Union Movement? " And he insisted that it must be the purpose of the LRC to bring the spirit of the class war into politics. But the whole discussion was killed by one well-delivered blow from J. Sexton of the Dock Labourers. He reminded the conference " that the initial purpose of this movement was to bring the scattered elements of the Labour Movement to agree on a common platform of independent representation of Labour. Personally he was in favour of the resolution, but he would not vote for it because he thought that in these Conferences no one side should ram their principles down the throats of the other side." A majority of the conference clearly agreed and the previous question was moved and carried without a formal vote. [2]

But there were to be further attempts by both sides to " ram their principles down the throats of the other," and, surprisingly, on one occasion the Socialists were to succeed in their purpose. They had returned to the attack at the 1903 conference when the West Ham Trades Council supported by the ILP moved that: " This annual conference of the (LRC) hereby declares that its ultimate object shall be the obtaining for the workers the full results of their labour by the overthrow of the present competitive

[1] *Labour Party Documents*, Part I, folio 125.
[2] *1901 LRC Annual Conference Report*, pp. 20-1.

system of Capitalism and the institution of a system of Public Ownership of all the means of production, distribution and exchange." The West Ham delegate demanded to know, " If that was not the object of the Committee, what was? " He received no answer; there was no debate; but the resolution was narrowly defeated on a card vote by 295,000 to 291,000.[1] Two years later an identically worded resolution appeared on the agenda. Again there was no debate; but amazingly enough, the conference report records: " the resolution was agreed to without discussion." [2]

No attempt was made, however, to incorporate this resolution into the section of the party constitution entitled " Object". The constitution as revised at the 1905 conference still committed the LRC to do no more than " To secure, by united action, the election to Parliament of candidates promoted, in the first instance, by an Affiliated Society or Societies in the constituency . . ." There were further provisions about the independence to which the elected M.P.s must pledge themselves, but there was no hint in the constitution that either the LRC-sponsored M.P.s or the LRC itself sought to establish a socialist form of society.[3]

At the same conference (1905) the final attempt was made by the foes of socialism in the trade union movement to rid the LRC of the socialist societies. A resolution submitted in the name of the General Union of Carpenters and Joiners proposed in effect that the trades councils, the ILP and the Fabian Society should be forced to quit the LRC. The seconder argued that ". . . Trade Unionists should be quite sufficient for their movement . . .", although co-operative societies, he conceded, should be eligible for membership. He claimed that few individuals would, in effect, be expelled since most members of the trade councils and the ILP were in practice also members of a trade union. In opposing the resolution, G. N. Barnes (of the Engineers) asked the Trade Unionists " to emphatically and overwhelmingly reject the resolution, so emphatically as to prevent its reappearance at any subsequent Conference." He conceded that " the Trade Unionists and the Socialists had slightly different objects, but five years ago they decided to come together for the purpose of making a common effort for the benefit of their common cause. . . . They had been remarkably successful, and he failed to see why they should turn round upon one section of their comrades in the movement and seek to turn them out. . . . To say

[1] *1903 LRC Annual Conference Report,* p. 36.

[2] *1905 LRC Annual Conference Report,* p. 52.

[3] Jennings (*Party Politics,* Vol. II, pp. 234 ff.) warns against the tendency on the part of some historians of the Labour Party (including as authoritative a writer as Henry Pelling) to exaggerate the importance of " socialism " as a factor in the growth of the Party.

the least, the proposition which they were considering was lacking in a spirit of gratitude." He warned the movers that if they succeeded they might in future find trade union candidates endorsed by the LRC facing rival socialist nominees. When it was put to a vote the resolution " was defeated by a large majority "; the report adds " the chairman not thinking it worth while to count." [1] Three years later (at the 1908 conference) Pete Curran, of the Gasworkers, was to recall that in 1900 " the Socialist Trade Unionist and what might be called the old-time Trade Unionist joined hands in an open and honourable alliance . . ." [2] The phrase is not inappropriate; by dint of hard work and restraint by sensible men on both sides, " the open and honourable alliance " had been maintained intact through the six years in which the foundations of the Labour Party were laid.

At the constituency level, however, these foundations were not as yet very substantial. In its first year the LRC had set up a committee to recommend what form of organization they should promote. The committee reported to an LRC Executive in January 1901: " We do not think it advisable to start as yet any uniform system of organization for the whole of the country . . ." They noted that ". . . some of our affiliated societies are already organized in certain constituencies. We think that these attempts should be encouraged by us, and be made the basis of a complete organization later on." It was recommended that the LRC's first efforts " should be directed to the constituencies fought by us at the recent (1900) general election. . . . That letters (should) be written to the secretaries of the trade councils, trade unions, socialist and other affiliated organizations . . . in these constituencies, asking them to get together as soon as possible a joint meeting, for the purpose of devising means for letting it be known that a Labour Candidate will be run again in the constituency . . ." [3] Out of these joint meetings there emerged a number of local LRCs. The " Basis and Constitution " of the Leicester LRC (adopted in 1901) gives an indication of the nature and scope of their work.[4] The object of the committee was declared to be " to unite the forces of Labour in order to secure the election of Independent Representation on all Local and National Governing bodies." And membership was to be open to " delegates from the Trades Council, Trade Unions, Co-operative Societies, ILP and other Labour and Socialist organizations that are willing to work for the objects, and conform

---

[1] *1905 LRC Annual Conference Report,* pp. 45-6.
[2] *1908 Labour Annual Conference Report,* p. 59.
[3] *Labour Party Documents,* Part I, folio 23.
[4] *Ibid.,* Part I, folios 83-6.

to the rules of this and the National Labour Representation Committee." It was further provided that " the Methods of Working shall be that affiliated societies shall be invited to send in nominations, both for Candidates and Wards to a General Meeting of the Committee, held at least three months before the election (except in cases of by-elections, when the Executive Committee shall have power to act). Candidates who are approved or selected at this meeting must be willing to stand as ' Labour Candidates,' independent of either political party, and to form distinct Labour Groups reporting periodically, or by request to this Committee." There was the further significant provision that " The Committee shall have power, if it thinks advisable, to run Candidates of its own, where no Candidate is nominated by an affiliated society." [1]

Local LRCs under varying names grew in number until there were almost one hundred in existence by 1906. An attempt was made at the 1903 conference to permit them to affiliate directly to the national LRC. Speaking in favour of the proposal, John Quinn (of the Builders Labourers) argued that as ". . . these committees were doing a useful work in educating people as to the necessity of Labour Representation, and that they were the direct outcome of conferences that have been held by (the LRC), he thought it was only fair and reasonable that . . . they should be allowed to be affiliated to the National body itself." [2] The proposal was defeated apparently on the grounds that such local work should be mainly the responsibility of the trades councils. Subsequently, however, at a meeting of the Executive of the LRC, Henderson moved that the Executive should propose to the 1905 conference " that in Constituencies which are not covered by a Trades Council the Labour Association for the whole Constituency will be eligible for affiliation if it accepts the constitution and policy of the National LRC." [3] The proposal was adopted by the Executive and in its report to the 1905 conference it stated: " We have been aware during the last twelve months of the remarkable growth of local Labour Representation Committees, which, on the whole, are modelled upon our Constitution, and are doing locally what we are doing nationally. . . . Before they were formed our only points of contact with constituencies were Trades Councils." The Executive

---

[1] For the purpose of local government elections only a number of " Municipal Workers Committees " were set up in some areas. The *1901 LRC Annual Conference Report*, Appendix, pp. 22-4, gives the constitutions of such committees set up in seven main cities.

[2] *1903 LRC Annual Conference Report*, p. 26.

[3] Minutes of the EC of the LRC, 27th September, 1904, *Labour Party Documents*, Part I, folio 266. The voting on Henderson's proposal is given as seven for, two against.

therefore recommended the affiliation of local LRCs and the revised constitution adopted by the 1905 conference made this provision.[1] Every effort was subsequently made to ensure that these local LRCs should preserve the " honourable alliance " between the socialist and trade union wings of the movement. Local LRCs which broke this alliance were refused affiliation. Thus the minutes of an Executive Committee meeting in 1906 record that an application for an affiliation had been received from the Leytonstone LRC but the Committee decided " that as none but Socialists can become Candidates under its Constitution, we cannot affiliate the (Leytonstone) committee." [2] It is important to note, however, that the great majority of these local LRCs retained the federal character of the national body; it was not possible for individuals to become members of the local LRCs; they could only associate themselves with its work by joining one of its constituent bodies. But in a few areas local Labour Associations were established on the basis of individual membership and these were the true forerunners of the present-day local Labour Parties. The most notable pioneer associations of this sort were Arthur Henderson's Labour and Progressive Association at Barnard Castle and similar organizations at Poplar and Woolwich.[3]

It would perhaps be inaccurate to describe the organization which existed nationally and in the constituencies on the eve of the 1906 elections as a political party in the sense that the Liberal and Conservative organizations of the day could be so described. As MacDonald later wrote, the LRC still conceived of itself as a *committee* to promote the election of Labour members to Parliament; and he added that the LRC still had " the limited mind of a Committee." [4] But however limited the LRC's conception of its rôle may have been, it is important to emphasize that by the eve of the 1906 election they had laid virtually the entire groundwork of the modern Labour Party. A parliamentary party had already been called into being and outside Parliament a mass organization of a strange and complex sort numbering well over 900,000 adherents was firmly established.

[1] See *1905 LRC Annual Conference Report,* p. 31, and Appendix II, p. 73. There can be little doubt that the original architects of the LRC had hoped sooner or later to encourage such local developments. Snowden in his *Autobiography* (Vol. I, p. 225) remarks that Keir Hardie never regarded the trade union basis of the Labour Party " as the permanent form of Labour representation."

[2] *Labour Party Documents,* Part II, folio 11.

[3] See, for example, *Fifty Years History of the Woolwich Labour Party* (1903-53), pp. 11 ff. See also Cole, G. D. H., *British Working Class Politics 1832-1914,* p. 231.

[4] MacDonald, J. R., *A Policy for the Labour Party,* p. 27.

There is little ground for surprise that the LRC managed to return 29 candidates in January 1906; they had polled, it is true, only 323,195 votes, a figure not much more than one-third of their total membership. But the explanation lies in the fact that only 50 seats were contested; in these seats the party polled 37 per cent. of the votes cast.[1]

There were comparatively few changes in the structure of the Labour Party during the twelve years that elapsed between the election of 1906 and the adoption of the new party constitution in 1918. The formal definition of the party's " Object " as set forth in the constitution as amended at the 1906 conference had read: " To organize and maintain a Parliamentary Labour Party, with its own Whips and policy," and to secure the election of candidates for this purpose.[2] Eleven years later, on the eve of the adoption of the new constitution, the official " Object " of the party had been modified merely by the addition of a single phrase. It read: " To organize and maintain in Parliament *and the country* a political Labour Party." [3] During the intervening years persistent efforts were made by various groups in the party to secure the adoption of either a specific programme or a broader statement of objectives. Thus, for example, at the 1907 conference a resolution was moved in very similar terms to the one which had been so surprisingly adopted without debate at the 1905 conference. It read: " This annual conference of the Labour Party hereby declares that its ultimate object shall be the obtaining for the workers the full results of their labour by the overthrow of the present competitive system of capitalism, and the institution of a system of public ownership and control of all the means of life." But on this occasion there was vigorous opposition; Bruce Glasier and Keir Hardie of the ILP both spoke against the motion, mainly on the ground that it would alienate many trade union supporters who were not socialists. The amendment to the constitution was overwhelmingly rejected by a vote of 98,000 to 835,000.

The supporters of the move were quite unabashed by their defeat and a year later they again proposed an alteration of the constitution in the same sense; again they were rebuffed, 91,000 to 951,000. It seems clear, however, that the basic objection of the Labour

[1] *1906 Labour Annual Conference Report*, pp. 5-6. It should also be noted that 24 of the 29 candidates who were elected faced no Liberal opponent; this was by far the most important explanation of their success. The way in which a Lib-Lab understanding was negotiated has now been fully examined in Bealey, F. and Pelling, H., *Labour and Politics 1900–1906*, Chapter VI.

[2] *Ibid.*, p. 72.

[3] *1917 Labour Annual Conference Report*, p. 152. [Italics mine.]

conference was not to the sense of the motion but to the proposal that it should be incorporated into the party constitution, for before it adjourned the same conference passed the following resolution: " That in the opinion of this Conference the time has arrived when the Labour Party should have as a definite object the socialization of the means of production, distribution, and exchange, to be controlled by a democratic State in the interest of the entire community; and the complete emancipation of Labour from the domination of capitalism and landlordism with the establishment of social and economic equality between the sexes." D. J. Shackleton, M.P., of the Textile Workers (who, it will be recalled, had been runner-up to Keir Hardie in the contest for the leadership in 1906) vehemently opposed the resolution because he said that it would convert the Labour Party into a socialist party; he believed that if the resolution was passed " it would put a hindrance in the way of (the Labour Party's) success. It would be breaking away from the federal understanding and making it possible for any member of a Trade Union to say, ' Are you a Socialist? ' And if the answer was ' No,' to reply, ' Then you do not represent the Labour Party '." Despite this warning the resolution was passed by 514,000 to 469,000. It had not, however, been proposed as a formal amendment to the party constitution and it was not included in the revised version of the constitution appended to the conference report.[1]

Periodically in succeeding years the conference rejected demands that the party should either formulate a specific programme or modify its constitution to incorporate a specifically socialist " Object". Yet the socialist element in the party had comparatively little difficulty in passing general resolutions reasserting that the party intended to work toward an ultimate socialist goal. Thus, for example, Bruce Glasier secured the adoption by the 1914 conference of a resolution which read in part: ". . . (the conference) again affirms that the aim of the Labour Movement is to abolish poverty and class oppression by bringing land and industrial capital under the ownership and control of the community for the collective good of all . . ." [2] Against this background, the action of the 1918 conference in incorporating into the party constitution a statement of socialist objectives is perhaps less surprising than is sometimes suggested. On a number of occasions before 1918 the conference had been willing to declare its general support for a socialist system of society. But even the sponsors of these resolu-

---

[1] *1908 Labour Annual Conference Report*, pp. 76-7, and Appendix III (Constitution as Revised under the Authority of the Hull Conference 1908), p. 102.

[2] *1914 Labour Annual Conference Report*, p. 113.

tions seem clearly to have realized that it would hinder their political purposes to force the incorporation of such a declaration into the party constitution.

Certainly during the years 1906–18 the " open and honourable alliance " between the socialists and trade unions seemed to be much too weak and precarious to stand the strain of a forcible conversion into a socialist party. The division of labour between the socialist societies and the trade unions was so strange that in retrospect it seems almost inconceivable that it should have proved workable at all. Throughout these years the total membership on which the socialist societies were affiliated ranged from 20,000 to 47,000, as against a trade union membership which ranged from approximately one million to almost 2½ million. Yet the socialist societies (and in particular the ILP) provided the overwhelming proportion of such proselytizing zeal as animated the Labour Party during these years; and in addition throughout a large part of the country the ILP was in effect the only real constituency organization of the party.

On the eve of the First World War the Labour Party still had no system of individual membership except in one or two areas. There were local LRC and trades councils carrying on the work of the party in a total of only 158 areas. The ILP on the other hand claimed in 1914 some 672 branches. Admittedly some of these were tiny organizations which in some towns were federated in a single urban organization and it is significant that only 244 ILP branches were represented at their 1914 conference.[1] But there can be no doubt that in many areas the ILP provided the only effective local Labour Party organization. It provided also an important influence in the formulation of party policy at the national level. A Standing Committee to co-ordinate the work of the ILP and the Fabian Society had been established in the years immediately before the war; of its work Beatrice Webb could write in October 1912: " The Standing Committee . . . is controlling the policy of the Labour and Socialist movement in this country—in so far as this movement has any policy." [2] But two years later she had to concede that the trade unions could still determine the pace at which the policies formulated and " controlled " by the ILP and the Fabian Society were formally adopted by the party in Parliament. " The middle and working-class Socialists (she wrote in February 1914) are in a quandary. They are hopelessly outnumbered within the Labour Party, and whenever they protest they are voted down. They have pledged themselves to working-class representation as part of the

---

[1] *1914 ILP Conference Report*, p. 8.
[2] *Beatrice Webb's Diaries 1912-24*, p. 6.

process of making the manual labourer conscious of his disinherited condition, and of arousing, in the working class, faith in the class struggle. But they are by their adhesion to the present Parliamentary Party bolstering up a fraud—pretending, to the outside world, that these respectable but reactionary Trade Union officials are the leaders of the Social Revolution."[1]

These two comments cast an important light on the relationship between the two elements in the honourable alliance. The socialist societies could generate as many ideas and as much energy as they wished. From time to time they could even secure the adoption of conference resolutions affirming broad socialist goals as the ultimate object of the Labour Party. But the trade unions provided the overwhelming proportion of the mass membership and the funds of the party; the Labour Party could move only as far and as rapidly as the trade unions were prepared to follow. One of the best definitions of the working relationship between the constituent elements of the party was given by G. J. Wardle (Chairman of the NEC for 1917), who said: " From the very first the ties which bound the party together were of the loosest possible kind. It has steadily, and, in my opinion, wisely, always declined to be bound by any programme, to subscribe to any dogma, or to lay down any creed. . . . On the contrary, its strength has been its catholicity, its tolerance, its welcoming of all shades of political and even revolutionary thought, providing that its chief object—the unifying of the workers' political power—was not damaged or hindered thereby." [2]

The only other major change in the party constitution during the period 1906–18 was the consequence of the Osborne judgment, given in the House of Lords in December 1909. W. V. Osborne, a member of the Amalgamated Society of Railway Servants, had sought an injunction to prevent his union from diverting a part of its funds to support the Labour Party. The issue was carried through the courts to the House of Lords and their decision sustained Osborne's contention; they ruled in effect that all political action by trade unions was *ultra vires*. Henceforth trade unions could not legally put forward their own candidates or subscribe funds to the work of the Labour Party. This, of course, was a body blow at the party and proved a grave hindrance to its work during 1910, the year of the double election. To meet the situation the NEC made two proposals to the 1911 conference.[3] They first attempted

---

[1] *Beatrice Webb's Diaries 1912-24*, p. 19.

[2] *1917 Labour Annual Conference Report*, p. 82.

[3] Manuscript minutes of the NEC, 29th September, 1910, and 20th December, 1910, *Labour Party Documents*, Part II, folios 153, 170-1.

to meet one of the principal criticisms of the party constitution which had frequently been made in the course of the Osborne litigation. It had been ruled that the pledge of the Labour M.P.s to abide by the decisions of the parliamentary party was " contrary to public policy." [1] After a heated debate the 1911 conference decided that candidates should no longer be required to sign such a pledge. The amended rule would henceforth read: " Candidates and Members must maintain this Constitution; appear before their constituencies under the title of Labour Candidates only; abstain strictly from identifying themselves with or promoting the interests of any other Party; and accept the responsibilities established by Parliamentary practice." Bruce Glasier led the attack on this proposed change and he was supported by Keir Hardie. Although Hardie was a member of the NEC he denounced the proposal; " the recommendation of the Executive meant (he said) that they had allowed themselves to be terrified by the dicta of the Law Lords." MacDonald and Henderson succeeded, however, in securing the adoption of the Executive's proposal. [2]

The other NEC recommendation made in response to the Osborne judgment was to the effect that the conference should pledge itself to secure the passage through Parliament of a new Act guaranteeing trade unions their political rights. When no action had been taken by the following year, the 1912 conference assembled in belligerent mood. The Sheffield Trades Council moved " That as Trade Unions have had the right, by a forty years' custom prior to the Osborne decision, to levy themselves for Labour Representation, we instruct the Labour Party Executive to take immediate action to obtain the complete reversal of that judgment and restore to Trade Unions the right to levy themselves for the support of direct representatives in Parliament and on public boards, should they so decide by a majority vote of their members." A. G. Cameron (of the Amalgamated Carpenters and Joiners) moved an

[1] *1911 Labour Annual Conference Report,* p. 23. Parliamentary candidates had been required to sign the following undertaking: " Candidates and Members must accept this Constitution; agree to abide by the decisions of the Parliamentary Party in carrying out the aims of this Constitution; appear before their constituencies under the title of Labour Candidates only; abstain strictly from identifying themselves with or promoting the interests of any Parliamentary Party not affiliated, or its Candidates; and they must not oppose any Candidate recognized by the National Executive of the Party."

[2] *Ibid.,* pp. 78-84. Snowden subsequently remarked drily: " I don't know that (this change) made such practical difference. I had never found the pledge to be an embarrassment to my independent judgment. Indeed I doubt if I ever signed it." Snowden, Viscount, *An Autobiography,* Vol. I, p. 224.

amendment which added: " and until it is reversed we advise all Trade Unions affiliated to our Party to defy the law, and in this way prove that we are determined to use our funds according to the decision of the majority of our members." The amendment was put and carried: and the resolution, as amended, was then " unanimously agreed to." [1] It is impossible in retrospect to discover what effect, if any, this recommendation that trade unions should take illegal action may have had. The Labour Party published no trade union membership figures for the year 1912–13; in all subsequent recapitulations of the history of the party membership a note appears stating: " Owing to the operation of the Osborne Judgment it was made impossible to compile membership statistics for 1913." [2]

The Liberal Government passed a new trade union act in 1913 which went a considerable way toward meeting the demands of the Labour Party. In addition to defining the industrial objects or trade unions it provided that they might legitimately adopt certain specific political objects. Political expenditure by trade unions was legalized, but it could be made only from a separate political fund. The fund could be set up only after a favourable ballot vote by the union membership. It was further provided that any member could claim exemption from payment of the political levy without thereby sacrificing any of his other union rights. The Osborne controversy appears to have had no lasting effect on trade union affiliation to the party. Affiliated membership had reached a high point of 1,800,000 by 1912. The report to the 1914 conference recorded a trade union membership of 1,500,000 and a recovery the following year to just over two million. No subsequent legal action was taken to destroy the " honourable alliance". It remained for the party itself to re-organize the basis of that alliance by the adoption of a new constitution in 1918.

The Labour Party, as Henderson told the annual conference which assembled in January 1918, " had never in the proper sense claimed to be a national political party." They had been no more than " a political federation " of trade unions and socialist bodies and a small number of local Labour Parties which had co-operated together to elect Labour representatives to Parliament. But, as Henderson warned the conference, without a broader organizational basis and a more clearly defined objective the party could not possibly take advantage of the enormous opportunities which were clearly opening before it at the close of the First World War. In the

[1] *1912 Labour Annual Conference Report*, pp. 90-1.
[2] See, for example, *1953 Labour Annual Conference Report*, p. 32.

course of the war the Labour movement had won full recognition as a major partner in the national effort; and it had taken the lead in a variety of campaigns to protect the standard of living and to advance the interests of the working population. With ample justification, the NEC could point (in its report to the January 1918 conference) to the development of a new " community consciousness " and could add that the Labour Party " has been definitely accepted by ever-increasing numbers of the public as its concrete expression." And many of these " ever-increasing numbers " were for the first time to be accorded the right to vote. As Henderson reminded the conference, " the last register made up in 1914 contained in round figures 8 million electors. The first register under the new (Representation of the People) Act ought to contain about 16 million electors." At least 12,500,000 of these stood outside the Labour Movement and under the party's present constitution they " could not enter . . . except through narrow gates." [1]

It was particularly doubtful whether the millions of newly enfranchised women (most of whom in any case were not eligible to join trade unions) would consider joining any of the tiny and somewhat sectarian socialist societies, whose membership after several decades of political activity numbered no more than 75,000. In any case, few of the party leaders were content to see the ILP continue as the main focal point of constituency activity. Its attitude to the war had rendered it suspect throughout wide areas of the Labour movement and, although the gulf was narrowing during the closing stages of the war, it was clear that most of the moderate party leaders were reluctant to see the ILP resume its old functions. There could be little doubt, as Henderson claimed, that millions of new voters would be prepared to consider supporting Labour candidates. Yet 78 was the highest number of candidates the party had ever run in a previous election.[2] There was clearly therefore a need for a new system of constituency organization which would cover the whole country.

As Henderson put it to the party conference of January 1918, there were two possibilities. They could scrap the whole of the existing party machinery and begin afresh. The Labour Party could cease to be a federation and they could " begin to build up from a new foundation a political organization depending only upon individual membership." Henderson confessed that the idea

[1] *The Book of the Labour Party*, Vol. I, p. 227.
[2] This was in the first election of 1910; if all of these candidates had been elected Labour would still have had smaller parliamentary representation than the Irish Party.

tempted him. " Speaking as an old electioneerer he did not mind saying that if he had to begin afresh that would be the ideal at which he would aim." But with a general election imminent, so drastic a reorganization would be unwise. And in any case he could not imagine the Executive " saying to the Trade Unions upon whom the Party had depended that they had no further use for them." The Executive had therefore decided " to stick by the Federation, but to graft on to it such a form of constituency organization, linked up with the local Labour Parties or Trades Councils, as would remove the (present) limitations (on the development of constituency organization)," and would ensure that " the Federation and the constituency organization (were brought) into close contact with the Annual Conference and the National Executive."

The new party constitution which Henderson laid before the conference (on behalf of the NEC) therefore proposed (section 2) that " the Labour Party shall consist of all its affiliated organizations, together with those men and women who are individual members of a local Labour Party and who subscribe to the constitution and programme of the Party." Provision was also made for representation of local Labour Parties at the annual conference and for their representation on the National Executive. Henceforth the Executive should consist of 23 members [1] composed as follows: (a) 13 representatives of the affiliated organizations; (b) five representatives of the local Labour Parties; (c) four women, and the Treasurer. Candidates for the latter post could be nominated by any affiliated organization and the nominees would be voted upon by the whole conference. The remainder of the Executive would be nominated as follows: the thirteen representatives of the affiliated organizations would be nominated by the " national organizations," a category which henceforth would include both the trade unions *and* the socialist societies; the local Labour Parties would nominate their representatives; and candidates for the four places reserved for women could be nominated by any affiliated organization. *The separate lists of nominations would, however, be voted upon by the entire conference.*

The new procedure for nomination and voting for the Executive was, of course, of major importance. It destroyed in one stroke the system of " reserved places " which had guaranteed that there

---

[1] Henderson originally proposed that the NEC should consist of 21 members (11 representing affiliated organizations; five for the Local Labour Parties; four women and the Treasurer), but on the insistence of the trade unions at the adjourned conference in February, 1918, (see below) the representation of the affiliated organizations was increased to 13 and the total NEC membership to 23.

should be three representatives of socialist societies, and one for the trade councils on the Executive. For the first time *it placed in the hands of the trade unions the power to determine the composition of the entire Executive.* In light of Henderson's comment (that he would have preferred ideally to have based the party organization solely on individual membership) there is not much reason to doubt that he must have been reluctant to place the control of the party organization so exclusively in the hands of the trade unions. But the reason why he made this proposal is evident enough. The trade union leaders were uneasy and suspicious about the new scheme for local Labour Party representation and they would almost certainly have flatly refused to accord the local parties separate representation on the NEC if this were to be offered in addition to the three reserved places for the socialist societies. Even in the form in which Henderson proposed it, the new constitution met considerable trade union resistance. J. Sexton (of the Dock Labourers) argued that the old constitution was sufficiently broad " to let anybody in who wanted to come in." The new constitution would destroy the whole basis of the alliance; " the only thing left (he said) appeared to be the name of the Labour Party."

Other trade union speakers expressed sympathy with Henderson's purpose but they were dubious and uneasy about the new constitutional arrangements. There were calls for delay in the adoption of the new constitution. In reply Egerton Wake reminded the conference that " The pamphlet containing the new proposals was issued to the affiliated organizations in November (1917): and by 15th December amendments were received from at least twenty affiliated organizations." But Robert Smillie (of the Miners Federation) had moved " that the whole question of the Constitution be referred back to the affiliated Societies and that a Conference be called at an early date finally to consider the same." Philip Snowden for the ILP was severely critical of Smillie's proposal. A general election would be upon them in a matter of months; " was it to be said of the Labour Party as had been said of the Government owing to its management of the War: always too late? . . . . The ILP begged the conference to sacrifice all else so that the recommendations of the Executive might be approved." Smillie's motion for delay was nevertheless carried (for: 1,337,000; against: 1,318,000). George Lansbury immediately proposed that the adjournment should be for a period of one month only, and this was agreed.[1]

The conference reassembled for a one-day session on 26th

[1] *January, 1918, Labour Annual Conference Report*, pp. 98-104.

February, 1918, and proceeded to adopt the new constitution with only a few comparatively minor amendments. Two of these have already been noted: the representation of the affiliated national organizations on the NEC was increased from 11 to 13 [1] and the Parliamentary Labour Party insisted upon and was granted joint responsibility with the NEC for formulating the party's election programme. [2] The conference also decided that Labour candidates should have rather less latitude than the Executive proposed in dealing with issues on which the party had not specifically pronounced. Candidates would be required (as the Executive suggested) to give prominence in their election addresses and constituency campaigns to the issues selected by the NEC and the PLP for incorporation in the party's national election programme; but the Executive had further suggested that they should " remain free to include, in addition, any other proposals not inconsistent therewith, and to discuss any other subjects at their own discretion . . ." The conference decided that this permissive clause should be dropped from the constitution, a decision which no doubt reflected the old view that Labour M.P.s must continue to be primarily servants of the movement.

The 1918 constitution also for the first time embodied a declaration of the Labour Party's ultimate objective. Hitherto, the constitution had declared the sole object of the party to be " to organize and maintain in Parliament and the country a political Labour Party." But the new constitution declared that one of the party's objects was " To secure for the producers by hand or by brain the full fruits of their industry, and the most equitable distribution thereof that may be possible, upon the basis of the common ownership of the means of production, and the best obtainable system of popular administration and control of each industry or service." Resolutions in a similar vein had been passed by other party conferences, but now for the first time this careful (if somewhat ambiguously phrased) definition of a socialist objective was incorporated into the party constitution. The decision to incorporate this clause no doubt reflected the influence of Webb [3]; it reflected also a growing acceptance within the trade union movement of the argument that Labour had won all it could hope to win as a pressure group devoted to extracting concessions from the capitalist parties. The speeches of some of the trade union delegates to the February conference suggest that they were uneasy about this

[1] See p. 477 above.
[2] See p. 407 above.
[3] See Middleton, J. S., " Webb and the Labour Party," in *The Webbs and Their Work* (ed. Margaret Cole), London, 1949, pp. 167 ff.

new socialist commitment. But their fears were no doubt lulled by the fact that the new constitution had placed overwhelming, and indeed, one might almost say, exclusive, control over the party in the hands of the trade union element.

At a further party conference held in June 1918 the party proceeded to adopt a more elaborate statement of its objectives based on the policy statement drafted by Webb entitled *Labour and the New Social Order*. The NEC did not submit the document itself to the conference but proposed instead 26 policy resolutions based upon *Labour and the New Social Order*. The resolutions dealt also with a number of points which had been omitted or treated very briefly in Webb's statement. The whole group of policy resolutions was adopted with few major amendments. During 1918 the Labour Party thus provided itself with a broad definition of its objectives and a specific set of policies which became the basis for its electoral programmes both in 1918 and to some extent in the campaigns which the party fought in later years. The transformation of the Labour Party was now complete. The " Committee " established in 1900 to secure the election of Labour Members of Parliament had fostered the formation of a new parliamentary party; it had transformed itself into a mass political party; and at long last it had formulated a statement of policy and declared its goals.

The functioning of the separate units of the new party organization established in 1918 is examined in some detail below, but several more general comments must also be made. First, it should be noted that the new constitution eliminated the representation of the trades councils from the Executive. The NEC reported to the January 1918 conference that " at the present moment " there were 146 trades councils associated with the party.[1] They had had a long and honourable association with the movement and had increased rapidly in number during the war when many new trades councils had been formed primarily for the purpose of providing trade union representation on the various local *ad hoc* organizations set up in connection with the war effort. Many national trade union leaders were inclined, however, to view the trades councils with suspicion on the ground that they had tended to become a focal point of left-wing militancy within the trade union movement. The trades councils therefore had few powerful friends to speak on their behalf when Henderson proposed in effect that they should cease to serve as the principal local agents in their areas for Labour Party political activity. Subsequent conference reports reflected a steady decline in the number of trades councils affiliated to the party.

[1] *January 1918 Labour Annual Conference Report* (Report of the NEC), p. 23.

The new constitution was ultimately to have an even more serious impact on the rôle of the ILP within the Labour Party, although its effects were not immediately evident. The NAC of the ILP did, however, sense danger. In its report to its own conference in April 1918, the NAC recalled that the ILP had " never regarded the constitution of the Labour Party as being satisfactory from the democratic point of view." Too much attention had had to be paid to what the NAC described as the " scruples and susceptibilities and jealousies of the Trade Unionists . . . (and, they added) A democratic party dependent upon the financial support of powerful and wealthy trade unions can never be a democratic party in the true sense of the word." The NAC hinted broadly that it would like to have seen a basic transformation in the structure of the party but conceded that Henderson's proposals were " probably as revolutionary as the powerful Trade Unions affiliated to the Party would accept." The NAC recalled that at the adjourned meeting of the party conference in February 1918 they had proposed an amendment designed " to maintain the federal representation on the Executive, and to restore the old system by which the Socialist bodies elected their direct representatives to the Executive." This proposal had been rejected (for: 345,000; against: 1,839,000) in favour of a 23-member Executive all of whose members would be elected by the whole conference. The NAC remarked bitterly, " Under this system the large Trade Unions will, as they have hitherto done, completely dominate the policy of the Party, without even the influence which the direct Socialist representation on the Executive has been able to exercise in the past." They warned that henceforth even if an ILP nominee should be elected to the Executive by the Labour conference, ". . . he will not be elected to represent the ILP, but to represent the Labour Party Conference."

The NAC also warned that the new local Labour Parties catering for an individual membership ". . . will come into competition with the branches of the Independent Labour Party." In part, this would be the result of the fact that the local Labour Parties would make much smaller demands on both the energies and the financial resources of its members. However, the ILP consoled itself by adding: " A large membership is not necessarily a source of strength. The strength of a Party depends upon the character and enthusiasm of its individual members, and we have no doubt that the ILP with its unceasing activities, its persistent propaganda and the inspiring idealism of its Socialism and Internationalism, will continue to attract all the men and women into its membership who are really of value to the effectiveness of a political party."

They therefore wished the new Labour Parties well in the hope that they would " stimulate rather than injure the local branches of the ILP." Certainly, the NAC decided, it ought to be possible for the new local parties to recruit many active workers from among the vast numbers of trade unionists affiliated to the party. " We shall be glad (the NAC report concluded) to see these two million nominal adherents beginning to do the active propaganda work for the Labour Party which hitherto has been done almost solely by the ILP." [1]

At first it seemed as if this combination of petulance and optimism might prove to be justified. The local Labour Parties grew rapidly in number and for some years after 1918 the ILP also reported a steady increase in its own membership. The figures concealed, however, a fundamental transformation which was taking place in the rôle of the ILP. Nothing could alter the fact that it was in the process of being superseded in the rôle it had played as the principal local propaganda agency of the Labour Party both between and during elections. The ILP itself became increasingly involved in furious internal ideological disputes; it was ultimately to become no more than a socialist debating society. The local Labour Parties inevitably became the real focal point of party activity in the constituencies and it is important to note that their life was qualitatively different from that of the ILP. They did not enjoy the national autonomy of the affiliated societies; they much more nearly resembled local branches of the national organization of the party. Their subservient status was a source of endless friction within the party and led to repeated demands that they should be accorded a greater share in the control of the affairs of the party.

This demand was finally met in 1937 when the only basic modification of the 1918 constitution was adopted. The NEC proposed to the 1937 conference that representation of the constituency parties on the Executive should be increased from five to seven; the further, more striking, recommendation was added that these seven representatives should be elected by the vote of the constituency delegates alone (and that the twelve trade union representatives and the one representative of the socialist societies should also be elected separately by their respective conference delegations). The first recommendation was carried by a vote of 1,408,000 to 1,134,000 and the second by the comfortable majority of 1,814,000 to 658,000.[2] Thus for the first time since before the adoption of the 1918 constitution the trade unions no longer had at their disposal all of the places on the NEC, although

[1] *1918 ILP Conference Report* (Report of the NAC), pp. 19-22.
[2] *1937 Labour Annual Conference Report*, p. 154.

they were still in effective control of 18 of the 25 elected places on the Executive.[1]

Only one other major event in the years after 1918 affected the rôle of the trade unions within the Labour Party organization. The Trade Union Act of 1913 had provided, it will be recalled, that a member of a trade union which was affiliated to the Labour Party could ensure that no part of the funds he subscribed to his union could be used for political purposes by signing a form " contracting-out " of the political levy.[2] Critics of this provision of the 1913 Act argued that it made it inevitable that the lethargic and the timid among the trade unionists could be too easily delivered into the hands of the Labour Party. It was thus provided in the Trade Unions and Trades Disputes Act passed by the Conservative Government in 1927 that the process should be reversed; henceforth members of trade unions affiliated to the Labour Party who wished some part of their subscription to be devoted to political purposes were required to sign a form " contracting-in". The factor of inertia thus no longer operated in favour of the Labour Party. It is difficult to see how it could be argued that a great issue of principle was involved,[3] but Labour Party leaders nevertheless maintained vehemently that this iniquitous provision in the 1927 Act should be reversed; within a year of taking office the 1945 Labour Government had done so.[4]

The effects of the 1927 Act and of the 1946 repeal of its provisions respecting the political levy are shown in the official party membership figures. In 1927, before the Act became operative, 3,238,939 party members were affiliated through their trade unions. In the following year the number fell by one-third to 2,025,139,[5] and until

[1] For a further discussion of trade union influence in the Executive, see p. 517 below.

[2] For a further discussion of the political levy, see Cole, G. D. H., *A History of the Labour Party from 1914*, Appendix IV.

[3] The Conservatives as well as the Labour Party, claimed there was. But Alfred Duff Cooper, then a Conservative M.P., recalls that when he discussed the issue privately with officials at Central Office they " confessed crudely that their object was to deplete the funds of the Labour Party." (Duff Cooper, *Old Men Forget*, London, 1953, p. 143.)

[4] During the 1951 election campaign Winston Churchill announced that " The Conservative Party has no intention of initiating any legislation affecting trade unions should we become responsible in the new Parliament " (*The Times*, 13th October, 1951). And Maxwell Fyfe added that " whether the political levy is paid by contracting in or contracting out is an internal matter which the unions should be permitted to settle for themselves " (*The Times*, 20th October, 1951).

[5] Part of this decline can be accounted for by the disaffiliation of the civil service unions who were forbidden under the Act to affiliate to any political party.

the end of the Second World War it hovered in the vicinity of the two million mark. Even with the return of Labour to power in 1945 it rose to only just over two and a half million. But when the 1946 legislation became operative the number of trade unionists affiliated to the party jumped spectacularly (in 1947) to almost 4,400,000.[1] It seems fairly clear from these figures that the contracting-out arrangement is worth between one and one and a half million members to the Labour Party. There could hardly be more convincing evidence of the lack of significance attached to their Labour Party membership by a large proportion of those who are affiliated through their trade unions.

Changes in the constitution of the Labour Party since 1918 have on the whole been surprisingly few. There has been no equivalent to the wholesale reorganizations of the mass party which have frequently taken place on the Conservative side following the defeat of the party at a general election. This may reflect the unconscious assumption by the Conservatives (which they state explicitly on only rare occasions) that they are the natural rulers of the country; other things being equal, the Conservatives appear to assume that their party will be in power. When they are defeated they seek, with an air of incredulity, for a possible explanation. They inevitably seem to assume that they have somehow been betrayed by the inefficiency of their own machinery. The active party workers demand and usually obtain an extensive reorganization of the National Union; heads roll, and there is a major transformation of the party. Perhaps because Labour is surprised by victory rather than defeat, there are fewer recriminations and less tendency to demand wholesale reorganization after the party has suffered a defeat.[2]

---

[1] Fourteen years later the NEC reported to the 1961 party conference that the total membership of affiliated trade unions was 5,512,688 (total party membership: 6,328,330). *1961 Labour Annual Conference Report* (Report of the NEC), p. 37. The total membership of unions affiliated to the TUC at that time was 8,299,393. It would therefore appear that approximately 63 per cent. of the TUC membership is affiliated to the Labour Party. The equivalent figure for the first twenty years of the party's history was about 50 per cent. rising to a previous high point in 1927 of approximately 65 per cent. While the 1927 Trades Disputes Act was operative the proportion of TUC members affiliated to the Labour Party ranged between 45 per cent. and 30 per cent. See Flanders, Alan, *British Trade Unionism*, p. 49.

[2] For a discussion of the Wilson Committee set up to examine the party's electoral machinery after the 1955 defeat, see McKenzie, R. T., " The Wilson Report and the Future of the Labour Party Organization," *Political Studies*, Vol. IV, No. 1, February, 1956.

II

THE MODERN STRUCTURE OF THE LABOUR PARTY [1]

The Annual Conference

Those who write and speak for the Labour Party customarily refer to the annual conference as if it were in every sense the governing body of the party. Clement Attlee's own conception of the conference was quoted in Chapter I; it will be recalled that he claimed that the Labour Party annual conference is " the final authority of the Labour Party . . . . a Parliament of the movement . . . . (It) lays down the policy of the Party, and issues instructions which must be carried out by the Executive, the affiliated organizations, and its representatives in Parliament and on local authorities." This same conception of the rôle of the party conference is to be found in much of the official party literature. Reference was also made in Chapter I to *The Rise of the Labour Party* (issued in 1948 by the party head office for use in discussion groups throughout the party) which stated (p. 14): ". . . in the Labour Party, the final word rests with the Annual Party Conference, and between Conferences the National Executive Committee is the administrative authority. The Parliamentary Party carries through its duties within the framework of policy laid down by the Annual Party Conference to which it reports each year. The Parliamentary Party has no power to issue orders to the National Executive, or the Executive to the Parliamentary Party. Both are responsible only to the Party Conference." [2]

These passages grossly exaggerate the rôle of the conference in the affairs of the Labour Party. They appear to imply that Labour M.P.s and hence, by implication, the PLP and even a Labour Government must be subject to the direction of the annual conference; but, as was shown in Chapter VII, the PLP is autonomous and the annual conference has no control whatever over the actions of a Labour Government. The party constitution states that " the work of the Party shall be under the direction and control of the Party Conference . . ." ; but this can only mean " the work of the Party *outside Parliament*." In other words the mass organization of the Labour Party is self-governing; but so is the National Union. There is only one significant difference between the parties in this respect: the professional organization of the Labour Party is responsible to the annual conference through the NEC, while the profes-

---

[1] See Table 7 at p. 487.
[2] See pp. 10–11 above.

sional organization of the Conservative Party is responsible only to the Leader through the Chairman of the Party Organization. There appears to be a further and important contrast in the rôle of the annual conferences of the two parties in that the Labour conference is nominally accorded the right to lay down the basic principles and long-range goals of the party. But, as was noted in Chapter VII, the list of " Party Objects " includes the significant phrase, " to give effect *as far as may be practicable* to the principles from time to time approved by the Party Conference." (Italics mine.) The constitution does not indicate which organ of the party has the right to determine the " practicability " of the principles approved by the conference. But it would seem fair to assume that in the first instance this is the responsibility of the NEC. And in any case it is perfectly clear that the PLP also has the right to refuse to attempt to apply any principle approved by the conference if, in the view of the PLP, it is not practicable.

The Labour annual conference is also formally accorded an important rôle in the formulation of the party programme. The constitution states: " The Party conference shall decide from time to time what specific proposals of legislative, financial or administrative reform shall be included in the Party Programme." But there is this important qualification: " no proposal shall be included in the Party Programme unless it has been adopted by the Party Conference by a majority of not less than two-thirds of the votes recorded on a card vote." This provision obviously represents a formidable hurdle for any minority group within the party which attempts to convert the conference to support a particular proposal for inclusion in the party programme. Since the trade unions normally cast five-sixths of the votes in the party conference it seems clear that under this clause no proposal can be included in the party programme unless it has the support of rather more than half the trade unions affiliated to the party. Even after a specific proposal has been adopted by the conference there is no assurance that it will be incorporated into the party's election manifesto. It has already been noted that the NEC and the PLP must *jointly* decide which items shall be included in the manifesto and there can be little doubt that the influence of the PLP in these joint discussions is preponderant, if for no other reason than that the NEC normally includes a majority of PLP members. And if the PLP is in office, the members of the Government, as has already been shown, have a decisive voice in determining what items shall be included in the election manifesto. Finally, as will be seen below, the system of voting at the conference helps to ensure that the NEC normally remains in effective control of the affairs of the conference.

TABLE 7

THE LABOUR PARTY

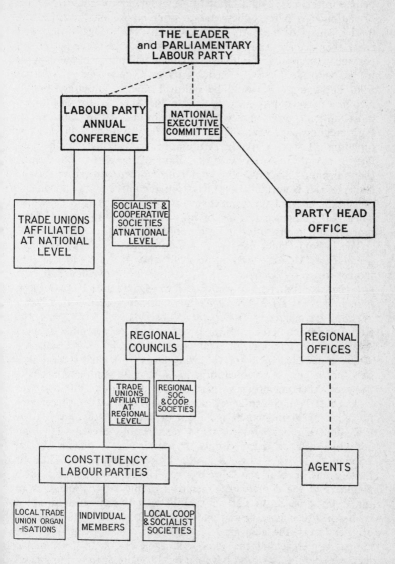

Despite their many differences the Conservative and Labour conferences have certain important functions in common. Both conferences provide an opportunity for the ardent partisans who belong to the mass organization to meet together to debate questions of national or party policy and to offer advice on these matters to the leaders of the party in Parliament. The delegates hear and cheer their leaders and, quite frequently, criticize them. It would be unconstitutional if either parliamentary party allowed itself to be controlled and directed by its own mass party organization, but equally it would be political suicide for either parliamentary party consistently to ignore the annual assembly of its most militant and hard-working supporters. The Conservative Party acknowledges that the conference has no more than advisory functions. Labour Party literature appears to imply that the conference has a decisive voice in the affairs of the party. But despite the enormous difficulties the conference sometimes makes for the leadership, it is normally kept in effective control by the adroit use of certain internal party mechanisms; and on the rare occasions when the conference gets out of control it usually succeeds in little more than demonstrating its own impotence.

The Labour conference normally meets once a year for four and a half days (Monday morning to Friday noon) usually in late September or early October. It is considerably smaller than the Conservative conference (averaging since 1945 about 1,100 delegates, plus approximately 200 *ex officio* members, compared with a membership averaging 3,600 for the Conservatives); but, like the Conservative conference, it is large enough to resemble a mass meeting rather than a serious deliberative assembly. Representation at the conference is on the following basis: (*a*) Each trade union or other affiliated national organization may send one delegate for each 5,000 members or part thereof on whom affiliation fees were paid; (*b*) Constituency parties may also send one delegate for each 5,000 individual members or part thereof and if their individual and affiliated women's membership exceeds 2,500 an additional woman delegate may be appointed; (*c*) Each Central Labour Party (in a divided borough) or Federation of Labour Parties may appoint one delegate; (*d*) The following are *ex officio* members of the conference: members of the NEC; members of the PLP; prospective Labour candidates who have been adopted by a constituency party and endorsed by the NEC; the Secretary of the Party; the chairman and one delegate appointed by the annual conference of the Labour League of Youth. *Ex officio* members do not, however, have the right to vote or to be nominated for office unless they have also been appointed as delegates. Local party agents are also customarily allowed to attend the conference although the constitution does not accord them even *ex officio* status. These arrangements provide a potential conference representation of over 2,500 delegates and *ex officio* members, but normally the total conference membership is only approximately three-fifths of this potential figure. Table 8 below shows the actual and potential membership at three representative post-war

TABLE 8

DELEGATES AT LABOUR PARTY CONFERENCES

	1948		1949		1950	
	Actual	Potential	Actual	Potential	Actual	Potential
Trade Unions .	501	933	547	1,004	567	1,048
Constituency and Borough Parties .	584	658	600	675	606	678
Federations . .	18	25	18	24	17	23
Socialist and Co-operative Societies	11	14	10	12	10	12
Totals . .	1,114	1,630	1,175	1,715	1,200	1,761
Ex officio Members	184	513	253	614	215	591
Totals . .	1,298	2,143	1,428	2,329	1,415	2,352
Agents . . .	85	157	. 92	204	146	252
Grand totals .	1,383	2,300	1,520	2,533	1,561	2,604
Difference between actual and potential . . .	−917		−1,013		−1,043	

conferences (1948, 1949 and 1950). It will be noted that in these years the trade unions sent approximately one-half the delegates to which they were entitled. The constituency parties and affiliated societies, on the other hand, took up almost all the places to which they were entitled; each year, indeed, they outnumbered the trade union delegates. This served to emphasize the disparity in voting strength between the constituency element in the party and the trade unions, since at the 1950 conference, for example, the 633 delegates from the constituency parties, the socialist and co-operative societies had a potential voting strength of approximately one million against a voting strength of just over five million for the 567 trade union delegates. In other words, rather less than half the delegates cast five-sixths of the votes.

The time of the conference is normally taken up as follows: the proceedings open with the election of a chairman (since 1904 the chairman of the NEC has normally been elected), and after speeches of welcome from the mayor of the town in which the conference is being held and by the chairman of the constituency Labour Party, the chairman of the conference gives his opening address. Thereafter the Conference Arrangements Committee makes a report outlining the order of business which it proposes for the week. The conference then receives a report from the NEC (which has been printed in advance) and which is subject to debate by the conference. Delegates may attempt to refer back sections of the report which do not meet with their approval, although such efforts are rarely successful. Thereafter the Leader of the Party speaks to the report of the PLP which has also been laid before the delegates and which is again subject to debate. Frequently one day or more of conference time is taken up by a debate on a major statement of policy presented by the NEC. For example, the 1945 conference spent the best part of three days discussing *Let Us Face the Future*; in 1949 two days were devoted to a discussion of *Labour Believes in Britain* and in 1953 a discussion of *Challenge to Britain* took up nearly four days of conference time. Normally, however, from two to two-and-a-half days are available for discussion of resolutions proposed by affiliated organizations or constituency parties.

Until 1947 affiliated organizations were permitted to submit two resolutions and two amendments for the conference agenda, but by a decision of the conference of that year they were limited to one resolution and one amendment with the further provision that they could submit an additional resolution and an amendment to the party constitution every third year when the constitution of the party is subject to review. In an ordinary year therefore it is theoretically possible for the conference to be faced with approximately 800 resolutions and 800 amendments and in a "constitutional" year as many as 1,600 resolutions and amendments. But a great many organizations do not avail themselves of the opportunity to submit resolutions or amendments; the following table shows the number actually submitted for the conferences of 1948, 1949 and 1950:

TABLE 9

	1948	1949	1950
Resolutions Submitted	303	217	361
Amendments to Resolutions	94	50	85
Amendments to Constitution	—	—	10

Inevitably the resolutions submitted tend to deal with perhaps ten or a dozen major subjects which are currently of concern to the party and the nation, and in the " preliminary agenda " the resolutions are grouped under broad topic headings. The following table shows the number of resolutions submitted to the 1948–49–50 conferences dealing with the subjects indicated:

TABLE 10

	Number of Resolutions		
	1948	1949	1950
Wages, Prices and Profits, Cost of Living	39	19	59
Housing and Building, Rents and Sale of Houses	20	33	30
Foreign Affairs	15	6	27
General Election Programme	1	17	11
Nationalized Industries	15	8	13
Distribution	6	3	18
Marginal, Rural and Backward Areas	4	—	15
Rating and Derating	5	8	6

The closing date for the receipt of resolutions at party head office is " not later than 12 clear weeks " before the conference meets. The resolutions are then dispatched to all affiliated organizations. If any organization wishes to submit amendments it must do so not later than six clear weeks before the opening of the conference. These again are classified, printed by the head office and returned to the affiliated organizations by approximately four weeks before the opening of the conference.

During this four-week period the affiliated organizations have an opportunity to discuss the final agenda and, if they wish, indicate to their delegates how they should vote when the resolutions and amendments come before the conference. The extent to which delegates are instructed by their organizations varies considerably. It is particularly difficult to generalize about the procedures followed by the unions in this regard since there is a wide variation from one union to another. If a particular union has had its own annual conference in the weeks or months preceding the Labour conference, and if the union conference has taken a stand on some important policy issue which also appears on the Labour Party agenda, then the union delegation to the party conference can be expected to press for the adoption of a similar policy by the party conference. On other issues, on which the union has taken no formal stand, either the union's executive committee or its delegation to the Labour Party conference will normally be left to decide how the union's influence and " block vote " [1] should be exercised in the conference debates. A prominent union official who has had wide experience of the political rôle of British trade unions has given the writer the following description of the process by which union delegations to the Labour conference arrive at these decisions. " On the eve of the Labour conference (he said) the union delegations meet, but what happens then depends upon the structure of the union. In some unions the permanent officials are only secretaries, but some officials are very powerful personalities." He then mentioned by name the delegation of one of the larger unions and added that their eve-of-conference meeting " becomes like another conference and with ' X ' (a prominent union official) in the chair, using his particular talents, he can play ducks and drakes with the union delegates. ' X ' can be very deaf at times and if he doesn't want to hear an amendment he won't . . . It all depends, you see, on the personalities involved." And he emphasized that in other delegations no single individual has predominant influence in the discussion or in the decision as to how the union's vote will be cast.

Union delegations may also meet periodically during the course of the conference sessions to decide what stand they should take on issues which may arise in the course of conference proceedings. But one serious weakness of conference procedure is the fact that even in debates of major importance the conference very rarely adjourns at the conclusion of the debate (before the vote is taken) to enable delegations to reach a decision on the resolution before the conference in light of the arguments that have been advanced

[1] For a discussion of the procedures by which trade unions determine their conference policies, see Harrison, M., *The Trade Unions and the Labour Party since 1945*, London, 1960, *passim*.

in the debate. As a result leaders of union delegations have occasionally protested that they found themselves in an impossible situation. Even Ernest Bevin, who was sometimes considered to be amongst the most domineering of trade union leaders, made such a protest at the 1936 conference. At the end of the very confusing debate on the international situation at that conference [1] when the vote was about to be taken Ernest Bevin came to the rostrum and said, " I want to put a point of procedure. Some of us are here with delegations and no decision. We (of the Transport and General Workers Union) are scattered right across the Hall and it is impossible for anybody to exercise the card one way or the other. I want to appeal to Conference to let us actually cast the vote in the morning, so as to give us a chance to consult." His proposal was seconded by Ben Smith, M.P., of the same union. The chairman announced (presumably after a hurried consultation) that " Conference Arrangements Committee are quite agreeable to (Mr. Bevin's suggestion) if Conference is also agreeable." But Conference was not; on a show of hands Bevin's proposal was defeated 264–271. [2]

After a review of the rôle of the trade unions at the Labour Party conference, D. E. McHenry wrote in 1938: " Few trade unions have devised any machinery for the discussion of issues brought up on Conference Agendas, and many leave important decisions to an Executive Committee of paid officials or to a single dominant individual." [3] After many discussions with trade union leaders it would appear that some such criticism is still justified. There can be little doubt that, generally speaking, no effort is made by most trade unions to conduct detailed discussions of the conference agenda in union branches of the sort which take place even at ward level in many constituency Labour Parties. It may be argued that this is unnecessary at least on major issues which have been reviewed by the union's own annual conference [4]; but on most other issues the union executive or the union delegation to the party conference is allowed to determine how the block vote of the union will be cast. Nor can there be much doubt that in many instances one or a very few influential figures in a particular union are likely to have a dominant influence in these discussions.

As has been suggested many local parties hold special meetings

[1] See p. 426 above.
[2] *1936 Labour Annual Conference Report*, pp. 206-7.
[3] McHenry, D. E., *The Labour Party in Transition, 1931-8*, p. 34.
[4] For a discussion of the procedure by which unions formulate policy in connection with their own conferences, see Allen, V. L., *Power in Trade Unions*, pp. 102 ff.

either at ward level or at constituency level at which members are given an opportunity to discuss the way in which their delegate should vote at the conference. Other parties leave their delegates comparatively free to decide how they should vote in light of the conference discussion.[1] As was noted in the discussion of the Conservative conference, the mandating of delegates to the Labour conference has been subject to severe criticism by their Conservative opponents. In reply, Clement Attlee has defended the Labour Party procedure: " It might be thought (he wrote) that (the) instruction of delegates meant that speeches and discussion would be ineffectual, the issues having been decided previously. This happens no doubt on some subjects, but generally speaking the circulated agenda becomes transformed in the course of business by consultations between groups in order to obtain support for essentials rather than wording, so that the delegate may find that in the result he has to interpret his instructions, and the light in which he interprets them is that of the discussion. Frequently, too, the issues which emerge at a Conference arise out of the Annual Report or from some circumstance which was not envisaged at the time of the instruction of the delegates. There is, therefore, an opportunity for the Conference to be swayed by argument, and in practice this often occurs."[2] In fact, however, on many major issues this is not possible. (See p. 613 ff. below.)

The "final agenda", with its resolutions and amendments numbering between four and five hundred, is subject to drastic revision and pruning before it is placed before the conference. This is the responsibility of the Conference Arrangements Committee and the procedure which they follow is of considerable interest. Where a comparatively small number of motions— perhaps three or four—have been submitted on the same subject the organization which submitted the first resolution received is asked to initiate a consultation by correspondence with other organizations submitting resolutions on the same subject. The latter are told that if they do not receive a communication from the initiating organization they should notify the party head office.

---

[1] Henry Pelling (in *The Origins of the Labour Party, 1880-1900*, p. 234) has drawn attention to the fact that Keir Hardie was opposed to the principle of mandating delegates. " . . . whenever (ILP) conference time came round (Pelling writes) he was careful to insert a note in the (*Labour Leader*) urging the branches not to follow the practice of binding their delegates to strict instructions, but to leave them free to be influenced by the debate, which would of course be dominated by himself and his colleagues."

[2] Attlee, C. R., *The Labour Party in Perspective—and Twelve Years Later*, p. 79.

If none of the organizations takes action as instructed all of the resolutions concerned fall from the agenda. But normally postal consultations do take place and they result in a considerable reduction in the number of resolutions and amendments on the preliminary agenda; one or other of the organizations concerned usually withdraws its motion in favour either of an agreed composite resolution or of one particular resolution which is acceptable to the whole group. Where agreement cannot be reached the Conference Arrangements Committee arranges to meet the delegates of the organizations concerned either just before or during the course of the conference; this meeting usually arrives at a mutually satisfactory arrangement.

Where a large group of resolutions have been submitted on each of a number of subjects, special group meetings dealing with each of these subjects are held on the Saturday afternoon prior to the opening of the conference on Monday. These group meetings are usually served by a member of the head office staff as secretary; a member of the NEC usually attends to present the views of the Executive. These meetings are almost invariably successful in reducing the resolutions and amendments on the subject concerned to manageable proportions. Sometimes the success of these operations is quite spectacular. Thus, for example, at the 1950 conference 44 resolutions and four amendments on wages, prices and profits were withdrawn in favour of one composite resolution. Where a fairly sharp difference of opinion prevents this sort of achievement the group meeting sometimes draws up two resolutions. One of these resolutions will be acceptable to the NEC and will receive their support in the conference debate; the other often takes the form of a composite resolution embodying a wide range of proposals all or most of which are unacceptable to the NEC but which reflect important currents of opinion within the party.[1]

The following table shows how resolutions were dealt with at the conferences of 1948–49–50:

[1] It is sometimes maintained by organizations whose resolutions have been composited into the " hostile " resolution that it becomes a ragbag collection of propositions which on one ground or another is bound to be unacceptable to most of the delegates. In other words it is suggested that the Conference Arrangements Committee has skilfully ensured that the omnibus resolutions unacceptable to the Executive are made to look ludicrous in the eyes of the conference by stuffing into them all manner of eccentric views in the party, with the result that NEC has an easy time in ensuring their defeat. The Executive can, of course, reply that there is no alternative procedure which would ensure that all currents of opinion in the party are allowed full expression at the conference.

TABLE 11

THE FATE OF RESOLUTIONS SUBMITTED FOR THE CONSIDERATION
OF LABOUR CONFERENCES

	1948	1949	1950
Total number of resolutions submitted	303	217	371*
Number composited	132	97	188
Number of composite resolutions	22	15	19
Number of composite resolutions debated by Conference	12	3	11
Number of other resolutions debated by Conference	7	1	16
Number of resolutions which fell or were withdrawn	50	38	72
Remaining resolutions remitted to NEC without conference discussion	124	93	103

* This total includes ten amendments to the Constitution.

Conference debates take place on the basis of proposals submitted either from the platform (in the form of resolutions, reports
or policy statements by the NEC) or from the floor (individual
or composite resolutions submitted by constituency parties or
affiliated organizations). If the initiative has come from the NEC,
the Executive nominates speakers to open and close the debate;
normally there is no time limit on the speeches by the Executive
nominees although other participants in the debate are limited to
a maximum of five minutes. When the party is in opposition the
NEC almost invariably nominates one of its own members (or
occasionally a party official) to make the opening or closing statements. When the party is in office Ministers are frequently invited
by the NEC to give either the opening or closing addresses even
though the Ministers themselves may not be members of the
Executive.

There have been periodic protests against Ministerial domination
of conference discussions. At the 1930 conference for example
a constituency delegate moved a resolution which stated in part
" that this Conference views with some concern the amount of
time which is again to be allowed to Cabinet Ministers . . ." In
support of the resolution the mover protested that at the previous
year's conference " nearly all the resolutions of a general character
(submitted by the constituency parties) . . . were referred (without

debate) to the Executive Committee . . ." An amendment was moved which welcomed " the allotment of a substantial part of the Conference time to the delivery and discussion of addresses by Cabinet Ministers as being of practical educational value alike for delegates and the public, and the most effective means of maintaining touch between the Parliamentary leaders and the Conference . . ." although the amendment also endorsed in rather vague terms the original motion's contention that " sufficient time should be given to the discussion of general Resolutions sent in by affiliated bodies." The mover of the amendment thought the delegates " would have been sorry to miss the addresses they had had from Cabinet Ministers, and they would have been sorrier still for the public to have lost the information, and the Movement the publicity value which the presence of these Ministers and their addresses had given." But he thought that " considering the weight of the business they had to get through, four Cabinet Ministers in a conference of one week was rather much . . ." The speaker hoped the Executive would take this into consideration in drawing up plans for the next conference. Replying for the Executive, Arthur Henderson argued that the conference could not have it both ways; they could not both hear statements from a number of Ministers and debate a long list of resolutions. The NEC, Henderson said, were quite prepared to look into the matter, but " he thought himself it would be a mistake to abandon the practice of putting Ministers up. They should use them as long as they had them. . . . Putting up Ministers had been an experiment (and in his view) it had been a huge success." After Henderson's statement the previous question was moved and carried.[1]

Allegations of Ministerial domination also echoed from time to time through the conferences of 1946–51, but no action was ever taken to limit the right of Ministers to appear before the conference. However much they may have grumbled about the time allowed to Ernest Bevin and other prominent figures in the post-war Labour Governments, delegates appear to have relished the opportunity to

---

[1] *1930 Labour Annual Conference Report*, pp. 251-2. In the same address Henderson made a rather surprising suggestion for the limitation of the conference agenda. He said he would ask the conference " to consider whether they ought to put down on the Agenda some of the resolutions which were there. They were becoming too big an institution to spend their time debating the same issues which had been decided at the Trades Union Congress. The matters discussed at the Conference ought to be strictly political and not industrial." Needless to say this view has never been accepted by the conference ; it has never abdicated its right to discuss industrial matters which have been " decided " by the Trades Union Congress.

hear full-dress expositions of Government policies from leading parliamentarians. No doubt it was also salutary for the Ministers to hear on these occasions criticisms of their work from conference delegates. But attendance at these debates left little doubt that, in this two-way process of communication, by far the most significant flow of information and opinion was from Minister to conference. Ministers seized and used the opportunity to brief their most active supporters in the country with arguments in favour of the Government's policies and achievements. In this respect both Labour and Conservative conferences serve an almost identical purpose when their respective parties are in power.

When debates take place on resolutions originating from the floor of the conference the mover of the resolution is normally accorded ten minutes and successive speakers five. Again, the NEC spokesman who closes the debate is not restricted by any time limit, and again this has led to periodic allegations by delegates that the Executive tends to monopolize the time of the conference. In Table 12 below the number of speeches given from the platform and from the floor and the proportion of conference time taken up by each is shown for two representative Labour conferences (with the party in opposition, 1953, and in office, 1948). For comparative purposes the same information has been included for Conservative conferences in the same years. It will be noted that whether Labour was in office or in opposition, platform spokesmen took up approximately the same proportion of conference time (37 per cent. in office, 35 per cent. in opposition), although in both cases a much larger number of speeches was given from the floor. It is also important to note the striking similarity in the platform-floor ratio between the Labour and Conservative conferences. With the Conservatives in opposition (1948) their platform took up a rather smaller proportion of the conference time (25 per cent.); but when the Conservatives were in office their platform took up 37 per cent. of conference time which is identically the same proportion as was taken by the platform at the Labour conference of 1948 when their party was also in office.

It is not surprising that constituency delegates at Labour conferences should feel themselves somewhat frustrated. As was already noted, they constitute approximately half the total membership of the conference, yet as Table 12 shows, they normally take up no more than 34–38 per cent. of conference time. They have traditionally tended to think of the conference as an opportunity for instructing their own Executive in the policies which it should pursue in governing the affairs of the party. Yet they find themselves (no doubt inevitably) confined for the most part to delivering

TABLE 12

SPEECHES FROM PLATFORM AND FLOOR AT CONSERVATIVE AND LABOUR CONFERENCES

PARTY IN OPPOSITION

	Conservative 1948	Labour 1953
Total Number of conference speeches	170	195
By constituency representatives	127	102
By Members of Parliament	18	29
By trade union delegates	—	35
Total from Floor	145	166
Total from Platform	25	29
Percentage of conference time taken up		
By constituency representatives	64%	34%
By Members of Parliament	11%	16%
By trade union delegates	—	15%
Total taken up by Floor	75%	65%
Total taken up by Platform	25%	35%

PARTY IN OFFICE

	Conservative 1953	Labour 1948
Total Number of conference speeches	94	214
By constituency representatives	65	117
By Members of Parliament	10	29
By trade union delegates	—	34
Total from Floor	75	180
Total from Platform	19	34
Percentage of conference time taken up		
By constituency representatives	51%	38%
By Members of Parliament	12%	11%
By trade union delegates	—	14%
Total taken up by Floor	63%	63%
Total taken up by Platform	37%	37%

Notes :

The proportion of time taken up by conference speeches has been calculated by counting the column-inches taken up by the speeches in the official conference reports.

In accounting for the difference in the number of speeches given at Conservative and Labour conferences it must be remembered that the former normally meets for two-and-a-half days, the latter for four-and-a-half.

a number of five-minute speeches which taken together represent not much more than a third of conference time. On the other hand constituency representatives can hardly complain about the relationship between their share of conference time and that of the trade unions. The latter constitute five-sixths of the mass membership of the party, yet the speeches of their delegates normally take up 15 per cent. or less of the time devoted to speech-making at the conference. Perhaps, however, this only serves to heighten the constituency delegates' sense of exasperation. They are more numerous than the trade union delegates; they do more of the speaking; yet at the end of each debate they find themselves hopelessly outvoted by their comparatively reticent yet all-powerful trade union comrades.

As has been explained, the final speaker in each conference debate is either a member of the NEC or a Minister (or occasionally a party official) nominated by the NEC. On behalf of the Executive this final speaker advises the conference as to how (in the view of the Executive) they should dispose of the resolution before them. Occasionally he may invite the conference to vote on the issue without benefit of advice from the Executive, but normally the NEC spokesman advises one of five courses of action. He may request the conference to take no vote at all on the understanding that the NEC will take note of the resolution. Such advice would appropriately be given if the resolution dealt with a matter which was already the subject of active negotiation by the Executive or by the Labour Government (if the party were in office). Alternatively the Executive spokesman may accept a resolution on behalf of his colleagues on the understanding that the Executive will take action to implement it; in such a case, of course, a conference vote is unnecessary. As a third alternative the Executive spokesman may invite the mover and seconder of a resolution to withdraw their proposal. He may argue either that the Executive is already implementing the policy advocated in the resolution or that the Executive or the Labour Government would be embarrassed by the adoption of the resolution. If the mover and seconder refuse to withdraw then the issue must be put to a vote. The fourth and fifth alternatives involve an outright recommendation by the Executive spokesman that the conference should either adopt or reject the resolution under discussion. In either case the NEC spokesman in closing the debate gives the reasons why the NEC recommends either course of action. Fairly frequently, after the spokesman has made a case against a resolution, the mover and seconder agree to withdraw the resolution. Sometimes they do so apparently because they are satisfied by having had the opportunity to ventilate their views, and are reluctant to see their resolution decisively defeated by the conference on the advice of the Executive. But if the mover and seconder insist, a vote is taken. In an overwhelming proportion of cases conference acts on the advice of the Executive.

Conference votes may be taken either orally, by show of hands or by card vote. If the first method is used the chairman merely asks: " Is that agreed? " and the conference responds (orally); if the response is decisively affirmative or negative the chairman declares the resolution to be carried or defeated. If a considerable number of delegates dissent from his decision the chairman then proceeds to one of the alternative methods of voting. If he calls for a show of hands the principle of " one delegate, one vote " is operative and (as will be evident from the discussion above of the proportion of trade union and constituency delegates who attend the conference), it is obvious that the latter are accorded much greater influence than they are entitled to wield on the basis of their membership. If the chairman or any considerable proportion of the delegates are dissatisfied with the result on a show of hands, then a card vote is taken. National and constituency organizations are allotted one thousand votes for each one thousand members (or part thereof) on whom affiliation fees have been paid, and federations and central Labour Parties are also allotted one thousand votes each regardless of the size of their membership. It will be evident that on this basis the affiliated trade unions cast an overwhelming proportion of the vote.

At recent conferences the proportion of voting strength has been approximately five million for the trade unions to one million for the constituency parties. At the 1950 conference, for example, the affiliated trade unions disposed of 5,014,000 votes compared with 985,000 for the constituency parties and a total of 61,000 for the socialist societies (plus the Royal Arsenal Co-operative). The voting strength of the six largest unions was as follows:

Transport and General Workers (T & GW)	830,000
National Union of Mineworkers (NUM) .	651,000
Amalgamated Engineering Union (AEU) .	595,000
General & Municipal Workers (G & MW)	400,000
National Union of Railwaymen (NUR) .	366,000
Union of Shop Distributive and Allied Workers (USDAW)	317,000

In addition, 74 other unions cast the remaining 1,855,000 votes. In the constituency section the largest party sending a delegate to the conference (South Lewisham) was entitled to cast 6,000 votes; four other parties had 5,000, and approximately 70 parties cast either

4,000 or 3,000 votes; but 216 were entitled to 2,000 and the largest single group (290) cast only 1,000 votes. The Transport and General Workers, it should be noted, disposed of very nearly as many votes as the whole group of constituency parties taken together; and the six largest unions, if they voted together, controlled more than half the voting strength of the conference. Three of the six largest unions (the AEU, the NUR and USDAW) have had, of course, a reputation of voting " left " on many issues, and on certain controversial matters they have by no means regularly voted with the other three big unions. But if the more conservatively minded trio, the Transport and General, the Miners and the General and Municipal, stand together they can carry any issue at the conference provided that they win two-thirds of the voting support of the unions outside the big six. They can do so even if the votes of the AEU, NUR, USDAW, plus the votes of every constituency party and socialist society are cast on the other side, which, of course, would be very unlikely.[1]

There is room for argument as to how far conference voting has reflected a clear-cut and consistent " trade union versus constituency party " split. A leading party official has claimed in private discussion with the writer that on no major issue in the past 15 years has a majority of the trade unions been opposed by a majority of the constituency parties. He argued that conference decisions have always been sustained by what could be termed a " concurrent majority". This assertion cannot be tested against the voting records in the official conference reports since the totals figure given of the vote for or against a particular resolution are not broken down to indicate how the unions or the constituency parties cast their ballots. But attendance at most of the post-war Labour conferences and a review of the debates and votes on major policy issues (and also of the votes in the elections to the NEC) suggest this conclusion: on the great majority of occasions the assertion stands: most of the unions and of the constituency parties usually find themselves allied against a minority of the constituency parties and of the unions.

But there can be little doubt that there have been some occasions of major importance where the assertion does not stand, where a clear-cut trade union versus constituency party split seems obviously to have occurred. Martin Harrison in his *The Trade Unions and the Labour Party since* 1945 (p. 240) concludes that such a split occurred in the debates on German rearmament and on SEATO in 1954. And after a very careful analysis of the estimated voting figures on a

---

[1] For recent changes in Union voting patterns, see p. 599 below.

number of other issues (a problematical business) he concludes
that there may also have been such splits on perhaps half a dozen
issues of varying importance since the war.

Normally trade unions, constituency parties, and socialist
societies cast the total vote to which they are entitled in a single
unit; this practice, known as " block voting," is one of the most
controversial aspects of the internal life of the Labour Party. It
should be noted that block voting is not prescribed in the constitution or standing orders of the Labour Party. It is merely a customary practice; there is no party regulation which prevents any of the
organizations affiliated to the party from splitting their votes in any
way they choose. On occasion, indeed, some organizations appear
to have done so; to take but one example, Beatrice Webb describes
how the miners' union split their vote in the elections for the NEC
at the 1920 conference (which she attended).[1] But such instances
appear to be extremely rare; almost invariably the unions and
constituency parties cast their votes *en bloc*. The practice appears
to date back to a decision of the Parliamentary Committee of the
Trades Union Congress in 1894 to adopt a system of card voting
at their annual congress. Until that time voting at Congresses had
been on the basis of " one delegate, one vote," but it was decided to
supersede this arrangement by a system of card voting by which the
leader of each union delegation cast a vote equivalent to the total
number of members on which his union was affiliated to the Congress.
This method of voting was adopted without debate at the inaugural
conference of the LRC in 1900 and has been used at Labour Party
conferences ever since. Constituency representatives have perenni-
ally grumbled about this voting system and on a few occasions have
put their case against the block vote before the conference itself.

Thus, for example, at the 1922 conference the delegates of the East
Lewisham Divisional Labour Party moved a resolution which
proposed that in view of the fact that trade unionists had ample
representation and opportunities for expressing their opinions in
local Trades and Labour Councils and in local Labour Parties, the
system of block voting by trade unions at annual conferences should
be suspended. Arthur Henderson on behalf of the Executive
vigorously opposed the resolution. The unions, he pointed out,
were paying 90–95 per cent. of party funds; they had been invited
to join in the work of the party on certain conditions and it would
be wrong to change the basis of their association. The motion was
declared lost without a recorded vote.[2]

[1] *Beatrice Webb's Diaries 1912–24*, p. 183.
[2] *1922 Labour Annual Conference Report*, pp. 220-1.

Not all of the critics of block voting seek to destroy the system outright and to return to a system of one delegate one vote. It is sometimes argued (and the case for this view would appear to be strong) that unions ought to divide their total vote in a proportion which reflects the division of opinion either within their own annual conference or within their delegation to the Labour Party confer-ence. If one returns to the vote on rearmament at the 1952 Labour conference discussed above, one can see how this modified system of block voting might be applied. Similar resolutions favouring a reduction in the arms programme had been debated either a few weeks or a few months earlier at the annual conferences of a number of the unions. If, in a particular trade union, a similar resolution had been defeated by a vote in the proportions of say 3 to 2 at their union conference, there would appear to be no reason why this union's block vote at the Labour Party conference should not be split in the same proportions. Or alternatively (if it were argued that the development of the international situation in the period since the union had held its conference made this desirable) the union's delegation to the Labour Party conference might review the situation at their private meeting on the eve of the conference; they could then agree on a division of their block vote which fairly reflected opinion within the delegation. But any change of this sort would obviously have to be made by the unions themselves and not by the Labour Party conference; otherwise it would be construed as an attempt to dictate to the unions how they should conduct their own business.[1] And from discussion with trade union officials it would appear that there is no enthusiasm whatever for any change in the present method of block voting. Most union officials argue that the present system reflects the tradition of trade union solidarity and they are in no way daunted if their voting methods are described as a variation of what the Communists call " democratic centralism".

Equally, there is no evidence of enthusiasm for any change in trade union voting methods amongst the parliamentary leaders who are usually the dominant figures in the party conference. They have rarely defended the block voting system in terms even as frank as those used by Arthur Henderson in the debate (quoted above) at the 1922 conference. But no doubt they would subscribe to the views he expressed. And in all probability they would warmly agree with an even stronger view once expressed in private by Sidney Webb. Beatrice Webb recorded in her diary a conversation which

---

[1] It would also be essential of course, that the constituency parties and other affiliated bodies should be prepared to split their votes on some similar principle.

she and her husband had with Oswald Mosley shortly after his break with the Labour Party. She wrote:

> " Looking in the future (Mosley) foresees a growing cleavage between the constituency parties led by the left-wing enthusiasts, and the Trade Unions led by rather dull-witted and conventional Trade Union officials. The keenest of the young Trade Unionists are in revolt against the Block Vote and the dictatorship of the well-established officers of the big Trade Unions. Sidney observed afterwards that the constituency parties were frequently unrepresentative groups of nonentities dominated by fanatics and cranks, and extremists, and that *if* the block vote of the Trade Unions were eliminated it would be impracticable to continue to vest the control of policy in Labour Party Conferences."[1]

This statement lays bare the realities of power within the Labour Party conference. It should be recalled that when Webb made this statement he was a member of the second Labour Government; there can be little doubt that he accurately reflected the conviction of the great majority of the parliamentary leaders of the Labour Party then *and now*. They would find it intolerable if the conference could be dominated or controlled by those (many of whom they consider " fanatics, cranks and extremists ") who turn up in large numbers as delegates from constituency parties. The conference could not be accorded even nominal authority in determining the long-range goals of the party if it were subject to the overriding influence of the constituency party delegates. But the parliamentary leaders have little to fear from the party conference as long as they retain the confidence (and the block vote support) of the traditionally moderate and conservative leadership of the majority of the big trade unions.[2] Indeed it is this bond of mutual confidence between the parliamentary leaders and a preponderant part of the trade union leadership which is an essential key to the understanding of the functioning of the Labour Party. Nowhere is this bond of confidence more effectively demonstrated than in the records of the debates and votes at the party conference.

This is not to say that the conference is inevitably and on all

[1] *Beatrice Webb's Diaries*, 19th May, 1930, folios 53-4.
[2] E. M. King, who had been a junior minister in the 1945 Labour Government, resigned from the party in 1954 and in an exchange of letters with Attlee he appeared to imply that the latter's " honest leadership " was hopelessly frustrated by the extremists who control the party conference. The conference, he wrote, " is undemocratic and increasingly appears as an annual appeal to the unwise by the unscrupulous which annually succeeds." Attlee, quite unruffled, replied blandly that, in his view, the conference " always sensibly turns down the kind of nonsense that is put up." (The *Manchester Guardian*, 14th May, 1954.)

occasions a captive organization which must obey the whims of a small, tight-knit and essentially undemocratic group composed of the leaders of the PLP and of a majority of the trade unions. While the leading parliamentarians and trade union leaders stand together, they do have almost overwhelming influence in determining the outcome of conference deliberations. But this is not necessarily an " undemocratic " situation. Each element in the controlling group wields great authority ; each is unquestionably buttressed by powerful oligarchic tendencies. But like the Conservative Leader, they exercise their authority *only with the consent of their followers*.[1] It may be that the mass membership of the constituency section of the Labour Party is almost powerless—perhaps even more so than its Conservative counterpart—in the face of the alliance between parliamentarians and trade union leaders. But it must be recognized that the constituency section of the Labour Party constitutes only a small fraction of the total membership of the party. It is no doubt irksome for them to find themselves consistently bludgeoned by the representatives of the " sleeping partners " of the Labour Party mass organization, the members affiliated through their trade unions. But the solution to this problem, if it is a problem, would appear to lie in an attempt to galvanize the rank-and-file members of the affiliated trade unions into insisting upon a more effective voice in deciding how the block vote of their union shall be cast at the party conference. Any attempt to rob the unions of that block vote would only wreck " the open and honourable alliance" which was so painstakingly established in 1900.

There have of course been occasions when the conference has played a decisive rôle in the affairs of the party. This has happened, for example, in certain rare instances when the PLP and the NEC have found themselves out of step. In November 1918, it will be recalled, the weak and somewhat discredited PLP wished to remain in the Lloyd George Coalition; but the NEC recommended to a special party conference that the party should withdraw and this recommendation was endorsed. Again, the 1935 conference might be said to have arbitrated in what was, in one sense, an internal dispute within the PLP over the sanctions issue.[2] As has already

[1] For a further discussion of oligarchical control of union block votes, see Chapter X, pp. 598-9 and 627-8.

[2] The 1954 conference also played a similar rôle when the parliamentary leaders were again divided, on this occasion over German rearmament. A sharp split within the unions left the issue in doubt. But the NEC faithfully reflecting majority opinion with the PLP managed to carry by a narrow majority a resolution which embodied the views of the PLP leaders. For a discussion of the issues raised by the 1960 and 1961 Conference decisions on unilateralism, see pp. 612 ff. below.

been suggested, the rôle of the Labour conference on this occasion closely resembled that of the Central Council of the Conservative Party during the great debate on India in the early 1930s. (See Chapter IV.) On other occasions the Labour conference, like its Conservative counterpart, has served as a vitally important sounding board of party opinion. Undoubtedly, for example, the discussions on Spain at the 1936 conference provided a dramatic demonstration of the depth of feeling on the subject throughout the Labour movement; it had the effect of stimulating both the NEC and the leaders of the PLP to adopt a somewhat stronger line both in their public statements and in Parliament.

The Labour conference has also on occasion played an important rôle in the formulation of the party programme. This was not the case on the occasion of the adoption of *Labour and the New Social Order* in 1918 or of *Labour and the New Society* in 1928; the policies set forth in both documents were adopted without any very important intervention by the conference. But in the preparation of Labour's 1945 programme, *Let Us Face the Future* (published in April 1945), the conference made at least one important contribution. The NEC had laid before the previous party conference in December 1944 several broad statements of policy which were to become the basis on which Labour's electoral programme was to be prepared. The most important of these statements (dealing with economic and financial policy) reaffirmed the party's " Socialist faith," its support for a " planned economy " and for " the transfer to the state of power *to direct the policy* of our main industries, services and financial institutions." The wording of these phrases was, of course, highly significant. To some it implied that the Executive was evading the issue of public ownership. In moving the adoption of the statement on behalf of the NEC, Emanuel Shinwell emphasized that the party stood " as always, for the abolition of a vicious competitive system and for the establishment of the highest possible standard of living based on collective organization and the ownership of indispensable national industries and services." But the fact remained that there was no indication in the Executive statement that any specific industry would be brought into public ownership.

Ian Mikardo (for the Reading Labour Party) drew attention to this omission, saying " we are deeply disturbed that the resolution of the Executive which has just been moved does not mention public ownership in any part . . . . (and he warned that) our rank and file comrades, to whom Socialism still means a great deal, will be appalled and disappointed at its un-Socialist character." Therefore, " to clarify the position " Mikardo moved a resolution which stated in part:

"This Conference welcomes the recommendation of the National Executive Committee that the Party should contest the next General Election with a programme based on the Socialist principles of the Party, and make it clear that this programme will include: . . . the transfer to public ownership of the land, large-scale building, heavy industry, and all forms of banking, transport and fuel and power . . . "

In the debate that followed several speakers picked up the point that Mikardo had made. James Callaghan (then a prospective candidate at South Cardiff) said, " I think we are entitled to an explanation from the Executive Committee as to why the issue of public ownership was not included in the Report. It may be said that as it is such a cardinal feature of Labour Party policy there is no need to say anything about it. That may be true so far as the delegates here are concerned and the Executive Committee, but there are millions of men in the Forces who do not understand that public ownership is a part of Labour Party policy. I think it is high time that we should re-state our fundamental principles in a document of this sort." Nevertheless, in replying to the debate for the Executive, Philip Noel-Baker asked that Mikardo should not press his resolution to a vote. " Of course (said Noel-Baker), we are in general agreement with it, but in some particulars, especially about building, we are not certain that it is quite in agreement with the statement which the Conference accepted two days ago. We undertake to examine that point and others with great care. We think that the resolution should be neither accepted nor rejected to-day." But Mikardo refused to withdraw and the conference ignored the advice of Noel-Baker and carried the Reading resolution without a recorded vote.[1]

This incident illustrates both the strength and limitations of the influence of the conference. *Let Us Face the Future*, when it appeared four months later, contained a strong statement of the party's intention to bring certain industries into public ownership; indeed a categorical list of such industries was included. It may be, as has sometimes been claimed, that the pledge to nationalize the iron and steel industry might never have been included had it not been for the adoption of Mikardo's resolution " making it clear that . . . heavy industry" would be transferred to public ownership. On the other hand *Let Us Face the Future* included no specific pledge to nationalize large-scale building or any of the other " forms of banking" apart from the Bank of England. In addition there was no promise to nationalize the land within the lifetime of the 1945

[1] *1944 Labour Annual Conference Report*, pp. 160-8.

Parliament. Obviously the NEC and the PLP were entirely within their rights in weeding out conference decisions for the purposes of preparing an election statement. But it seems fair to assume that in drafting the passages referring to nationalization they were probably influenced by the resolution adopted by the conference of December 1944.

The conference of 1953 also played an important, although by no means a spectacular rôle in the final formulation of *Challenge to Britain*, a policy statement adopted by the Labour Party as a foundation for its subsequent electoral programme. The previous year's conference had instructed the National Executive to prepare such a policy statement, and *Challenge to Britain*, in a somewhat novel departure, was subject to the detailed consideration of the 1953 conference. In presenting the document on behalf of the NEC, James Griffiths described the procedure as " a very great democratic venture."

> " We have (he said) submitted a statement of policy to you ; we have asked you to read it, to study it, to put your suggestions to us, to table your amendments . . . . When I have concluded this opening statement we shall proceed to what I would describe as the committee stage. We shall take " Challenge to Britain " section by section. (And) shall take your amendments in conjunction with the appropriate sections. Members of the Executive will speak to you and give Conference their advice upon the amendments that have been put forward. It will be for you then to decide and at the close of the debate our leader, Clem Attlee, will commend the document as amended (if it is amended) to the Conference and to the country."[1]

In the course of the four-day debate which ensued, 54 amendments (many of them " composite " amendments embodying several separate amendments submitted by constituency parties or affiliated organizations) were moved. Of these, 25 were defeated by the conference on the advice of the NEC or withdrawn at the request of the NEC; the supporters of 13 resolutions agreed to remit their resolutions to the NEC for their further consideration. Sixteen of the original 54 were adopted by the conference. In no instance, it should be noted, did the conference accept an amendment against the advice of the NEC. Each of the 16 amendments was adopted after the NEC had agreed to accept them (or, in one instance, without any comment from the NEC). In most instances the amendments which were passed by the conference urged, in effect, that the Executive should expand the policy statements along lines sug-

---

[1] *1953 Labour Annual Conference Report*, p. 85.

gested by the amendment, or alternatively that some item should be included which the mover of the amendment felt would repair an omission in *Challenge to Britain*. In no instance could it be claimed that the conference insisted upon a major change of policy against the wishes of the Executive. Amongst the defeated amendments were several which would have had this effect; but in every such instance the NEC, with the support of the block vote, ensured their overwhelming defeat. James Griffiths's " democratic venture " may have marked a modest innovation in Labour Party policy-making, but it could hardly be described as revolutionary. Certainly, Attlee (in his concluding statement for the Executive immediately before *Challenge to Britain*, as amended, was declared to be " carried almost unanimously ") made no such claim. ". . . the National Executive (he said) has shown no undue pride of authorship. Where we thought the matter was put better in the amendments, we have accepted the amendments, and Conference has accepted them." The proceedings were as unexciting as Attlee's statement suggests.[1]

The rôle of the conference with Labour in office has been remarkably similar to the relationship between the conference of the National Union and a Conservative Government. Neither party conference has had even the faintest vestige of direct control over its Government; in each case conference debates serve mainly as an opportunity for active party members to hear authoritative expositions of government policy. And, in turn, the debates give Ministers the opportunity to judge the temper of their more militant supporters. If anything, Labour conferences have tended to view Labour Governments with even more awe and pride than characterizes the Conservative attitude to their Governments [2] (possibly because Labour Governments are a rarer phenomenon). Nevertheless Labour conference debates have on occasion echoed the spirit of the delegate to the National Union conference of 1925, who, it will be recalled, warned Stanley Baldwin: " our loyalty is the same as ever, but it has got to be ' On, Stanley, On.' "

Certainly this was the mood of the 1929 Labour conference during the course of a long debate on unemployment. The debate took place on the reference back of a passage in the report of the PLP concerning the unemployment policies of the recently elected Labour Government. The report explained that there had been " no opportunity for the Minister of Labour to deal with administrative questions " in connection with unemployment benefits, and

---

[1] *1953 Labour Annual Conference Report*, p. 207.

[2] This was particularly true of Conservative conferences during the inter-war years; Conservative conferences after 1951 tended to be somewhat less critical of their Government.

added that it had been decided that " questions of general legislation (respecting unemployment) should be left over until the autumn and spring." W. T. Kelly, M.P., moved the reference back with a ringing challenge to the contention that there had been " no opportunity . . . to deal with administrative questions." The full-scale debate which ensued appears to have occupied at least four hours of conference time. In the course of the debate, J. H. Thomas, the Minister responsible for unemployment policy, gave a lengthy address and was closely questioned by a number of delegates, including Ernest Bevin. The Government's position was defended by Clynes, and George Lansbury (in a final speech for the Executive) warned that if the conference carried the reference back it would be " in effect a vote of censure upon (Margaret Bondfield, the Minister of Labour) and upon the administration—upon the Party generally, because you are dealing not with a Cabinet Report, but with a Report of the Labour Party in the House of Commons. . . . (the conference would be) censuring the whole of the Members of the Parliamentary Party in the House of Commons (cries of ' No ')." The conference chairman (Herbert Morrison) concluded the debate by warning that " If Mr. Kelly and his friends persist in this matter, and (the reference back) is carried, the people who will rejoice more than anybody else will be the Conservative newspapers and the Opposition in the House of Commons." Kelly refused to relent; the reference back was put to a vote; and it was narrowly defeated, 1,027,000 to 1,100,000.[1]

Again, at the 1930 conference, there were heated discussions of the Government's unemployment policy; and again the Government could be left in no doubt about the deep uneasiness of its followers over its record in handling the problem.[2] Appeals to party loyalty, plus the support of a considerable proportion of the trade union block vote, narrowly saved the second Labour Government from outright repudiation by the party conference of 1929 and 1930; but like the delegates to the Conservative conference of 1925, the Labour delegates could congratulate themselves on having played the part of goad and stimulant to the Cabinet.

During the lifetime of the 1945 and 1950 Labour Governments, the party conference played a remarkably modest rôle. At each of the conferences during the period 1946 to 1951 the NEC invariably acted as a watchdog for the Government; they never once advocated, or were even prepared to tolerate, a proposal which differed in any significant particular from the policies of the Labour Government.

[1] *1929 Labour Annual Conference Report*, (Parliamentary Report), pp. 83-4 and 171-90.
[2] *1930 Labour Annual Conference Report*, pp. 186-204.

And, on the whole, the conferences acted upon the advice of the NEC with surprising docility. On a total of only nine occasions during the six party conferences (1946–51) was the advice of the NEC rejected by the conference. In 1946 the conference passed four resolutions which were opposed by the NEC. Two of these criticized the Government's publicity; a third criticized its agricultural policy, but was adopted despite a plea by the Minister of Agriculture that it should be rejected; a fourth (criticizing certain items of educational policy) was adopted despite a plea by the NEC and the Minister of Education that it should be rejected.[1] The 1947 conference overrode the advice of Aneurin Bevan, the Minister of Health and a member of the NEC, by passing a resolution favouring the abolition of tied cottages. The same conference overwhelmingly insisted on adopting a resolution favouring equal pay for equal work for women despite a plea from the NEC that the resolution should be withdrawn.[2] The 1948 conference renewed the demand for the abolition of tied cottages, again overriding Aneurin Bevan and the NEC; and the same conference passed a resolution opposing " any reduction or withdrawal of food or clothing subsidies . . ." despite a plea by Dr. Edith Summerskill on behalf of the National Executive " to leave this (matter) to the discretion of the Chancellor of the Exchequer." [3] During the conferences held in the three years 1949–51 inclusive, the Executive's advice was rejected on only one issue involving a major matter of policy. The NEC asked the Union of Shop, Distributive and Allied Workers to withdraw a resolution proposing a certain course of action with respect to food distribution. The union refused and the resolution was put to the conference and carried.[4] This one instance apart, the NEC had not the slightest difficulty in restraining the conference from taking action which would in any way embarrass the Labour Government. On the whole, the Attlee Governments were as nearly immune as any Conservative Government can expect to be from outright condemnation by its annual conference.

A few of the militant spirits in the constituency parties tried early in the lifetime of the 1945 Government to stimulate the party to redefine the relationship between the conference, the Executive and the Government. Nat Whine, then chairman of the St. Maryle-

[1] *1946 Labour Annual Conference Report,* pp. 128-30, 182-4 and 191-5.
[2] *1947 Labour Annual Conference Report,* pp. 125-7 and 157-9. It is interesting to note that after the party had gone into opposition in 1951, at the party conference the following year the NEC accepted a resolution in favour of equal pay. See *1952 Labour Annual Conference Report,* p. 177.
[3] *1948 Labour Annual Conference Report,* pp. 150-2 and 212-4.
[4] *1950 Labour Annual Conference Report,* pp. 154-7.

bone Borough Labour Party, wrote of the 1947 conference (which he attended) that it had been "impossible to distinguish between NEC and Government policy, and delegates were . . . asked to vote for or against resolutions, not because of their socialist content . . . but because the resolutions would be accepted as a declaration of confidence in the policy of (a particular) Department or of the ruling Minister. No distinction was made, in voicing these demands, between those aspects of Government policy which arose directly out of approved Labour Party policy and those which were expedients to gain time. . . . It is becoming increasingly but reluctantly accepted within the Labour Party that every (conference) issue is an issue of confidence (in the Labour Government)." But the writer revealed singularly little understanding either of Cabinet Government, or of the relationship between the PLP and the mass organization of the party, when he added: " The consequence of this procedure has been for the NEC and the Conference to abdicate from their historic rôle and to surrender to the Cabinet the initiative in the determination of Party policy."

Whine proceeded, however, to outline an interesting set of suggestions for dealing with the problem he had described. He urged that the order of business of the conference should be " so arranged as to distinguish clearly between discussions on the Parliamentary Report and on General Policy." He apparently intended that the discussions of the parliamentary report should revert to the status they had occupied during the lifetime of the second MacDonald Government when these discussions sometimes became the occasion for a full-dress review of various aspects of the Government's record. He proposed that " This phase of the Conference shall belong to the Government, and shall provide an opportunity for an exchange of views between the Government and the Party, and to determine whether and in what measure the Government retains the general support and confidence of the Party." The parliamentary report as a whole would be introduced by the Prime Minister and senior Cabinet Ministers would be invited to reply to criticisms of the work and policy of departments for which they were responsible. " In order to provide conditions suitable for liberty of speech by the delegates, free from contingent embarrassments to the Party, in respect of specific aspects of Government policy, the general discussion on the Parliamentary Report (should) be held in open sessions, and a vote taken, and the discussions on the work of individual Ministers and their Departments (should) be held in secret session." The sessions devoted to a discussion of general policy would " belong to the Party and . . . provide an opportunity for delegates to express freely their views on long term aims and current problems not covered by the Parliamentary Report." During these discussions Ministers would be entitled to speak only if they were members of the NEC or in the capacity of delegates or *ex officio* members of the conference.[1]

There are obvious difficulties in connection with Whine's proposal. It would be nothing like so easy as he seems to imply to distinguish between a debate on the record of the Government and a discussion of the party's long-range policies. And in light of the Labour Party's record in the matter of maintaining the secrecy of its " confidential " discussions, Ministers might in effect find themselves virtually on trial in public. But whatever the merits or demerits of Whine's proposal it has found no serious support at any authoritative level within the party. Throughout the lifetime of the 1945 and 1950 Labour Governments, the parliamentary and trade union leaders appeared satisfied with the increasing docility of the Labour conference; there is no evidence that they were disturbed by the fact that it had come to play a very modest rôle indeed in its relations with the Labour Government.

With the return of the party to opposition in 1951, the Labour conference was considerably revitalized, though it did not then play, nor has it ever in the modern history of the party played, the rôle which Attlee assigns it in the passage quoted at the beginning of this section. The party conference has never been and cannot be " a Parliament of the movement," not, at least, if the PLP and a Labour Government are counted part of " the movement". This is not to say that the conference has ever been the totally meaningless affair which Philip Snowden appeared to imply when he wrote:

> " My experience of Conferences has taught me to attach very little importance to their resolutions. Of the hundreds of resolutions I have seen passed by Labour Conferences outlining a drastic programme of reform, I can hardly call to mind one which has had any practical result. Conferences will talk; let them talk. Governments, including Labour Governments, dispose of Conference resolutions. There is all the difference in the world between the licence and irresponsibility of a Conference and the position of a Government which has to face practical difficulties and knows that no Government can move far ahead of public opinion. Nobody knows that better than members of the Labour Cabinets. The rank and file of the Labour Party ought to

[1] Whine, N., " Government and Party," *Fabian Quarterly*, No. 57. Spring 1948, pp. 8-12. Some of the same issues are discussed in two articles by Ian Mikardo, M.P., and Morgan Phillips under the general title, " Do we need a New Constitution? " in *Labour Forum*, Vol. I, No. 7, April-June, 1948, pp. 10 ff.

have learnt that lesson by now. They have had enough experience of the futility of Conference resolutions."[1]

The Labour conference has rarely behaved in the silly irresponsible way which Snowden here suggests; it has been too tightly controlled for that. Under the careful tutelage of the NEC (with its preponderant representation of parliamentary leaders) and of the representatives of the trade unions (with their block votes) the conference has rejected the advice of the leaders of the party on only the rarest of occasions. It has often been a thorn in their flesh; but the conference of the National Union has, on occasion, served the same function with respect to the Conservative leaders.

Aneurin Bevan, long the favourite of the constituency parties, on several occasions undertook to define for the conference its rôle in the formulation of policy. Inevitably perhaps, he was more generous in attributing authority to the conference than the actual circumstances justified; but his statements were basically sound. On the first occasion he was urging the rejection of a conference resolution respecting tied cottages at the 1947 conference. The resolution read in part: " This Conference . . . instructs the National Executive Committee to approach H. M. Government with a request for the introduction of legislation having for its purpose the immediate abolition of the tied cottage system. . . . That further the Government shall take immediate steps to ensure that no worker, whether on a contract of service or a basis of tenancy, shall be evicted without suitable alternative accommodation is first proved (sic)." In reply to the debate Bevan reminded the conference of the tremendous legislative burden which had been undertaken by the Labour Government. And he added, " There is such a thing as parliamentary priorities. . . . If this resolution were carried it would mean that the Movement would immediately have to embark on a campaign against the Government. That is what the resolution says. . . . But if you say that the Government has an obligation to carry out immediately all the resolutions passed in the last forty years that would be imposing on us a task impossible to carry out. . . . It is impossible for the Conference not know-

[1] Snowden, An Autobiography, Vol. I, pp. 87-8. For an illustration of Snowden's attitude to Labour conferences when he was still a member of the party, see his comments on the proposal of the Labour conference of 1927 with respect to surtax. The Times, 12th December, 1927. Perhaps the culminating evidence of Snowden's disregard for the Labour conference and its policy declarations was provided in a speech in the House of Commons on 2nd October, 1931, when he stated (three years after the adoption of Labour and the Nation): " I must confess I have never read Labour and the Nation." House of Commons Debates, 2nd October, 1931.

ing the Parliamentary situation to determine the Parliamentary timetable. All the Conference can do is to record its views on principle, and ask that they be implemented at the earliest possible moment." The conference overrode the advice of Bevan by a narrow majority in favour of the resolution (for, 1,558,000; against, 1,555,000).[1]

A year later, when no action had been taken by the Government to implement the decision of the 1947 conference, a delegate of the National Union of Agricultural Workers moved another composite resolution which stated in part, " That this Conference urges the Government to introduce legislation abolishing the tied cottage system . . ." Again Aneurin Bevan warned the delegates: " It is quite impossible for a conference of 1,100 people, even if it were constitutionally proper, to determine the order in which the Parliamentary Labour Party and the Government introduces legislation into the House of Commons. It is for the Conference to lay down the policies of the Parliamentary Party, and for the Parliamentary Party to interpret those policies in the light of the Parliamentary system. Any other procedure would merely confuse the whole situation." But despite Bevan's advice the resolution was again carried, this time without a recorded vote.[2]

On this occasion, the conference had exercised its undoubted right to ignore the advice of its leaders; but they in turn exercised their undoubted right to ignore the advice of the conference. All the latter succeeded in doing was to prove itself as impotent as was the Conservative conference during the inter-war years when it repeatedly insisted that successive Conservative Governments should set about the task of reforming the House of Lords. In both cases the parliamentary leaders professed that they shared the objectives of the conference. But in both cases the leaders insisted on their own ultimate right to choose the most suitable moment in which to act upon the advice of the conference. And if the parliamentary leaders judge it necessary to do so they may postpone " the moment of action " to the Greek kalends. No parliamentary party and certainly no Government can forswear the right to judge the " practicability " of the decision of its mass organization; this fact the Labour Party has wisely recognized in its constitution.

The National Executive Committee

The constitution of the Labour Party provides that the National Executive Committee " shall subject to the control and directions

[1] *1947 Labour Annual Conference Report*, pp. 125-7.
[2] *1948 Labour Annual Conference Report*, pp. 212-14.

of the Party Conference, be the Administrative Authority of the Party." [1] No distinction is made in this clause between the PLP and the Labour Party, but clearly the intention is that the NEC should be responsible for the work of the Party *outside Parliament*, subject of course to the overriding authority of the annual conference. The NEC is composed of 28 members, two of whom are *ex officio:* the Leader (since 1929) and the Deputy Leader (since 1953). A third member of the NEC, the Treasurer of the Party, may be nominated by any affiliated organization and is elected by vote of the whole party conference. For the purpose of nomination and election of the remaining 25 members of the committee, the NEC is divided into four divisions: Division I consists of 12 members nominated and elected by the affiliated trade unions from among their members; Division II consists of one member nominated and elected by the socialist, co-operative and professional organizations affiliated to the party; Division III includes seven members nominated and elected by the constituency Labour Parties, Federations and Central Labour Parties. Division IV consists of five women members of the party who may be nominated by any affiliated organization and who are elected by a vote of the whole party conference. [2] In addition, the Secretary of the Party is also a member of the NEC and may take part in its deliberations although it is the custom that he should not exercise a vote. The NEC elects its own chairman and vice-chairman and the Executive normally elects to these offices the individual with longest service on the Executive who has not yet served in the office.

Ever since the formation of the Labour Representation Committee the trade unions have been in a position to control a majority of the places on the NEC. Under present arrangements they have 12 direct representatives among the 28 members of the committee. In addition, however, they cast an overwhelming preponderance of the vote for the five women members and for the Treasurer. In effect therefore they can determine, if they wish, who shall occupy 18 of the 28 places on the Executive. It need not be implied that the trade unions have on all occasions insisted that the places they control should be occupied by individuals who are completely subservient to their own point of view. Indeed, during the period 1918–29 when the trade unions and affiliated societies voted jointly for 13 places on the Executive the trade unions tolerated the election of a number of non-trade unionists from the ILP and the Fabian Society. Similarly they have supported the election of women

[1] *Labour Party Constitution* (1953), p. 9.
[2] *Ibid.*, pp. 21–2. For the composition of the Executive during earlier periods see Table 13 on p. 518.

members to the NEC who were not active in the trade union movement, and Arthur Greenwood was re-elected Treasurer for many years although he was a parliamentary rather than a trade union figure. But there can be little doubt that few members of the Executive elected in the categories in which the trade unions have a preponderant vote will long survive in office if he or she falls foul of majority opinion among the leaders of the trade unions affiliated to the party.

TABLE 13

THE COMPOSITION OF THE NEC

Date	Trade Unions	Trade Councils	Treas- urer	Social- ist Societ- ies	Consti- tuency Parties	Women	Leader	Total
1900	7	—	—	5	—	—	—	12
1901	7	1	—	5	—	—	—	13
1902–8	9	1	—	3	—	—	—	13
1909–11	11	1	—	3	—	—	—	15
1912–17	11	1	1	3	—	—	—	16
1918–29	13*	—	1	—	5	4	—	23
1930–36	12	—	1	1	5	5	1	25
1937–52	12	—	1	1	7	5	1	27
1953–	12	—	1	1	7	5	2†	28

* Called " National Societies " section.
† Includes Deputy Leader.

Notes :

Up to 1918 each section nominated and voted for its own representatives on the Committee (*i.e.* ILP elected their own two, and Fabian Society their one).

1918-36 each section nominated its own representatives but they were voted upon by the whole conference (except women members who could be nominated by any section of the conference).

Since 1937 each section has nominated and voted its own representatives (except in the case of the women's section, which is nominated and voted upon by the whole conference).

The Secretary of the Party is not included in the above table.

A review of the record of the NEC shows that it has never attempted to move in any direction in which a majority of affiliated trade unions were not prepared to follow. This is not to say that the trade unions have consistently determined an agreed policy among themselves and then foisted it upon the NEC and the party as a whole. It has much more frequently been the case that the initiative has come from the parliamentary leaders of the party who, as has already been explained, have invariably been well represented on the NEC and during long periods have constituted a majority of its members. So long as the leading parliamentarians have been able, as individuals, to retain the confidence of the leading figures in the trade union world, and so long as they have been able to convince these trade unionists of the wisdom of the policies they propose, the NEC has inevitably fallen into line. To recall a phrase which was used in the discussion of the Conservative Party, this is a process of " leadership by consent "—that is, by the consent largely of the trade unions, since frequently in the history of the party the minority of constituency representatives on the NEC have found themselves out of sympathy with the remainder of the Executive and the parliamentary leaders.

The authority of the Leader and of other prominent parliamentarians on the NEC who share his views has been enhanced (in a negative sense) by the provision of the Labour Party constitution which prohibits members of the General Council of the Trades Union Congress from being nominated for the NEC. Occasionally leading figures in the trade union movement have chosen to seek membership of the NEC rather than the General Council of the TUC, but this is not the general rule; in a majority of unions the most influential and powerful figures have chosen to serve on the General Council. As a result, at almost every stage in the modern history of the party the trade union representation on the NEC has consisted of second and sometimes third rank union leaders. A description of NEC meetings by those who have attended them suggests that as a rule most trade union representatives are prepared to play a modest rôle and to support the initiative of the Leader of the Party and his parliamentary supporters. Votes taken in the NEC on issues of policy may find trade union representatives divided, just as the constituency representatives may find themselves voting on opposite sides. But whenever the Leader of the Party and those of his colleagues who represent majority opinions in the PLP have been challenged by rebel opinion (which is usually based in the constituency section of the Executive) a majority of the trade union representatives have almost invariably voted overwhelmingly on the side of the Leader and his friends.[1]

[1] This analysis of divisions of opinion within the NEC has inevitably had to be based largely on discussion with present and former members of the Executive since there is very little published evidence concerning the history of the NEC's deliberations. However, this interpretation of recent NEC developments is to some extent sustained by a passage in Beatrice

It is therefore misleading to speak of " trade union control of the NEC," if by that phrase it is intended to imply that the trade unions have invariably taken positive action to manipulate the Executive for the purpose of fulfilling a concerted and agreed trade union programme. Leadership and initiative within the NEC has almost invariably been retained by the Leader and the representatives of majority opinion within the parliamentary party. Indeed, in the 1931 crisis, as was shown in the analysis of the fall of the second Labour Government in 1931,[1] the non-M.P. section of the NEC abdicated all attempt to control the course of events. But even in less dramatic circumstances, the trade union element in the NEC is normally prepared to accept and follow the leadership of the PLP leaders on the NEC. The latter have normally been able to control the affairs of the party so long as they retained the confidence of a majority of the trade union representatives on the Executive.

A discussion of the composition of the NEC must also include some reference to the striking continuity of its membership. In the annual elections for the NEC during the period 1900–53, some 1,125 places were filled. A total of 199 people filled these places with an average length of service of just over five years. Forty-six individuals served for only one year; 115 served for under five years; and the remainder, 84 (or 42 per cent. of those who served on the NEC) held office for five years or more. And of these, 42, or 21 per cent. of those who served, did so for ten years or more. The hard core of long-service veterans consisted of five who served from 20 to 24 years (C. R. Attlee, Ben Turner, Mrs. B. Ayrton-Gould, Mrs. J. L. Adamson, Susan Lawrence) and five others who served 25 years or over (J. R. Clynes, Arthur Henderson, J. R. MacDonald, Hugh Dalton, and Herbert Morrison). These figures do not necessarily suggest that there has ever existed a tight-knit oligarchical control of the Executive; there has clearly been a fairly steady recruitment of new members from year to year. But equally there was never in the course of NEC elections a sudden or dramatic transformation in the membership of the Executive. A hard

---

Webb's diary in which she records a conversation with Susan Lawrence after the latter's re-election to the NEC in 1925: " Susan (she wrote) who is now back again on the Executive of the Labour Party is depressed with its commonplace Trade Union composition—says that it means the dominance of [MacDonald] and a moderate and timid policy . . . there being no one but Lansbury to stand up to him, the Executive will be silent and not protest—until it is too late . . . " *Beatrice Webb's Diaries,* 12 October, 1925, folios 89–90. For a further comment on this issue, see p. 599-600 below.

[1] See pp. 443-4 above.

core of members who enjoyed the confidence of the party retained office for long periods of time and thereby helped to ensure continuity of policy; they also helped to ensure the development of certain conventional relationships between the NEC, the party conference and the PLP.

The functions of the NEC [1] may be classified in two broad divisions: first, to supervise the work of the party outside Parliament at every level; second, to report on its own work to the conference and to submit to the conference " such resolutions and declarations affecting the Programme, Principles and Policy of the Party as, in its view, may be necessitated by political circumstances." The first of these functions involves a very wide range of responsibilities. The NEC must " ensure the establishment of and . . . keep in active operation " Constituency Labour Parties, Central Labour Parties and Federations in every appropriate political area throughout the country. It must ensure that all the officers and members of the party at every level conform to the constitution, rules and standing orders of the party. The NEC is given powers to enforce these regulations by taking " any action it deems necessary for such purpose, whether by way of disaffiliation of an organization or expulsion of an individual, or otherwise." Any such action must be reported to the next annual conference of the party when it is subject to review and to possible reversal by the conference itself.

The NEC has never hesitated to use its powers of disaffiliation and expulsion when it deemed such action to be necessary; its annual reports bristle with illustrations of the procedure followed in proscribing organizations and movements which have attempted to win the support of Labour Party members or of the party itself for particular sets of objectives which were frowned upon by the NEC. [2] The procedure followed in the disaffiliation of recalcitrant constituency parties is nowhere better illustrated than in the publication entitled *The NEC Versus the Widnes Labour Party: The Facts* (London, 1939), which contains the full text of the correspondence exchanged between the Divisional Labour Party concerned and

---

[1] For a detailed list of the " Duties and Powers " of the NEC see Clause VIII of the Party Constitution (1953).

[2] It is not possible to review NEC procedure in any of these instances in detail, but an account of the procedure followed in dealing with one of the most explosive issues of the 1930s, the Popular Front campaign, can be found in the following sources: *The Report of the NEC* to the 1939 party conference, and in the report of the conference itself. For a description of the rôle of the principal figure in this dispute see Strauss, P., *Cripps—Advocate and Rebel*, pp. 111-14; Estorick, E., *Stafford Cripps : Master Statesman*, pp. 143-8 ; and Foot, M., *Aneurin Bevan*, Vol. I, Chapter 9.

the officials of party head office acting on behalf of the NEC. Disciplinary action culminating in expulsion has also been taken against a number of individuals in the party, including Members of Parliament. The Parliamentary Labour Party can do no more than withdraw the whip from recalcitrant M.P.s and exclude them from meetings of the PLP. It cannot force an M.P. to resign his seat nor prevent him from attempting to secure re-election. The NEC, however, can expel the M.P. from the Labour Party and refuse to approve his readoption as a Labour candidate. If his local party insists on readopting him despite NEC disapproval (as sometimes happens) then the NEC can and usually does proceed to disaffiliate the party. It can then be expected to form another Constituency Labour Party which adopts a candidate acceptable to the NEC.[1]

Perhaps the most striking feature of the whole history of NEC disciplinary action, whether against movements, constituency parties or individuals, has been this: in almost every case the action of the NEC has been overwhelmingly approved by the subsequent annual conference. The record would suggest that when the leaders of the parliamentary party find themselves embarrassed by an individual or an organization they can rely with confidence on the NEC to rid them of the troublemakers concerned. The NEC in turn can almost invariably depend upon the conference to sustain its action.

The second main responsibility of the NEC (to report on its work to the annual conference and to present policy statements to the conference) has already been dealt with in some detail. The importance of its rôle in this regard was best expressed by Herbert Morrison in the course of an address to the 1937 annual conference in which he said: " This Executive is the servant of the Conference, but it has a duty to lead the Conference, to advise the Conference in the way it ought to go, and I hope every Executive that has responsibility will never hesitate to give Conference firm advice as to what it ought to do." [2] As has already been shown, the Executive has almost invariably fulfilled the rôle Morrison here assigns it. On rare occasions, as for example in the foreign affairs debate at the 1936 conference, the voice of the NEC has been muffled or confused,[3] but on almost every other important issue of policy the

---

[1] A variation of this procedure occurred in 1949 in the case of Konni Zilliacus, a Labour M.P. who had been elected in 1945. For the NEC's account of its action in his case see their report to the 1949 conference, p. 18, and the conference report for that year, pp. 119-26.

[2] *1937 Labour Annual Conference Report*, p. 163.

[3] See p. 426 above.

NEC has made a forthright recommendation as to the action the conference ought to take.

Whatever divisions may exist within the NEC itself, it now speaks in conference with a single voice. This was not always the case; there are instances in earlier conference reports when prominent members of the Executive have spoken on opposite sides in important debates. Thus, for example, at the 1908 conference MacDonald, then Secretary of the Party, spoke against a resolution calling on the Government " to establish a legal minimum wage in selected trades, on the lines suggested in the Sweated Industries Bill introduced into Parliament by Mr. Arthur Henderson, M.P." Henderson, in reply, defended his action and warned the conference not to embarrass the PLP by defeating the resolution; the conference accepted his advice and passed it.[1] There is no clear indication as to when a principle akin to Cabinet solidarity first became accepted in the councils of the NEC, but the last important conference demonstration of disunity within the NEC occurred when Lansbury disagreed with his colleagues on the issue of sanctions at the party conference of 1935. After 1951, a small minority of the NEC vigorously dissented from the views of the majority on several major issues. In political speeches between conferences the dissenters did not attempt to conceal their differences, but at the conference itself no member of the NEC has given any hint that he disagreed with his colleagues on any issue discussed by the conference. In May 1954, however, the NEC decided that all its members would be bound by the principle of Cabinet solidarity except on issues which the NEC itself might from time to time specify. The resolution read as follows: " Decisions arrived at by a majority vote are binding upon the National Executive Committee unless otherwise decided by the National Executive Committee itself. Any infringement of this rule shall be dealt with at the next subsequent meeting." [2]

The dispute within the NEC which followed the resignation of Aneurin Bevan and two of his Ministerial colleagues from the Labour Government on 22nd April, 1951, led to an important controversy over the policy-making functions of the NEC. Three days after the resignations the NEC held a meeting at which one of Bevan's supporters proposed that the NEC should convene a special party conference to enable the party as a whole to debate the issue of rearmament (which had been the principal subject of

---

[1] *1908 Labour Annual Conference Report*, pp. 73-4.

[2] One week later the NEC ruled " That the issue of German rearmament shall be declared to be exempt as regards individual expressions of opinion, from the implications imposed by the (above) resolution . . . " *Labour Press Service*, June, 1954.

dispute between Bevan and his Cabinet colleagues). This proposal was rejected by the NEC which issued a statement reaffirming its wholehearted support for the Government's defence and budgetary policies. On the following day Bevan and three of his supporters on the NEC wrote to Morgan Phillips claiming that by taking sides in the controversy arising out of the Ministerial resignations the NEC had, in their view, " exceeded its proper function".

> " The NEC (the letter added) is the servant not of the Government but of the Party. Its primary task is to carry out the decisions of the Annual Conference. Its relations even with a Labour Government—though, naturally, close and friendly—are second to its obligations to the Party. It has, rightly, no power to issue directives to the Government: in turn, it should not be called on automatically to endorse Government policies, even major policies, which have not been pronounced upon by the Party Conference.
>
> " A serious situation would arise if it came to be thought that the NEC was merely an extension of the machinery of Government. The NEC's activities might well be crippled in such a situation, and the Government itself embarrassed—if, for instance, Party delegates to Socialist Parties and conferences in other countries were to be regarded as agents of the Government.
>
> " Equally serious is the opposite danger that could arise from the disturbance of this constitutional balance—the danger that the Government could come to be regarded as the instrument of the Party Executive. It is in order to stress the undesirability of any such tendency that a Labour Prime Minister always presents to the Annual Conference of the Party a separate report on the work of the Parliamentary Labour Party.
>
> " The distinction between Government and Party has always been jealously maintained in British Constitutional practice. It is one of the important safeguards of the rights of the individual who seeks to express a minority view within the framework of the Party constitution. The statement just issued by the NEC tends to blur this constitutional distinction and to weaken this safeguard. . . . We cannot agree that the NEC was within its powers in issuing this statement or has the right to prevent us from discussing, in Parliament or elsewhere, the issues on which it hastened to take sides. . . . "

The Party Secretary said in reply that he accepted the view set forth by Bevan and his colleagues that the NEC and the Government " must preserve their separate identities and that the National Executive Committee has no obligation automatically to endorse Government policy . . ." But he added that this nevertheless

> " leaves the National Executive Committee free to comment on the work and policies of any Government—Labour no less than

Tory . . . . Such statements are, of course, reported to the subsequent Annual Conference where they are open to discussion like every other activity of the National Executive Committee . . . . I cannot believe that you would wish to confine National Executive Committee statements to problems of internal Party organization, since some of you have in the past subscribed to statements by the National Executive Committee on political issues which were not foreseen at the previous Party Conference. As the elected authority responsible for representing the Labour Party between Conferences the National Executive Committee has not only the right but the duty to publish its views, especially on matters which might be the subject of controversy and confusion in the Movement."[1]

Undoubtedly Bevan and his friends were on weak ground in challenging the right of the NEC to make a statement on a major matter of public controversy. As Morgan Phillips quite rightly pointed out, the NEC has never hesitated in the past to make such statements even though the issue involved had not hitherto been discussed by a party conference; a subsequent conference would have the opportunity to review and, if it wished, to repudiate the action of the NEC. The Bevan group did not choose to raise a quite different question: whether the NEC had not in the six years since 1945 abdicated its responsibility to maintain a viewpoint of its own, independent from that of the Labour Government of the day. As has already been noted, not once in the lifetime of the Labour Governments of 1945 and 1950 did the NEC give any public indication that it disagreed with any item of Government policy. No doubt it was late in the day to raise this issue, but certainly the protest which was made on this occasion carried little weight, since Phillips could point out that members of the group had themselves subscribed to statements by the NEC on issues which had not been discussed by a previous party conference.

During the inter-war years especially, the NEC's function in declaring and affirming Labour Party policy between conferences was of much greater importance than it has been since 1945. The NEC met much more frequently then than it does now. (To take but a few examples at random: it met 41 times during the year 1918–19, 34 times during 1923–4, 39 times during 1935–6; whereas during the years since 1945 it met no more than 10 to 12 times a year.) During the 1930s, and especially when the party was at its weakest in the years 1931–5, the decisions of the NEC, and the policy declarations which it issued, were undoubtedly on many occasions of greater public interest than were the deliberations

[1] See *1951 Labour Annual Conference Report*, (Report of the Executive), pp. 5-6.

and decisions of the PLP. But with the formation of a Labour Government in 1945 and the emergence of a powerful PLP the deliberations of the NEC sank into comparative insignificance. It is doubtful whether they were of much greater importance than those of the Executive Committee of the National Union. There was some revival in the importance of the work of the NEC after Labour returned to opposition in 1951 but it appeared unlikely that the NEC would recapture the limelight which it held in the 1930s and earlier. It is abundantly clear that the real centre of day-to-day policy-making within the Labour Party is to be found in the deliberations of the Parliamentary Committee and of the PLP. However, it is important to note that during the bitter quarrels of the 1950s and early 1960s the NEC became a forum in which the dissident minority, defeated in the PLP, could renew its battle against the parliamentary leaders.

The Sub-Committees of the NEC

The NEC has five major sub-committees and, in addition, it appoints a number of special sub-committees and advisory committees which deal with particular problems of current concern to the party. The major committees are as follows: organization, international, commonwealth, policy and publicity, finance and general purposes. The Leader and Deputy Leader, the Chairman, Vice-Chairman and the Treasurer of the NEC are *ex officio* members of each committee; the remaining members of each committee are recruited from the NEC itself by the following procedure: after the election of a new NEC the Secretary of the party sends to the members of the NEC a list of the sub-committees which are to be established and invites them to indicate (in order of preference) the committees to which they wish to belong. The Secretary himself then allocates individuals to particular committees (NEC members may not always find themselves allocated to the committees which they would prefer). The Secretary's draft list of committee memberships is then submitted to a meeting of the NEC and it is normally approved without debate.

Reference has been made to Table 6 (p. 424) which shows that, since 1945 especially, the composition of the sub-committees of the NEC has reflected much the same preponderance of M.P.s (and of Ministers and ex-Ministers) as has the NEC itself. In allocating NEC members to the sub-committees the Secretary may have deliberately sought to reflect a balance similar to that which exists in the parent committee; but whatever the reason there can be little doubt that the preponderance of members of the PLP on the three major committees (policy, organization and international) has helped to ensure that the views of these committees are unlikely to be at variance with those of the majority of the PLP itself. This is particularly the case since the leaders of majority opinion in the PLP can usually rely upon the support of a majority of trade union members of the NEC. The sub-committees work closely with the principal departments of the party head office; their work will therefore be examined more fully in Chapter IX. Reports of the work of the sub-committees are incorporated in the NEC report which is presented to the annual conference. It is therefore possible for conference delegates to move back the reference of particular passages in sub-committee reports to which they object, although such moves have been successful only on the rarest occasions.

There is one other sub-committee of the NEC which should be bracketed with the five major sub-committees referred to above; but the NEC itself seems rather reticent about its work. This is the elections sub-committee. Its principal duty is to consider in the first instance whether the approval of the NEC ought to be given to prospective candidates whom constituency parties wish to adopt.[1] On comparatively rare occasions when the NEC has proposed to withhold endorsement of sitting Labour Members reference has been made in the report of the NEC to the work of the elections sub-committee.[2] In such instances the action of the sub-committee is, of course, subject to debate by the party conference.

[1] See p. 550 below.

[2] The following excerpt from the NEC report to the 1949 conference (p. 18) gives an indication of the functions of the elections sub-committee: "In March, 1949, Mr. L. J. Solley, M.P., was selected by the Thurrock Trades Council and Constituency Labour Party to be their Parliamentary Candidate at the next General Election. The Constituency Party's application for the National Executive Committee's endorsement of the Candidature was referred to the Elections Sub-Committee of the Executive and considered by them at their meeting on 26th April. At this meeting it was decided to defer making a recommendation to the National Executive Committee pending a further meeting of the Sub-Committee which Mr. Solley was invited to attend.

"In accordance with this decision, Mr. Solley attended the meeting of the Sub-Committee held on 16th May. Mr. Solley was given an opportunity to comment and to answer questions on a document outlining his activities and attitudes during the last three years. In the course of the interview, not only was the endorsement of his candidature considered but also his membership of the Party.

"This interview was reported to the National Executive Committee at their meeting on 18th May, when after full discussion it was decided to expel Mr. Solley from membership of the Labour Party. This decision was immediately conveyed to Mr. Solley and also to the Thurrock Trades Council and Constituency Labour Party who were at the same time informed that it would be necessary to proceed with the selection of a prospective Parliamentary Candidate for the next General Election."

But in contrast to the fairly full reports of the work of other NEC sub-committees which are regularly incorporated in the NEC Report, there is usually little or no information concerning the activities of the elections sub-committee. Certainly there is no indication of the number or names of prospective candidates from whom approval has been withheld. By omitting any full report of the work of its elections sub-committee the NEC no doubt manages to avoid a great many tiresome conference debates. The NEC is thus able to handle the delicate matter of candidatures with a minimum of interference from the mass organization of the party. The arrangement which it has evolved is strikingly similar to that which operates within the National Union. It will be recalled that the National Union's Standing Advisory Committee on Candidates, unlike the other advisory committees of the National Union, does not report to the party's annual conference.[1]

The NEC participates in a number of joint committees with other sections of the Labour movement. The most important of these is the National Council of Labour, a body which is composed of seven representatives of the Trades Union Congress, seven representatives of the Co-operative Union and seven representatives of the Labour Party (of whom four are nominated by the PLP and three by the NEC). One representative attends for the Labour Peers and the editor of the *Daily Herald* is also permitted to do so. In addition, the secretaries of the TUC, the Labour Party and the Co-operative Union serve as joint secretaries of the Council. For some years during the 1930s the Council served as a policy-making body on behalf of the trade unions and the Labour Party (the Co-operative Union did not formally join the Council until 1941). But it has now ceased to do so; it serves primarily a liaison function and is of little political significance. Each of the constituent bodies presents a report on its major activities to each meeting in order that the organizations represented may be kept informed of each other's work. Some of the Council's meetings are given over to an exchange of views on current problems of common concern. Thus the Council's report presented to the 1953 Labour Party conference records that during the eight meetings held in the previous year there were discussions of such matters as the future of the iron and steel industry, agricultural marketing boards, the co-operative movement in the colonies and the International Confederation of Free Trade Unions.

---

[1] Since this passage was written the work of approving prospective candidates has been transferred to the organization sub-committee. It conducts its work in much the same way.

The NEC is represented on two other joint committees which bring it into close association with organs of the co-operative movement. One of these is a joint committee of the NEC and the National Policy Committee of the National Co-operative Authority; the other is a joint committee of the NEC and the National Organization Committee of the Co-operative Party. The work of the latter organization cannot be dealt with in detail, but some further reference must be made to its relations with the Labour Party. Over a thousand retail, wholesale and producer co-operative societies with a total membership of approximately 11 million are affiliated to the *Co-operative Union*; and approximately two-thirds of these societies (with a membership of over eight million) are affiliated to the *Co-operative Party*,[1] which was founded in 1917. The Co-operative Party has repeatedly refused to affiliate nationally with the Labour Party although it has negotiated an agreement with the latter which is designed to promote close relations between the two bodies both in Parliament and outside. Under this agreement local Co-operative Society Parties are encouraged to affiliate with Constituency Labour Parties and to run joint candidates both for Parliament and local government bodies, usually under the title " Co-operative and Labour." These candidates commit themselves in advance to joining the Parliamentary Labour Party and to conforming to its regulations. In the 1951 elections 38 such candidates were jointly sponsored, of whom 16 were returned to Parliament. The Co-operative Party meets separately in annual conference and its work outside Parliament is synchronized with that of the Labour Party through the joint committee referred to above. In every important respect the " Co-operative and Labour " M.P.s are indistinguishable from other members of the PLP.

Although the NEC does not maintain formal links with the Fabian Society through a joint committee as it does with the co-operators and the trade unions, some reference must be made to the Fabian Society's unique rôle in the Labour Party. The Society was, it will be recalled, one of the sponsoring bodies which helped to form the LRC in 1900 and it has been affiliated to the Labour Party since the party's inception. The Fabian Society has never sought power for itself; it has never had an electoral programme of its own; it has reserved its right to encourage research and discussion within the Labour movement of all issues which, in the Society's own judgment, are worthy of study. The Society as a whole is not committed to support the views of any of the authors whom it publishes. Groups or factions within the Labour Party have there-

---

[1] See Bailey, J., *The Co-operators in Politics*, pamphlet, n.d. (c. 1949).

fore never been able to use the Society's name to win support for their policies.

It is not possible to recount the history of the Society[1]; but it should be noted that it has at present 6,400 members who are affiliated either nationally or through the 115 local societies. The then president of the Society, G. D. H. Cole, defined its rôle in 1953 when the Labour Party was sharply divided on the issue of " Bevanism ". Cole said:

> " It is at times like these that the value of the Fabian Society as a research organization open to Socialists who differ sharply about some aspect of immediate policy appears most plainly. The Fabian Society cannot take sides either for or against the Bevanites: it has to hold the allegiance of Bevanites and anti-Bevanites and of those larger sections of the movement which reject both labels, or it cannot carry on with the tasks it has set itself. Its great task is to work out, not policies to throw at the Labour Party's head but projects based on careful thought, which commit no one but their authors and are open to be taken or left, or altered for adoption, as the responsible bodies to which they are offered see fit. The Society is there to enable its members to offer considered advice to the Labour Party, to the Trade Unions, to the Co-operators— indeed to any Labour body that cares to take notice of them." [2]

The Society has sometimes been formally requested by the Labour head office to undertake particular pieces of research. After the Labour Party's return to opposition in 1951, for example, the research department at head office invited the Fabian Society to examine some of the problems which had faced the two post-war Labour Governments. Arthur Skeffington, M.P. (a Fabian who was elected in 1953 as the representative on the NEC of the socialist, co-operative and professional organizations), has described the Society's response to this request: " A number of expert groups were formed (by the Society). Reports were forwarded on the social services, housing policy, on education and on nationalization. By agreement these findings have not been published but we know they were of assistance to the sub-committees preparing *Challenge to Britain*, and we received the thanks of the NEC." [3] Normally

---

[1] See Pease, E. R., *History of the Fabian Society*, London, 1925, and Margaret Cole's definitive account, *The Story of Fabian Socialism*, London, 1961. See also *Fabian Journal*, No. 12, April 1954, reviewing the work of the Society on its 70th anniversary, and Milburn, J. F., " The Fabian Society and the British Labour Party," *The Western Political Quarterly*, Vol. XI, No. 2, June, 1958.

[2] Cited in *Fabian Journal*, No. 12, April, 1954, pp. 26-7.

[3] Skeffington, A., " The Fabian Society and the Labour Party," *Fabian Journal*, No. 12, April, 1954, p. 27.

the results of the Society's research are made available more generally and informally throughout the Labour movement. The critics of the Society sometimes argue that with the development of large-scale research resources at Labour head office it no longer serves a useful purpose, but there is a large enough body of opinion in the Labour movement which disagrees with this view to ensure that the Society should continue to play its present modest but important rôle in encouraging research into and discussion of problems of socialist policy.

III

THE REGIONAL ORGANIZATION OF THE LABOUR PARTY

The Labour Party was much slower than the Conservative in devising a system of regional organization; but, like the Conservatives, Labour has been careful to ensure that its regional organizations acquire very little authority in the affairs of the party. As early as 1886 the National Union had recognized the wisdom of devolving some of its work on a set of Provincial Unions and from these beginnings the present elaborate area organization has evolved. The first two regional councils of the Labour Party were those established in 1938, one for Lancashire and Cheshire, and the other for Wales. Subsequently 11 such councils in all have been established covering England, Wales and Scotland. [1]

The Labour Party has adopted at the regional level a principle which is to be found in the Conservative Party at both national and regional levels. The professional organization of the Labour Party in the regions (the regional organiser and his staff) are responsible *not* to the elective regional council or its executive but to the National Agent and the party head office in London. The head office in turn is of course responsible to the NEC and the party conference, an arrangement which contrasts with the Conservative

[1] The following is a list of the Regional Councils and the counties which they represent: EAST MIDLANDS: Derbyshire, Leicestershire, Lincolnshire, Northamptonshire, Nottinghamshire; EASTERN: Bedfordshire, Cambridgeshire, Isle of Ely, Essex, Hertfordshire, Huntingdonshire, Norfolk, Suffolk; LONDON: Administrative County of London and Middlesex; NORTHERN REGION: Cumberland, Durham, Northumberland, North Riding except Scarborough and Whitby; NORTH-WESTERN: Cheshire, part of Derbyshire, Lancashire, Westmorland; SCOTLAND; SOUTHERN: Berkshire, Buckinghamshire, Hampshire, Kent, Surrey, East Sussex, West Sussex, Isle of Wight; SOUTH-WESTERN: Cornwall, Devon, Dorset, Gloucestershire, Somerset, Wiltshire; WALES: Wales and Monmouthshire; WEST MIDLANDS: Herefordshire, Oxfordshire, Shropshire, Staffordshire, Warwickshire, Worcestershire; YORKSHIRE: East Riding, Scarborough and Whitby, West Riding, York.

chain of command; but at the regional level of the Labour Party, the relationship between the professional party workers and the mass organization of the party is identical with that in the Conservative Party. If anything, the regional councils of the Labour Party tend to be even less influential than the area councils of the National Union. They meet more rarely (once a year compared with two to four times a year) and Labour's regional councils, unlike the Conservative area councils, are forbidden to debate national or international affairs. They have a few drastically limited functions (which are discussed below) but they are so nearly powerless that it is difficult to understand how they succeed in holding the interest of those who attend their meetings. Ostrogorski's cynical comment on the Conservative area organization of his day (". . . without even resorting to much wire-pulling, the central office ensures the organization of the party a complete unity of management which makes all the threads converge in the London office and utilizes the popular Associations for its own ends . . .") could be as aptly applied to the regional organizations of the Labour Party to-day.

The initiative in the formation of regional councils came in the first instance from the NEC rather than from the regions themselves. Thus, for example, the report of the first annual meeting of the East Midlands Regional Council recorded: " The proposal of the NEC to establish the East Midlands Regional Council was approved unanimously at a conference of 88 Trade Union and Labour Party organizations, represented by 360 delegates held . . . at Nottingham, 5th December, 1942 . . . . Mr. Shepherd (the National Agent) placed the proposal of the National Executive before the conference, which agreed to appoint a provisional committee to draft the constitution, rules and standing orders for the consideration of a Second Conference," etc. [1] The constitution subsequently adopted is typical of those in effect in other regions. It outlines a very modest set of objectives. Membership of Labour regional councils is open to the following bodies: constituency parties and borough (or central) parties affiliated to the Labour Party nationally, county federations of Labour Parties, and federations of trades councils recognized by the TUC; individual trade unions (if their entire membership is within the region) or, alternatively, area or district committees of national trade unions (whose membership extends over more than one region); co-operative societies and area

[1] *Report of the Provisional Executive Committee to the First Annual Meeting of the East Midlands Regional Council of the Labour Party*, 26th June, 1943, p. 2.

or district committees of co-operative organizations; area or district committees of socialist societies affiliated to the Labour Party nationally; women's advisory councils. All of these affiliated organizations are entitled to send delegates to the annual meeting of the regional council; and in addition the following may attend the annual meeting as *ex officio* members without voting rights: members of the NEC who reside in the region, M.P.s and candidates for the region and two representatives from each Labour Group on county councils within the region.

The major function of the annual meeting is to elect an executive committee which, like the NEC, is composed on a federal basis, ensuring representation for the trade unions, constituency parties and women's advisory councils and each other type of organization affiliated to the regional council.[1] The executive committee meets on an average of six or seven times a year and attends to the work of the council in the intervals between the latter's annual meetings. The members of the executive may also be called on for other duties: thus, for example, the 1953 Lancashire and Cheshire Report notes: " Executive members have also co-operated with the Regional Organizer to an increasing extent in the work in the constituencies by acting at local enquiries, deputizing at selection conferences and at other meetings of vital importance to the Party." [2] The executive elects its own chairman and treasurer and in some instances these offices have been occupied by the same individual for very long periods of time. On the death of George Tomlinson the Lancashire and Cheshire Report recalled that: " From the inception of the Regional Council in 1938, George Tomlinson has been Chairman of the Council . . ." [3] According to Tomlinson's biographer [4] he cherished the office with paternal concern: ". . . the Lancashire and Cheshire Regional Council was very near to his heart. . . . It was one of the positions he wanted to keep all his life." His biographer concedes that " he sometimes annoyed delegates by his adroit manœuvring of controversial items on the agenda . . ."; but Tomlinson " had his wish "; he died in harness, although his achievement is somewhat tarnished by the fact that a resolution from a constituency Labour Party appeared on the agenda for the subsequent annual meeting proposing " That this Regional Council

[1] See for example the composition of the Executive Committee of the Southern Regional Council, *Report of the Executive Committee of the Council*, 1953, p. 1.
[2] *Report of the Executive of the Lancashire and Cheshire Regional Council*, 1953, p. 4.
[3] *Ibid.*, p. 3.
[4] Blackburn, F., *George Tomlinson*, p. 198.

adopts the same procedure as the National Executive with regard to the chairmanship of the Regional Council, e.g. that a different chairman should be appointed each year." [1] Leaving nothing to chance, the constitutions of most regional councils provide that the regional organizer " shall act as Secretary to the Regional Council."

The primary functions of the regional councils are to ensure the establishment of constituency and borough Labour Parties; " to co-operate with the National Executive Committee, the General Council of the Trades Union Congress, the Co-operative Union Limited, or other Kindred Organizations, in joint political or other action . . ."; and to encourage the work of county federations of Labour Parties and other party organizations in connection with local government. The Executive Committee of the West Midlands Regional Council underlined in its annual report for 1953 the limited functions of its council: " (Its) primary work . . . must remain the strengthening and further development of the organization and activity of the Constituency Parties." [2]

Official party literature has occasionally hinted that the councils might have a broader function. Thus, for example, a party pamphlet published in 1948, *The Rise of the Labour Party*, stated (p. 14): " The Regional Councils (also serve) as groupings which can be consulted by the National Executive on issues of policy, and means whereby the currents of opinion within the Party can be measured and taken account of in formulating national programmes." But such consultation has occurred on only the rarest of occasions; and even then it has been concerned not at all with " currents of opinion within the party " but merely with internal problems of administration. Thus the 1944 East Midlands Report notes that ". . . (the) Executive was consulted by the NEC concerning a number of proposals it was considering placing before the next Annual Conference. Subjects covered included the ' Year of Party Development ' campaign, the fixing of a common minimum membership subscription for all parties . . . authority and procedure concerning the nomination and selection of Parliamentary candidates . . . the opening of a General Election Fund." [3]

There have been occasional exasperated protests both on the regional and national level against the comparative impotence of

---

[1] *Report of the Executive of the Lancashire and Cheshire Regional Council*, 1953, p. 18.

[2] *Report of the Executive Committee to the 10th Annual Meeting of the West Midlands Regional Council*, 1953, p. 13.

[3] *1944 Annual Report of the East Midlands Regional Executive Committee*, p. 9.

the councils. At the 1949 national party conference Harold Davies, M.P., moved the rererence back of the section of the NEC report dealing with regional councils: ". . . some of us (he said) believe that the Party machine needs revitalizing. . . . The time has come . . . to see if we can make Regional Councils really effective. I believe that if the Regional Councils had a first-class Conference some time before this main one the results of the main Conference discussion would be thereby improved. The Regional Councils have not got enough power within the constitution of the Party." He urged that " individual voices " must be made to " feel that they are helping to polish and implement Labour Party policy." The reference back was seconded; but there was no debate and in reply to Davies's proposal Morgan Phillips, the party Secretary, redefined the function of regional councils in a sentence that gave no encouragement to the hope that they might be permitted to play a more effective rôle in the affairs of the party: " We established the Regional Councils (he said) for the purpose of getting in every part of the country a complete liaison between Co-operatives, Trade Unions and the Constituency Labour Parties." The reference back was lost without a recorded vote.[1]

Harold Davies's plea has frequently echoed through the meetings of the regional councils themselves. At the annual meeting of the West Midlands Regional Council in 1953 a constituency Labour Party delegate moved the following resolution:

> " That this Conference welcomes meetings where prominent members of the Labour Movement are in attendance, but deplores the present habit of designating as ' Conferences ' meetings which are in fact devoted to a lecture with questions and discussion if time permits, and particularly objects to the practice of bringing a ready-made resolution before such a meeting, thus denying the local Movement a share in policy-making; and accordingly calls upon the Regional Party to organize in addition to these lectures, some genuine Conferences where discussion may be initiated by the rank and file, as it is only at such a meeting that a two-way traffic of ideas between leadership and membership is possible, and as only when both sides have a chance of listening to the other misunderstandings and divisions can be avoided."

Another delegate moved an amendment to add: " That the National Executive Committee of the Labour Party should give powers to Regional Councils to discuss policy matters." The secretary of the regional council (who, as was noted above, is invariably the regional organizer and thus a representative of the

---

[1] *1949 Labour Annual Conference Report*, p. 134.

party head office) warned that these proposals would "need a decision of National Conference and would necessitate recasting the whole structure of the Party nationally and regionally." He appealed for the withdrawal of the resolution but after a lively debate the issue was carried to a vote. The amendment was defeated by 92 votes to 58 but the resolution was carried on a show of hands.[1] Presumably this resolution found its way to party head office and was called to the attention of the NEC. But there is no reason to believe that it met with a favourable response at the national level; certainly no action was taken to implement the proposal.

Despite occasional outbursts of impatience with their comparative impotence the councils seem content for the most part to function within the areas of activity allotted to them. Where policy matters are concerned they are permitted to discuss resolutions submitted by affiliated organizations " dealing with" (as the constitution of one regional council puts it) " political and social aspects of public, legislative and administrative affairs *within the regional area*." Under this provision the council and its executive can of course deal with a wide range of social problems with a specific regional application. A characteristic resolution submitted to the 1953 meeting of the Lancashire and Cheshire Regional Council read: " This Conference views with alarm the growing unemployment problem throughout the N.W. Region and urges the NEC to formulate an immediate policy for submission to H.M. Government to ensure full employment within the textile industry and textile machinery industry." And of narrower application, another resolution submitted to the same annual meeting read: " That this Regional Council strongly urges the Ministry of Transport to take immediate action to alleviate the very serious traffic congestion in Cheadle, Cheshire, by allowing the Kingsway Extension to proceed." [2] But where resolutions are submitted that contravene the regulations which limit discussion to matters of regional interest they are firmly ruled out of order. The report of the Yorkshire Regional Council for 1953 notes that the standing

[1] *Report of the Annual Meeting of the West Midlands Regional Council,* 7th-8th March, 1953, (duplicated), pp. 10-11. It is significant that when in 1954 the NEC found itself in difficulties with many sections of the party because of its support for German rearmament, it decided to arrange a special series of regional " conferences." Clement Attlee commented: " I have great hopes that the regional conferences the Labour Party is organizing will help to persuade our comrades in the country that the official (NEC) view is right and that Labour common sense will prevail." (The *News Chronicle,* 3rd June, 1954.)

[2] *Report of the EC of the Lancashire and Cheshire Regional Council,* 1953, pp. 20-1.

orders committee rejected resolutions which had been submitted dealing with the national health service, the denationalization of road transport and the Vienna Peace Congress.[1]

A minor but persistent concern of some of the regional councils has been the appointment of magistrates. A report of the Northern Regional Council records that: " As a consequence of the resolution carried at the last Annual Meeting, it was decided to make a census of Magistrates with Labour and Trade Union affiliation in comparison with the number from other political parties. This revealed that in 13 County and Municipal Boroughs, Labour had 111 against 300 others. . . . Representation was made and the figures sent to the Lord Chancellor, and Mr. Morgan Phillips was asked to raise the question with the Lord Chancellor's Office. A promise was given to give sympathetic consideration to future recommendations. Constituency Parties were asked to submit names, and these have been sent to Head Office and passed to the Lord Chancellor's Office for consideration." [2] Apart from policy issues in the region and the problem of the appointment of magistrates, regional councils and executives deal mainly with the standard range of political activity in their region. They encourage the co-ordination of policy among Labour Groups elected to the various local government bodies within the region and play an active rôle in local government elections. They organize schools and conferences, propaganda demonstrations, and conduct recruiting campaigns for the party.

In conclusion, it must be emphasized that the regional organization of the Labour Party, like its counterpart on the Conservative side, plays an insignificant part in the life of the party. In each party, the central organizations appear to conceive of the work of the regions as a useful but harmless outlet for the energies of those apparently tireless people who seem never to overlook an opportunity to form themselves into committees for the advancement of the cause in which they believe. The party bureaucracy must obviously have a system of regional offices to attend to the affairs of the party in various parts of the country. The regional officials act under the direction of the party head office; but it is useful to provide that they should serve alongside some democratically elected group of party enthusiasts in the regions. It would be irksome and inconvenient if these local enthusiasts were permitted to direct the work of the regional officials. They are therefore prohibited from doing so in both the Conservative and Labour Parties. And in the process of keeping its regional councils out of mischief, the Labour Party goes one step further. Unlike the

[1] *Report of the EC of the Yorkshire Regional Council*, 1953, p. 27.
[2] *Report of the EC of the Northern Regional Council*, 1953, pp. 7-8.

Conservatives, it prohibits its regional bodies from concerning themselves with national and international issues. In both parties the central headquarters is eager as always to tap new sources of voluntary labour and enthusiasm; but they are equally eager as always to devise means of ensuring that this enthusiasm is not misdirected into efforts to determine or control the policies of the party.

IV

THE CONSTITUENCY ORGANIZATION OF THE LABOUR PARTY

The Labour Party at constituency level duplicates to some extent the federal principle which is operative nationally; as a result, Labour's constituency organization is very much more complicated than that of the Conservatives. In a fairly typical type of constituency organization (in a single borough, undivided for the purpose of parliamentary elections)[1] the structure of the party, on broad lines, is as follows: in each ward or polling district of the borough there will be a ward committee composed of individual members, and there may also be a women's section, and possibly a Young Socialist Group. At the constituency level these ward organizations combine with a number of affiliated bodies, the most important of which are trade unions; less frequently a trades council, a co-operative society or local branch of the Fabian Society or other socialist society may also be affiliated. Individual members of the Labour Party participate solely through their ward organizations; unlike the Conservatives, they do not meet together at the constituency level. At that level the affairs of the party are controlled by a General Management Committee (which is discussed below) composed of delegates from the wards and the affiliated organizations.

The constituency parties are, as one Labour publication puts it, " the operative units of party activity,"[2] and like the Conservative constituency associations, they are in most respects self-governing.

[1] It is impossible in brief compass to deal with the multifarious forms of local Labour Party structure. This account therefore confines itself to a characteristic type of organization, the constituency Labour Party in a single and undivided borough.

[2] *The Labour Party*, a duplicated document produced by the party head office, October, 1950, p. 6. See also Hanham, H. J., " The Local Organization of the Labour Party," *Western Political Quarterly*, Vol. IX, No. 2, June, 1956, pp. 376–388; Blondel, J., " The Conservative Association and the Labour Party in Reading," *Political Studies*, Vol. VI, No. 2, June 1958, p. 110 ff. For a perceptive analysis of the work and problems of local parties, see McKitterick, T., " The Membership of the Party," *Political Quarterly*, July–September, 1960, p. 312.

They administer their own affairs, they elect their own officers, raise and administer their own funds, undertake their own programme of publicity and propaganda and conduct election campaigns in the constituency on behalf of the party; subject to the approval of the NEC, they also select their own candidates and appoint their own agent. If anything, however, the Labour constituency parties are subject to rather more detailed control by the central organs of the party than are the Conservative associations. The latter are " recommended" to adopt certain model rules; but the Labour Party constitution (clause III, section 2) requires that: " Each Constituency Labour Party, Central Labour Party, and Federation *must* . . . . adopt the Rules laid down by the Party Conference." The NEC has the authority " to sanction modifications in the . . . Rules where local circumstances render it necessary." But parties are warned in advance that any proposed modifications " must not alter the objects, the basis or conditions of affiliated and individual membership, vary the procedure for the selection of Parliamentary Candidates . . . or effect a change in the relationship of Central Labour Parties or Constituency Labour Parties with the National Labour Party."[1]

The NEC also keeps a much closer check than does the National Union on possible constitutional manipulations by the constituency parties. According to the Model Rules (although this provision is often ignored) the constituency parties must apply annually for renewal of their affiliation to the Labour Party and when they do so they are required " to deposit a copy of the Rules approved by the National Executive Committee in their case with the application." The stern warning follows: " Affiliation to the National Labour Party will be deemed to be severed unless this requirement is carried through." Even the standing orders which parties may devise for themselves must be submitted to the NEC for approval. From long experience the NEC has no doubt become convinced of the need to scrutinize the inner life of constituency parties with minute care, but none the less the phraseology of these provisions seems strangely rigorous. The atmosphere is somewhat mellowed by a passage in the principal handbook for local party work supplied by the head office (*Party Organization*), which states: " A party should insist on a commonsense and straightforward observance of the constitution and rules by all officials, members and sections. To say this does not mean that narrow-mindedness over

---

[1] *Constitution and Rules for Constituency Labour Parties in Single and Undivided Boroughs* (henceforth referred to as Model Rules Set A), p. 3. [Italics mine.] These model rules were laid down by the party conferences of 1929 and 1930; they have not been fundamentally altered since.

detail is commonsense. Rules are not intended to be red tape, but a secretary should realize that carelessness in applying them is often the cause of strains and trouble growing in a party." The head office concludes paternally: " Be wise and keep a party constitutionally in order." [1]

There is provision for two classes of members at constituency level: those who belong through affiliated organizations, and individual members who belong through ward committees. Organizations which may affiliate to constituency parties include trade unions, co-operative societies and branches of the Co-operative Party, branches of socialist societies or professional organizations which are affiliated to the Labour Party nationally, trades councils, and " any other organization or branch thereof which the National Executive Committee deems eligible for affiliation." [2] The trade unions, of course, constitute by far and away the most important category of affiliated organizations. Members of affiliated trade unions are not, however, entitled to take an active part in the affairs of the constituency party unless they become enrolled as individual members. They may do so by asking their trade union branch secretary to forward their names and addresses to be recorded in the register of party members kept by the party secretary. In some instances the initiative is taken by the party secretary himself who approaches the union branch secretary to obtain a list of his members paying the political levy. The party secretary may then make a direct personal appeal to the individuals concerned. This appeal may invite the " indirect " union member to enrol as a direct member and in that capacity pay a full membership fee. But this is to invite the trade unionist to pay a duplicate fee and he may refuse to do so; he may be unwilling to pay more than the political levy which he has already subscribed through his union. [3]

The second category, individual membership, is open to anyone of 16 years of age or over on the following conditions: the applicant must " accept and conform to the Constitution, Principles, Programme and Policy of the (national) Labour Party and the Rules of (the particular constituency) Party "; in addition, individual members must, if eligible, belong to a trade union affiliated to the

[1] Croft, H., *Party Organization*, 1950, p. 7.

[2] *Model Rules* Set A, p. 5. As an illustration of the extent of affiliation in a highly organized Central Labour Party in a divided borough see Appendix VI, "Affiliated Organizations 1953," *Fifty Years History of the Woolwich Labour Party*, 1903-53, pp. 80-1.

[3] Normally a union affiliated nationally to the Labour Party pays to the party one shilling per year for each of its members paying the union's political levy. The membership fee for an individual member of a local party is six shillings per year.

TUC and if the union is affiliated to the Labour Party he must contribute to its political fund. An additional clause bars anyone " who is a member of a Political Party or organization ancillary or subsidiary thereto declared by the Annual Party Conference or National Executive Committee . . . to be ineligible for affiliation to the Labour Party . . ." [1] (This provision is primarily intended, of course, to bar members of the Communist Party and of Communist-inspired " front " organizations from joining in the work of the Labour Party.) Clearly the conditions of membership of the Labour Party are hedged round with a great many more qualifications and restrictions than are operative in the case of membership of Conservative associations. It is only fair to add, however, that some of the provisions (such as that requiring all members who are eligible to join a trade union) are not enforced by many local parties.

The affairs of the constituency party are controlled by a body usually known as the General Management Committee (hereinafter GMC), which consists of delegates elected by the affiliated organizations mentioned above and representatives of ward committees (see below), women's sections and branches of the Young Socialists. The basis of representation on the GMC for affiliated organizations and other party units is determined by the constituency party itself; again, however, they must secure approval of their arrangements from the NEC. And, again, there are provisions designed to exclude heretics from appearing as delegates from affiliated organizations. The GMC is in full control of the affairs of the party; the executive and all other committees are subject to it.

The GMC takes corporate action in some matters such as the guaranteeing of expenses in elections; but the individual members of the GMC are also entitled to " act as delegates when expressing the opinions of their societies or when bringing resolutions from their organizations." In addition to supervising the whole range of party work, the GMC has power of expulsion. Acting on the advice of the executive committee it may " take all necessary steps to safeguard the Constitution, programme, principles and policy of the Labour Party within the Borough." It may take action " involving the punishment or expulsion of any organization or individual " with the proviso that the latter " shall have the right of appeal . . . to the National Executive Committee which Committee shall have power to confirm, vary, or reverse the action taken by the General Management Committee." [2]

At its annual meeting the GMC elects from among its own members an executive committee which directs the work of the

[1] *Model Rules* Set A, p. 6.
[2] *Ibid.*, p. 12.

party under the general supervision of the GMC. The executive committee normally consists of the officers of the party—the president (or chairman), two vice-presidents, treasurer, financial secretary and secretary (who are annually elected by the GMC from among its members)—and as many additional members as the GMC shall decide. (In the case of a very small party it is sometimes provided that the general management committee should itself serve as an executive committee.) The executive normally meets once a month; it receives financial statements and reports from the lower echelons of the party, and generally supervises and stimulates the development of party activity. It usually sets up a number of sub-committees concerned with the social life of the party and the usual range of political activity.

Special reference must be made to one of the officers of the party, the secretary, who is often the most important single individual in the organization. If the constituency party employs an agent[1] he is normally elected to serve also as secretary. In addition to the duties usually attached to such a post, the secretary is encouraged " to keep contacts with and consult frequently with all officials. . . . To keep an oversight on all activities in the party. . . . To watch for opportunities of development and promote organization to secure this. . . . To be the disinterested servant of the party and to encourage all members to work harmoniously together for the good of the cause." [2] The secretary would appear indeed to require the virtues of a paragon, although it is added hopefully " there is no reason why a person of ordinary abilities should not become a good secretary, providing he has zeal and tact . . ."

When the secretary is in fact also the agent of the party he often emerges as the key figure in the constituency organization. The agent is encouraged to think of himself as " the managing director of the party "; but there is this stern enjoinder: " He is . . . not a dictator." The agent is responsible for " organizing the societies and individuals in the movement into a collective unity for the achievement of the party's aims. He must cultivate the art of getting people interested in the work of the party. He will always be looking out for likely individuals and assessing their qualities." These passages clearly invite the secretary-agent to adopt an almost paternal rôle, nursing, guiding, encouraging the voluntary party workers. With this encouragement, a headstrong or self-centred individual sometimes finds himself tempted to convert his party into

---

[1] On the work of the Labour Party agents, see Comfort, G., *Professional Politicians*, p. 59 ff. See also *The Mechanics of Victory*, Fabian Society, 1962, p. 14 ff.

[2] *Party Organization*, pp. 8–9.

a one-man organization; worse still, he may find himself undertaking to manage and manipulate jobs that should be left to others. Hence the warning that it is "a great mistake (for the agent) ... to undertake individual work himself except on special occasions to set an example. He is expected to inspire and impel members to engage in the multifarious activities of the party, and to plan, organize and direct the work. There is a type of man who is an 'omnibus official'; he is so occupied in doing every job he can lay his hands on that he never notices that other people cannot get a look in, and when they become apathetic he is loud in his complaints that no one ever does anything in that party but himself. The most useful thing an (agent) can do is to stand behind his officials and secretaries. Help and encourage them, but let them have real responsibility and the praise for good work."[1]

After a great many meetings and discussions with Labour Party agents, one is forced to observe that the party has not been notably successful in recruiting the sort of person envisaged in the passages quoted above. The pay for the work is poor and the chances for promotion to more responsible positions within the party are not good. A considerable part of the time of many agents is taken up with raising their own salaries by means of specially organized football pools and other money-making devices.[2] This inevitably detracts from the time available for political activity. It would seem evident that there must be a major overhaul of Labour Party policy with respect to the employment of agents if the party hopes to effect any real improvement in its constituency organization.

That such improvement is necessary in the party's interests is abundantly clear from a review of the membership figures for constituency parties. If total membership figures are a reliable evidence of the health of these parties then there is an extraordinary range in their degree of well-being. Table 14 at p. 544 shows the relationship between Party membership and Labour vote in 20

[1] *Party Organization*, pp. 8-10.

[2] If for any reason it became impossible to resort to these methods of raising funds it has been estimated that as many as one-third of the constituency parties employing full-time agents would have to dispense with their services. In 1951 the party employed 296 agents; ten years later it had only 210. See *Mechanics of Victory*, Fabian Society, 1962, p. 14.

The distribution of these agents is also of interest. In the 81 constituencies in the Lancashire and Cheshire area, for example, the party has 34 agents. Of these 8 are employed by borough parties (covering two or more constituencies); 15 agents are employed in constituencies with trade union sponsored candidates (there is a total of 20 such constituencies); and 11 agents are employed in the 47 constituencies in which the candidates are sponsored by the constituency party rather than by a trade union.

TABLE 14

RELATIONSHIP BETWEEN LABOUR PARTY MEMBERSHIP AND THE
LABOUR VOTE IN TWENTY CONSTITUENCIES IN LANCASHIRE
AND CHESHIRE *

Constituency	Member-ship	Labour Vote	Member-ship as Percent-age of Labour Vote	Majority (Labour = + Cons. = −)
Ten Parties with largest Membership:				
Salford West	6,012	27,542	22%	+ 3,487
Nelson and Colne	4,500	25,611	18%	+ 4,400
Wythenshawe	4,250	22,045	19%	− 6,566
Salford East	3,724	27,729	13%	+ 3,487
Farnworth	3,715	26,297	14%	+ 8,185
Bury and Radcliffe	3,361	28,058	12%	− 1,897
Clayton	3,200	27,985	11%	+ 11,863
Rochdale	3,188	27,343	12%	− 454
Stretford	2,865	25,694	11%	− 9,725
Leigh	2,821	33,881	8%	+ 14,296
Ten Parties with smallest Membership:				
Ince	675	32,148	2%	+ 19,843
Warrington	631	26,225	2%	+ 8,602
Crosby	537	10,251	5%	− 14,783
Wavertree	535	19,702	3%	− 8,477
Southport	502	12,535	4%	− 17,853
Blackpool North	456	12,727	4%	− 17,229
Scotland	354	28,558	1%	+ 15,214
Kirkdale	350	19,637	2%	+ 758
South Fylde	350	12,408	3%	− 23,318
North Fylde	282	11,284	2%	− 14,135

* The Labour vote given in this table is that which the party received in
the 1951 general election, when Labour held 37 of the 81 seats in the region.
The membership figures are those presented to the 1953 annual meeting of the
Lancashire and Cheshire Regional Council of the Labour Party.

Lancashire and Cheshire constituencies (this area was chosen
because at the time the relative strength of the two major parties in
the area was similar to their relative strength throughout the country
as a whole; of the 81 constituencies in the area, Labour held 37, the

Conservatives 43 and the Liberals one). For the purposes of this table, the ten constituency Labour Parties which had the largest membership and the ten which had the smallest were chosen. It will be noted that there is a remarkable range in the percentage of Labour voters recruited into the party (22 per cent. at Salford West as against 1 per cent. at the Scotland division of Liverpool). The largest number of parties in the area had a membership representing between 5 and 10 per cent. of the Labour vote in the constituency. It will be further noted that the size of the party membership appears to bear no relation to whether the constituency is " safe " Labour, " safe " Conservative, or marginal. Four of the ten largest parties are in Conservative-held seats; four of the ten smallest are in Labour-held seats. The strength of a constituency party would appear to depend on the calibre of its GMC and its agent or secretary and on the amount and quality of the work they are prepared to undertake.[1]

V

THE WARD COMMITTEES OF THE LABOUR PARTY

It is the aim of the Labour Party to establish a ward committee in each ward of the constituency with the primary purpose of maintaining " the necessary machinery for elections within its area, and, with the approval of the Executive Committee of (the constituency) Party (undertaking) propaganda work." [2] Individual members of the party are attached to the appropriate ward committee and in addition (as was noted above) members of affiliated societies who choose to enrol themselves as members of a ward committee may do so.

The party head office gives this advice to those engaged in promoting ward activity: " The ward committee or association should be an influential body in its district. There must be enterprise and determination to develop ward committees into large associations capable of impressing and coping with the population in their areas. The old-fashioned complacency with a ward committee of a dozen people must give way to a modern conception of a ward association of some hundreds of members and an activity which surpasses the whole energy of the original central party, if the cause of Socialism

---

[1] A subsequent constituency analysis of the national situation in 1959 suggests, however, that "on average . . . the larger the Labour majority, the smaller the Labour Party membership." *The Mechanics of Victory* (Fabian Society, 1962) p. 17.

[2] *Model Rules* Set A, p. 9.

is to be organized for victory with 15 to 20 million votes sustaining it." This passage is clearly directed against a fairly persistent tendency (to be found everywhere in the party) for a small group of party stalwarts to convert the ward organization into a tight-knit band of the faithful who are content to elect each other in turn to serve on the GMC and to manipulate the affairs of the ward without too much interference from a large-scale membership. For those who take this view, head office explains: " There is no need to fear big ward committees; the power and prestige of a general management committee of a party rises and increases in proportion to the size and influence of its ward committees and sections." And there is a reminder that there is a reward for those who take this view: " There is more glory in directing the strong than in dominating the weak." [1]

If a ward contains two or more polling districts within its boundaries the ward committee is advised to form sub-committees to undertake organizational work within such districts. These sub-committees are not to become " detached groups "; they are to be subject to the control and authority of the ward committee. The duties of the sub-committee are as follows:

" 1. To see that a street captain or leader is fixed for every street or group of streets.

" 2. To create a body of helpers to be under the direction of each leader :

(a) for distribution of literature,
(b) for collection of subscriptions,
(c) for electoral canvassings, etc.

" 3. To codify information about the residents :

(a) for the party electors' index or marked register,
(b) for securing the franchise for eligible persons at registration times,
(c) for special appeals for membership." [2]

From a study of ward organization this would appear to be a somewhat idealized description of how ward sub-committees should function; it is doubtful if this standard of performance has been achieved in very many instances. The nearest most parties appear to get to this ideal is an arrangement whereby individual members act as " collectors " for particular streets; they also help to prepare a marked register and distribute literature and voting cards at elections. During elections most of this work is done voluntarily, but the collectors who carry on the work between elections are

[1] *Party Organization*, p. 19.
[2] *Ibid.*, p. 21.

allowed, in a great many constituencies, to retain a prescribed percentage of the sums they collect.

It is important to note that it is only at ward level that individual members of the Labour Party have an opportunity for regular participation in the affairs of the party. Ward meetings open to all members are held on the average once a month, and at these meetings there is an opportunity for discussion of local party affairs and for the formulation of proposals and resolutions which may be submitted to the GMC for debate and, if they are adopted, for forwarding to the NEC and the party head office. Inevitably only a small percentage of the total party membership within the ward is likely to attend such meetings. Estimates of the proportion of total membership which is continually active in party affairs between elections range from one to five per cent. Certainly it would be agreed that ten per cent. would be an unusually high proportion. A group of members of the Manchester Fabian Society undertook a detailed study by questionnaire and interview of Labour Party activity in nine of Manchester's 36 wards. They found that " attendance at ordinary monthly meetings (of the ward committees) varies between five and 35 people, though each ward (has) several hundred subscribing members; there was an average of 18 (in attendance) at the nine meetings answering our questionnaire." [1]

The Manchester survey showed that there is some tendency for the regularly active part of the membership to include a higher proportion of members with more extreme views on matters of public policy. This largely accounts for the fact that resolutions on matters of policy which flow from the wards to the constituencies to the national organization tend to reflect a more militant point of view than would have been likely to have emerged from a fuller meeting of the party membership; certainly the views expressed are unlikely to be typical of the general body of voters who support the Labour Party at elections. The national officials of the party are well aware of this and in conversation they consistently tend to minimize the importance of the policy resolutions which emerge from the constituency parties. They view these manifestations of opinion with much the same cynicism that Conservative officials adopt toward the " diehard " resolutions which by an almost exactly similar process emerge (although very much less frequently) from Conservative associations.

It must be emphasized of course that only a very small part of the time of monthly ward meetings tends to be taken up with the discussion of national or international issues. The Manchester survey

[1] " Put Policy on the Agenda," *Fabian Journal*, February, 1952, pp. 27 ff.

has a useful account of ward activity based on first-hand observation of a large number of ward meetings:

> " A great deal of time is taken up with the reading of minutes
> from previous meetings. Every decision of the officers and the
> committee is open to discussion and, if necessary, to reversal, and
> the secretary cannot reply to any letter received in his official
> capacity without authority from the ward. Thus there is often
> little space on the agenda for anything but business items, and
> business items are frequently of a non-political nature—'How
> much should be spent on cakes for the children's party?' . . . .
>
> " However, in some cases there is time for politics as well, and
> discussion then usually turns to local issues. If the ward is repre-
> sented by Labour councillors they will probably be present at the
> meeting and liable to pretty close questioning. 'Why is the Council
> unable to provide proper school meals for our children?' . . . ."

As the Manchester report adds, " This highly democratic tradition
makes the conduct of business very slow and cumbersome. It
makes for dull meetings and sparse attendance; indeed, it is only
by keeping their meetings small that some wards are able to curtail
discussion of business sufficiently to get anything done at all. On
the other hand, it is a tradition which provides lively, effective
debate of local issues, and sometimes of national issues too, when
the opportunity arises." But the report concludes that, on the
whole, ward parties ". . . are social rather than political organizations, particularly in districts where the Party is assured of a majority.
Between elections, people attend meetings rather as they would go
to a club, to meet their friends and discuss the business of running a
club. Their interest turns to politics only when this is forced upon
them by local conditions or by a group of more enthusiastic
members." [1]
It seems fair to conclude that, between elections at least, the
great proportion of party members are content to play no part at
all in the work of their ward or constituency party. Those who
do take an active part are mainly concerned with the pleasantly
complex task of maintaining the party organization in being, a task
which involves an extensive social programme and a great deal of
routine internal party administration. Discussion of public issues
is likely to be focused mainly on local government affairs and to
turn to national issues only under provocation of dramatic events

---

[1] " Put Policy on the Agenda," *Fabian Journal,* February, 1952,
pp. 28–32. See also McKitterick, T., " The Membership of the Party," *Political
Quarterly,* July–September, p. 312 ff. on the frequently " unrepresentative nature
of the active minority of party members."

or on the insistence of a few enthusiasts who are eager that the party should express its views on some question of public policy.

One other major function of the party organization at ward and constituency level must also be mentioned; indeed, for the purpose of this study it is the most important function: the selection and adoption of candidates for parliamentary elections. In this matter, as in so many aspects of constituency and ward activity, the national organs of the Labour Party play a more prominent rôle than does the National Union or the Central Office in the adoption of Conservative candidates. Even the initial decision as to whether a constituency party should contest an election must be " considered by the Executive Committee of (the constituency) Party in consultation with the National Executive Committee or its officers . . . (and) if it is thought expedient to contest the constituency the General (Management) Committee shall be asked to give authority to the Executive Committee . . . in co-operation with the National Executive Committee to secure nominations for the candidature." [1] Normally these provisions requiring consultation and co-operation with the NEC are no more than a formality; they do not in practice involve any limitation on the right of the constituency party to contest an election. But the existence of these provisions may become important when it is decided at the national level (as it was in the Second World War) that there should be " an electoral truce " between Labour and its political opponents.

When the decision has been taken to contest an election and to select a candidate, a procedure prescribed in detail by the NEC must be rigorously followed. It should be noted in the first instance that individuals who wish to become Labour candidates are not permitted to raise their own names for consideration as can be done by those seeking a Conservative nomination. Aspiring Labour candidates may, of course, communicate privately with the executive committee, a ward committee or an affiliated organization in an attempt to secure their sponsorship; but every potential candidate must be nominated by one or other of these bodies. Any individual member of the Labour Party or a member of an affiliated organization " who is not disqualified under the Constitution of the Party, or under the decisions of its Party Conference " is eligible for nomination either by the executive committee or by one of the bodies entitled to send representatives to the general management committee of the party. A person who is so nominated must give his consent in writing and in the event that his name appears on the

[1] *Model Rules* Set A, p. 9.

official panel of available parliamentary candidates of an affiliated organization (such as a trade union), " the consent in writing of the Executive Committee (of the affiliated organization) must also be obtained and sent in with the form of nomination." This provision is intended, of course, to ensure that the affiliated organization is currently prepared to provide financial assistance for the particular nominee in that particular constituency. (It is conceivable, for example, that a trade union might be prepared to sponsor a member of its panel of available candidates in a safe or marginal seat but might be unwilling to provide funds for the candidature of the same individual in a " hopeless " seat.)

In addition, the executive committee of the constituency party may itself make nominations. In the course of doing so it may invite the party head office to propose names from amongst the lists of available candidates maintained at head office. Alternatively, the NEC itself may take the initiative and propose names from its lists[1] to the executive of the constituency party, although if it does so the NEC is usually careful to propose more than one name in order to avoid giving the appearance of throwing its weight behind a particularly favoured individual. Before the meeting of the party's GMC to consider nominations, the executive committee consults with the NEC or its officers " to determine the validity of the nominations received." This provision is intended to give the NEC an opportunity to express its views on an individual whose qualifications have not hitherto been reviewed by the NEC; if the NEC indicates at this stage that the individual concerned will not receive their subsequent approval if he is selected by the GMC, then, of course, the executive committee will convey this information to the GMC and under normal circumstances the individual concerned would have no prospect of selection by the GMC.

The executive committee may submit a questionnaire to the " outsiders " who have not been locally nominated, to determine their views on various matters of party policy; alternatively (or in addition) it may interview them personally. It then proposes a short list composed of the outsiders who in the view of the executive would be suitable candidates; this list, along with the locally nominated names, goes before a " selection conference " of the GMC called for the purpose of choosing a prospective candidate. This meeting is attended by a representative of party head office (frequently the regional organizer) who supervises the procedure of the selection

---

[1] There is an " A list " of possible candidates who have trade union sponsorship and a " B list " of those who have not. Individualists on these lists are not, however, assured of automatic endorsement by the NEC, should they be adopted as prospective candidates.

meeting to ensure that it conforms to the regulations laid down by the NEC. The individuals whose names appear on the executive's short list or who have been nominated by ward committees or affiliated organizations are usually invited to make brief speeches (often of only ten minutes in duration) and to answer questions put by members of the GMC. These speeches in themselves would seem to provide an absurdly inadequate basis on which to judge the personal qualifications and political opinions of a potential candidate. But in many circumstances they provide the only opportunity for such judgments to be made. When the speech-making has been completed, delegates to the GMC vote (on the basis of one vote per delegate) in a series of ballots until one potential candidate has secured a clear majority of the votes cast. The procedure is not yet, however, completed; the party rules require that " the selection of a prospective Parliamentary candidate shall not be regarded as completed until the name of the member selected has been placed before a meeting of the National Executive Committee, and his or her selection has been duly endorsed. Until such endorsement has been received (the Constituency) Party shall not introduce its prospective candidate to the public." [1] Before it grants its endorsement the NEC satisfies itself that suitable financial arrangements have been made for the candidate concerned and in addition that the nominee is prepared to " accept and conform to the Constitution, Programme, Principles and Policy of the Party."

Under certain circumstances the procedure which has been outlined may be jettisoned. As the party rules put it: " Where no valid nominations are received, or when an emergency arises, or when the Executive Committee of (the particular Constituency) Party or the National Executive Committee are of opinion that the interests of the Labour Party demand the suspension of (this) procedure . . . (it) may be dispensed with after consultation and agreement between the Executive Committee of (the) Party and the National Executive Committee." And apart from this rather vague provision for the suspension of the normal selection procedure, there is a specific arrangement that the procedure will in any case be suspended in the event of a parliamentary by-election in the constituency. In such circumstances " the National Executive Committee shall co-operate with the Executive Committee of (the Constituency) Party in the nomination of a candidate. The National Executive Committee may, if it deems it necessary in the interests of the Labour Party, advise the Executive Committee of (the)

---

[1] *Model Rules* Set A, p. 10. Since 1950 there have been at least five cases when the NEC has refused such endorsement.

Party to select a nomination it may submit to it." [1]   In fairness it should be noted that the NEC, despite its sweeping power to suspend nomination procedures in either of the circumstances described above, almost invariably avoids acting in high-handed fashion which might alienate active party workers in the constituency organization.   These clauses should be understood as emergency powers which have been carefully included in the model rules of constituency parties as a protection for the national party against the possibility that a constituency party may be captured by irresponsible or undesirable elements at a critical moment in the affairs of the national party.

Even when normal procedures are followed, party regulations nevertheless appear to require extraordinarily detailed supervision by the NEC of the process of selection of candidates; inevitably this raises the question as to whether or not the constituency parties have any real autonomy in this matter.   Some observers appear to have concluded that they do not.   Writing in *Parliamentary Affairs*, Mark Abrams stated that head office control of nominations had produced ". . . a state of affairs not unlike the era of rotten boroughs before 1832; but with one difference—where the great Whig and Tory families disposed of dozens of safe constituencies, Transport House now has under its patronage hundreds of safe seats." [2]   There can be no doubt that this judgment is totally unjustified.   It may be, as Ivor Bulmer-Thomas (who has had experience as a candidate for both major parties) has claimed, that the Labour Party head office can, as he puts it, " probably do more " for a particular individual whom it wishes to see returned to the House of Commons than can the Conservative Central Office; [3] but it must be emphasized that in either party effective influence from the centre is limited and that, in most circumstances, it is greatly resented.   Indeed there is good reason to believe that a potential candidate usually finds himself at a disadvantage if it becomes generally known in the GMC that he has strong support from party head office or the NEC.

It may of course happen that a local party is prepared to fall in line with a recommendation from party head office, although even then it is probable that a vocal minority within the constituency party will object on principle.   The Woolwich Labour Party gives a brief and rather elliptical account of the process by which Ernest Bevin was adopted as the candidate for Woolwich East in the

---

[1] *Model Rules* Set A, p. 10.

[2] Abrams, M., (reviewing *Public Opinion 1935-46* by Mildred Strunk) in *Parliamentary Affairs*, Vol. V, No. 1, Winter 1951, p. 232.

[3] Bulmer-Thomas, I., *The Party System in Great Britain*, p. 208.

election of 1950 following the retirement of the sitting member (Bevin's former seat had disappeared as a result of the redistribution of constituency boundaries): " the National Agent sought an interview with the Party on the question of a prospective Parliamentary candidate for East Woolwich." And he asked the Woolwich Labour Party " to consider (Ernest Bevin) in connection with the East Woolwich candidature. *After considerable discussion*, a special General Council Meeting was called to consider a recommendation by the Executive, that Mr. Bevin be invited to become the prospective Parliamentary candidate for East Woolwich. This was accepted and Mr. Bevin was invited to attend the next General Council meeting at which he accepted the candidature." [1] The phrase " after considerable discussion " would imply that there must have been at least some opposition to the proposal although clearly the majority view was in favour of accepting the National Agent's advice. It should be emphasized that the party had every right to reject his advice; but in the Labour Party as in the Conservative Party the national headquarters can usually (but not invariably) find a constituency which is willing, and even in some instances eager, to select a prominent national figure as its candidate. There is nothing sinister in this and it in no way implies that constituency parties can fairly be described (as Abrams suggests) as " rotten boroughs".

A more serious criticism of the method of selecting candidates arises out of the financial aspect of the process. As was noted above, the Conservative Party prohibits candidates from contributing more than £25 a year to constituency party funds; M.P.s may contribute a maximum of £50 a year. Neither may contribute " directly or indirectly " to the constituency party's election fund, and it is forbidden for a selection committee to ask questions of potential candidates concerning the financial contribution (within the prescribed limit) which he is likely to be able to make. It often happens at Labour selection meetings that the NEC representative will declare that members of the GMC must not ask questions concerning the financial contribution which nominees or their sponsoring organizations can provide. But the GMC is inevitably aware that if they select a candidate who has been specifically endorsed by his union a considerable financial contribution will almost certainly be forthcoming. The maximum contributions which sponsoring organizations may make if a candidate is chosen from their panel of available parliamentary candidates is as follows: at parliamentary elections they may contribute up to

[1] *Fifty Years History of the Woolwich Labour Party*, 1903-53, p. 43. [Italics mine.]

80 per cent. of the maximum expenditure permitted under the Representation of the People Act; in addition the sponsoring organization may contribute a maximum annual grant to the funds of the constituency party of £250 in borough divisions and £300 in county divisions.[1]

Naturally there is a strong tendency for trade unions to agree to sponsor candidates in safe Labour seats. At the 1951 election, for example, of the 613 Labour candidates, 139 were sponsored by trade unions and of these 105 (or 75 per cent.) were elected. In contrast, only 40 per cent. of candidates sponsored by constituency Labour Parties were elected (173 out of 436); 16 of the 38 candidates sponsored by the Co-operative Party were elected, as was the one candidate sponsored by the Royal Arsenal Co-operative Society. As might be concluded from these figures, the unsponsored contender for a nomination in a safe Labour seat (or a marginal seat which seems particularly promising from a Labour point of view) may face stiff competition indeed from a trade union sponsored rival. It is always tempting for a constituency party to adopt the latter and thus lift from its own shoulders a great many of the financial worries otherwise associated with the campaign. There may also be a strong tendency for an unsponsored contender for a nomination, if he has private personal resources, to let it be known that he will make a heavy contribution (within the prescribed limits) either to the election expenses of the constituency or towards the payment of its annual operating costs. If, as seems probable, one can now assume that the Conservative financial regulations are rigorously enforced, then there can be little doubt that a few well-to-do M.P.s in the Labour Party make a larger annual contribution to the funds of their constituencies than they would be permitted to make under the regulations of the Conservative Party.[2]

To the charge that the trade unions " collar the best places " a strong reply can of course be made. Mary Agnes Hamilton has emphasized that it must be remembered that " Trade Unionism has made these places good. Labour's strongholds are in the mining areas and the railway centres: in the constituencies where Trade Unionism has done the organizing work and built a powerful solidarity among the workers."[3]   Nevertheless, it cannot be doubted that trade union sponsorship of candidates is sometimes an insidious influence at selection conferences. The writer was present as an observer at a Labour selection meeting at which the

---

[1] *1948 Labour Annual Conference Report,* p. 10.
[2] For the changed situation since 1957, see p. 555, n. 2.
[3] Hamilton, M. A., *The Labour Party To-day,* p. 75.

following extraordinary incident took place.[1] The names of five duly nominated candidates came before the GMC. One of them was sponsored by his trade union, a large and comparatively prosperous union. For personal reasons he was unable to attend the meeting and it transpired that no member of the GMC present had ever met him or had any first-hand knowledge of his qualifications, other than the details included on his written nomination form. Even the Regional Organizer (who was present and represented the NEC at the meeting) had never met the individual concerned, although he undertook to give the GMC a description of what, from long experience, he thought the GMC could assume the trade union nominee was like. Each of the other four nominees made ten-minute speeches in turn and answered questions. On the face of it one would have thought that no rational GMC would have considered adopting the absentee contender whom no person present had ever seen. But when the successive ballots began, he proved to be a very strong contender; indeed, it was not until the fifth and final ballot that he lost out by a narrow margin to one of the four nominees who was present. The only possible interpretation of this procedure would seem to have been that the comparatively poor constituency Labour Party concerned must have been aware that by adopting the absentee trade unionist they were assuring themselves of a considerable contribution to their election funds and annual expenses. They were no doubt aware of this, if for no other reason than that their candidate at the previous election had been a member of the same union and that union had made a substantial annual contribution to their funds. It would seem evident that basic reform in the financial relations between candidates, M.P.s and their constituency parties is as overdue to-day in the Labour Party as it was in the Conservative Party before the adoption of the Maxwell Fyfe Report.[2]

It has already been shown that constituency parties have little influence in the formulation of the goals and programme of the Labour Party, less influence on the policies of the PLP, and only

[1] It should be noted that the constituency concerned was a " safe " Conservative seat, which may account in part for what might otherwise be considered the irresponsible behaviour of the selection meeting.

[2] Since this passage was written the Wilson Committee set up by the NEC in 1955 reported: " We are disturbed by the number of candidates who out of their own pockets are required to make annual contributions towards Constituency Party finances " and recommended that " early steps be taken to end this practice . . . " *Interim Report of the Sub-Committee on Party Organization*, London, 1955, p 16. And in 1957, the NEC decided that unsponsored candidates must not contribute more than £50 per year to constituency funds (twice the maximum sum permitted in the Conservative Party). 1957 *Labour Annual Conference Report*, p. 13.

a faint influence on the activities of a Labour Government. It is sometimes argued, however, that they have ultimate control over the parliamentary party since they determine its composition by their choice of candidates. In a sense this is a valid observation. Delegates to the GMC meeting which selects a prospective candidate have an opportunity during the course of the ten-minute speeches delivered by each nominee (and in the brief question period that follows) to judge whether or not the views he expresses are broadly in sympathy with their own. But it must be remembered that once the candidate has been elected he need not thereafter undertake to conform to the views of his constituency party on any matter of public policy. The Labour Party in practice subscribes to Burke's conception of the relationship between the M.P. and his constituents[1]. This does not mean, however, that M.P.s can consistently and with impunity ignore the opinions of their active local supporters; most M.P.s make a continuous effort to remain *en rapport* with their local parties. And if they establish a reputation for integrity and frankness with their local supporters it is very rarely indeed that they are subject to really severe pressures designed to force them to change their attitudes and opinions.

Official party memoranda to Labour M.P.s and prospective candidates repeatedly warn them against giving pledges to special interest groups or pledges to support particular policies which are not included in the election manifesto of the Labour Party. One such warning concluded by reminding candidates and M.P.s that if they did give such pledges they, as Members of Parliament, were subsequently " liable to find themselves in the position of instructed delegates rather than public representatives who have a duty to give their vote in Parliament after they have heard the pros and cons of debate." [2] The particular warning concerned was directed against giving pledges to outside (non-Labour) organizations; but it is equally clear that the party considers it unwise for candidates or members to offer to promote in Parliament every policy advocated by their own constituency party. Discussion of this issue with a number of Labour M.P.s points to the conclusion that (as one M.P. put it): " Most Members of Parliament consider the views of their constituency party as one of a number of considerations, and by no means the most important one, to be taken into account in determining how they shall vote in the House of Commons " (or, one might add, in party meetings).

It can be argued, of course, that a constituency party has one final sanction against its M.P.: it can refuse to readopt him. But

[1] See p. 253 above.
[2] *1949 Labour Annual Conference Report* (Report of the NEC), p. 5.

it is important to note that the procedure for readopting sitting members is heavily weighted in the member's favour. The model rules provide that if a constituency is represented in Parliament by a member of the PLP the " procedure for selection of a prospective Parliamentary candidate shall not be set in motion until an election is imminent "; when it is imminent the normal procedure for adopting a new candidate is dispensed with and the sitting member will automatically be readopted except in the following circumstances:

(a) if the Member intimates his intention to retire, or
(b) " The General (Management) Committee on securing a mandate from its affiliated and Party organizations intimates by resolution its desire that he or she must retire."[1]

In other words, the sitting member need not test his strength at an adoption meeting against other possible rivals in his constituency or against others from outside the constituency who might be considered by the executive committee to be a preferable candidate. Those who desire to unseat a sitting member are therefore forced to secure a hostile resolution calling for his retirement. Obviously this gives the member much greater security than he would enjoy if he were forced to test his strength against others as a preliminary to his readoption. It also helps to reduce even further the possibility that local parties will be able to bring to bear the threat of refusal to readopt as a weapon with which to bludgeon their M.P. into advocating the particular policies which they themselves may favour.[2]

It is evident from the preceding analysis that the activities of the mass organization of the Labour Party (including its trade union, local party and other elements) loom much larger in the affairs of the party as a whole than do the activities of the National Union on the Conservative side. In part this is because, with the Conservatives so continuously in office in this century, their leaders have usually constituted the government of the country. And (as Labour discovered in 1945–51) there can be no question in such circumstances of the party organization outside parliament directing the affairs of the party and its leaders in parliament: indeed to judge from the

---

[1] *Model Rules* Set A, p. 11.
[2] For a valuable discussion of the relationship of M.P.s to their local associations see Richards, P. E., *Honourable Members*, Chapter VII. He points out that in the case of the dispute over German rearmament in the 1950s the Labour Party headquarters intervened in the affairs of certain constituency Labour Parties to protect those M.P.s who supported rearmament against the wishes of their local parties. On the repercussions of the Suez affair, see Epstein, L., " British M.P.s and their Local Parties," *American Political Science Review*, Vol. LIV, No. 2, June, 1960, p. 374 ff.

record of the party conferences during the life-time of the two Attlee governments, if Labour had been in office as continuously as the Conservatives (or for that matter the Swedish socialists) the evident concentration of power in the hands of the parliamentary leaders would have been as obvious as it is in the Conservative party in Britain (or in the Swedish socialist party).

But not only has Labour been fairly continuously in opposition (and its leaders usually bereft of governmental office); it has also saddled itself with a party constitution which appears to vest control of party policy in the extra-parliamentary organs of the party. This has made it inevitable that the party leaders should devote a considerable part of their time to the complex task of carrying their supporters outside parliament with them. This they have almost invariably succeeded in doing so long as they have maintained the " working alliance " with a majority of the leading trade unionists which has been referred to throughout this chapter. And the significant fact is that the parliamentary leaders have almost continuously retained the initiative as the formulation and determination of policy; they have in no sense been the mere " mouthpieces " for policies determined for them elsewhere, although this has been the rôle traditionally cast for them by one element within the party.

Most of the time (but by no means all the time) the mass organization of the Labour Party exerts greater influence on the parliamentary leaders than does its Conservative counterpart. None the less its *primary* function is the same: to try to secure an electoral majority for its parliamentary party. The mass organization of each party has a special channel of communication to the party leaders (denied to its supporters and voters who are outside the party organization); and this means that the party activists have special opportunities to influence policy decisions. Obviously the parliamentary leaders of any party cannot afford to be either disrespectful or indifferent to the moods and aspirations of their active supporters outside Parliament. But it does not follow from this that the parliamentary leaders are in any direct sense subject to the will of their organized supporters; if they were, British parliamentary government, as presently conceived, would be unworkable.

CHAPTER IX

THE LABOUR PARTY HEAD OFFICE

FROM its earliest beginnings the Labour Party head office has operated under the direction of the National Executive Committee; neither the Leader himself nor the Parliamentary Labour Party has ever exercised formal control over the work of the professional organization of the party. This is in sharp contrast to the position in the Conservative Party; as was shown in Chapter V, the Conservative Central Office was originally the creation of the Leader of the Party and has always been responsible to him (during the earlier years through the Whips' Office and subsequently through the Chairman of the Party Organization). These arrangements have no doubt helped to ensure that the professional organization of the Conservative Party should not become a power in its own right or develop a primary allegiance to the mass organization of the party rather than to the parliamentary party. The Conservative Central Office has always been subservient to the parliamentary party; it has never developed the evils associated with the terms " boss " and " machine " in American politics. It has never become a centre of power and authority outside and beyond the control of the elected representatives of the party.

A formal reading of the Labour Party constitution might suggest that the party had laid itself open to these dangers; but in practice it has escaped them. There are many reasons why it has done so, and two are of particular interest. It is important to recall that, for the first thirty-four years of its existence, Labour head office was under the direction of only two Secretaries, MacDonald (1900–11) and Henderson (1912–34), and, of great importance, both of them (from 1906 onwards) were prominent figures in the PLP. MacDonald entered Parliament in 1906 and served for some years as Secretary both of the PLP and of the party outside Parliament. Henderson, during his years as Secretary at head office, was almost continuously in Parliament; he served in senior positions in the PLP (as Chief Whip, member of the executive committee of the parliamentary party, and briefly as Leader) and as a Cabinet Minister in the first two Labour Governments. Thus, throughout its early years, the Labour Party professional organization was continuously under the direction of leading parliamentarians who understood and respected the primacy and autonomy of the par-

liamentary element of the Labour Party. Both MacDonald and
Henderson were occasionally accused of manipulating the affairs
of party head office in autocratic fashion, but neither showed the
least inclination to attempt to use the professional organization
of the party as a means of controlling the parliamentary party.

A second factor which helps to account for the fact that the
head office has never threatened the autonomy of the PLP, arises
from a consideration which has already been reviewed in detail:
the fact that the NEC, under whose direction the party head office
operates, has never for any length of time been seriously out of
step with the PLP. As has been emphasized, the leading figures in the
PLP have almost invariably played a major and often a dominant
rôle in the affairs of the NEC. Thus while the Labour Party can
justly claim that its professional organization is subject to the control
and direction of the democratically-elected executive of the mass
party, it can with equal justice be pointed out that the parliamentary
leaders of the party have been able to wield very nearly as much
influence over the activities of the professional organization of the
party as have their opposite numbers among the leaders of the
Conservative Party. Thus both parties have escaped the evils of the
" boss " and the " machine " so far as their headquarters organizations are concerned.

I

THE HEAD OFFICE UNDER MACDONALD AND HENDERSON

The beginnings of the Labour Party head office could hardly
have been less auspicious. It will be recalled that at the 1900 LRC
conference the post of Secretary almost went begging. F. Brocklehurst (of the ILP) suggested the LRC should have two secretaries
—but the proposal found no support and another delegate nominated
Brocklehurst himself. The latter declined nomination and proposed
the name of Ramsay MacDonald, a fellow ILP delegate at the
conference. MacDonald accepted nomination and was elected
unanimously.[1] Snowden may well have been right when he subsequently recalled that most of those present thought of the job as
not much more than a secretarial or clerical post; MacDonald
alone, Snowden claimed, saw its potentialities.[2] Certainly there
could have been no immediate financial inducement to accept the

---

[1] *1900 LRC Conference Report,* p. 16.
[2] Snowden, *An Autobiography,* Vol. I, p. 92. Although it will be recalled
that Keir Hardie later claimed that much thought had been given to the
selection of MacDonald; cf. p. 343 above.

post. The office of Secretary carried no salary, although at the end of the first year's work MacDonald was voted twenty guineas " as an acknowledgment of his past services." The Committee also conceded the necessity for some sort of office accommodation and early in 1901 they hired a room in MacDonald's own flat at 3 Lincoln's Inn Fields at a rent of £25 per annum. It was, as MacDonald later recalled, a back room " so dark and unsuitable " that he and his wife could find no use for it.[1] The LRC also empowered MacDonald " to buy tables and other immediate requisites and report cost to next meeting." [2]

Half a century later, Sam Watson, the chairman of the NEC for 1949–50, boasted that in the head office staff and organization at Transport House ". . . we have the finest machine of any political party in Europe."[3] This remark was a gross exaggeration when it was made. But whatever the state of the Party machinery at that time there is no doubt that it deteriorated markedly in the 1950s. The Wilson Committee in 1955 declared itself " deeply shocked at the state of the party organization in many parts of the country . . . our machine . . . is rusty and deteriorating with age."[4] Seven years later a Fabian study group's report was almost as pessimistic.[5]

Perhaps the most striking feature of the party's attitude to its head office throughout its history has been its evident reluctance to provide funds for staff and facilities to enable head office adequately to fulfil its task. As was noted in Chapter VI, MacDonald threatened to resign early in 1903; the letter in which he indicated his intention did not take the form of an outright request for increased remuneration, but it is significant that before the end of the year the Executive had decided to recommend to the annual conference that the Secretaryship should carry a salary of £250 a year. Characteristically, the Committee added the proviso: " £250 a year, from which (the Secretary) finds his clerical assistant's salary." The Committee also decided to rent a two-room office in Victoria Street at £75 a year.

MacDonald was greatly aided during this period by Arthur Henderson, who was appointed Treasurer of the Party (an unpaid post) in 1904. According to Henderson's biographer, he had begun to undertake " the lion's share of the work " of the party office as

[1] *1924 Labour Annual Conference Report,* p. 115.
[2] Manuscript Minutes of LRC Executive, 7th March, 1901, *Labour Party Documents,* Part I, folio 49.
[3] *1950 Labour Annual Conference Report,* p. 175.
[4] Labour Party, *Sub-Committee on Party Organization. Interim Report,* (The " Wilson Report "), London, 1955, p. 7.
[5] *The Mechanics of Victory,* Fabian Society, 1962.

early as 1903.[1] This comment appears to minimize MacDonald's
own contribution; but there can be little doubt that Henderson
soon became greatly preoccupied with the detailed work of party
organization or that he was eager to trade posts with MacDonald
and take over the Secretaryship as he did in 1912. Meanwhile, in
1907, the NEC decided that in light of MacDonald's new parliamentary duties (following his election in 1906) he should be relieved
of responsibility for detailed office work " while retaining control
over the carrying out of the Party's policy in the constituencies,
advising re candidatures, conferences, etc." The assistant secretary
(James Middleton, who later served as Secretary 1934–44) was put
in charge of the office. An assistant to the whips in Parliament
(Scott Lindsay) was also appointed to help with the work of the
parliamentary party; and it was further arranged that during the
recess he should take part in the work of the head office.[2] It is
evident that the link between the parliamentary party and the head
office was extremely close. In Parliament MacDonald served as
Secretary of the PLP, and later in 1911–14 as Chairman, while outside
Parliament he was Secretary of the party organization from 1900 to
1911. Henderson was elected whip in 1906 and served as Chairman of
the PLP in 1908–10; while at head office he was Treasurer and deeply
concerned in the work of party organization until he succeeded
MacDonald as Secretary at head office in 1912.

It is not surprising that even MacDonald and Henderson found
the work too heavy and they managed to convince the Executive
of the need for the appointment of a National Agent. The EC
proposed such an appointment to the 1907 conference but their
recommendation was firmly rejected by a vote of 626,000 to 323,000.[3]
The Executive, pressed no doubt by its overworked head office
personnel, renewed its recommendation in the following year and
this time the conference acquiesced in the proposal by a narrow
majority.[4]

On the eve of the first world war the total employed staff of the
Labour Party consisted of only 11 persons: seven at head office,
with the part-time services of the Parliamentary Assistant, two
travelling organizers and a Scottish Secretary. Five years later,
in its report to the 1919 conference, the NEC could boast that the
staff had been more than quadrupled; 30 men and women were
employed at head office and 17 others were working for the party
in various capacities throughout the country. The NEC Report

---

[1] Hamilton, M. A., *Arthur Henderson*, p. 75.
[2] *1907 Labour Annual Conference Report*, (Report of the NEC), p. 9.
[3] *Ibid.*, p. 48.
[4] *1908 Labour Annual Conference Report*, pp. 54-5.

also described a fairly elaborate departmental organization at head office; the latter had been sub-divided to include the Secretary's office, the Assistant Secretary's office, the National Agent's department, the Chief Woman Officer's department, a Press and Publicity department, an Information Bureau and an enquiry office.[1] The work of the various sub-divisions of head office conformed roughly to the present arrangements which are discussed below.

In the pages of the NEC Report the head office organization looked impressive enough; but it seemed less so to the ruthless gaze of Beatrice Webb. In March 1918 she wrote in her diary:

> "The Labour Party is the most ramshackle institution in its topmost story. Henderson sits alone in the untidy office . . . no member of the Executive or of the Parliamentary Party ever comes near him except Sidney (Webb). J. R. MacDonald, the Treasurer, supposed to be his fellow Executive officer, is conspicuous by his absence. Neither the pacifist nor the pro-war M.P.s trouble him with their advice or take counsel with him as to their own action. Snowden, the Chairman of the ILP—the leading Socialist organization within the Labour Party—never loses an opportunity of sneering at Henderson or denouncing the ' official Labour Party.' The fair-minded and gentle-natured Middleton, the Assistant Secretary, sits in another tiny room and supervises two seedy male clerks—ex-trade union workmen—and as many somewhat inferior female typists. There is the little dwarflike Gillies—an honest over-sensitive and obstinate-minded but well-informed little Glasgow Fabian—as intelligence officer, and a certain journalist—Tracey—a pleasant and, I think, competent young man as publicity officer. Upstairs, superintending the women's section, sits the redoubtable Marion Phillips—hardly an element of solidarity in an office. There are some one hundred Parliamentary agents, most of whom I saw yesterday at a Fabian Research Department reception—old men, unkempt men, half-educated men—an inferior brand of the Trade Union branch official—with no alertness and little organizing capacity. The chief Parliamentary agent—Peters—is of the Sunday-School type, who trudges through his work with a sort of mechanical persistence, carrying out Henderson's orders."

Alongside what she calls " this decrepit staff," Mrs. Webb noted the presence of a " circle of rebellious spirits and idealist intellectuals " who gathered round G. D. H. Cole and the Webbs themselves. She lists as the most notable of this group R. H. Tawney,

[1] *1919 Labour Annual Conference Report,* (Report of the NEC), p. 44. Subsequently during the period 1921-6 the Labour Party and the TUC merged their press and publicity and their research and information services, and operated them under joint auspices. The arrangement was terminated in 1926 on the initiative of the General Council of the TUC. See *1926 Labour Annual Conference Report,* (Report of the NEC), p. 34.

J..J. Mallon, Delisle Burns, Arthur Greenwood, Arnold Toynbee and H. J. Gillespie.

> "These young men have formed themselves into a sort of informal advisory committee, sometimes presided over by Sidney as Henderson's representative, sometimes left to their own devices. This morning I found them foregathered in the Fabian Common Room engaged in constituting a series of Advisory Committees to the Labour Party on some half a dozen subjects, whilst two of them—Tawney and Arnold Toynbee—were drafting a leaflet . . . . The ILP leaders seem altogether out of it. I suggested, when called in to advise as to the membership of the Advisory Committees, that J. R. MacDonald and W. C. Anderson should be asked to be Chairmen of the two principal committees. The suggestion was accepted, but without enthusiasm."

After her cynical review of the head office personnel, Mrs. Webb decided that "Unless the two old parties have completely lost their cunning, it is difficult to imagine that such a crazy piece of machinery as the existing Labour Party will play a big part in the reconstruction of the UK and the British Empire after the war." [1]

There was some rumbling of discontent at the 1919 party conference. One delegate attempted to refer back the whole of the National Agent's report in order to draw attention to what he described as the inefficiency of the National Agent. But Henderson rose to the defence of the head office staff and the motion was defeated.[2] That there were serious weaknesses, there can be little doubt. G. D. H. Cole, with his intimate knowledge of the party organization in this period, attributed these weaknesses in part to "under-staffing and even lack of appreciation of the need for workers of first-class quality in (the Labour Party's) central and regional offices. There was no development until much later of an adequate International Department; there was hardly any research work, as distinct from the day to day services of information—and even these were on an inadequate scale . . ." One difficulty was lack of funds (the party, it must be recalled, had to meet the cost of the four electoral campaigns which were fought in the first six years after the war); but Cole adds: "This . . . was not the whole explanation: there was also a failure to appreciate brains and a suspicion of 'cleverness' which prevented service in the Party machine from offering attractions to the younger people who could have helped to provide it with the driving force that it manifestly lacked." [3]

[1] *Beatrice Webb's Diaries 1912–24*, pp. 116–17.
[2] *1919 Labour Annual Conference Report*, pp. 124-5.
[3] Cole, G. D. H., *A History of the Labour Party from 1914*, pp. 123-4.

Even Henderson himself appears to have been conscious of the inadequacies of the head office staff. When he entered the 1924 Labour Government as Home Secretary he had relinquished his party salary but had continued for a time in charge of party administration. In August, 1924, Middleton was made Acting Secretary and Henderson took the title Honorary Secretary, continuing to make himself available, as the NEC report put it, " for consultation and advice on questions of election policy, organization and finance." [1] But, in private conversation with Beatrice Webb, Henderson admitted that without his own services the party head office was in a bad way. Beatrice Webb wrote in her diary (after a conversation with Henderson in July 1924) that he " was deploring the absence of brains at (head office) now he could no longer be there. ' I sometimes wonder whether I should not have done better in the interests of the Party to have refused Office and stuck to my job of Party organization.' " [2]

The head office was in further difficulties following the return of the second Labour Government in 1929. Again Henderson became Honorary Secretary and Middleton was named Acting Secretary. In addition, no less than five senior officials of head office were elected to Parliament. One of them (Arthur Greenwood, secretary of the Research Department) joined Henderson in the Government. The others who were elected included W. W. Henderson (the son of the Secretary), who was in charge of the Press and Publicity Department; W. G. Hall, secretary of the Finance Department; J. F. Shillaker, the Pensions Officer; and Dr. Marion Phillips, the Chief Woman Officer. All of them solemnly assured the NEC (according to its report) " that their Parliamentary duties (would) not prevent the efficient fulfilment of their Party work," and the NEC, innocently one would have thought, agreed " for the present " that they should continue to give " full-time service " at head office.[3] But not every member of the party was so readily prepared to accept this situation. Halford Knight, M.P., said in a public speech: " No other political party in the country could, or would, tolerate the absence of paid officials from duty to serve in Parliament. Secretaries and organizers should be required to elect in which direction their abilities were to be applied. The big Trade Unions had long recognized this separation, and feeling on the matter was widespread and growing in the political movement." [4]

---

[1] *1924 Labour Annual Conference Report,* (Report of the NEC), p. 75.
[2] *Beatrice Webb's Diaries,* 21st July, 1924, folio 78.
[3] *1929 Labour Annual Conference Report,* (Report of the NEC), p. 57.
[4] Cited in *Gleanings and Memoranda,* November, 1929, p. 438.

An absurd twist was added to the situation in the following year. MacDonald resigned his position as Treasurer in June 1930 after provision had been made that the Leader should be an *ex officio* member of the Executive, and the NEC proceeded to appoint in his place Arthur Henderson, who was already Foreign Secretary in the Government and Secretary of the Party.[1] On the fall of the second Labour Government Henderson, it will be recalled, became for a year Leader of the Party and carried on his work as chairman of the Disarmament Conference of the League of Nations at Geneva, while still retaining the posts of Secretary and Treasurer. There could hardly be a more vivid demonstration of the party's pathetic dependence on Henderson; but clearly at this stage the situation, to many, had become intolerable. Henderson resigned the post of Leader in 1932, and two years later vacated the office of Secretary. On the latter occasion the NEC reviewed the situation created by his resignation and reported that "while it is felt undesirable that there should be any change in the existing right of the Secretary to enter Parliament it is proposed, however, that the office should not be held by anyone holding Ministerial rank in a Labour Government." At the 1934 conference Clynes moved an amendment to incorporate this provision into the standing orders governing the election of Secretary. However, a constituency party delegate proposed a further amendment which provided that " the Secretary of the Party shall not be eligible to sit in the House of Commons, but that he shall devote the whole of his time to the organization of the Party." The NEC resisted this amendment and, although there is no specific indication to this effect, it seems fair to assume that they may have felt that the presence of the Secretary in Parliament would help to ensure that the direction of the mass organization remained in the hands of someone who was thoroughly familiar with the problems and limitations of parliamentary action. The conference overrode the NEC and adopted the amendment precluding the Secretary from becoming a M.P. by a vote of 1,449,000 to 841,000.[2] At the 1935 conference J. S. Middleton was formally confirmed as successor to Arthur Henderson. He remained in office until 1944, when he was succeeded by Morgan Phillips. Phillips in turn served until he retired through ill health in 1961 and he was succeeded by his deputy, Len Williams, in the following year.

---

[1] *1930 Labour Annual Conference Report,* (Report of the NEC), p. 4.

[2] At the same conference it was further decided that the Secretary should not be subject to annual re-election but should remain in office so long as his work proves satisfactory to the NEC and the annual conference. *1934 Labour Annual Conference Report*, p. 208.

II

THE HEAD OFFICE: THE MODERN STRUCTURE

After Henderson's resignation the office of Secretary considerably changed in character. As a prominent parliamentarian with enormous personal prestige in the party, Henderson had exerted an almost paternal control over the affairs of head office and had played a prominent part at successive annual conferences. As his biographer has shown, he played an active part in conference discussions even where major issues of policy were concerned, and rarely failed to get his own way.[1] He was much more than managing director of the professional organization of the party; in a sense he combined the functions which in the Conservative Party have been divided between the Chairman of the Party Organization and the General Director of the Conservative Central Office. There was probably no one who could have taken his place after 1935; and there is strong evidence that the conference was anxious that no one should attempt to do so. Certainly his successor Middleton did not. A modest man of limited ability, Middleton did no more than administer the affairs of the professional organization under the direction of the NEC. He rarely intervened in conference discussion and never on an occasion when major policy issues were under review. His successor Morgan Phillips, like Middleton, had never been a Member of Parliament and for a time he, too, served as no more than managing director of the professional staff supervising the work of the departments of head office and carrying out the decisions of the NEC. An examination of Phillips's contributions to conference debates during the years 1945–52 (inclusive) shows that he intervened mainly when technical aspects of the work of the NEC or of head office were under discussion. At the 1949 conference, for example, he dealt with the procedure for compositing resolutions and spoke briefly on party propaganda, the League of Youth, proscribed organizations, the work of regional councils and on party finance.[2]

Meanwhile, however, Phillips had been playing an increasingly prominent part in the international socialist movement and when the Socialist International was formally reconstituted in 1951 he was elected its first Chairman. At the 1953 Labour annual conference Phillips emerged in a rôle which the Secretary had not played since the heyday of Arthur Henderson's authority.

The explanation of the Secretary's new rôle is to be found part in

[1] Hamilton, M. A., *Arthur Henderson*, pp. 268-70.
[2] *1949 Labour Annual Conference Report, passim.*

the fact that a number of long-standing NEC members including Morrison, Dalton and Shinwell had been overthrown in recent NEC elections, and the "loyalist" majority on the NEC, while secure in its ascendancy over the Bevanite rebels, was deficient in debating skills and therefore recruited the Secretary's support.

Perhaps the most remarkable feature of Phillips's seventeen years as secretary is that he survived both the withering criticisms of the state of the party organization made by the Wilson Report in 1955 and the disastrous series of electoral failures suffered by the party in the 1950s. It is obvious that in similar circumstances the Conservatives would have sacked a whole series of Party Chairmen. But again Hugh Dalton's remark is apposite: Labour has " a strong sense of social security near the top. To do a man out of his job, at that eminence, is against good followership."

After illness forced Phillips to retire in 1961, the Labour Party was strongly urged to adopt the Conservative practice of appointing a major parliamentary figure to head up the party's central office, with a General Director serving under him.[1] The NEC considered the proposal, then dropped it and attempted to achieve the same purpose by indirect means. Len Williams who had been Phillips's deputy was promoted to the post of Secretary; but George Brown, the Deputy Leader of the PLP (who had become chairman of the Organization Sub-Committee of the NEC), also became in effect "over-lord" of Transport House and did not hesitate to invite comparison of his rôle in preparing the party machinery for the forthcoming election with that of Iain Macleod as the Conservative Party Chairman. There was a precedent here (of sorts) in the rôle of Herbert Morrison during and after the 1945 election; but it is curious that the inbred conservativism of the Labour Party seems to inhibit so completely its capacity to re-examine its own structure.

These considerations aside, and despite the *ad hoc* nature of George Brown's new rôle, the arrangements seemed to ensure that the parliamentary leadership would be in effective control of the work of Transport House.

The structure of the head office has varied remarkably little since 1918. It is at present composed of seven departments:

(1) Secretary's
(2) Organization
(3) Women
(4) International
(5) Research
(6) Press and Publicity
(7) Party Finance

[1] See *The Mechanics of Victory*, Fabian Society, 1962.

The Secretary works immediately under the direction of the NEC and the Women's Department is closely linked to the National Labour Women's Advisory Committee which advises the NEC on questions concerning the organization and work of women in the party; each of the other five departments works in close relation to one of the major sub-committees of the NEC which were described in Chapter VIII.

The relationship between the professional staff of a department and the relevant NEC sub-committee may be illustrated in this way: If the NEC has decided, for example, that a comprehensive statement of policy should be produced, they would first indicate the general lines on which the statement should be prepared. The Research Secretary would then draft a statement which would be reviewed by the Secretary and then laid before the Policy and Publicity sub-committee for discussion at a series of meetings of the committee.   Sections of the statement would perhaps be referred for more detailed examination to *ad hoc* sub-committees on which experts who are members of (or friendly to) the Labour Party may be co-opted. Each of these sub-committees would be serviced by a member of the staff of the Research Department in the capacity of secretary. When these special sub-committees had reported, the Research Secretary would redraft the policy statement in light of their findings. It would then be submitted again to the Policy and Publicity sub-committee which after further revision would forward the report to the NEC. After the latter body had reviewed the report it would probably be discussed with representatives of the Economic Committee of the TUC and possibly revised. The policy statement would then be laid before the annual conference. In the early stages of these discussions the secretary of the Research Department serves in a relationship to the chairman of the Policy and Publicity sub-committee somewhat analogous to the relationship between the permanent head of a Ministry and his Minister. There is, however, this difference: the Research Secretary is answerable to the whole of the Policy sub-committee which will probably include individuals with divergent viewpoints on important issues. At the meetings of the sub-committee the Research Secretary might conceivably argue on some matters against the views of his chairman; it is also possible of course that a majority of members of the committee might over-ride the views of the chairman.

It is impossible to make a categorical statement on the degree of influence exercised by a particular member of the professional staff of head office. Much depends, of course, on the personality and ability of the person concerned. There can be no doubt, however, that ultimately the members of the professional staff are the servants of the NEC and its sub-committees. If they are sufficiently persuasive and able they may succeed in exerting personal influence on the formulation of policy; but it would be inaccurate to suggest that the professional staff in any sense dominates or controls policy-making within the party.

The staff of the *Secretary's Department* serve as executive officers for the Secretary himself, and they are concerned therefore with the entire work of the party. The reports of the work of the Secretarial Department (which are incorporated like those of the other departments in the report of the NEC to the annual conference) touch upon an extraordinarily wide range of subjects; any topic which may have engaged the attention of the Secretary (acting in his own right or on behalf of the NEC) is likely to be included. Thus the Secretary's report to the 1953 conference deals with such matters as the ceremonies connected with the seventieth birthday of the Leader of the Party; the appointment of fraternal delegates to a variety of annual conferences; political broadcasting; the question of televising the annual party conference; the decision to produce a Labour weekly newspaper; party summer schools; the work of the special sub-committees appointed to deal with the denationalization of industry by the Conservative Government, and a wide variety of other matters.[1]

The work of the *Organization Department* is subject to the supervision of the Organization sub-committee of the NEC and under the immediate direction of the National Agent, who serves as the secretary of the sub-committee. The department deals with the work of the entire party organization outside Parliament. It is concerned with the training of agents and other key party workers; it provides postal and other courses in electoral law and party organization; it organizes membership campaigns and through its regional staff supervises on behalf of the Elections sub-committee and the NEC the adoption of prospective parliamentary candidates. In this connection it conducts negotiations with constituency parties which find themselves at odds with the NEC in the matter of the adoption of candidates. The Organization Department is also particularly concerned with by-elections and is responsible for ensuring that the resources of the party are fully organized in such campaigns by recruiting extra professional talent to assist the constituency Labour Party concerned. The Organization Department also directs the work of the party's regional staff and exerts a fairly rigorous control over the work of the regional offices.

The Organization Department is responsible for one of the

---

[1] *1953 Labour Annual Conference Report*, (Report of the NEC), pp. 5 ff.

most controversial features of the party's work, the activities of its youth organization formerly known as the League of Youth. It is impossible to review its stormy history, which is to be found in the annual reports of the party during the inter-war years. The principal source of controversy revolved round the right of the League of Youth to adopt independent attitudes on major policy questions. The NEC always preferred that the League of Youth should be primarily a recreational and educational body and that it should not concern itself with debating policy issues. But during the 1930s the leading spirits in the League resented any attempt to restrict its activities; they acted in defiance of the wishes of the national party on a number of occasions and succeeded at one point in getting the League disbanded.

The League of Youth was subsequently re-established, but party literature is careful to indicate the limited nature of its functions:

> " The League of Youth is not a separate political party. It is an integral part of the Labour Party. Its primary function is to foster interest among young people in the policy of the Party. In addition, the League is responsible for recruiting youth into Labour's ranks. Through the League of Youth young people acquire knowledge and experience of Party work and enjoy fellowship in joint educational, recreational and social activities . . . . League of Youth branches are sections of their local Labour Parties. As individual members, young people are encouraged to play a full part in the normal life of their Constituency Labour Party through local Parties or Ward Associations."[1]

The clear intention was to discourage the League of Youth from debating national and international issues, since they might adopt policy resolutions at variance with those of the parent party itself. League branches named delegates to Area Federations of the League of Youth and to a Regional Advisory Committee whose purpose it is " to advise the (Regional) Council on the co-ordination and development of League activities throughout its Region." The regional councils in turn elected two representatives to sit on a National Consultative Committee of the League of Youth. This Committee met at least quarterly " to consider the national administration of the League of Youth and to advise the National Executive Committee of the Labour Party on youth matters." [2] The 1953 report of the Organization Department notes that this Consultative Committee met on five occasions during the previous year and adds that " its work has been hampered by the great number of changes which have taken place in its membership. Of the

---

[1] *Handbook of Labour's League of Youth,* (n.d.) p. 2.
[2] *Ibid.,* p. 2.

22 League representatives serving on the Committee, only seven have held office for a period exceeding twelve months."[1] No doubt this turnover in membership was attributable in part to the effects of national service; but neither can there be any doubt that it reflected a widespread dissatisfaction among young people in the Labour Party with the work of the League of Youth itself. The 1953 report claimed a total of 538 League of Youth branches, a figure which represented, the report admits, " a net overall reduction of 132 " during the previous year. The report added brightly that newly-established branches " are formed at the rate of approximately one hundred each year," but there is no doubt that the Labour Party has been remarkably unsuccessful in its attempts to build a stable and contented youth organization.[2]

The *Women's Department* is headed by the Chief Woman Officer, who reports directly to the NEC rather than to one of its sub-committees. The NEC in turn, however, is advised by the National Labour Women's Advisory Committee which was established by the NEC in 1951. It is composed of the five women members of the NEC plus two women named by each of the eleven regional councils. The representatives of the Women's Sections (along with women members of trade unions, socialist and co-operative societies) had met for some years in an Annual Conference of Labour Women, and the delegates from the Women's Sections of Constituency Labour Parties to the 1951 meeting of this conference discussed and approved the NEC's proposal to establish the Advisory Committee. The Women's Department stimulates, assists and supervises the whole range of women's work within the party organization. It sponsors special campaigns to recruit women members and conducts conferences and residential schools to train women in party work and for service in public life.

Two sub-committees of the NEC (International and Commonwealth) are concerned with the work of the *International Department*. The department itself, under the direction of the International Secretary, is responsible for maintaining contacts with socialist parties in other countries and in the Commonwealth. Under the direction of the NEC it arranges for delegations of party representatives to attend meetings of the Socialist International and of individual socialist parties in other countries. It conducts research on international problems and publishes periodicals and special documents

[1] *1953 Labour Annual Conference Report,* (Report of the NEC), p. 11.

[2] The League of Youth was subsequently dissolved in 1955 and succeeded by the Young Socialist organization. They have been permitted to debate policy questions at their first two national conferences in 1961 and 1962 and in 1961, in particular, reached a number of decisions which proved embarrassing to the party leadership.

for use throughout the party. In 1953 the department undertook a new departure in its work when it organized what it called a " Fact-Finding Mission " to West Africa. Three members of the NEC and one member of the staff of the International Department visited British territories in West Africa and had discussions with members of public bodies, trade unionists, co-operators, and political leaders. This, the department claims, was " the first time that the Labour Party or indeed any political party had sent a visiting mission to the Colonies." [1] The findings of the Mission were reported to the NEC and taken into account in the formulation of the Executive's statements on Colonial policy.

The *Research Department* and the *Press and Publicity Department* work under the direction of the Policy and Publicity sub-committee of the NEC. The work of the Research Department in the formulation of policy has already been reviewed and its reports contain detailed descriptions of the way in which the department has contributed to the preparation of the major policy statements the party has issued. [2] The department also undertakes research activities on behalf of special sub-committees set up by the NEC to deal with particular problems, and in addition, as a recent department report puts it, it supplies " a steady stream of background material to the Parliamentary Party." Pamphlets and leaflets are published on matters of current concern to the party and they are made available to local parties and individuals; the latter may also make requests for information to the department. The staff includes an Education Officer whose duty it is to visit ward and constituency parties to encourage the development of party education. The party itself has expressed dissatisfaction with the extent to which its local organizations have responded to these efforts. The 1953 report admits that " education activity is only being undertaken by a minority of Constituency Parties."[3]

The duties of the *Press and Publicity Department* are indicated by its title. In addition to providing a press service for all local and national papers, it also makes particular effort to assist local Labour Party publications. The department also publishes a wide range of pamphlets, leaflets, posters and special printed material for elections.[4]

[1] *1953 Labour Annual Conference Report,* (Report of the NEC), p. 24.

[2] See for example a review of the procedure followed in the preparation of *Challenge to Britain,* in the *1953 Labour Annual Conference Report*, (Report of the NEC), p. 26.

[3] *1953 Labour Annual Conference Report,* (Report of the NEC), p. 27.

[4] The Labour Party's public relations activities have come under heavy fire in recent years. See for example Rowland, C., " Labour Publicity," *Political Quarterly*, July–September, 1960, pp. 348–60; *The Mechanics of Victory*, Fabian Society, 1962, pp. 8 ff.

The NEC's Finance and General Purposes sub-committee supervises the work of the *Finance Department* of head office. The finances of the Labour Party are considered at Appendix B and it is necessary here to note only that the Finance Department is responsible for supervising the general funds of the party and a number of special funds which are established for general elections, for party development, and for superannuation and pensions for employees of the Labour Party.

III

THE REGIONAL OFFICES OF THE LABOUR PARTY

As was noted in the discussion of regional councils, the regional staff of the party is responsible not to the councils themselves but to the party head office. Until 1951 the NEC made annual grants to regional councils and allowed them responsibility for providing from these funds accommodation and clerical assistance for the use of the regional staff. In that year it was decided, however, that the NEC itself should take over full responsibility for the regional offices; they were to become henceforth the regional offices of the Labour Party. One, at least, of the regional councils resisted this change and the reaction of the NEC and head office to this resistance is worth noting. The Report of the Executive Committee of the Lancashire and Cheshire Regional Council to the 1953 meeting of the Council (p. 10) explains that the Executive had taken the view that " the best interests of the Party would be served by the (regional) office remaining the office of the Regional Council and under its direction." In the course of the negotiations with the NEC the regional council was notified that the annual grant from the NEC would be stopped unless the regional executive agreed that the office should become the property of the NEC. The regional executive's report explains that " a deputation from the Regional Council met the Finance Committee of the Labour Party at Morecambe during the (1952) annual conference to put the regional point of view, and on 17th January, 1953, Mr. W. J. Webber, Chairman of the Finance Committee, and Mr. Len Williams, National Agent, met the Regional Executive Committee. It was clear following these meetings that the National Executive Committee was not prepared to alter its point of view and the Regional Executive Committee therefore decided to adopt the conditions as set out in the Head Office memorandum." It seems evident from this report that the Organization Department (with the co-operation of the Finance Committee) has not hesitated to use economic sanctions to ensure that it retains full control of the affairs of the regional offices.

The regional organizers themselves are appointed by the Organization sub-committee of the NEC, subject to the approval of the full NEC; each organizer becomes, in effect, the representative of the NEC and of the head office in the region. He is responsible to and reports directly to the National Agent. He is charged with maintaining the party machinery in the region at a high state of efficiency and co-ordinating the activities of local parties at regional level. The regional organizer has no direct concern with policy questions; policy resolutions passed by constituency parties are sent directly to the NEC and are not channelled through his office (although some constituency parties may, out of courtesy, send the regional organizer a copy of their resolutions).

As was shown in the discussion of the selection of candidates, the regional organizer usually represents the NEC at selection conferences and his report on the procedure followed normally provides the basis on which the NEC decide whether or not to approve the actions of the constituency party. In matters other than the selection of candidates the regional organizer has no direct authority over either the constituency party or its agent. Much depends on the personalities involved in the relationship and the regional organizer must rely upon the goodwill of the local parties to ensure that they act upon his advice and instructions. The constituency parties in turn, of course, cannot be unaware that the advice of the regional organizer to the NEC will carry great weight with the latter in the event that the constituency organization through misbehaviour finds itself threatened with disaffiliation.

In addition to the regional organizer, the staff of the regional office normally includes an assistant regional organizer, a women's organizer and a small clerical staff. In a by-election the regional organizer is normally appointed to act as constituency agent and he is, of course, expected to be the authority on problems of electioneering within the region. He also maintains contact with the regional group of M.P.s; he may attend their meetings at the House of Commons and present the views of the regional council on parliamentary issues which are of particular concern to the region.

In summary, it must be noted that the professional staff of the Labour Party plays a very similar rôle to that of the Conservative Party. It provides certain research services for the parliamentary party and for the policy-making bodies of the party outside Parliament. It encourages and supervises the work of the mass organization and canalizes the energies of the voluntary party workers into channels which are approved by the party leaders. Labour head office, in contrast to the Conservative Central Office, is the servant of the annual conference and the NEC, while, as has already been noted, the Conservative Central Office is directly responsible to the Leader. But in practice this makes much less difference than one might expect. The Conservative Leader has never dared to use the professional organization of the party for purely personal ends, while in practice the Labour head office has invariably served the purposes of the Leader of the parliamentary party and his colleagues. There is no concentration of power and authority in head office which in any sense threatens either the autonomy of the parliamentary party or the authority of a Labour Government. Inevitably the professional staff of the party acquires some influence in the formulation of party policy. This influence has perhaps been greatest in the international work of the party. Here the Secretary of the party and staff of the International Department have been permitted to speak for the Labour Party to an extent which is only dimly realized by most members of the party. But it must be emphasized that they have been permitted to do so by the NEC itself, and that body has almost always faithfully reflected the views of the majority of the parliamentary party on foreign affairs. It could not therefore be argued that even in this field the officials of party head office have acquired independent authority in formulating the policies of the party. To the militants of the constituency Labour Parties, head office may often seem the master and not the servant of the mass organization; but it cannot be denied that the NEC has never in the history of the party lost its ability to call the professional staff to heel. The latter has served for the most part as a faithful civil service, counselling and guiding its masters on the NEC but ultimately obedient to the latter's instructions. The NEC itself (for reasons that have been analysed above) has usually followed faithfully in the footsteps of the parliamentary leaders and this in turn has ensured that head office has consistently served the purposes of the PLP.

PART III

CHAPTER X

EPILOGUE: THE CONSERVATIVE AND LABOUR PARTIES SINCE 1955

[This chapter deals mainly with the evolution of the Leadership of the two major parties since 1955; the other important changes in structure and practice have been taken into account in the revisions to the text and footnotes of Chapters I–IX.]

THE CONSERVATIVE PARTY SINCE 1955

THE changes in the Conservative Leadership since 1955 have illuminated in an important way the institutional position of the Leader of the Party (discussed in Chapters II and III). The transfer of power from Sir Winston Churchill to Sir Anthony Eden (later Lord Avon) in 1955 was as uneventful and " inevitable " as any in the party's history. Yet during Eden's term of office (even before the disastrous climax of Suez) he was in trouble of the sort which suggested that he might not have long survived as Leader. The succession of Harold Macmillan instead of R. A. Butler was as unexpected as Baldwin's preferment over Curzon in 1923 and cast important new light on the process by which Conservative Leaders " emerge " or, as in R. A. Butler's case in 1957, may fail to do so.

British party Leaders have tended to enjoy a striking degree of security of tenure. Once the Conservatives have chosen their Leader he can stay in office (as was shown in Chapters II and III) until he himself decides to retire or, as has happened on at least three occasions in this century, he is forced from office by a revolt among his followers. The Labour Leader is in theory subject to annual re-election (while the party is in opposition, although not while it is in office); but no Labour Leader, once he was clearly established in office, was ever challenged for re-election until Harold Wilson stood against Hugh Gaitskell following the Scarborough Conference decision in favour of unilateral nuclear disarmament in 1960 (see p. 621 below). It can be argued that in both parties there have been periods when the Leaders have clung too long to office, thus contributing to the difficulties of their successors and to a general " stagnation at the top ". Certainly it would seem that Baldwin, despite the great (and largely under-estimated) work he did for his party and for the country, clung to office several years too long. Attlee's case is more debatable. He led the Labour Party for twenty years, a longer period than any party Leader has held office since Gladstone. It may be that Attlee was wise to have carried on through the 1951 Parliament, since this went far to ensure that Gaitskell rather than Morrison (who by then was probably too old) would get the Leadership. (Morrison has since declared that he is convinced that this was Attlee's deliberate purpose.)[1] Yet there is a debit entry in the account: Labour after 1951 needed as fundamental an overhaul of its organization and policies as that undertaken by the Conservatives after 1945; but after eleven years in high office Attlee seemed too tired or indifferent to undertake such an operation.

Certainly it would seem incontestable that by clinging to the leadership into his 81st year, Sir Winston Churchill contributed to the difficulties of his successor. Throughout the fifteen years Churchill led the party Eden had been acknowledged as his *heir apparent*. According to Eden, as early as December 1940, Churchill had told him " firmly that in his judgment [Eden] . . . must succeed him if he was incapacitated from any cause during the war ".[2] There seems little doubt that the nervous strain involved in serving as perpetual understudy to an apparently indestructible chief helped to aggravate Eden's already considerable emotional and physical difficulties. He might well have failed as Leader in any case; but his chances would surely have been better had he inherited the Leadership either immediately after 1945 (if Churchill had recalled his own view that Lloyd George unwisely clung to office beyond his moment of war-time triumph) or soon after the Conservatives were returned to office in 1951.

Had it not been for Eden's own ill-health he might, of course, have succeeded Churchill when the latter suffered a serious stroke

---

[1] Morrison, Lord, *An Autobiography*, London, 1960, p. 293.

[2] Eden, Sir Anthony, *Full Circle*, London, 1960, p. 266. One of Eden's biographers has written: " When . . . Chamberlain resigned the Conservative leadership in 1940, and Churchill was appointed to succeed him, there was a move to elect Anthony Eden as Deputy Leader—an appointment that had never been made in the Party's history. The move originated with a few Conservative M.P.s who thought it might be wise if a somewhat safer Party man were at hand to keep an eye on the erratic genius of the new Leader. It failed to secure general support and no such motion was put to the election meeting. Nevertheless, there were few who did not realize that Anthony Eden was from that time Leader-designate." Broad, C. L., *Sir Anthony Eden*, London, 1955, p. 239. In addition, in 1942, when the King asked Churchill whom he would recommend as his successor in the event of Churchill's own death in the course of his war-time travels, the Prime Minister named Eden. See Wheeler-Bennett, J. W., *King George VI*, London, 1958, p. 543 ff.

in 1953. Randolph Churchill has written of the events of that summer when Eden underwent an operation and spent some months recuperating abroad:

> "It is probable that, if Eden had been in England and in good health, Churchill would have resigned and Eden would have become Prime Minister. As it was, the general view was held in high governing circles that it would be wrong if Eden, who had waited so long to be Prime Minister, should forfeit his reversionary rights by the strange misfortune that he and the Prime Minister were ill at the same time. Various expedients were debated, including that of a 'caretaker' Government under Lord Salisbury, to hold the fort till Eden should be recovered. Friends wrote and told Lady Eden that her husband's interests were being constantly borne in mind and that he should think of nothing save getting well."[1]

However, Sir Winston "fought his way back to health with a Roman mastery of mind over flesh" (in his son's words), celebrated his 80th birthday in office in November 1954 and (with what prompting from his colleagues it is not yet possible to establish)[2] finally tendered his resignation to the Queen on 5th April, 1955. It had been expected in some quarters that with Eden's claim to the succession so overwhelming he would be called to the Palace in a matter of hours. But, no doubt to underline the Royal prerogative on these occasions (as the *Manchester Guardian* suggested),[3] Eden was not called to the Palace until the following day. Subsequently, on 21st April, he was unanimously elected Leader of the Party at a meeting attended by Conservative M.P.s and Peers, prospective candidates and the Executive of the National Union.[4] In conformity with established practice the meeting was presided over by the party Leader in the House of Lords (Lord Salisbury), who nominated Eden; the principal supporting speech was made by the man generally considered to be second in authority to Eden in the

[1] Churchill, R. S., *The Rise and Fall of Sir Anthony Eden*, London, 1959, p. 190. See also Broad, C. L., *Sir Anthony Eden*, p. 238, and Eden's own account in his *Full Circle*, p. 52.

[2] Randolph Churchill remarks: "His [Eden's] friends were loud-mouthed in calling for Churchill's departure and suggested that if Eden's succession were to be long delayed he might become so frustrated that he would have passed the peak of his powers by the time that he entered the joy of his inheritance." Churchill, R. S., *The Rise and Fall of Sir Anthony Eden*, p. 192.

[3] *Manchester Guardian*, 6th April, 1955. Owing to a newspaper strike the *Guardian* was the only national paper to record these events.

[4] The *Manchester Guardian* calculated that those entitled to attend this meeting included "the 320 Conservative Members of the House of Commons, about 280 Peers who take the Conservative Whip, the 250 officially adopted Parliamentary Candidates and the 150 members of the Executive of the Conservative and Unionist Association". *Manchester Guardian*, 6th April, 1955.

party (and his putative successor), R. A. Butler, who thereafter deputized for Eden and presided over the Cabinet when he was absent from the country.

Eden's subsequent career as Leader was probably the most disastrous in the modern history of the party. One could debate Neville Chamberlain's claim to this particular distinction; certainly his inadequacy as war leader was of potentially greater menace to his country. Yet Eden's failure was in a sense more complete; the disaster that brought him down (the Suez fiasco) was more nearly of his own contriving than was the comparable event (the bungling of the Norwegian campaign) that ruined Chamberlain. And further, Eden had already revealed, in the fifteen months he held office before the Suez storm broke, a notable incapacity for leadership.

The crisis during the summer and autumn of 1956 was so spectacular that the events of the earlier months of Eden's Premiership have since been largely overshadowed. Eden had taken office to the widespread plaudits of the editorial writers and political commentators who, for the most part, predicted for him a distinguished career as Prime Minister. This expectation was based primarily on his outstanding record as Foreign Secretary (a post he held in all for eleven years, a record unequalled in modern parliamentary history). But Eden's political experience had in fact been more " one-sided " than that of any modern Prime Minister. It is almost true to say that his sole political concern, since he became parliamentary Private Secretary to Austen Chamberlain (then Foreign Secretary) in 1925, two years after he had entered Parliament, had been with external affairs; whereas, in contrast, every Prime Minister (except Attlee and MacDonald) during the past half-century had served as Chancellor of the Exchequer (as well as in a variety of other posts) *en route* to 10 Downing Street. When the Conservatives had returned to office in 1951 it had been expected in some quarters that Eden would take either a senior domestic ministry or a non-departmental post which would leave him free to deputize for Churchill over the whole range of governmental affairs. But Eden himself was said to have insisted on returning to the Foreign Office.[1] He had been accorded the title " Deputy Prime Minister ", but it seems probable that his duties as Foreign Secretary were so onerous during the early 1950s that he could have devoted comparatively little attention to home affairs.

Certainly, in office, Eden and his government soon faced serious

---

[1] Broad, C. L., *Sir Anthony Eden*, p. 198. On this point Eden himself merely states: " At Mr. Churchill's invitation I became Foreign Secretary once again . . . " *Full Circle*, p. 9.

domestic difficulties. The new Prime Minister had decided to go to the country almost immediately and, *after* the date of the election was announced (26th May), R. A. Butler, as Chancellor, introduced what was widely described as an " election budget "; it provided for cuts in taxation of the order of £150,000,000. The Eden government was returned with an increased majority (this was the first time in almost a century that a party had improved its position at the end of a full term in office); but by the autumn it was necessary to introduce a much sterner special budget to deal with the mounting problem of inflation, which may well have been stimulated by the budget of the previous spring. Apparently for this and other reasons Eden's personal popularity thereafter slumped sharply; the Gallup Poll reported that between the autumn of 1955 and the spring of 1956, the proportion of the electorate approving of the Prime Minister's work fell from 70 to 40 per cent.[1]

During the Parliamentary Recess of Christmas 1955 a number of articles appeared in the press assessing Eden's performance to date and speculating about his future. The most striking of these appeared in the *Daily Telegraph* (3rd January, 1956) over the signature of Donald McLachlan, then the paper's deputy editor. It was sharply critical of the Prime Minister's performance and complained of " changes of mind by the Government; half-measures; and the postponement of decisions. . . . " The article carried added weight because the *Telegraph* was among the most faithful supporters of the Conservative Party. Other papers of every shade of opinion joined in a flurry of speculation about Eden's future (a not unusual development during a Parliamentary recess when there is little " hard " political news). The climax came, however, when *The People* (a paper not primarily noted for its sober assessments of political realities) predicted that Eden was about to resign. The Prime Minister's response to this newspaper chatter was without parallel in the history of party leadership. Although he had been in power for only nine months, his office issued a formal denial that he intended to resign.[2] R. A. Butler, surprisingly enough, also issued a statement denying all knowledge of the supposed resignation and pledging himself, in a perhaps characteristic phrase, " to support the Prime Minister in all *his* difficulties " [italics added]. As the *Manchester Guardian* remarked, " Whatever rumours were circulating before, [these denials were] bound to increase them a hundredfold."[3]

---

[1] Cited in Butler, D. E., *The British General Election of 1959*, p. 36.
[2] Curiously enough, Eden himself makes no reference to this incident in *Full Circle*, the volume of his autobiography covering this period.
[3] *Manchester Guardian*, 2nd January, 1956.

This incident may be of interest primarily in suggesting that by this time Eden's temperamental instability had rendered him unfit for the strains of high office.[1] But it also throws some light on the extent to which a Prime Minister and party Leader may, in certain circumstances, be very vulnerable to serious criticisms from " his own side ". The rash of press articles would probably have had little consequence had it not been initiated by the solemn article criticizing Eden's leadership in the " loyalist " *Daily Telegraph*. An ineffective Leader whose Government is already in trouble may soon feel his authority to be in jeopardy if there are open demonstrations of discontent among those who normally offer unswerving support.

Eden's difficulties began in earnest with the abrupt dismissal by King Hussein of Jordan of his British Chief of Staff, General John Glubb (known as Glubb Pasha), on 1st March, 1956. This event apparently convinced Eden that Nasser, who he believed had inspired the dismissal, represented an irreconcilable threat to Britain's position in the Middle East. And to " appease " Nasser would, he felt, be as fatal as the appeasement of Hitler had proved before 1939. Indeed, this parallel seems to have become an obsession with Eden during the months that followed the seizure of the Canal in July. Meanwhile, in the Parliamentary debate on the events in Jordan on 7th March, Eden's own performance was very badly received both by the House and the press. Ian Waller, in a syndicated political column, wrote with extraordinary insight and (in his final comment) prescience:

> " His performance can be summed up in one word: Deplorable! It was inept and inconclusive. Even if Sir Anthony had restated his old policies with firmness and conviction, he might have held the House.
>
> " Instead, he met an outburst of barracking and contemptuous roars of disapproval and disgust such as a Premier has not been subjected to for many years. Sir Anthony, looking ill and exhausted, was quite incapable of overcoming it, and had to be rescued at one stage by the Speaker restoring order.
>
> " It was a shocking scene, and it was hard to believe that Sir Anthony who has, on foreign affairs, always held the House, was the centre of it. The Government won the vote, but Sir Anthony suffered a blow to his prestige that was clearly reflected in the silent, devastated ranks on the Conservative benches behind him.
>
> " Inevitably, these episodes start one asking the question: 'How long can Eden go on for?' . . . Events may save Sir Anthony, but it

[1] In discussing Eden's handling of his Cabinet, J. P. Mackintosh writes: " Nervous and tense, he was always poking into the departmental affairs of his colleagues and could not brook opposition." Mackintosh, J. P., *The British Cabinet*, London, 1962, p. 435.

is hard to avoid the feeling that the cards are mounting and that, if the year goes on as it has begun, it will not be Sir Anthony Eden but Mr. Harold Macmillan who reigns in Downing Street in 1957." [1]

It is difficult to dissent from Randolph Churchill's harsh judgment: " The [Jordan] debate marked the beginning of the disintegration of the personality and the character that the public thought [Eden] to possess."[2]

It is unnecessary to recount in detail the Suez story, already the subject of a half-dozen books and scores of polemical articles.[3] For the purposes of this brief analysis of Eden's rôle as party Leader, the fundamental question is this: How far was his downfall due to a failure of political leadership and an undertow of rebellion among his supporters? It will be many years before one can hope to attempt a final assessment of the importance of these considerations. Officially Eden resigned because of physical illness (which was obviously aggravated by the nervous strain of the Suez adventure and the bitter criticism of Eden's rôle in it). But if Eden's physical condition had remained unimpaired could he have carried on as Leader? Superficially the main body of his party appeared to be almost completely united in support of the Prime Minister and his Suez policies; but there can be little doubt that in fact there were large elements of the party who were forced to recognize either that it was madness to have launched the military attack on Egypt in the first place or that, once the attack was launched, it was folly to have called a halt before the operation was completed.

The Bromberger brothers in their book, *Secrets of Suez*, have argued (p. 159) that the Suez operation was halted partly as a result of a threat by a group of 40 Conservative M.P.s to vote against the Government in the House of Commons. It certainly is the case that some such group met privately on two occasions during the course of hostilities, as Nigel Nicolson, a leading Conservative opponent of Suez, has testified.[4] But in the critical vote

[1] Cited in Churchill, R. S., *The Rise and Fall of Sir Anthony Eden*, p. 227.

[2] Churchill, R. S., *The Rise and Fall of Sir Anthony Eden*, p. 228.

[3] Eden has provided his own account in *Full Circle*, Book III. See in addition Childers, E., *The Road to Suez*, London, 1962; Johnson, P., *The Suez War*, London, 1957; Foot, M. and Jones, M., *Guilty Men*, London, 1957; Utley, T. E., *Not Guilty: The Conservative Reply*, London, 1957.

[4] Nicolson, N., *People and Parliament*, London, 1958, p. 133. Nicolson maintains, incidentally, that the pressure from the Conservative Associations for a militant policy against Nasser was a major influence in determining the Eden Government's course of action during the summer and autumn of 1956. (The General Purposes Committee of the National Union passed a resolution on 6th November expressing support for the " resolute action that is being taken in meeting the crisis in the Middle East".) Public opinion generally also appeared to be strongly anti-Nasser.

on 8th November (after the hostilities had ceased) there were no more than eight known Conservative abstentions.[1] And there is no firm evidence as to what part the anti-Suez Conservatives played in helping to bring the hostilities to a stop.[2] Undoubtedly, the most important immediate consideration was the run on sterling on 6th November. It seems likely that this factor, combined with the United Nations, American and Commonwealth pressures, would have proved decisive in any case. But without these pressures it is doubtful if the Government would have been deterred by such opposition as it encountered from its own back-benchers, provided of course that the military action had been quickly completed. Eden himself subsequently wrote of the period 1st–7th November:

> " There were reports at this time of a dissident minority in the Conservative Party in the House of Commons. I was told that if a cease-fire were not announced that day (6th November), some of them would not vote with us. I was not influenced by these reports, or by knowledge that there had been some contacts between one or two members of our party and the Opposition Leaders. The overwhelming majority was firmly loyal. . . . "[3]

Granted, however, that the operation had been bungled in both its planning and its execution, could Eden's followers have long ignored the evidence that was provided of his personal incapacity for high political leadership, whatever his physical condition? It may well be that, beneath the public façade of loyalty to Eden, pressure was in fact brought to bear on him by certain of his senior colleagues, even before the diagnosis of renewed physical illness was made public in early January.

In any event, Eden returned on 14th December from his enforced rest at Jamaica (where he had gone to recuperate from " overstrain " after the military activities had ceased) and declared his intention to carry on as Prime Minister.[4] Then on 9th January came the announcement, intensely surprising in the absence of any previous press speculation that it might occur, that Eden had tendered his resignation to the Queen. In the hours that elapsed

[1] For a further analysis, see Epstein, L., " British M.P.s and their Local Parties: The Suez Case ", *American Political Science Review*, Vol. LIV, No. 2, June, 1960, p. 377.

[2] Peter Richards in his valuable book, *Honourable Members*, London, 1959, p. 249, rather too readily accepts the Brombergers' estimate of their influence.

[3] Eden also adds: " There are always weak sisters in any crisis and sometimes they will be found among those who were toughest at the outset of the journey." Eden, Sir Anthony, *Full Circle*, p. 557.

[4] *The Times*, 15th December, 1956.

before Eden's successor was called to the Palace the next day most political commentators continued to assume, as they had done for some years, that Butler was the "inevitable" successor.[1] Indeed, as recently as 22nd December, *The Economist* had committed itself to the remarkable view that, "If Sir Anthony were to lay down the Premiership tomorrow, there is really no doubt that the Queen would be constitutionally bound to send for Mr. Butler." But in fact Harold Macmillan, the Chancellor of the Exchequer under Eden, was invited to take office after the Palace had consulted Lord Salisbury and Sir Winston Churchill. (The latter subsequently stated publicly that he had recommended Macmillan to the Queen.)[2] On 22nd January Macmillan was unanimously elected Leader of the Party with R. A. Butler again in the (now somewhat unenviable) rôle of seconder of the nomination—this time of the man who had snatched the prize from him.

There is no documentary evidence as to how and why Macmillan won preferment over Butler. But an investigation of the circumstances suggests the following interpretation: When Eden returned from Jamaica there was much private speculation within the party as to whether he could in fact continue as Leader (whether for physical or other reasons). Those M.P.s who held strong views on the question of the succession began conveying them privately to the party's Chief Whip. This was subsequently revealed in an important exchange of correspondence between Conservative M.P.s in the *Daily Telegraph*. One of the younger M.P.s, T. L. Iremonger (first elected in 1954), wrote on 12th January 1956:[3]

> "Matters were handled so that the Sovereign has in effect chosen the Party's Leader for it without the will of the Party itself having found expression. Had arrangements been made for the Party to elect its new Leader before the Sovereign made her choice, it might have seemed to have made the Sovereign's choice for her, an even less acceptable position.
>
> "The Prime Minister's resignation, which no one claims was subject to any inexorable immediate compulsion, should I suggest have been so timed as to allow the general feeling of Conservative

[1] On the morning of 10th January the following national papers predicted with more or less certainty that Butler would be chosen: *Daily Mail, Daily Express, Daily Herald, Daily Mirror, News Chronicle*. The *Manchester Guardian* hoped that a "fresh" name (i.e. neither Butler nor Macmillan) would emerge. *The Times* and *Daily Telegraph* made no prediction. However, the early editions of the *Evening Standard* on 10th January carried an article by Randolph Churchill suggesting that Macmillan would probably be called.

[2] The *Manchester Guardian Weekly*, 8th January, 1959.

[3] For a fuller statement of Iremonger's views see the report of the speech in *The Recorder* (Ilford), 17th January, 1957.

M.P.s about his successor to be assessed and passed on to the Sovereign's advisers.

"It is said that the Leader of the Conservative Party is never elected, he emerges. No question arises, therefore, of anything more than informal soundings having been required, but such soundings should have been taken and from my knowledge were signally not taken. The status of all those members of the Party who have been elected to the Commons is thereby diminished, and I question whether this is desirable.

"You, Sir, say that 'soundings were taken among Conservative backbenchers'. If you are right and some backbenchers were sounded out and others ignored, then here is intolerable oligarchy, and I protest against it. I hope you are wrong. Lest I be misunderstood, I should say that in the event no one is personally better pleased at the choice of Mr. Macmillan than I am."

On 15th January Dame Irene Ward, M.P., replied:

"... Mr. Iremonger has been singularly out of touch with his colleagues if he has been unaware of the 'Empire-building' during the weeks after the Suez intervention. I would have preferred to have served under Sir Anthony Eden to the end of the road, but as a realist I took steps to inform our most admirable Whips before the Christmas recess that in the event of a change of Prime Minister I preferred Mr. Macmillan.

"A party meeting with opinion even partially divided on the Party Leadership would have been both impractical and undignified. The country has adequate protection in the powers of the monarch, and for Parliament or a party to seek to weaken them because of even exceptional difficulties would be a blunder of the highest magnitude."

On the same day, another Conservative M.P., Martin Lindsay, wrote:

"My colleague Mr. T. L. Iremonger is quite wrong in stating that the views of Conservative M.P.s on the choice of Prime Minister were not known or considered.

"It was quite apparent to the majority of us that Sir Anthony was a very sick man when he returned from Jamaica. Most of us, therefore, anticipated the situation which we considered was likely to arise during the Parliamentary recess and wrote to the Chief Whip expressing our individual opinions as to whom the Queen should send for.

"To my knowledge Mr. Heath [the Chief Whip] received a large number of such letters and was therefore in a position to state authoritatively that the greatest measure of agreement would be found in support of Mr. Macmillan."

Mr. Iremonger, unrepentant, insisted (18th January) that in his complaint he had reflected the views of "younger Tory M.P.s generally" when he complained that:

> " Capricious lobbying by individual Members is no substitute for an orderly and responsible sounding of opinion by those whose function it is to investigate all views and not merely to receive notes from the more impulsive. . . .
>
> " Let us not blink the fact, however embarrassing, that an unfortunate precedent has been set."[1]

But of course the failure to conduct more formal soundings (even Iremonger did not propose that the new Leader should be elected) conformed to long-established precedents in the history of the Conservative Leadership. The Iremonger correspondence demonstrates, however, that the " soundings " may (as in this case) be so subtly conducted that many M.P.s—and especially those who are new to the Party and the House—may be entirely unaware that they are taking place.

What does seem to have been unprecedented in the transfer of power in 1957 was that, on this occasion, members of the Cabinet were individually invited to express a preference as to who should succeed Eden as Prime Minister and Leader of the Party.[2] It appears that this operation was conducted by Lord Salisbury, the Leader of the Party in the House of Lords, and by Lord Kilmuir, the Lord Chancellor (neither of whom as peers could be considered to be in the running). It is important to note that the members of the Cabinet appear to have been polled separately, and not jointly and openly in a meeting of the Cabinet. Again, as on all previous occasions, the Conservatives sought to avoid a formal counting of heads, whether by Conservative M.P.s generally or within the Cabinet. The Conservative elder statesmen who conduct these operations are vividly aware of the dangers of "one man, one vote" and majority decisions in these matters. It could certainly be argued that the most important question to be decided on this occasion was not who would have obtained the most votes in a formal contest, but who had the best chance of re-uniting the party after the Suez debacle.[3] This second question would not necessarily have

---

[1] For some reason, which is not altogether obvious, *The Times* thought that: " . . . clearly it is almost an impossibility for the younger members of the dominant party to be consulted . . . ", *The Times*, 11th January, 1957.

[2] This was first reported by Randolph Churchill in the *Evening Standard*, 11th and 15th January, 1957. The *Sunday Times* on 13th January put the matter less positively, stating that Salisbury and Kilmuir " made informal soundings of Ministers " and the paper also added that " on the side of the party organization, leading members of the national body had informal exchanges about opinion in the constituencies."

[3] *The Economist*, 19th January, 1957, seemed to see a novel danger in this procedure (of choosing the man who would divide the party least). Would it not lead (the paper wondered) to the emergence in high office of " sheep " (i.e., those least willing to offend any section of the party)? But surely this is a

produced the same answer as would a counting of heads (or ballots).

In theory (although in practice this would almost certainly not have been the case) Butler might have won a formal contest with, say, 52 per cent. of the votes of Members of Parliament to Macmillan's 48 per cent. But if the 48 per cent. were more bitterly opposed to Butler than the 52 per cent. were to his rival, Macmillan, then Macmillan might well be considered the preferable Leader.   In other words the Conservative system of selecting Leaders tries to take into account both intensity of feeling roused by the potential rivals for the Leadership and the " political weight " of their supporters *and* opponents. It is because Conservative elder statesmen and party managers clearly understand that, even among Conservatives, some men are " more equal " than others that they are so reluctant to count heads in determining who should lead the party (or indeed in determining any other issue facing the party: as was shown in Part I, voting almost never takes place in any of the organs of the Conservative parliamentary party).[1]

Butler appears, then, to have lost the chance to succeed Eden because there was a powerful minority (at least) in the party who distrusted him deeply as a prospective Leader and preferred Macmillan. It was reported by *The Economist* [2] that the first reaction of the anti-Butler M.P.s, when they heard of Eden's resignation, was to call for a party meeting to choose a new Leader, but that this was resisted by leading figures in the party. There is no doubt however that Butler's bitterest opponents organized a campaign by word of mouth and by telephone on the evening of 9th January urging those opposed to his succession to notify the party Whips immediately. Butler had earned the dislike of some right-wing Conservatives for his eager championship of welfare legislation. While Minister of Education he had been responsible for the Education Act of 1944; but, in addition, he had played the major rôle after 1945 in remodelling Conservative policy and ensuring that the party accepted, both formally and in practice, the broad outlines of the Welfare State.   He was thus clearly labelled as a " left-

long-standing danger in any parliamentary system, at least in peace-time. It took a war emergency to produce the only two Prime Ministers of unquestioned greatness in this century, Winston Churchill and Lloyd George. The former certainly (and the latter quite possibly) would not otherwise have reached the highest office.

[1] The propensity of the Parliamentary Labour Party to vote on almost every issue has the effect of identifying and isolating minorities. It may also be the case that the Labour Party leadership, when it is sure of its majority, may be less likely to make concessions to the minority.

[2] 12th January, 1957.

wing " Conservative so far as domestic social policies were concerned.

But there was a more important consideration: he was suspect as an alleged " appeaser " who was believed to be reluctant to support the use of British military power to restrain the vaulting ambitions of foreign dictators who challenged British interests. He first earned this reputation in 1938 during the crisis over Chamberlain's handling of foreign affairs. When Eden resigned as Foreign Minister in February of that year, his Under-Secretary of State at the Foreign Office, the then Lord Cranborne, also quit office. And when Lord Halifax succeeded Eden, it was the comparatively youthful R. A. Butler who took Lord Cranborne's place. Now, almost 20 years later, it was the same Lord Cranborne (who had meanwhile succeeded to the title of Marquis of Salisbury) who played the leading rôle in sounding out party opinion as to whether Butler or Macmillan should succeed Eden.

It might have been assumed that this old quarrel would play no part in determining Butler's prospects in January 1957. But unfortunately for him the appeasement allegations were revived as a result of the Suez crisis in the autumn of 1956. There is no firm evidence that Butler actively opposed Eden's policy (certainly there is no proof of the allegation in the Brombergers' *Secrets of Suez*, page 159, that Butler threatened to resign unless the operation were halted). Indeed, Eden's own account of the attitude of his Cabinet towards the Suez policy would seem to preclude the possibility that Butler had opposed it in any way: " There was no friction of any kind between us. When we were in council no marked divergences were revealed. I have been a member of many Governments in times of nominal peace. I have not known one more united on an issue of the first importance. There were, of course, shades of opinion, but these did not obtrude." [1] And in the House of Commons Butler spoke for, and voted with, the Government throughout the many divisions forced by the Opposition. None the less, a considerable number of Conservative M.P.s appear to have become convinced that Butler's attitude to the Suez initiative was at best equivocal.

By contrast, Macmillan appeared in public (whatever his private doubts may have been) to support the operation whole-heartedly. And there was the further fact that Macmillan in the 1930s had been a forthright critic of the appeasement policies.[2] In domestic

[1] Eden, Sir Anthony, *Full Circle*, p. 520.

[2] Eden, it was suggested above (p. 584), became obsessed by the parallels he saw between Hitler and Nasser; Macmillan may have been tempted to accept this dubious analogy because of his own record of strong opposition to appeasement in the 1930s.

matters Macmillan had been at least as far to the " left " as Butler. Indeed in the pre-war years he had probably been more so. He had made his main reputation after 1951 as a very successful Minister of Housing and Local Government, who easily reached the target of 300,000 houses per year which had been urged in the Conservative Party by its own Conference in 1950 (see p. 197–8). He had left little mark in his subsequent brief appearances as Minister of Defence (1954–55), Foreign Secretary (April–December, 1955), and Chancellor of the Exchequer (1955–57). But, in the nightmare world in which the Conservatives found themselves after the failure of their Suez policies, Macmillan seemed a far more forthright, self-possessed and dynamic figure than R. A. Butler.

Did the Queen " choose " the new Leader of the Conservative Party in January 1957? Sir Ivor Jennings, in his *Cabinet Government* (3rd edition, p. 28) appears to conclude that she did. He states, that the " Party was prepared to follow either Mr. Butler or Mr. Macmillan and was ready to accept the Queen's choice ". But this remark surely gives a very misleading impression. The Queen's only direct consultations were, of course, with two of the most senior figures in the Party, Lord Salisbury and Sir Winston Churchill; but the former, in particular, had taken extensive " soundings " in the Party through his consultations with ministers and with the Chief Whip who, as was shown above, had an extensive knowledge of back-bench opinion. Salisbury (like Churchill) had without doubt recommended that Harold Macmillan would have the best chance of any of the leading figures in the Party of forming a strong united government. The Queen thereupon called Macmillan to the Palace as the strongest prospective Prime Minister in the majority Party; subsequently he was elected Leader of the Party. But it would seem obvious that Macmillan became Leader not because he was, in any meaningful sense of the term, " the Queen's choice ", but because he was the " Party's choice ", always allowing for the fact that the Party determines its preference by a unique method which does not involve a formal vote.

As Prime Minister and Party Leader Macmillan, up to a point, continued to demonstrate the qualities of self-assurance and purposefulness which appear to have won him the Leadership. He weathered the post-Suez storms with remarkable calm; he was quite unshaken when in May 1957 eight Conservative M.P.s resigned the Party Whip in protest when the Government " capitulated to Nasser " (by agreeing that British ships could use the Suez Canal again, even though it remained under Egyptian control). On 30th March, 1957, less than three months after he became Prime Minister, Macmillan had accepted Lord Salisbury's resignation which the

latter offered in protest against the Government's decision to release
Archbishop Makarios from exile in the Seychelles. (This incident
had the useful effect of quashing the absurd suggestion made in
some quarters that Macmillan was in some sense the creature of
Lord Salisbury, because Salisbury had played the leading rôle in
advising the Queen to call him to the office of Prime Minister.)
When, in January 1958, the Chancellor of the Exchequer and two
other Treasury ministers resigned in protest against the Government's failure to place a rigid ceiling on public expenditure,
Macmillan (who was about to leave the next day on a Commonwealth tour) dismissed the matter as " a little local difficulty ".

During his earliest period as Leader, Macmillan had one enormously important source of strength. This was the fact that the Party
had been very close to the brink of disaster and knew it. It appeared
to want above all else a Leader of utter self-assurance who could
not be deflected from his purpose by the impulsive actions of lesser
men around him. In such circumstances Macmillan was to turn
the resignations referred to above to excellent advantage; by accepting them without apparent hesitation he provided an effective
demonstration that he was master of both the Cabinet and the
Parliamentary Party.

Another of Macmillan's major assets was the loyalty of R. A.
Butler; no one since Curzon had more obvious grounds for being
disgruntled with the treatment Fortune (and his Party colleagues)
had accorded him. Butler might understandably have been tempted
to throw his weight behind one or other of the discordant elements
in the Party. But so far as all public evidence was concerned,
he gave Macmillan unquestioning support. Butler was rewarded
(without precipitate haste) when it was announced in July, 1962,
that, thereafter, he would act as Deputy Prime Minister, a title
rarely accorded in peace time. But by then it was inevitably being
asked whether Butler was not being forced to play Morrison to
Macmillan's Attlee.

During the first eighteen months of Macmillan's leadership,
by-elections and public opinion polls appeared to point to the
probability of a savage Conservative defeat at the general election
due to be held not later than 1960. But from the summer of 1958
onwards the Government's and Mr. Macmillan's personal fortunes
steadily improved. His public image of steadfast calm and his
bold pursuit of the idea of a Summit Conference appear to have
increased his stature as a national leader.[1] He was aided by a

---

[1] By 14th March, 1959, *The Economist* could write: " British politics are now
more heavily overlaid by a single personality [Mr. Macmillan] than at any
time since Sir Winston Churchill's heroic wartime days."

marked up-turn in economic affairs in 1958 and by the continued difficulties of the Labour Party arising out of its bitter dispute over defence policy. There can be no doubt, however, that under Macmillan's leadership the Conservative Party was far more adroit than its Labour opponents in adjusting its policies to the social and economic changes in Britain in the late 1950s. It was therefore a combination of both good luck and good management that enabled Macmillan to carry his party to one of its greatest victories in October 1959.[1]

For some two years thereafter Macmillan seemed as secure and ascendant in the affairs of the party as any peacetime Conservative Leader had ever been, as he enjoyed the rewards of a successful Leader who had saved his party from the ruin it thought it faced after the failure of Sir Anthony Eden's leadership. Macmillan launched a number of bold new policies of which by far the most important was his government's application, in October 1961, for full membership of the European Economic Community. This application was to fail because of the French government's virtual veto in January 1963; but in the course of the negotiations Macmillan succeeded brilliantly in winning the support of the Conservative Party in Parliament and in the country for this radical departure in policy.

Meanwhile, however, the Prime Minister had run into acute domestic difficulties which began with the renewed economic crisis of the summer of 1961. To meet the situation the Government introduced certain restrictions on consumption and, in addition, for the first time an attempt was made to introduce a " wages policy " designed to ensure that wage increases would henceforth be directly related to increases in production. In its first stages, this involved the Government in a highly unpopular attempt to maintain a " wages pause " which appeared to bear particularly harshly on certain occupations, such as the nursing profession.

The popularity of Harold Macmillan and his government slumped dramatically during the winter of 1961–62, and in the spring the party faced a disastrous series of by-elections, in which the total vote cast for the Conservatives fell not only below that of the Labour Party, but also below that of the Liberals (the latter a party which still held only seven seats in Parliament). As a direct consequence, or so it seemed, Macmillan undertook in July 1962 the most drastic re-organization of his Government ever undertaken within the life-time of a Parliament in modern times, replacing one-third of the

---

[1] For a discussion of the factors which may have contributed to the Conservative victory in the 1959 election, see Butler, D. E., and Rose, R., *The British General Election of 1959*, London, 1960, Chaps. II and IV.

Cabinet. The Gallup Poll subsequently reported that only 36 per cent. of the electorate now expressed approval of Macmillan's performance as Prime Minister, and added that support for a British Prime Minister had sunk to so low a level only once before: in 1940 during the closing days of the Chamberlain Government.[1]

By the winter of 1962–63 there were persistent reports of dissatisfaction with Macmillan's leadership in the Conservative Party in Parliament. A few Conservative M.P.s had stated more or less explicitly that they believed the Prime Minister should make way for a younger Leader and a much larger number were prepared to state privately that they held similar views.

In the gloom following the collapse of the Brussels negotiations there was a growing demand for a new Leader, particularly after the accession of Harold Wilson, twenty-two years Harold Macmillan's junior, as Leader of the Labour Party, in February 1963. It was widely reported at the time that it took the strenuous combined effort of the Chief Whip, Martin Redmayne, and the Chairman of the 1922 Committee, John Morrison, to hold the Conservative Parliamentary Party in line behind the Prime Minister.[2]

In April 1963, Macmillan attempted to quash rumours that he would soon retire by telling a private 1922 Committee luncheon (open to all Conservative back-bench M.P.s) that he fully intended to lead the Party into the next election.[3] But the Leadership issue exploded suddenly again in early June when the Secretary of State for War, John Profumo, resigned after admitting that he had lied to the House of Commons about a personal matter which, however, involved the possibility of a breach of military security. The subsequent House of Commons debate on the security aspects of the affair on June 17 ended in a division which became, in effect, a vote of confidence in the Prime Minister personally, as the Minister ultimately responsible for security matters. The Government's majority fell to 69 with 27 Conservative M.P.s who were present deliberately abstaining. It immediately became apparent that Macmillan's position was in grave jeopardy. There was little inclination on the part of his Conservative critics to demand his immediate resignation in the midst of the Profumo scandal since it was widely felt that this would blacken the Prime Minister's reputation most unfairly and might also prove permanently damaging to the Party's prospects. But it was widely assumed that in a matter of weeks or months Macmillan would have to make way for a new Leader. On June 28th, however, Mr. Macmillan repeated his

[1] *Gallup Political Index* No. 31, July 1962, p. 114.
[2] Margach, J., " The Great Gamble," *Sunday Times*, 14 April, 1963.
[3] *The Times*, 12 April, 1963.

declaration that he expected to lead the Party in the next election.[1] And in the same statement he referred to evidence he had received of the widespread popular support he continued to enjoy among Conservative Party members outside Parliament.   This remark particularly incensed some of the Prime Minister's opponents among back-bench M.P.s, who felt that he was attempting to appeal over the heads of M.P.s to their constituency militants.

Harold Macmillan was now engaged in a tremendous struggle for survival in circumstances even more difficult than Baldwin had faced at critical moments in his career. The situation provided yet another reminder that the Conservative Leader's security of tenure is not absolute; the panoply of his formal powers in no way protects him from the vicissitudes of political leadership which are the concomitant of democratic politics.

THE LABOUR PARTY SINCE 1955

Any examination of the rôle of the Leader of the Labour Party since 1955 is, first and last, a study of the career in that office of Hugh Gaitskell; he succeeded Attlee in December 1955 and seven years later, after he had survived perhaps the most tempestuous crisis in the Party's history, he died in office in January 1963.

What accounts for the troubles he and his Party endured during the period of his leadership? In some measure they are to be explained by Gaitskell's personal shortcomings as Leader.   An

[1] *The Times*, 29 June, 1963.

intensely sensitive man (in no sense the "desiccated calculating machine" Bevan once suggested), he none the less lacked the delicate political antennae which are perhaps the prerequisites of the really skilful party leader. There is considerable evidence to suggest that, as a result, he frequently found himself in difficulties through a failure to anticipate the consequences of his own initiatives as Leader. The most spectacular example was the strange "Clause Four" quarrel (discussed on pp. 607 ff. below); but there were a number of other less dramatic illustrations of difficulties which could be attributed in part at least to Gaitskell's curious insensitivity to the mood and attitude of his own followers.

But whoever had led the Labour Party during this period would almost certainly have had to face a comparable series of problems. In part these sprang from the disastrous series of electoral set-backs the Party faced during the four elections of the 1950s. If Labour had won these with working majorities it might well have been as free of serious internal conflict as, for example, the Swedish Socialists have been during almost three decades in power.[1] Whatever a party's domestic arrangements, a series of defeats are likely to breed rebellions against the leadership of the party and bitter recriminations among politicians starved of office and power. This is as true of Conservative parties, which allegedly vest all authority in their Leader, as it is of parties like Labour which claim that control of their party's affairs lies ultimately with the party's annual Conference. It is important to recall that on the last occasion when the Conservatives lost three successive elections (those of 1906 and the two elections of 1910) they repudiated the leadership of Balfour and became involved in violent quarrels over questions of policy.

Labour's difficulties during the past decade cannot be attributed solely, however, to its electoral failures. By the 1950s the party could no longer evade the "ideological" dilemma which every Social Democratic party had to face in the post-war period. In reality the issue was this (although it was rarely formulated in these terms): can a Socialist party accept, as permanent, a mixed economy (with something like the present balance of public and private ownership) and content itself with controlling and planning that economy, and with introducing further social legislation designed to increase "social justice" and "social equality"? Or must any Socialist party press on, stage by stage, until it has

[1] There are of course important differences in the constitutions of the British and Swedish socialist parties, but unquestionably when any party is in office for long periods the fact that its Leader is Prime Minister and his chief colleagues constitute the Cabinet, goes far to ensure that they are likely to remain in effective control of the party's affairs.

achieved a society " based on the common ownership of the means of production, distribution and exchange " (the declared aim of the Labour Party which had been written into its Constitution). This debate, common to Socialist parties everywhere, was bedevilled in Britain during the early 1950s by the bitter personal battle between Aneurin Bevan and Hugh Gaitskell for the succession to Clement Attlee. This quarrel reached such a pitch that for a time it became almost impossible for the rivals and their supporters to discuss any issue on its own merits. In addition, the argument over domestic policy also became entangled with a parallel dispute over foreign affairs and defence. Could a party of the Left advocate full member- ship of collective defence pacts which—in the case of NATO, for example—were bound to be based on the ultimate threat of the use of nuclear weapons and which involved both the rearmament of Western Germany and the presence of American bases in Britain?

A further factor in Labour's difficulties was the breakdown of the system of decision-making on policy questions which had been evolved over the first half-century of the party's existence. In the preceding analysis (in Part II) it was shown that Labour's Parlia- mentary Leadership was largely successful in escaping from the principle of rigid extra-Parliamentary control which was implicit in the party's formal constitutional arrangements. These arrange- ments were in fact based on a theory of " inner-party democracy " which, if applied literally, would have made it impossible for the PLP to accept the conventions of Cabinet and Parliamentary Government. This problem arose partly from the fact that most of the founders of the Labour Party assumed, understandably enough, that political parties were (or at least ought to be) similar forms of organization to trade unions or co-operative societies. In such organizations it is considered to be obviously desirable that the " leaders " should hold themselves ultimately responsible to their " followers ", that is to the mass membership of the organization. In most trade unions and co-operative societies the representatives of the mass membership, meeting in annual conference, are therefore recognized as the ultimate governing body of the association. This same principle was incorporated into the constitution of the Labour Party, and its Annual Conference was therefore entitled, in theory, to issue binding instructions to the Parliamentary Labour Party (Chapters I and VIII above).

By a variety of devices which have been analysed in Part II the Parliamentary leadership managed, in practice, to acquire sufficient initiative in policy-making, and immunity from external " direction " by the Party Conference, to enable the Parliamentary Party to act as a reasonably coherent and responsible Opposition; in addition they were able to form two Governments (in 1945 and 1950) which were as effectively in control of the affairs of the nation as were previous Conservative and Liberal Governments. But it should be emphasized that this was accomplished without any formal attempt either to amend the Party constitution to bring it in line with the Party's practice, or to modify Party rhetoric which continued to insist on the uniquely " democratic " nature of Labour's internal structure. It should also be noted that the success of the informal arrangements which secured the authority of the Parliamentary leadership depended on the subtle understanding between the chief parliamentarians and a few leading trade unionists who were prepared to act, in effect, as a kind of " Praetorian guard ", protecting the Parliamentary Party from overt attempts by the " activist " element among the unions and the constituency parties to drive the PLP in directions in which it did not wish to go. (Martin Harrison in his valuable study *Trade Unions and the Labour Party since 1945* [1] has demonstrated that the trade unions have not acted in the Party Conference as a homogeneous political group arrayed against a uniform block of constituency delegates. This analysis corresponds closely to the argument advanced in this book [see p. 502 above] to the effect that on most important occasions in the modern history of the party there has been a " concurrent majority " behind Conference decisions, with a preponderant group of *both* trade unions *and* constituency parties voting on one side, and a minority of each element—usually on the Left—voting on the other.)

Even in the early 1950s, this arrangement had begun to run into sporadic difficulties. After the resignation in 1951 of Aneurin Bevan, Harold Wilson and John Freeman from the second Attlee Government, a struggle began to determine who should succeed Clement Attlee as Leader of the Party, as it became increasingly likely that he would soon retire. It became evident that the main protagonists were Hugh Gaitskell, Chancellor of the Exchequer in the second Attlee Government, and the rebel leader, Aneurin Bevan, who had resigned in 1951 giving as his immediate reason the decision by Gaitskell and the Cabinet to impose certain new charges on the users of the National Health Service.[2] The two main rivals

---

[1] *Trade Unions and the Labour Party since 1945*, London, 1960, *passim*.

[2] It is difficult not to conclude that the real reason for Bevan's resignation in 1951 was that he had been passed over by Attlee when the offices of Chancellor of the Exchequer and Foreign Secretary in turn fell vacant. (Cripps resigned in 1950 and was succeeded by Gaitskell; in the following year Bevin was replaced by Morrison. The two who were thus promoted were Bevan's only possible rivals for the Leadership.) For the views of Hugh Dalton on the consequences of this development see his *High Tide and After*, pp. 358 ff. For an economist's comment, see Mitchell, J., *Crisis in Britain, 1951*, London, 1963, Chapter VI.

also became, in effect, the spokesmen for the conflicting views within the party both on the nature of Socialism and on the defence and foreign policies which the Labour Party should adopt.

In the years that followed, the struggle was fought out within each section of the Labour Party, in the Parliamentary Committee, in the Parliamentary Party itself, in the National Executive and in the Annual Conference. Throughout this period, the centre and right-wing elements, led first by Attlee and then by Gaitskell, always had on their side a majority of the Parliamentary Party; they consistently defeated the Bevanite faction, which in the Parliamentary Party usually numbered 50 to 60 M.P.s (or about one-fifth of the total).

The Parliamentary leadership came closest to defeat on the issue of the rearmament of Germany at the 1954 Party Conference, when the Left managed to rally more support than it had on any comparable issue for a generation. In the course of the conference debate, the then Parliamentary Leaders (Attlee and the Deputy Leader, Morrison, who were both soon to retire) gave an extraordinary hostage to fortune; in appealing to the Conference to reject a resolution opposing German rearmament, they re-affirmed, by implication, the hoary doctrine that the Conference had the right to issue instructions both to the Parliamentary Party and to a *future* Labour Government. Attlee warned that if the resolution were passed it would leave a future Labour Foreign Secretary "tied and bound".[1] It was known that the vote would be close (the resolution was actually defeated by 3,270,000 to 3,022,000) and it may be that the leaders resorted in desperation to this dangerous argument. But in practice no one had been clearer than Attlee himself (for example in his exchanges with Churchill during the 1945 election; see pp. 330–1 above) that a Labour Government would not, and could not, be subject to external direction. None the less the incident was vivid proof of the extraordinary muddle-headedness of Labour leaders on the issue of inner-party democracy. It suggests that even the most experienced of the Labour parliamentarians had given very little thought to the process by which they had escaped from the traps provided by their own party constitution.

Labour's difficulties in the 1950s were further complicated by the almost simultaneous death, or retirement from office, of most of those who had learned by experience (even if they had never tried to regularize their methods) how to reconcile Labour's complicated internal machinery to the requirements of Parliamentary Government. Because of Labour's rapid growth in the 1920s the

[1] *Labour Annual Conference Report, 1954*, p. 94.

Party had acquired and trained a group of parliamentarians, most of whom belonged roughly to the same age group. In the early 1950s almost all of them either died (Cripps, Bevin) or, for age or other reasons, left the Party's Front Bench in Parliament (Attlee, Morrison, Dalton, Shinwell, Arthur Greenwood, Chuter Ede, Tom Williams).

During roughly the same period a number of leading trade unionists left office, of whom Arthur Deakin,[1] Bevin's successor as head of the Transport and General Workers' Union, was by far the most important, since he understood better than anyone else the importance of the " Praetorian guard " function which certain of the major union leaders must fulfil if Labour was to play its Parliamentary rôle with any hope of success. These trade unionists were succeeded, for the most part, by men who were either inexperienced in the working of Labour's machinery at the highest level, or who were largely antipathetic to the seemingly endless political squabbles which marked these years. In particular, Deakin's own successor, who might have been prepared to carry on his work within the Labour Party, also died in 1955 following a very brief term of office. And a new head of the Transport Workers emerged in 1956 in the person of Frank Cousins, who stood well to the left both of his own predecessors and of the Parliamentary leaders on most issues in domestic and foreign affairs. (There is not the slightest reason to believe that the sudden and unexpected accession of a militant left-winger to the leadership of Britain's largest union represented a " lurch to the left " within the membership of that union. Yet the huge weight of the union within the Party organization gradually swung against the Parliamentary leaders on a number of major issues in the years after Cousins took office. This was primarily because the internal power structure of the union makes it possible for a strong-willed General Secretary—whether Deakin or Bevin on the right or Cousins on the left—to exert enormous influence on union decisions.)

One other development played havoc with the balance of forces within the Party structure. For the first time in the history of the Party almost all of the seven " constituency " places on the NEC (most of which had been held for many years by M.P.s who were in broad agreement with Attlee and the other Parliamentary

[1] Deakin died in May, 1955. For a discussion of the rôle of Deakin as trade union leader, see Allen, V. L., *Trade Union Leadership* (Based on a Study of Arthur Deakin), London, 1957. Chapter 8 analyses Deakin's political attitudes and his condemnation of what he called " the antics of disruptionists within the Labour Movement ", a phrase he used to describe the Bevanite minority within the Party.

leaders) were captured by " rebel " M.P.s who supported Aneurin Bevan, both in his bid for the leadership and in his campaign to swing Party policies to the Left. This helps to account for the fact that during the struggles of the 1950s the presence of a majority of M.P.s on the NEC no longer in itself operated as a factor tending to ensure that the NEC's views conformed to those of the Parliamentary leaders, as it certainly had done during the period 1937–51 (see pp. 516 ff. above).

Since these changes had occurred almost simultaneously within the unions, the Parliamentary Party, and the National Executive, each in turn became an open battleground for the personal and ideological clash between the forces grouped around Gaitskell and Bevan. During this period the leaders of the PLP had to fight a more sustained and open battle to retain their control of Party policy than ever before in the modern history of the Party. Not that their control was ever effectively broken throughout the 1950s; Party policy remained moderate and reformist in domestic affairs (the Parliamentary leaders were prepared to agree, perhaps against their better judgment, to a pledge to renationalize the Steel industry, but they made no other major concessions on the issue of public ownership); and in foreign affairs Labour remained throughout the 1950s firmly committed to collective security and to the British retention of nuclear weapons until general disarmament was achieved. But the policies advocated by the Parliamentary leaders were continually in dispute in one organ or another of the Party organization. The public spectacle of bitter internecine conflict unquestionably damaged Labour's standing with the electorate, and contributed to the defeats of 1955 and 1959.[1]

The Gaitskell-Bevan clash was first formally fought out, strangely enough, in contests between them for the Party Treasurership. This is a post which, in itself, carries little real power or influence within the Party, but its importance lay in the fact that it is voted upon by all sections of the mass organization (trade unions, constituency parties and the other elements represented at the Conference). Aneurin Bevan had for several years headed the poll in the elections for the constituency section of the National Executive; but he apparently felt that he must prove himself acceptable to a wider spectrum of Party opinion. Thus, when Gaitskell was nominated for the Treasurership in 1954, Bevan withdrew from the constituency section and stood against him. He was

---

[1] With respect to the 1959 election, see Abrams, M. and Rose, R., *Must Labour Lose?*, Chaps. I, IV and V. On the basis of a survey of voter opinion one of the authors concludes that a major factor counting against Labour was " the impression of weak, divided leadership " (p. 100).

defeated then and again in the following year when he stood against Gaitskell a second time.[1]

After the Party was defeated in May 1955, Attlee carried on as Leader, apparently with some reluctance, until on 7th December he resigned abruptly and went to the Lords. Three candidates for the Leadership entered the field:[2] Gaitskell, who clearly had the support of most of the leading parliamentarians, and a number of powerful trade union leaders; Herbert Morrison, the Party's Deputy Leader, who appeared not to realize that Gaitskell had pre-empted his own natural constituency within the Party; and Aneurin Bevan, who could be presumed to have the assured backing of no more than his usual 60-odd supporters. In the event Gaitskell won a clear victory on the first ballot, with 157 votes to Bevan's 70 and Morrison's 40. In this contest Gaitskell clearly had had little to fear from Morrison. He was 19 years younger than Morrison who, at 68, was widely considered too old for the post. In addition Morrison's star had been in the descendant; he had been a failure as Foreign Secretary in 1951; he had been defeated for the NEC in 1952 after serving on that body for over twenty years; and his rather uninspired attitude to the future of Labour policy and the need for " consolidation " had also proved a liability. Bevan did rather better in the contest than had been predicted although his total vote was not much higher than the usual figure of support for Left causes within the PLP. Clearly, however, he had jeopardized his own prospects by resigning from the Shadow Cabinet in early 1955 and by quarrelling publicly with Attlee at that time. His turbulent record over a quarter of a century in the PLP was no doubt considered by most of his colleagues to disqualify him as

[1] The figures in the 1954 contest were: Gaitskell 4,338,000, and Bevan 2,032,000. Harrison estimates that Bevan got just over one-fifth of the union votes and approximately two-thirds of the constituency votes. In 1955, after Bevan's near expulsion from the Party in the spring, the figures were: Gaitskell 5,475,000, and Bevan 1,225,000, with Bevan's share of the union's votes falling to one-tenth and of those of constituency parties to one-half. Harrison, M., *Trade Unions and the Labour Party*, p. 316. In the following year *after* Gaitskell had been elected Leader, Bevan was elected Treasurer in the hope, it would seem, that this would contribute to party unity.

[2] For accounts of the events leading up to the ballot on 14th December, 1955, see Morrison, Lord, *An Autobiography*, pp. 292 ff; Dalton, H., *High Tide and After*, pp. 429 ff; Krug, M., *Aneurin Bevan*, pp. 231 ff. The most striking incident in the period immediately before the balloting was Bevan's unsuccessful public appeal to Gaitskell urging that they both should stand down in favour of Morrison; Bevan clearly realized that he would have a better chance of preventing Gaitskell from obtaining the leadership if their own contest were postponed during a presumably brief Morrisonian *interregnum*. Bevan's proposal recalled the action of Austen Chamberlain and Walter Long in 1911 when they jointly agreed to make way for Bonar Law. (See p. 30 above.)

Leader of the Party, despite his unquestioned superiority over Gaitskell as an orator and parliamentarian.

Gaitskell's election, the fourth contest for the leadership in the Party's history (the others were in 1906, 1922 and 1935), had given him the clearest margin of victory any Leader had ever secured. But this fact in itself could have proved misleading. The wholesale exodus from the Party's Front Bench by its elder statesmen was for some time to leave Gaitskell almost completely bereft of reliable supporters of outstanding parliamentary skill. Numbers, in terms of votes within the PLP, were on the side of Gaitskell, but many of the most adroit and skilful parliamentarians had been supporters of Bevan. Outside Parliament, within the mass organization of the Party, Gaitskell had no one even remotely resembling Ernest Bevin or Arthur Deakin (who had died six months before Gaitskell became Leader) to rally the steady support of a majority of the trade union block votes at the Annual Conference. And Gaitskell could hardly expect the assured support of the Constituency Party section of the organization which had so steadily elected " Bevanites " to the National Executive in the early 1950s.

Against this background Gaitskell's accomplishments over the next four years until the election of 1959 were striking indeed. In matters of policy, as has already been suggested, the parliamentary leadership made no really major concessions to the militant Left within the Party; the Party programme on which the election of 1959 was fought reflected in almost all major respects the views of Gaitskell and his supporters with respect both to domestic and foreign policy. (Indeed, immediately after the election, Bevan was to remark that " Socialism " had not been defeated because Labour had not stood on a Socialist programme during the campaign; it was, he said, a programme of " pre-war Liberalism brought up to date ".) But what was even more striking, all of the leading rebels within the Party, who had fought bitterly against Gaitskell's accession to the Leadership, made their peace with him and campaigned loyally by his side in the 1959 election. The most remarkable of all the " converts " was Aneurin Bevan himself.[1] To the consternation of some of those who had fought with him during the years in the wilderness in the early 1950s, he came fully to terms with Hugh Gaitskell; for the time being at least,[2] he dropped

---

[1] For a gossip-ridden but interesting discussion of how and why Bevan came to terms with Gaitskell, see Hunter, L., *The Road to Brighton Pier*, London, 1959, Chap. XXIII.

[2] Some of Bevan's loyal supporters during this period argued that, in the nature of things, the struggle against Gaitskellism would continue " now hidden, now revealed ". At the moment it was presumably hidden.

his campaign to destroy his former rival and even played a leading part (at the Labour Party Conference at Brighton in 1957) in defeating the first great effort to win the Party round to a policy of unilateral nuclear disarmament.

These events, taken together, throw additional light on the analysis (in Chapter VI) of the powers of the Labour Party Leader. Once Gaitskell had been chosen as Leader in 1955, two considerations appear to have occurred to his former rivals: the first was that, if they were to persist in their efforts to overthrow the Party's chosen Leader, this would almost certainly destroy the possibility that Labour might win the next election. Even the most ideologically preoccupied members of the Parliamentary Labour Party could hardly ignore the evidence which suggests that in a British general election the voters are primarily concerned, not so much with the choice of a particular individual to represent their constituency, but rather with deciding which of two rival teams should form a Government. If by persistent internecine conflict the Labour Party were to succeed in destroying its " team image ", then its prospects of victory would disappear almost completely.

The second consideration which almost certainly served to win the rebels of yesterday round to support for Gaitskell was this: he was clearly not only Leader of the Labour Party, he was also the " Shadow Prime Minister "; and if Labour did manage to win, then there was not the slightest doubt that he would become Prime Minister and have within his gift the 80-odd offices which taken together constitute a Ministry. These factors unquestionably account for Gaitskell's striking success during the years 1955–59 in holding the Labour Party to a line of policy in both home and foreign affairs which reflected in almost every respect the view of the majority of the PLP who had elected him. And it can be confidently added that, had Gaitskell won the election of October 1959, he would have formed a Government which would have ruled the country in the succeeding years with at least as great authority as the Attlee Governments demonstrated in the period 1945–51. It would again have become as clear to the active supporters of the Labour Party, as it has been almost continuously to the Conservative Party members while their leaders are in office, that in practice the Parliamentary system makes it inevitable that authority should be concentrated in the hands of the group who lead the Parliamentary Party.

Gaitskell's achievement during his first four years as Leader is all the more impressive because he was far more isolated than Attlee, for example, had been during his most successful period as Leader. Those who at that time most strongly shared Gaitskell's personal views on home and foreign affairs tended either to be "intellectuals-in-politics", who carried comparatively little weight in the Parliamentary Labour Party, or, if they were men of some political substance (such as Alfred Robens, M.P., now Lord Robens) they simply proved unequal to the tasks of covering off the principal "Shadow Ministries" on Gaitskell's Front Bench. Gaitskell therefore found it increasingly necessary to rely on his former rivals and political enemies, such as Bevan and Harold Wilson (who became respectively his Shadow Foreign Minister and Shadow Chancellor), primarily because they were vastly abler as parliamentarians than were the more moderate or right-wing figures in the Party. (In addition, of course, Gaitskell no doubt wished to ensure that his Front Bench team represented a reasonable spectrum of opinion in the Parliamentary Party, a wise objective for any parliamentary leader provided that the extremists of the Left or Right are prepared loyally to defend the collective decisions of the parliamentary leadership, as Bevan and Wilson were at this time)[1]. There was no evidence during this period that Gaitskell was in any sense the "prisoner" of his leading left-wing colleagues; indeed, to the public gaze it seemed almost precisely the other way round, especially after Bevan had broken with many of his former rebel colleagues and stood with Gaitskell as a firm opponent of unilateral nuclear disarmament.

It must be noted, however, that conditions within the trade unions, which had so seriously deteriorated from the point of view of Labour's parliamentary leaders since the days of Ernest Bevin and Arthur Deakin, helped to tarnish the public image of Hugh Gaitskell as a prospective Prime Minister on the eve of the election of 1959. In May of that year, the Annual Conference of the General and Municipal Workers Union, which hitherto had almost invari-

---

[1] R. H. S. Crossman has persuasively argued that the Labour Party would be well advised to drop the system of electing to the Parliamentary Committee when in opposition, and instead conform more closely to the Conservative practice of allowing the Leader to choose a Shadow Cabinet in much the same way as he is permitted to choose a Cabinet when the party is in power. The present system of election to the Parliamentary Committee (see p. 412 ff.) ensures, in effect, that the majority of the PLP can determine the composition of the entire Parliamentary Committee, and in periods of acute conflict within the Party, the Left minority in the PLP is likely to be seriously under-represented or not represented at all. If, on the other hand, the Leader were allowed a free hand in selecting his entire Shadow Cabinet, he would almost certainly try to ensure that it fairly reflected the balance of opinion within the PLP. It should be noted however (see p. 413 n. 3) that since 1955 the Labour Leader has named certain additional shadow ministers, who in effect supplement the work of the Parliamentary Committee. This modification in the practice of the Party has undoubtedly strengthened the authority of the Leader.

ably adopted a moderate and orthodox line on both domestic and foreign affairs, suddenly and unexpectedly voted in favour of unilateral nuclear disarmament.[1] (According to Martin Harrison's account this had happened because a number of delegates were absent from the Conference Hall, " either sunning themselves, drinking tea, or on their way home ".)[2] For the next eleven weeks, until a special conference of the General and Municipal Workers Union could be recalled to reverse this decision (which they did by 194 votes to 139), it looked to many as if the current defence policy statement [3] supported by Gaitskell might be defeated, especially since Frank Cousins, who personally supported unilateral nuclear disarmament, was taking a prominent part in the campaign to get the official statement either basically modified or rejected.

There was in fact no real likelihood that the official policy would have been overthrown in favour of unilateral nuclear disarmament, had the Party's regular Conference been held in the autumn (it was in fact postponed because of the general election). But day by day the newspapers dramatized the conflict as a personal contest between Hugh Gaitskell (then Labour's prospective Prime Minister) and Frank Cousins and the unilateralist forces. Thus, with the old processes of policy decision within the Party so obviously in disarray, Labour presented to the electorate the spectacle of a Party badly split on a major question of national importance, whose Leader was struggling desperately to assert his authority against certain " rebel barons " of the trade union movement. To an extent that was underestimated in the first edition of this book, Labour's policy-making procedures, especially after long periods in opposition (and by the early 1960s Labour had set a modern record in this regard), can prove fatally damaging to its electoral prospects. Even though the parliamentary leadership has remained in effective control, the *public* struggle to retain that control has sometimes given the impression that the Party was about to lapse into anarchy.

The two years after Labour's electoral defeat in October 1959 were, in some respects, the strangest period in the entire history of the Party. After its third successive rebuff by the electorate, Labour might have been expected to have taken to heart some of the lessons the Conservatives learned after 1945 from their one great

[1] The resolution was passed by 150 votes to 126, with 75 abstentions.
[2] *Trade Unions and the Labour Party since 1945*, p. 51.
[3] It had been drawn up jointly by the NEC, the PLP and the TUC General Council.

defeat in modern times. Then, it will be recalled, the Conservatives set up a Party commission (under Sir David Maxwell Fyfe, now Lord Kilmuir) to re-examine the party organization from top to bottom; under R. A. Butler, various party committees redrafted party policies to bring them into line with the changing social conditions of post-war Britain; and the party machinery at Central Office was drastically reorganized by Lord Woolton as Chairman of the Party Organization.

Labour's only remotely comparable action in the 1950s had been taken after the election defeat of 1955 when the NEC set up what came to be known as " the Wilson Committee ". It was given terms of reference much more narrowly drawn than those governing the work of the Maxwell Fyfe Committee. (It was instructed by the Executive " to enquire into all aspects of party organization which directly affect the efficiency of our electoral machinery at National, Regional, Constituency, and Ward [or Village] level ".) The Maxwell Fyfe Committee, on the other hand, had been invited to examine, in addition to electoral machinery, the question of party finance, the constitution of the National Union and its relationship to the party in Parliament. The Wilson Committee declared, after its survey was completed, that it was " deeply shocked at the state of Party organization in many parts of the country . . . compared with our opponents [they added] we are still at the penny-farthing stage in a jet-propelled era, and our machine, at that, is rusty and deteriorating with age ". Various proposals were made by the Committee, mainly with a view to improving electoral machinery.[1] But no attempt was made, since it would have been outside the terms of reference of the Committee, to re-examine the Party's constitutional structure which had always been ill-adjusted to the Party's parliamentary rôle and which, in the changing circumstances of the 1950s, had been working less well than ever before. The Party did produce during the decade a fairly continuous stream of policy documents; but taken together, they certainly did not represent as drastic a re-examination of the Party's aims and basic objectives as the Conservatives had undertaken after 1945. And the headquarters of the Labour Party at Transport House were never subject to anything remotely resembling the overhaul of the Conservative Central Office undertaken by Lord Woolton.

It seemed obvious, after the defeat of October 1959, that Labour

---

[1] See *Interim Report of the Sub-committee on Party Organization*, London, 1955, and an article by the present writer entitled " The Wilson Report and the Future of the Labour Organization ", *Political Studies*, Vol. 4, No. 1, February, 1956, pp. 93–7.

must now at last address itself to these tasks. At the very least Labour might have been expected to appoint a Party commission, with terms of reference similar to those of the Maxwell Fyfe Committee, to undertake a complete and thorough overhaul of the Party constitution.[1] But instead the Leader of the Party, Hugh Gaitskell, personally undertook one of the most maladroit operations in the modern history of party politics. At the postponed Party Conference (held in abbreviated form on 28th and 29th November, 1959, at Blackpool), acting, as it appeared, largely on his own, he launched a full-scale attack on the single clause in the Party Constitution (Clause Four) which pledged the Party to work for the establishment of a society based on " the common ownership of the means of production, distribution, and exchange . . . " During the succeeding months a bitter and sterile debate ensued and ultimately dissolved into a second and even more fateful quarrel over the issue of unilateral nuclear disarmament.

It is wholly understandable that Gaitskell should have attempted to demonstrate to the British electorate the fact that the Labour Party no longer intended to bring the whole economy into public ownership. He claimed with considerable justification [2] at the Conference in November 1959 that confusion on this point (exploited naturally enough by the Conservatives) had been a serious electoral liability for Labour. One way of meeting this problem, therefore, was either to remove from the Constitution or to rewrite the archaic Clause Four. A public debate on this issue followed by a victory for the " revisionists " would no doubt have helped to convince the electorate that Labour accepted a mixed economy. But what is extraordinarily difficult to understand is why Gaitskell undertook the operation in the way he did.

Under existing Party rules it was necessary to have some sort of Conference before the end of 1959, to take the place of the annual gathering which would have been held, had it not been for the election, in late September. It was apparently decided by the NEC to hold as brief a conference as possible and, further, to use it as an occasion largely for " blowing off steam ". For this reason there were no Executive resolutions presented to the Conference and for some curious reason it was also decided that each of the principal executive spokesmen should speak solely for himself, rather than

---

[1] This proposal was urged on the Party from several quarters. See the Fabian pamphlet *Whither* of November 1959, and an article by the present writer in *The Observer*, 25th October, 1959.

[2] See for example the findings of a survey of voter opinion, in Abrams, M., and Rose, R., *Must Labour Lose?*, Chap. II.

for any collective or agreed NEC policy. (Thus Gaitskell began his remarks by saying, " This afternoon I speak for myself alone." And Aneurin Bevan, who had just been elected Deputy Leader, following the retirement of James Griffiths, said, in winding up the election post-mortem, " I am talking for myself.") But it was not merely that Gaitskell was "speaking for himself "; he does not appear to have taken the precaution of ensuring that the leading members of the NEC and the Deputy Leader would *publicly* support his campaign with respect to Clause Four. The opening speech by that year's Party Chairman, Mrs. Barbara Castle, M.P. (a long-standing left-wing rebel and associate of Aneurin Bevan) and the closing Conference speech by Bevan himself were in the great tradition of passionate socialist rhetoric. Both addresses revolved round the theme that large-scale common ownership (very much of the sort envisaged in Clause Four) should remain the centrepiece of Labour's political programme. Indeed both speakers went out of their way to pour scorn on any suggestion that wholesale public ownership was either outmoded, irrelevant, or a political liability.

Thus Gaitskell's speech, which opened the formal debate on " the lessons of the election ", was, in effect, sandwiched between the speeches of Mrs. Castle and Aneurin Bevan. Gaitskell began with a tough-minded review of the social and economic changes of recent years which had militated against Labour's electoral success. But the nub of his speech was his warning that " nationalization was a vote-loser " because of " the confusion in the public mind about our future policy ".[1] Gaitskell acknowledged that it might still be necessary to extend the public sector of the economy, but he insisted that " public ownership is not itself the ultimate objective; it is only a means of achieving the objective ".

> " [Since] our goal is not one hundred per cent. State ownership . . . we should clear our minds on these fundamental issues and then try to express in the most simple and comprehensive fashion what we stand for in the world today. The only official document which embodies such an attempt is the Party Constitution, written over 40 years ago. It seems to me that this needs to be brought up to date. For instance, can we really be satisfied with a statement of fundamentals which makes no mention at all of colonial freedom, race relations, disarmament, full employment or planning? The only specific reference to our objectives at home is the well-known phrase:

> To secure for the workers by hand or by brain the full fruits of their industry and the most equitable distribution thereof that may be possible, upon the basis of the common ownership of the means of production, distribution and exchange. . . . "

[1] *1959 Labour Annual Conference Report*, p. 110.

The Conference listened in silence as Gaitskell continued, but there were cries of dissent toward the end of the following passage:

> " Standing as it does on its own, this [clause] cannot possibly be regarded as adequate. It lays us open to continual misrepresentation. ... It implies that the only precise object we have is nationalization, whereas in fact we have many other Socialist objectives. It implies that we propose to nationalize everything, but do we? Everything? —the whole of light industry, the whole of agriculture, all the shops —every little pub and garage? Of course not. We have long ago come to accept, we know very well, for the foreseeable future, at least in some form, a mixed economy; in which case if this is our view— as I believe it to be of 90 per cent. of the Labour Party—had we better not say so instead of going out of our way to court misrepresentation?"

In the debate that followed Gaitskell was bitterly attacked by many left-wing speakers, including among others, Frank Cousins of the Transport and General Workers Union, who said:

> " I was a bit disturbed by Hugh's reference that ... there may be need to revise the Constitution. ... It seemed a bit peculiar that there had been no consultation with the NEC. I think I am a fairly powerful man in my own organization, but if I were going to give a public airing to a change in the constitution of my union I should wait until I had talked to the Executive before doing it . . . if, as I gather, Rule Four is likely to be revised to make a different reference to our attitude towards public ownership, I would suggest, with the greatest respect to our Leader, that no way (*sic*) . . . is going to change that one."

Within hours of the end of the Conference Aneurin Bevan had stated publicly that he was not in favour of getting rid of " the ultimate objective " pledging the party to bring the means of production, distribution and exchange into common ownership. (For curious reasons [1] his statement did not become widely known and some observers, in the course of the Clause Four argument, were to remark on Gaitskell's " bad luck " in not having Bevan —who was soon to become fatally ill—at his side.)

Before he made the Blackpool speech Gaitskell had in fact shown the text to Bevan, who apparently did not indicate his disagree-

---

[1] This remark was made in an interview which appeared on BBC Television News (29th November, 1959) and which was one of Bevan's last public appearances. It had been filmed earlier in the day and was broadcast while Gaitskell, Bevan and other delegates were *en route* back to London. On investigating this issue the present writer has been told by a leading left-wing colleague of Bevan's (who travelled with him back to London from Blackpool) that Bevan said of Gaitskell's attack on Clause Four Socialism: " He's our prisoner now."

ment with the passage concerning Clause Four nor did he demur in any way about the contents of the speech. This probably misled Gaitskell into assuming that Bevan would publicly support his efforts. But it is difficult to see why he did not ensure that he had *specific* assurances of such support from Bevan (as Deputy Leader) and from other leading members of the party, in view of the fact that he was about to ask the party to re-examine the only specific objective to which it was pledged in its constitution. No theory of party leadership expounded either in this book or, so far as one is aware, in any other serious study of democratic political parties, would suggest that such an operation, conducted in this way, would be likely to succeed. And in fact it failed almost completely. After months of acrimonious quarrelling, the National Executive on 16th March, 1960, " reaffirmed " the Party's present objectives (including Clause Four) and then proceeded to propose an "amplification and clarification " of them along the lines that Gaitskell had suggested in his speech at the Party Conference at Blackpool. The relevant passage of these expanded aims dealing with public ownership stated that the Labour Party

> " is convinced that [its] social and economic objectives can be achieved only through an expansion of common ownership substantial enough to give the community power over the commanding heights of the economy. . . . Recognizing that both public and private enterprise have a place in the economy it believes that further extension of common ownership should be decided from time to time in the light of these objectives and according to circumstances, with due regard for the workers and consumers concerned." [1]

This statement might have been counted a modest victory for Gaitskell, had it been formally adopted to replace Clause Four, since it would have been the first acknowledgment in the Party Constitution that the Labour Party recognized that private enterprise, in some form at least, has an enduring place in the economy. But after this NEC decision in March, the battle continued for several months during which it seemed increasingly likely that these new proposals might be rejected at the forthcoming Party Conference. In a final humiliating defeat for Gaitskell the NEC decided on 13th July 1960 " not to proceed with any amendment or addition to Clause Four of the Constitution ", although the Executive added " that the statement which it adopted on 16th March is a valuable expression of the aims of the Labour Party in the second half of the twentieth century and commends it to the Conference accordingly ".

[1] Cited in *1960 Labour Annual Conference Report*, p. 13.

Shortly before this rebuff for Gaitskell the attacks on his leadership reached a new pitch of virulence. Frank Cousins declared at the Scottish conference of his union (which had unanimously reasserted its belief in Clause Four) that in his opinion Gaitskell was mistaken in his philosophies and his beliefs were not " socialist ".[1] And the executive council of " Victory for Socialism ", a left-wing organization headed by Sidney Silverman, M.P., had called upon Gaitskell to resign. In response to this challenge, the NEC had passed a unanimous vote of confidence in Gaitskell and the Parliamentary Committee laid a motion before the PLP on 30th May, 1960, expressing " full confidence in the Leader of the party " and condemning " in the strongest possible terms all personal attacks in whatever form and from whatever quarter ". During the debate on this motion, Sydney Silverman himself was the only speaker who called for Gaitskell's resignation and the motion was carried by 179 to 7 with perhaps 12 to 18 deliberate abstentions (according to the varying press estimates)[2]. Hopelessly though he had botched his Clause Four campaign it was clear that Gaitskell's position as Leader was not at stake.

The whole sorry business of Clause Four was drawn to a conclusion at the 1960 Party Conference on the day after the tempestuous debate on nuclear disarmament (discussed below). Despite the opposition of Frank Cousins and the Transport and General Workers Union the Conference approved the declaration as " a valuable expression of the aims of the Labour Party ". In his speech for the Executive at the end of the debate, Gaitskell claimed that his speech to the previous year's Blackpool Conference had been misrepresented in that some of his critics within the Party had claimed that he was opposed to public ownership. He reminded the Conference that he had said " we have no intention of abandoning public ownership and accepting for all time the present frontiers of the public sector ". He went on to claim (and a re-reading of his speech bears this out) that he had not at Blackpool specifically called for the deletion of Clause Four from the Party Constitution. He now insisted that his " original proposal " was that " we should leave Clause Four but add the new statement of aims in the Constitution ". However, no one listening to his speech at Blackpool could have helped but conclude that his essential purpose was to wean the Party away from its commitment to work for a society based on the common ownership of all the major economic processes. And it is almost impossible to see how this could have been accomplished without deleting the old wording of Clause Four.

[1] *The Times*, 30th May, 1960.
[2] *The Times* and the *Manchester Guardian*, 30th May, 1960.

In his 1960 Conference speech, Gaitskell gave the following account of the Party's reaction to his Blackpool suggestion:

> " ... it became obvious that there was throughout the Party and the Movement very strong feelings about this 1918 Constitution. It might be misleading to call them sentimental, and if I used a term of that kind it would not be in any derogatory sense; but there was an attachment to that Constitution, and we in the National Executive felt bound to take note of the obvious feelings that existed."

He even went so far as to claim that " ... It was never an issue of principle; it was an issue of presentation. ... " Since the matter was therefore of such modest importance " and in view of the reaction, not only ... of people who would ordinarily be regarded as left-wing ... but of many other people in the Movement who ... would probably describe themselves as right-wing, we decided to drop the idea." But then with considerable frankness Mr. Gaitskell added the further explanation: " It was quite clear that we were going to have a major division over defence, and we did not wish to add to the divisions in the Party unnecessarily." [1]

In other words Gaitskell had dropped his efforts to alter the Party Constitution when it became clear that Clause Four in its original form was going to be defended not merely by the minority (which he estimated at Blackpool to be perhaps 10 per cent. of the Party) who, in effect, accept an essentially Marxist definition of the goals of Socialism, but also by a great many party stalwarts who were outraged by the suggestion they should re-examine what they considered to be the most essential single tenet of their Socialist faith.[2]   And there were many of these stalwarts whom Gaitskell could hope to (and indeed had to) carry with him if he were to have any prospect of winning his fight against unilateralism at the 1960 Conference.

This shadowy compromise over Clause Four took place the day after the Party Conference decided (against the combined advice of the Leader of the Party, the NEC, the PLP, and the General Council of the TUC) to adopt, in effect, a policy of unilateral nuclear disarmament, a policy which carried with it the fairly clear implication that Britain should take no part in any alliance based on the possible use of nuclear weapons.   The history (and the nuances) of this argument over defence cannot be re-examined

---

[1] *1960 Labour Annual Conference Report*, pp. 218–19.

[2] Others on the " intellectual Left " found new beauty in the venerable phrases written so long ago: " The more I study this formula (Clause Four) ", wrote R. H. S. Crossman, " the more admiration I feel for Sidney Webb and Arthur Henderson who drafted it in 1918." From " The Spectre of Revisionism ", *Encounter*, Vol. XIV, No. 4, April, 1960, p. 25.

here, although the events which led up to the decision taken at Scarborough must be sketched in broad outline. In March 1960, the Conservative Government announced that it would not proceed with its attempt to develop the Blue Streak rocket as a means of delivering Britain's own nuclear weapons, although it would continue to make " an independent contribution " to the nuclear deterrent power of the West by maintaining its " V Bomber " Force and ultimately by using the new American Skybolt as a means of delivering British nuclear weapons. Gaitskell was out of the country at the time, attending a Socialist Conference in Israel, but in his absence the Party spokesmen in the debate declared that it had now become clear that Britain could no longer attempt to be an independent nuclear power.

In April, May and June, 1960, there were consultations between the Trades Union Congress, the National Executive and representatives of the Parliamentary Labour Party who together produced a new joint defence statement in July. The key passages of this statement declared that Britain should continue to remain a loyal supporter of NATO, but that she could no longer maintain herself as an independent nuclear power; in future Britain must leave to the United States the provision of the thermo-nuclear deterrent. The statement also re-affirmed Labour's opposition to the establishment of the Thor (fixed site) missile bases in Britain, although there was no reference to the other sorts of American bases then in Britain from which nuclear weapons might be delivered against an enemy. The statement did not oppose the equipment of NATO forces (with the exception of Germany) with tactical nuclear weapons, although it stated that they too should be manufactured exclusively by the Americans and " deployed only under strict NATO control ". (There were a number of other suggestions in the statement as to how NATO's dependence on nuclear weapons might be reduced and the effectiveness of political control over NATO military forces might be increased.)

This new statement of defence policy was endorsed by the Parliamentary Labour Party in June, and by the Annual Conference of the Trades Union Congress in September 1960 (although the latter body also adopted what was generally considered to be a contradictory resolution, sponsored by the Transport and General Workers Union, which would have carried Britain some way in the direction of unilateralism by requiring the removal of all bases equipped with nuclear weapons from this country).[1] Much of the subsequent confusion that surrounded the debate on these issues at the Party Conference on 5th October arose from the fact that a

[1] *TUC Report*, 1960, p. 396.

number of the leading unions had already taken up their stand on the defence issue *before* the new joint policy statement was published; their conference delegations had therefore to vote on proposals which in their present form had never been discussed by their respective union conferences.

In these circumstances two of these unions, the Transport and General Workers Union and the Amalgamated Engineering Union, pressed their own resolutions before the Conference, as did the Amalgamated Society of Woodworkers. The Conference therefore had to vote on four proposals: the first was the official defence policy statement; the second, the Woodworkers' resolution which accepted the official statement, and specifically added that " the realities of international politics make imperative our continued membership of NATO "; the third, a resolution of the Transport and General, which called, in part, for " a complete rejection of any defence policy based on the threat of the use of strategic or tactical nuclear weapons "; and finally the Engineers' resolution which demanded " the unilateral renunciation of the testing, manufacture, stock-piling and basing of all nuclear weapons in Great Britain ".

It was never made completely clear by the sponsors of the Transport Workers' motion and the Engineers' resolution whether they accepted the interpretation, widely placed upon them, that they would have involved British withdrawal from NATO and from its military alliance with the United States. Gaitskell, in winding up the debate, insisted that they did and pointed out that, among the very many resolutions withdrawn in favour of these two, were no less than sixty which specifically advocated withdrawal from NATO. When challenged on this point, Frank Cousins replied, in the final, extraordinarily ambiguous passage of his speech:

> " When I am asked if it means getting out of NATO, if the question is posed to me as simply saying, am I prepared to go on remaining in an organization over which I have no control, but which can destroy us instantly, my answer is Yes, if the choice is that. But it is not that." [1]

This would appear to have left the matter entirely unclarified, but earlier in his speech he had said:

> " There is only one simple issue of difference between us [on the defence policy statement]: the NEC believe that *the policies of the Western Alliance* and our own country are to be based on the theory of having the bomb; we think they ought to be based on the opposite theory of not having the bomb." [2] [Italics mine]

[1] *1960 Labour Annual Conference Report*, p. 180.
[2] *Ibid.*, p. 179.

It therefore seems fair to conclude that Cousins's position at that time was that a British Labour Government should not only itself give up the bomb but should also insist that both NATO and the United States do likewise; and if these requests were refused then Britain should presumably withdraw from these alliances.

Certainly this was the view of a number of those who supported his resolution, including, for example, the then Chairman of the General Council of the TUC, Ted Hill (of the Boilermakers' Society) who said: " We find the Russians on the one hand and the Americans on the other, like grizzly bears wanting to get at each other. We should pull out of this bear garden and form a third world force. Bring together the British Commonwealth of Nations. Let them act as mediators between these two gorillas." And Michael Foot held up the example of India and other non-aligned powers, presumably as proof of the fact that Britain, were she to withdraw from her military alliances, would still be able to wield great influence in world affairs.[1]

Even before the debate began it was generally accepted that the resolutions of the Transport Workers and the Engineers would be carried, because a sufficiently large number of unions had already taken decisions committing them to unilateralism, or because of last-minute decisions by Conference delegations, such as that of the Amalgamated Engineering Union (which decided it would not vote both for unilateralism and for the Executive statement as it had done at the TUC conference). Despite this the debate was intensely dramatic. There were strong warnings from leading members of Parliament such as George Brown, the Party's defence spokesman, and Dennis Healey, a leading foreign affairs spokesman, that should the Conference vote for unilateralism, they personally could not accept the decision but would campaign for its reversal.

Gaitskell's final speech was one of the boldest and most forthright in the whole history of British party leadership. After reviewing the arguments on both sides in detail, he made it crystal clear that he believed that a vote for either the Transport Workers' or the Engineers' resolutions would be a vote for both unilateral nuclear disarmament and for neutralism. He acknowledged that the resolutions would probably be carried and that the Executive statement would be defeated. But then he added:

> " It is not the end of the problem because Labour Members of Parliament will have to consider what they do in the House of Commons. What do you expect of them? You know how they voted in June—overwhelmingly for the policy statement. It is not in

[1] *1960 Labour Annual Conference Report*, p. 188.

dispute that the vast majority of Labour Members of Parliament are utterly opposed to unilateralism and neutralism. So what do you expect them to do? Change their minds overnight? To go back on the pledges they gave to the people who elected them from their constituencies? And supposing they did do that. Supposing all of us, like well-behaved sheep, were to follow the policies of unilateralism and neutralism, what kind of an impression would that make upon the British people?... I do not believe that the Labour Members of Parliament are prepared to act as time-servers ... because they are men of conscience and honour. ... What sort of people do you think we are? Do you think we can simply accept a decision of this kind? Do you think that we can become overnight the Pacifists, Unilateralists and Fellow-Travellers that other people are?...

" I say this to you: we may lose the vote today and the result may deal this Party a great blow. ... [But] there are some of us ... who will fight and fight and fight again to save the Party we love. We will fight and fight and fight again and bring back sanity and honesty and dignity, so that our Party with its great past may retain its glory and its greatness. ... I ask delegates who are still free to decide how they vote to support what I believe to be a realistic policy on defence, which yet could so easily have united the great Party of ours, and to reject what I regard as the suicidal path of unilateral disarmament which will leave our country defenceless and alone."

Amidst great excitement the vote was taken with the results that had been foreseen; the Executive statement and the Woodworkers' resolutions were both defeated and the Transport Workers' and Engineers' resolution carried, although each decision was taken by an extremely narrow majority.[1] A careful analysis of the voting figures [2] points to the strong probability that the constituency delegates had voted in proportions of about two to one in support of Gaitskell and the official defence policy (with perhaps one-fifth of constituency votes withheld by deliberate abstentions). The platform was defeated primarily because four of the six biggest unions had voted against it, including the T&GWU, the AEU, the USDAW, the NUR, and the ETU; only the NUM and the NUGMW had remained " loyal ". The bond of mutual confidence between the leaders of the PLP and the necessary majority of the biggest unions was broken and this ensured Gaitskell's defeat, despite his remarkable success in securing approximately 67 per

[1] The actual votes were as follows: the Executive statement was defeated by 3,339,000 to 3,042,000; the Woodworkers' resolution was defeated by 3,331,000 to 2,999,000; the Transport and General resolution was carried by 3,282,000 to 3,239,000; and the AEU resolution by 3,303,000 to 2,896,000. *1960 Labour Annual Conference Report*, p. 202.

[2] See Hindell, K., and Williams, P., " Scarborough and Blackpool ", *Political Quarterly*, Vol. 33, No. 3, July–Sept. 1962, pp. 306 ff.

cent. of the constituency votes. Some of the constituency delegates may have been " unmandated " on the defence issue; others almost certainly " broke their mandates " under the influence of Gaitskell's passionate appeal to " save the party ".[1]

One other debate at the 1960 Conference must be noted, since it has an important bearing on one of the central issues examined in this book. In the course of the summer preceding the Conference, as it began to seem increasingly likely that the party leadership would be defeated and the unilateralists would win the day, it was urged upon Gaitskell in some quarters that he should do exactly what in fact he did: that is, call upon the Parliamentary Labour Party to refuse to accept the Conference decision in favour of unilateralism and neutralism. Since this possibility was " in the wind " a number of constituency parties submitted resolutions designed to determine beyond question the right of the Conference to decide policy and to " issue instructions " to the Parliamentary Party. Two of these resolutions were considered by the Conference the day before it was to debate the defence issue. One resolution read as follows:

> " This Conference reaffirms its belief that in a democratic organization decisions should be the result of the majority vote by the membership and *instructs* the Parliamentary Labour Party to carry out fully the decisions arrived at by the Party Conference. It also resolves that, in future, Parliamentary Candidates must reaffirm their belief in this principle and promise to fulfil it. Between Conferences when *snap decisions* must be taken, the Parliamentary Labour Party must be guided by the general principles accepted at the previous Conference." [2] [Italics mine]

The mover of the resolution insisted that:

> " Members of Parliament have only the same rights as you and I. . . . Their only special privilege is that we have selected them to represent us in Parliament to be the spokesmen for the policies decided on at Annual Conference. . . . We do not want our so-called Leaders to show, in the guise of paternalism, the contempt for the very people who elected them. Some may say that what we are seeking to do in our resolution is to bind our Parliamentary Party hand and foot. Yes, indeed, that is exactly what we want." [3]

But this meat was too strong for all but the most militant of dele-

---

[1] Martin Harrison, incidentally, has concluded from his analysis of the 1954 debate on German re-armament that on that occasion the NEC won only 24 per cent. of the constituency vote. *Trade Unions and the Labour Party Since 1945*, p. 229.

[2] *1960 Labour Annual Conference Report*, p. 161.

[3] *Ibid.*, pp. 161–162.

gates and this particular resolution was rejected by a vote of 5,627,000 to 767,000.

The other resolution placed before the Conference was more moderate in wording although not diametrically different in spirit:

> " This Conference reaffirms that the policy of the Labour Party to be pursued nationally and in Parliament on questions of principle shall be determined by Annual Conference. While acknowledging that *the day to day tactics* in Parliament must be the job of the Parliamentary Labour Party, this Conference declares that Labour policy is decided by the Party Conference which is the final authority."
> [Italics mine]

It will be noted that the main difference between these two resolutions is that the former would leave to the Parliamentary Party the right to make " snap decisions " while the latter would allow it to determine " day to day tactics in Parliament ". The difference in intention between the resolutions would not have seemed to be very great.

John Stonehouse, M.P., the mover of the second (the " day to day tactics ") resolution, said that he regretted the necessity for presenting it to the Conference, but he and others had been " deeply concerned by the inspired rumours which had been appearing over the past few months indicating that the Parliamentary Party could be divided from the Annual Conference " and by the fact that " there are many prominent Members of the Labour Party who have also been advocating this course ". He then proceeded to restate the traditional Labour view of the Conservative Party:

> " Over and over again we have criticized the Conservatives because they have an undemocratic structure. When the Tory Party meet in this hall next week it will be merely a demonstration. Mr. Macmillan, and Mr. Macmillan only, decides the policy of the Conservative Party. Even when the Conservative Party is in opposition, that is the Leader's prerogative. The Tories do not have a party democracy; they have a Leader dictatorship."

But for the Parliamentary Labour Party to resist " the will of the members of the Labour Party as expressed through Annual Conference " would be " to jettison the tested democracy of this Movement and replace it with the esoteric wisdom of a small élite." [1]

Stonehouse made it clear that he did not wish to go quite as far as the advocates of the other resolution, and stated that " it is not our wish that M.P.s should be subjected to detailed instruction—that would be unconstitutional." [2] But none the less they must not

---

[1] *1960 Labour Annual Conference Report*, pp. 159–60.
[2] *Ibid.*, p. 160.

defy " the will of the Annual Conference "; since if that were to happen the democratic Labour Movement would " commit suicide ".

The strategy of the NEC (which, it is understood, was decided by a narrow majority) was not to oppose the Stonehouse resolution, but to accept it on conditions which were fairly clearly intended to emasculate its basic intention. The Party's Deputy General Secretary, A. L. Williams, was put up to reply for the NEC and he stated that they would accept Stonehouse's resolution provided that it was clearly understood by everybody that it involved no change whatever in the long-established principles governing the relationships between the Conference, the NEC and the PLP. In outlining these " long-established principles " he stressed in the most uncompromising fashion that the PLP is " an autonomous body " and added: " Nowhere in the Constitution is authority given to the Party Conference to instruct the Parliamentary Labour Party." He granted that the Party Conference had the right to decide the programme, principles and policy of the Labour Party, although he also reminded the Conference that according to the Constitution, " no proposal shall be included in the Party Programme unless it has been adopted by the Party Conference by a majority of not less than two-thirds of the votes recorded on a card vote." He also acknowledged that it is the duty of the NEC and the Parliamentary Committee of the PLP, meeting jointly, to decide which items from the Party Programme shall be included in the Manifesto to be issued at an election. And he noted that the NEC has the right to confer with the PLP at the opening of each Parliamentary Session and at any other time when the Parliamentary Labour Party may desire a meeting.

Williams emphasized (and, indeed, anyone explaining the working of the Conservative Party would have to acknowledge the same point) that " the Parliamentary Party cannot function satisfactorily unless it does take account of the views expressed by the Party Conference." But again he insisted that " [the PLP] could not under any circumstances be in the position of having to act upon instructions of the National Executive Committee, this Party Conference or by any other body. . . . " Here he was developing a theme which had been expounded by the General Secretary of the Party, Morgan Phillips, earlier in the summer in a document entitled *Constitution of the Labour Party*. Phillips had written:

" . . . The Parliamentary Party could not maintain its position in the country if it could be demonstrated that it was at any time or in any way subject to dictation from an outside body which, however representative of the Party, could not be regarded as representative of the country. In any event, constitutionally, the British Government is responsible to Parliament whether that Parliament votes along Party lines or across them. Nothing can alter this."

Phillips had gone on to plead for " mutual trust and confidence " between the various organs of the Party and had conceded that " the Parliamentary Party could not for long remain at loggerheads with Annual Conference without disrupting the Party " (a proposition that is as true of any party with a mass organization as it is of the Labour Party). Williams closed his address with the appeal that " in a democratic movement we do not even talk about instructions; we meet new situations by consultation, by an attempt to get the greatest measure of agreement."

After Williams had spoken there was a protest from the floor on the ground that the NEC had agreed to accept this composite resolution only with strings attached. When Stonehouse was asked whether he accepted the conditions Williams had laid down, he replied: "I believe that the position, although it is complicated, as explained by Mr. Williams is the correct one. But I do ask that the National Executive Committee, as I understand they have already done, will accept the meaning of the words as explained in [my resolution]." On the following day, in its vote for unilateralism, the Conference was to decide the sort of issue that Stonehouse must have had in mind when he referred in his resolutions to " questions of principle ". And Gaitskell in his defiant reply made it abundantly clear that he was *not* prepared to devote himself to deciding on " the day to day tactics " which would be required to implement the policy. The impasse now appeared complete; and it was not to be resolved until a year later when the conference reversed itself and fell in line with the defence policy supported by the majority of the PLP.

The intervening year was one of high drama in the annals of the Labour Party. The first crisis came in November on the occasion of the annual election of the Party Leader. On 14th October, Anthony Greenwood, a well-known unilateralist, resigned from the Shadow Cabinet and announced that, unless a stronger candidate came forward, he would stand against Gaitskell (in the somewhat unlikely rôle of a " unity " candidate). After some hesitation Harold Wilson, the Party's " Shadow Chancellor ", took up the challenge a week later and Greenwood withdrew; " under strong pressure from many colleagues, [and] with the greatest possible regret and . . . reluctance," Wilson said he had decided that he had " no alternative " to accepting nomination against Gaitskell.

Wilson insisted that he was " as conscious as any other Labour M.P. of the great qualities and sincerity of Hugh Gaitskell " but he had become convinced that Gaitskell " and his friends on the extreme right wing of the Party " were " uncompromising and resolute " in their determination to fight against the Scarborough Conference decision. Wilson had on other occasions made it plain that he was not personally a unilateralist; but apparently he could see no issue of principle involved on the Scarborough decision since, as he put it, " defence policy . . . by the very nature of things changes from year to year and even from month to month." His own suggestion as to how the gap between the PLP and the Conference on defence should be bridged was not notably precise; the first pre-requisite in re-establishing the unity of the Party, he said, was " a willingness to re-state the National Executive Committee's defence policy on a basis which could be accepted with dignity by Labour M.P.s but which, at the same time, *reflected the fact* that important pronouncements had been made by the Scarborough Conference " [italics added]. This, it will be noted, was a far cry from the spirit of the resolution which John Stonehouse had moved and the Scarborough Conference had accepted which had declared that " Labour policy is decided by the Party Conference which is the final authority," although Wilson had clearly intended to appeal to those who held this view when (in his statement declaring his intention to stand against Gaitskell) he called on the Party " to repudiate the campaign now being waged . . . for a major change in the democratic and Socialist basis of the movement."

Briefly, Wilson's position appeared to be that Gaitskell had provoked an utterly needless and potentially disastrous quarrel; nothing of great importance was at stake and Wilson seemed confident that a form of words could be found which could bridge the gap between a conference committed in favour of unilateralism and a Parliamentary Party equally firmly committed against. He had decided therefore to accept Greenwood's cue and he offered himself as a " unity " candidate against a Leader who was so senselessly threatening to wreck his own party. " . . . if Hugh Gaitskell [were] returned unopposed ", Wilson declared, " . . . this will be taken as a mandate from his parliamentary colleagues to defy conference, to ignore the National Executive Committee and to plunge the movement into still worse conflict."[1]

Gaitskell now became the first Leader of the Party who, con-firmed by an initial contest for office, was subsequently challenged for re-election. When the result of the contest was announced on 3rd November, 1960, Wilson scored slightly more than the traditional

[1] *The Times*, 21st October, 1960.

number of Left votes in the PLP but he was decisively beaten by 166 to 81. Gaitskell apparently took this, as Wilson had predicted he would, as " a mandate to defy conference " or rather as a signal to launch a campaign to secure the reversal of the Scarborough decision. Gaitskell had already reminded the Left of the PLP that they had never in the past acted as if they felt themselves to be slavishly bound by conference decisions with which they disagreed; nor had they hesitated to campaign for their reversal. This time it was the majority of the PLP who were at odds with the conference and they proposed to exercise the same privilege. " ... The right to dissent" he argued, "is not something that can be made to depend on the fewness of those who dissent. It must be allowed to a majority."[1]

In subsequent months Gaitskell faced many hectic party meetings in the country (he was sometimes drowned out by pickets shouting " Gaitskell must go "); a great many party members, whatever their views on defence, were undoubtedly deeply perplexed by the unique internal party struggle which Gaitskell now waged. And he had to fight long and often very bitter verbal battles within the labyrinthine committee system of the Labour movement. But Gaitskell had certain impregnable sources of strength. He had the backing of a Parliamentary Committee which gave him over- whelming support. Of the twelve members elected to the new Committee after the Leadership contest only two—Harold Wilson (who fell from his place the previous year at the top of the poll to ninth) and Fred Lee—were opposed to his efforts to reverse the Scarborough decision. And George Brown, who on the eve of the Scarborough Conference had seemed to be on the point of backing away from the struggle, was elected to the Deputy Leadership as a " Gaitskellite ". (It was not generally known that his own view was that Gaitskell could never lead a united Labour Party.)

In early defence debates in the House of Commons it became clear that at least two-thirds of the Parliamentary Party would support Gaitskell's position on defence. In addition, he had majority support on the NEC (the Executive adopted the somewhat curious line that it was the " custodian " of the Conference decision; but like the PLP it did nothing whatever to implement the decision). Gaitskell could also rely on the consistent support of a majority on the General Council of the TUC.

In addition, it gradually became clear that there was far more widespread support throughout the party for Gaitskell and the position he had taken at Scarborough than had perhaps been realized at the time. To mobilize this support an organization called the Campaign for Democratic Socialism (CDS) was formed within

[1] *The Guardian*, 24th October, 1960.

the party with W. T. Rodgers (a former secretary of the Fabian Society) as executive secretary. CDS began systematically to rally key party workers in the local Labour parties; they tried, wherever possible, to secure the defeat of unilateralists in local party elections and also to win local support for the campaign to reverse the Scarborough decision. By June 1961 the supporters of CDS claimed to have over 3,000 members in small and large " cells " throughout the party; they also predicted that at the autumn Party Conference 80 per cent. of the local parties would support Gaitskell.[1] This prediction was to be falsified; it is almost certain that the share of constituency support backing Gaitskell and the NEC defence policy fell from 67 per cent. in 1960 to 63 per cent. at the conference in the following year.[2] However it must be kept in mind that the 67 per cent. who had voted against unilateralism in 1960 must have included a great many who had been won over to Gaitskell by the sheer power and courage of his defiance of the Conference, and the warning that he and other prominent members of the PLP had given that they would in no circumstance abide by the Conference decision but would fight to get it reversed. Many, in other words, were responding to the appeal to " save the Party " rather than to the intellectual case against unilateralism, a policy which inevitably must have its powerful attractions for the constituency militants. In addition, the unilateralists themselves mounted a considerable campaign during 1960–61. In light of these considerations it might be counted a modest success for CDS (but no more) that they were able to retain very nearly the same constituency support in 1961 that they had won in 1960.

But, as in the previous year (and on all important occasions), the decisions taken by the big unions were of crucial importance. And in 1961, as in most of the critical debates in the modern history of the Party, a majority of the big unions swung behind the Parliamentary leadership. The CDS activists, and the anti-unilateralists generally, were intensely busy within certain of the key unions. It seemed for a time that a muffled compromise on defence, worked out by R. H. S. Crossman (chairman of the NEC during 1960–61) and Walter Padley, might attract some union support, especially since Padley himself was President of the USDAW which had voted for unilateralism in 1960. But Padley was prevailed on by the anti-unilateralists to drop his own " compromise " and both his own union and the AEU reversed their positions in May, 1960. The NUR also swung over by a narrow margin. Among other

[1] *The Times*, 12th June, 1961. See also the CDS monthly publication *Campaign*.
[2] Hindell, K., and Williams, P., " Scarborough and Blackpool ", *Political Quarterly*, July–December, 1962, p. 331.

unions joining the band-wagon were a number of medium and smaller unions representing the Builders, Foundrymen, Locomotive men, Vehicle-builders and so forth. In all, thirteen unions casting 1,551,300 votes changed sides. (There was also a considerable upsurge of anti-unilateralism in several other unions which did not change over, including the mighty TGWU.) Remarkable as it may seem, incidentally (as Hindell and Williams point out), not one of the unions which reversed its position thought it necessary to explain to the 1961 conference why it had done so.

By mid-June *The Times* had declared: " Gaitskell has won. He has not only beaten the unilateralists . . . [he] has put them to rout." [1] The writer predicted that he would have a majority of at least two million. In the event it was nearer to three million (4,526,000 to 1,756,000).[2] In addition to the " switch-overs ", the unilateralist forces had lost the support of the traditionally left-wing ETU which had been disaffiliated from the Labour Party during 1960–61, because of the revelations in a court action of illegal practices used by certain Communist officials to maintain control of the union. (Incidentally, although there is no suggestion that they are maintaining their positions by illegal means, Communists continue to wield grossly disproportionate influence in certain other unions. For example they, along with certain fairly consistent fellow-travellers, compose very nearly half of the main policy decision-making organ of the AEU.)

Although the 1961 conference reversed itself on unilateralism it proceeded to pass two further resolutions which the parliamentary leadership viewed with disfavour. One demanded the removal of the American " Polaris " submarine base from Britain; the other objected to the training of German troops in this country. But again Gaitskell and the PLP refused to be bound by either resolution and they made no move to advocate these policies in Parliament.[3] And interestingly enough when Harold Wilson succeeded Gaitskell

---

[1] *The Times*, 12th June, 1961.

[2] *1961 Labour Annual Conference Report*, p. 194.

[3] This goes some way to answer a point raised by Leon Epstein in an article entitled " Who Makes Party Policy: British Labour 1960–61 ", *Midwest Journal of Political Science*, Vol. VI, No. 2, May 1962, pp. 165–82. He arrives at conclusions broadly similar to those of the present writer but raises the question as to whether the PLP could have ignored a second decision in favour of uni-lateralism if the 1961 Conference had failed to reverse itself. The evidence suggests that Gaitskell and a majority of the PLP had no intention of accepting direction from its Conference and they therefore defied the 1961 resolutions as flatly as they had those of 1960. On the other hand it is highly doubtful if any parliamentary party could remain permanently at odds with its party conference on major matters of policy; the likely consequence would be the break-up of the Party.

as Leader he made it clear that he stood with the PLP in refusing to be bound by the Conference decision on the Polaris base.[1] The great defence dispute of 1960–61 seems to have carried the parliamentary leadership further than it had gone before in insisting that, even in opposition, it cannot be subject to external direction.

The reversal of the Scarborough Conference decision was, above all else, a personal triumph for Hugh Gaitskell. His open defiance of the Conference in 1960 was one of the boldest acts in the history of party leadership in Britain. He had determined the line he would take without seeking the formal approval of either the National Executive or the Parliamentary Committee. Among the trade unions he had no one backing him with the commanding authority of an Ernest Bevin (indeed the most powerful single figure in the trade union world, Frank Cousins, had inherited Bevin's block vote—if not his influence with other trade unionists—and was implacably determined to use it against Gaitskell's policies). In the PLP Gaitskell had the loyal support of a solid majority; but he had no front-bench team which wielded the authority within the party once at the disposal of Attlee and his principal colleagues. Indeed Gaitskell's " Shadow Chancellor ", Harold Wilson, deserted him after the Scarborough defeat and attempted to unseat him as Leader; and that year's Party chairman, R. H. S. Crossman, declared it a " disaster " when Gaitskell refused to accept the Crossman–Padley compromise and insisted on maintaining an unambiguous opposition to unilateralism. These could have proved serious defections (since neither Wilson nor Crossman belonged to the " irreconcilable " Left) and Gaitskell might have been tempted to try to avoid them by trimming his sails. But this he did not do at any point in the controversy.

It can well be argued that Gaitskell's victory did not in itself prove that he understood the art of political leadership, since this may well consist, in considerable part, in avoiding knock-down battles like that of 1960–61 (or certainly like that of the previous year over Clause Four). But it can equally be argued that moments arrive in the history of any party when a great issue of principle must be fought through to a finish. Baldwin's battle with his party over India (see p. 138 ff.) and Austen Chamberlain's struggle with the 1921 Party Conference over the Irish Treaty (see p. 85 ff.) rank among such moments. And so, without question, does Gaitskell's struggle against unilateralism in 1960–61.

The course of events in that year would not seem to have been wholly incompatible with the basic argument advanced in this

[1] In a BBC Television interview on the day Wilson became Leader, 14th February, 1963.

book about the distribution of power within the Labour Party. As *The Times* remarked: " Mr. Gaitskell and his loyalist majority in the Parliamentary Party have surely exploded the theory that the Party Conference is the policy-making body which issues orders to the M.P.s and their chosen leader. None of last year's exaggerated claims for the powers of the Conference can be seriously made for years to come—until, in fact, the Labour rank-and-file have a total lapse of memory." [1] But *The Times* underestimated the almost infinite capacity for wilful self-deception, even in the higher reaches of the Party. Within a month after it had become clear that the Conference would reverse itself and fall in line with the majority of the PLP the Chairman of the NEC, R. H. S. Crossman, could write, in the light of these events, that it was clear that " the extra-parliamentary party ... [is] the final authority on policy issues ... " [2] And after presiding over the actual conference that reversed itself he declared in an interview that this proved " yet again " that the Conference had final authority in matters of policy.

It was shown above how frequently Labour Party leaders have demonstrated their confusion on this issue. (See, for example, Attlee and Morrison in the German rearmament debate in 1954, p. 598 above.) It is doubtful if Hugh Gaitskell himself had thought through the nature of the problem until he found himself caught in the trap in 1960. In the previous year (on 17th July, 1959), when of course there was no real prospect that the Labour Conference would " go unilateralist ", he had been asked in an interview about his views of the powers of the conference. He had said that the conference should not try to " dictate to a future Labour government exactly what it should do "; but he added: " Of course the great issues of principle must be settled by the conference." The transcript of this interviewer continued as follows:

Interviewer: " Well, if it can settle great issues of policy, suppose the Conference carried a resolution in favour of unilateral nuclear disarmament ... would that not bind a future Labour government?"

Gaitskell: " I think that would, yes."

Interviewer: " And therefore that would be a clear statement of principle? "

Gaitskell: " Yes, I would certainly accept that." [3]

[1] *The Times*, 12th June, 1961.

[2] See the exchange of correspondence on this issue with the present writer in the *New Statesman*, 30th June, 7th, 14th, 21st, 28th July, 1961. Subsequently, Crossman seems to have changed his ground completely ; see his Introduction to the Fontana edition of Bagehot, W., *The English Constitution* (1963), pp. 41-2, and also p. 641 below.

[3] This interview was reproduced in part in the *Observer*, 8th October, 1961.

Yet at Scarborough in 1960 Gaitskell seemed finally to realize that it is precisely on the great issues of principle that a major Parliamentary Party cannot be forced to reverse itself at the behest of its extra-parliamentary organization, unless that Parliamentary Party is prepared to surrender all claims to electoral respect. This indeed was the very core of Gaitskell's argument in his great speech at the 1960 Conference; and it was, in effect, the basis of his successful claim to the loyalty and support of the PLP in the struggle to reverse the conference decision.

Keir Hardie revealed a clear understanding of these matters (and rather more courage than many of his successors). When the 1907 Conference passed a resolution on women's suffrage with which Hardie, then Parliamentary Leader, did not agree, he startled the Conference (it will be recalled) by saying that " . . . if the motion they had carried that morning was intended to limit the action of the Party in the House of Commons, he would have seriously to consider whether he remained a member of the Parliamentary Party." And a few years later he wrote:

> " In the House of Commons the membership of the Party decide their own policy without interference from the Executive or any outside authority. This is the right which the Parliamentary Party has always claimed, and which has never been seriously challenged." [1]

There is a further comment to make on the events of 1960–61: the comparative ease with which the CDS and the anti-unilateralists recaptured support within the unions is a reminder of the fact that the Labour Party machinery (including the vitally important trade union element) is manipulated by a tiny handful of political activists whether of the right, centre or left. The unilateralists had captured enough of the machinery to win in 1960. They were put to rout in the following year by a very modest (if highly skilful) effort by a small group of dedicated anti-unilateralists. In each case a small " stage army " was claiming to speak for the millions of union and local party members, over 90 per cent. of whom play no part whatever in arriving at the decisions taken in their name.

The defeat of unilateralism in 1961 may well have been a more accurate reflection of the views of the whole party membership (or at least of the whole body of Labour voters) than was the Scarborough decision of the previous year, so far as can be gathered from the evidence of the public opinion polls. One opinion survey conducted in September 1960 reported that only 16 per cent. of union members favoured unilateral nuclear disarmament; yet

---

[1] Cited in Hughes, E., *Keir Hardie*, London, 1956, p. 208.

despite this fact both the TUC and the Labour Party were simultaneously " converted " to this view.[1] The Gallup Poll also found at roughly the same time that about 24 per cent. of Labour voters supported unilateral nuclear disarmament.[2]   Indeed throughout the swaying battle over nuclear disarmament in the Labour Party the proportion of Labour voters backing such a policy hovered around 20–25 per cent. (and did not vary significantly beyond that range).[3] The fact remains, however, that the two struggles of 1960 and 1961 were no more than " stage-army battles " conducted in the name of the huge majority of politically inactive members of the trade unions and constituency parties. Neither victory could be deemed a triumph for " inner-party democracy ".   But the 1961 victory *was* a triumph for the view that if a political party accepts the Cabinet and Parliamentary system, final authority in policy-making is bound to reside in the hands of the parliamentary party and its leadership. This is self-evidently the case when the party is in power; and when the party is in opposition its " Shadow Cabinet ", whatever weight it may give to the views of its extra-parliamentary supporters, cannot allow itself to become merely the mouthpiece for opinions formulated by the tiny band of activists which normally controls its "mass" organization outside Parliament.

A tragic postscript to the chronicle of the Labour Leadership and its problems since 1955 was provided by the death of Hugh Gaitskell on 18th January, 1963. After his victory over unilateralism he had by 1962 acquired commanding authority within the Labour Party; indeed it is doubtful if anyone in the Party's history, with the possible exception of MacDonald in the 1920s, enjoyed a comparable position of ascendancy in the Parliamentary Party.   Gaitskell's stature had increased, in a perhaps surprising way, as a result of his last major appearance before the Party Conference in October 1962. In a powerful speech he all but committed the party to outright opposition to Britain's entry into the Common Market, at least on any terms that might conceivably have been available.[4] Whatever

[1] *Report of the Survey of Opinions concerning Nuclear Disarmament*, London, Odhams Press, 1960.
[2] The Gallup Political Index, No. 9, September 1960.
[3] S. M. Lipset also draws attention to the significance of these figures in his introduction to Michels' *Political Parties*, Collier Books edition, 1962, p. 31.
[4] Gaitskell told the present writer in July 1962 that he had originally hoped that the issue of Britain's entry into the Common Market could have been kept " above party ", but that he had become convinced that the Macmillan government had hoped from the beginning to turn the issue into an election-winning " gimmick ". He added that his own attitude toward entry had gradually hardened into one of opposition the more he examined the economic and political implications of such action.

the merits of the arguments Gaitskell set forth there is little doubt that he had arrived at his position by a long and careful consideration of the economic and political factors involved. None the less the speech came as a great shock to those of his usual supporters, mainly on the Right and in the Centre of the Party, who favoured Britain's entry into the European Economic Community: equally, it delighted Gaitskell's old enemies on the Left. But above all else, this Brighton speech served to demonstrate, to anyone who could still have doubted it, that Gaitskell was his own man, that he did not hesitate to take up a position on a major issue which angered some of his staunchest friends and pleased his left-wing foes. As a result Gaitskell was now more than ever the unassailable Leader of the Labour party. Within three months he was dead.

With Gaitskell's death, following two and a half years after that of Aneurin Bevan, the Party had lost the two great figures of the post-Attlee period. It is a sad comment on the condition of the Party during this period that the two men had spent the best years of their political lives locked in internecine political conflict. They had negotiated a truce and worked together for a time in the period before the election of 1959; but the fragments of evidence available (see p. 609 and n. 1) suggests that their contest might well have been renewed had Bevan survived into the era of bitter quarrelling which followed the Blackpool Conference of 1959. Certainly, the " Bevanites " of yesterday were Gaitskell's main opponents during the Clause Four and unilateralist disputes.

The long struggle between Gaitskell and Bevan was in part no doubt the consequence of their temperamental incompatibility. But, in addition, as was suggested above (pp. 595–8), they became the symbolic representatives of two conflicting views of the future of democratic socialism. Such views found expression in every other socialist party in the democratic world. But what was unique in the experience of British Labour was the apparent inability of the Party either to contain or to resolve its ideological conflicts. This almost certainly was the direct consequence of the Party's unique constitutional arrangements with the almost unlimited opportunity they provide for the perpetuation of internal party disputes. During most of the Party's history its Leaders had managed (by the devices analysed in Part II) to reconcile the requirements of their party constitution with the necessities of parliamentary government. But during the long conflict of the 1950s and early 1960s they had to pay what would seem to have been an intolerably high price for doing so.

Yet, strangely enough, even after the worst series of electoral defeats suffered by a major party in modern times no move was made to re-examine the Party's decision-making machinery. Arthur Henderson had undertaken a drastic overhaul of the party organization at the end of the First World War but he found no successor in the troubled years after 1951.

With the exception of the bizarre incident of the Clause Four controversy, Gaitskell and his supporters won every major battle in the twelve years after the fall of the second Attlee government. There is therefore a certain irony in the outcome of the contest to determine who should succeed Gaitskell as Leader. The nominees for the first ballot included George Brown, the Deputy Leader, Harold Wilson, the Shadow Foreign Secretary, and James Callaghan, the Shadow Chancellor of the Exchequer. The results, announced on 7th February 1963 were as follows:

Harold Wilson	115
George Brown	88
James Callaghan	41

According to the PLP rules, which require that if no candidate secures a majority the bottom man must retire, Callaghan withdrew. In the final ballot announced on 14th February, the outcome was:

Harold Wilson	144
George Brown	103[1]

Harold Wilson had been Aneurin Bevan's principal lieutenant in the rebel campaign which they led against the Party leadership following their resignations from the Labour Government in 1951. Subsequently, Wilson had made his peace with the parliamentary leaders much sooner than Bevan and as a result he tended to be viewed as a somewhat equivocal figure by both the Party's Right and Left wings. By 1960 he was again a leading figure in the Party's interminable civil war and attempted to unseat Gaitskell as Leader, a move which earned him the deep enmity of a considerable part of the PLP.

Why then did Wilson win the leadership in February 1963? Not, certainly, because the Party had " swung to the Left "[2]; there was no evidence whatever that such a swing had occurred. The first explanation is that Wilson was incomparably the ablest parliamentary performer in a party no longer very rich in such talents after so many years in opposition. And the second explanation is that Wilson's strongest rival, George Brown, who had a

[1] For the fullest press account of the contest see the *Observer*, 17th February, 1963.

[2] This was, for example, the mistaken interpretation placed on his election in an editorial in the *New York Times*, Overseas Edition, 17th February, 1963.

greater public reputation for loyalty to the parliamentary leadership, did not, for purely personal reasons, inspire widespread confidence among the members of the PLP. The Party by this time was convinced that it would win the forthcoming election; it believed therefore that it was choosing not merely a Leader of the Party but also the next Prime Minister. George Brown had a reputation for impulsiveness, truculence and insensitivity which more than offset his other qualities. And so to the eighty votes which Wilson had won when he challenged Gaitskell in 1960 were added another sixty who, it is fair to assume, felt that he would be more likely to prove an effective Leader and possible Prime Minister than the highly unpredictable George Brown.

And so Harold Wilson, who had played a leading rôle in the Party's civil wars for over a decade, became the leader of George Lansbury's " band of brothers ", the Parliamentary Labour Party.

THE CONSERVATIVES AND THEIR MILITANTS SINCE 1955

THE Conservative Party also had difficulties with its Party activists in the years under review, although they took a very different form from those of the Labour Party. The Conservative difficulties arose mainly from a series of " disciplinary " actions taken by local Associations against those Conservative M.P.s who had been bold enough to make publicly known their disapproval of the Eden Government's attack on Egypt in November 1956. The eight known " abstainers " in the critical division on 8th November (which took place after hostilities had ceased) ran into varying degrees of trouble with their local Conservative Associations.[1]

---

[1] For a detailed and valuable analysis of their individual cases see Epstein, L., " British M.P.s and their local parties: the Suez case ", *American Political Science Review*, Vol. LIV, No. 2, June 1960, pp. 374–90. For understandable reasons, in view of the condition of the party system in the American Congress, even the most sophisticated American observers of British politics are so enchanted with the " coherence " of British parliamentary parties that they tend to be enamoured of *every* factor which can be held to contribute to it. During the Suez crisis the local Conservative Associations certainly helped to dragoon the deviant " anti-Suez " M.P.s into line, and therefore Epstein can find no real fault even in the harshest of cases of constituency pressures on M.P.s. He also quotes with apparent approval an article by Attlee in which the latter argued that, when an M.P. finds himself in disagreement with his party, he should submit the issue to his local association and then resign from Parliament if the association so wishes (" Party discipline is paramount ", *The National and English Review*, Vol. 148, January 1957). Significantly enough, Attlee did not, so far as one can tell, promote so disastrous a view during the twenty years he led the Labour Party.

It must be remembered that the Eden Government's attack on Egypt had been condemned by the United Nations (very nearly unanimously), by preponderant opinion in the Commonwealth, by the main body of the serious press in the United Kingdom, as well as by both Opposition Parties. If ever there were a moment, one might have thought, when M.P.s were entitled to place their conscience or their own judgment above the demands of their Party Whips, surely it was at this time. Yet only eight M.P.s did so, and they did no more than abstain in a vote of confidence (*after* the hostilities had ceased). Those local associations which took disciplinary action against their M.P.s would seem to have acted on the view that party loyalty must at all times and in all circumstances take priority over every other consideration in a parliamentary system.

It is difficult to determine exactly what part constituency association pressure played in determining the subsequent fate of the " rebel eight " but it is certainly clear that several were, in effect, driven from political life. The most interesting case was that of Nigel Nicolson (one of the most forthrightly anti-Suez Conservatives) at Bournemouth East and Christchurch.[1] One aspect of this case has provided a largely neglected but important piece of evidence regarding the supposed tendency of local political associations to throw up leaders whose views are more extreme than those of the general membership of the association. The fifty-five-member executive of Nicolson's association was unanimously[2] against him; a meeting of his local association voted its lack of confidence in him by 298 to 92;[3] yet, when a series of fortuitous circumstances resulted in a postal ballot being taken of the members of the association on the issue of Nicolson's re-adoption, he was defeated by the narrowest of majorities (3,762 to 3,671).[4] This ballot was taken more than two years after the Suez crisis when passions had cooled; but it should be noted that they had not cooled so far as the executive of the association was concerned and it remained bitterly hostile toward Nicolson.

The contrasting fate of the " pro-Suez " rebels among Conservative M.P.s is of importance. (There were twenty in all who

[1] He has provided a detailed account of the early stages of his own case and a valuable examination of the problems it involved in his *People and Parliament*, London, 1958. See also Martin, L., " The Bournemouth Affair: Britain's First Primary Election ", *The Journal of Politics*, Vol. 22, No. 4, November 1960.

[2] Epstein, L., " British M.P.s and their Local Parties: The Suez Cases ", *American Political Science Review*, Vol. LIV, No. 2, June 1960, p. 385.

[3] Martin, L., " The Bournemouth Affair: Britain's First Primary Election ", *The Journal of Politics*, Vol. 22, No. 4, November 1960, p. 661.

[4] *Ibid.*, p. 675.

deliberately abstained in one or other of two votes in the House of Commons to demonstrate their disapproval of the Government's " softness " toward Nasser; and of these eight went so far as to resign from the Conservative whip.) After examining the subsequent experience of these M.P.s Epstein concludes that for the most part " . . . pro-Suez abstention, unlike anti-Suez abstention, was . . . not even controversial " so far as the M.P.s' local associations were concerned.[1]

Too much should not be made of what one can only assume was the totally unique combination of circumstances at the time of Suez. But when it is kept in mind that a number of Conservative M.P.s also endured considerable difficulties with their local associations because they dared to vote in favour of the abolition of capital punishment in a *free vote* (with the whips off)[2] there is now ground for a very real concern about the extent to which independently-minded M.P.s on the Conservative side may hesitate to express " advanced " views on any political issue which might clash with those of the most active members of their constituency associations. Unlike the Labour " rebels ", they are unlikely to have serious trouble with the Party Whips. (Edward Heath, a former Chief Whip, has said that on re-examining Party records he could find only one instance since the First World War in which the Conservative whip was withdrawn from a Tory rebel.) But if the independently-minded Conservative M.P. now has little to fear from the Whips in Parliament he may have a good deal to fear from the scorpions in the constituency associations. One curious consequence of Lord Woolton's " democratization " of the Conservative local associations is that they are now much more likely to attempt to " bully " their M.P.s. This was a less serious problem during the " bad old days " when many M.P.s might almost have been said to buy their nominations (in that they frequently offered to pay most of if not all of local constituency expenses).[3] It is too easy now for local associations who pay almost all of the Member's constituency expenses to look upon him as their employee. Momentarily at least there has been a trend in the Conservative Party towards what Bagehot called " constituency government "; as he warned:

" Constituency government is the precise opposite of parliamentary government. It is the government of persons far from the scene of action, instead of the government of moderate persons close to the

[1] Epstein, L., " British M.P.s and their Local Parties: The Suez Cases ", *American Political Science Review*, Vol. LIV, No. 2, June 1960, p. 382.

[2] *Ibid.*, p. 375.

[3] It should not be forgotten that some of the most independently-minded M.P.s in the Unreformed Parliament sat for " rotten boroughs ".

scene of action; it is the judgment of persons judging in the last resort and without a penalty, in lieu of persons judging in fear of a dissolution and ever conscious that they are subject to an appeal." [1]

The Leaders of the Conservative Party are no doubt aware of the dangers of " constituency government " and would not deliberately encourage it. But while they boast of the leniency and tolerance of their parliamentary discipline, they do not appear to have taken very active steps to warn their constituency zealots against exceeding their legitimate rôle in the political system.

[1] Bagehot, W., *The English Constitution*, Fontana edition (1963), p. 161.

or other organs of the party. The Assembly is thus responsible for determining the broad outlines of party policy.

The Liberal *Council* (which corresponds to the Conservative Central Council) meets quarterly; it includes thirty representatives elected by the Assembly, along with representatives of the party in the Commons and the Lords and members elected by the Area Federations, the Women's Liberals, the Young Liberals, and all members of the Executive. According to Liberal Party literature, the first duty of the Council is " to stimulate militant Liberalism in every part of the country " and to express the views of Liberals on current political questions as they arise. The Council is also responsible for maintaining the party headquarters, for raising funds, for securing that candidates are adopted in as many constituencies as possible, and for publicity and propaganda work. In addition, it appoints a smaller body, the *Executive Committee*, which meets at least once a month, to look after the day-to-day affairs of the party.

Liberal strategy during the 1959 general election was controlled from Party Headquarters by a small standing committee set up by the party Leader under the Chairmanship of Frank Byers (a former Liberal M.P.). This five-member Standing Committee continued to function after the election and was responsible for a further centralization of control of the Party and the consequent upheavals in organization (which included the departure from office of two successive General Directors of the party organization). The Committee also played an important part in reorganizing the procedures of the party Assembly, after that body had had a particularly chaotic session in 1958. Eventually after much internal criticism of the Committee's power, the Committee was legitimized, so to speak; its composition was changed to include three *ex officio* members plus six others; its official status henceforth was that of a subcommittee on organization. Yet it unquestionably continued to wield great power in determining the broad directions of the Party's affairs.

The constituency associations are banded together into a number of Area Federations to co-ordinate and extend the work of the party within their respective areas. The constituency associations themselves are responsible for their own organization, working arrangements and finance. They also undertake the usual educational and propaganda work and, of course, they sponsor Liberal candidates in local and national elections. An unusual feature of the Liberal Party constitution is the wide range of additional responsibilities laid on the constituency associations. According to the party constitution, they must " keep watch upon the legislative and administrative work of the Government especially as it affects the needs and interests of the district and to direct the attention of local authorities, the public and the press to the importance of these subjects, and to the methods by which Liberals believe they should be handled." They must " help all citizens *without respect of party*, creed or race, to secure their rights, and to protect them against oppression." (Italics added.) They must, finally, " demonstrate that Liberals desire to help their neighbours by providing, wherever possible, such social services as are not otherwise available." This is a surprising outburst of radical idealism to be found in a party constitution; on paper at least, it appears to set the Liberal Party rather apart from the narrower political pre-occupations of the other two parties, although in practice the Liberal Associations play a rôle very similar to those of the Conservative and Labour parties.

The *Party Headquarters* is responsible to the Executive and the Council and through them to the Assembly. It provides secretarial and executive assistance to all the national organs of the party and their committees, and in addition the headquarters is responsible for publicity, propaganda and research.

The Liberal Party's endemic financial difficulties have arisen from the fact that, unlike the Conservative and Labour Parties, it could rely on the assured financial support of no great interest group. The then Chairman of the Liberal Party Executive wrote in 1948 that the party was poor, " only because it has no wealthy pressure group to finance it."[1] In addition, during the party's long decline electoral failure bred further financial difficulties and these difficulties helped to ensure renewed failure. In the late 'fifties and early 'sixties the converse also proved to be true; a rise in the party's electoral fortunes helped to bring about an improvement in its financial position. In 1951 the Liberal Party annual income was barely £11,000. It rose very gradually until by 1959 it was £23,573; after the 1959 election the figure rose to £43,932 and in 1961 it was £46,879. In 1962 according to the Party's Treasurer, Col. Gardner-Thorpe, the Liberal Party funds were keeping pace with the increased poll at the by-elections of that year. In the first six months of 1962 the Liberal Party received £50,346—more than its income for the whole of 1961.[2]

---

[1] Cited in Fothergill, P., " Political Party Funds: The Liberal View," *Parliamentary Affairs*, Vol. I, pp. 52 ff.

[2] *The Guardian*, 24th August, 1962.

PARTY FINANCE [1]

THE CONSERVATIVE PARTY

THE Maxwell Fyfe Committee on Party Organization undertook an extensive review of the Conservative party's financial methods. This committee warned of the dangers of the party's policy of secrecy in financial matters: " In the past no information about the expenditure or income or requirements at the Centre has been available to responsible Constituency Officers, Members of Parliament, Candidates or ordinary members of the Party. The advantages of secrecy," the committee argued, " are outweighed by the disadvantages of failing to tell Conservative supporters frankly what bill they must foot if they want the country properly governed. . . . The Treasurer of the Party should publish an annual financial statement . . . People will subscribe more generously when they can see how their contributions are spent." [2] In moving the adoption of the interim report of the Maxwell Fyfe Committee at the 1948 conference, Henry Brooke added the further warning that " lack of information . . . engenders suspicion." [3]

In launching his appeal for a £1,000,000 fighting fund in 1947, Lord Woolton admitted: " It is a new thing for the Conservative Party to make a public appeal for money. . . . In the past the Party has been shy of asking for money, and it has collected for its Central Fund from a few hundred people." [4] It would not seem unreasonable to assume that these were the people who responded to the famous appeal by Mr. Baldwin in 1926: " We need funds and I look to the City of London to give a lead in providing that support which as business men they should be prepared to give, in view of our efforts to make their business safe." [5]

Lord Woolton warned at the 1947 conference, however, that the Conservatives were not " the rich man's Party " and he claimed

---

[1] This Appendix is a revised version of " A Note on Party Finance," by the present writer which originally appeared in Bailey, S., (ed.), *The British Party System*, London, 1952. It is republished by kind permission of the Hansard Society.

[2] *Maxwell Fyfe Report*, p. 15.

[3] *1948 Conservative Annual Conference Report*, p. 37.

[4] *1947 Conservative Annual Conference Report*, p. 77.

[5] *Daily Telegraph*, 2nd February, 1926.

indeed " we are over-spending ourselves five times". The Maxwell
Fyfe Committee estimated " the gap " in national party finances
(i.e., the difference between assured annual income and what the
party " ought to be able to spend ") at £200,000. The committee
argued that this sum should be raised by the constituency associations through a " voluntary quota scheme " related to the Conservative voting strength in each constituency at the immediately preceding general election. The Maxwell Fyfe Committee subsequently reported that " a great many Associations are accepting
freely and generously their new responsibility." However, since
the party still does not publish its accounts, it is impossible to
know how far the constituency contributions have helped in the
closing of the £200,000 annual " gap " in the party's funds.

As was noted in Chapter IV the Conservative Party in opposition
after 1945 also re-examined another financial problem: the question
of contributions to party funds by candidates and M.P.s. Lord
Woolton admitted at the 1947 annual conference: " In the past it
has cost a good deal of money to be a Conservative candidate,"
and he added the warning, " We cannot afford only to draw our
candidates from the people with money." [1] To meet this problem
the Maxwell Fyfe Committee recommended, first, that the entire
election expenses of Conservative candidates should be the
responsibility of the constituency associations ; second, that
candidates should not be permitted to contribute to the funds of
their association more than £25 per year and M.P.s should not be
permitted to contribute more than £50 per year. In any case, the
question of an annual subscription to the funds of the party must
not henceforth be mentioned by any constituency selection committee
to any candidate before he has been selected. These provisions
were to apply to all candidates selected after 31st December, 1948.
After a spirited debate this report was adopted by the annual conference in October 1948. [2]

In March 1962 The Conservative Central Council decided not to
adopt a proposal that the legal ceiling on election expenditure by
all parties at constituency level should be raised. The limit—£450
a candidate plus an additional 1½d. for each elector in borough
constituencies and 2d. in the counties—was fixed fourteen years
earlier, when Labour was in power. Since then all costs involved in
electioneering have soared. It is possible the Conservatives may have
decided not to open the question of local expenses for fear the demand
might grow for a wholesale revision of the law respecting all forms
of political expenditure.

[1] *1947 Conservative Annual Conference Report*, p. 77.
[2] *1948 Conservative Annual Conference Report*, pp. 35-44.

The officials of the Conservative Party have continued to argue against the publication of party accounts. A former General Director of the Conservative Central Office put the argument in this way: " The idea of publishing the accounts of political parties is superficially attractive. It arises from the instinctive curiosity about other people's affairs which we all share." He claimed, however, that the public welfare would not be advanced in any way by such publication because " the publication of comparative figures . . . would be completely misleading. There can be no standard form of comparison owing to the fundamental differences in the composition and functions of the different party organizations and their relations with quasi-political bodies." [1]

In the same vein, the Conservative *Campaign Guide* for 1950 argued that in fact the Labour Party is only a section of the socialist movement as a whole and therefore the money which it confesses to spending is only a small part of the funds expended on propaganda for socialism. " In 1948," the *Guide* claims, " the combined income of the political funds of the trade unions amounted roughly to £399,000, of which £113,000 went to the Socialist Party in affiliation fees. The whole of the balance of £286,000 was also available for the propagation of Socialism." In the same year, the *Campaign Guide* pointed out, the subscriptions of the Retail Societies to the Co-operative Union amounted to over £100,000 and of this sum a " substantial part ", it is claimed, was applied to the furtherance of the Socialist cause. In addition, the *Guide* argued that the £370,000 a year spent by the Retail Societies themselves on educational work, " cannot be anything but a powerful auxiliary of the Socialist propaganda machine." The Conservative handbook therefore concluded that " the Socialist Movement has at its disposal an income little less than £1,000,000 a year quite apart from what is raised and spent by the Constituency Labour Parties." [2]

Because the publication of party accounts would be liable to be " highly misleading ", the Conservative Party opposed the motion, moved by Mr. Geoffrey Bing, a Labour M.P., and accepted by the House of Commons on 15th December, 1949, " that in the opinion of this House, political parties and all other organizations having political action as one of their aims should publish annually full and adequate statements of their accounts." [3]

In parliamentary debates in July 1960 and in March 1961 the Conservatives again opposed the publication of party accounts. On the latter occasion Sir Toby Low, M.P. (Vice-Chairman of the

[1] *Parliamentary Affairs,* Autumn, 1948, pp. 49 ff.
[2] *Conservative Campaign Guide,* 1950, (Supplement), pp. 93-6.
[3] *House of Commons Debates,* 15th December, 1949.

Conservative Party Organization) said: " I know the honourable Members opposite are under the curious illusion that the Labour Party publishes its accounts . . . . Its accounts include sums varying between £220,000 and £280,000 a year, but those sums do not show, first, constituency revenue and expenditure . . . which Mr. Ian Mikardo told us in 1955 amounted to £1 million. The accounts do not include two-thirds of the trade union funds—two-thirds which amount to £500,000. They do not include the fund which the Co-operative Party uses for political purposes. Nor do they include any money value, because I do not see how they could, for the reason of the fact that many trade union branches and shop stewards' meetings form nuclei of political organizations. They include none of those things."[1] He claimed in conclusion: " We have no meaningful account from any political party in this country ". It was " hypocritical " for any political party to pretend otherwise.[2]

THE LABOUR PARTY

The National Executive Committee report to the annual conference includes a statement showing the Labour Party's current financial position. The 1961 report showed a credit balance at the end of 1960 of over £323,000. The statement indicates that for that year the Trade Unions provided £206,000 in affiliation fees, while the constituency Labour Parties contributed £30,000 in affiliation fees.[3]

Constituency parties are responsible for their own financial arrangements, including election expenses, although various forms of assistance in money and in kind (printed material, etc.) are provided in certain circumstances from central party funds. Where a candidate is specifically endorsed by a particular trade union or co-operative society, it is customary for the sponsoring organization to make a money grant to the funds of the constituency party and to contribute a special sum towards election expenses. As was noted above (p. 554), the maximum a sponsoring organization may contribute to the constituency party's funds is an annual grant of £300 and 80 per cent. of the legal maximum election expenses.

The trade unions have of course been the financial mainstay of the Labour Party. Martin Harrison in his survey of trade union finance has commented:

[1] *House of Commons Debates* (1961), Vol. 636, p. 1427.
[2] *Ibid.*, p. 1430.
[3] When a General Election is due a special fund-raising appeal is made by the party. Thus, for example, in 1949 the trade unions contributed £148,000 towards the General Election Fund and £27,000 towards the party's Development Fund, in addition to their annual affiliation fees for that year of £124,000.

" By any British standard the unions' political income is formidable. Now running at about three-quarters of a million pounds per year—and backed by reserves equal to two years expenditure—it has almost quadrupled since the war. In 1945 the total income of union political funds was £219,000. Increased membership and the return to contracting-out brought it up sharply to £465,000 by 1948. Then, after a more gradual rise, a general increase in contributions after 1956 raised it rapidly to £770,000 in 1958." [1]

Harrison estimates that union political funds were dispersed in 1958 in the following way: £364,000 to the national level of the Labour Party; £12,000 at the regional level; £161,000 to the constituencies; in addition £154,000 was spent internally by the unions.[2]

Two years later it was reported that during 1959 (an election year) the trade unions had spent £891,000 from their political funds, easily the largest sum in the history of the movement.[3] (In their reserve political fund that year they held £1,234,000.) The average expenditure amounted to 2s. 8d. for each of the 6,770,000 members paying the levy. (11.9 per cent. of union members contracted out of the political levy).

But despite the rich financial resources of the trade unions the Labour Party in recent years has found itself in increasing financial difficulty. Individual membership declined steadily after 1957 and there was also a slight decline in trade union membership. By 1961 the party reported an accumulated deficit of £94,952.[4] In order to meet this problem it was decided that the the sum contributed to central party funds by local parties and by affiliated trade unions should be raised (in two stages) from 6d. to 1s. a head per year. But even this increased rate produces a comparatively modest sum if one takes into account the cost of modern electioneering and propaganda techniques.[5] In addition it would seem remarkable that the individual membership subscription of 6s. a year has not been increased in over 20 years although in the same period there has been a three-fold increase in prices and a four-fold increase in wages.[6]

But the party is not as poor as its deficit would lead one to believe. The party has a Reserve Fund which, beginning with a balance of £113 in 1943, reached £327,428 in 1961. This is treated however as

---

[1] Harrison, M., *The Trade Unions and the Labour Party*, p. 60.

[2] *Ibid.*, p. 95.

[3] *The Times*, 14th November, 1960. In previous election years they spent £638,000 (1955) and £583,000 (1951).

[4] *1961 Labour Party Annual Conference Report*, p. 48.

[5] Rowland, C., " Labour Publicity ", *Political Quarterly*, Vol. 31, No. 3, July–September, 1960.

[6] *The Mechanics of Victory*, Fabian Pamphlet, 1962, p. 18.

an emergency fund—to be dipped into only at elections. As the *New Statesman* has commented, in a survey of Labour finances, " the sum is an extraordinarily large nest-egg for a party that is always pleading poverty..." The paper adds that the " general election fund is seen as something sacred—only to be touched in the actual emergency of a general election campaign...." The *New Statesman* concluded that the evidence suggests that " Transport House still believes that British General Elections are won or lost in three weeks."[1]

The weakness of the Labour Party's publicity efforts in the past appeared to be due not primarily to a lack of money so much as to a waste of resources and a myopic view as to how elections are won. During the 1959 election campaign itself the Conservative Party spent not much more than the Labour Party (the Conservatives spending £475,915 to the Labour Party's £437,725 and the Liberals' £114,949).[2] But according to David Butler and Richard Rose, who analysed the costs of campaign expenditures in their study of the 1959 election, the Tory expenditure for the two years *before* the election was approximately £468,000 (that is five times Labour's expenditure during the same period).[3] This pre-election expenditure is of course in no way controlled by election law; the law is entirely " pre-psephological," in that it takes no account of the findings of recent election studies which suggest that political activity and propaganda during the 200 weeks between elections is far more important than the propaganda activity during the three weeks of the campaign itself.[4] Clearly the law ought to be re-examined (perhaps by a Royal Commission) and changed to take into account the importance of expenditure between elections. Meanwhile the Labour Party in its own interest might come to terms with the fact that there is no use hoarding its considerable financial resources until too late (i.e. until the election campaign proper begins).[5]

[1] *New Statesman*, 15th September, 1961.

[2] Butler, D. and Rose, R., *The British General Election of 1959*, London, 1960, Chapt. III.

[3] *Ibid.*, p. 281.

[4] Trenaman, J. and McQuail, D., *Television and the Political Image*, London, 1961, *passim*.

[5] See also McKenzie, R. T. " Voting, Spending and the Law ", *Observer*, 18th March, 1962. Since the criticisms of Labour's attitude towards election spending (in the text above) were written, the party's policy has changed dramatically. In May 1963 it launched a massive campaign of press and poster advertising estimated by *The Times* (20th May, 1963) to cost approximately £200,000. For a valuable criticism of the British electoral law see Newman, F. C., " Money and Elections in Britain—Guide for America?" *The Western Political Quarterly*, Vol. X, No. 3, Sept., 1957 and " Reflections on Money and Party Politics in Britain," *Parliamentary Affairs*, Vol. X, No. 3, Summer 1957.

The Labour Party certainly does not have at its disposal the funds which the Conservative Party can probably command. But in its inquest into the 1955 electoral defeat the Wilson Report commented (regarding the party's financial situation) that they " thought it dangerously misleading to think exclusively in terms of Tory money and to ignore the efficiency of the voluntary organization which explains a great deal of their success and which it is not beyond (the Labour Party's) power to rival."[1]

In comment on their opponents finances the Labour Party *Handbook* (*Facts and Figures for Socialists*, 1951) argued vehemently that " the nation should know what groups and organizations are specially anxious to have a Conservative Government." The *Handbook* met the Conservative charge that Labour has powerful financial allies whose support is not reflected in the party's budget by alleging that " big business is actively helping the Tories . . . The Aims of Industry and the Economic League are two organizations engaged in anti-socialist propaganda. They have the strong support of the powerful Federation of British Industries." The Economic League, it was claimed, had at that time 92 permanent full- and part-time speakers and during 1948 it distributed $9\frac{1}{2}$ million leaflets and secured over 25,000 inches of press publicity. The Aims of Industry is described as " a propaganda body in the interests of big business ", and the *Handbook* quotes the organization's 1948 report in which reference is made to the fact that in that year the press gave the Aims of Industry over 78,000 column inches of space (" worth no less than £780,000 ").[2]

---

[1] *Interim Report of the Sub-Committee on Party Organization*, London, 1955, pp. 7 ff.

[2] *Labour Party Handbook*, 1951, pp. 304–6.

STANDING ORDERS OF THE PARLIAMENTARY LABOUR PARTY

As Revised, Session 1945–6

" The Parliamentary Party have the authority to withdraw the Whip on account of things said or done by Members of the Party in the House, such decision to be reported to the National Executive Committee.

" Outside activities, whether in writing or speech, which are contrary to the discipline or constitution of the Party shall be dealt with by the National Executive Committee."

STANDING ORDERS

" 1. For the purpose of securing concerted action in the House, Members shall consult the Officers of the Parliamentary Party before tabling any Motion, Amendment or Prayer, or other proposal which may involve Party policies or decisions and shall not vote for any Motion, Amendment or Prayer contrary to the decision of the Party Meeting.

" 2. Where there is a persistent refusal to observe the decisions of the Parliamentary Party, it shall be the duty of the Liaison Committee to bring a recommendation to the Party Meeting to report the Member to the National Executive Committee, who shall consider the matter in its constituency and other aspects with which the National Executive Committee is concerned. The Member concerned shall have the right to be heard both by the Parliamentary Party and the National Executive Committee.

" 3. It is recognized that on certain matters, for example religion and temperance, Members may have good grounds for conscientious scruples, and in such cases they may abstain from voting.

" (The above Standing Orders may be amended, rescinded, altered, added to or suspended for such period and under such conditions as may be determined upon by a duly constituted meeting of the Parliamentary Labour Party.)

" NOTE.—Members should take advantage of Party Meetings in suitable instances to raise questions of Party policy concerning which they may have doubts." [1]

---

[1] *1946 Labour Annual Conference Report*, Appendix I, p. 221.

As Revised, March 1952

" 1. The privilege of membership of the Parliamentary Labour Party involves the acceptance of the decisions of the Party Meeting. The Party recognizes the right of individual Members to abstain from voting on matters of deeply held personal conscientious conviction.

" 2. The Parliamentary Party have the right to withdraw the Whip on account of things said or done by Members of the Party in the House. The Member or Members concerned shall have the right to be heard at the Party Meeting before the Whip is withdrawn.

" 3. The National Executive Committee shall be informed of any decision to withdraw the Whip.

" 4. It is the duty of the Parliamentary Committee to bring before the Party Meeting cases of serious or persistent breaches of Party discipline, and in appropriate cases to recommend to the Party Meeting that the Member or Members concerned shall be reported to the National Executive Committee. The Member or Members concerned shall have the right to be heard by the Parliamentary Committee and the Parliamentary Party.

" 5. For the purpose of securing concerted action in the House, Members shall consult the Officers of the Parliamentary Party before tabling any motion, amendment or prayer, or other proposal which may involve Party policies or decisions.

" These Standing Orders may be amended, rescinded, altered, added to, suspended or reinstated for such period and under such conditions as may be determined, after due notice, by a duly constituted meeting of the Parliamentary Labour Party." [1]

As Revised, December 1961

After the 1959 election the PLP agreed to rescind its Standing Orders in favour of a " gentlemen's agreement " to maintain a voluntary discipline within the Parliamentary Labour Party. But during the two years that followed there were bitter disputes on defence which culminated in the withdrawal of the Whip from five M.P.s in March 1960. It was subsequently decided in December 1961 to reimpose Standing Orders in somewhat more stringent form. The Standing Orders follow:

" 1. If the party is to be an effective force politically, its activities must be co-ordinated and collective decisions taken. The privilege

---

[1] *1953 Labour Annual Conference Report,* Appendix IV, p. 215. For a discussion of these standing orders see Morrison, H., *Government and Parliament,* Chapter VIII.

of membership of the Parliamentary Labour Party involves the acceptance of these decisions.

" 2. The party recognizes the right of members to abstain from voting in the House on matters of deeply held personal conscientious conviction, but this does not entitle Members to cast votes contrary to a decision of the party meeting.

" 3. It is the duty of the Parliamentary Committee to bring before the party meeting cases of serious or persistent failure by members to act in harmony with the Parliamentary Labour Party, including a bad record of attendance in the division lobbies.

" 4. The Parliamentary Party has the right to withdraw the Whip on account of things said or done by members of the party in the House. The Member or Members concerned shall have the right to be heard at the party meeting before the Whip is withdrawn.

" 5. The NEC shall be informed of any decision to withdraw the Whip.

" 6. In appropriate cases the Parliamentary Committee may recommend to the party meeting that a Member or Members concerned shall be reported to the NEC. The Member or Members concerned shall have the right to be heard by the Parliamentary Committee and by the parliamentary party.

" 7. For the purpose of securing concerted action in the House Members shall consult the officers of the parliamentary party before tabling any motion, amendment or prayer. The tabling of such motion, amendment or prayer shall be delayed for one sitting day should the officers so request. Where the officers are unable to give approval to the tabling of any motion, amendment or prayer, this must be made known by the sponsor or sponsors to such other Members as may be approached in seeking support of the notice of motion.

" 8. These standing orders may be amended, rescinded, altered, added to, suspended or reinstated for such period and under such conditions as may be determined after due notice by a duly constituted meeting of the Parliamentary Labour Party."

APPENDIX D

PLP EXECUTIVE (excluding representatives of Peers) SHOWING OVERLAPPING OF MEMBERSHIP WITH NEC.

	EXECUTIVE COMMITTEE					ADMINISTRATIVE COMMITTEE					LIAISON COMMITTEE						PARLIAMENTARY COMMITTEE		
	1935	1936	1937	1938	1939	1940	1941	1942	1943	1944	1945	1946	1947	1948	1949	1950	1951	1952	1953
Alexander, A. V.	×	×	×	×	×	×	×	×										⊗	⊗
Ammon, C. G.	⊗	⊗	⊗	⊗	⊗	⊗	×	⊗	×[2]	⊗							⊗	⊗	⊗
Attlee, C. R.									×	○	○	○	○	○	○	○			
Barnes, A.									×	○	○	○	○	○	○	○	×	×	×
Bevan, A.						×	×	×	×			×	×	×[4]					
Bowles, F.												○	×	×	○		×	×	×
Callaghan, J.						×													
Clynes, J. R.	⊗	○	○	○															
Dagger, G.	⊗	⊗	⊗	⊗	⊗	⊗	×[3]	×	×	○			×[3]	×	○		⊗	×	×
Dalton, H.	⊗	⊗	⊗	⊗	⊗	×	⊗	⊗	×	○			○	×[3]	○		⊗	×	×
Davies, Rhys																	×	×	×
Dobbie, W.								×[3]	×	×						×[5]			
Ede, Chuter	×[6]	×[6]	×[6]	×[6]	×[6]	×[6]	×[4]												
Edwards, C.																			
Gaitskell, H.																×			
Garro-Jones, G. M.						×	×	×	×	×							×	×	×
Gibson, C.																×			
Greenwood, Anthony	×	×	×	×	×	×	×	×	⊗	⊗	○	○	○	○	× ○	× ○	× ○	○	○
Greenwood, Arthur	×	×	×	×	×	×	×	×	×	×	○	○	○	○	○	○	⊗	⊗	⊗
Grenfell, D. R.	×	×	×	×	×	×	×	⊗	⊗	⊗	○	○	○	○	○	○	⊗	⊗	×
Griffiths, J.			○	×	×	×	⊗	×						×[3]			×	×	×
Hall, G. H.																			
Hall, W. G.															×[3]				
Henderson, A. (Jnr.)					×														
Hicks, G.					×														
Johnston, T.																			
Jones, A. Creech	×	×	×	×		×	×	×											
Jones, M.	×	×	×	×		×													

Kennedy, T.
Key, C.
Lawson, J. J.
Lees-Smith, H. B.
Lunn, W.
MacDonald, G.
MacLean, N.
Milner, J.
Montague, F.
Morrison, H.
Noel-Baker, P.
Parker, J.
Pethick-Lawrence, F.
Pritt, D. N.
Robens, A.
Shinwell, E.
Silkin, L.
Smith, Ellis
Smith, Tom
Soskice, Sir F.
Stokes, R. R.
Summerskill, E.
Walkden, A.
Williams, T.
Webb, M.
Wedgwood-Benn, W.
Westwood, J.
Whiteley, W.
Wilmot, J.
Woodburn, A.

NOTES: O = Member of NEC. X = Member of (Executive) Committee of PLP.
[1] Died during term of office.
[2] Became Peer.
[3] Filled vacancies.
[4] Resigned.
[5] As Leader of the House.
[6] As Chief Whip.

BIBLIOGRAPHY

This bibliography includes the principal manuscript and printed sources consulted in the course of this study. Only the most important periodical material has been included. Other newspaper and periodical references are indicated in footnotes throughout the text.

I. THE CONSERVATIVE PARTY

A. PRIMARY SOURCES AND OFFICIAL PARTY LITERATURE

The most important sources of information on the history of the mass organization of the Conservative Party are the annual reports of the Executive Committee, Central Council and annual conferences of the National Union. For the early years after 1867 these are in manuscript form. Subsequently in the 1870s a few were printed by the National Union. Thereafter until 1947 the reports were compiled in scrap book and manuscript form and are available only in the library at the Conservative Central Office; the library also contains a great deal of other relevant manuscript, printed, and press-clipping material. Since 1947 the National Union has published verbatim conference records.

The most important additional source of information on the history of the mass organization is a monthly record of speeches and news of party developments which was published from 1893 to 1912 as *National Union Gleanings,* and under the revised title *Gleanings and Memoranda* from 1912 to 1933. This publication was superseded for the period 1934-9 by a quarterly periodical entitled *Politics in Review* and, since 1946, the Central Office has published *Notes on Current Politics.* Extensive use has also been made throughout this study of the pamphlet material published by the National Union and the Central Office since 1867. The most important literature on the party organization published since 1945 include *The Interim and Final Reports of the Committee on Party Organization 1948 and 1949* (the Maxwell Fyfe Report); Central Office *Organization Series* which includes the following titles: (1) *The Party Organization;* (2) *Duties of Officers;* (3) *Model Rules;* (4) *Procedure at Business Meetings;* (5) *The Young Conservative and Unionist Organization;* (6) *Constituency Finance;* (7) *Electoral Registration;* (8) *Organization of Indoor and Outdoor Meetings;* (9) *The Voluntary Worker and the Party Organization;* (10) *Local Government and the Party Organization;* (11) *The Young Britons Organization.* Other official party publications of importance include *The Rules and Standing Orders of the National Union* (1951);

Bailey, R., *The Practice of Politics* (1950) ; *Political Education Handbook* (1951) and the reports of " The Two-way Movement of Ideas " published by the Conservative Political Centre.

B. HISTORICAL AND GENERAL STUDIES OF THE CONSERVATIVE PARTY

Beer, Samuel, "The Conservative Party of Great Britain," *Journal of Politics,* Vol. XIV, No. 1, February 1952.

Biffen, J., "The Constituency Leaders," *Crossbow,* Vol. IV, No. 13, 1960.

Birch, Nigel, *The Conservative Party,* London, 1949.

Blondel, Jean, "The Conservative Association and the Labour Party in Reading," *Political Studies,* Vol. VI, No. 2, June 1958.

Butler, A., " 1951–59 The Conservatives in Power," *Political Quarterly,* Vol. 30, No. 4., Oct.–Dec. 1959.

Epstein, L. D., "British M.P.s and their Local Parties: The Suez Cases," *American Political Science Review,* Vol. LIV, No. 2, June 1960.

Epstein, L. D., " Politics of British Conservatism," *American Political Science Review,* Vol. XLVII, No. 1, March 1954.

Feiling, K., *The History of the Tory Party 1640-1714,* Oxford, 1924.

Feiling, K., *The Second Tory Party 1714-1832,* London, 1938.

Gorst, H., *The Fourth Party,* London, 1906.

Hayter, L. H., *An Outline of the History of the Conservative Party,* Taunton, 1925.

Hearnshaw, F. J. C., *Conservatism in England : An Analytical Historical and Political Survey,* London, 1933.

Herrick, F. H., "Lord Randolph Churchill and the Popular Organization of the Conservative Party," *Pacific Historical Review,* No. 15, June 1946.

Hill, R. L., *Toryism and the People 1832–46,* London, 1929.

Hogg, Quintin (Lord Hailsham), *The Case for Conservatism,* London, 1947.

Labour Research Department, *Tory M.P., 1955,* London, 1955.

McDowell, R. B., *British Conservatism 1832-1914,* London, 1959.

Martin, L. W., " The Bournemouth Affair: Britain's First Primary Election," *The Journal of Politics,* Vol. 22, No. 4, Nov. 1960.

Petrie, C. A. (Sir), *The Carlton Club,* London, 1955.

Political Quarterly, " Special Number—The Conservative Party," April-June, 1953.

Political Quarterly, " Special Number—The Conservative Party," July–Sept., 1961.

Potter, Allen, " The English Conservative Constituency Association," *The Western Political Quarterly,* Vol. IX, No. 2, June 1956.

Raymond, J. (ed.), *The Baldwin Age,* London, 1960.

Riley, E. S., *Our Cause,* Exmouth, 1948.

Rose, R., " The Bow Group's Rôle in British Politics," *The Western Political Quarterly,* Vol. XIV, No. 4, Dec. 1961.

Shore, Peter, *The Real Nature of Conservatism* (A Labour Party Publication), London, 1952.

Tooting Conservative and Unionist Club, *Tooting Conservative and Unionist Club, 1886–1956*, London, 1956.

Utley, T. E., *Not Guilty: The Conservative Reply*, London, 1957.

White, R. J., *The Conservative Tradition*, London, 1950.

Woods, Maurice, *History of the Tory Party*, London, 1924.

C. BIOGRAPHIES, AUTOBIOGRAPHIES AND MEMOIRS

Amery, L. S., *My Political Life*, London, 1953–55 (3 vols.).

Baldwin, A. W., *My Father, The True Story*, London, 1955.

Balfour, A. J., *Chapters of Autobiography*, London, 1930.

Beaverbrook, Lord, *The Decline and Fall of Lloyd George*, London, 1963.

Beaverbrook, Lord, *Men and Power 1917–1918*, London, 1956.

Birkenhead, Earl of, *Life of Frederick Edwin, Earl of Birkenhead*, London, 1933.

Birkenhead, Frederick, Second Earl of, *F. E. Smith, First Earl of Birkenhead*, London, 1959.

Blake, R. N. W., *The Unknown Prime Minister: The Life and Times of Andrew Bonar Law, 1858–1923*, London, 1955.

Boothby, R., *I Fight to Live*, London, 1947.

Boyd, F., *Richard Austen Butler*, London, 1956.

Broad, C. L., *Sir Anthony Eden*, London, 1955.

Cecil, Lady Gwendolen, *The Life of Robert, Marquis of Salisbury*, London, 1921-32 (4 vols.)

Chamberlain, Sir Austen, *Down the Years*, London, 1935.

Chamberlain, Sir Austen, *Politics from Inside*, London, 1936.

Churchill, R. S., *The Rise and Fall of Sir Anthony Eden*, London, 1959.

Churchill, R. S., *Lord Derby*, London, 1959.

Churchill, W. S., *Lord Randolph Churchill*, London, 1906·(2 vols.).

Churchill, W. S., *The Second World War*, London, 1948-54 (6 vols.).

Driberg, T., *Beaverbrook*, London, 1956.

Dugdale, Blanche, *Arthur James Balfour*, London, 1936 (2 vols.).

Eden, Sir Anthony, *Full Circle*, London, 1960.

Feiling, K., *The Life of Neville Chamberlain*, London, 1946.

Fox, A. W., *The Earl of Halsbury*, London, 1919.

Garvin, J. L., *The Life of Joseph Chamberlain*, London, 1932-4 (4 vols.).

Gollin, A. M., *The Observer and J. L. Garvin 1908–14*, Oxford, 1960.

Harris, R., *Politics Without Prejudice: a Political Appreciation of Rt. Hon. R. A. Butler*, London, 1956.

Hemingford, Lord, *Back-Bencher and Chairman*, London, 1946.

Hewins, W. A. S., *Apologia of an Imperialist*, London, 1929 (2 vols.)

Holland, B., *The Life of Spencer Compton, Eighth Duke of Devonshire*, London, 1911.

James, R. R., *Lord Randolph Churchill*, London, 1959.

Jenkins, R., *Mr. Balfour's Poodle*, London, 1954.

Jones, W. D., *Lord Derby and Victorian Conservatism*, Oxford, 1956.

Kennedy, A. L., *Salisbury, 1830–1903: Portrait of a Statesman*, London, 1953.

Macleod, Iain, *Neville Chamberlain*, London, 1961.

Mendelssohn, P. de, *The Age of Churchill*, Vol. 1, "Heritage and Adventure, 1874–1911," London, 1961.

Monypenny, W. F., and Buckle, G. E., *The Life of Benjamin Disraeli, Earl of Beaconsfield*, London, 1910-20 (6 vols.).

Newton, Lord, *Lord Lansdowne, A Biography*, London, 1929.

Nicolson, H., *Curzon, The Last Phase*, London, 1934.

Nicolson, Nigel, *People and Parliament*, London, 1958.

Norwich, Viscount, *Old Men Forget, the Autobiography of Duff Cooper*, London, 1953.

Petrie, Sir Charles, *Joseph Chamberlain*, London, 1940.

Petrie, Sir Charles, *The Chamberlain Tradition*, London, 1938.

Petrie, Sir Charles, *The Life and Letters of the Rt. Hon. Sir Austen Chamberlain*, London, 1939–1940 (2 vols.).

Petrie, Sir Charles, *Life and Times of Walter Long*, London, 1936.

Rentoul, Sir Gervais, *Sometimes I Think*, London, 1946.

Ronaldshay, Earl of, *The Life of Lord Curzon*, London, 1928.

Salvidge, S., *Salvidge of Liverpool*, London, 1934.

Steed, Wickham, *The Real Stanley Baldwin*, London, 1930.

Templewood, Viscount (Sir Samuel Hoare), *Nine Troubled Years*, London, 1954.

Winterton, Earl, *Orders of the Day*, London, 1953.

Woolton, Earl of, *The Memoirs of the Rt. Hon. The Earl of Woolton*, London, 1959.

Wrench, Sir J. E. L., *Geoffrey Dawson and our Times*, London, 1955.

Young, G. M., *Stanley Baldwin*, London, 1952.

Young, K., *Arthur James Balfour*, London, 1963.

II. THE LABOUR PARTY

A. PRIMARY SOURCES AND OFFICIAL PARTY LITERATURE

From its inception in 1900 the Labour Representation Committee (and after 1906, the Labour Party) published an annual report incorporating the report of the Executive Committee of the party and, after 1907, a report of the party in Parliament. These documents constitute the most important source of information on the evolution of the party organization. In addition, for the purpose of this study the annual reports of the Trade Union Congress, the Independent Labour Party and the Co-operative Party have also been consulted. Use has also been made of the manuscript minutes of the Executive Committee of the LRC and of the Labour Party for the period prior to the First World War, which are to be found in the British Library of Political and Economic Science under the title *The Infancy of the Labour Party* (2 vols.), and which have been referred to throughout the text as *Labour Party Documents*. Through the kind permission of the Passfield Trustees the writer was accorded access to the unpublished diaries of Beatrice Webb for the period 1924-31.

The most important official party publications dealing with the structure and organization of the party include the following: *The Constitution and Standing Orders of the Labour Party* (revised 1953); *Constitution and Rules* for various types of constituency parties (*Model Rules* sets A to E inclusive); annual reports of the executive committees of regional councils of the Labour Party; Croft, H., *Party Organization* (revised 1950); *Trades Councils Guide* (TUC, revised 1953); *Labour Year Book* (issued under the auspices of the TUC, the Labour Party and the Fabian Research Department), 1916 and subsequent editions; *Handbook : Facts and Figures for Socialists,* 1950 and subsequent editions; *The British Labour Party* (a duplicated publication " prepared for the guidance of foreign visitors desiring to know more about the structure of our movement ") 1950; *The Rise of the Labour Party* (Labour Discussion Series, No. 1, 1948); the Committee of the International Socialist Conference also published a *Report* of the international socialists' experts conference on propaganda and organization in 1950 (circular No. 235/50) which compares the structure of the Labour Party and continental Social-Democratic parties.

Several constituency Labour Parties have published pamphlets which are of interest in a study of the party organization, *e.g. Fifty Years' History of the Woolwich Labour Party 1903–53; The National Executive Committee versus the Widnes Divisional Labour Party* (published by the Widnes Party in 1939, incorporating their exchange of correspondence with the NEC and officials of the party head office which culminated in the disaffiliation of the Widnes Party).

B. HISTORICAL AND GENERAL STUDIES OF THE LABOUR PARTY AND AFFILIATED ORGANIZATIONS

Abrams, M. and Rose, R., *Must Labour Lose?*, London, 1960.

Allen, V. L., *Power in Trade Unions*, London, 1954.

Allen, V. L., " The Reorganization of the TUC 1918–1927," *British Journal of Sociology*, Vol. XI, No. 1, March 1960.

Allen, V. L., *Trade Union Leadership*, London, 1957.

Allen, V. L., *Trade Unions and the Government*, London, 1960.

Attlee, C. R., *The Labour Party in Perspective—And Twelve Years Later*, London, 1949.

Bassett, R., *1931 Political Crisis*, London, 1958.

Bealey, F. and Pelling, H., *Labour and Politics 1900–1906*, London, 1958.

Beer, Max, *History of British Socialism*, London, 1948.

Bonnor, J., " The Four Labour Cabinets," *Sociological Review*, Vol. 6, No. 21, July 1958.

Burns, J. M., " The Parliamentary Labor Party in Great Britain," *American Political Science Review*, Vol. XLIV, No. 4, December 1950.

Cole, G. D. H., *Fabian Socialism*, London, 1943.

Cole, G. D. H., *A Short History of the British Working Class Movement, 1789-1947*, London, 1948 (3 vols.).

Cole, G. D. H., *British Working Class Politics, 1832-1914*, London, 1941.

Cole, G. D. H., *A History of the Labour Party from 1914*, London, 1948.

Cole, Margaret, *The Story of Fabian Socialism*, London, 1961.

Crosland, C. A. R., *Can Labour Win?* (Fabian Pamphlet), London, 1960.

Crossman, R. H. S., *Labour in the Affluent Society* (Fabian Pamphlet), London, 1960.

Crowley, D. W., *The Origins of the Revolt of the British Labour Movement from Liberalism*, (unpublished thesis presented for the degree of Ph.D. in the University of London), 1952.

Epstein, L., " Who Makes British Party Policy: British Labour, 1960–61," *Midwest Journal of Political Science*, Vol. VI, No. 2, May 1962.

Fabian Journal (70th Anniversary Number), No. 12, April 1954.

Fienburgh, Wilfred, " The Future of Labour's Organization," *Fabian Journal*, No. 17, Nov. 1955.

Guttsman, W. L., " Changes in British Labour Leadership," in Marvick, D., *Political Decision-Makers*, Glencoe (Ill.), 1961.

Hall, W. G., *The Labour Party*, London, 1949.

Hamilton, M. A., *The Labour Party To-day*, London, (n.d., 1938?).

Hanham, H., " The Local Organization of the Labour Party," *The Western Political Quarterly*, Vol. IX, No. 2, June, 1956.

Harrison, M., *Trade Unions and the Labour Party*, London, 1960.

Hennessy, B., " Trade Unions and the British Labour Party," *The American Political Science Review*, Vol. XLIX, No. 4, Dec. 1955.

Hindall, K. and Williams, P., " Scarborough and Blackpool," *The Political Quarterly*, Vol. 33, No. 3, Sept. 1962.

Hitchner, D., " The Labour Government and the House of Commons," *The Western Political Quarterly*, Vol. V, No. 3, Sept. 1952.

Hobhouse, L. T., *The Labour Movement*, London, 1912.

Humphrey, A. W., *History of Labour Representation*, London, 1912.

Labour Party, *Constitution of the Labour Party*, London, 1960.

Labour Party, *Sub-Committee on Party Organization. Interim Report*, (The " Wilson Report "), London, 1955.

Loewenberg, G., " The British Constitution and the Structure of the Labour Party," *American Political Science Review*, Vol. LII, No. 3, Sept. 1958.

Lyman, R. W., *The First Labour Government 1924*, London, 1957.

MacDonald, J. R., *The Socialist Movement*, London, 1911.

McHenry, D. E., *The Labour Party in Transition, 1931–38*, London, 1938.

McKenzie, R. T., " Policy Decision in Opposition: A Rejoinder ", *Political Studies*, Vol. V, No. 2, June 1957.

McKenzie, R. T., " The Wilson Report and the Future of the Labour Party Organization," *Political Studies*, Vol. IV, No. 1, Feb. 1956.

Miliband, R., *Parliamentary Socialism*, London, 1961.

Pease, E. R., *History of the Fabian Society*, London, 1925.

Pelling, H., *The Origins of the Labour Party*, London, 1954.

Pelling, H., *A Short History of the Labour Party*, London, 1961.

Poirier, P. P., *The Advent of the Labour Party*, London, 1958.

Political Quarterly, " Special Number—The Labour Party," Vol. 31, No. 2, July–Sept., 1960.

Powell, J. Enoch, " 1951–59 Labour in Opposition", *Political Quarterly*, Vol. 30, No. 4, Oct.–Dec. 1959.

Reid, J. H. S., *The Origins of the British Labour Party*, Minneapolis, 1955.

Roberts, B. C., *Trade Union Government and Administration in Great Britain*, London, 1956.

Roberts, B. C., " Trade Unions and Party Politics," *Cambridge Journal*, Vol. 6, April 1953.

Rogow, A. A. and Shore, P., *The Labour Government and British Industry 1945–51*, Oxford, 1955.

Rose, S., " Policy Decision in Opposition," *Political Studies*, Vol. IV, No. 2, June, 1956.

Shanks, M., " Politics and the Trade Unionist," *Political Quarterly*, Vol. 30, No. 1, Jan.–March 1959.

Shepherd, Lord, *Labour's Early Days*, Tillicoultry, Scotland, n.d.

Shinwell, E., *The Labour Story*, London, 1963.

Tillett, B., *Is the Parliamentary Labour Party a Failure?* London, 1908.

Tracey, H., (ed.), *Book of the Labour Party*, London, 1925 (3 vols.).

Webb, Sidney, " The First Labour Government," *Political Quarterly*, Vol. 32, No. 1, Jan.–March 1961.

Wertheimer, E., *Portrait of the Labour Party*, London, 1930.

Williams, F., *Fifty Years' March: The Rise of the Labour Party*, London, 1949.

C. AUTOBIOGRAPHIES, BIOGRAPHIES AND MEMOIRS

Attlee, C. R., *As It Happened*, London, 1954.

Blackburn, F., *George Tomlinson*, London, 1954.

Blatchford, R., *My Eighty Years*, London, 1931.

Brockway, F., *Socialism Over Sixty Years*, London, 1946.

Brockway, F., *Inside The Left*, London, 1942.

Bullock, Alan, *The Life and Times of Ernest Bevin*, Vol. I. *Trade Union Leader 1881–1940*, London, 1960.

Clynes, J. R., *Memoirs*, London, 1937 (2 vols.).

Cole, Margaret, *Beatrice Webb*, London, 1946.

Cole, Margaret (ed.), *Beatrice Webb's Diaries 1912-24*, London, 1952.
Cole, Margaret, *Growing Up Into Revolution*, London, 1949.
Cole, Margaret, (ed.), *The Webbs and Their Work*, London, 1949.
Cole, Margaret, *Makers of the Labour Movement*, London, 1948.
Cooke, C. A., *The Life of Richard Stafford Cripps*, London, 1957.
Dalton, H., *Call Back Yesterday : Memoirs 1887-1931*, London, 1953.
Dalton, H., *The Fateful Years Memoirs 1931-1945*, London, 1957.
Dalton, H., *High Tide and After Memoirs 1945-1960*, London, 1962.
Elton, Lord, *Life of James Ramsay MacDonald*, London, 1939.
Estorick, E., *Stafford Cripps*, New York, 1949.
Evans, T., *Bevin*, London, 1946.
Foot, M., *Aneurin Bevan*, London, 1962.
Graham, T. N., *Willie Graham : The Life of the Rt. Hon. W. Graham*, London, (n.d. c. 1948).
Haldane, Richard Burdon, *An Autobiography*, London, 1929.
Hamilton, M. A., *Arthur Henderson*, London, 1938.
Hamilton, M. A., *Sidney and Beatrice Webb*, London, 1933.
Hodge, J., *Workman's Cottage to Windsor Castle*, London, 1931.
Hughes, Emrys, *Keir Hardie*, London, 1956.
Hunter, L., *The Road to Brighton Pier*, London, 1959.
Hyndman, H. M., *Further Reminiscences*, London, 1912.
Iconoclast, (Mary Agnes Hamilton), *J. Ramsay MacDonald, 1923-1925*, London, 1925.
Jenkins, R., *Mr. Attlee*, London, 1948.
Johnston, T., *Memories*, London, 1952.
Kirkwood, D., *My Life of Revolt*, London, 1935.
Krug, M., *Aneurin Bevan: Cautious Rebel*, New York, 1961.
Lansbury, G., *My Life*, London, 1928.
Martin, K., *Harold Laski*, London, 1953.
Morrison, Lord, *Herbert Morrison, An Autobiography*, London, 1960.
Murphy, J. T., *Labour's Big Three: A Biographical Study of Clement Attlee, Herbert Morrison and Ernest Bevin*, London, 1948.
Postgate, R., *The Life of George Lansbury*, London, 1951.
Shinwell, Emmanuel, *Conflict without Malice,* London, 1955.
Smillie, R., *My Life for Labour*, London, 1924.
Snell, Lord, *Men, Movements and Myself*, London, 1936.
Snowden, Viscount, *An Autobiography*, London, 1934 (2 vols.).
Stewart, W., *J. Keir Hardie*, London, 1925.
Strauss, P., *Bevin and Co.*, New York, 1941.
Strauss, P., *Cripps—Advocate and Rebel*, London, 1943.
Thomas, J. H., *My Story*, London, 1937.
Thorne, W., *My Life's Battles*, London, 1925.
Tillett, B., *Memories and Reflections*, London, 1931.
Tiltman, H. H., *James Ramsay MacDonald*, London, 1930.
Tsuzuki, C., *H. M. Hyndman and British Socialism*, Oxford, 1961.
Turner, B., *About Myself*, London, 1930.
Vankataramani, M. S., " Ramsay MacDonald and British Domestic Policy and Foreign Policy 1919–1931," *Political Studies*, Vol. VIII, No. 3.

Webb, Beatrice, *Diaries, 1924–32*, London, 1956.

Weir, L. MacNeill, *The Tragedy of Ramsay MacDonald*, London, 1938.

Williams, Francis, *A Prime Minister Remembers (The War and Post-War Memoirs of the Rt. Hon. Earl Attlee)*, London, 1961.

Williams, F., *Ernest Bevin*, London, 1952.

III. GENERAL WORKS ON POLITICS

(Dealing in part or in whole with British political parties)

Amery, L. S., *Thoughts on the Constitution*, Oxford, 1948.

Bagehot, W., *The English Constitution*, with an introduction by R. H. S. Crossman, London (Fontana Edition), 1963.

Beer, S. H., " Great Britain: From Governing Elite to Organized Mass Parties," in Neumann, S. (ed.) *Modern Political Parties*, Chicago, 1956.

Beer, S. H., " The Future of British Politics," *Political Quarterly*, Vol. 26, No. 1, Jan.–March 1955.

Beer, S. H., " Pressure Groups and Parties in Britain," *American Political Science Review*, Vol. L, No. 1, March 1956.

Beer, S. H., " The Representation of Interests in British Government: Historical Background," *American Political Science Review*, Vol. LI, No. 3, Sept., 1957.

Belloc, H., and Chesterton, C. K., *The Party System*, London, 1911.

Beloff, Max, " The Leader of the Opposition," *Parliamentary Affairs*, Vol. XI, No. 2, Spring 1958.

Beloff, Max, *The Party System*, London, 1958.

Benney, M., Gray, A. P., and Pear, R. H., *How People Vote*, London, 1956.

Birch, A. H., *Small Town Politics*, Oxford, 1959.

Booth, A. H., *British Hustings 1924–1950*, London, 1957.

Bullock, Alan and Shock, M. (eds.), *The Liberal Tradition, From Fox to Keynes*, London, 1956.

Butler, D. E., *The British General Election of 1951*, London, 1952.

Butler, D. E., *The British General Election of 1955*, London, 1955.

Butler, D. E., *The Electoral System in Britain, 1918-51*, Oxford, 1953.

Butler, D. E., " Some Notes on the Nature of British Political Parties," *Occidente* (Anglo-Italian Review of Politics), Vol. X, No. 2, March-April 1954.

Butler, D. E., " The Paradox of Party Difference," *The American Behavioral Scientist*, Vol. IV., No. 3, Nov. 1960.

Butler, D. E. and Rose, R., *The British General Election of 1959*, London, 1960.

Butler, J. R. M., *The Passing of the Great Reform Bill*, London, 1914.

Cambray, P. G., *The Game of Politics: A Study of the Principles of British Political Strategy*, London, 1932.

Campion, Lord (and others), *Parliament : A Survey*, London, 1952.

Carter, B. E., *The Office of Prime Minister*, London, 1956.

Childers, E., *The Road to Suez*, London, 1962.

Comfort, G. O., *Professional Politicians, a Study of the British Party Agents*, Washington, 1958.

Cross, C., *The Fascists in Britain*, London, 1961.

Crossman, R. H. S., *The Charm of Politics*, London, 1958.

Duverger, Maurice, *Les Partis Politiques*, Paris, 1951.

Eckstein, H., *Pressure Group Politics*, London, 1960.

Eckstein, H., " The Government of Britain," in Beer, S. H. and Ulam, A. B. (eds.), *Patterns of Government*, New York, 1958.

Emden, C. S., " The Mandate in the 19th Century," *Parliamentary Affairs*, Vol. XI, No. 3, Summer 1958.

Emden, C. S., *The People and the Constitution*, (2nd edition), Oxford, 1956.

Epstein, L. D., " Cohesion of British Parliamentary Parties," *American Political Science Review*, Vol. L, No. 2, June 1956.

Epstein, L. D., " Partisan Foreign Policy: Britain in the Suez Crisis," *World Politics*, Vol. XII, No. 1, January 1960.

Finer, S. E., *Anonymous Empire*, London, 1958.

Finer, S. E., *Private Industry and Political Power*, London, 1958.

Finer, S. E., Berrington, H. B., and Bartholomew, D. J., *Back-bench Opinion in the House of Commons, 1955–59*, London, 1961.

Foot, Michael, *Parliament in Danger*, London, 1959.

Fothergill, P., " Political Funds: The Liberal View," *Parliamentary Affairs*, Vol. I, 1947–48.

Gaitskell, Hugh, *In Defence of Politics*, Foundation Oration delivered at Birkbeck College, 1954.

Galloway, G. B., *Congress and Parliament*, Washington, 1955.

Gash, N., *Politics in the Age of Peel*, London, 1953.

Gollan, J., *The British Political System*, London, 1954.

Grainger, G. W., " Oligarchy in the British Communist Party," *British Journal of Sociology*, Vol. IX, No. 2, June 1958.

Greaves, H. R. G., *The British Constitution*, (3rd edition), London, 1955.

Grimond, J., *Liberal Future*, London, 1959.

Gwyn, W. B., *Democracy and the Cost of Politics*, London, 1962.

Hanham, H. J., *Elections and Party Management, Politics in the Time of Disraeli and Gladstone*, London, 1959.

Harman, N., " Minor Political Parties in Britain," *The Political Quarterly*, Vol. 33, No. 3, July–Sept., 1962.

Harrison, W., *The Government of Britain*, (4th edition), London, 1957.

Heasman, D. J., " The Monarch, the Prime Minister and the Dissolution of Parliament", *Parliamentary Affairs*, Vol. XII, No. 1, Winter 1960–61.

Heberle, R., *Social Movements: An Introduction to Political Sociology*, New York, 1951.

Jennings, Sir Ivor, *Party Politics*, Vol. I, *Appeal to the People*, Cambridge, 1960; Vol. II, *The Growth of Parties*, Cambridge, 1961; Vol. III, *The Stuff of Politics*, Cambridge, 1962.

Jennings, W. I., *Cabinet Government*, London, 1936.

Jennings, W. I., *Parliament*, Cambridge, 1948.

Jones, T., *A Diary with Letters*, London, 1954.

Laski, H. J., *Parliamentary Government in England*, London, 1938.

Lavau, G., *Partis Politiques et Réalité Sociale*, Paris, 1953.

Leiserson, A., *Parties and Politics*, New York, 1958.

Lewis, G. K., "The Present Condition of British Political Parties," *Western Political Quarterly*, June 1952.

Lipson, L., "Party Systems in the United Kingdom and the Older Commonwealth: Causes, Resemblances, and Variations," *Political Studies*, Vol. VII, No. 1, Feb., 1959.

Livingston, W. S., "British General Elections and the Two-Party System, 1945–55, *Midwest Journal of Political Science*, Vol. III, No. 2, May, 1959.

Lowell, A. L., *The Government of England*, New York, 1908 (2 vols.).

McCallum, R., and Readman, A., *The British General Election of 1945*, Oxford, 1947.

McDonald, N. A., *The Study of Political Parties*, New York, 1955.

McElwee, W., *Britain's Locust Years 1918–1940*, London, 1962.

McKenzie, R. T., "Parties, Pressure Groups and the British Political Process," (Special Number on Pressure Groups), *Political Quarterly*, Vol. 29, No. 1, Jan.–March, 1958.

McKenzie, R. T., *The 'Political Activists' and some Problems of Inner-Party Democracy in Britain*. Paper delivered at 5th World Congress International Political Science Association, Paris, 1961.

Mackintosh, J. P., *The British Cabinet*, London, 1962.

Martin, E. W., *The Tyranny of the Majority*, London, 1961.

Mathiot, A., *The British Political System*, London, 1958.

Michels, R., "Some Reflections on the Sociological Character of Political Parties," *American Political Science Review*, Vol. XXI, No. 4, November 1927.

Michels, R., *Political Parties*, with an introduction by S. M. Lipset (Collier Books Edition), New York, 1962.

Milne, R. S., and Mackenzie, H. C., *Marginal Seat*, London, 1958.

Milne, R. S., and Mackenzie, H. C., *Straight Fight: A Study of Voting Behaviour*, London, 1954.

Morrison, H., *Government and Parliament*, Oxford, 1954.

Mowat, C., *Britain between the Wars 1918–1940*, London, 1955.

Namier, L. B., *Monarchy and the Party System*, Oxford, 1952.

Newman, F. C., "Money and Elections in Britain—Guide for America?" *The Western Political Quarterly*, Vol. X, No. 3, Sept., 1957.

Newman, F. C., "Reflections on Money and Party Politics in Britain," *Parliamentary Affairs*, Vol. X, No. 3, Summer 1957.

Nicholas, H. G., *The British General Election of 1950*, London, 1951.

Nicolson, Sir H., *King George the Fifth, His Life and Reign*, London, 1952.

Northedge, F., "British Foreign Policy and the Party System," *American Political Science Review*, Vol. LIV, No. 2, June, 1960.

O'Leary, C., *The Elimination of Corrupt Practices in British Election (1868–1911)*, Oxford, 1962.

Ostrogorski, M., " The Introduction of the Caucus into England," *The Political Science Quarterly*, Vol. VIII, No. 2, June 1893.

Ostrogorski, M., *Democracy and the Organization of Political Parties*, London, 1902 (2 vols.).

Overacker, L., " The British and New Zealand Labour Parties: A Comparison, *Political Science*, Vol. 9, No. 1, and Vol. 9, No. 2 (1957).

Pelling, H., *The British Communist Party*, London, 1959.

Petrie, Sir Charles, *The Powers behind the Prime Minister*, London, 1959.

Pierssené, S. H., Fothergill, P., and Greenwood, A., " Political Party Funds," *Parliamentary Affairs*, Vol. I, No. 4, Autumn 1948.

Pike, E. R., *Political Parties and Policies*, London, 1934.

Political Quarterly, " The Selection of Parliamentary Candidates," Vol. 30, No. 3, July–Sept. 1959.

Pollock, J. K., " British Party Organization," *Political Science Quarterly*, Vol. XLV, June 1930.

Pollock, J. K., *Money and Politics Abroad*, New York, 1932.

Pollock, J. K., " The British Party Conference," *American Political Science Review*, Vol. XXXII, No. 3, June 1938.

Potter, A. M., " British Party Organization (1950)," *Political Science Quarterly*, Vol. LXVI, No. 1, March 1951.

Potter, A. M., *Organized Groups in British National Politics*, London, 1961.

Rae, W. Fraser, " Political Clubs and Party Organizations," *The Nineteenth Century*, Vol. III, No. XV, May 1878.

Ranney, J. C., and Carter, G. M., *The Major Foreign Powers*, New York, 1949.

Richards, P. G., *Honourable Members*, London, 1959.

Robbins, C., " Discordant Parties—A Study of the Acceptance of Party by Englishmen," *Political Science Quarterly*, Vol. LXXIII, No. 4, Dec. 1958.

Rose, Richard, " Money and Election Law," *Political Studies*, Vol. IX, No. 1.

Rose, R., *The Policy Rôle of English Party Militants*, Paper delivered at International UNESCO Seminar, Bergen, 1961.

Schattschneider, E. E., *Party Government*, New York, 1942.

Schumpeter, J. A., *Capitalism, Socialism and Democracy*, London, 1952.

Self, Peter, and Storing, H., *The State and the Farmer*, London, 1962.

Seymour, C., *Electoral Reform in England and Wales*, Yale, 1915.

Smellie, K. B., *A Hundred Years of English Government*, London, 1950.

Spearman, D., *Democracy in England*, London, 1957.

Stephenson, T. E., " The Leader-Follower Relationship," *Sociological Review*, Vol. 7, No. 2, Dec. 1959.

Stewart, J. D., *British Pressure Groups*, Oxford, 1958.

Stewart, M., *The British Approach to Politics*, (3rd edition), London, 1955.

Stout, Hiram, *British Government*, New York, 1953.

Symons, J., *The General Strike*, London, 1957.

Taylor, E., *The House of Commons at Work*, (2nd edition), London, 1955.

Thomas, J. Alun, " The System of Registration and the Development of Party Organization 1832-1870," *History*, Vol. XXXV, February and June, 1950.

Thomas, J. A., " The House of Commons, 1832-1867: A Functional Analysis," *Economica*, Vol. V, No. 13, March 1925.

Thomas, N. P., *History of British Politics from the Year 1900*, London, 1956.

Tivey, L., " The System of Democracy in Britain," *Sociological Review*, Vol. 6, No. 1, July 1958.

Trenaman, J., and McQuail, D., *Television and the Political Image; a Study of the Impact of Television on the 1959 General Election*, London, 1961.

Twentieth Century, " Special Number—Who Governs Britain?", Oct. 1957.

Waller, I., " Pressure Politics," *Encounter*, Vol. XIX, No. 2, Aug. 1960.

Wilson, E. D. J., " The Caucus and its Consequences," *The Nineteenth Century*, Vol. IV, No. XX, October 1878.

Wilson, H. H., *Pressure Group: The Campaign for Commercial Television*, London, 1961.

Young, R., *The British Parliament*, London, 1962.

INDEX

ACLAND-HOOD, Sir A., 65, 73, 181, 184–5

Adamson, Mrs. J. L., 520

Adamson, William, 306, 346, 405–6, 409

Advisory Committee on Policy, Conservative Party's, 65–6, 210–13, 284, 285, 288

Agents, Conservative, 197, 219, 246–8

Agents, Labour, 488–9, 542–5, 570

Agricultural Workers, National Union of, 516

Aims of Industry, The, 659

Akers-Douglas, A. (Lord Chilston), 73, 77 *n* 4, 265, 266

Alexander, A. V. (Lord Alexander of Hillsborough), 361, 414, 415

Amalgamated Engineering Union, 410 *n* 1, 501–2, 614–6, 623, 624

Amery, L. S., on reasons why Baldwin succeeded Bonar Law, 40 *n* 3; and downfall of Lloyd George Coalition, 95, 96 *n* 2, 93; explains election of 1923, 111 *n* 1; supports Baldwin's India policy, 204–5, 137; comment on N. Chamberlain, 44; denounces Chamberlain Government (1940), 47

Anderson, W. C., 316, 564

Anti Corn Law League, 13

Area Organization (Conservative), 195, 206, 207, 214, 215, 219, 231–41; Area Agent, 233, 293; Area Chairman, 233–5, 293; Area Councils, 233, 235–6, 241, 244; Area Executive Committee, 236; Area Offices, 233, 236, 274, 293; Area Political Officer, 293

Ashbury, J., 164

Asquith, H. H. (1st Earl of Oxford and Asquith), 42, 77, 82, 302, 303, 396, 400–1

Assheton, Ralph, 273

Astor, Lady, 277

Atkinson, W., 466

Attlee, C. R., early career and emergence to leadership, 320, 356–65; in Labour Government of 1924, 358, 363; in Labour Government of 1929, 358–9; elected Vice-Chairman of PLP, 356, 359, 413; acting-Leader, 360; elected Leader, 299 *n* 2, 300, 360–3, 383; as member of PLP (Executive) Committee, 414; as member of NEC, 520; attempts to remove from leadership, 326, 328, 369 *n* 1; and formation of Churchill Coalition (1940), 325, 429; and break-up of Coalition (1945), 328–30; becomes Prime Minister, 331–2, 429; ignores Conference decisions intended to restrict powers of Labour Prime Minister, 323, 332–4; as Prime Minister, 323, 331, 332–4, 383–4, 446, 450, 580; in opposition after 1951, 334, 384, 503, 510; on origins of Labour Party, 300 *n* 1; attitude towards MacDonald, 363–4; on rôle of NEC Chairman, 330 *n* 2; on rôle of Labour Party Conference, 10, 12, 419–20, 427, 485, 494, 505 *n* 2, 598; exchanges with Churchill on Labour Party organization (1945), 13–14, 330–1; criticizes Conservative Party organization, 10; on party discipline, 631 *n* 1

Australian Labour Party, 309, 316, 332

Ayrton-Gould, Mrs. B., 520

BAGEHOT, Walter, 633–4

Baker, J., 394

Balcarres, Lord, 29 *n* 2, 77

Baldwin, Oliver (2nd Earl Baldwin of Bewdley), 442

Baldwin, Mrs. Stanley, 112

Baldwin, Stanley (1st Earl Baldwin of Bewdley), 17, 23 *n* 1, 192, 198–9, 202, 222, 268, 270–1, 276, 299, 314, 366, 579–80; rôle in downfall of Austen Chamberlain, 39, 103; seconds resolution offering leadership to Bonar Law, 37; emergence as